Learning from Covid-19 in Southeast Asia

The **ISEAS – Yusof Ishak Institute** (formerly Institute of Southeast Asian Studies) is an autonomous organization established in 1968. It is a regional centre dedicated to the study of socio-political, security, and economic trends and developments in Southeast Asia and its wider geostrategic and economic environment. The Institute's research programmes are grouped under Regional Economic Studies (RES), Regional Strategic and Political Studies (RSPS), and Regional Social and Cultural Studies (RSCS). The Institute is also home to the ASEAN Studies Centre (ASC), the Singapore APEC Study Centre and the Temasek History Research Centre (THRC).

ISEAS Publishing, an established academic press, has issued more than 2,000 books and journals. It is the largest scholarly publisher of research about Southeast Asia from within the region. ISEAS Publishing works with many other academic and trade publishers and distributors to disseminate important research and analyses from and about Southeast Asia to the rest of the world.

Learning from Covid-19 in Southeast Asia

Restriction, Relief, Recovery

EDITED BY

LEE HWOK AUN • SIWAGE DHARMA NEGARA • JAYANT MENON

ISEAS YUSOF ISHAK INSTITUTE

First published in Singapore in 2025 by
ISEAS Publishing
30 Heng Mui Keng Terrace
Singapore 119614
E-mail: publish@iseas.edu.sg
Website: http://bookshop.iseas.edu.sg

This publication is made possible with the support of Konrad-Adenauer-Stiftung.

KONRAD
ADENAUER
STIFTUNG

ISEAS Library Cataloguing-in-Publication Data

Name(s): Lee, Hwok Aun, editor. | Negara, Siwage Dharma, editor. | Menon, Jayant, 1965–, editor.
Title: Learning from Covid-19 in Southeast Asia : restriction, relief, recovery / edited by Lee Hwok Aun, Siwage Dharma Negara and Jayant Menon.
Description: Singapore : ISEAS – Yusof Ishak Institute, 2024. | Includes bibliographical references and index.
Identifiers: ISBN 9789815203806 (soft cover) | ISBN 9789815203813 (ebook PDF) | ISBN 9789815203820 (epub)
Subjects: LCSH: COVID-19 Pandemic, 2020-—Economic aspects—Southeast Asia. | COVID-19 Pandemic, 2020-—Government policy—Southeast Asia.
Classification: LCC RA644 C87L43

Cover design by Lee Meng Hui
Index compiled by Raffaie Nahar
Typeset by Superskill Graphics Pte Ltd
Printed in Singapore by Markono Print Media Pte Ltd

CONTENTS

LISTS OF TABLES

LIST OF FIGURES

ACKNOWLEDGEMENTS

The breadth and depth of the chapters in this book testify to the collective effort and industry of multiple contributors. This project germinated in the middle of 2021, when Covid-19 infections were resurging and starkly reminding us that the pandemic was far from over after one and a half years. Similarities and differences in Southeast Asia had also emerged, and data were becoming more available, sparking interest in a regionwide inquiry with country-specific and comparative elements. Literature on Covid-19 had also been published by then, providing empirical investigation and policy analysis amid the unfolding crises. To make an original and substantive contribution, we formulated thematic trios of Southeast Asian country studies to give each chapter a focus and to facilitate more cohesive inter country comparison, as explained in Chapter 1.

This work progressed under the banner of the ISEAS – Yusof Ishak Institute's Regional Economic Studies (RES) programme, for which we thank RES Coordinator Cassey Lee. ISEAS Director and CEO, Choi Shing Kwok, and Director of the Research Division and Deputy CEO, Terence Chong, gave valuable support and encouragement. Between October 2021 and February 2022, we held a webinar series at which authors presented conceptual frameworks and preliminary findings. Research papers were presented at a 28–29 July 2022 conference at ISEAS. We thank discussants Sanchita Basu Das and Dean Dulay for providing incisive and constructive feedback on the draft papers presented, and conference moderators and participants for lively and fruitful interactions.

The July 2022 conference was the first international hybrid event organized by ISEAS after the wide reopening of cross-border travel. We are hugely indebted to Foo Chen Nee, Nurul Iffah Johar, Daron Hoon and Lee Ling Ling for their administrative and logistical support, which made the conference an enjoyable and seamless affair despite the many challenges. We thank ISEAS interns Hafiz Nasruddin, Koh Jun Ming and Ang Tze Xin for their assistance with data sourcing and various project tasks.

This project's team of contributors channelled their expertise, empirical research and policy analyses into the chapters that form this volume. We extend our hearty gratitude to them for coming on board the project and investing time and effort into producing twelve informative, insightful and engaging country studies, and two studies with regional scope. We hope that the comparative synthesis essays we have written do justice to their work.

We are grateful to Katherine Demopoulos for her sharp and meticulous copyediting, which refined the manuscript. Our ISEAS Publishing colleagues, especially Ng Kok Kiong and Rahilah Yusuf, ensured that the final product lives up to ISEAS's high standards.

Konrad Adenauer Stiftung (KAS) provided financial support for the July 2022 conference and for publishing expenses, without which this book would not have been possible. We thank KAS for their generosity.

Lee Hwok Aun
Siwage Dharma Negara
Jayant Menon

ABOUT THE CONTRIBUTORS

Editors and Comparative Synthesis Essay Authors

Lee Hwok Aun (PhD) is a Senior Fellow and Co-Coordinator of the Malaysia Studies Programme at the ISEAS – Yusof Ishak Institute. He was previously a Senior Lecturer and Head of the Department of Development Studies at the University of Malaya. His research and publications focus on inequality, affirmative action, labour, social protection and public policy.

Siwage Dharma Negara (PhD) is a Senior Fellow, Co-Coordinator of the Indonesia Studies Programme, and Coordinator of the Singapore APEC Study Centre at the ISEAS – Yusof Ishak Institute. Before joining ISEAS in 2014, he was a researcher at the Indonesian Institute of Sciences (LIPI). He has also worked for the Education Team at the World Bank Office in Jakarta.

Jayant Menon (PhD) is a Senior Fellow at the ISEAS – Yusof Ishak Institute. His last post was at the Asian Development Bank (ADB) as Lead Economist in the Office of the Chief Economist. He was also at the ADB Institute in Tokyo from 2005 to 2008. He started work as an academic in Australia, spending almost a decade at the Centre of Policy Studies at Monash University at its original campus in Clayton, Melbourne. He has also worked at the University of Melbourne, Victoria University, and the American University in Washington, DC.

Authors (by Chapter Order)

Teng Delux (PhD) is a Research Fellow at the Cambodia Development Research Institute. (CDRI).

Pen Socheata is a Policy Researcher at the General Secretariat of the Digital Economy and Business Committee. She is a former Research Assistant at the Centre for Development Economics and Trade (CDET), Cambodia Development Resource Institute (CDRI).

Phouphet Kyophilavong (PhD) is a Professor in the Faculty of Economics and Business Management, National University of Laos. He has been a visiting scholar at Pukyong National University, Nagoya University, University of Laval, Kobe University and Nanyang Technological University, as well as Fulbright US-ASEAN Visiting Scholar at Harvard University. He is editor-in-chief of the *Lao Journal of Economics and Management*.

Khaysy Srithilat (PhD) is a Lecturer in the Faculty of Economics and Business Management, National University of Laos.

Sandii Lwin (DrPH) is the Founder and Managing Director of the Myanmar Health and Development Consortium (MHDC) overseeing programmes including communicable diseases, research and evaluation, health financing, pandemic preparedness, nutrition, environmental health, renewable energy, and water and sanitation. She previously worked for the Global Fund to Fight AIDS, Tuberculosis and Malaria, the World Bank, and UNDP.

Kyaw San Wai is a Researcher with the Myanmar Health and Development Consortium (MHDC). He has fifteen years of experience in policy-related research on Myanmar and ASEAN-related issues as well as public health project implementation in Myanmar since 2016. He was formerly an analyst with the S. Rajaratnam School of International Studies (RSIS), Singapore and the Myanmar Institute of Strategic and International Studies (MISIS).

Nilar Win is an Economist with the Myanmar Health and Development Consortium (MHDC). She has over six years of experience working in Myanmar with various development organizations such as the World Bank and INGOs.

Arief Ramayandi (PhD) is a Senior Research Fellow/Economist at the Asian Development Bank Institute (ADBI). Prior to joining ADBI, Arief was a Principal Economist in ADB's Economic Research and Development Impact Department. He has published in the field of macroeconomics and development and was part of the team preparing the Asian Development Outlook reports for ADB.

Ronald U. Mendoza (PhD) is a governance and institutional reforms specialist with over twenty-five years of experience in development policy and public administration reforms. He is presently a Senior Economist with the Ateneo Policy Center and a Member of the United Nations Committee of the Experts on Public Administration (UN CEPA). Ron served as Dean and Professor with the Ateneo de Manila University, School of Government from 2016 to 2022.

Sheena A. Valenzuela (MPM) is a public policy research and programme management professional, focusing on national security, the blue economy, health governance, and renewable energy. She was a policy researcher at the Ateneo Policy Center, School of Government, Ateneo de Manila University in the Philippines from 2016 to 2023. Sheena was previously a research consultant to UNDP Philippines and UPPAF-RESPOND.

Nguyen Thu Huong is a Researcher at the Centre for Analysis and Forecasting which recently merged into the Vietnam Institute of Economics under the Vietnam Academy of Social Sciences. She has contributed to various projects with the World Bank and the United Nations Development Programme (UNDP). Huong's work focuses on enhancing educational systems and policies, aiming to drive positive change and development within educational institutions globally, including the Young Lives study by University of Oxford and UNDP's Vietnam National Human Development Report.

Yanuar Nugroho is a Visiting Senior Fellow with the ISEAS – Yusof Ishak Institute, Senior Lecturer at Driyarkara School of Philosophy Jakarta, and Expert Coordinator at the National Secretariat of SDGs Implementation, Indonesia. His research interests and publications revolve around innovation and social change, knowledge dynamics, sustainability, public policy, state capacity, and foresight. Having first-hand experience as a high-level policymaker when appointed as Deputy Chief of Staff to the Indonesian President in 2015–29, Yanuar now aspires to bring knowledge closer to policy by promoting evidence-based policy.

Sofie Syarief is an Indonesian television journalist with fifteen years of experience covering issues on politics, democracy, and public policy, as well as a PhD student in the Department of Media, Communications and Cultural Studies of Goldsmiths, University of London, with research on power and the alternative news media in Indonesia. Her works mainly revolve around media and democracy, and based on a belief that journalism is a form of activism, she is interested in contributing to the creation of a more democratic media landscape in Indonesia.

Tricia Yeoh (PhD) is the CEO of the Institute for Democracy and Economic Affairs (IDEAS) Malaysia, Senior Adjunct Research Fellow at Monash University Malaysia and Visiting Fellow at the ISEAS – Yusof Ishak Institute. She writes and speaks widely on federalism, subnational opposition politics and institutional reforms. She has previously worked in the Chief Minister's Office of the Selangor State Government.

Punchada Sirivunnabood (PhD) is an Associate Professor in the Faculty of Social Sciences and Humanities, Mahidol University, Thailand and a former Visiting Fellow at the ISEAS – Yusof Ishak Institute. Her research focuses on political parties, election, party finance, Indonesian politics and Thai politics. She recently published a book on the Political Finance Assessment of Thailand with International IDEA.

Melati Nungsari (PhD) is an Associate Professor at the Asia School of Business (ASB) and a Research Affiliate at the Massachusetts Institute of Technology. She has consulted for and worked on research projects with the UN High Commissioner of Refugees, the UN Development Program, and the World Health Organization. She is also the Research Lead for the Rapid Youth Success in Entrepreneurship Program, and the Faculty Director of the ASEAN Research Center, at ASB. Before joining ASB, Dr Melati was an economics professor at Butler University and Davidson College in the US.

W.L. Terence Ho is Deputy Executive Director of the Institute for Adult Learning and Associate Professor (Practice) at the Singapore University of Social Sciences. He has held policy, research and leadership positions in the Singapore Public Service in a career spanning over twenty years. While at the Ministry of Manpower, he was involved in designing and implementing measures to protect jobs and livelihoods in the early phase of the Covid-19 outbreak.

Archanun Kohpaiboon (PhD) is an Associate Professor in the Faculty of Economics, Thammasat University, Bangkok, Thailand and a member of the International Competitiveness and Development Research Center (ICDRC), Faculty of Economics, Thammasat University.

Juthathip Jongwanich (PhD) is an Associate Professor in the Faculty of Economics, Thammasat University, Bangkok, Thailand. She is the chief editor of Thailand and the World Economy and a member of the International Competitiveness and Development Research Center (ICDRC), Faculty of Economics, Thammasat University.

Mayoon Boonyarat is Director of Social Protection Strategy and Development Division, Division of Financial Inclusion Policy Development, Fiscal Policy Office, Ministry of Finance, Thailand.

Tham Siew Yean (PhD) is Visiting Senior Fellow at the ISEAS – Yusof Ishak Institute and Emeritus Professor at Universiti Kebangsaan Malaysia. She works mainly on foreign direct investments, industrial development, and trade agreements in Malaysia and the region. She is also a board member of the Global Development Network (GDN) and Institute of Strategic and

International Studies (ISIS), Malaysia, as well as a Non-Resident Senior Research Fellow at Wong MNC Centre in California.

Andrew Kam Jia Yi (PhD) is an Associate Professor and Senior Fellow at the Institute of Malaysian and International Studies (IKMAS), Universiti Kebangsaan Malaysia. He is also Head of the Centre for Latin American Studies at IKMAS. He works mainly on international trade, global production networks, productivity analysis, industrial economics and econometrics.

Sara Abdullah is the Head of Political Cooperation, ASEAN Secretariat. She previously worked on regional policies on education and youth development at the Secretariat. Prior to joining the ASEAN Secretariat, she taught English Language, Literature, and Drama in Singapore.

1

INTRODUCTION

Covid-19 Impacts and Responses across Southeast Asia

Lee Hwok Aun, Siwage Dharma Negara and Jayant Menon

THREE DISTINCT YEARS: 2020, 2021, 2022

Covid-19 shook the globe at the dawn of a new decade. The scale and speed of viral transmission, and the concurrent health and economic crises resulting from border closures and mobility restrictions, posed unprecedented policy and political challenges. Southeast Asia shared the global experience of Covid-19, with distinct national and regional features.

At the onset of the pandemic in early 2020, the world gravitated towards "flattening the curve" by minimizing human contact, which shut down economies except for essential services. As the year progressed and countries experienced waves of Covid-19 infection, mobility restrictions and border closures were maintained in much of Southeast Asia. Governments extended economic relief and stimulus to protect jobs, mitigate income losses and keep businesses afloat. Governments also grappled with the challenges of coordinating security, health and economic policies, creating and managing mobile applications for recording movement and tracing the contacts of infected persons, and communicating information between agencies and to the public. The region performed relatively well in containing Covid-19 infection, but almost all economies significantly contracted. The adverse consequences were mitigated for some segments, especially those able to shift to online work and formal entities supported by public assistance, but swathes of society experienced great socio-economic hardship.

The storyline of 2021 was markedly different. The more transmissible Delta variant surged across the region but, having gained experience, including in contact tracing applications and public communication channels, governments shifted towards more localized mobility restrictions and adopted mechanisms for gauging the severity of the pandemic and applying commensurate measures for physical distancing. Countries stumbled along the way, with some incapacitated by political instability and others undermined by vested interests. Cross-border travel remained tightly controlled, with quarantine protocols widely in place. As vaccines were approved, procurement and mass roll-out were pursued as the highest priorities. Most countries accelerated Covid-19 inoculation from the second half of 2021. Southeast Asia broadly shifted into recovery mode, while public expenditure and indirect income supplements continued to provide relief and stimulus, and increasing attention was placed on job creation and reviving business activity. Cross-border travel resumed in late 2021 after an almost two-year hiatus, bringing relief to the strains placed on business, leisure and personal ties, although onerous screening and testing requirements were also introduced.

The momentum of economic recovery was sustained into 2022, marking the third leg in the Covid-19 odyssey. As vaccination rates passed critical majority thresholds, the momentum of domestic and international reopening continued amid the outbreak of the Omicron variant. Tourism and services, among the most adversely impacted sectors in 2020–21, re-emerged from their protracted downturn. The general optimism at the dawn of the year, however, was soon diminished by Russia's war in Ukraine, which exacerbated supply chain disruptions and stoked global instability and inflationary pressures. Though new challenges have risen to the forefront of policy priorities, looking back remains important as societies move on.

The pandemic was also a period of accelerated data flow, with many countries conducting daily briefings on Covid-19 cases, hospitalizations, deaths and other public health indicators. The frequency and transparency of such disclosures were necessary to update the public and to provide assurance that decisions were based on the numbers. Of course, amid the immersion in data, we must not forget that the pandemic inflicted the ultimate cost in lives lost. Time plots of Covid-19 infections and mortality are perhaps the most used visualization. While helpful for outlining Covid-19 waves and the magnitude and timing of public health impact and policy progress, multiple country graphics are too cluttered for the printed page. The chapters of this book illustrate these chronologies by individual country and also underscore the distinctiveness of each country's experience.

To set some regional context, it is perhaps useful to provide a brief overview of the cumulative health and economic impacts of the pandemic. We observe in Table 1.1 that Covid-19 cases and deaths varied across countries, though the figures may be biased by a health system's capacity to track Covid-19 infections and deaths. Nonetheless, a general assessment of the region's efficacy in containing infections, especially in 2020, is borne

TABLE 1.1
Southeast Asia: Cumulative Covid-19 Cases and Deaths (as of September 2023)

	Total Cases	*Total Cases per Million Population*	*Total Deaths*	*Total Deaths per Million Population*
Brunei	310,522	691,583	163	363
Cambodia	138,941	8,286	3,056	182
Indonesia	6,813,429	24,731	161,918	588
Laos	218,853	29,066	671	89
Malaysia	5,127,712	151,090	37,187	1,096
Myanmar	641,225	11,835	19,494	360
Philippines	4,111,331	35,578	66,681	577
Singapore	2,573,565	456,547	1,872	332
Thailand	4,757,049	66,349	34,471	481
Vietnam	11,623,372	118,380	43,206	440
Southeast Asia	36,315,999	53,449	368,719	543
Rest of World	725,452,996	99,436	6,415,449	879

Source: Our World in Data's Covid-19 dataset at https://ourworldindata.org/coronavirus (accessed 12 May 2023).

out in the overall outcomes across three years. The regionwide averages of cases and deaths per million are lower than the figures for the rest of the world.

The economic disruption of the pandemic looms large in the gross domestic product (GDP) figures, which capture total economic activity and output (Table 1.2). Although Southeast Asia generally curbed Covid-19 contagion quite well in 2020, the region concurrently suffered steep economic downturns. This was expected because economic shutdowns were extensive and protracted, and external and uncontrollable factors such as supply chain disruptions and the total collapse of tourism hit

TABLE 1.2
Selected Countries and Regional/World Averages: GDP and Annual Growth, 2010–22

	GDP per Capita (Constant Dollar)[a]	*GDP Real Annual Growth (%)*				
	2020	*2010–18*[b]	*2019*	*2020*	*2021*	*2022*
Southeast Asia						
Cambodia	4,276	7.2	7.1	–3.1	3.0	5.2
Myanmar	4,947	7.0	6.8	3.2	–17.9	3.0
Laos	7,764	7.4	5.5	0.5	2.5	2.7
Philippines	7,773	6.3	6.1	–9.5	5.7	7.6
Vietnam	10,451	6.5	7.4	2.9	2.6	8.0
Indonesia	11,516	5.4	5.0	–2.1	3.7	5.3
Thailand	16,866	3.3	2.1	–6.1	1.5	2.6
Malaysia	25,831	5.2	4.4	–5.5	3.1	8.7
Brunei	61,604	–0.2	3.9	1.1	–1.6	–1.6
Singapore	94,910	4.3	1.3	–3.9	8.9	3.6
East Asia						
China	16,297	7.5	6.0	2.2	8.4	3.0
South Korea	42,397	3.0	2.2	–0.7	4.1	2.6
Region/World						
East Asia and Pacific[c]	10,780	5.3	5.0	–3.2	2.6	5.8
All Countries Worldwide	16,204	3.5	2.8	–2.9	6.2	3.3

Notes:
a. 2017 international dollar adjusted for purchasing power parity (PPP);
b. compound annual growth rate;
c. excluding high-income countries and China.
Source: World Bank's World Development Indicators at https://databank.worldbank.org/source/world-development-indicators (accessed 22 May 2023).

hard, although economic stimulus had some mitigating effect. Vietnam, which averted widespread lockdown, fended off a recession in 2020—as did Myanmar, but the latter suffered a cataclysmic collapse in 2021 in the aftermath of the coup.

Covid-19 has been a defining experience that demands research attention to investigate what happened and what lessons we can learn, particularly in the socio-economic and public policy spheres. This book provides retrospective and critical examinations of the Covid-19 period in the region, spanning the key policy responses of restrictions to contain the virus, provision of economic relief and stimulus, and measures to facilitate recovery. The complexity of policy challenges is shown in Figures 1.1 and 1.2, which respectively attempt to encapsulate the Indonesian and Malaysian cases.[1] Alongside the headline data series of Covid-19 cases and vaccinations, as exhibited in the composite graphics summarizing the two countries' pandemic experience, the imperative to protect human life led countries to closely monitor hospitalization rates and deaths related to Covid-19. These other aspects are covered in the country chapters of this book.

The complexities of pandemic responses, of course, extend beyond the contents of summaries, such as those in Figures 1.1 and 1.2. The formulation of action plans encompassing mobility restrictions, economic shutdown and medical treatment, and the decision to shift between different phases of tightening control or reopening required unprecedented levels of coordination. The concurrent health and economic crises, and the magnitude of self-imposed shutdowns, also demanded clear communication across administrations and stakeholders and expansive assistance to households and businesses. Such challenges were distinct to 2020–22, in a region that had experienced the massive Asian financial crisis in 1997–98 and other economic downturns, and various epidemics that were more localized, albeit also more virulent. These factors reinforce the relevance of studying the journeys of Southeast Asian countries through the pandemic.

APPROACH AND CONTRIBUTION

The pandemic generated great interest and prolific social science publications from as early as 2021. The cumulative literature on the

FIGURE 1.1
Indonesia's Covid-19 Experience: Cases, Mobility Restrictions, Stimulus Packages, Recovery and Vaccination Programmes

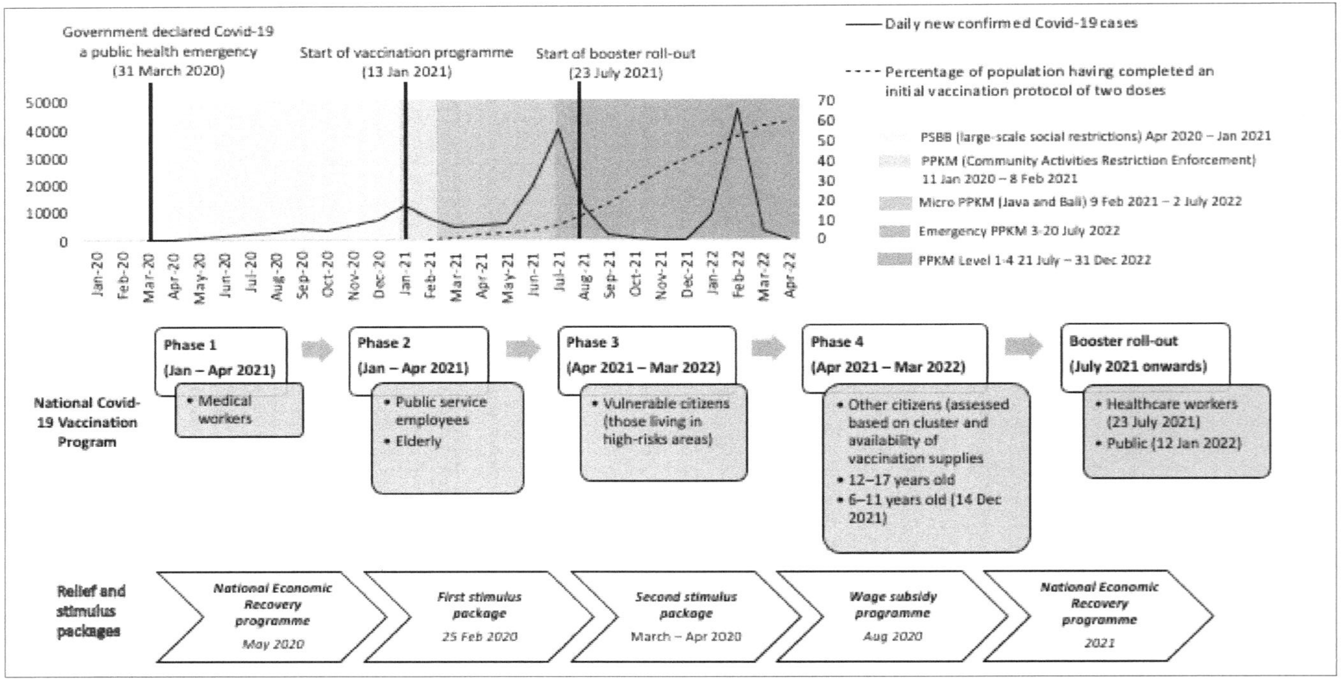

Sources: Authors' compilation from news articles.

FIGURE 1.2
Malaysia's Covid-19 Experience: Cases, Mobility Restrictions, Stimulus Packages, Recovery and Vaccination Programmes

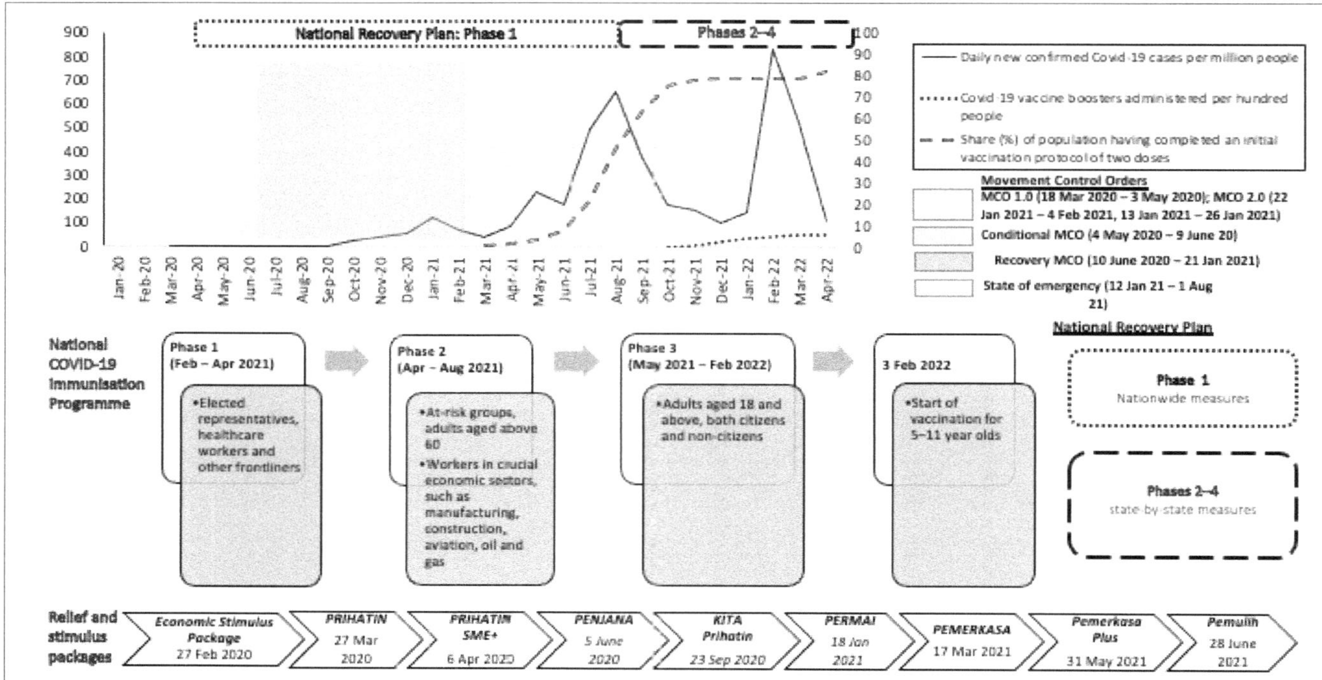

Sources: Authors' compilation from news articles.

subject matter is voluminous, even when narrowing down the search to Southeast Asia. Some of these works are based on research conducted in the early stages of the pandemic as rapid, in-the-moment responses to provide insights for managing the crises and transitioning towards recovery. A substantial literature focused on a single Southeast Asian country; prominent among these are edited volumes published in 2021 on Indonesia (Lewis and Witoelar 2021) and Malaysia (Louis, Kaur and Cheong 2021; Pandian, Kaur and Cheong 2021; Lim, Kaur and Cheong 2021). The books provided wide-ranging insights into these two countries' experiences in the economic, educational and psychological realms. More recently, the chapters in Indrawati et al. (2023) explain how Indonesia handled the Covid-19 pandemic and its effects on the economy and social life during 2020–21, from the perspective of policymakers who were involved in the design of the National Economic Recovery Programme and scholars who closely monitored and evaluated the policy responses. Singapore's stories of coping with the pandemic, from the onset of restrictions to the reopening in 2022, were collated by Yee and Tambyah (2022).

The gravity and universality of the pandemic inspired various multi-country publications spanning Southeast Asia. These edited volumes, primarily consisting of individual country studies on a specific subject, build on both the uniqueness of country experiences and the need for specialized focus among the numerous topics pertinent to Covid-19. Shin, McKenzie and Oh (2022) assembled country studies on an array of topics—from digitalization to migration to community-level responses—to survey pandemic responses and derive post-pandemic lessons. Aslam and Gunaratna (2022), who cover South, West and Southeast Asia, examine policies in various spheres as well, notably the security dimensions, recognizing that the restrictions imposed to contain the pandemic have involved security forces and may have acute effects on marginalized and politically volatile communities. The papers compiled in Sciortino (2023) focus on the social protection offered by Southeast Asian countries to citizens and residents, and emphasize biases and limitations that omitted swathes of the population, especially the informally employed and migrant workers. Tan and Chan (2023), another notable compendium, probed migration, demographic and educational impacts of Covid-19.

This book is the product of a research project that started in mid-2021. From the outset, we place high priority on comparative analysis, and set out to formulate a multi-country study project that addressed key challenges of the pandemic thus far and facilitated cross-country learning. The pandemic had been unfolding for a year and a half. Countries had gained experience in mitigating Covid-19 infection and extending social assistance while grappling with the more contagious Delta variant, procuring vaccines and planning inoculation roll-outs. The prospect for recovery was brightening. Similarities and differences had emerged among Southeast Asian countries' pandemic management, and the diversity of economic development levels, geography and political systems provided frameworks for organizing comparative study.

We deemed that the most valuable contribution this book could make, as the research progressed over a few months along with vaccination roll-outs and an increasing momentum of economic recovery, would be to investigate the full experience of pandemic impacts and responses. In conceptualizing the potential chapters to be written, we were cognizant of the breadth of subjects and the distinctiveness of country experiences, as evidenced by the richness of the edited volumes cited earlier in this chapter.

Meeting our objectives entailed grouping countries by subject matter and assembling contributors from the region. Instead of collating generic overviews of each country's Covid-19 experience that could lack depth, or openly inviting contributions that would yield disparate topics, we formulated study themes that encapsulated specific phenomena and policy challenges regarding Covid-19, and assigned countries especially suited for drawing out comparative lessons within each theme. We also strove to include as many countries from the Association of Southeast Asian Nations (ASEAN) as possible.

The chapters in this final product, covering nine of ASEAN's ten members, address the specificities of each country's experience and discuss policy implications. To further enhance the lessons learnt, the book includes comparative synthesis essays that critically engage with the country studies, drawing out key similarities and differences in five thematic groups and policy lessons for the future.

SOUTHEAST ASIAN DIVERSITY AND DISPARITY: DESIGNATING COVID-19 RESEARCH THEMES

We formulated four themes to optimize Southeast Asia's diversity of geography, demography, economic development and political systems, and a fifth that takes a regional perspective. These themes are derived from economic, demographic and geographic criteria that warrant a brief discussion, with reference to economic, demographic and governance indicators. Comparisons across the region, especially on this subject, which encompasses public health, economic and security apparatus of the state, must place in context the disparities in income levels, economic structure and geography (Coxhead 2018), as well as the range of political regimes—with mixes of monarchy, parliamentary systems, presidential republics and centralized and federal systems, and varying levels of democratic freedom (Croissant and Lorenz 2018).

The first theme, Covid-19 in the transition economies, is defined by developmental conditions. Similarities across the transition economies of Cambodia, Laos and Myanmar are apparent. The countries flanking Thailand to the east and west have the lowest GDP per capita of the region (Table 1.3) and lesser financial resources on the whole, although they qualify to a greater extent for international development assistance. Lower urbanization and a higher share of agriculture in employment exert varying impacts on pandemic response; viral contagion is higher in densely populated areas and in services and industry jobs. However, the mitigating factors must also be juxtaposed with the exceedingly large informal economy and low social protection, while deficiencies in internet and broadband access in Cambodia, Laos and Myanmar hindered their ability to perform contact tracing, online work and learning, and other adaptations (Table 1.4). The Myanmar coup of February 2021 also impacted adversely on governance in a singular manner, distinguishing the country from all others.

Governance of these countries is also regarded as less effective, although these are perception-based evaluations and we must be circumspect when drawing causal links between political systems and pandemic response measures (Table 1.5). Relatively autocratic regimes may be able to implement lockdowns—and create compliance with mandates in general,

TABLE 1.3
Southeast Asian Countries (Lowest to Highest GDP per Capita): Economic and Demographic Profile, 2020

	GDP per Capita (Constant US$)[a]	*Share of Total Employment (%)*[b]			*Population (Millions)*	*Urban Population (Percentage of Total)*	*Health Spending (Percentage of GDP)*
		Agriculture	*Industry*	*Services*			
Cambodia	4,276	38.9	25.4	35.7	16.40	24.2	7.5
Myanmar	4,947	46.5	18.6	35.0	53.42	31.1	4.6
Laos	7,764	58.1	10.8	31.1	7.32	36.3	2.7
Philippines	7,773	24.3	18.7	57.0	112.19	47.4	5.1
Vietnam	10,451	29.0	33.1	37.8	96.65	37.3	4.7
Indonesia	11,516	29.0	21.8	49.3	271.86	56.6	3.4
Thailand	16,866	31.6	22.5	45.9	71.48	51.4	4.4
Malaysia	25,831	9.6	28.3	62.1	33.20	77.2	4.1
Brunei	61,604	1.3	24.3	74.4	0.44	78.3	2.4
Singapore	94,910	0.3	14.4	85.3	5.69	100.0	6.1

Notes:
a. 2017 international dollar adjusted for purchasing power parity (PPP);
b. sectoral shares of GDP do not necessarily total one hundred, due to differences in categorization.
Source: World Bank's World Development Indicators at https://databank.worldbank.org/source/world-development-indicators (accessed 22 May 2023).

TABLE 1.4
Southeast Asian Countries (Lowest to Highest GDP per Capita): Structural Features Relevant to Pandemic Management

	Informal per Total Employment (%)[a]	*Population Covered by Social Protection (%)*[b]	*Internet Use (Percentage of Population), 2021*[c]	*Fixed Broadband Subscriptions (per Hundred People), 2021*[d]
Cambodia	89.4 (2019)	3.1 (2013)	60.15	2.03
Myanmar	81.0 (2020)	13.8 (2017)	44.02	1.66
Laos	88.8 (2017)	2.2 (2018)	62.00	2.03
Philippines	62.8 (2018)	40.6 (2015)	52.68	8.45
Vietnam	68.6 (2022)	34.9 (2014)	74.21	19.83
Indonesia	80.2 (2022)	44.6 (2019)	62.10	4.54
Thailand	65.0 (2018)	71.9 (2018)	85.27	17.35
Malaysia	8.3 (2019)	76.7 (2016)	96.75	11.12
Brunei	31.0 (2021)	—	98.08	17.83
Singapore	—	—	91.10	25.69

Notes:
a. Informal employment as defined by country;
b. percentage of population participating in social insurance, social safety net, unemployment benefits and active labour market programmes. Estimates include both direct and indirect beneficiaries.
Sources:
a. Department of Statistics Malaysia. 2020; all other countries: ILOSTAT's compilations from national labour force surveys;
b, c, d. World Bank's World Development Indicators at https://databank.worldbank.org/source/world-development-indicators (accessed 22 May 2023).

TABLE 1.5
Southeast Asian Countries (Lowest to Highest GDP per Capita): Indicators of Democracy and Governance

	V-Dem Electoral Democracy Index Ranking (2022)[a]	*Worldwide Governance Indicators (2021) Percentile*[b]		
		Political Stability[c]	*Government Effectiveness*	*Control of Corruption*
Cambodia	146	43.9	36.1	11.5
Myanmar	173	4.7	8.7	15.9
Laos	167	69.8	30.3	15.4
Philippines	100	17.0	57.7	34.1
Vietnam	161	44.8	62.0	47.1
Indonesia	74	27.8	65.4	38.5
Thailand	147	27.4	60.6	35.1
Malaysia	97	50.9	81.3	61.1
Brunei	–	92.9	91.4	86.1
Singapore	101	97.6	100.0	98.6

Notes:
a. 179 countries ranked;
b. figures indicate the country performs better than *x* per cent of the total countries surveyed;
c. political stability and absence of violence.
Sources. V-Dem Institute (2023), World Bank's Worldwide Governance Indicators at http://info.worldbank.org/governance/wgi/Home/Reports (accessed 24 May 2023).

such as vaccination—with less resistance from citizens, but they may also be less responsive to popular issues and grievances compared to democratic systems. In view of the lesser data access and fewer research resources to investigate specific questions, the country studies of Cambodia, Laos and Myanmar in this project provide an overview of the pandemic impacts and responses. This project was, however, also able to incorporate findings of a survey conducted in Cambodia and Laos.

Southeast Asia's most populous countries—Indonesia, the Philippines and Vietnam—faced pandemic management challenges arising from their demographic conditions, with the added features of archipelagic geography in Indonesia and the Philippines (Table 1.3). This project thus grouped the three under the theme of managing and mismanaging the pandemic, with a focus on mobility restrictions and efforts to curb contagion. This assignment of subject and country case studies also aimed to juxtapose the differing strategies that had already emerged in the first year of the pandemic. The

Philippines' stricter and longer lockdown contrasted starkly with Vietnam's policy of refraining from extensive lockdowns in 2020, while Indonesia's approach was somewhere in between. Vietnam's high levels of internet access and exceptionally high broadband subscription rate also suggested that the country's digital infrastructure potentially enabled effective contact tracing and compiling and disseminating information—possibilities that were worth investigating (Table 1.4).

The extensive coordination required in national pandemic management warranted a specific investigation. Covid-19 coordination encompassed two dimensions. Horizontally, government departments in different domains—especially those overseeing finance, health, industry, education and labour—had to align their information, communication and actions. Vertically, national and subnational governments had to interact and cooperate in new ways to align interventions at the central and local levels. The geographic and political diversity of Southeast Asia translates into potentially insightful cross-country variations in coordination.

Indonesia, Malaysia and Thailand were chosen as case studies for exploring the theme of horizontal and vertical coordination. The more decentralized structures of Indonesia and Malaysia, and the centralized polity of Thailand, have shaped policy coordination horizontally between agencies and vertically between national and subnational governments. While perception of government effectiveness was not a criterion for selecting the three countries, it is notable that all register similar World Governance Indicator scores (Table 1.5). As the three country chapters took shape, mobility restrictions, economic stimulus and vaccination emerged as the more salient areas of coordination to be researched. The chapters also consider communication, among government agencies and layers of administration as well as between authorities and the public, and evaluate the clarity and consistency of government conduct in these respects.

Mobility restrictions and economic shutdowns were imposed by fiat and far exceeded the magnitude of those put in place during past epidemics. It should be noted that nothing has remotely come close to Covid-19, but Southeast Asia can claim some experience in containing deadly flu outbreaks, most obviously in the mid-2000s with SARS, avian flu and the Nipah virus. The Asian financial crisis of 1997–98, which triggered massive economic contraction across the region, also exposed deficiencies in the provision of economic relief and social assistance that have since been significantly addressed through the expansion of social protection. The global financial crisis of 2008–9, which did not cause economic recession in all Southeast Asian countries, nonetheless prompted actions such as job protection schemes in Singapore.

A fourth theme is the design and implementation of economic relief and stimulus measures. The selection process settled on the countries with abundant financial resources and comparatively developed institutions: Singapore, Malaysia and Thailand. The development levels of Singapore, a high-income economy, and upper-middle-income Malaysia and Thailand (Table 1.3), clearly correspond with lower informality and greater social protection outreach (Table 1.5), and the countries are also well regarded for government effectiveness. At the same time, the greater proportion of services employment possibly augmented the proportion impacted by lockdowns, given the sector suffered relatively greater impacts from restrictions on both domestic mobility and cross-border travel. The economic relief and stimulus measures in Singapore, Malaysia and Thailand were conspicuously extensive and responsive. Research findings enable us to synthesize the three countries' policy priorities and approaches and their achievements and shortcomings, which show striking similarities and differences. The focus of public measures has predominantly operated through the formal economy, although interventions such as household cash transfers can also be extended to the informally employed.

The project was rounded out with regionwide perspectives and an effort to conduct research spanning all countries. As the regional platform of multilateral cooperation, ASEAN's initiatives warranted some attention. The opportunities and challenges surrounding vaccination, which was key to reopening and recovery, also merited in-depth coverage. These issues merged in this volume's fifth thematic group, country-level and ASEAN experiences of vaccination and reopening.

Vaccine procurement and ASEAN's Covid-19 interventions took place behind the scenes, but yield important lessons. All countries sourced vaccines from multiple countries, and encountered constraints to varying extents, as well as domestic challenges in roll-out and public participation. By mid-2022, when vaccination figures were publicized by all countries, six out of the ten ASEAN member states had vaccinated more than 70 per cent of the population, the minimum threshold recommended by the World Health Organization. Combatting the coronavirus, a borderless menace, clearly could have benefited from regional coordination. ASEAN's efforts in this regard are notable, albeit constrained by levels of funding and participation. While the vaccine procurement of the regional bloc amounted to a fraction of total vaccine requirements, and its travel corridor initiative was not implemented, the experience suggests there is potential for more effective responses.

LIMITATIONS AND CONTRIBUTIONS

We should reiterate that this project has focused on economic impacts and public policy implications of Covid-19. Issues related to the medical profession and epidemiology, while fundamental, lie beyond our scope. Within our social science ambit, we also provide limited coverage of the psychological and educational ramifications of the pandemic.

We have placed more emphasis on retrospective and rigorous analyses to address particular thematic questions. Accordingly, the chapters provide focused and contextualized answers, rather than prescriptions on the question of whether to impose lockdowns or not, or formulas on the right mix of protecting health and protecting the economy. This book shows the uniqueness of Covid-19 and of each country's experience in handling the crisis, which underscore that the next one will surely have unique features that demand a measured and circumspect approach when drawing lessons from 2020–22.

While we assigned a thematic focus to the country chapters, each can be read on its own and particular insights will stand out for each reader. At the same time, we have endeavoured to collate and extract comparative lessons, in the form of synthesis essays appended to the back of each thematic group. Those essays offer specific insights and are concise enough that we can direct readers there rather than provide summaries here.

Nonetheless, we conclude this opening chapter with a few general remarks. The Covid-19 experience offers vast lessons on preparedness for future pandemics that may again require coordinated public health, security and economic responses. In grappling with Covid-19, the world gravitated towards lockdowns and social distancing in a climate of uncertainty and in view of the unprecedented magnitude of the threat. The next pandemic will assuredly have its own confounding elements, but the experience of 2020–22 offers immense insight for balancing efforts to contain deadly contagion while keeping the economy running. To cushion the socio-economic fallout of future financial crises or severe recessions, countries can also draw lessons from the relief and stimulus measures rolled out in 2020–22. The pandemic experience should spur further discussion on the Covid-19 responses that should be recorded as ad hoc, one-off interventions and those that should be institutionalized. Some protocols or special programmes could also be placed on standby, to be activated when crises strike.

Notably, growth in the digital economy accelerated during the pandemic, as applications were deployed to trace contacts, disseminate information, deliver retail goods and services, and disburse social assistance. Further expansion and advancements will surely continue, with the promise of new growth engines and increased access to finance and ease of transactions. However, governments must be vigilant in regulating the sector and checking against monopolistic behaviour to safeguard personal privacy and the public interest.

The pandemic has also highlighted systemic issues that are interwoven throughout the chapters of this book. A robust, nimble and well-resourced public healthcare system is crucial to meeting the challenges of a public health crisis. The importance of maintaining the education system must be underscored. Learning disruptions due to missed school days or migration to online platforms that educators are ill-equipped for and households unable to use, due to lack of computing devices or inadequate internet connection, can have long-term consequences on children's development. The injection of fiscal spending and stimulus measures also depends on stable macroeconomic management and government capacity to run deficits or draw on reserves, along with responsive governance that is attuned to the needs of vulnerable communities. The pandemic's prolonged scarring effects, notably in exacerbating inequality and compounding socio-economic disadvantage, may not yet be fully apparent and warrant further research. However, there is ample evidence that the disadvantaged and vulnerable have borne greater and more lasting harm. The Covid-19 pandemic has highlighted the need for societal and policy resets, and reaffirmed the imperative of economic justice and equitable distribution.

Note

1. The authors thank ISEAS interns Hafiz Nasruddin and Koh Jun Ming for compiling news articles and data, and Ang Tze Xin for designing Figures 1.1 and 1.2.

References

Aslam, Mohd Mizan, and Rohan Gunaratna, eds. 2022. *COVID-19 in South, West, and Southeast Asia: Risk and Response in the Early Phase.* London: Routledge.

Coxhead, Ian, ed. 2018. *Routledge Handbook of Southeast Asian Economics.* Abingdon and New York: Routledge.

Croissant, Aurel, and Philip Lorenz. 2018. *Comparative Politics of Southeast Asia: An Introduction to Governments and Political Regimes*. Cham: Springer.

Department of Statistics Malaysia. 2020. *Informal Sector Work Force Survey Report 2019.* Putrajaya: Department of Statistics Malaysia.

Indrawati, Sri Mulyani, Suahasil Nazara, Titik Anas, Candra Fajri Ananda, and Kiki Verico, eds. 2023. *Keeping Indonesia Safe from the COVID-19 Pandemic: Lessons Learnt from the National Economic Recovery Programme.* Singapore: ISEAS – Yusof Ishak Institute.

Lewis, Blane D., and Firman Witoelar, eds. 2021. *Economic Dimensions of Covid-19 in Indonesia: Responding to the Crisis*. Singapore: ISEAS – Yusof Ishak Institute.

Lim, Weng Mar, Surinderpal Kaur, and Huey Fen Cheong, eds. 2021. *COVID-19, Business, and Economy in Malaysia: Retrospective and Prospective Perspectives*. London: Routledge.

Louis, D. Gerard Joseph, Surinderpal Kaur, and Huey Fen Cheong, eds. 2021. *COVID-19 and Psychology in Malaysia: Psychosocial Effects, Coping, and Resilience*. London: Routledge.

Pandian, Ambigapathy, Surinderpal Kaur, and Huey Fen Cheong, eds. 2021. *COVID-19, Education, and Literacy in Malaysia: Social Contexts of Teaching and Learning*. London: Routledge.

Sciortino, Rosalia, ed. 2023. *Who Cares?: COVID-19 Social Protection Response in Southeast Asia*. Chiangmai: Silkworm Books.

Shin, Hyun Bang, Murray McKenzie, and Do Young Oh, eds. 2022. *COVID-19 in Southeast Asia: Insights for a Post-Pandemic World.* London: LSE Press.

Tan, Kevin S.Y. and Steve K.L. Chan, eds. 2023. *Populations and Precarity during the COVID-19 Pandemic: Southeast Asian Perspectives.* Singapore: ISEAS – Yusof Ishak Institute.

V-Dem Institute (Varieties of Democracy Institute). 2023. *Democracy Report 2023: Defiance in the Face of Autocratization.* V-Dem Institute, University of Gothenburg.

Yee Sin Leo and Paul Tambyah, eds. 2022. *Covid-19 Pandemic in Singapore.* Singapore: World Scientific.

Theme 1

COVID-19 IN THE TRANSITION ECONOMIES

Cambodia, Laos, Myanmar

2

CAMBODIA'S COVID-19 IMPACTS AND ECONOMIC RECOVERY PATHWAYS

Aspects and Perspectives[1]

Teng Delux and Pen Socheata

INTRODUCTION

Covid-19 wreaked suffering and death on millions across the world and, by 19 December 2022, it had infected 138,438 people in Cambodia and claimed 3,056 lives in the country (Ministry of Health 2022). The pandemic, a public health crisis that precipitated economic shocks, negatively affected economies around the world, triggering a significant decline in earnings and output and pushing millions into extreme poverty. Cambodia's economy was heavily affected by the pandemic, and the number of people living below the poverty line increased; around 4.5 million people remain near-poor and are vulnerable to falling into poverty when exposed to economic and other external shocks (World Bank n.d.). The tourism, garment and construction sectors, which together account for more than 70 per cent of Cambodia's economic growth and employ nearly 40 per cent of the workforce, suffered staggering job losses (Kunmakara 2020). At the onset of the pandemic, it was estimated that poverty could increase between 3 and 11 percentage points in the event of a 50 per cent income loss that lasted six months for households engaged in those sectors (World Bank 2020).

Not surprisingly, Cambodia was severely hit by health and economic crises arising from the pandemic. The country was under-equipped to contain viral infections due to the lack of public and private funding and its limited healthcare system and thus imposed a strict and extended lockdown from April to August 2021. Economic growth turned negative, registering −3.1 per cent in 2020, the first contraction after three decades of continuous expansion (World Bank 2021a). Covid-19 disrupted Cambodia's growth trajectory and also threatened its competitiveness and the well-being of its people.

The Cambodian government introduced various public health and social protection measures to support households and workers in need, and through 2022 continued to implement fiscal, monetary and policy responses to sustain the country's economic recovery. Complementing the Covid-19 containment policies and social assistance, the vaccination roll-out played a significant role in mitigating Covid-19 impacts. The country registered fifty-two days of zero Covid-19 cases in the first half of 2022, followed by a slight re-emergence of nineteen cases in late June 2022 (Yalirozy 2022). By 8 July 2022, 14.4 million Cambodians had received two doses of the vaccine, accounting for 86.8 per cent of the Cambodian population (Our World in Data n.d.). The Asian Development Bank (2022b) praised Cambodia for its successful vaccination roll-out and acknowledged its strong political leadership and its rapid purchase, distribution and deployment of vaccines as the driving factors for the success. Additionally, in 2021, Cambodia's readiness for emergencies, as evaluated by the Operational Readiness Index,[2] increased by 10 percentage points from only 42 per cent in 2018 (ADB 2021, p. 4). The government's quick roll-out of vaccinations contributed to its ability to reopen the country. Normal economic activities resumed on 1 November 2021, bolstering the post-pandemic recovery pathway.

The purpose of this chapter—which details a survey of experts and policymakers conducted from April to June 2021, and June to August 2022—was to examine the impact of Covid-19 in Cambodia and identify the economic recovery pathways. We set out two objectives: (1) to identify risks the economy faced due to the pandemic and the responses of the government, private sector and other stakeholders to mitigate them and (2) to seek opinions from experts on the state of recovery of Cambodia's economy from the pandemic.

The study generated four main findings. First, Cambodia is expected to return to pre-pandemic economic growth later than 2024, not only because of ongoing Covid-19 impacts but also due to global inflation exacerbated by the Russia–Ukraine war. Cambodia's industrial sectors, especially the manufacturing of high value-added products, remain the priority for economic recovery, followed by tourism and agriculture. Second, government interventions have been effective, but Cambodia needs to develop an identification system that effectively locates excluded and disadvantaged people. It also needs to enhance the public health system. Third, the country faces risks from weakened growth in trading partners (the United States and European Union), the ongoing household debt crisis and global energy inflation due to the Russia–Ukraine war. Fourth, an inclusive and sustainable Covid-19 recovery relies on social protection policies, notably cash transfers, that effectively target beneficiaries, and other policies such as tax relief, loan restructuring and low-interest loans. In addition, Cambodia must also prioritize long term policies, including diversification of the economy, particularly into agribusiness and industries other than garments and textiles, and encourage technology adoption.

CAMBODIA'S COVID-19 IMPACT AND RESPONSE

On 28 January 2020, Cambodia confirmed its first case of Covid-19 in a Chinese tourist visiting Sihanoukville. However, the government believed the virus situation was controllable and therefore allowed a cruise ship stranded at sea to dock in Cambodia on 11 February 2020 after it had been turned away by four countries (Thailand, Taiwan, Japan and the Philippines). Cambodia arguably managed the pandemic well during 2020 by introducing public health measures including safety standards and protocols, vaccination campaigns and restrictions on mass gatherings and all state-organized events, alongside efficient fiscal and monetary measures such as the cash relief programme. Cambodia experienced different waves of Covid-19 infection, including one prolonged community spread in early 2021, known as the "February 20 incident". The disease quickly spread across the country, triggering school closures, lockdowns and other measures to slow the virus transmission.

For most of 2021, Cambodia had its hands full dealing with increased cases and deaths, a race between the vaccine and the virus. Between April to August 2021, a high infection rate continued, triggered by 1,919 cases of migrant returnees who arrived home with the Delta variant, in addition to cases among domestic healthcare workers and community infections (ADB n.d. a). The cumulative case count increased from 13,402 in April 2021 to 93,055 in August 2021; daily cases reached a maximum of 1,130 (67.39 per million) on 30 June 2021. The numbers were possibly related to the mass testing policy, which recorded 1.36 million tests (81.88 per 1,000 people) cumulatively by 30 June 2021. The cumulative deaths increased from 11 people (0.66 per million) on 31 March 2021 to 1,397 people (83.31 per million) by 31 July 2021, which was higher than the world average (Figure 2.1).

A series of infection waves continued to impact different sectors that had contributed significantly to Cambodia's economy before the pandemic. During the pandemic, the lockdown, social distancing, travel and shipping restrictions and disruptions to the supply chain triggered a substantial decline in earnings and outputs and displaced 100 million people from the global labour market (ILO 2020a, 2020b). While countries adopted policy measures with unprecedented speed and scope, the *ILO Monitor* (ILO 2020a, 2020b) highlighted some key challenges: finding the right balance of interventions (health, economic and social policies) to produce optimal sustainable labour market outcomes; implementing and sustaining policy interventions at the necessary scale when resources are likely to be increasingly constrained; protecting and promoting the working conditions of vulnerable, disadvantaged and hard-hit groups to make labour markets fairer and more equitable; securing international solidarity and support, especially for emerging and developing countries; and strengthening social dialogue and respect for rights.

FIGURE 2.1
Cambodia's Daily New Covid-19 Cases and New Deaths

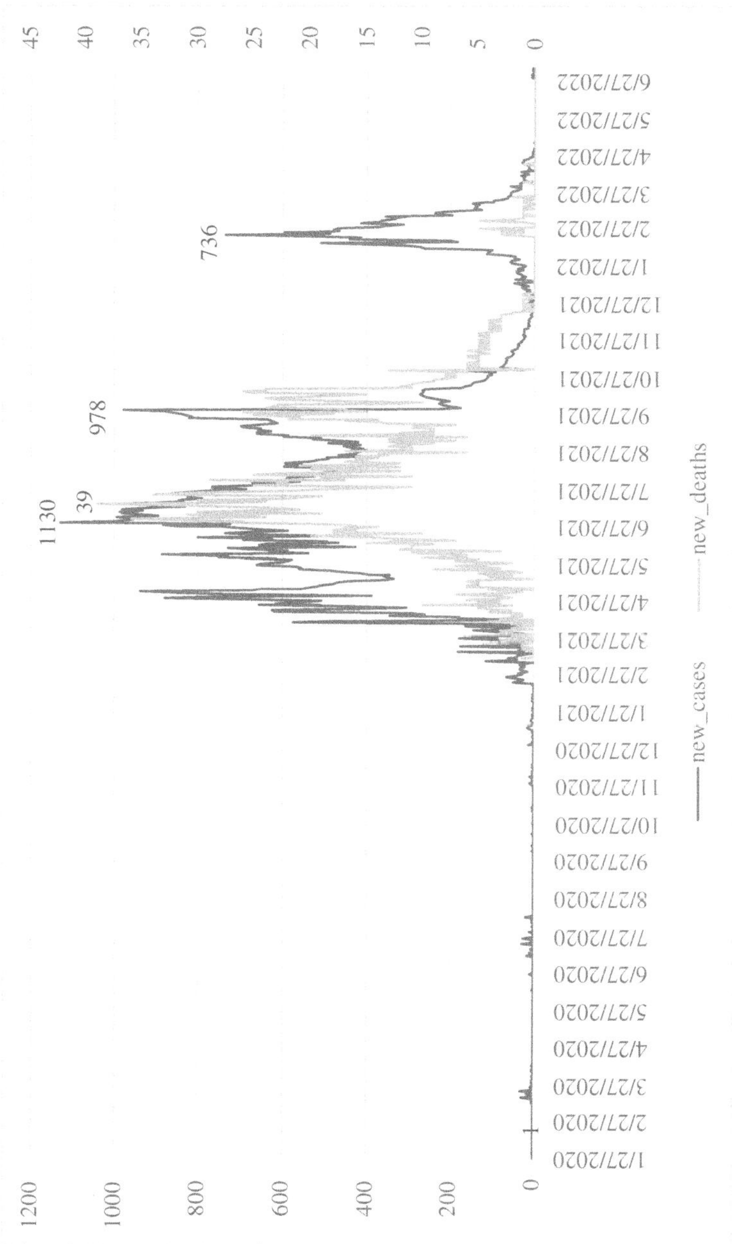

Source: Our World in Data (n.d.).

COVID-19 IMPACTS ON SOCIO-ECONOMIC DEVELOPMENT

The global economy entered 2022 in a weaker position than had been expected. As the new Omicron variant spread and the Russia–Ukraine war escalated, countries reimposed mobility restrictions and faced higher inflation. The Covid-19 pandemic had unprecedented social, political and economic effects on the economies of developed and developing countries. The impact was also disproportionately distributed across countries, with small and low-income countries facing more severe consequences given their weak health systems, limited fiscal and monetary policy options and relatively strong reliance on external trade.

Cambodia's economy has experienced structural change in the past two decades (NIS 2022; ADB n.d. b). The impact of Covid-19 is broadly reflected in changes in sectoral composition in 2020. Services have since 2000 contributed the largest share to gross domestic product (GDP), although the share of agriculture has in some years inched closely to that of services. From 2011, Cambodia's industrial sector experienced sustained growth; its share of GDP surpassed agriculture in 2015 and is approaching that of services (Figure 2.2). Agriculture, formerly the dominant sector, has generally become proportionately less significant, with its production share dipping below one-quarter of national output since 2017. There was a slight reversal of this trend in 2020, when the share of agriculture increased from 22.1 per cent in 2019 to 24.4 per cent in 2020, while the share of industry also increased but by a much slighter margin (36.5 per cent to 37.0 per cent). The decline in the share of services, from 41.4 per cent to 38.6 per cent, captures the reality that service activities bore the heaviest consequences of the Covid-19 restrictions (Figure 2.3). According to the Ministry of Economy and Finance (MEF 2022a), Cambodia's growth was expected to recover in 2021 at a low rate of 3.0 per cent supported by economic intervention measures and the recovery of industry (7.4 per cent) and agriculture (1.1 per cent), while the service sector, especially the hotel and restaurant sectors, continued a downward trend, with negative growth of −0.4 per cent. The Ministry of Economy and Finance projected GDP growth in 2024 at 6.6 per cent, supported by growth in industry (8.5 per cent), agriculture (1.1 per cent) and services (6.9 per cent) (MEF 2024).

FIGURE 2.2
Cambodia's Economic Output (Percentage of GDP at Current Basic Prices)

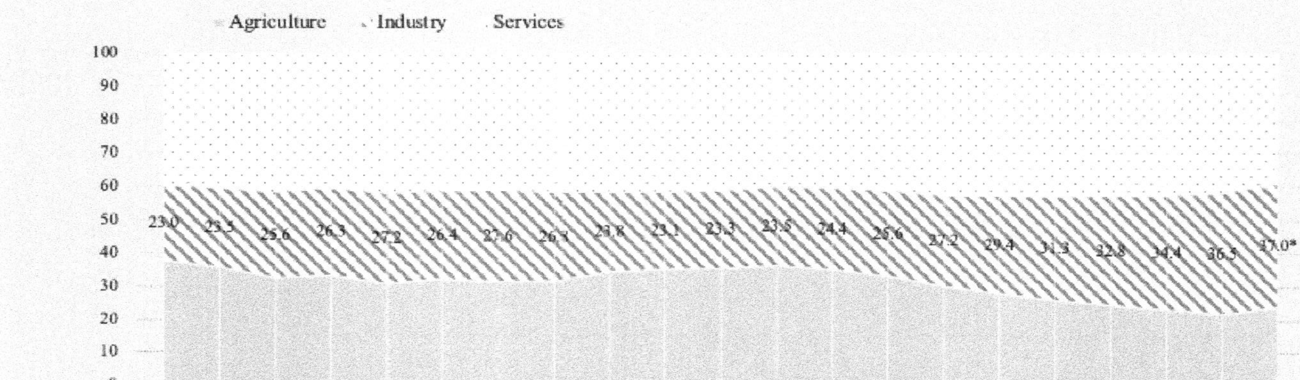

	2000	2001	2002	2003	2004	2005	2006	2007	2008	2009	2010	2011	2012	2013	2014	2015	2016	2017	2018	2019	2020
Services	39.1	40.4	41.5	40.1	41.7	41.2	40.8	41.3	41.3	41.3	40.7	39.8	40.1	40.9	42.2	42.3	42.4	42.3	42.1	41.4	38.6*
Industry	23.0	23.5	25.6	26.3	27.2	26.4	27.6	26.8	23.8	23.1	23.3	23.5	24.4	25.6	27.2	29.4	31.3	32.8	34.4	36.5	37.0*
Agriculture	37.8	36.1	32.9	33.6	31.2	32.4	31.7	31.9	34.9	35.7	36.0	36.7	35.6	33.6	30.7	28.2	26.3	24.9	23.5	22.1	24.4*

Sources: NIS (n.d.) and ADB (2021a).

FIGURE 2.3
Growth of Cambodia's Economic Output by Sector, 2000–20 (Percentage Annual Change)

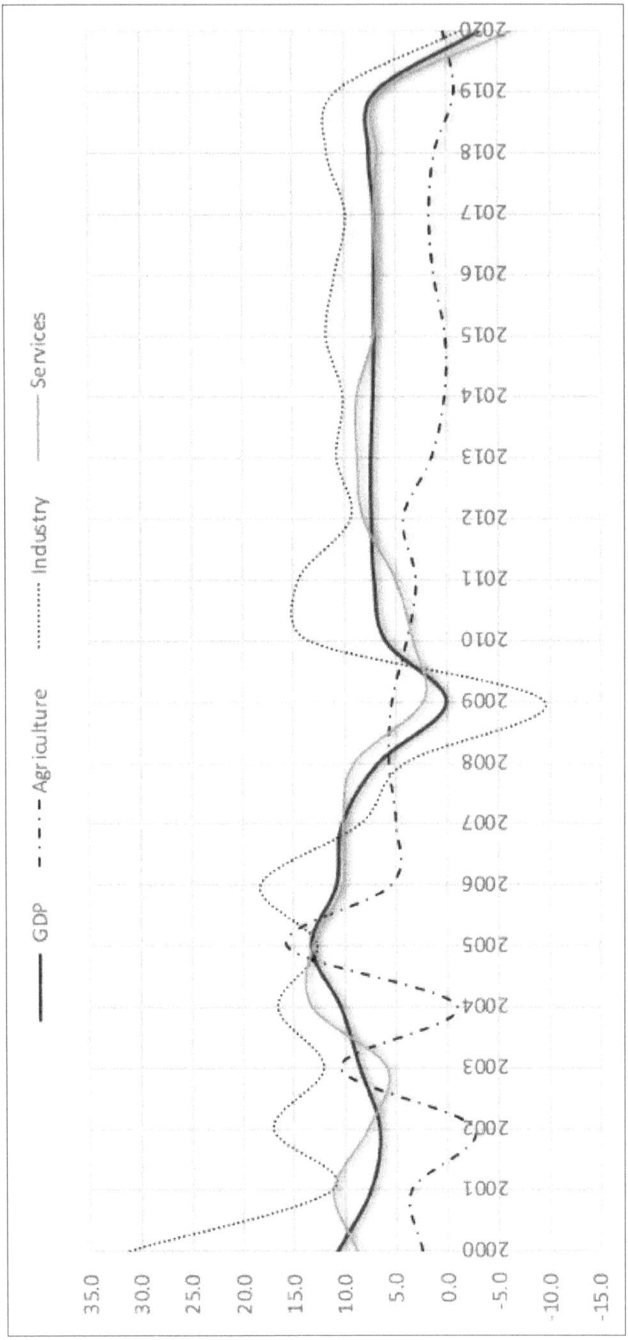

Sources: NIS (n.d.) and ADB (2021a).

Cambodia's economy registered negative growth in 2020 (–3.1 per cent), with tourism, manufacturing and construction especially affected.[3] The tourism sector suffered the biggest contraction, as international arrivals plunged over 90 per cent in 2021 due to the halt in most international travel. A collapse in revenue at up to 3,000 businesses resulting from the suspension of operations caused 45,000 people to lose their jobs (Kunmakara 2020). In 2021, factory closures and logistics disruptions reduced exports from the garment sector by 6.5 per cent. Internal and external demand dropped significantly as consumers stayed at home, stores closed, and orders were cancelled, especially those from the European Union. These factors significantly affected the manufacturing industry in Cambodia, which relies on an export-led growth model. Lastly, the informal sector experienced a huge loss of income due to the pandemic (Kunmakara 2020). Despite the critical Covid-19 impact on other sectors, the agriculture sector remained positive. However, risks from weakened growth in trading partners (the United States and European Union), a household debt crisis and global energy inflation were the other major constraints to economic recovery.

In Cambodia, the most significant impacts of the pandemic were those on employment and income, and households' coping strategies, although these are areas of limited research. Among the resources is a report from the United Nations Children's Fund and partners (UNICEF et al. 2021), which drew on six rounds of a survey (carried out from August 2020 to March 2021) and informed the employment and income discussion of this chapter. In August 2020, the survey found that around 10 per cent of workers had obtained a job since the beginning of the pandemic, but 18 per cent of workers had lost their jobs, while 33 per cent had enjoyed a wage increase compared to 50 per cent suffering a wage reduction. Wage precarity worsened in late 2020, with around 80 per cent reporting income reduction in October 2020. The adverse impact continued into 2021: in March 2021, 68 per cent of workers reported wage reductions, in part due to Covid-19 outbreaks in the wake of the February 20 incident. In general, coping strategies revolved around two main options: selling goods and assets and borrowing money. Expectedly, but still concerning nonetheless, poor households were more likely to borrow for emergency needs and for consumption rather than for investment. Gender impacts are also worth mentioning. In the Mekong Subregion, the formal garment sector and informal sectors are female-dominated and vulnerable as both come with fewer social benefits. When restrictions on movement were imposed, women more acutely struggled to meet basic needs, faced mental deterioration, experienced gender-based violence and were burdened with more caring duties in households than men (CARE, UN Women and UNICEF 2020).

POLICY MEASURES AND RESPONSES

From January 2020 to December 2021, Cambodia implemented around 2,200 policy responses.[4] Efforts to contain the spread of the virus took the form of highly stringent measures, such as closing the border with importing countries and imposing strict quarantine in provincial areas near borders (ADB 2022b). The restrictions began in early 2020: the government closed schools, universities, bars, karaoke and night clubs; limited mass gatherings; cancelled public holidays including the Khmer New Year and the water festival; enforced social distancing and sanitation measures; introduced new lockdown measures by defining red zones, orange zones and yellow zones and applying different levels of restrictions; and closed borders with neighbouring countries to prevent the spread of the new Covid-19 variants. A curfew was imposed on all non-essential travel within Phnom Penh in April 2021. On 4 June 2021, the Ministry of Health announced it would improve medical infrastructure and medical waste management to curb the spread of Covid-19.

Opinions on the implementation of containment policies are divided. Bunthea et al. (2022) argued that the measures in the containment policies were harsh, giving a punishment of up to three years' imprisonment for anyone breaking a curfew and twenty years' imprisonment for those breaking the rules applicable in their particular zone. Besides the negative impacts of the containment measures, Bunthea et al. (2022) also praised the measures for preventing Covid-19 from having a significant impact on vulnerable groups in 2020. Dahles (2022) supports the government's policy responses and praises the containment mechanisms as a path towards recovery.

Cambodia's government rolled out various measures to deal with the economic impacts of Covid-19; these included public health initiatives, a vaccination campaign and pragmatic economic policies. The measures supported economic recovery, helping GDP growth to rebound to a positive 3 per cent in 2021 and 5.2 per cent in 2022 and is forecast at 5.6 per cent in 2023 and 6.6 per cent in 2024, boosted by an increase in merchandise exports and foreign direct investment (ADB n.d; MEF 2024). At the end of the third quarter of 2022, Cambodia's total public debt stock was US$9.47 billion or 24.9 per cent of GDP, which was "sustainable" and at "low risk" of causing debt distress (MEF 2022b). Challenges remained; the economy's slow recovery in 2022 was expected to extend beyond the year and a return to pre-pandemic growth rates was expected to be stalled by global uncertainty, mainly due to global energy inflation, the weakened growth of trade partners (the United States and European Union) and a household debt crisis (Kang 2022). The International Monetary Fund (IMF 2022) also highlighted risks associated with private debt. For several years, credit growth has outpaced nominal GDP growth. As a result, outstanding private sector credit reached 170 per cent of GDP by the end of 2021, much higher than the ratios in other economies in the region, while restructured loans were expected to reach around 13 per cent of GDP in June 2022, and non-performing loans had soared to about 4.5 per cent of GDP in 2022.

The World Bank and ADB also underlined risks linked to the global economy. In particular, the United States and the European Union projected a 2022 slowdown that would adversely affect Cambodia's export-oriented manufacturing sectors. The zero-Covid policy and the 2022 structural slowdown in China, Cambodia's main source of foreign direct investment, are also projected to limit investment. With regard to Cambodia's competitiveness, the need for export diversification and progress beyond the country's labour-intensive and low value-added export model requires policies that boost firm and worker productivity and harness domestic investment, and that also reduce the reliance on foreign direct investment (World Bank 2021b, 2022; ADB 2022a).

In December 2021, as part of post-pandemic economic recovery efforts, the Cambodian government launched a strategic policy with programmes to promote economic recovery for the next two years. The policy focused on recovery, reform and resilience. First, regarding recovery, the government focused on solving structural issues, normalizing socio-economic activities and stabilizing macroeconomic and work conditions for employers and employees. The top four top-priority sectors were agriculture and agro-industry, tourism, garment manufacturing and non-garment manufacturing (Royal Government of Cambodia 2021). Policy measures, roadmaps, strategic plans and strategies were created to facilitate the recovery effort in each sector. In the tourism sector, three main documents facilitated the recovery phases: (1) a Roadmap for the Recovery of Cambodia Tourism During and Post Covid-19, (2) Policy Measures to Encourage Local Tourism 2021–2023 and (3) a Strategic Plan for Vaccination Tourism. In the garment sector, a fundamental document remains the Cambodia Garment, Footwear, and Travel Goods Sector Development Strategy 2022–27; the aim is to develop resiliency in this sector with high-added-value products and competition.

Second, in the reform elements of the strategic policy, the government focuses on reforming trade and investment, including regulations and enforcement, to maximize trade benefits that contribute to economic growth, diversification and competitiveness. Third, to build resilience, the government aims to prepare and create a sustainable and inclusive socio-economic environment through social protection, a green economy, human development and productivity, development of small and medium-sized enterprises (SMEs), and climate change resilience (Royal Government of Cambodia 2021).

FISCAL AND MONETARY RESPONSES

As of May 2021, the Cambodian government had allocated a package worth US$60 million for virus testing, containment and treatment and US$762 million for social assistance funding. The latter comprised US$502 million for a new monthly cash transfer programme for poor and vulnerable households and US$260 million cash for a work programme to absorb workers who had lost employment in factories/enterprises abroad and had returned home. This would support the workers and also bring about socio-economic achievements through the construction of small-scale physical infrastructure to support agriculture and the broader economy. The Cambodian government also provided targeted financial support of US$40 per month for each worker occupied in the garment/textile, footwear, travel accessories and bags sectors, and in tourism (e.g., hotels, guesthouses, restaurants and travel agents) from January to March 2021. The government spent US$123 million on wage subsidies and training programmes for the unemployed and for those who had been suspended from work in the garments sector and tourism. Tax relief measures worth around US$200 million were introduced (IMF n.d.). The government allocated US$600 million in one batch of support: low-interest loans to certain banks (US$200 million in the Credit Guarantee Fund and US$270 million in the Additional Financing Facility) and packages to SMEs in manufacturing (US$50 million) and agriculture (US$80 million). Financial institutions in Cambodia had restructured some US$4.2 billion in loans for 285,074 borrowers as of 31 December 2020. In the first half of 2021, Cambodian banking and financial institutions restructured US$5.5 billion in loans for 367,239 borrowers (IMF n.d.).

Over US$3 billion has been spent by Cambodia to address the social and economic impacts of the Covid-19 crisis. In a macroeconomic policy framework and public financial policy created in preparation for a draft report on the 2023 Law on Financial Management, the Ministry of Economy and Finance stated that US$824 million and US$1.29 billion were spent in 2020 and 2021, respectively, and an additional US$989 million was allocated to implement the intervention measures in 2022 (Kunmakara 2022).

SOCIAL PROTECTION AND POLICY RESPONSES

The Cambodian government has paid very close attention to social protection programmes under its National Social Protection Policy Framework 2016–25, which focuses on social assistance and social security. Covid-19 and its impacts shone the spotlight on Cambodia's nascent social protection, raising awareness that some programmes needed to be extended or expanded in the post-pandemic era. The IDPoor system was created before the Covid-19 pandemic to identify poor households and reach them through governmental and non-government organizations.[5] The government had also introduced the Equity Card, which entitles holders to three main benefits: (1) healthcare support under the Health Equity Fund, (2) cash transfers for children and poor pregnant women and

(3) scholarships for primary and secondary students (Theng, Cerceau and de Riel 2021). The National Social Protection Policy Framework was launched in 2017 to better integrate social security and social assistance (ibid.). During the pandemic, the IDPoor system was designated as a mechanism through which to provide social assistance offered under the National Social Protection Policy Framework. The Ministry of Planning identified the beneficiaries, and the Ministry of Social Affairs, Veterans and Youth Rehabilitation facilitated the registration of beneficiaries, calculation of benefits and provided the payments (Ministry of Planning 2020).

Cambodia implemented several rounds of relief and stimulus packages, commencing July 2020. Among the measures were cash transfers to around 700,000 of Cambodia's 2.8 million in the IDPoor scheme (UNDP 2022, p. 24). By end-June 2022, US$714.9 million had been provided in cash handouts (Dara 2022). Overall, Covid-19 social protection responses were estimated to have benefited all 2.8 million IDPoor households over two years, with 108,000 households given support post-lockdown. Further, as of February 2022, Cambodia had provided cash transfers to an additional 5,576 laid-off workers who did not qualify for protection under the IDPoor scheme.

The major driving forces for the successful expansion of cash transfers were the accelerated methods of identifying IDPoor households at the commune level, with major support from the United Nations Development Programme, the United Nations Children's Fund (UNICEF) and the German Agency for International Cooperation (GIZ). The latter, on behalf of the German and Australian governments, provided 1,700 tablets to the Cambodian Ministry of Planning in order to expedite the IDPoor programme and enable it to conduct mobile, online registration (Sopheavatey 2020). Therefore, the government was able to swiftly identify the new Covid-19-impacted households (Theng, Cerceau and de Riel 2021). On the beneficiary side, the Garment Workers Survey (2021), with 2,000 respondents, found that government support programmes were the third most common coping mechanism for garment workers to mitigate Covid-19 impacts and stay afloat (Bossba and Socheata 2022; Roth and Bossba 2023). Given the continuing economic vulnerabilities, social protection must continue to be prioritized.

VACCINATION CAMPAIGN

Cambodia's vaccination campaign started in early 2021 with donations of 600,000 Sinopharm vaccines from China and nearly 1.3 million doses of the AstraZeneca vaccine through the Covid-19 Vaccines Global Access (COVAX) initiative (Badzmierowski 2021). In February 2021, the Ministry of Health authorized the emergency use of these vaccines. The first Covid-19 vaccination drive began in February 2021 and the campaign for second doses started in April 2021. By 8 July 2022, the total Covid-19 vaccine doses administered per hundred of the global population reached 154.24, while Cambodia was at 249.42 doses, compared to only 4.05 on 1 April 2021 and 43.71 on 30 June 2021. Ninety-one per cent of the population (15.1 million people) had received at least one dose, while 14.4 million people had received two. The figure for administered booster doses, at 57.4 per 100 persons, was double the world average (Figure 2.4).

The vaccination campaign accelerated through 2021 as the government leveraged bilateral ties to secure additional vaccine supplies from different sources. Of the total vaccines administered, Sinovac accounted for 60 per cent, Sinopharm 18 per cent, AstraZeneca 11 per cent, Pfizer 8 per cent, Moderna 2 per cent and Janssen 1 per cent (Figure 2.5). By 14 August 2022, vaccination progress for the adult population (≥18 years) of ten million was ahead of the target at 103.5 per cent, with marked progress in the children and youth populations as well. For young people aged twelve to eighteen, the government was at 100.91 per of its target, for children aged six to twelve the figure was 109.81 per cent, for five-year-old children, 137.56 per cent, and for children aged three to five it was 74.06 per cent. Clear public communication, a rapid expansion of vaccinations to include younger children and providing vaccinations at strategic locations all contributed to a quick roll-out. By 14 August 2022, about 7.78 million people had received a fourth dose, and more than half a million a fifth.

Despite the successful vaccination campaign, Cambodia's health system capacity remains among the lowest in Asia. For instance, there are currently only 0.7 hospital beds per 1,000 people. This suggests that a surge in cases of a new Covid-19 variant, where people require hospitalization, could quickly overwhelm the healthcare system. The low capacity of the healthcare system is a key factor in the draconian response

FIGURE 2.4
Covid-19 Vaccine Doses, Cambodia and World

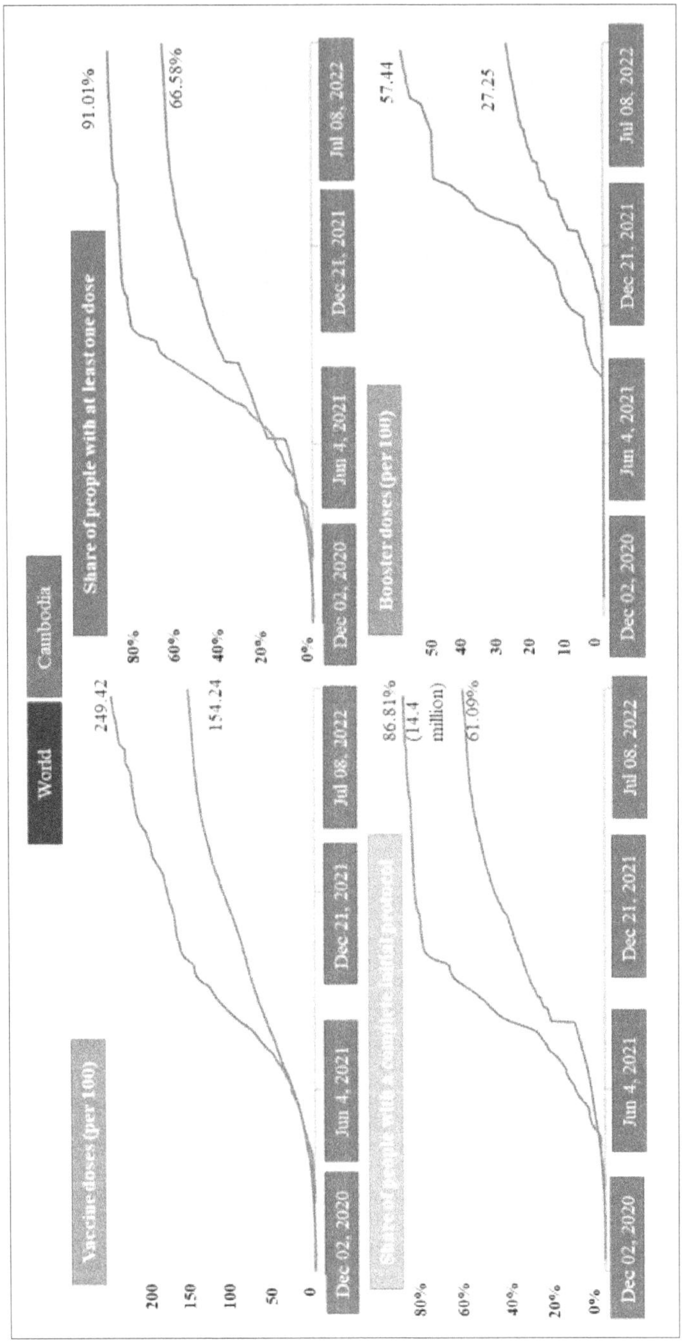

Source: Our World in Data (n.d).

FIGURE 2.5
Covid-19 Vaccines Used in Cambodia, 14 February 2021 to 14 August 2022

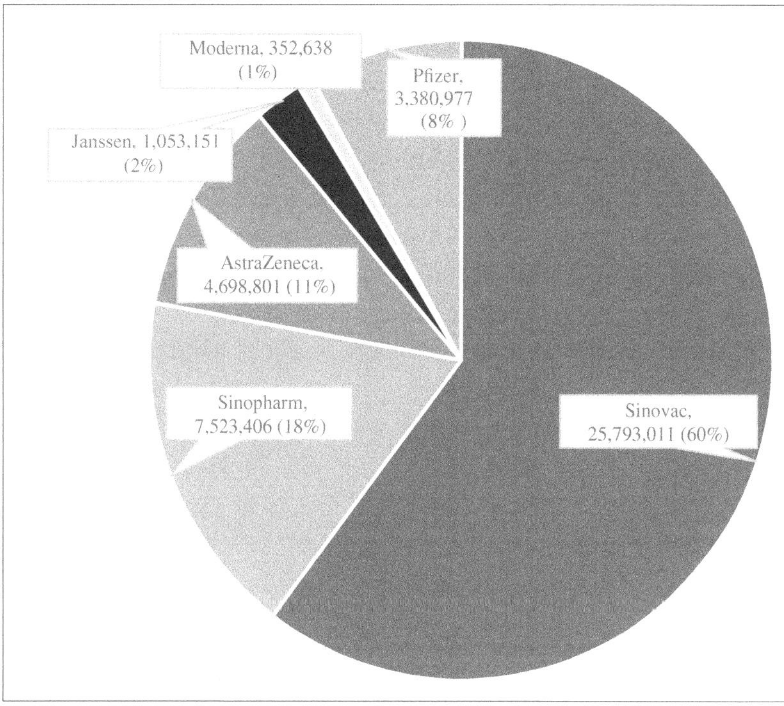

Source: Ministry of Health (2022).

to the February 2020 community outbreak. Had there been more capacity, the government may have had more space to take a more nuanced and targeted approach to manage the outbreak, thereby reducing the toll on the economy and livelihoods. One of the key lessons from the pandemic is the need to increase the quantity and quality of the healthcare system (Menon 2022).

RESEARCH DESIGN AND METHODOLOGY

The Covid-19 pandemic pushed Cambodia's growth targets further into the future and also acts as a threat to the country's competitiveness and the well-being of its people. The research we conducted to inform this chapter aims to understand the state of recovery and the possible pathways to economic recovery. We also investigate the bottlenecks in implementing interventions and explore potential solutions or policies. The results from our research can be valuable input for policymakers. The authors conducted an expert panel survey in April–June 2021 and June–August 2022, and key informant interviews with stakeholders on themes related to economic recovery, social protection, gender-sensitive policy and risks related to Covid-19. The findings shed interesting light on attitudes

Cambodia's Covid-19 response and the outlook for recovery during the time of the crisis.[6] With financial and technical support from the International Development Research Centre, Canada and to contribute to the understanding of short- and long-term effects of this pandemic, a consortium of research institutes in Cambodia, Laos, Myanmar and Vietnam was formed. The Delphi technique was used to explore the recovery pathways for Cambodia during and after Covid-19 (Hilbert, Miles and Othmer 2009). For the purpose of this study, the Delphi technique was used to form a consensus evaluation of the recovery pathways/policies from a group of experts in a structured iterative manner:

- *Identifying and forming an expert panel:* We created a list of key experts from the government, NGOs and civil society organizations, development partners, academia and the private sector in Cambodia.
- *Reviewing and compiling possible policies:* We reviewed literature, policy documents and reports in order to identify potential recovery pathways and policies suitable for Cambodia. These potential recovery pathways and policies were used to design the questionnaire for the online expert opinion survey and the key informant interviews with individual experts, which were conducted either face-to-face or online.
- *Online expert opinion survey:* The research team used the questionnaire to conduct two rounds of online opinion surveys with experts to obtain their evaluations of the pathways and policies. Responses to each recovery policy were formulated as a Likert-scale item. The survey was administered and data was collected using the Kobo Toolbox.
- *Analysis and feedback to expert panels:* The research team conducted a preliminary analysis of the data collected and provided feedback to each key expert, asking them to re-evaluate the policies. After this, the research team conducted the analysis again using descriptive

statistics to choose the policies that had the highest scores based on three criteria: importance, relevance and reliability.

- *Key informant interviews:* The authors conducted interviews with thirteen experts. The research team purposively selected business associations, policymakers and practitioners from government, NGOs and civil society organizations, development partners and academia.
- *Policy dialogue:* Stakeholders from public and private sectors exchanged views in group policy discussions.
- *Data management and analysis:* Microsoft Excel and SPSS or STATA were used to manage and analyse survey data.[7] The research team generated descriptive statistics in the form of tables or graphics.

FINDINGS AND DISCUSSION

Over 50 per cent of experts regarded Cambodia's control of Covid-19 and its contribution to the international fight against Covid-19 as "somewhat good" or "very good". Fundraising by the government or private entities, public donations and Cambodia's record on gender equality were rated low in the first round of the expert opinion survey (Figure 2.6). On Cambodia's economic prospects, the first round of the expert opinion survey was more pessimistic, with 53 per cent considering them as "somewhat bad". In the second round, in 2022, 67 per cent thought the current economy was "somewhat good". This move towards a more positive view aligns with the perceptions of the government's control over Covid-19: in the first round of the survey (2021), 52 per cent of respondents deemed the government effective, compared to 89 per cent in the second round (Figure 2.7). The successful vaccination campaign, with 15.1 million vaccinated and 249.4 doses per 100 people by 8 July 2022, was a good sign for public health resiliency.

However, when asked about the most likely year that Cambodia's economy would reach its pre-pandemic growth, in the first round, the largest share of experts, 31 per cent, chose 2023. In the second round, expectations had moved further into the future: the largest share of experts, 41 per cent, chose 2025 (Figure 2.8). Despite the evidence of some recovery (from negative growth in 2020 to positive growth in 2021), experts in the key informant interviews also stated that Cambodia needed a few more

FIGURE 2.6
First Round of Expert Opinion Survey: Please Assess the Listed Issues

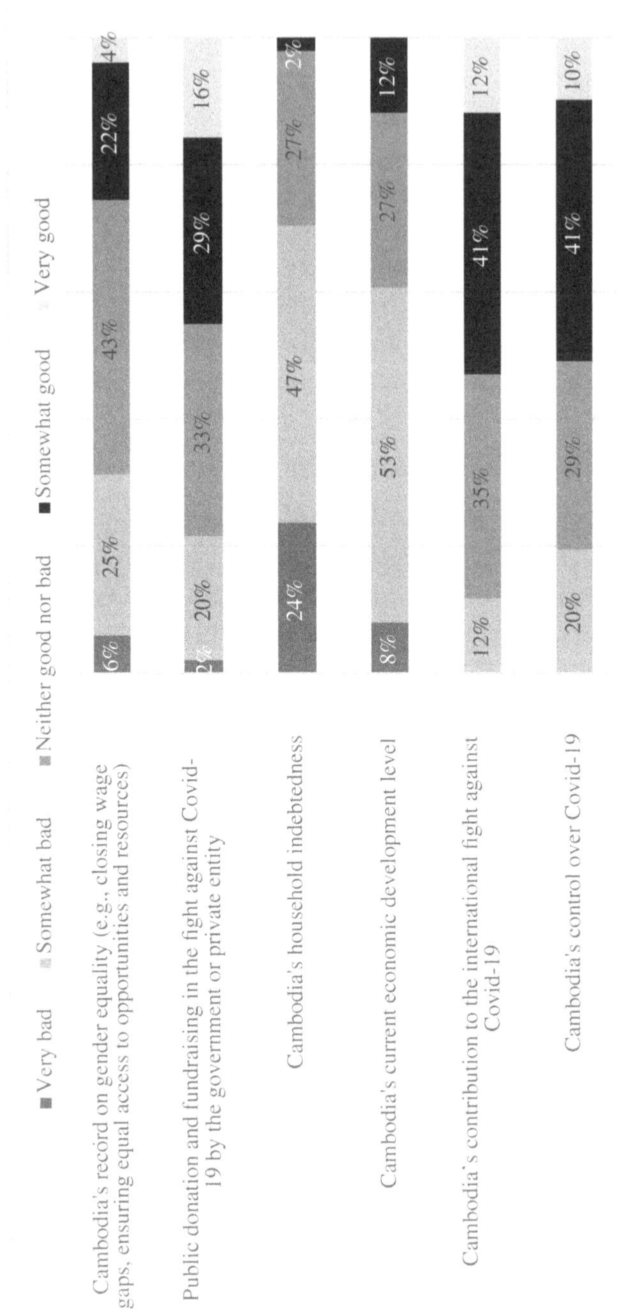

Source: First round of expert opinion survey.

FIGURE 2.7
Cambodia's Economic Development and Control of Covid-19

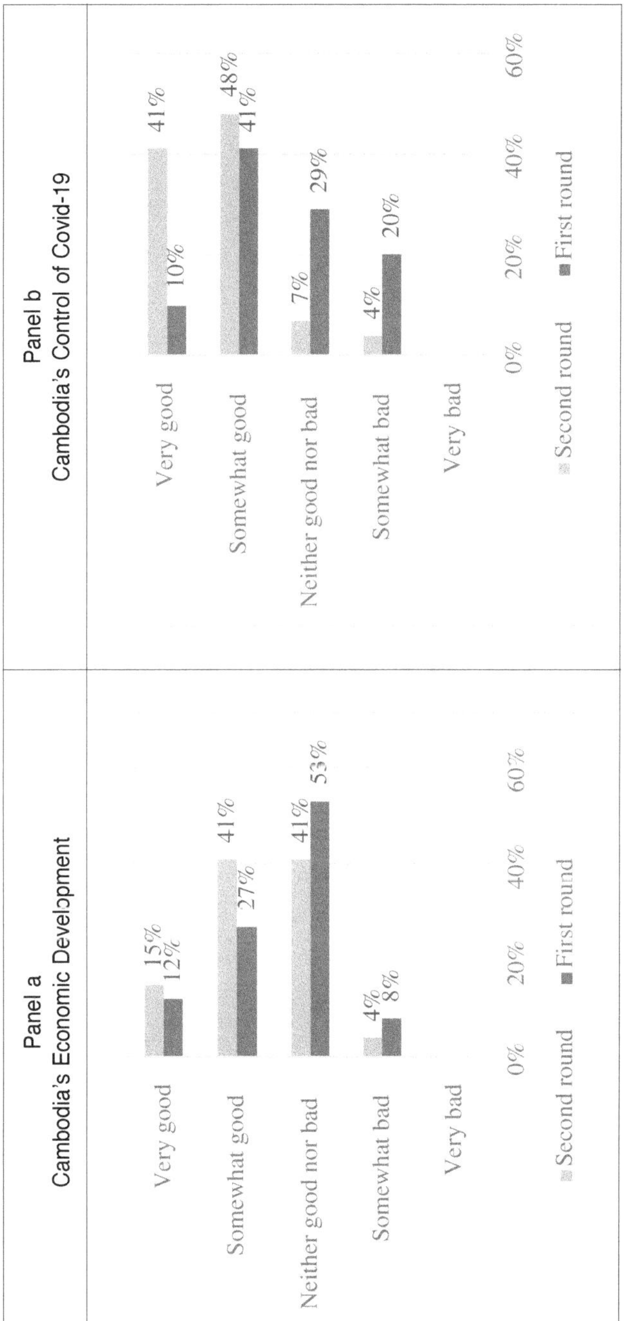

Sources: First and second rounds of expert opinion survey

FIGURE 2.8
Likeliest Year of Cambodia's Economic Recovery to Pre-pandemic Levels

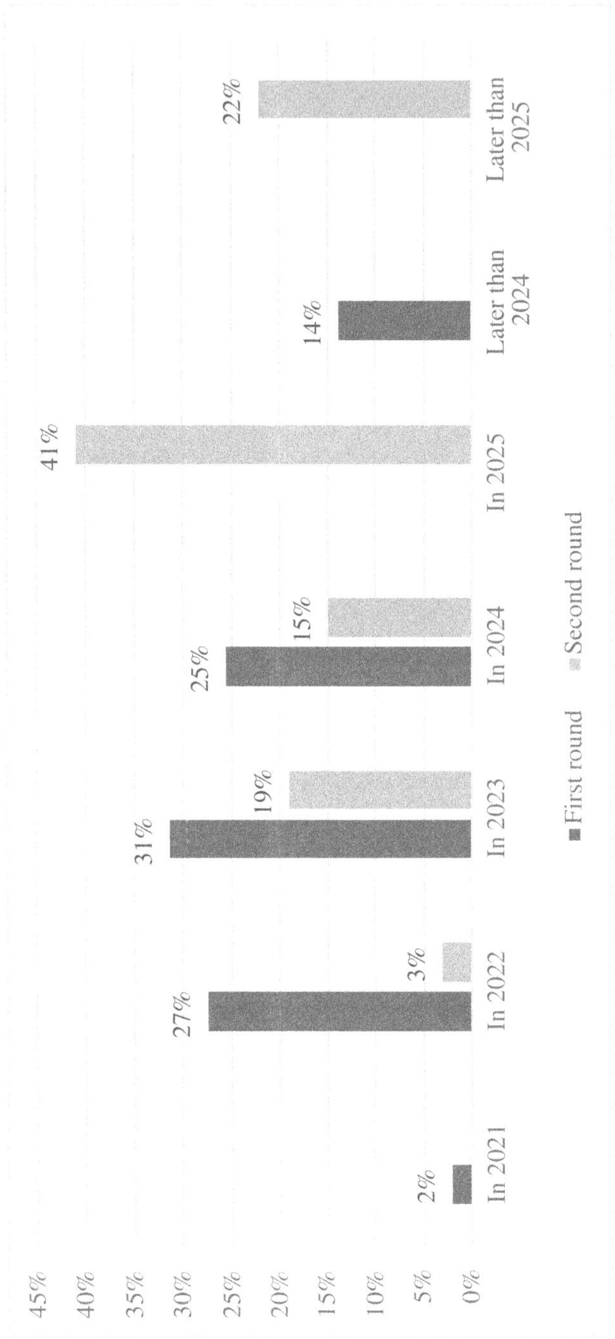

Sources: First and second rounds of expert opinion survey.

years to achieve its target of an average 7 per cent growth rate, because the country also faced inflation related to the Russia–Ukraine war, which was likely to hinder growth. Concerning potential risks (Table 2.1), experts were very optimistic about Cambodia's public health situation: their scores

TABLE 2.1
Survey Question: How Likely to Occur Are the Following Risks to Cambodia's Economy?

Risk	*First Round of Survey*	*Second Round of Survey*
Household debt crisis	4.16	3.74
Increase in education disparity	3.90	3.70
Youth unemployment	4.10	3.70
Overburdening of households, and particularly women in those households, with education responsibilities	3.92	3.63
Healthcare breakdown in health facilities	3.92	3.52
Increased overall prices due to the expansion of fiscal and monetary policy measures	3.47	3.52
Overburdening of households, and particularly women in households, with healthcare responsibilities	3.88	3.44
Climate change and extreme weather conditions	3.12	3.41
Commodity shocks	3.24	3.37
Gender inequality in wages, employment and access to other opportunities and services	3.39	3.33
Digital inequality/divide	3.47	3.22
Property bubble	3.18	3.22
Sovereign debt crisis	3.53	2.93
Growing practices of protectionism (inward-looking policy agenda)	3.14	2.85
Partial lockdown due to another outbreak of Covid-19 or new variants	4.04	2.70
Complete lockdown due to another outbreak of Covid-19 or new variants	3.65	2.59

Note: Scores range from 1 (the lowest likelihood) to 5 (the highest likelihood): 1.0–1.8 (very low likelihood of occurrence); 1.81–2.6 (low likelihood); 2.61–3.4 (medium likelihood); 3.41–4.2 (high likelihood); 4.21–5.0 (very high likelihood).
Sources: First and second rounds of expert opinion survey.

on the likelihood of occurrence of both total and partial lockdowns fell, respectively, from 3.65 and 4.04 in the first round to 2.59 and 2.7 in the second round. Other macroeconomic risks that experts were concerned about included the household debt crisis and inflation.

Regarding government intervention to support the economy since the Covid-19 outbreak, 59 per cent of experts (in EOS1) believed that somewhat more could be done, and 70 per cent of experts considered Cambodia's fiscal stimulus packages were too small. The experts' impressions had slightly improved by the second round. In the second round, the proportion who regarded the fiscal stimulus as too small declined to 44 per cent (Figure 2.9).

All experts from the key informant interviews believed that health interventions (vaccinations) and non-health interventions, such as cash transfers and financial assistance schemes, were not only preventing people from sliding into poverty but also helping to stimulate and reopen the economy, especially local businesses. They also emphasized the importance of the cash transfer programme, which only became large-scale in Cambodia because of Covid-19 and required extension due to high oil prices, which posed a threat to livelihoods. However, other experts acknowledged gaps in the implementation of the cash transfer programme. The programme's budget was small compared to that of other countries, and many disadvantaged people were excluded due to the limitations of the identification system, resulting in some underprivileged, especially those working in the informal sector and those unregistered with IDPoor, being excluded.

Gender equality is the focus of the United Nations' Sustainable Development Goal 5. The policy measures implemented in Cambodia during the pandemic were of unprecedented scale, but few measures were gender-responsive, aimed at addressing the pandemic by supporting women's attachment to the labour market and improving their working conditions, including the quality of their earnings and their security in the labour market (ILO 2021). Urgent policy actions for gender-responsive policy (Table 2.2) should focus on protecting essential workers and any worker exposed to health risks in their job, with special attention paid to women in the most precarious forms of employment (i.e., informal, domestic paid workers); to ensuring adequate investment in healthcare in general and specifically to promoting quality and affordable sexual

FIGURE 2.9
Sufficiency of Government Interventions and Fiscal Stimulus Package

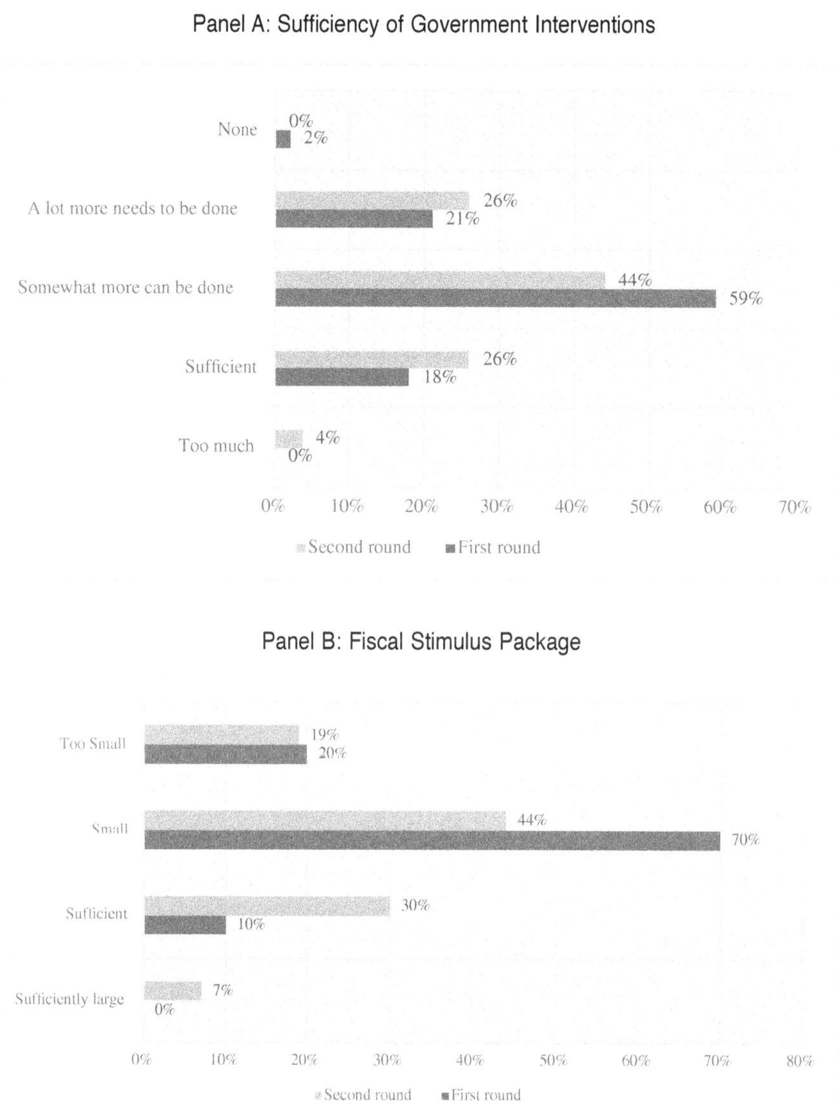

Source: First and second rounds of expert opinion survey.

TABLE 2.2
Urgent Actions for Gender-Responsive Policies

	Policy Action Is Urgently Needed to …	*First Survey Round*
1	Ensure adequate investment in healthcare in general, and promote quality and affordable sexual and reproductive health for all women.	3.86
2	Protect essential workers and any worker exposed to health risks in their job, with special attention to women in the most precarious forms of employment (i.e., informal domestic paid workers).	3.99
3	Introduce economic support packages for vulnerable women.	3.84
4	Introduce measures to reduce and redistribute unpaid care work. These measures especially include universal childcare to enable women to better combine work with family responsibilities.	3.75
5	Implement measures to reduce:	
5.1	– occupational segregation;	3.52
5.2	– gender pay gaps;	3.68
5.3	– inadequate access to affordable childcare.	3.86
6	Close glaring gaps in social protection. (Long-term investments in social protection systems that reach all women and girls are key to economic recovery and future resilience. In particular, Cambodia needs social protection systems that help families and businesses restore income, preserve livelihoods and compensate for price hikes.)	3.81
7	Prioritize prevention and redress of violence against women and girls in Covid-19 responses. (Ensure that services for survivors of violence are deemed essential and remain accessible and adequately funded.)	3.82
8	Improve sex-disaggregated data collection and expand research on the gendered impacts of Covid-19, particularly on those most marginalized. (Sex-disaggregated data on socio-economic effects and related policies are also crucial.)	3.46

Note: 1 (least urgent) to 5 (most urgent).
Source: First round of expert opinion survey.

and reproductive health for all women; to introducing economic support packages for vulnerable women; and implementing measures to reduce inadequate access to affordable childcare.

The survey also sought out expert opinion on the importance and relevance of key policy responses to deal with Covid-19 economic impacts.

Policies on cash transfers, low-interest loans and loan restructuring are crucial in supporting the recovery effort in the long term. On monetary measures implemented in response to Covid-19, experts rated the government's response "very good" in loan restructuring, lowering required reserves that banking and financial institutions must maintain at the National Bank of Cambodia both for the riel and for foreign currencies, and cutting the interest rate in its Liquidity-Providing Collateralized Operations scheme. The loan restructuring was initially targeted at sectors directly impacted by Covid-19 but was quickly expanded to cover all private lending. By the end of 2021, debts of US$5.2 billion had been restructured, equivalent to 12.9 per cent of total private sector lending and 19.9 per cent of GDP. Private sector lending increased by 52.9 per cent during 2020–22, with loans to businesses rising 47.6 per cent and personal loans by 73.6 per cent. The forbearance measures related to the pandemic and growth slowdown have increased the indebtedness of banks and households (Menon 2022). Household credit growth and a heavy reliance on formal and informal borrowing to address financial difficulties remain macroeconomic stability concerns and require close monitoring and assessment. Financial literacy has been and will be relevant to addressing this issue: the government could increase financial literacy and awareness, particularly on the use of loans and the importance of saving during good times.

In both rounds of the survey, most experts rated all the main economic sectors as important for economic recovery. The subsector of agriculture, including crops, livestock and poultry, and fishery, is essential to generating growth. In industry, priority subsectors—those that would speed up economic recovery—included manufacturing (textiles, clothing and footwear, and food, beverages and tobacco), electricity, gas and water, and construction. In the services sector, trade, finance, transport and communication were rated by the experts as being of high importance in accelerating economic recovery. Industry, especially subsectors creating high value-added products, was the priority sector for economic recovery. Productivity improvement and upgrading of agriculture, manufacturing and other services were rated as vital for sustaining competitiveness. These sectors require continued investment in infrastructure and human resources development. The construction and real estate sectors stagnated significantly in 2020–22. The close links between construction, real estate and the financial sector mean that further corrections in the property market could spill over to the rest of the economy. The construction and real estate sectors are unlikely to be major sources of growth in the medium term (Menon 2022).

Experts from the key informant interviews pointed out that the manufacturing sector, especially the high value-added subsectors, would play the most significant role in driving sustained high growth in the Cambodian economy. Therefore, it is essential to diversify the existing manufacturing sector and move up the value chain; this requires significant investment in reskilling and upskilling employees so they become highly productive workers. The tourism sector was considered the second priority sector for generating growth. The government could lean on tourism-related policies to attract all types of tourists (from low- to high-end), diversify tourist destinations, ensure hospitality quality and extend the average length of stay to maximize tourism income. Lastly, agriculture is still an important sector, given the Cambodian agricultural endowment. However, the agro-processing subsector should be the main focus rather than traditional agriculture. These sectors have the potential to generate better and well-paid jobs for both women and men in the current context of Cambodia's economy.

When questioned about the policies most needed to strengthen the economic recovery (Table 2.3), the experts from the two rounds of the survey rated certain policies of high importance: social protection policies related to cash transfers, wage subsidies, developing effective social protection mechanisms, and other policies such as tax relief, loan restructuring and low-interest loans. In addition, both they and the experts from the key informant interviews also valued some long-term policies to diversify the economy, particularly related to agribusiness and industries other than garments and textiles, and policies to encourage technology adoption. Further diversification of the economy will require greater connectivity and investments in rural and urban infrastructure, the fostering of entrepreneurship, an expansion in the use of technology and the building of new skills to address emerging labour market needs.

TABLE 2.3
How Necessary Are the Listed Policies for Inclusive, Sustainable and Resilient Covid-19 Recovery?

Policy	*Mean Score*
Continuing cash transfers for poor and vulnerable households.	3.89
Further developing effective mechanisms for targeting social protection.	4.26
Promoting equal access to good jobs with adequate pay for men and women.	4.52
Adopting a more environmentally friendly policy agenda for public and private sectors.	4.33
Encouraging efforts to adopt technologies for the Industrial Revolution 4.0.	4.22
Implementing more tax and non-tax support for micro, small and medium-sized enterprises (MSMEs).	4.33
Implementing more tax and non-tax support for women-led MSMEs.	4.19
Continuing public investment in IT infrastructure and connectivity and ensuring access to, and use of, digital technologies for women and men equally.	4.37
Continuing to diversify the economy, particularly to agri-business and industries other than garments and textiles.	4.67
Other.	3.4

Note: 1 (least necessary) to 5 (most necessary).
Source: Second round of expert opinion survey.

CONCLUSION AND RECOMMENDATIONS

Although Cambodia was able to contain the health impact of the pandemic, it was heavily impacted by the direct effects of containment measures and by socio-economic issues related to unemployment, lost income and inflation. However, a successful vaccination campaign and pragmatic economic policies helped position the government to reopen the economy. While the economy returned to positive growth of 3 per cent in 2021, rising to 5.6 per cent in 2023, long-term growth will depend on public policy choices. To achieve the high pre-pandemic rates of growth, Cambodia will need to implement a well-targeted programme of investments and reforms, enhance competitiveness through efficiency and effectiveness of resource allocation and wealth redistribution, and improve the quality of public services.

We suggest three policies based on the findings of this study.

- Cambodia could address risks associated with household indebtedness, unemployment, disruptions to health facilities caused by the outbreak of illness, and the overburdening of households with requirements for them to spend money and time on healthcare. The government could establish strategies to raise public awareness of healthcare and health protection. With healthcare capacity constraint in dealing with a health crisis like Covid-19, Cambodia needs more investment in the healthcare system. The government could also enhance the social protection system by developing effective mechanisms to get social protection to those in need.
- It is necessary for the government to closely monitor inflation, as rising oil and food prices have put pressure on workers' earnings and the economy as a whole. The government could maintain fiscal and monetary policies that encourage cash transfers, low-interest loans and loan restructuring. The government could provide more tax and non-tax support for micro, small and medium-sized enterprises. The government could diversify the economy and improve technology adoption. It could continue public investment in IT infrastructure and connectivity and ensure equal access to, and use of, digital technologies among the public.
- Cambodia could focus on potential growth sectors, including manufacturing, crops, livestock and poultry, and fishery, and could diversify in the services sector, namely in services related to trade, finance, tourism, transport and information and communications technology. These subsectors are crucial in supporting the long-term recovery. Those high value-added subsectors play a significant role in driving a sustained and high-growth economy. The government could also diversify the existing manufacturing sector, move up the value chain, improve competitiveness, invest in reskilling and upskilling programmes, promote domestic tourism, diversify tourist destinations and ensure hospitality quality.

Notes

1. The views expressed in this chapter are those of the authors. They do not necessarily represent the views of the Cambodia Development Resource

Institute (CDRI) or its funder, the International Development Research Centre. Topics discussed in this chapter were introduced by the authors at the CDRI Monthly Research Seminar on 25 August 2021, "Cambodia Economic Priorities During Covid-19 Pandemic: Opinions and Perspectives". The authors also brought the topics to a panel discussion at a national policy forum convened by the Asia Foundation on 23–24 November 2021, "Cambodia Post Covid-19 Economic Recovery: Aspects and Perspectives". Similar topics were presented at three further events: the ADB–Asian Think Tank Development Forum 2021, "Unlocking the Economic Potential of the Tourism Industry Post-Covid-19"; "Covid-19 in Southeast Asia, 2020-2022: Restriction, Relief, Recovery" on 28–29 July 2022, ISEAS – Yusof Ishak Institute; and the 2022 HDCA Conference, "Capabilities and Transformative Institutions" on 19–22 September 2022.

A consortium of research institutes in Cambodia, Laos, Myanmar and Vietnam was formed with financial and technical support from the International Development Research Centre, Canada to contribute to the understanding of short- and long-term effects of the pandemic. The consortium consists of research think tanks in the Greater Mekong Subregion, namely the CDRI, the Faculty of Economics and Business Management, the National University of Laos, the Centre for Economic and Social Development (CESD) and the Centre for Analysis and Forecasting, Vietnam Academy of Social Sciences (CAF-VASS). The objectives are: (1) to provide a rapid response to and deeper assessment of the socio-economic impacts of the Covid-19 pandemic, focusing on, but not limited to, the effectiveness and efficiency of macroeconomic responses (fiscal and monetary), the impact on business operations and the profitability of enterprises, and enterprises' mitigation strategies, with the focus on women-led establishments, female-headed households, the poor and vulnerable. Findings will be provided to government ministries and institutes, development partners, women business associations and civil society organizations for evidence-based and informed decision- and policymaking; and (2) to enhance partnerships and cooperation among research institutions in the Greater Mekong Subregion, encouraging the sharing of information and lessons learnt on Covid-19 responses and building the capacity of researchers of the institutes involved in the project.

2. See Kandel et al. (2020). The index helps to assess the status of national readiness across each of the World Health Organization (WHO) regions. According to the WHO, high-level operational readiness to respond to emergencies will allow a timely, effective and efficient response.

3. Kunmakara (2020) reported that the manufacturing sector shrank by 11 per cent year-on-year, and the growing oversupply of real estate and the absence of foreign buyers were big challenges. Tourism was the worst affected sector as international arrivals plunged 55 per cent in the first half of 2020. Only agricultural output increased, by 21.7 per cent year-on-year due to an ecologically questionable expansion of cultivated areas and the absence of major natural disasters. Cambodia's garment, footwear and travel goods industries are the largest export sectors, employing about 750,000 people in approximately 1,100 factories. Unemployed workers receive a monthly stipend of US$30 from their factory and US$40 from the government. Tourism minister Thong Khon said that nearly 3,000 tourism-related establishments such as hotels, guesthouses, restaurants, massage parlours, karaoke clubs, nightclubs and tour and travel companies had been either suspended or closed, affecting 45,405 workers (Xinhua 2020).
4. It is difficult, and rather subjective, to quantify the policy responses. Nonetheless, one estimate put the number of measures introduced at 2,200 (Bunthea et al. 2022).
5. There are two poverty categories to which poor households can be assigned: Poor Level 1 (very poor) and Poor Level 2 (poor). These poverty categories are assigned based on questionnaire scores and consideration of the circumstances of households. All IDPoor households (Level 1 and Level 2) live below the national poverty line.
6. The first round of the expert opinion survey, Stimulating Economy and Employment, Supporting Jobs and Income, drew fifty-one respondents. Ten were women, eighteen were experts with a PhD or postdoctoral experience and twenty-seven were experts with a master's degree. The respondents dropped to only twenty-seven in the second round, which was conducted from June to August 2022; twenty respondents were men, fourteen held a master's degree, and almost half were from domestic and international NGOs. The survey used a multiple-choice approach. We also conducted key informant interviews with open-ended questions, which allowed the interviewees to explain their opinions freely and offer greater insights on themes related to economic recovery, social protection, gender-sensitive analysis and risks. Thirteen respondents were interviewed, including government representatives, academic professionals and international development partners.
7. SPSS: Statistical Package for the Social Sciences; STATA is a general-purpose statistical software package developed by StataCorp.

References

ADB (Asian Development Bank). N.d. a. "Economic Forecasts for Cambodia". www.adb.org/countries/cambodia/economy (accessed December 2022).

———. N.d. b. "Key Indicators Database". https://kidb.adb.org (accessed December 2021).

———. 2021. "Kingdom of Cambodia: Covid-19 Active Response and Expenditure Support Program: First Quarterly Monitoring Report (July–September 2020)". March 2023. https://www.adb.org/sites/default/files/project-documents/54195/54195-001-dpta-en.pdf

———. 2022a. *Asian Development Outlook 2022 Update: Entrepreneurship in the Digital Age*. Manila: Asian Development Bank, September 2022. https://www.adb.org/sites/default/files/publication/825166/ado2022-update.pdf

———. 2022b. "Kingdom of Cambodia: Covid-19 Active Response and Expenditure Support Program Second and Third Quarter Monitoring Report for October–December 2020, and January–March 2021". https://www.adb.org/sites/default/files/project-documents/54195/54195-001-dpta-en_2.pdf

Badzmierowski, Brian. 2021. "AstraZeneca Vaccines Arrive Tuesday". *Khmer Times*, 1 March 2021. https://www.khmertimeskh.com/50819072/astrazeneca-vaccines-arrive-tuesday/ (accessed 1 April 2021).

Bossba, Benghong Siela, and Pen Socheata. 2022. "Types and Implementation of Social Assistance under the Context of Covid-19: A Case of Garment and Textile Manufacturing in Cambodia". In *National Policy Forum: Cambodia's Covid-19 Recovery Pathways*, pp. 49–60. Paper presented at the National Policy Forum, 23–24 November 2021, Phnom Penh, Cambodia. https://policypulse.org/wp-content/uploads/2021/11/NPF-Booklet-Final-small.pdf

Bunthea, Keo, Eric Kasper, Mina Chiang, and Sharlene Chen. 2022. "Cambodia's Covid-19 Response and Migrant Workers". IDS Policy Briefing 193, Institute of Development Studies. https://www.ids.ac.uk/publications/cambodias-covid-19-response-and-migrant-workers/

CARE, UN Women and UNICEF (United Nations Children's Fund). 2020. "Rapid Gender Analysis during Covid-19 Pandemic: Mekong Sub-Regional Report–Cambodia, Lao People's Democratic Republic, Myanmar, Thailand and Viet Nam (September 2020)". https://reliefweb.int/report/cambodia/rapid-gender-analysis-during-covid-19-pandemic-mekong-sub-regional-report-cambodia

Dahles, Heidi. 2022. "Groundhog Day for Cambodia's Economic Rebound". *East Asia Forum*, 12 January 2022. https://eastasiaforum.org/2022/01/12/groundhog-day-for-cambodias-economic-rebound/

Dara, Voun. 2022. "Cash Assistance for Poor Continues". *Phnom Penh Post*,

26 June 2022. https://www.phnompenhpost.com/national/cash-assistance-poor-continues (accessed 30 June 2022).

Hilbert, M., I. Miles, and J. Othmer. 2009. "Foresight Tools for Participative Policy-Making in Inter-governmental Processes in Developing Countries: Lessons Learned from the eLAC Policy Priorities Delphi". *Technological Forecasting and Social Change*, 76, no. 7: 880–96. http://dx.doi.org/10.1016/j.techfore.2009.01.001

ILO (International Labour Organization). 2020a. *ILO Monitor: Covid-19 and the World of Work.* 3rd ed. Geneva: International Labour Organization.

———. 2020b. *ILO Monitor: Covid-19 and the World of Work.* 5th ed. Geneva: International Labour Organization.

———. 2021. "Building Forward Fairer: Women's Rights to Work and at Work at the Core of the COVID-19 Recovery". Policy Brief, 19 July 2021.

IMF (International Monetary Fund). N.d. "Policy Responses to Covid-19". https://www.imf.org/en/Topics/imf-and-covid19/Policy-Responses-to-Covid-19 (accessed 9 December 2022).

———. 2022. "IMF Staff Completes 2022 Article IV Mission to Cambodia". 20 September 2022. https://www.imf.org/en/News/Articles/2022/09/20/pr22312-cambodia-imf-staff-completes-2022-article-iv-mission-to-cambodia

Kandel, Nirmal, Stella Chungong, Abbas Omaar, and Jun Xing, 2020."Health Security Capacities in the Context of COVID-19 Outbreak: An Analysis of International Health Regulations Annual Report Data from 182 Countries". *The Lancet* 395, no. 10229: 1047–53.

Kang Sothear. 2022. "ADB Re-projects Cambodia's GDP down for 2023, Inflation up for 2022". *Khmer Times,* 22 September 2022. https://www.khmertimeskh.com/501155416/adb-re-projects-cambodias-gdp-down-for-2023-inflation-up-for-2022/ (accessed 22 September 2022).

Kunmakara, May. 2020. "NBC: Economic Growth Stagnant in First Half, to Shrink 1.9% in 2020". *Phnom Penh Post*, 13 July 2020. https://www.phnompenhpost.com/business/nbc-economic-growth-stagnant-first-half-shrink-19-2020 (accessed 15 July 2021).

———. 2022. "Over $3B Spent in Two Years to Combat Covid-19". *Phnom Penh Post*, 20 June 2022. https://www.phnompenhpost.com/business/over-3-b-spent-two-years-com-bat-covid-19 (accessed 20 June 2022).

MEF (Ministry of Economy and Finance). 2022a. "Budget in Brief 2022". https://mef.gov.kh/documents/%e1%9e%90%e1%9e%9c%e1%9e%b7%e1%9e%80%e1%9e%b6%e1%9e%9f%e1%9e%84%e1%9f%92%e1%9e%81%e1%9f%81%e1%9e%94-%e1%9e%86%e1%9f%92%e1%9e%93%e1%9e%b6%e1%9f%86-%e1%9f%a2%e1%9f%a0%e1%9f%a2%e1%9f%a2/

———. 2022b. "Cambodia's Public Debt Bulletin as of End-Q3 2022". Vol. 16.

https://mef.gov.kh/documents/%e1%9e%96%e1%9f%92%e1%9e%9a%e1%9e%b9%e1%9e%8f%e1%9f%92%e1%9e%8f%e1%9e%b7%e2%80%8b%e1%9e%94%e1%9e%8f%e1%9f%92%e1%9e%9a%e2%80%8b%e1%9e%9f%e1%9f%92%e1%9e%90%e1%9e%b7%e1%9e%8f%e1%9e%b7%e2%80%8b%e1%9e%94-3/

———. 2023. "Budget in Brief 2024". 27 December 2023. https://mef.gov.kh/documents/budget-in-brief-2024/

Menon, Jayant. 2022. "Three Key Challenges Facing Cambodia's Post-pandemic Recovery and Future". Paper presented at Cambodia Outlook Conference, 6 October 2022, Phnom Penh, Cambodia. https://coc2022.cdri.org.kh/three-key-challenges-facing-cambodias-post-pandemic-recovery-and-future-growth/

Ministry of Health. 2022. "Covid-19 Vaccination Progress Report in Cambodia: Covid-19 Vaccines Used in Cambodia, 14 February 2021 to 14 August 2022". https://www.facebook.com/MinistryofHealthofCambodia

Ministry of Planning. 2020. "Cambodia's Social Protection Response to Covid-19". Paper presented at "Global e-conference: Turning the COVID-19 Crisis into an Opportunity: What's Next for Social Protection", 5–8 October 2020. https://socialprotection.org/sites/default/files/publications_files/Cambodia_IDPoor Presentation - socialprotection.org e-conference Asia final.pdf

NIS (National Insitute of Statistics). N.d. "National Accounts 2018". https://www.nis.gov.kh/index.php/en/21-na/41-national-accounts (accessed 10 October 2021).

———. 2020. "Cambodia Socio-Economic Survey". https://nis.gov.kh/index.php/km/14-cses/12-cambodia-socio-economic-survey-reports (accessed 1 December 2022).

Our World in Data. N.d. "Coronavirus (Covid-19) Vaccinations in Cambodia". https://ourworldindata.org/covid-vaccinations?country=KHM (acccseed July 2022).

Royal Government of Cambodia. 2021. "Strategic Framework and Programs for Economic Recovery and to Promote Cambodia's Economic Growth in Living with Covid-19 in the New Normal for 2021–2023". https://data.opendevelopmentcambodia.net/km/dataset/eb201d47-7b34-4ed3-9ecc-ef9a8a5b6254/resource/6a300ed7-acca-4b74-a410-43f8cc989bef/download/strategic-framework-and-programs-for-economic-recovery.pdf

Roth, Vathana, and Benghong Siela Bossba. 2023. "Impacts on the Lives and Livelihoods of Factory Workers during COVID-19: A Gender-Sensitive Analysis". Working Paper Series no. 140, June 2023, Cambodia Development Resource Institute, Phnom Penh. https://cdri.org.kh/storage/pdf/WP140_Lives%20and%20livelihoods%20of%20workers_Final_1689653380.pdf

Sopheavatey, Lay. 2020. "UNDP Donates Tablets to Catalyze Identification of Poor Households". *Cambodianess*, 15 July 2020. https://cambodianess.com/article/undp-donates-tablets-to-catalyze-identification-of-poor-households

Theng, Pagnathun, Sabine Cerceau, and Emily de Riel. 2021. "Cambodia's Social Protection Response to Covid-19". In *Policy in Focus: What's Next for Social Protection in Light of COVID-19: Country Responses* 18, no. 1: 40. https://ipcig.org/sites/default/files/pub/en/PIF47_What_s_next_for_social_protection_in_light_of_COVID_19.pdf#page=40

UNDP (United Nations Development Programme). 2022. "Cambodia's Covid-19 Cash Transfers Show Significant Benefits, Says a New Report". News release, 27 July 2022. https://www.undp.org/cambodia/press-releases/cambodias-covid-19-cash-transfers-show-significant-benefits-says-new-report

UNICEF, World Food Programme, UNAIDS (Joint United Nations Programme on HIV/AIDS), UNFPA (United Nations Population Fund) and UN Women. 2021. "Covid-19 Socio-Economic Impact Assessment". July 2021. https://docs.wfp.org/api/documents/WFP-0000135808/download/?_ga=2.145550900.1646168537.1642951024-1453324245.1626620143

World Bank. N.d. "The World Bank in Cambodia". https://www.worldbank.org/en/country/cambodia/overview (accessed 12 December 2020).

———. 2020. "Cambodia Economic Update: Cambodia in the Time of Covid-19". May 2020. http://pubdocs.worldbank.org/en/357291590674539831/pdf/CEU-Report-May2020-Final.pdf

———. 2021a. *Cambodia Economic Update, June 2021: Road to Recovery*. 15 June 2021. Phnom Penh: World Bank. https://openknowledge.worldbank.org/handle/10986/35783

———. 2021b. "Resilient Development. A Strategy to Diversify Cambodia's Growth Model". December 2021. World Bank Group. https://documents1.worldbank.org/curated/en/099925001262213662/pdf/P1719580f183f60bb0ac1e01e64a9c905ea.pdf

———. 2022. "Cambodia Economic Update: Weathering the Oil Price Shock". June 2022. World Bank Group. https://documents1.worldbank.org/curated/en/099315006282226217/pdf/P1773400c74b8e06308c8a00ff3a41dd50c.pdf

Xinhua. 2020. "Cambodia Allocates 1.16 Bln USD for Economic, Social Supports during Covid-19". 8 July 2020. http://www.xinhuanet.com/english/2020-07/08/c_139197388.htm (accessed 30 June 2022).

Yalirozy, Teng. 2022. "PM Urges Vigilance as Covid Re-Emerges". *Cambodianess*, 29 June 2022. https://cambodianess.com/article/pm-urges-vigilance-as-covid-re-emerges (accessed 29 June 2022).

3

LAOS'S COVID-19 RECOVERY PATHWAYS

Phouphet Kyophilavong and Khaysy Srithilat

INTRODUCTION

The Covid-19 pandemic has caused significant damage to the socio-economic development of the Lao People's Democratic Republic (Laos). Before the Covid-19 pandemic, Laos had maintained high economic growth for about two decades, while also facing a number of economic challenges, including high external debt, and trade and fiscal deficits. The growth slowdown due to Covid-19 was compounded by increased deficits, largely due to public spending to mitigate the impacts of the pandemic.

Over the period 2020–21, the Covid-19 pandemic resulted in the deployment of lockdown and social distancing measures across the globe. Strict lockdown measures impacted immensely on economies and livelihoods, with economic activities constrained or halted, causing massive contractions in output and income. Stringent measures to limit travel further harmed businesses, leading to the closure of many firms, particularly in services and service-related sectors. The inability of business owners in these sectors to sustain their operations led to serious unemployment as many firms had to lay off their employees.

Like every country, Laos also faced the socio-economic and health impacts of Covid-19. Even though the number of transmissions was kept low compared to many countries, the global nature of the pandemic and the international travel restrictions seriously impacted the Lao economy and its healthcare and education systems. To mitigate the damage caused by the pandemic, the Government of Laos implemented several policies, including fiscal and monetary responses. The economic recovery pathway from the pandemic has become an important debate in Laos.

This chapter investigates the policies and strategies for economic recovery in Laos. First, we provide some context for Laos's economic situation and recent development record, with attention paid to macro-economic factors that affected the country's capacity to respond to and recover from the Covid-19 pandemic. We then provide an overview of the impacts of the Covid-19 virus on Laos and the country's responses. We also discuss Laos's long-term economic challenges. Further, this chapter incorporates an expert survey conducted in 2021 to gather opinions about Covid-19 policy measures and priorities and expectations for economic recovery. Laos's recovery can be observed in retrospect, but the survey findings are useful for shedding light on opinions towards public policy and the recovery outlook while the country was amid the pandemic. Laos's further progress hinges on broader policies that help maintain macroeconomic stability, mitigate devaluation of the domestic currency, moderate inflation and avoid a debt crisis.

RECENT ECONOMIC DEVELOPMENT AND FUTURE PRIORITIES

Laos has experienced rapid economic development in recent decades. From 2001 through 2018, the average annual increase in real gross domestic product (GDP) was more than 7 per cent. The economy of Laos has evolved away from agriculture and towards services and industries. Agriculture's contribution to GDP decreased from 46 per cent in 1990 to less than 20 per cent in 2019. In addition, international trade in products and services has increased significantly, from 31 per cent of GDP in 1990 to 80 per cent in 2018 (LSB 2019), showing that Laos's economy is interconnected with the global economy.

By 2030, Laos aims to have shifted from a less-developed, lower-middle-income country to an upper-middle-income status (Government of Laos 2020). Poverty eradication and income inequality are vital issues that Laos needs to address in order to achieve its sustainable development goals. Even though the poverty rate has dropped dramatically, the number of people living in poverty remains high, particularly in rural areas (Table 3.1). The poverty headcount rate has decreased steadily but remained at a relatively high level of 18 per cent at the latest measurement, taken in 2018–19, demonstrating that economic growth has inadequately trickled down. The resources sectors, while responsible for the recent economic boom, did not translate commensurately into job creation or income gains for Lao society (Kyophilavong 2016). Furthermore, inequality has risen (Table 3.2): the Gini coefficient of expenditure rose from 36 per cent in 2012/13 to 38.8 per cent in 2018/19 (World Bank 2020). Many studies have shown that high inequality has a negative impact on economic growth in the long run. As a result, addressing inequality is also a major concern for Laos.

Laos faces a number of challenges as it strives towards long-term economic growth, poverty reduction, equitable distribution of income and environmental protection (Government of Laos 2020). However, the country also faces budget deficits and trade imbalances, which have forced

TABLE 3.1
Laos: Households below the Poverty Line

	LECS1	*LECS2*	*LECS3*	*LECS4*	*LECS5*	*LECS6*
	1992/1993 (%)	*1997/1998 (%)*	*2002/2003 (%)*	*2007/2008 (%)*	*2012/2013 (%)*	*2018/2019 (%)*
Laos	64.0	39.1	33.5	28.0	24.6	18.3
Urban	27.0	22.0	20.0	17.0	7.9	7.0
Rural						
With road[a]	43.0	32.0	31.0	30.0	31.4	23.8
Without road[b]	61.0	51.0	46.0	43.0		
Lowlands	—	—	28.0	20.5	—	—
Midland	—	—	36.5	29.0	—	—
Uplands	—	—	34.0	33.0	—	—

Notes: Calculations are based on the Lao Expenditure and Consumption Survey (LECS).
a. "With road" refers to villages with road access all year round, during both dry and rainy seasons.
b. "Without road" refers to villages without year-round road access.
Sources: World Bank and Department of Statistics (2009); World Bank and LSB (2020).

TABLE 3.2
Laos: Gini Coefficient of Expenditure Inequality

	LECS1	*LECS2*	*LECS3*	*LECS4*	*LECS5*	*LECS6*
	1992/1993	*1997/1998*	*2002/2003*	*2007/2008*	*2012/2013*	*2018/2019*
Laos	30.5	34.9	32.6	35.4	36	38.8
Urban	30.9	39.7	34.8	36.3	35.2	38.6
Rural						
With road[a]	29.3	32.1	30.3	33.2	31.5	34.5
Without road[b]	27.5	30.9	29.4	33.3		
			Region			
Vientiane	29.3	36.9	36.0	38.0	–	–
North	26.9	34.5	30.7	35.2	–	–
Central	31.5	32.5	31.0	34.0	–	–
South	32.3	32.4	31.4	32.2	–	–

Notes: Calculations based on the LECS (Lao Expenditure and Consumption Survey).
a. "With road" refers to villages with road access all year round, during both dry and rainy seasons.
b. "Without road" refers to villages without year-round road access.
Sources: World Bank and Department of Statistics (2009); LSB (2004); World Bank and LSB (2020).

it to borrow a large amount of money from outside sources, resulting in massive foreign debt (World Bank 2020).

COVID-19 HEALTH, SOCIAL AND ECONOMIC IMPACTS

Laos was arguably quite successful in controlling Covid-19. From the beginning of the pandemic to 23 May 2022, Laos registered 209,823 cumulative cases and 754 deaths, relatively low for a population of 7.4 million. There were 59 new cases and no deaths from 15 February 2020 to 14 April 2021. The first case of Covid-19 arrived in Laos at the beginning of March 2020. Remarkably, as of 3 June 2020, Laos had tested around 7,249 patients, confirming 19 cases, of which 16 were hospitalized. From 3 June 2020 to the beginning of April 2021, Laos recorded no Covid-19 cases. The successful control of Covid-19 was due to measures imposed by the Lao government, including the nationwide lockdown and strict enforcement of mobility restrictions. Covid-19 containment measures began with a nationwide lockdown and imposition of social distancing and domestic lockdown for three weeks from 1 to 19 April 2020 (Prime Minister's Order No. 6, 29 March 2020). These measures were extended to

3 May 2020. The measures involved: a ban on travel to other localities or areas with infection or risk of infection; closure of all border checkpoints (only transport of goods was allowed); a shutdown of most factories (except for those producing certain items including consumer goods and medical equipment) and large projects; and the temporary suspension of mining activity at one mine and of construction in the power sector.

The second wave of Covid-19 occurred in April 2021 (during Lao New Year). Laos experienced a high infection rate—around 100,000 cases cumulatively to December 2021—and a higher fatality rate. During this period, the Lao government imposed measures including partial lockdowns and travel restrictions.

Subsequently, the Omicron variant of Covid-19 rapidly spread around the world and inevitably reached Laos, becoming the country's third wave of Covid-19 infection. The number of infections and deaths increased in this third wave. On 23 February 2022, the National Taskforce Committee for Covid-19 Prevention and Control confirmed the first infection in the community and a total of twenty-seven cases of the Omicron variant. From February 2022, Laos's lockdown measures and its most strict policies were removed, but the government retained various restrictions, including social distancing, limitations on gatherings and the requirement that face masks be worn. Nonetheless, the highest daily infections of the entire pandemic experience occurred during this phase, with 2,819 cases recorded on 24 March 2022.

Vaccination was the key to controlling the infection rate while rolling back the mobility restrictions. By 6 May 2022, 67 per cent of the population had received two initial vaccinations and one booster shot. The vaccination rate, up to that point, was slightly higher than in Indonesia and the Philippines but far behind rates in Thailand, Vietnam and Cambodia (World Bank 2022a). Vaccination rates varied considerably across the provinces, although at end-2022 the Lao government claimed to have vaccinated 80 per cent of the population. This vaccination rate was sufficient to allow the government to gradually ease containment measures. Some restrictions, such as shortened quarantine times for certain groups of visitors and home isolation, had been relaxed from mid-2022. Several other measures remained in place, but compliance levels varied greatly across different measures (World Bank 2022a).

The Covid-19 pandemic has had a tremendous effect on the Lao economy. Before Covid-19, hydropower, construction and the wholesale and retail industries all contributed significantly to GDP growth, but their contributions began to erode when Covid-19 arrived in 2020. At the same time, natural disasters and low productivity have impeded agricultural growth (Rasphone 2020; World Bank 2020). Real GDP growth declined significantly, from 5.5 per cent in 2019 to 0.5 per cent in 2020, before rebounding to 2.5 per cent in 2021 and 3.8 per cent in 2022 (World Bank 2022b). The services sector contracted significantly: growth declined from 6.9 per cent in 2019 to −3.5 per cent in 2020, improved slightly to −2.2 per cent in 2021 and only turned positive again in 2022, reaching 2.9 per cent (World Bank 2022b).

When the pandemic hit in early 2020, many micro and small businesses lost revenue due to containment measures. This resulted in layoffs and income losses across industries. According to a survey by the Lao National Chamber of Commerce and Industry (LNCC 2020), as a result of the April 2020 nationwide lockdown, 70 per cent of companies laid off some employees, 40 per cent laid off more than 50 per cent of staff and 13 per cent laid off more than 90 per cent. The UN and MPI (2020) predicted that Covid-19 would cause 321,700 people in Laos to lose their jobs; this figure was expected to comprise 191,200 citizens and 130,532 migrant workers. Moreover, the UNDP estimated that the increase in unemployment would force 361,000 individuals into poverty. Socio-economic needs and the outlook for economic stimulus and recovery were pressing issues, especially in late 2021 as the world decisively shifted to recovery mode.

RECOVERY PATHWAYS: EXPERT SURVEY FINDINGS

Economic recovery from the Covid-19 pandemic was a major concern. Therefore, we conducted an expert opinion survey from August to November 2021 on Laos's Covid-19 recovery pathways. The pool of experts, all based in Laos, included high-level government officials, academics, experts from international development agencies and NGO representatives. The study collected eighty responses. This section summarizes the major findings.

Economic Condition and Government Support

Government support was crucial during the economic recession brought on by Covid-19. However, fiscal space remains limited; Laos has large budget deficits and high external debts. More than 53 per cent of experts surveyed said the country's economic situation was fairly bad and 12 per cent said it was very bad (Figure 3.1). The responses indicated that the respondents believed Laos was experiencing a serious economic slowdown by early 2021.

Just over half of the experts surveyed expected Laos's economy to recover no later than 2024—meaning that the country would take three years to return to pre-pandemic income levels (Figure 3.2). Further, 72 per cent of experts thought that the government should make additional interventions to support the economy (Figure 3.3), while around 50 per cent described Laos's fiscal stimulus packages as small (Figure 3.4). These results reflect a substantial concern towards the socio-economic adversities faced by Laotian society and the government's challenges in dealing with the economic downturn. The low vaccination rate at the time of the survey possibly contributed to the rather pessimistic outlook.

FIGURE 3.1
How Would You Rate Laos's Economy Now? (in percentage)

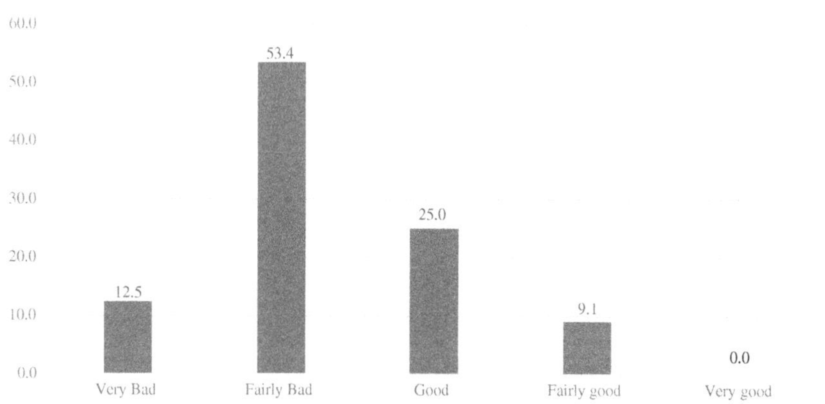

Source: Survey of experts conducted by the authors in 2021.

FIGURE 3.2
When Will Laos's Economy Recover to Pre-pandemic Levels? (in percentage)

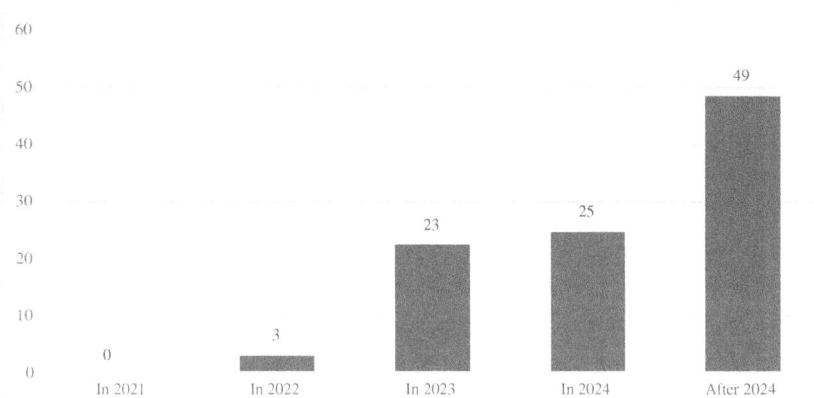

Source: Survey of experts conducted by the authors in 2021.

FIGURE 3.3
Has the Lao Government Intervened Sufficiently to Support the Economy since the Covid-19 Outbreak? (in percentage)

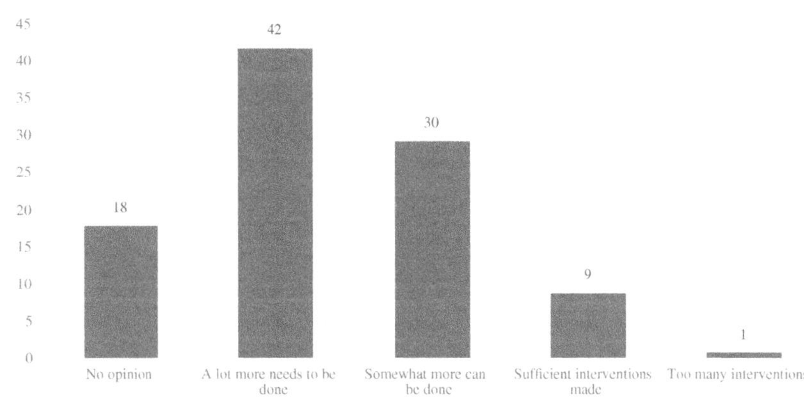

Source: Survey of experts conducted by the authors in 2021.

Policy Responses to Risks Exacerbated by Covid-19

The Covid-19 pandemic also exacerbated various risks faced by Laos. Experts widely expressed concern about the likelihood of debt crises (sovereign debt and household debt) and commodity shocks, as well as

FIGURE 3.4
What Do You Think of Laos's Fiscal Stimulus Packages? (in percentage)

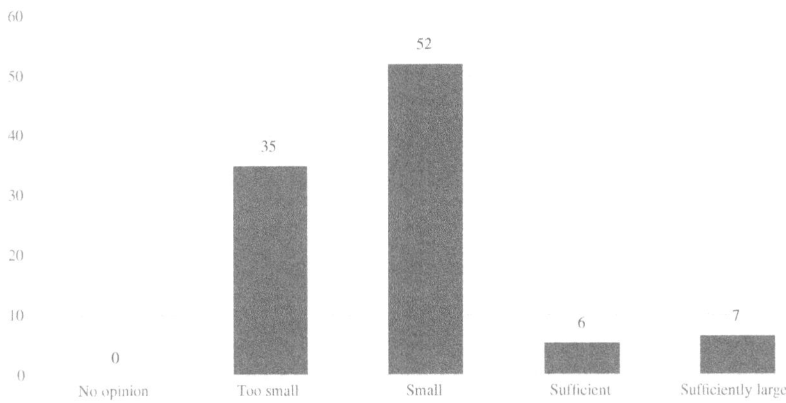

Source: Survey of experts conducted by the authors in 2021.

youth unemployment and inflation (Table 3.3). Respondents provided answers on a scale of 1 (lowest likelihood) to 5 (highest likelihood). It is noteworthy that macroeconomic issues register high scores, suggesting that Laos's international economic vulnerabilities weigh heavily in the minds of the country's opinion leaders. The survey then inquired about opinion towards the policy responses, in terms of their importance and viability (Table 3.4).[1] Experts deemed that the policy response should focus on low-interest loans for small- and medium-sized enterprises, income tax exemption, reduced electricity prices and donations from the public. Interestingly, the survey respondents ranked direct government assistance as a lower priority; such assistance includes cash transfers for households and business subsidies. This may be due to the timing of the survey—it took place in late 2021 after the worst of the pandemic had passed—or questions about the viability of the government providing these transfers and subsidies.

The survey also sought opinion towards sectoral priorities for Laos's economic recovery. Experts rated infrastructure of various forms—health, education, physical—and services as highly important, especially hospitals, schools or education facilities, roads and information communication technology (ICT) (Table 3.5). The focus on these sectors aligns with long-

TABLE 3.3
How Would You Rate These Risks to Laos's Economy in 2021?
(Scale: 1–5)

Risks	*Likelihood of Occurrence*	*Severity of Effects on the Economy, Society and Geopolitics*
Complete lockdown due to another wave of Covid-19	3.50	3.92
Partial lockdown due to another wave of Covid-19	3.99	3.78
Household debt crisis	3.90	3.92
Sovereign debt crisis	4.13	4.13
Increased prices due to expansionary fiscal and monetary policy	3.94	3.95
Property bubble	3.63	3.57
Commodity shocks	4.18	4.25
Youth unemployment	4.15	4.09
Erosion of social cohesion	3.27	3.39
Gender inequalities in wages, employment and access to other opportunities	3.22	3.16
Digital inequalities	3.43	3.20
Cybersecurity failure	3.19	3.15
Climate change and extreme weather	3.35	3.36
Growing protectionism (inward-looking policy agenda)	3.52	3.72
Breakdown in healthcare facilities	3.50	3.67
Overburden of healthcare on households	3.67	3.76
Increase in education disparity	3.66	3.64
Overburden of education responsibilities to households	3.76	3.69
Other, specify	0	0

Source: Survey of experts conducted by the authors in 2021.

term priorities but also arises from the health and education inadequacies exposed by Covid-19. These sectoral rankings possibly also derive from Laos's limited financial sources, which means it is reliant on foreign direct investment for growth. In the past, foreign direct investment was concentrated in the resources sectors such as mining and hydroelectricity, which neither provided sustained growth nor significantly reduced poverty.

The survey also investigated views on the delivery mode for development projects in the context of recovery from Covid-19, probing respondents' views on public-private partnerships (PPPs). These were generally viewed

TABLE 3.4
How Important Are These Policy Responses in Helping Recovery Efforts?

Policy Responses	*Importance*	*Viability*
Cash transfers	3.5	2.6
Cash-for-work programmes	3.8	3.0
Subsidies to business	3.5	2.6
Skill training programs	4.0	3.3
Low-interest loans from SME fund	4.1	3.3
Income tax exemption	4.2	3.7
Profit tax exemption	4.0	3.5
Duty fee exemption	4.1	3.8
Deferring loan payment	4.0	3.6
Reducing electricity prices	4.3	3.6
Unemployment allowance	4.0	3.0
Reducing administrative expense	3.8	3.5
Facilitating donations and charity work	4.3	3.9

Source: Survey of experts conducted by the authors in 2021.

TABLE 3.5
How Would You Rate these Sectors for Their Importance, Relevance and Viability for the Post-Covid-19 Recovery?

Sector	*Importance*	*Relevance*	*Viability*
Airports	3.8	3.7	3.4
Electricity	4.3	4.3	3.8
ICT	4.4	4.3	4.0
Railways	4.2	4.0	3.9
Roads	4.5	4.3	4.0
Water Supply	4.2	4.0	3.8
Hospitals	4.6	4.5	4.1
Schools/Universities	4.4	4.3	4.0

Note: In the questionnaire, the authors used a rating scale of one to five, with one being the lowest and five the highest.
Source: Survey of experts conducted by the authors in 2021.

positively (Table 3.6) and considered crucial, especially for developing ICT, roads and hospitals (Table 3.5). A directive on PPPs was issued in 2021: the main objectives were promoting, regulating and monitoring PPPs to ensure efficiency, productivity, fairness, transparency, accountability and compliance with the national socio-economic development plan. The

TABLE 3.6
How Do You Rate Public-Private Partnerships in these Sectors for Ensuring Efficient and Smooth Covid-19 Recovery?

PPP Projects	*Importance of PPPs*	*Relevance of PPPs*	*Viability of PPPs*
Airports	3.8	3.7	3.4
Electricity	4.3	4.3	3.8
ICT	4.4	4.3	4.0
Railways	4.2	4.0	3.9
Roads	4.5	4.3	4.0
Water Supply	4.2	4.0	3.8
Hospital	4.6	4.5	4.1
Schools/Universities	4.4	4.3	4.0

Note: In the questionnaire, the authors used a rating scale of one to five, with one being the lowest rating and five the highest.
Source: Survey of experts conducted by the authors in 2021.

broader aim was to build confidence and attract private investment into public projects. In the past, PPPs were mainly involved in hydropower. This decree could promote PPP projects in other sectors such as ICT, roads and hospitals.

STRUCTURAL AND LONG-TERM ECONOMIC CHALLENGES

Maintaining Economic Stability and Managing External Debt

The Covid-19 crisis exacerbated long-standing macroeconomic weaknesses. From the beginning of the pandemic, Laos struggled to manage huge fiscal budget deficits and current account deficits. Due to fears of increased debt burdens, the government continued to restrict its expenditure, decreasing overall spending from 20.2 per cent of GDP in 2019 to 17.8 per cent in 2020. At the same time, government revenue decreased by 23 per cent in the first half of 2020 as compared to the same period of 2019. The reduction in total income triggered additional borrowing to cover the shortfall, which raised overall public debt. According to the World Bank (2021), the budget deficit was 5.2 per cent in 2017 and was anticipated to decline to 4.7 per cent in 2021. At the same time, overall public debt increased from 58.2 per cent in 2019 to 62.1 per cent in 2020 and reached 66.4 per cent in 2021 (World Bank 2022b).

The macroeconomic impact of the pandemic, combined with continuing structural issues, pushed Laos into debt difficulties (World Bank 2022a). Due to a high debt service burden, inadequate tax collection, limited financing choices and low foreign currency reserves, Laos continues to experience liquidity and solvency issues. External borrowing and public and publicly guaranteed debt reached US$14.5 billion (89 per cent of GDP) at the end of 2021, up from US$13.3 billion (73 per cent of GDP) in 2020 (World Bank 2022b). High levels of public debt augment the financial sector's vulnerabilities (IMF 2017). Laos's debt sustainability will largely hinge on the outcome of bilateral debt negotiations with major creditors.

Laos's Covid-19 experience demonstrated that mobility restrictions and containment measures have a negative impact on people's well-being and living standards. More broadly, large swings in economic activity, high inflation, currency devaluation and financial market volatility can cumulatively increase unemployment and poverty (UN and MPI 2020), jeopardizing Laos's progress towards sustainable development and its graduation from least developed country status by 2026. Food prices, particularly meat prices, increased as a result of the lockdown and a rise in fuel prices, which was due in part to Russia's war on Ukraine. Food inflation rose from 2.4 per cent in January 2021 to 6.25 per cent in January 2022 (Figure 3.5). In addition, a shortage of foreign earnings resulted in the depreciation of the kip against the US dollar and the Thai baht, which increased the cost of imports and exacerbated Laos's inflation (Figure 3.6).

Maintaining economic stability is a challenging task for Lao policymakers. To stabilize domestic prices and the external balance, the Lao government needs policy space to deploy macroeconomic tools flexibly. These tools include fiscal and monetary policy restrictions, exchange rate regime management and strong regulation and supervision of the banking sector.

Avoiding a Debt Crisis

Even before Covid-19, the World Bank and the IMF had, in 2017, identified Laos as a country with a high risk of debt distress (IDA and IMF 2017).

FIGURE 3.5
Consumer Price Index (CPI), Dec 2015=1)

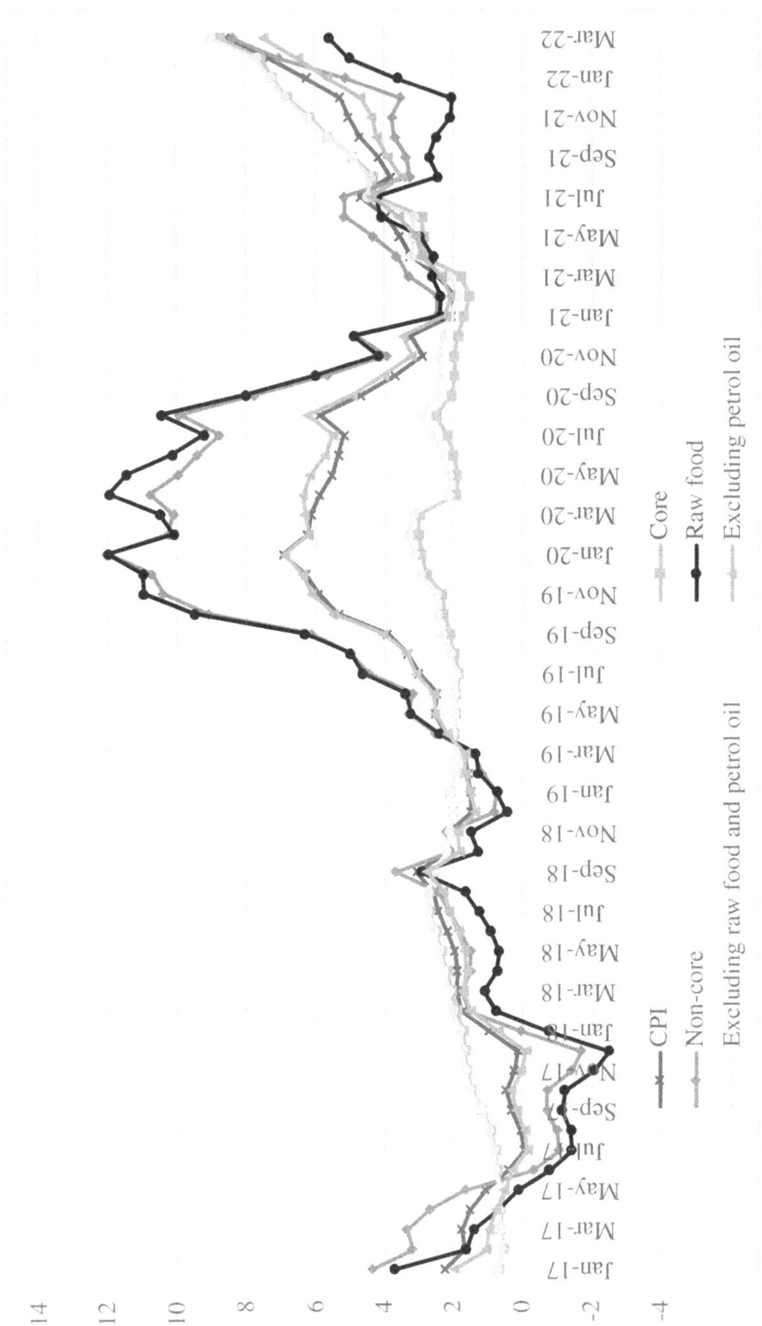

Source: IMF (2023).

FIGURE 3.6
Laos Exchange Rate (kip per US dollar and per Thai baht)

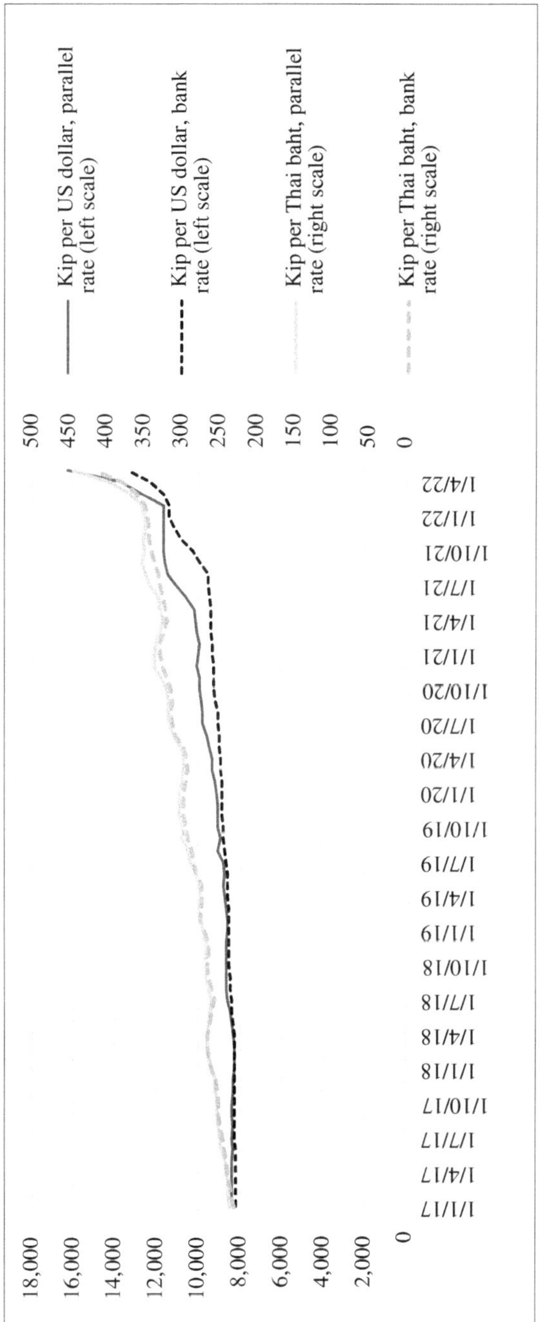

Source: IMF (2023).

The mismatches between the short-term maturity of debt obligations and the longer-term mobilization of state revenue were identified as the reason (IMF 2019). Much of Laos's debt is denominated in foreign currency, which exceeds the country's foreign exchange reserves, thereby jeopardizing its financial situation (Barney and Souksakoun 2021).

At end-2021, the external borrowing and public and publicly guaranteed debt increased from US$13.3 billion (73 per cent of GDP) in 2020 to US$14.5 billion (89 per cent of GDP). This is one of the highest levels in the region (World Bank 2022b). The liabilities of Laos's state-owned utility Électricité du Laos (EDL) alone were estimated to be up to US$8 billion in 2020, or around 41 per cent of GDP.

Laos's infrastructure-led economic growth has been financed through significant financial leveraging[2] and the accumulation of national debt (Barney and Souksakoun 2021). According to Barney and Souksakoun (2021), the government was in danger of defaulting on its debt. Over the decade prior to their report, they investigated the origins of the debt issue, focusing on the relevance of hydropower and the Laos-China railway project.[3]

Laos could implement a variety of restructuring measures, including privatizing state assets and renegotiating debt with China. It could also renegotiate or restructure its sovereign debt and propose energy sector reforms. The government could participate in the multilateral and bilateral Covid-19 support programmes, including the G20 Debt Service Suspension Initiative (Barney and Souksakoun 2021). Direct negotiations with China, Laos's main bilateral creditor (including a China–Laos currency swap arrangement), are crucial.

Maximizing Gains from the High-Speed Train

The Lao government has prioritized transforming physical connectivity, particularly given its landlocked geography, by constructing high-speed rail, which was to be in operation by end-2021. The Laos-China railway connects Laos to the network of the Belt and Road Initiative, which, by creating time and cost savings, has the potential to improve the comparative advantage of Laos. It also provides Laos with better access to regional and global value chains, which can make the country more attractive to investors (World Bank 2020).

The Laos-China railway could enable the formation of a logistics hub in the region. If logistics costs can be lowered substantially and to competitive levels, Laos's neighbours might switch from sea transport to the Laos-China railway. According to the Laos-China railway report of January 2023, the line has transported more than 2.89 million metric tons of cargo since it first opened and more than 1.79 million passengers. However, the transit trade via Laos along the railway route could reach 3.9 million metric tons per year by 2030, with a 1.5 million metric ton shift from sea to railway (LCRC 2023). Undoubtedly, these are optimistic projections, possibly driven by Laos's need to service the hefty debts incurred to build the railway. Nonetheless, the reality remains that increased use of this railroad and expansion of Laos's logistics services sector, in combination with the implementation of cutting-edge integrated logistics techniques, could enable Laos to maximize the gains from this massive national project (World Bank 2020).

Promoting Digital Transformation

Promoting the digital economy is a priority for the Lao government. The National Assembly approved the National Digital Strategy Plan 2021–30 in November 2021 (MPT 2021). Moreover, the laws and regulations related to the digital economy have been approved (MPT 2021). The rapid spread of digital technologies disrupts production, trade and investment, generating opportunities and challenges for sustainable development (UNCTAD 2019). The promotion of the digital economy and technology adaptation is a key engine of growth, but it is also accompanied by challenges in developing countries, including Laos.

Promoting the digital economy can promote economic growth (Rong Li and Gospodarik 2021) and the development of fintech (Chen, Yan, and Chen 2022). However, the main challenges are creating the necessary infrastructure and building human resources, setting and adhering to new regulations and expanding firms' capacities to adapt to digital technology (MPT 2021). The digital economy can change trade structures, investment patterns, employment and skills, but it also brings the risk that inequalities within countries and regions may increase. Therefore, the promotion and implementation of the National Digital Strategy Plan 2021–30 is a key priority for economic recovery from the Covid-19 pandemic (Kyophilavong, Sayvaya, and Soukchalern 2024a and 2024b).

Improving the Business Climate

As Laos integrates further into regional and global economies through the ASEAN Economic Community, the East Asia Free Trade Area and the World Trade Organization, competition with other member countries may increase. The Lao government is trying to improve the business climate to promote small and medium-sized enterprises and economic growth, but there remain challenges. Although the prime minister issued Decree 2 in 2018 on improving regulations and coordination for the business sector, the ease of doing business remains poor. The 2020 World Bank (2020) Ease of Doing Business Index ranks Laos 154th out of 190 countries. This reflects the country's complicated and sometimes opaque economy and trade and integration hurdles that limit its attraction as an investment destination. Investors complain about excessive transaction costs and an opaque, sluggish and complex business environment. Overall, the economy remains inward-looking (only 2.9 per cent of companies directly export [World Bank 2020]), with little investment or innovation among local businesses. The improvement of the business climate is crucial for economic recovery.

Developing Human Resources

Human capital is the engine of economic growth. The endogenous growth theory maintains that the human capital accumulated through education facilitates technological progress—through improvements in existing or new technologies (Romer 1986, 1990; Lucas 1988). However, according to an empirical study by Gylfason (2001), resource-rich countries tend to invest less in human resources. Gylfason found that, as a result, resource-rich countries had low rates of enrolment in education. This has far-reaching implications for long-term development.

Human resources development is relatively weak in Laos. According to the Human Development Index, Laos ranked 137th out of 189 countries in 2020, the lowest among the ASEAN countries (UNDP 2020). In addition,

Laos suffers from poor nutrition, and school enrolment is relatively low. Despite increased consumption and reduced poverty, malnutrition remains a serious problem. In 2006, the percentage of underweight and stunted children under five was 37 per cent and 40 per cent, respectively (World Bank and Department of Statistics 2009). These numbers show that nutrition is one of the most severe problems in Laos, though stunting has declined in recent years, from 44 per cent in 2011 to 33 per cent in 2017. However, there are significant regional differences. The World Bank and Department of Statistics report found that stunting affected one out of every three children under five in Laos, and that substantial regional disparities persist. In 2017, the capital, Vientiane, had the lowest stunting rate (13.8 per cent), while Phongsaly had the highest (54 per cent) (NIPN 2020).

Fostering human resources is crucial for economic development in Laos (Kyophilavong, Lassachack, and Volavong 2016; Kyophilavong et al. 2018). In particular, supporting the poor to improve nutrition for children and implementing the early childhood development programme are two of the most important tasks facing the country (Heckman, Pinto, and Savelyev 2013; Belfield et al. 2006).

CONCLUSION

This chapter has surveyed the impacts of the pandemic and Laos's policy responses, with a focus on economic recovery measures and criteria for sustained, long-term progress. Before the Covid-19 pandemic, the Lao economy faced a number of challenges, including high external debt, budget and trade deficits and high poverty and inequality rates; these were all exacerbated by the pandemic. Covid-19 caused significant damage to the socio-economic development of Laos, requiring serious attention to be paid to the country's economic recovery pathway. Based on the expert opinion survey, pandemic policy measures were inadequate, although the country also lacked the financial means to implement extensive assistance. Laos's economy will take time to recover to pre-pandemic levels and will also require decisive action to mitigate risks, promote foreign direct investment and strengthen public-private partnerships, particularly in service sectors. In addition, the policy responses, such as improving access to finance, tax exemptions and reductions in utility prices, are also crucial elements for economic recovery. Laos suffered a steep slowdown in growth and negative growth in the services sectors during the Covid-19 pandemic, on top of rising fuel prices, domestic currency devaluation, inflation and increased debt.

The literature and expert opinion surveys highlighted some key requirements if Laos is to maintain growth and development. First, due to the Covid-19 pandemic and the increase in fuel prices, the domestic currency (kip) has devalued and inflation has increased. Controlling these is a priority. Second, Laos must avoid a debt crisis. The country had heavy external debt before Covid-19 but the adverse impacts of the pandemic have compounded its macroeconomic vulnerability and increased the importance of averting a debt crisis. Third, Laos needs to maximize the use of the Laos-China railway. In order to do so, improving trade facilitation, reducing non-tariff barriers and liberalizing trade in services are key. Fourth, the country must improve the business climate, human resource development and conservation of natural resources and the environment, all of which are crucial to its competitiveness and sustainability. Progress in these areas can support Laos towards reaching its goal of graduating from least developed country to upper-middle-income country by 2030.

Notes

1. Some policies score high in importance but low in viability.
2. The financing of infrastructure and its impact on macroeconomic stability was discussed by Kyophilavong and Lamphayphan (2014).
3. Construction of the Laos-China railway began in December 2016. It was opened on 3 December 2021. The line is 427.201 km long and requires 150 new bridges and 76 new tunnels (Jianguo, Youding, and Ying 2016). It cost US$6 billion, 70 per cent of which was provided by China, and is the largest and most expensive project to date in Laos. The cost is equivalent to one-third of Laos's GDP.

References

Barney, K., and K. Souksakoun. 2021. "Credit Crunch: Chinese Infrastructure Lending and Lao Sovereign Debt". *Asia & the Pacific Policy Studies* 8, no. 1: 94–113.

Belfield, C.R., M. Nores, S. Barnett, and L. Schweinhart. 2006. "The High/Scope Perry Preschool Program: Cost-Benefit Analysis Using Data from the Age-40 Followup". *Journal of Human Resources* 41, no. 1: 162–90.

Chen, X., D. Yan, and W. Chen. 2022. "Can the Digital Economy Promote FinTech Development, Growth and Challenge?". *Growth and Change* 53, no. 1: 221–47.

Government of Laos. 2020. "Lao PDR's Development Policy Priorities for the Next 5 Years: High-Level Consultation on the 9th NSEDP under the Roundtable Process". Ministry of Planning and Investment. News release, 11 December 2020. https://laopdr.un.org/en/105110-lao-pdr%E2%80%99s-development-policy-priorities-next-5-years-high-level-consultation-9th-nsedp-under

Gylfason, T. 2001. "Natural Resources, Education, and Economic Development". *European Economic Review* 45 no. 4–6: 847–59.

Heckman, J., R. Pinto, and P. Savelyev. 2013. "Understanding the Mechanisms through Which an Influential Early Childhood Program Boosted Adult Outcomes". *American Economic Review* 103, no. 6: 2,052–86.

IDA (International Development Association) and IMF. 2017. "Lao People's Democratic Republic: Joint World Bank–IMF Debt Sustainability Analysis". Report prepared jointly by the staff of the International Development Association (IDA) and the International Monetary Fund (IMF). https://www.imf.org/external/pubs/ft/dsa/pdf/2017/dsacr1753.pdf

IMF (International Monetary Fund). 2017. "Lao People's Democratic Republic: Staff Report for the 2016 Article IV Consultation—Debt Sustainability Analysis". International Monetary Fund 2017, no. 053. https://www.elibrary.imf.org/view/journals/002/2017/053/article-A002-en.xml

———. 2019. *Lao People's Democratic Republic: Staff Report for the 2023 Article IV Consultation.* Country Report No. 2019/267. Washington, DC: International Monetary Fund. https://www.imf.org/en/Publications/CR/Issues/2019/08/08/Lao-Peoples-Democratic-Republic-2019-Article-IV-Consultation-Press-Release-Staff-Report-48577

———. 2023. *Lao People's Democratic Republic: Staff Report for the 2023 Article IV Consultation.* Country Report No. 2023/171. Washington, DC: International Monetary Fund. https://www.imf.org/en/Publications/CR/Issues/2023/05/22/Lao-People-s-Democratic-Republic-2023-Article-IV-Consultation-Press-Release-Staff-Report-533636

Jianguo, C., X. Youding, and Z. Ying. 2016. *New Boten-Vientiane Railway-Feasibility Study: General Report.* China Railway Eryuan Engineering Group Co., Ltd.

Kyophilavong, P. 2016. "Mining Booms and Growth in Laos: Empirical Result from CGE Model". *International Journal of Development Issues* 15, no. 1: 51–61.

———, and T. Lamphayphan. 2014. "Lao PDR Country Report". In *Financing ASEAN Connectivity*, edited by F. Zen and M. Regan, pp. 131–65. ERIA Research Project Report FY2013, No. 15, Jakarta: ERIA (Economic Research Institute for ASEAN and East Asia).

———, X. Lassachack, and T. Volavong. 2016. "Do Cash Transfers Help the Poor during Trade Liberalization? Evidence from Laos". *International Area Studies Review* 19, no. 4: 355–71.

———, I. Sayvaya, and P. Soukchalern. 2024a. *The Impacts of Digital Technology Adaption on Micro, Small and Medium Enterprises (MSMEs) Before Covid-19 in Laos*. Research report, ERIA, forthcoming.

———, I. Sayvaya, and P. Soukchalern. 2024b. *The Strategies and Policies for Digital Transformation in Laos*. Research report, ERIA, forthcoming.

———, K. Ogawa, B. Kim, and K. Nouansavanh. 2018. "Does Education Promote Economic Growth in Lao P137DR? Evidence from Cointegration and Granger Causality Approaches". *Journal of Developing Areas* 52, no. 2: 1–11.

LCRC (Lao–China Railway Company Limited). 2023. *The Lao-China Railway Company Limited Report* (various issues).

LNCC (Lao National Chamber of Commerce and Industry). 2020. *Survey Report on Impact of Covid-19 on Businesses*. Lao National Chamber of Commerce and Industry. https://lncci.la/documents-for-impacts-of-covid-19/

LSB (Lao Statistics Bureau). 2019. *Statistical Yearbook 2022* (various issues). https://laosis.lsb.gov.la/board/BoardList.do?rootId=2103000&menuId=2103101&lang=en&bbs_bbsid=B404&keyword=&searchType=undefined

Lucas, Robert E. Jr. 1988. "On the Mechanics of Economic Development". *Journal of Monetary Economics* 22, no. 1: 3–42.

MPT (Ministry of Post and Telecommunications). 2021. "National Digital Strategy Plan 2021–2030". Laos: Ministry of Posts and Telecommunications.

NIPN (National Information Platform for Nutrition). 2020. "Nutrition Policy Landscape Analysis". Policy Analysis Unit, National Information Platform for Nutrition.

Rasphone, S. 2020. "The Impact of Covid-19 on Socio-economic Development in Lao PDR. Preparation for Updating Vulnerability Profile Report for Lao PDR under the Situation of Covid-19 Pandemic Crisis". National Information Platform for Nutrition.

Romer, P.M. 1986. "Increasing Returns and Long-Run Growth". *Journal of Political Economy* 94, no. 5: 1002–37.

———. 1990. "Endogenous Technological Change". *Journal of Political Economy* 98, no. 5 (Part 2): S71–S102.

Rong Li, R. and C.G. Gospodarik. 2021. "The Impact of Digital Economy on

Economic Growth Based on Pearson Correlation Test Analysis". *International Conference on Cognitive based Information Processing and Applications (CIPA 2021)* 10: 19–27.

UN (United Nations) and MPI (Ministry of Planning and Investment). 2020. *Socio-economic Impact Assessment of Covid-19 on Lao PDR*. https://laopdr.un.org/en/124250-socio-economic-impact-assessment-covid-19-lao-pdr

UNCTAD (United Nations Conference on Trade and Development). 2019. "Digital Development: Opportunities and Challenges, Trade and Development Board, Sixty-Sixth Session". Geneva, 24–28 June 2019. https://unctad.org/system/files/official-document/tdb66_d5_en.pdf

UNDP (United Nations Development Programme). 2020. *Human Development Report: The Next Frontier: Human Development and the Anthropocene*. New York: UNDP. https://hdr.undp.org/content/human-development-report-2020

World Bank. 2020. *Lao PDR Economic Monitor: Lao PDR in the Time of Covid-19*. Washington, DC: World Bank. https://www.worldbank.org/en/country/lao/publication/lao-pdr-economic-updates

———. 2021. *Lao PDR Economic Monitor: A Path to Recovery*. Washington, DC: World Bank.

———. 2022a. *Lao PDR Economic Monitor: Restoring Macroeconomic Stability to Support Recovery*. Washington, DC: World Bank. https://www.worldbank.org/en/country/lao/publication/lao-pdr-economic-updates

———. 2022b. *Lao PDR Economic Monitor: Tackling Macroeconomic Vulnerabilities*. Washington, DC: World Bank.

World Bank and Department of Statistics. 2009. Poverty in Lao PDR 1992/3–2007/8. Washington, DC: World Bank; Vientiane, Department of Statistics. https://documents.worldbank.org/pt/publication/documents-reports/documentdetail/698651468044953908/poverty-in-lao-pdr-2008-lao-expenditure-and-consumption-survey-1992-03-2007-08

World Bank and LSB. 2020. *Poverty Profile in Lao PDR: Poverty Report for the Lao Expenditure and Consumption Survey 2018–2019*. https://thedocs.worldbank.org/en/doc/923031603135932002-0070022020/original/LaoPDRPovertyProfileReportENG.pdf

4

CAPABILITIES, "COUP-VID" AND CATACLYSM

Myanmar's Responses to Covid-19

Sandii Lwin, Kyaw San Wai and Nilar Win

INTRODUCTION[1]

As with other countries, Myanmar's response to Covid-19 was shaped by its own social and economic contexts, and, perhaps more than in any other Southeast Asian country, by its political history and climate. The role of the autonomous, powerful military or Tatmadaw in the post-independence national political landscape influenced how Myanmar responded to the pandemic in 2020, while the multi-faceted political crisis affected the response from February 2021 onwards.

On 1 February 2021, the military (a.k.a. the Tatmadaw) seized power alleging major irregularities in the November 2020 general election. It instated a state of emergency that was still in place as of early 2024. Myanmar now has two entities claiming to be the country's legitimate government. The military formed the State Administration Council (SAC) which exercises de facto control over all major economic and policy infrastructures. Lawmakers loyal to the overthrown civilian government formed the National Unity

Government (NUG). The country has since seen renewed civil war between the SAC and its various opponents, including the NUG.

This chapter outlines the Covid-19 response and coordination measures implemented in Myanmar. It provides an overview of the four Covid-19 waves in the country between 2020 and mid-2022, and associated response measures including testing and vaccination, stay-at-home orders, quarantine in community facilities, economic responses including cash and non-cash transfers, and civil society, community and private sector responses. We analyse the effects of and responses to Covid-19 in two time periods—before the 2021 coup and after it. We draw on official government publications, but, due to the dearth of reliable official sources, also use media articles.

Myanmar reported its first confirmed case in March 2020. Stay-at-home orders and requirements for people to quarantine in community facilities under a zero-Covid approach were implemented during the first two waves with varying efficacy. The coordination efforts of the National League of Democracy (NLD) government were considered to be one of the leading factors in Myanmar's success in handling the first two waves. However, as the second wave was petering out, the military seized power (February 2021) and the country's Covid-19 response was disrupted. The health system, including testing and vaccination facilities, was incapacitated as healthcare staff spearheaded strikes, protesting against the coup (Nachemson 2021). Vaccinations resumed in March 2021 but were hampered by the political crisis and a ban put in place by India on exports of its vaccine. There was a heavy death toll during the third wave, the Delta variant (June to October 2021), due to continuing health system disruptions and challenges (Figure 4.1). However, by the time the fourth Omicron wave arrived, vaccination rates had increased, and most people opted to self-test and treat themselves at home.

On the economic front, the buoyant growth of the preceding decade was deflated by lockdowns, travel restrictions and plummeting trade, which was hit by border closures. Myanmar faced supply chain disruptions, with order cancellations particularly acute in the manufacturing sector. Unemployment surged and the urban poor reported dangerous coping strategies: for example, turning to sex work (Lovett and Nay Chi Nway 2020). However, service industries and start-ups were able to weather the lockdowns by taking their businesses online and offering home delivery.

FIGURE 4.1
Myanmar: New Cases and New Deaths (per Million), January 2020 to May 2023

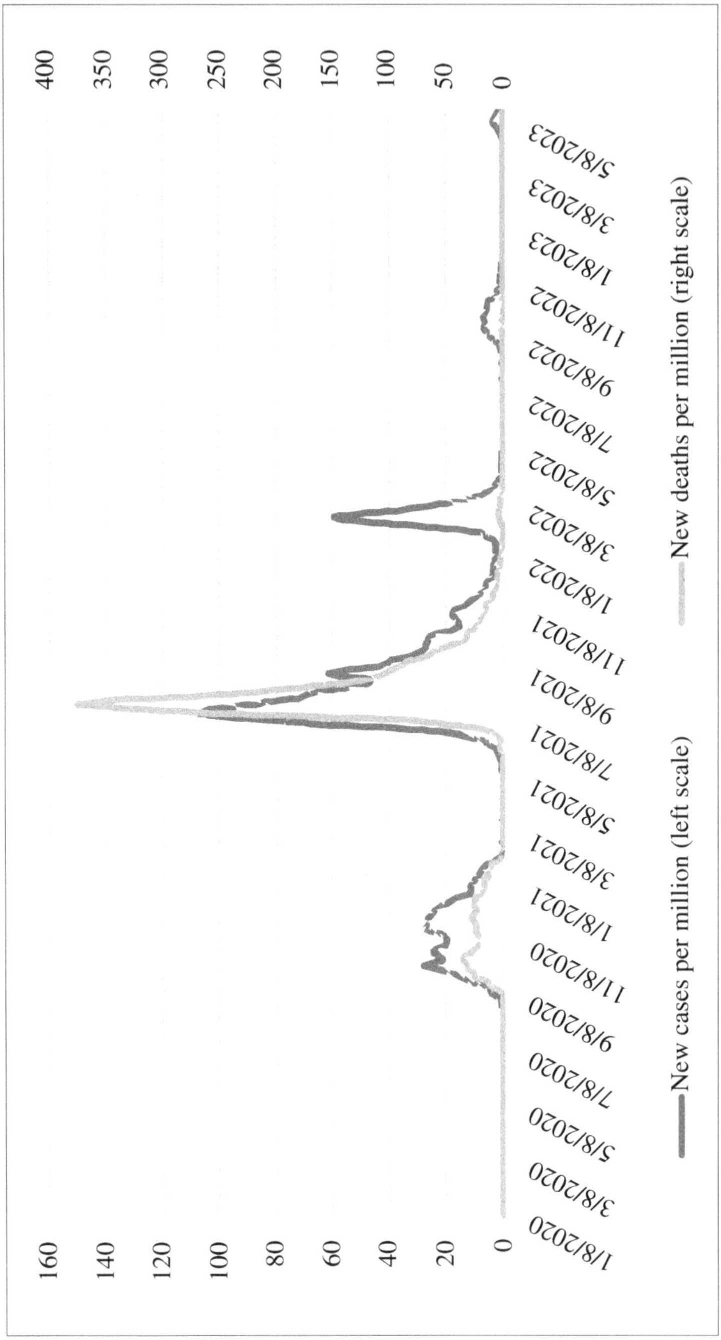

Source: ourworldindata.org.

Improved yields in the agricultural sector as a result of favourable weather conditions contributed to Myanmar's economic growth of 1.7 per cent in the financial year from October 2019 to September 2020 (World Bank 2020a). The coup jeopardized a quick and robust rebound, but by mid-2022 Myanmar was exhibiting signs of recovery.

Myanmar's two-part Covid-19 experience demonstrates how low-resource countries can respond to emergencies with political resolve and multi-stakeholder participation, but also how political turmoil can cause a decline in crisis management and exacerbate the negative impacts.

OVERVIEW OF COVID-19 IN MYANMAR

Myanmar witnessed four distinct Covid-19 waves between early 2020 and mid-2022. Each wave prompted different policy and community responses reflecting the evolving global Covid-19 situation alongside domestic political developments. Up to the end of June 2022, Myanmar had reported around 613,600 confirmed cases and nearly 19,450 confirmed deaths (Table 4.1) (Ministry of Health 2022). Given the country's weak health system, the post-coup crises and areas without government control, reported figures capture only a fraction of the true figures. Amid the political chaos, there were various claims around cases and deaths but all remain difficult to substantiate (Callahan 2021; Walker 2021a). According to Wang et al. (2022), Myanmar may have experienced around 101,000 direct Covid-19 deaths based on global excess mortality estimates. The bulk of the undercounted deaths probably occurred during the third wave, the Delta variant, which was the most devastating wave, with the capacity of the state to respond also the most limited. The third wave officially accounted for 57 per cent of confirmed cases and 82 per cent of reported deaths between March 2020 and June 2022 (Table 4.1).

A note on data and information sources is pertinent at this juncture. Reliable data has always been relatively scarce in Myanmar, and this problem is now exacerbated by widespread strife. Newly available information, analyses and commentary are also influenced by post-coup political developments. Various organizations still collect data and information but now operate in vastly different settings. Evaluation of Myanmar's Covid-19 response strategies is confounded by the military

TABLE 4.1
Covid-19 Waves in Myanmar

Wave	*Timeline*	*Reported Cases*	*Share of Total Covid Cases (%)*[a]	*Reported Deaths*	*Share of Total Covid Deaths (%)*[b]	*Notes*
1	March to May 2020	~250	0.04	6	0.03	
2	August 2020 to January 2021	~140,000	22.8	~3,100	15.9	
	February to June 2021	~20,000	3.3	~250	1.28	Post-coup health system crises
3	June to October 2021	~350,000	57.1	~16,000	82.05	Delta variant
4	February to March 2022	~75,000	12.2	~120	0.62	Omicron variant
	March to June 2022	~28,500	4.6	<10	0.05	
Total		*~613,750*		*~19,486*		

Notes: Percentages may not total 100 due to rounding. After the coup, the SAC reconstituted the Ministry of Health and Sports as the Ministry of Health and created the Ministry of Sports and Youth Affairs.
Total Covid cases for the period March 2020 to June 2022.
Total Covid deaths for the period March 2020 to June 2022.
Sources: Ministry of Health and Sports (2020–21); Ministry of Health (2021–22).

takeover and subsequent crises making it difficult to disentangle the impact of Covid-19 from that of the coup as data collection, media coverage and academic analysis decreased while the political situation consumed attention. Notably, data and policy documents were more widely available under the NLD government than the SAC.

First Wave (March to May 2020)

The first case was confirmed on 23 March 2020 in a repatriated national who subsequently returned to his home region near the Indian border (Reuters 2020). This set the context for the stigmatization of Covid-19 as an "imported disease" and for the government and health authorities to adopt a zero-Covid stance to prevent the virus from spreading to major cities. Misinformation, such as fake voice messages, contributed to panic buying in the weeks leading up to the first case (Lwin 2020a).

The government implemented targeted stay-at-home orders, given Myanmar's limited resources and the need to minimize economic impacts. Persons suspected of having Covid-19 were mandated to receive treatment only in government hospitals and their contacts were required to undergo mandatory community quarantine facilities. The government also began inspecting labour-intensive worksites such as garment factories to mitigate Covid-19 risks, and this worked well until the highly transmissible Omicron variant arrived two years later.

Second Wave (August 2020 to January 2021)

The second wave began in mid-August 2020 after a case was detected in Rakhine State bordering Bangladesh. This reinforced the imported disease mindset. Efforts were made to contain the outbreak in Rakhine but Yangon and other major cities soon reported cases. The government continued with mandatory treatment at public hospitals, expanding facilities and leveraging non-health, private sector and civil society resources to create a coordinated response. Similar to the first wave, those who had been in contact with an infected person, those who were exhibiting symptoms and those who were suspected of having Covid-19 were required to quarantine in a community facility.

Broader developments—efforts to hold Myanmar's first general election overseen by a civilian government in sixty years and peace talks—dominated political and popular discourses. There was an upsurge in cases after the November 2020 election but not to the scale seen in post-election surges elsewhere. Anecdotal evidence indicates cases were spreading undetected and unreported, due in part to people's fears that they would be forced to quarantine in a community facility leading them to keep their Covid-19 status private.

The country was at the tail end of the second wave when the military seized power on 1 February 2021. Covid testing, and the health system in general, collapsed as health staff began strikes, initiating civil disobedience against the coup. The large protests, peaceful at first, and the chaos and violence of the subsequent months meant that Covid-19 was likely spreading but remaining undetected and was of lesser concern to the public. Public anger against the coup was such that protesters chanted that the coup was "worse than Covid-19" (Thant 2021, p. 3).

Third Wave (May to September 2021)

In late May 2021, cases driven by the Delta variant began spiking in towns near the Indian border, reinforcing the imported disease framing. The weakened public health system was barely functioning, with very little treatment or resources available (Tsoi and Myint 2022). Private hospitals were finally allowed to treat Covid-19 cases; they demanded hefty fees but were nonetheless overwhelmed.

The military deployed its medical corps to reinforce the strained health system but they too were unable to cope with the surge. Striking doctors covertly provided home treatment, often risking arrest. Many people had no option but to test themselves with commercially available kits and resort to home treatment, though they needed to be hospitalized.

There were widespread shortages, with family members queuing for hours to refill oxygen canisters and tanks (*Irrawaddy* 2021; Reuters 2021a). The SAC was accused of restricting oxygen and mismanaging the response, while rumours of border and pharmacy closures saw panic buying of essential medicines (Radio Free Asia 2021c). Despite the many challenges, the third wave subsided by August 2021, but the populace was left traumatized.

Fourth Wave (February to March 2022)

The fourth wave, which was caused by the Omicron variant, began in early February 2022. Unlike earlier waves, one of the first reported outbreaks was at a Yangon factory (Mizzima Staff 2022). The milder nature of Omicron infections, alongside wider availability and uptake of vaccinations, and fatigue from the third wave meant that government and community attitudes towards the fourth were vastly different and responses less robust. Most people opted to test and treat at home, leading to under-reporting of cases. With very little intervention, the wave had subsided by early March 2022.

Vaccination

Vaccinations commenced in late January 2021 using the Serum Institute of India's Covishield version of the Oxford/AstraZeneca vaccine. The COVID-19 Vaccines Global Access (COVAX) facility did not initially ship vaccines to Myanmar over concerns regarding transparency and cold-chain integrity; COVAX vaccines began arriving in late 2021 (Ministry of Health 2021b). After the initial batches of Covishield ran out, the SAC procured vaccines from a range of sources, spanning China, Russia and India.[2] In May 2022, Myanmar started using Myancopharm, a domestically produced, licensed version of the Sinopharm vaccine, with over 1 million doses delivered in May 2022 (Myanmar News Agency 2022a, 2022b).

Frontline health workers and government leadership received vaccines a week before the coup of 1 February 2021. The coup led to political uncertainty and widespread walkouts of healthcare staff, and others, which disrupted vaccinations. Efforts resumed in March 2021 but were hampered by the continuing chaos and India's vaccine export ban from April 2021 to October 2021.

The SAC trained and mobilized non-striking auxiliary health staff, Red Cross volunteers and the military's medical directorate to roll out vaccinations, but staffing gaps remained for months. The overall vaccination effort was hostage to the highly polarized political landscape as some citizens boycotted vaccines in solidarity with protesters. Political disinformation attacking the SAC's vaccination programme was also rampant. However, the third wave changed attitudes and uptake increased.

The SAC's Ministry of Health oversaw Myanmar's main Covid-19 vaccination programme though parallel efforts also existed, organized by ethnic armed organizations and the private sector. Continuing their political boycott, some citizens resorted to the private sector (Liu 2022). Non-governmental organizations and armed ethnic organizations operating in areas that were not SAC controlled implemented their own vaccination programmes, relying on doses donated by China (*Channel NewsAsia* 2021; Macan-Markar 2021). The National Unity Government also established a task force to access COVAX vaccines and coordinate vaccination delivery in areas controlled by sympathetic ethnic armed organizations. However, by end-June 2022 National Unity Government vaccinations had not begun.

By end-June 2022, the SAC Ministry of Health reported 65 million vaccine doses given, with 35.4 million people having been vaccinated at least once and 30 million having received two doses. This translates to 64.4 per cent of the total population having received at least one dose and 50.6 per cent having received two, while 13.3 per cent had received only one. By June 2022, Myanmar's vaccination rate ranked last among countries of the Association of Southeast Asian Nations (ASEAN) even though it was one of the first to begin.

RESPONSES

This section covers four main components of Myanmar's response measures to Covid-19: (1) stay-at-home orders, (2) quarantine in community facilities, (3) civil society, community and private sector responses and (4) economic responses. Both the NLD and SAC administrations deployed other measures and thus, this list is not exhaustive.

Stay-at-Home Orders

During the first three waves of Covid-19, authorities implemented stay-at-home orders to mitigate transmissions. They were effective during the first and second waves but fatigue and broader political currents started to sap implementation by late 2020. During the third wave the orders mostly existed only on paper and by the fourth they had been abandoned. The term stay-at-home order was used instead of lockdown to mitigate public panic and prevent misinterpretations—the term "lockdown" was widely associated with much stricter measures.

Stay-at-home orders were placed on townships with active community transmissions, with a focus on urban townships, transit hubs and keeping Naypyitaw Covid-free (Aung 2020). At the township level, government offices and essential businesses remained open albeit with lower capacity, while food outlets were only permitted to sell takeaway (Lwin 2020b). Travel within the township was partially restricted, with residents requiring permits from ward or village administrators to cross township boundaries. The General Administration Department, which oversees townships and is a crucial part of subnational governance, set up checkpoints, while health posts were erected along main roads to screen travellers in rural townships and at state/regional borders. Below the township level, stay-at-home orders were more stringent for streets or buildings with reported cases. The specific location was cordoned off, with confirmed and suspected cases sent to health facilities and contacts subjected to mandatory facility quarantine. Red Cross or community volunteers staffed checkpoints to oversee the localized lockdown and coordinated delivery of food and essential supplies. During the first wave, a village in Chin State, the location of Myanmar's first confirmed case, and ten townships in Yangon were placed under stay-at-home orders. During the second and third waves, 75 and 119 townships respectively were placed under stay-at-home orders.

This two-tier system allowed a targeted approach, sparing most residents from stringent procedures and facilitating efficient use of sparse resources. Stay-at-home orders were complemented by measures such as curfews, school closures and travel restrictions. All international commercial flights were halted for two years (March 2020 to April 2022) except for government-arranged relief and special cargo flights. Domestic flights were suspended during the first three waves, and domestic inter-city buses were instructed to run at half capacity. The government implemented health guidelines for all factories in mid-April 2020; factories were closed in April 2020 and only allowed to reopen after inspection and certification by local health and labour authorities.

Community-Based Facility Quarantine

During the first and second waves, the government used quarantine to support its zero-Covid approach. Returnees, contacts of confirmed/suspected cases, and people displaying symptoms were subjected to mandatory quarantine for two to three weeks. The approach initially relied on existing quarantine facilities but they were quickly overwhelmed even before any case was confirmed. By late March 2020, the government began a new system of using community facilities across the country to enable each township or district to organize quarantine locally.

Government buildings such as stadiums, military camps, public housing complexes, schools and community centres, as well as community buildings and religious institutions, were mobilized as quarantine centres. The government reported having the capacity to quarantine 100,000 people at any given time. Hotel quarantine was also available but pricey, leaving most to choose community facilities. Around 200,000 people were quarantined in different facilities between mid-August and end-October 2020, based on data from the Ministry of Health and Sports.

Civilian-run quarantine facilities were mostly staffed by civil society volunteers organized under the government's National Volunteer Steering Unit. In border and transit states, the government established larger facilities to process and quarantine returning migrants (Weng 2020). As the number of returnees dramatically increased, many were bussed to their townships of residence for localized community quarantine.

Civil society and local communities contributed food, material and personnel to facilities in their vicinity as government resources became overstretched (Naing S. 2020). In the aftermath of the coup, most quarantine facilities could not function due to a lack of staff and a refusal by civil society organizations to work with the SAC. Military facilities and hotels continued to function as quarantine centres but health enforcement became weak in the latter, with stories of people paying to evade or leave earlier.

Civil Society, Community and Private Sector Responses

Under earlier periods of military rule and an underperforming state, a strong culture of civic collaboration and communal solidarity in the face of shared adversity emerged in Myanmar. The role and space of civil society, community and private sector involvement in responding to major crises grew following cyclone Nargis in 2008, and more so after 2010, with the change from military to civilian rule. Civil society organizations (CSOs), local communities and businesses helped fill critical gaps both before and after the coup to address issues such as staffing health checkpoints in townships under stay-at-home orders, operating quarantine centres, donating and operating Covid treatment centres and rolling out vaccinations.

The coup, the subsequent political crisis and the SAC's responses threw the entire architecture of civil society, community and the private sector into disarray. Measures taken against striking medical staff eroded trust and willingness to coordinate and cooperate with the military government, which was seen as further exacerbating the deadly impact of the Delta variant-driven third wave. Many volunteers and organizations continued to operate but under increasingly challenging conditions. Despite the insecurity and multiple crises, civil society, communities and the private sector rallied once again to respond to Covid-19.

CIVIL SOCIETY AND COMMUNITY

Civil society made three key contributions: personnel, ambulances and distribution of aid. In June 2020, the then minister of social welfare said more than 45,000 volunteers were staffing quarantine centres, with 15,000 in the Yangon region alone (Htwe 2020a and 2020b). While they provided much-needed support for the public health workforce, the volunteers came under increasing strain. Some CSOs operated community ambulances using repurposed vans, some provided critical care and delivered meals to Covid centres, quarantine facilities and locations under stay-at-home orders. They also organized fundraisers and distributed dry goods and cash aid to low-income families—these case transfers were independent from government transfers. During the third wave, CSOs became the sole responders in many areas (Radio Free Asia 2021b). Community ambulances and rescue crews were often the only source of oxygen and lifesaving treatment, and also the only party to take away the deceased (Reuters 2021c).

Some local communities took matters into their own hands out of fear or lack of state support. During the first and second waves, some neighbourhoods in major cities erected barricades to prevent outsiders from entering, based on the view of Covid-19 as an imported disease; others saw stay-at-home orders as too weak and sought collective action to create more stringent cordons sanitaires (Kyaw and Heijmans 2020).

Rural areas and villages required returnees and visitors to quarantine in community facilities such as the village monastery or school, with the community providing meals and other support. Communities along the border also mobilized to receive their members, kin returning from overseas and those transiting, overseeing community quarantines and processing the returnees, among other tasks (Hkawng, Awng and Fishbein 2020).

In areas not controlled by the state, parallel health systems run by ethnic health organizations provided well-established, community-based health networks that filled in the critical gaps both before and after the coup (Brennan 2021). This was especially visible in the roll-out of vaccination drives, and the response to escalating local community needs after 2020, including support for those affected by increased conflict and mass displacements.

PRIVATE SECTOR

The business sector became a major response pillar, mobilizing resources to buttress government efforts. When Myanmar's first dedicated Covid-19 treatment centre was established in the Yangon region, private hospitals contributed staff and equipment, supplementing the resources of the Ministry of Health and Sports and the military's medical directorate (Mon, Thar and Kean 2020).

Notably, in April 2020, one of the largest pharmacy firms, AA Pharmacy, procured and donated the diagnostic equipment that formed the basis of the country's testing capacity for the first few months. Myanmar's largest private bank, KBZ Bank, was a consistent donor to different response measures. Its subsidiaries, including two airlines, were mobilized to airlift emergency medical supplies into the country from abroad and to regional cities. AYA Bank's Ayeyarwady Foundation established 500-bed field hospitals in Yangon and Mandalay that helped relieve the burden on government hospitals. Other businesses also contributed facilities for similar use. Private banks, construction companies, private hospitals and importers of medical products also pooled resources to support endeavours (*Irrawaddy* 2020b).

The Union of Myanmar Federation of Chambers of Commerce and Industry, the country's largest private sector body, was involved both before and after the coup in working to stabilize the cost and availability of basic foodstuffs (for example, rice, edible oil and onions) by selling at subsidized rates. It also oversaw the first post-coup vaccination programme on behalf of the Ministry of Health and Sports, while the Myanmar Chinese Chamber of Commerce launched its own vaccination programme in August 2021 (Xinhua 2021). Many state/region and township-level business associations also donated oxygen plants in collaboration with charities and local health departments.

ECONOMIC RESPONSES

Covid-19 Economic Relief Plan

The NLD government announced the Covid-19 Economic Relief Plan in April 2020 to coordinate and guide the country's immediate economic response (Lwin 2020c). The plan had seven key goals (Table 4.2), some of which include clear and concrete action points, while other aspects were criticized as being vague (Karen Peace Support Network 2020; Bello, Franco and Vervest 2020).

Business Loans

Under the Covid-19 Economic Relief Plan, the government created an MMK100 billion pool (around US$71 million, 0.1 per cent of gross domestic product [GDP]) for low-interest (1 per cent) one-year soft loans to businesses. The pool was later increased to MMK200–500 billion (US$140–350 million), with the government later saying it was prepared to use up to 5 per cent of GDP in stimulus spending. The government also extended MMK59.5 billion in loans to forty-four microfinance institutions at 2 per cent interest rates, with small businesses eligible.

These loans were offered in sectoral batches such as to tourism, garments and agriculture. The first round (July 2020) went to 3,393 businesses and the second (September and October 2020) to 3,276. In October 2020, the

TABLE 4.2
Components of the Covid-19 Economic Relief Plan

Goal	*Key Activities*
1. Improve macroeconomic environment through monetary stimulus	Reduce interest rates, implement low minimum reserve requirements for banks, and reduce treasury bond/bill sales.
2. Ease impact on the private sector through improvements to investment, trade and banking sectors	Low-interest loans; credit guarantees; tax/fee deferrals, waivers and credits; loan restructuring; expediting investment approval; trade financing and facilitation.
3. Ease impact on labourers and workers	Extend labour benefits.
4. Ease impact on households	Waive some tariffs and taxes; cash and in-kind transfers.
5. Promote innovative products, such as mobile applications and platforms	Promote mobile financial payments and e-commerce.
6. Strengthen the health system	Improve quarantine facilities, import medical products, and upgrade facilities.
7. Increase access to Covid-19 response financing	Reallocate the budget to the Covid-19 Fund, and increase access to external development financing.

Source: Adapted from Government of the Republic of the Union of Myanmar (2020).

government unveiled the long-term Myanmar Economic Recovery and Resilience Plan, which replaced the Covid-19 Economic Relief Plan. It was reported that the government had spent more than MMK4 trillion or 3.4 per cent of GDP on the Covid-19 Economic Relief Plan.

After the coup, the SAC faced a severe tightening of fiscal space, broader political challenges and economic malaise, among other issues. These factors limited its ability to roll out existing and new interventions, even as businesses faced greater headwinds. Some economic response activities resumed by late 2021, with further loans disbursed from the existing allocation of funds to 998 businesses as of end-June 2022. The SAC revised the Myanmar Economic Recovery and Resilience Plan as the Myanmar Economic Recovery Plan, but little information on the contents has been made public. In mid-2022, the SAC announced a new MMK400 billion fund for economic recovery, repurposing leftover monies from the Natural Disaster Management Fund.

Cash and Non-cash Transfers

Under the Covid-19 Economic Relief Plan, the civilian government implemented cash and non-cash transfers (Table 4.3) in 2020 to soften the impact of stay-at-home orders and broader economic constrictions. Under the first round, in April 2020, the government provided essential foodstuffs to households with no regular income. This was followed by four rounds of cash transfers. These transfers relied on regional governments and administrators from the General Administration Department at township, ward and village level to identify and compile the lists of eligible recipients and disburse the aid.

There were also more targeted cash transfer efforts. In October 2020, the government announced plans to provide an additional MMK14,000 to each person in low-income families in townships under stay-at-home orders during the second wave. In mid-May 2020, the Social Welfare Department announced a collaboration with the Livelihoods and Food Security Fund, a Yangon-based international donor fund, of a one time MMK30,000 (US$22.25) payment to each of around 440,000 women and all elderly in five states (Nyein 2020a).

The Social Security Board under the Ministry of Labour, Immigration and Population (the Ministry of Labour after 2021) paid eligible insured workers 40 per cent of their wages as financial assistance during stay-at-home order periods and factory inspections for Covid-19 compliance, postponed the deadlines for employers and employees to make social insurance payments, and also announced plans to pay MMK30,000 to each uninsured worker (Thazin Hlaing 2020; Thiha Ko Ko 2020). In September 2020, the government announced an interest-free loan scheme for the 1 million-plus permanent government employees; they were eligible to borrow a sum twice their monthly salary (Naing A. 2020). An annual agricultural loan made during the monsoon season was modified: the interest rate was reduced from 8 per cent to 5 per cent (Democratic Voice of Burma 2020).

TABLE 4.3
Cash and Non-cash Transfers Implemented in 2020

No.	*Date*	*Support Given*	*Amount per Household*	*Recipients*	*Target Number of Households*	*Estimated Cost*
1	April 2020	Essential foodstuffs (non-cash)	MMK15,000	Households with irregular income	More than 4 million	MMK50 billion
2	May and June 2020	Cash for essential foodstuffs	MMK15,000	Households not awarded in the first round	1.4 million	MMK21.1 billion
3	July 2020	Cash transfer	MMK40,000	Low-income households	5.4 million	MMK218.1 billion
4	September 2020	Cash transfer	MMK20,000	Low-income households	5.6 million	MMK113.5 billion
5	November 2020	Cash transfer	MMK20,000–40,000	Low-income households	6.1 million	MMK164 billion +

Source: Based on government reports and media articles.

From April 2020, the government did not charge households for the first 150 units of electricity they used each month, translating to around MMK12,000 in monthly relief. This measure was intended to encourage households' compliance with stay-at-home orders, and residents posted on social media about donating their savings back to the government (Tha 2020). This relief continued monthly and remained in place as of July 2022. The government also coordinated with the private sector to stabilize the price of essential foodstuffs such as rice, pulses, cooking oil and onions (BBC Burmese 2020).

Following the coup, the SAC was unable to continue cash and non-cash transfers due to a severe contraction of fiscal space and the political crisis and insecurity, among other challenges (*Irrawaddy* 2021). However, it coordinated with the private sector to have essential foodstuffs sold at affordable prices in areas with higher poverty rates, such as peri-urban areas of Yangon and Mandalay. As of July 2022, the Social Security Board payments were continued, though payment of electricity tariffs had become politicized (Radio Free Asia 2021a).

PRE-COUP MONETARY POLICY RESPONSES

The government and the Central Bank of Myanmar enacted fiscal responses early in 2020. The CBM lowered its interest rate three times by one percentage point each time between mid-March 2020 and May 2020, decreasing from 10 to 7 per cent. This was the first adjustment in decades. Other interest rates, including those for bank deposits, collateralized and unsecured loans, were also lowered. The CBM had already been scaling back deposit auctions prior to Covid-19 due to weak demand given the higher inflation, and they were suspended from March 2020. Private banks were permitted to restructure or reschedule their loans as well, since trust in banks has remained relatively low since the 2003 banking crisis (triggered by US sanctions) and it can take very little to trigger a large problem. An August 2020 deadline for banks to sanitize their non-performing loans, turning them into overdrafts, was extended to August 2023.

The CBM also cut the reserve requirement or cash reserve ratio from 5 per cent to 3.5 per cent in April 2020 and issued a directive allowing banks to adjust their liquidity ratio calculation by increasing the weight of

CBM-issued treasury bonds from 50 per cent to 90 per cent. Money supply growth had been moderating prior to the pandemic, with an 11.23 per cent year-on-year increase in FY2018/19 but accelerated to 17.27 per cent over 2020, growing from MMK19.1 trillion in 2019Q4 to MMK22.4 trillion in 2020Q4, and reaching MMK23.2 trillion in 2021Q1.

On the foreign exchange front, the CBM continued its overall trend of purchasing US dollars in 2020, buying US$287.4 million between January 2020 and January 2021. This was an effort to maintain export competitiveness by stabilizing the kyat, which had been regaining against the dollar and other currencies since early 2019 after losing 15 per cent in 2018.[3] The kyat had appreciated against the dollar over 2020 at a rate faster than other currencies in the region. In its December 2020 report, the World Bank indicated that there was little data available to explain the strength, but listed a slight trade surplus and capital account investments alongside stronger kyat demand based on the expectations that its recovery in 2019 would continue. In this context, as foreign currency savings bore little or no interest whereas kyat-denominated savings did accrue some, citizens who had bought US dollars as a hedge during the earlier 2018 devaluation, as well as those who had dollar savings, converted their funds back into kyat. The World Bank also noted that Myanmar's shallow foreign exchange market made it extremely sensitive to small trades and speculation.

POST-COUP MONETARY POLICY RESPONSES

There have been no interest rate adjustments since mid-2020. However, the political uncertainty caused fears of a bank run and banking crisis, and these fears were exacerbated by rumours on social media. Consequently, the Central Bank of Myanmar (CBM) lowered the reserve requirement for private banks from 3.5 per cent to 3 per cent in April 2021. The liquidity ratio was also amended in May 2021, allowing banks to increase the weighting of treasury bonds from 90 per cent to 100 per cent. In December 2021, the reserve requirement was adjusted such that three-quarters of the 3 per cent could be kept as current account deposits at the CBM and the remaining quarter as cash. Money supply grew by 66.93 per cent over 2021, rising from MMK23.2 trillion in 2021Q1 to MMK38.71 trillion in

2022Q1, though this moderated over 2022Q2, when it fell 7.8 per cent to MMK35.69 trillion. These responses arguably were more a response to the political crisis than to Covid-19, but nonetheless influenced the post-coup economic trajectory.

Between February 2021 and March 2022, the CBM sold US$553.8 million to maintain the kyat (Figure 4.2), which nonetheless lost around half of its value between February 2021 and June 2022. In April 2022, the CBM imposed a fixed exchange rate of MMK1,850 to the dollar, which was revised to MMK2,100 in August 2022. Despite consecutive trade surpluses in the period covered, partly due to import restrictions, the currency's black-market value dipped (Figure 4.3). This reflects capital flight as some foreign investors exited Myanmar and locals turned to the US dollar, gold and real estate to hedge. Private sector sources have also pointed to speculation as a major source of currency volatility even before the coup, a problem that was exacerbated by political rumours and a lack of confidence in the SAC.

ASSESSING THE RESPONSES

Myanmar's stay-at-home orders were initially stringently enforced and communities, fuelled by fear, were not only compliant, but in some cases over-responded by implementing their own more stringent rules. With time, however, implementation petered out due to fatigue and complacency. There were shows of compliance where officials and community members portrayed adherence during checks and for photographic records. There were also allegations that during stay-at-home orders different rules were applied to different communities, such as the Rohingyas and other internally displaced people (Mann 2020; Nachemson 2020). After the coup, the stay-at-home orders mostly existed on paper only. The Ministry of Health and Sports faced severe human resource shortages, while the General Administration Department was hampered by local administrators resigning or being assassinated by anti-SAC resistance groups. That said, insecurity and fear of the Delta variant propped up stay-at-home orders during the third wave.

Afraid of quarantine, some travellers bypassed Covid checkpoints. Notably, at the onset of the second wave, thousands of domestic flight passengers failed to report on arrival to health authorities, who were

FIGURE 4.2
Net Balance of US Dollar Purchases and Sales by the Central Bank of Myanmar from October 2019 to March 2022

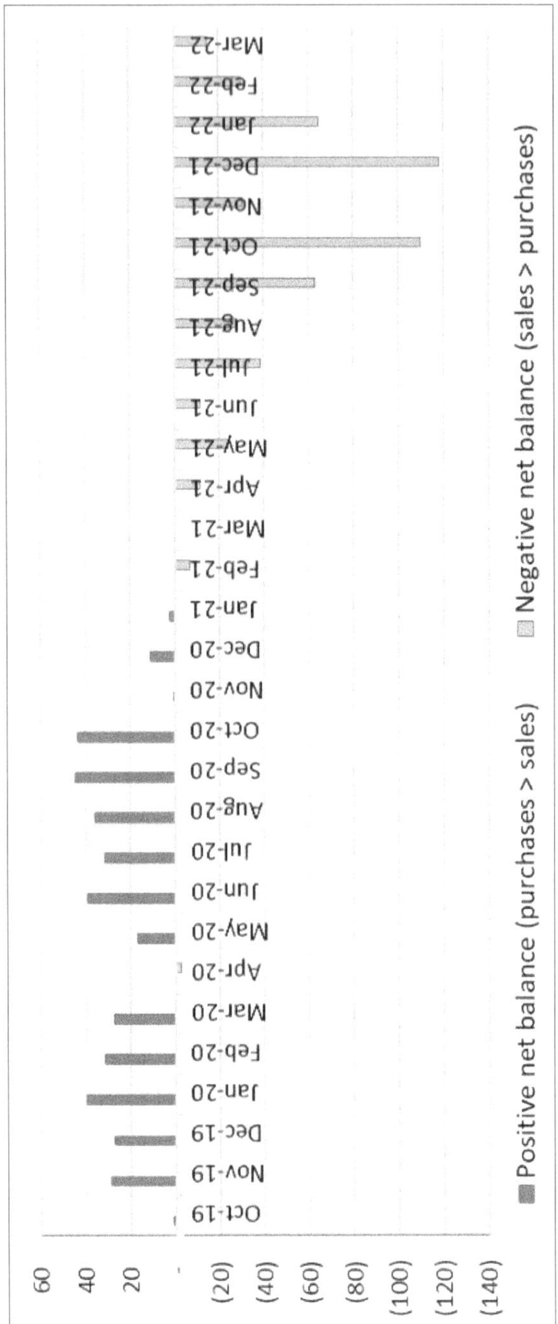

Source: Central Bank of Myanmar.

FIGURE 4.3
Reported Black-Market Rate of Kyat to US Dollar in Kyat, October 2019 to July 2022

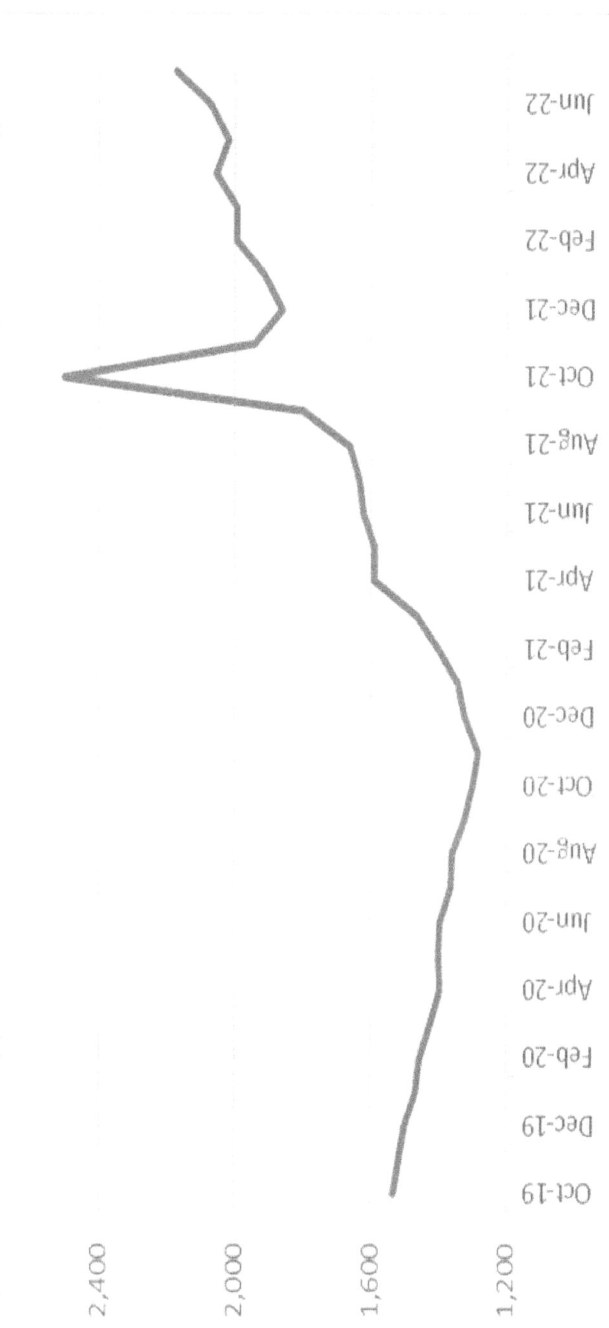

Sources: News outlets and money changer web pages.

scrambling to trace contacts (Htun 2020). Similarly, travellers are believed to have bypassed checkpoints around Naypyitaw by entering via minor roads. Interstate/region health checkpoints were also not stringent at times; for example, sometimes only the temperature of a vehicle's driver was checked, and not the passengers.

The system of community quarantine facilities had mixed results. On one hand, it complemented the stay-at-home orders in dampening the spread of Covid-19. The government aggressively quarantined people using broad criteria, such as all family members and people sharing office space. However, the mandatory and facility-based nature also caused significant panic. Fear of mandatory quarantine led to under-reporting of suspected cases and people avoiding treatment until symptoms worsened to the point of needing serious intervention.

The cash and non-cash transfers depended on the capacity and discretion of the administrators of wards (in cities and towns) and villages. This caused implementation challenges, such as recipients not getting the full amount, delays, disbursements to some less-poor families instead of those more in need, and accusations that the village and ward administrators showed favouritism in the disbursements (Phu 2020). Some administrators also lacked the competency to disburse the transfers. The cash transfers and loans also became politicized in the run-up to the election and more so after the coup. The National Unity Government declared repayments of the monsoon agricultural loans indefinitely suspended. The SAC faced challenges when farmers initially boycotted repaying both interest and capital. It later increased the loan amount to MMK150,000 (~US$70) per acre of rice in 2022, subject to farmers repaying earlier loans.

The Covid-19 Economic Relief Plan was a key policy document guiding economic response. When it was unveiled, the reaction was mixed because of its small fiscal envelope and lack of clarity (*Irrawaddy* 2020a). The business community described the plan as weak, as the package initially represented around 0.1 per cent of Myanmar's GDP. Going into the pandemic, Myanmar had built up some fiscal reserves that would have allowed a more robust response. Civil society and policy commentators pointed out that the document lacked details on the prioritization of measures and lacked a logical framework, making it harder for stakeholders to coordinate (Bello, Franco and Vervest 2020). Businesses' poor adherence to regulatory frameworks, such as not keeping proper financial records, limited their eligibility and undermined the impact of the loan scheme.

The NLD administration had a big advantage in State Counsellor Daw Aung San Suu Kyi's popular appeal. She assumed a central, visible role in the response and public outreach (Kyaw 2020b). Despite various hurdles, her involvement generated a huge reservoir of public trust in government responses and tolerance for shortcomings. It also galvanized civil society across the country to become involved and that in turn served as a multiplier for the government's response measures. Sentiment soured after the coup and subsequent political violence, with most citizens and CSOs actively boycotting the SAC, thereby limiting the impact of the interventions.

POLICY COORDINATION AND IMPLEMENTATION

This section covers the government policy coordination framework, including committees formed and factors affecting the implementation of the framework.

Coordination

Both before and after the coup, overall policy coordination was very centralized and top-down. In 2020, the national-level government took the lead with state and region ministers involved. Given Myanmar's political landscape and the 2020 general election, the NLD government brought in the autonomous military, but it had limited involvement and visibility.

Responses to Covid-19 were managed at three levels. Between January 2020 and April 2020, six committees were formed to coordinate the overall Covid-19 response: two inter-ministerial policy coordinating committees, one economic response committee and three committees that oversaw implementation (Table 4.4). At the national level, one of the inter-ministerial committees was chaired by the State Counsellor and coordinated national responses. A civil-military committee (the fourth committee in Table 4.4) chaired by Vice President-1 U Myint Swe was responsible for overseeing quarantine efforts. These two committees were replicated at the state, regional and township levels with corresponding administrative heads, such as chief ministers or township administrators

TABLE 4.4
Covid-19 Response and Coordination Committees Formed in 2020

No.	*Name*	*Date Established*	*Details*
1.	Central Committee on Prevention, Control and Treatment of the 2019 Novel Coronavirus	30 January 2020	Leadership: co-chaired by Minister of International Cooperation and Minister of Health and Sports. Duties: high-level coordination; screening and tracking international arrivals and suspected cases; health education and public service announcements; overseeing health, quarantine and response activities in ports of entry; coordinating the procurement of medical commodities and arranging the repatriation of citizens stranded in Wuhan, China.
2.	National-Level Central Committee on the Prevention, Control and Treatment of Coronavirus Disease 2019 (Covid-19)	13 March 2020	Leadership: co-chaired by State Counsellor. Composition: Ministers for International Cooperation and Health and Sports as joint secretaries; fifteen union ministers and social welfare ministers from each state and region. Duties: oversee Covid-19 control and response; oversee ports of entry and quarantine; procurement of medical commodities; coordinate with foreign embassies and issue notifications (government or ministry-level notices that act as official updates to laws and ordinances).
3.	Working Committee to Address the Impact of Covid-19 on the Country's Economy	13 March 2020	Leadership: chaired by Minister of Investment and Foreign Economic Relations. Composition: Ministry of Planning, Finance and Industry; Ministry of Commerce; Ministry of Labour; the Central Bank of Myanmar; and the Ministry of Hotels and Tourism. Duties: address negative impacts of Covid-19 on the economy; draft, implement and coordinate the Covid-19 Economic Relief Plan.

4.	Coronavirus Disease 2019 (Covid-19) Control and Emergency Response Committee	31 March 2020	Leadership: Chaired by Vice President 1 Composition: this is a civil-military committee, with all three military-controlled ministries represented. Duties: oversee Covid-19 quarantine efforts.
5.	National Volunteer Steering Unit	25 April 2020	Leadership: chaired by State Counsellor Composition: Minister of Social Welfare, Relief and Resettlement; the Union Government Ministry; state and region chief ministers; permanent secretary of the Ministry of Health and Sports. Duties: organize and coordinate civil society and community volunteers; monitor the needs of quarantine centres; oversee the welfare of volunteers; arrange food, transportation and safety equipment for volunteers.
6.	Committee to Coordinate National Covid-19 Response with Ethnic Armed Groups	27 April 2020	Leadership: chaired by senior NLD officials from the National Reconciliation and Peace Centre. Duties: share information on Covid-19 prevention and response; coordinate and collaborate on processing returning migrants; organize medical treatment; liaise and coordinate with ethnic armed groups and state and regional governments.

Sources: Based on government announcements and notifications.

from the General Administration Department. These structures stopped operating after the coup.

Implementation

The Covid-19 Control and Emergency Response Committee (CERC) was replicated at the state and regional level through coordination committees led by the Ministry of Social Welfare. Under these committees, township-level emergency response committees monitored potential Covid-19 cases, managed community quarantine facilities and food distribution, organized volunteers, supported public communications and oversaw the stay-at-home orders.

The level of coordination between the township committees, CSOs and local residents depended on the willingness of the township administrators (Brancati, Minoletti, and Riambau 2020). Townships such as Taunggyi and Kalaw were noted for effective measures supported by inclusive coordination processes and these served as models for Covid-19 response elsewhere in the country. Ethnic armed organizations administered areas along the Thai and Chinese borders, and their involvement was essential in ensuring that workers returning were quarantined and that the centres had enough support (Nyein 2020c).

After the coup, the military assumed a more visible central coordination role for Covid-19 and overall governance. SAC Deputy Prime Minister Vice Senior General Soe Win became chair of the CERC. The National Central and Economic Response committees (numbers 2 and 3 in Table 4.4) continued operations, but members were replaced with individuals from the SAC and officials appointed by the SAC. No formal declarations were made but it is almost certain that the other committees were scrapped. The SAC did publish updates from the coordination bodies, but it gave fewer details and announcements were often ignored. Consequently, businesses and communities were at times caught off guard when changes or new regulations were finally implemented.

Amid the evolving political and security situations, and alongside the fragile public health system, ethnic armed organizations and their health wings assumed a more active role in the overall public health response in non-state-controlled areas. The involvement of CSOs and communities in coordination efforts in state-controlled and non-state-controlled areas also withered away after the coup, though these groups continued to operate independently in serving communities facing multiple crises.

CONTEXT OF MYANMAR'S COVID-19 RESPONSES

Political Context

With the country's political history and looming elections, the civilian NLD government had to balance leveraging the military's institutional strength and resources, against using soldiers to enforce curfews and lockdowns (Kyaw 2020a). The General Administration Department had recently been transferred to civilian control and was being reformed. This led the NLD administration to use it as the main coordinating and implementing body for Covid-19 measures. It was supported by other civilian-controlled ministries such as the Ministry of Social Welfare, Relief and Resettlement and the Ministry of Health and Sports, alongside civil society.

Broad acceptance that the country's under-resourced health system would struggle to tackle Covid-19 also helped justify a zero-Covid approach, and raised public acceptance of stay-at-home orders and mandatory quarantines. The medical community had been maligned by pre-2020 malpractice scandals, but it saw a huge groundswell in public support in 2020 given its frontline Covid-19 role. The civil disobedience movement was then begun by medical staff in Covid centres, which further bolstered the public support.

After the coup, many of the response and coordination mechanisms developed and fine-tuned through 2020 collapsed almost overnight. The space for civil society shrank dramatically, with volunteers and CSOs caught in the spiralling crisis (Liu 2021). The political turmoil particularly affected the General Administration Department, which reverted to direct military control. Meanwhile, ward and village administrators either resigned—with their replacements rejected by communities—or were assassinated by anti-SAC forces. Trust of the public towards public institutions evaporated and post-coup Covid-19 disappeared from public attention—until it resurfaced with a vengeance as the third wave. The political violence against protesters and striking medical staff further inflamed defiance and public anger. Hospital staffing levels had been hollowed out by the strikes, and there was also stigma against using it, as this was perceived as supporting the SAC.

Economic Context

A 2018 study estimated that Myanmar's informal economy was "one of the largest in the world", representing around 50 per cent of economic output (Stokke, Vakulchuk, and Overland 2018; Chau 2019). Major unregulated revenue-generating components include jade mining, the transnational drug trade, illegal gold mining and smuggling and a sizeable, rare earth metals sector. Money laundering is also a major challenge, especially in non-state-controlled areas. It is facilitated by illegal casinos (Tower and Clapp 2020) and shadowy real estate practices in Yangon and Mandalay (Associated Press 2018; Lintner 2019).

For size comparison, the jade industry is estimated at US$30–40 billion a year, more than Myanmar's entire officially reported trade in all commodities and services (Global Witness 2015). There is no dollar figure for the drug trade, but, for scale, Myanmar authorities destroyed around US$840 million in seized illegal drugs in June 2020 (Xinhua 2020). Myanmar's rare earth exports to China in 2021 were estimated at over US$800 million (Radio Free Asia 2023) These figures rival if not eclipse economic activity from the formal sectors, especially the export industries.

These figures indicate that the national and local economies are affected by spillovers and patterns from sizeable irregular revenue streams (Stokke, Vakulchuk and Overland 2018). Social media, which played an outsized role in the country both before and after the coup, amplified rumours, affecting consumer behaviour and market patterns. These factors may also help to explain Myanmar's irregular currency and economic trajectories during the Covid-19 pandemic and after the coup.

Strong Head Start

Riding on a decade of economic liberalization and reforms, Myanmar's economy was in a comparatively healthy state in 2019 and early 2020 before the first Covid-19 wave struck in late March 2020 (Figure 4.4). In the financial year 2018/19 (see Appendix Table A4.1 for a brief guide to

FIGURE 4.4
Quarterly Change in Real GDP (Year-on-Year Growth, 2015/16 Constant Prices)

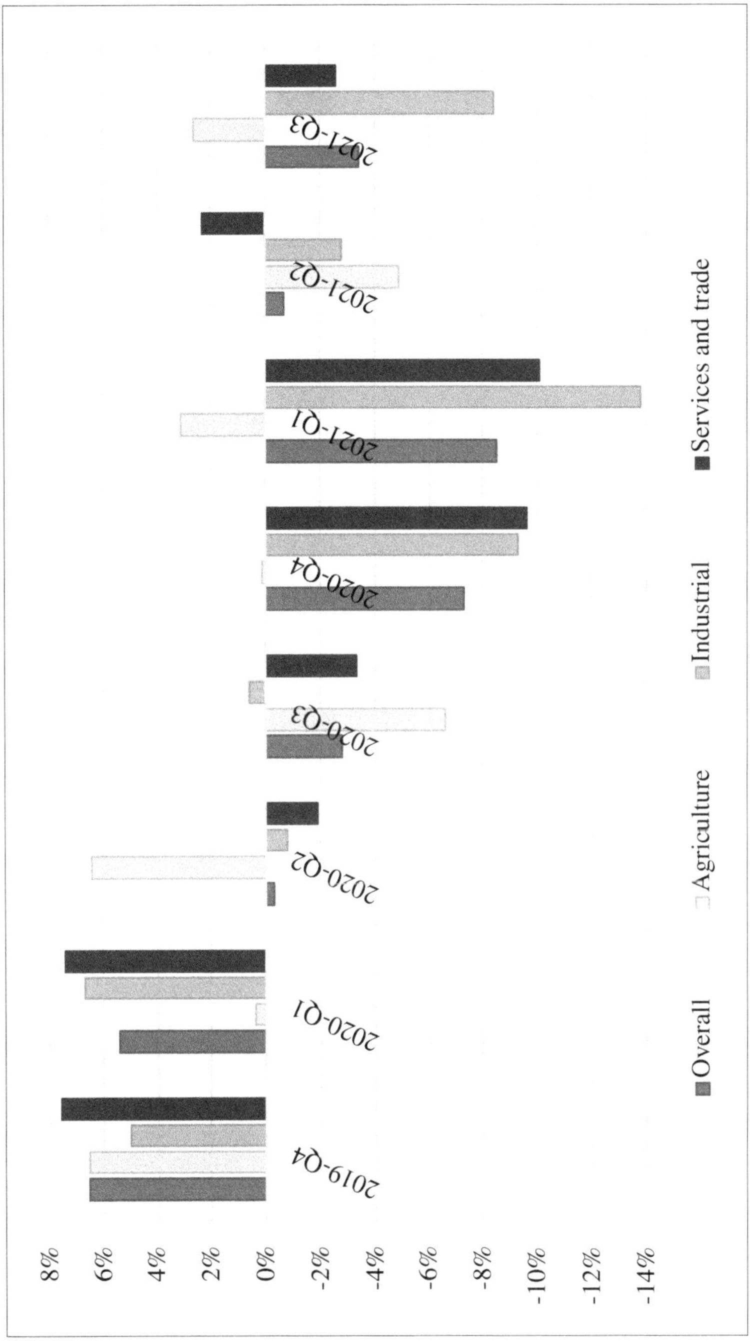

Sources: Ministry of Planning and Finance; Central Bank of Myanmar.

Myanmar's fiscal year timelines) Myanmar registered 6.8 per cent GDP growth (World Bank 2020b). Seasonal and political factors led to high output and growth in 2019Q4 and 2020Q1. Most of Myanmar's major export crops are harvested between October and April, and these accounted for 11.5 per cent of exports for FY2019/20, or US$2 billion. October to April is also the main travel season, and therefore tourism receipts for the fiscal year were frontloaded before global travel collapsed. The government had also begun rolling out increased infrastructure and social welfare spending in preparation for the November 2020 general elections.

Starting from 2019, the government was also aggressively courting and fast-tracking investment approvals given the reputational fallout and activists' calls for divestment following the 2017 Rohingya humanitarian crisis. In FY2018/19, the government approved US$4.63 billion and MMK1.69 trillion in domestic and foreign investments combined, while 2019Q4 and 2020Q1 saw approvals of US$2.96 billion and MMK1.07 trillion in investments.

However, increasing macroeconomic volatility, inflationary pressures, a widening current account deficit, lagging connectivity and business environment restrictions curtailed growth for 2019/20 somewhat.

Effects of the Coup

The 2021 coup has fundamentally transformed Myanmar's political, social, economic and security landscapes. In response to the military's heavy-handed responses to peaceful protests, armed resistance erupted across various areas starting in May 2021. The SAC is opposed by an array of armed groups including the new People's Defense Force militias and a number of major ethnic armed organizations. The National Unity Government nominally leads many People's Defense Forces, while others operate independently. Just as the Delta wave subsided in September 2021, the National Unity Government launched what it termed a "defensive resistance war" against the SAC (Walker 2021b).

Myanmar continues to experience widespread strife with daily reports of political violence and armed incidents alongside rampant disinformation. The humanitarian situation also continues to spiral, displacing over 0.76

million people due to conflict between February 2021 and end-June 2022. One tracking initiative estimates over 22,150 deaths, including 14,000 conflict deaths, during the same period (AAPP 2022).

Civil disobedience has resulted in major impacts on state revenue collection, notably on the heavily subsidized electricity sector.[4] Boycotts against electricity tariffs owed to the state electricity company cost the SAC an estimated US$1 billion in the six months after the coup. This compounded electricity generation problems caused by the depreciating kyat, resistance attacks on electricity infrastructure and a shrunken fiscal space for repairs. Electricity generation on average fell by 10 per cent between the 2019/20 and 2022/23 financial years. With increasingly erratic electricity supply, firms resorted to more expensive diesel generators, which cut margins and productivity across the board. Communities experienced a decline in living standards and safety due to frequent blackouts, with street lights and security cameras often not working.

Finally, data collection and reporting are excruciatingly difficult, with increased risks to personal security. The populace has become highly polarized and is generally less interested in objective or data-driven analyses as political content dominates traditional and social media. Trust in state-controlled media has plummeted, media regulations have been tightened, some operating licences have been revoked and lawfare used to target journalists and social media users. Platforms sympathetic to anti-coup groups have become more politicized. Research firms have either stopped functioning or have modified their output to better meet community needs, for example, publishing the locations of oxygen refill stations. All these factors mean that data and information have become less available, and the date that is produced is more likely to be coloured by risk or political considerations.

ECONOMIC IMPACT OF COVID-19

This section discusses the economic impacts of Covid-19, highlighting differences between the pre-coup (January 2020 to January 2021) and post-coup (February 2021 up to July 2022) periods. The section examines economic output, trade and investment and the monetary and fiscal situation.

Economic Output

Pre-coup

The economy had a strong start in the financial year 2019/20. The World Bank projected 6.4 per cent growth for FY2019/20 based on domestic demand and infrastructure spending in the run-up to the 2020 elections (World Bank 2019). Nonetheless, the economy began contracting from 2020Q2. While the first Covid-19 case was confirmed only at end 2020Q1, Myanmar was already experiencing knock-on effects from the pandemic, as China was its main trading partner and had started imposing lockdowns, causing supply chain disruptions in manufacturing. This was followed by cancellations of travel and orders from Asian and European countries, which were also imposing lockdowns.

Tourism-related services, natural gas exports and the crucial garment sector were the hardest-hit sectors in the pre-coup phase. Travel-related and travel-dependent services suffered, and many companies went out of business. However, as Myanmar's tourism receipts formed one of the lowest portions of GDP contribution in ASEAN, the decline in tourism had a less dramatic effect than it had on Myanmar's neighbours. A sudden drop in demand for major cash crop exports to China and weak transport and storage infrastructure pushed down the prices of many agricultural products, affecting rural communities. Supply chain disruptions initially affected the garment sector, but later stay-at-home orders took their toll. Global disruptions and impacts on seasonal order patterns also affected the factories. Nonetheless, the garment sector was able to maintain export volumes from the previous year.

The Asian Development Bank estimated that Myanmar lost between 1.2 million and 2.1 million jobs in 2020 (ADB 2020). The International Labour Organization reported that the unemployment rate doubled from 0.5 per cent in 2019 to 1.05 per cent in 2020, though average labour productivity increased in 2020 (Figure 4.5) (ILO 2020). It should be noted that a credible picture of Myanmar's labour situation is difficult to obtain, given that around 80 per cent of employment is in the informal economy (De et al. 2020).

In its December 2020 report, the World Bank found that stay-at-home orders and containment measures caused a weakening of domestic consumption, investment and trade, as well as disruptions to business

FIGURE 4.5
Employment and Labour Productivity in Myanmar

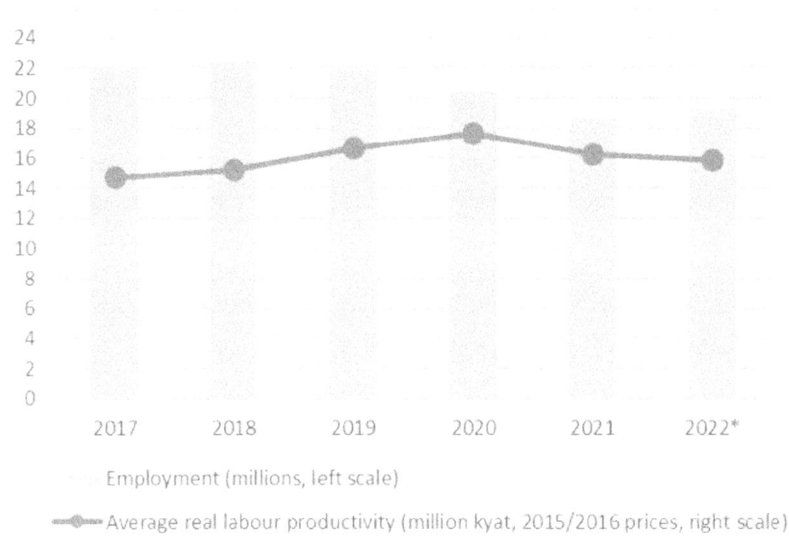

Note: For 2022, the data is for the first half of the year. Labour productivity is measured as real GDP per worker.
Source: ILO (2022).

operations and labour input. However, this was partially offset by a major increase in public consumption though procurement of medicines and cash and non-cash transfers.

Post-coup

After the coup, output further decreased due to mass protests, strikes and widespread disruptions to various economic sectors during the remainder of the 2020/21 financial year. This was exacerbated by the third Covid-19 wave, leading the World Bank to forecast an 18 per cent contraction in the economy in the 2020/21 financial year. (For comparison, the Ministry of Planning and Finance and the CBM both reported a 5.9 per cent contraction for the same period.) The World Bank projected relatively modest GDP growth of 3 per cent for the October 2021 to September 2022 period. (For comparison, the Ministry of Planning and Finance reported 2.4 per cent growth for the October 2021 to March 2022 mini-budget period.) In its January 2022 *Myanmar Economic Monitor*, the World Bank (2022a) reported that the Myanmar economy was 30 per cent smaller due to both the Covid-19 pandemic and the impacts of the coup, in contrast to some counterfactual projections, though it did not disaggregate the two factors.

The post-coup political crisis morphed into renewed civil war, and the third wave of Covid-19 caused significant constraints on supply and demand. Private consumption declined dramatically due to a broad collapse in consumer confidence, a reported decline in real household incomes (UNDP 2021) and overall uncertainty, which affected firms' sales and revenue (IHS Markit 2021, 2022; S&P Global 2022a). The situation was exacerbated by high commodity prices, which were caused by import restrictions, exchange rate volatility driven by restrictive policy responses, a loss of trust in state institutions, and speculation and rumours on social media. The International Labour Organization (ILO) estimated that 1.8 million jobs were shed in 2021, with unemployment rate reaching 2.17 per cent. Employment slightly recovered in the first half of 2022 but was 1.1 million below the 2020 level (ILO 2022). There was also a continued decline in productivity linked to a shift among workers towards lower productivity and informal sectors (Figure 4.5).

Manufacturing was notably impacted, with the purchasing managers' index showing mostly contractions until 2022Q2 (Figure 4.6). That said, the garment and agricultural sectors in particular were resilient and exports were close to pre-2021 levels. The construction sector in Myanmar's major cities also recovered quickly, as consumers tried to hedge against the kyat's weakness due to a weaker regulatory environment owing to the political crisis.

The SAC adopted a neo-mercantilist business policy, restricting imports of consumer goods and putting in place capital controls in an effort to control the foreign exchange rate and shore up foreign exchange reserves. This resulted in trade surpluses, but the impact of growing electricity disruptions, political and security uncertainty and a deficit of trust in state institutions continued to impact productivity and the black-market exchange rate (World Bank 2022b).

The overall economy began to show tentative signs of stabilization during 2022Q1. Liquidity constraints eased as private banks improved

FIGURE 4.6
Myanmar's Manufacturing Purchasing Manager's Index

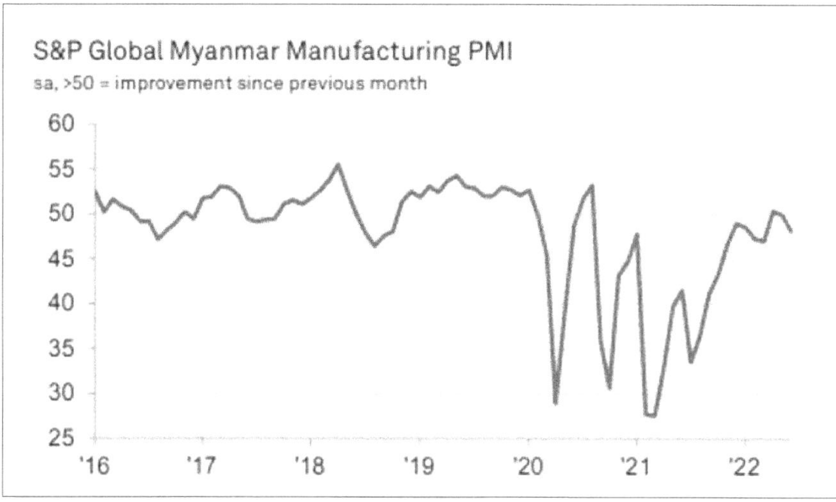

Note: Data were collected from 13 to 22 June 2022.
Source: S&P Global.

cash availability. However, growth was constrained by the imposition of a fixed exchange rate by the CBM in an effort to stabilize commodity prices.

Trade and Investment

Pre-coup

Covid-19 caused a relative contraction of Myanmar's trade volume compared to 2019 and 2020Q1 (Figure 4.4). Myanmar registered a 2020Q2 drop in both exports and imports, though this trend reversed during the next quarter. Rising imports for Covid-19 response and weak natural gas exports due to plummeting global energy prices in 2020 affected the trade deficit. However, the country posted a trade surplus in 2020Q3 that continued even after the coup until at least 2022Q2. The trade-to-GDP ratio went from 50.49 per cent in 2019 to 42.76 per cent in 2020.

Pre-coup, Covid-19 also appears not to have impacted domestic and foreign investment (Figure 4.7). In the 2019/20 financial year, a record US$5.9 billion and MMK1.9 trillion in investment was approved for 375

FIGURE 4.7
Approved Investment, by Quarter (US$ million)

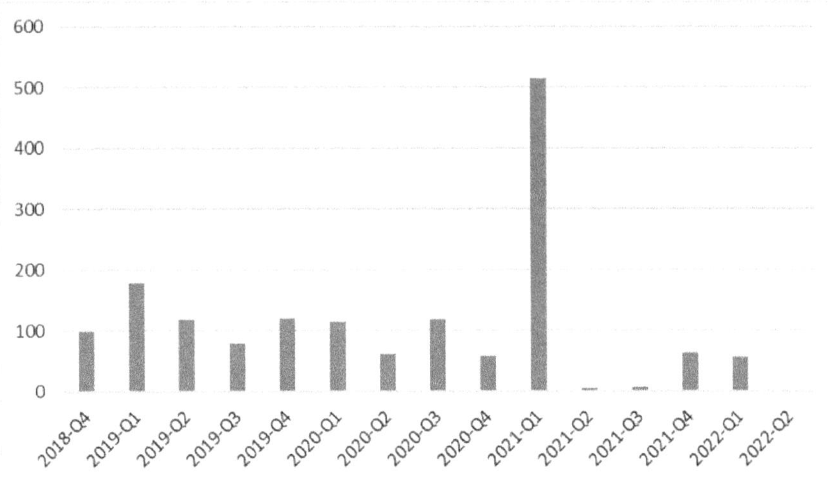

Note: There was an irregular spike in January 2021 as the then-government fast-tracked work to clear a backlog, anticipating the inauguration of the next administration. This did not occur due to the coup on 1 February 2021.
Source: Ministry of Planning and Finance.

projects, compared to US$4.6 billion and MMK1.69 trillion across 451 projects in the 2018/19 financial year (Ministry of Planning and Finance 2018–22). Notably, there was a spike in approved investments in January 2021, reflecting the fast-tracking by the then-civilian government of backlogged applications before the planned inauguration of the next administration in February 2021.

Post-coup

After the coup, there was another reduction in trade volume in 2021Q2 and Q3 but it had generally recovered in 2022Q1 (Figure 4.8). The trade-to-GDP ratio was 46.32 per cent in 2021 and 64.77 per cent for 2022Q1 and 2022Q2 combined. There was a trade surplus after the coup until 2022Q2 (Figure 4.8). Two possible factors may explain the positive balance of trade. With the weakening of the kyat but with the cost of certain local factors of production relatively stagnant, Myanmar's exports could have become

FIGURE 4.8
Myanmar International Trade Balance (US$ million)

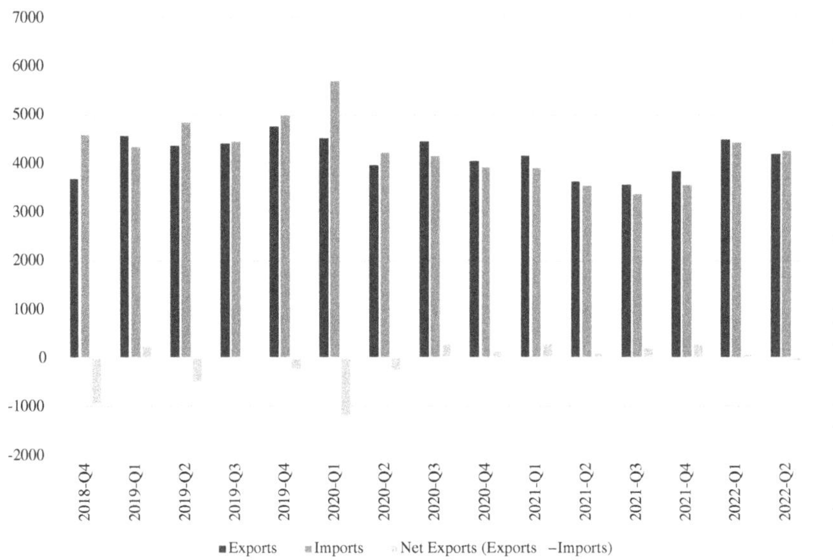

Source: Ministry of Planning and Finance (2018–22).

more competitive. The SAC authorities had also shifted the country's trade posture towards import substitution, with the argument that earlier trade deficits had caused macroeconomic issues. This was coupled with increased hurdles to foreign exchange access for importers compared to exporters. That said, exporters were required to surrender a proportion of their foreign exchange, while some importers from prioritized sectors such as fuels and edible oil were able to procure a limited amount of foreign exchange at the overvalued exchange rates.

With foreign investors in Myanmar facing reputational risks and demands to divest, investment cooled after the coup. The SAC nonetheless reported a one-off spike in investment approvals in 2021Q2, of more than US$2.7 billion across six large projects that were delayed by the coup and the subsequent turmoil. In the first four full quarters after the coup, investment was reported at US$3.5 billion and MMK514 billion across 112 projects (Ministry of Planning and Finance 2018–22). These are notable declines in both capital and project numbers. Further, as with the pre-coup figures, it is unclear how many of the approved projects progressed and how much of the capital investment was realized.

Banking Sector and Fiscal Health

Private Banking Sector

Weighed down by non-performing loans that at their peak formed 75 per cent of bank lending, there were concerns that the economic impact of Covid-19 would trigger a cascade of widespread defaults. Rumours of liquidity issues also appeared several times in 2018 and 2019, sapping trust that was already low due to overhang from Myanmar's 2003 banking crisis. The CBM had imposed a three-year deadline in mid-2017 for banks to sanitize their non-performing loans, but this was pushed back to August 2023, giving breathing space and assuaging fears for the wider economy. Further, the visible involvement of major private banks in the pre-coup Covid-19 response helped to dispel distrust.

The private banks were particularly affected by the coup and ensuing civil disobedience. Staff shortages and strikes, consumer boycotts and Covid-19 cases led most private banks to suspend operations across many branches.[5] The reduced number of operating branches impacted service provision, resulting in delayed cash transfers and triggered concerns around cash availability. From March 2021, rumours and a collapse of trust in state institutions resulted in citizens rushing to withdraw cash from ATMs.

The CBM imposed capital controls, requiring international and domestic non-governmental organizations to report all financial transactions involving international organizations or individuals from abroad. In an effort to stem bank runs, the CBM contributed to the cash shortage by limiting banks' access to physical cash. Private banks were ordered to reopen and did so in April and May 2021. Each imposed their own withdrawal limits, often less than CBM-mandated amounts. Customers had to wait in line to withdraw cash, the maximum withdrawal being between MMK200,000 (US$120) and MMK500,000 (US$300) per day or MMK2 million (US$1,200) per week, depending on the bank. Cash was preferred for all transactions—merchants imposed premiums on digital transfers—and banks organized advance bookings to secure withdrawals, while scalpers sold tokens for bank queues. There were also many anecdotal stories of staff at private banks arranging cash withdrawals in exchange for kickbacks. The cash shortage was particularly damaging during the third wave of the virus as people struggled to afford the rapidly escalating prices.

In April 2022, the SAC introduced a fixed exchange rate of US$1 to MMK1,850, with inbound dollars required to be converted at that rate (Nikkei Staff Writers 2022). This was done to conserve depleted foreign reserves and to cushion the impact of the global rise in edible and fuel oil prices that followed the Russian invasion of Ukraine. After appeals from the private sector, the regulation was gradually relaxed in the weeks after its promulgation, with foreign companies, investors in special economic zones and logistics operators given exemptions.

In early May 2022, the CBM attempted to encourage people to place deposits with banks by introducing special accounts with unlimited withdrawals on the newly deposited funds (Nikkei Staff Writers 2021). Banks reported uptake of these accounts, partly as people became fearful that cash would be stolen from their homes. Cash withdrawals were further relaxed in May 2022, with higher limits or no more advance bookings required. By June 2022, the banking sector remained weak but had improved compared to 2021 (World Bank 2022c).

Fiscal Health

The capacity of governments to weather crises depends significantly on extending economic stimulus, spending on public social assistance and sustaining government revenue collection. In contrast to the situation in the 2019/20 financial year, which included the first and second Covid-19 waves and during which tax revenues were sustained, tax revenue for the quarter immediately after the coup (2021Q1) dropped (Figure 4.9). Based on reports issued by the SAC’s Ministry of Planning and Finance, tax revenue had recovered by mid-2022. However, it should be noted that the depreciation of the kyat against foreign currencies means that overall tax revenue in dollar terms declined in comparison to the pre-coup era.

Based on figures from the Ministry of Planning and Finance, the World Bank reported that Myanmar’s fiscal gap widened after the Covid-19 pandemic, and did so to a greater degree after the coup (World Bank 2022a). In the financial year 2018/19 the fiscal gap was MMK3.86 trillion

FIGURE 4.9
Quarterly Tax Revenue (kyat trillion)

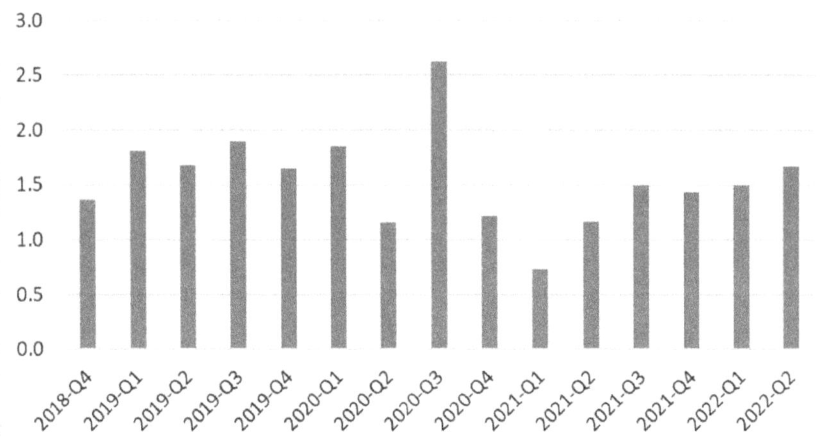

Source: Ministry of Planning and Finance.

or 3.7 per cent of the GDP; in the 2019/20 financial year, when Covid-19 began, it widened to MMK7.84 trillion or 6.9 per cent of GDP, and in the financial year 2020/21 it widened again to MMK8.88 trillion or 9.2 per cent of GDP. From October 2021 to April 2022 the deficit improved to MMK2.6 trillion, representing an annualized 5 per cent of GDP. This was due to improved revenue performance and lower spending.

The state of money supply, especially currency in circulation and savings, provides further reference points for assessing confidence in public institutions. It is instructive to compare money supply and savings data for three successive twelve-month periods beginning February 2019 and ending January 2022: the first twelve months from February 2019 is the period before Covid-19, followed by twelve months of Covid-19 under the civilian government, and then twelve months after the coup. Data from the Central Statistical Organization and the Ministry of Planning and Finance show that between February 2019 and January 2020, currency in circulation and savings in private banks grew by 6.5 per cent and 13.9 per cent, respectively (Ministry of Planning and Finance 2018–22). Taking the year prior to the coup as the baseline, and considering the economic downturn of 2020, the change in the twelve-month period—with currency in circulation expanding by 21.5 per cent and savings by 15.2 per cent (Ministry of Planning and Finance 2018–22)—arguably mirrors a flight to the security of cash alongside increasing consumption needs, while trust in the banking system remains. In stark contrast, the period from February 2021 to January 2022 saw currency circulation burgeon by 52.7 per cent and savings in private banks shrink by 29.5 per cent (Ministry of Planning and Finance 2018–22). These steep changes capture the collapse of confidence in the financial system and panic withdrawals. The money supply shock may also have compounded real economy bottlenecks, thus possibly exacerbating inflation.

Inflation, based on the rate of change in the consumer price index computed by the Ministry of Planning and Finance, steadily diminished from 9.5 per cent in December 2019 to 0.74 per cent in January 2021. However, it began to rise after the coup (Figure 4.10). It climbed steadily in 2021, when the liquidity crisis dampened the effects of currency volatility and consumer demand. However, once the banking sector stabilized and a degree of liquidity returned; inflation climbed more aggressively in 2022 and reached a deleterious 19.4 per cent in June 2022.

CONCLUSION

Across 2020–22, Myanmar's public health and economic adversities were compounded by political turmoil. The acute triple crisis underscores

FIGURE 4.10
Year-on-Year Inflation Rate from October 2019 to June 2022

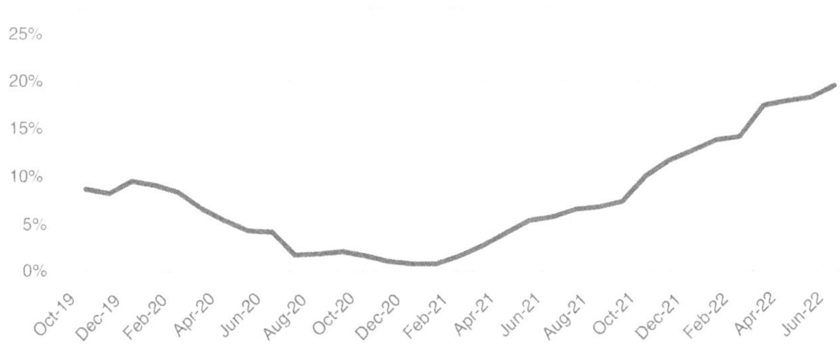

Source: Ministry of Planning and Finance.

the relevance and importance of disaggregating Myanmar's Covid-19 experience into a pre-coup phase corresponding roughly to 2020 and a post-coup phase from 1 February 2021 onwards. The 2020 general election was another key political event that helped explain the pandemic's consequences and the government's responses. Chronologically, the impact of the post-coup crisis is easier to discern during the February 2021 to June 2021 phase, when Covid-19 infections were lower and hence the economic woes can be firmly attributed to failures of governance. However, with the Delta wave of June 2021 to August 2021, the effects of Covid-19 and the coup on the economy are much harder to disaggregate. Lack of human resources due to walkouts in different economic sectors (e.g., banking and manufacturing) and the impact of the Delta wave in amplifying hospitalization and death rates led, through a complex of triggering factors, to reduced economic activity.

A gradual and continuing decline in the security situation, particularly after armed opposition to the coup began in May 2021 and after the declaration by the National Unity Government of a People's Defensive War in September 2021, also continues to affect economic productivity as of early 2024. Attacks on infrastructure and key trade nodes, as well as reduced state investment, continues to further sap economic productivity alongside the ongoing impacts of the banking crisis and restrictive foreign exchange policies.

Myanmar's response to Covid-19 began with promise but it was severely affected by the events of 2021. During 2020, the country was able to wade through different challenges leveraging the collective resources of the state, civil society and the private sector. It therefore was able to mount decent responses. The measures, such as stay-at-home orders and community-based facility quarantines, as well as the active involvement of civil society, had setbacks but were nonetheless effective to a degree during the first and second waves. Coordination was centralized but there was some effort to consult different stakeholders.

Myanmar was one of the few countries that posted positive growth during 2020, but the economy took a significant hit after the coup, with estimates of a contraction of nearly one-fifth in 2021 (World Bank 2021). While there were signs of relative economic stabilization in 2022, both domestic and international factors meant that recovery was uncertain.

After the coup, the response efforts and coordination structures underwent massive shocks due to the varying crises. The third wave was Myanmar's deadliest due to a confluence of factors, including the nature of the Delta variant, the collapse of the health system, the political turmoil and violence, weak governance and the decline of trust and coordination between stakeholders. The trauma of the third wave propelled vaccine uptake through both public and private means and vaccination coverage increased, though as of mid-2022 Myanmar lagged behind its neighbours.

The political crisis negatively affected data collection and analysis, and the dominance of commentary on the post-coup political conflict created significant gaps in knowledge on the economic dimensions of Covid-19. The deteriorating media landscape and a highly charged social media atmosphere also contributes to this dearth. And finally, the impact of rumours, currency speculation and disinformation—a long-standing toxic cocktail—were exacerbated by the coup, injecting broader uncertainties into the economy.

By mid-2022, the economy appeared to be on a gradual path towards some recovery. With orders gradually returning, employment had picked up again for the first time in twenty months (S&P Global 2022b). But blackouts and the high price of diesel continued to place constraints while border closures continued to contribute to supply chain challenges, slowing recovery in the manufacturing sector. The economy was expected to reap benefits from the reopening of the Chinese and Thai borders, which would allow inflow of inputs and outflow of agricultural products.

The pandemic finally appears in the rear-view mirror for most of the world, but Myanmar remains perilously adrift amid a multi-faceted, multi-causal tempest previously unseen in the country's recent history. As of mid-2022, communities continued to navigate a highly polarized, traumatic and emotionally charged environment, and the full impact of Covid-19 and the responses to it remained unclear.

APPENDIX

TABLE A4.1
Fiscal Years in Myanmar

Name	*Start*	*End*
FY 2018–19	1 October 2018	30 September 2019
FY 2019–20	1 October 2019	30 September 2020
FY 2020–21	1 October 2020	30 September 2021
Mini-budget FY 2021–22	1 October 2021	30 March 2022
FY 2022–23	1 April 2022	30 March 2023

Source: Authors.

Notes

1. This paper was written in the interests of academic research and does not imply or represent any political position or view of the authors individually or collectively. The original terminology used in the sources cited is retained solely for ease of reference.
2. The SAC bought Sinopharm and Sinovac vaccines from China and Sputnik vaccines from Russia (Reuters 2021b). Up to end-June 2022, China had delivered 54.34 million doses of Sinopharm and Sinovac vaccines, including 21.9 million donated doses (authors' compilation from "China Covid-19 Vaccine Tracker", Bridge Beijing, https://bridgebeijing.com/our-publications/our-publications-1/china-covid-19-vaccines-tracker). India delivered 21.2 million doses of Covishield and Covaxin, of which 17.5 million were bought and 3.7 million donated (authors' compilation from "Covid-19 Updates: Vaccine Supply", Ministry of External Affairs of the Government of India, 22 June 2022, https://www.mea.gov.in/vaccine-supply.htm). In March 2022, Myanmar received 2.2 million doses of CoronaVac (Sinovac) Covid-19 vaccines through the COVAX Facility. The SAC announced both plans to purchase seven million Sputnik V vaccines in June 2021 and domestic production plans (Myanmar News Agency 2022b).
3. The kyat weakened by around 15 per cent over 2018, going from MMK1,350 to the US dollar in 2018Q1 to around MMK1,550 by the end of the year.
4. Myanmar's electricity subsidies were projected to reach US$1 billion or around 4 per cent of the government budget in 2020.
5. The aim of the strikes and boycotts was to cause a bank run and bring down the military government.

References

AAPP (Assistance Association for Political Prisoners). 2022. "Daily Briefing in Relation to the Military Coup". 1 July 2022. https://aappb.org/?p=22168 (accessed 27 May 2024).

ADB (Asian Development Bank). 2020. "Proposed Countercyclical Support Facility Loan Republic of the Union of Myanmar: COVID-19 Active Response and Expenditure Support Program". Asian Development Bank, August 2020. https://www.adb.org/sites/default/files/project-documents/54255/54255-001-rrp-en.pdf

Associated Press. 2018. "How A Massive Influx of Chinese Migrants Has Changed Myanmar's Second-Largest City Mandalay". *South China Morning Post*, 1 May 2018. https://www.scmp.com/news/asia/southeast-asia/article/2144154/how-massive-influx-chinese-migrants-has-changed-myanmars (accessed 12 May 2024).

Aung, S.Y. 2020. "Yangon Extends Lockdown Measures for Myanmar's COVID-19 Hotspots". *Irrawaddy*, 13 May 2020. https://www.irrawaddy.com/specials/myanmar-covid-19/yangon-extends-lockdown-measures-myanmars-covid-19-hotspots.html (accessed 15 June 2022).

BBC Burmese. 2020. "Basic Commodities such as Rice and Edible Oil to be Sold to Basic Workers near Industrial Zones at Cheapest Prices". 26 March 2020. https://www.bbc.com/burmese/burma-52013182 (accessed 10 April 2024).

Bello, Walden, Jennifer Franco, and Pietje Vervest. 2020. "How to Improve Myanmar's Covid-19 Emergency Relief Program". Transnational Institute, 9 June 2020. https://www.tni.org/en/article/how-to-improve-myanmars-covid-19-emergency-relief-program (accessed 25 June 2022).

Brancati, Emanuele, Paul Minoletti, and Guillem Riambau. 2020. "Coping with Covid-19: Protecting Lives, Employment, and Incomes in Myanmar". International Growth Centre, 2020. https://www.theigc.org/publications/coping-covid-19-protecting-lives-employment-and-incomes-myanmar-0 (accessed 24 June 2022).

Brennan, E. 2021. "Community and Health Governance in Myanmar during and after COVID-19". *Georgetown Journal of International Affairs*, 28 January 2021. https://gjia.georgetown.edu/2021/01/28/community-and-health-governance-in-myanmar-during-and-after-covid-19/

Callahan, M. 2021. " 'Everyone Is Dying': Myanmar on the Brink of Decimation". *Asia Times*, 17 July 2021. https://asiatimes.com/2021/07/everyone-is-dying-myanmar-on-the-brink-of-decimation/ (accessed 4 June 2022).

Central Bank of Myanmar. *Monetary Policy Implementation Report.* Various dates. https://cbm.gov.mm/index.php/content/7023 (accessed 3 June 2022).

Central Statistical Organization and Ministry of Planning and Finance. "Selected Monthly Economic Indicators". Various dates. https://www.csostat.gov.mm/PublicationAndRelease/MonthlyPublication (accessed 3 June 2022).

Channel NewsAsia. 2021. "Myanmar Rebel Group Says It Received Covid-19 Vaccines from China". 24 July 2021. https://www.channelnewsasia.com/asia/myanmar-rebel-group-says-it-received-covid-19-vaccines-china-2066286 (accessed 5 May 2022).

Chau, T. 2019. "Myanmar Looks to Legalize Its Informal Economy". *Asia Times*, 9 October 2019. https://asiatimes.com/2019/10/myanmar-looks-to-legalize-its-informal-economy/ (accessed 10 April 2024).

De, Loveleen, De Quynh Nguyen Anh, Ippei Tsuruga, and Markus Ruck. 2020. "An Assessment of the Social Protection Needs and Gaps for Workers in Informal Employment in Myanmar". International Labour Organization. https://www.social-protection.org/gimi/Media.action;jsessionid=xwuWF0Sr05Xa5sp08xHj3TmXwodqk6NKHOPRN99pLIu692IO76b8!-765179005?id=18152

Democratic Voice of Burma. 2020. "Myanmar Agriculture Development Bank Reduces Agriculture Loan Interest Rates". 1 May 2020. http://ftp.dvb.no/post/385418 (accessed 10 April 2024).

Global Witness. 2015. "Jade: Myanmar's 'Big State Secret'". 23 October 2015. https://www.globalwitness.org/en/campaigns/oil-gas-and-mining/myanmarjade/ (accessed 10 April 2024).

Government of the Republic of the Union of Myanmar. 2020. "Overcoming as One: COVID-19 Economic Relief Plan". https://faolex.fao.org/docs/pdf/mya201762.pdf

Hkawng, Jaw Tu, Naw Awng, and Emily Fishbein. 2020. "Kachin Communities Rally to Receive Thousands of Workers Returning from China". *Frontier Myanmar*, 24 April 2020. https://www.frontiermyanmar.net/en/kachin-communities-rally-to-receive-thousands-of-workers-returning-from-china/ (accessed 5 May 2022).

Htun, Z. 2020. "Aung San Suu Kyi Vows to Sort Out Covid-19 Relief Snags For Myanmar's Poor". *Radio Free Asia*, 17 November 2020. https://www.rfa.org/english/news/myanmar/relief-snags-11172020200328.html (accessed 6 May 2022).

Htwe, Z.Z. 2020a. "COVID-19 Frontline Volunteers in Myanmar in Need of Protective Equipment and Safety Training". *Irrawaddy*, 5 June 2020. https://www.irrawaddy.com/news/burma/covid-19-frontline-volunteers-myanmar-need-protective-equipment-safetytraining.html (accessed 21 June 2022).

———. 2020b. "Myanmar Volunteers Play Vital Role in Yangon's Battle Against

COVID-19". *Irrawaddy*, 29 October 2020. https://www.irrawaddy.com/specials/myanmar-covid-19/myanmar-volunteers-play-vital-role-yangons-battle-covid-19.html (accessed 21 June 2022).

IHS Markit. 2021, 2022. "Myanmar Manufacturing PMI". IHS Markit (merged with S&P Global in February 2022). https://www.pmi.spglobal.com/Public/Release/PressReleases?language=en

ILO (International Labour Organization). 2021. "The Impact of COVID-19 in Myanmar: A Study of Workers Laid-Off in the Garment Sector". 27 July 2021. https://www.ilo.org/wcmsp5/groups/public/---asia/---ro-bangkok/---ilo-yangon/documents/publication/wcms_815349.pdf

———. 2022. "Employment in Myanmar in the First Half of 2022: A Rapid Assessment". 1 August 2022. https://www.ilo.org/asia/publications/issue-briefs/WCMS_852682/lang--es/index.htm

Irrawaddy. 2020a. "Myanmar's COVID-19 Economic Relief Plan Attracts Mixed Reactions from Industrial Insiders". 6 May 2020. https://www.irrawaddy.com/news/burma/myanmars-covid-19-economic-relief-plan-attracts-mixed-reactions-industrial-insiders.html (accessed 25 June 2022).

———. 2020b. "Myanmar's KBZ Bank Donates Nearly $1M to Coronavirus Efforts". 6 April 2020. https://www.irrawaddy.com/specials/myanmar-covid-19/myanmars-kbz-bank-donates-nearly-1m-coronavirus-efforts.html (accessed 10 April 2024).

———. 2021. "Abandoned by Junta, Myanmar People Forced to Rely on Each Other". 6 August 2021. https://www.irrawaddy.com/news/burma/abandoned-by-junta-myanmar-people-forced-to-rely-on-each-other.html (accessed 29 June 2022).

Karen Peace Support Network. 2020. "A Critique of Burma's Covid-19 Economic Relief Plan". 23 September 2020. https://www.karenpeace.org/wp-content/uploads/2021/02/CERP-critic_English.pdf (accessed 11 April 2024).

Kyaw, Khine Lin, and Philip Heijmans. 2020. "Myanmar's Poorest Take Virus Fight Into Their Own Hands". Bloomberg, 14 May 2020. https://www.bloomberg.com/news/articles/2020-05-13/diy-lockdowns-and-barricades-how-myanmar-is-fighting-the-virus#xj4y7vzkg (accessed 22 June 2022).

Kyaw San Wai. 2020a. "Myanmar and Covid-19". *The Diplomat*, 1 May 2020. https://thediplomat.com/2020/05/myanmar-and-covid-19/ (accessed 26 June 2022).

———. 2020b. "Myanmar's Covid-19 Response Banks on Aung San Suu Kyi". *East Asia Forum*, 31 July 2020. https://www.eastasiaforum.org/2020/07/31/myanmars-covid-19-response-banks-on-aung-san-suu-kyi/ (accessed 27 June 2022).

Lintner, B. 2019. "China Bids to Bring Yangon into a Modern Age". *Asia Times*, 1 June 2019. https://asiatimes.com/2019/06/china-bids-to-bring-yangon-into-a-modern-age/ (accessed 12 May 2024).

Liu, J. 2021. "CSOs after the Coup: Operations Squeezed, Funding Crunched". *Frontier Myanmar*, 28 September 2021. https://www.frontiermyanmar.net/en/csos-after-the-coup-operations-squeezed-funding-crunched/ (accessed 6 May 2022).

———. 2022. "Why People in Myanmar Don't Want the Junta's Jabs". *Frontier Myanmar*, 8 January 2022. https://www.frontiermyanmar.net/en/why-people-in-myanmar-dont-want-the-juntas-jabs/ (accessed 5 May 2022).

Lovett, Lorcan, and Nay Chi Nway. 2020. "'I Have to Do This': Myanmar Garment Workers Forced into Sex Work by Covid". *Guardian*, 22 October 2020. https://www.theguardian.com/global-development/2020/oct/22/i-have-to-do-this-myanmar-garment-workers-forced-into-sex-work-by-covid (accessed 11 April 2024).

Lwin, N. 2020a. "Combating Fake News in the Time of Coronavirus in Myanmar". *Irrawaddy*, 20 March 2020. https://www.irrawaddy.com/news/burma/myanmar-combating-fake-news-time-coronavirus.html (accessed 5 May 2022).

———. 2020b. "Myanmar Orders Quarantine, Monitoring for Arrivals from Countries Hit by Coronavirus". *Irrawaddy*, 16 March 2020. https://www.irrawaddy.com/news/burma/myanmar-orders-quarantine-monitoring-arrivals-countries-hit-coronavirus.html (accessed 15 June 2022).

———. 2020c. "Myanmar's Economic Year in Review". *Irrawaddy*, 25 December 2020. https://www.irrawaddy.com/business/myanmars-economic-year-review.html (accessed 20 July 2022).

Macan-Markar, M. 2021. "Myanmar Ethnic Armies March to China's Tune amid Covid Spike". *Nikkei Asia*, 18 August 2021. https://asia.nikkei.com/Spotlight/Myanmar-Crisis/Myanmar-ethnic-armies-march-to-China-s-tune-amid-Covid-spike (accessed 5 May 2022).

Mann, Z. 2020. "Different Laws Applied to Myanmar Covid-19 Restrictions Lead to Inconsistent Punishments for Violators". *Irrawaddy*, 13 May 2020. https://www.irrawaddy.com/specials/myanmar-covid-19/different-laws-applied-myanmar-covid-19-restrictions-lead-inconsistent-punishments-violators.html (accessed 5 May 2022).

Ministry of Health. 2021–22. "Coronavirus Disease 2019 (COVID-19) Surveillance Dashboard (Myanmar)". Ministry of Health and Sports. https://mohs.gov.mm/Main/content/publication/2019-ncov

———. 2021b. "Press Release on Updated Status of Cooperation with the Ministry of Health and the Gavi Covax Facility on COVID-19 Vaccination". 5 October 2021. https://www.moi.gov.mm/moi:eng/news/4795

———. 2022. "Covid-19 ရောဂါစောင့်ကြပ်ကြည့်ရှုမှု အခြေအနေ (29-6-2022, 8:00 PM)" [COVID-19 situation update 29 June 2022, 8:00 PM]. 30 June 2022. https://moh.gov.mm/page/18302

Ministry of Health and Sports. 2020–21. "Coronavirus Disease 2019 (COVID-19) Surveillance Dashboard (Myanmar)". https://mohs.gov.mm/Main/content/publication/2019-ncov

Ministry of Planning and Finance. 2018–22. "Selected Monthly Economic Indicators". https://www.mopf.gov.mm/en/page/planning/central-statistical-organization-cso/748

Mizzima Staff. 2022. "Covid-19 Outbreak at Mingaladon Industrial Zone Lens Factory". *Mizzima*, 3 February 2022. https://mizzima.com/article/covid-19-outbreak-mingaladon-industrial-zone-lens-factory (accessed 5 May 2022).

Mon, Ye, Hein Thar, and Thomas Kean. 2020. "Inside Phaunggyi, Myanmar's Ambitious Response to Covid-19". *Frontier Myanmar*, 23 April 2020. https://www.frontiermyanmar.net/en/inside-phaunggyi-myanmars-ambitious-response-to-covid-19/ (accessed 22 June 2022).

Myanmar News Agency. 2022a. "Myancopharm Covid-19 Vaccine Introduced to Targeted Groups". *Global New Light of Myanmar*, 5 May 2022. https://www.gnlm.com.mm/myancopharm-covid-19-vaccine-introduced-to-targeted-groups/ (accessed 30 June 2022).

———. 2022b. "Myanmar Receives COVAX Facility-Donated CoronaVac (Sinovac) Vaccines". *Global New Light of Myanmar*, 31 March 2022. https://www.gnlm.com.mm/myanmar-receives-covax-facility-donated-coronavac-sinovac-vaccines/ (accessed 30 June 2022).

Nachemson, A. 2020. "Racism is Fueling Myanmar's Deadly Second Wave of Covid-19". *The Diplomat*, 11 September 2020. https://thediplomat.com/2020/09/racism-is-fueling-myanmars-deadly-second-wave-of-covid-19/ (accessed 2 May 2022).

———. 2021. "Medics in Myanmar on Strike against Military amid Covid-19 Crisis". *Al Jazeera*, 3 February 2021. https://www.aljazeera.com/news/2021/2/3/medics-in-myanmar-on-strike-against-military-amid-covid-crisis (accessed 2 May 2022).

Naing, A. 2020. "Civil Servants to be Loaned Two Months' Salary at No Interest". *Myanmar Now*, 2 September 2020. https://myanmar-now.org/mm/news/4386/ (accessed 10 April 2024).

Naing, S. 2020. "Finding Community at a Covid-19 Quarantine Centre in Myanmar". Reuters, 24 December 2020. https://www.reuters.com/article/

us-health-coronavirus-myanmar-quarantine-idINKBN28Y0C3 (accessed 19 June 2022).

Nikkei Staff Writers. 2021. "Myanmar's Cash Shortage Casts Shadow Despite Rise in Activity". *Nikkei Asia*, 18 June 2021. https://asia.nikkei.com/Spotlight/Myanmar-Crisis/Myanmar-s-cash-shortage-casts-shadow-despite-rise-in-activity (accessed 4 June 2022).

———. 2022, "Myanmar's Forced Currency Conversions Seen Making Few Exceptions". *Nikkei Asia*, 7 April 2022. https://asia.nikkei.com/Business/Markets/Currencies/Myanmar-s-forced-currency-conversions-seen-making-few-exceptions (accessed 5 June 2022).

Nyein, N. 2020a. "Myanmar Govt, LIFT Fund Announce Extra Cash Payments to Help Most Vulnerable During COVID-19". *Irrawaddy*, 27 May 2020. https://www.irrawaddy.com/specials/myanmar-covid-19/myanmar-govt-lift-fund-announce-extra-cash-payments-help-vulnerable-covid-19.html (accessed 29 June 2022).

———. 2020b. "Myanmar Pharma Firm Donates Device to Massively Increase COVID-19 Testing". *Irrawaddy*, 6 April 2020. https://www.irrawaddy.com/specials/myanmar-covid-19/myanmar-pharma-firm-donates-device-massively-increase-covid-19-testing.html (accessed 3 May 2022).

———. 2020c. "Myanmar Sets Up Covid-19 Committee with Rebel Armies". *Irrawaddy*, 29 April 2020. https://www.irrawaddy.com/specials/myanmar-covid-19/myanmar-sets-covid-19-committee-rebel-armies.html (accessed 10 April 2024).

Phu Ei Ei New. 2020. "Complaints Made over COVID-19 Cash Assistance Programme for Poor People," *Mizzima*, 21 November 2020. https://www.mizzima.com/article/complaints-made-over-covid-19-cash-assistance-programme-poor-people (accessed 10 April 2024).

Radio Free Asia. 2021a. "Electricity Bill Boycott Denies Myanmar Military US $1 Billion in Power Revenues Since Coup". 15 September 2021. https://www.rfa.org/english/news/myanmar/power-09152021192918.html (accessed 10 April 2024).

———. 2021b. "Funeral Service Volunteers Lay Lives on The Line as Myanmar COVID Deaths Surge". 4 August 2021. https://www.rfa.org/english/news/myanmar/funeral-08042021183624.html (accessed 22 June 2022).

———. 2021c. "Hoarding of Covid Drugs in Myanmar Causes Prices to Soar". 13 August 2021. https://www.rfa.org/english/news/myanmar/covid-drugs-08132021180542.html (accessed 3 May 2022).

———. 2023. "Illegal Mining of Rare Earth Metals Surges in Northern Myanmar". 8 August 2023. https://economictimes.indiatimes.com/news/

international/world-news/myanmar-emerges-as-key-source-of-rare-earth-minerals-for-china/articleshow/92925855.cms?from=mdr (accessed 10 April 2024).

Reuters. 2020. "Myanmar Reports First Cases of Coronavirus". 24 March 2020. https://www.reuters.com/article/us-health-coronavirus-myanmar-idUSKBN21B0HB (accessed 4 May 2022).

———. 2021a. "Desperate Myanmar Residents Queue for Oxygen as COVID-19 Cases Surge". 12 July 2021. https://www.reuters.com/world/asia-pacific/myanmar-military-says-ramp-up-oxygen-supply-covid-19-cases-surge-2021-07-12/ (accessed 3 May 2022).

———. 2021b. "Myanmar Aims to Buy More Russian, Chinese COVID-19 Vaccines as Cases Rise". 1 July 2021. https://www.reuters.com/world/asia-pacific/myanmar-aims-buy-more-russian-chinese-covid-19-vaccines-cases-rise-2021-06-30/ (accessed 30 June 2022).

———. 2021c. "Myanmar's COVID Crisis Worsens as Mistrust of Junta Infects Health System". 14 July 2021. https://www.reuters.com/world/asia-pacific/myanmars-covid-crisis-worsens-mistrust-junta-infects-health-system-2021-07-13/ (accessed 10 April 2024).

S&P Global. 2022a. Myanmar Manufacturing PMI. S&P Global, 2022. https://www.pmi.spglobal.com/Public/Release/PressReleases?language=en

———. 2022b. "Myanmar's Manufacturing Sector Expands for First Time since August 2020". News Release, 2 May 2022. https://www.pmi.spglobal.com/Public/Home/PressRelease/1341b48b63a14187be0eec28ad626d1d

Stokke, K., R. Vakulchuk, and I. Overland. 2018. "Myanmar: A Political Economy Analysis". Norwegian Institute of International Affairs, 6 February 2018. https://www.nupi.no/en/publications/cristin-pub/myanmar-a-political-economy-analysis

Tha, K.P. 2020. "Myanmar Citizens Give Up Power Subsidy to Aid COVID-19 Fight". *Irrawaddy*, 8 April 2020. https://www.irrawaddy.com/specials/myanmar-covid-19/myanmar-citizens-give-power-subsidy-aid-covid-19-fight.html (accessed 21 June 2022).

Thant, Aye Min. 2021. "Myanmar: A Coup Is Worse than Covid. I've Lived through Three". *The Economist*, 5 February 2021. https://www.economist.com/1843/2021/02/05/myanmar-a-coup-is-worse-than-covid-ive-lived-through-three (accessed 1 May 2022).

Thazin Hlaing. 2020. "Myanmar Govt Offers to Pay Factory Workers 40% during COVID-19 Inspection Closures". *Irrawaddy*, 30 April 2020. https://www.irrawaddy.com/news/burma/myanmar-govt-offers-pay-factory-workers-40-covid-19-inspection-closures.html (accessed 21 June 2022).

Thiha Ko Ko. 2020. "Myanmar Govt to Distribute Cash to Workers without Social Security". *Myanmar Times*, 27 September 2020. https://www.mmtimes.com/news/myanmar-govt-distribute-cash-workers-without-social-security.html (accessed 21 June 2022).

Tower, J., and P.A. Clapp. 2020. "The Dangers of Myanmar's Ungoverned Casino Cities". United States Institute for Peace, 6 August 2020. https://www.usip.org/publications/2020/08/dangers-myanmars-ungoverned-casino-cities (accessed 12 May 2024).

Tsoi, G., and M. Myint. 2022. "Covid and a Coup: The Double Crisis Pushing Myanmar to the Brink". *BBC*, 30 July 2021. https://www.bbc.com/news/world-asia-57993930 (accessed 3 May 2022).

UNDP (United Nations Development Programme). 2021. "People's Purse Survey: Socio-economic Impact of the Events Since 1st February 2021 on Households in Myanmar". September 2021. https://themimu.info/sites/themimu.info/files/assessment_file_attachments/MYANMAR_PEOPLES_PULSE.pdf

Walker, T. 2021a. "Myanmar Faces Covid Vaccination Woes as Health System Under Threat". *Voice of America*, 11 September 2021. https://www.voanews.com/a/6222519.html (accessed 4 June 2022).

———. 2021b. "Myanmar's Shadow Government Announces 'Defensive War'". *Voice of America*, 8 September 2021. https://www.voanews.com/a/east-asia-pacific_myanmars-shadow-government-announces-defensive-war/6219380.html (accessed 6 May 2022).

Wang, Haidong, Katherine R. Paulson, Spencer A. Pease, Stefanie Watson, Haley Comfort, Peng Zheng, Aleksandr Y Aravkin, et al. 2022. "Estimating Excess Mortality due to the Covid-19 Pandemic: A Systematic Analysis of Covid-19-Related Mortality, 2020–21". *The Lancet* 399, no. 10334: 1,513–36. https://doi.org/10.1016/S0140-6736(21)02796-3

Weng, Lawi. 2020. "Myanmar's Mon State Consolidates Quarantine Centres for Returning Migrants". *Irrawaddy*, 6 April 2020. https://www.irrawaddy.com/specials/myanmar-covid-19/myanmars-mon-state-consolidates-quarantine-centers-returning-migrants.html (accessed 19 June 2022).

World Bank. 2020a. *Myanmar Economic Monitor: December 2020*. World Bank Group. December 2020. http://documents.worldbank.org/curated/en/906171608086222905/Myanmar-Economic-Monitor-Coping-with-Covid-19

———. 2020b. "Myanmar's Economy Severely Impacted by COVID-19: Report". World Bank Group. 25 June 2020. https://www.worldbank.org/en/news/press-release/2020/06/25/myanmars-economy-severely-impacted-by-covid-19-report

———. 2021. *Myanmar Economic Monitor: Progress Threatened; Resilience Tested.* Washington, DC: World Bank Group, July 2021. https://documents.worldbank.org/en/publication/documents-reports/documentdetail/884011627285477076/myanmar-economic-monitor-progress-threatened-resilience-tested

———. 2022a. *Myanmar Budget Brief.* World Bank Group, June 2022. https://documents1.worldbank.org/curated/en/099005009122231111/pdf/P1770020e598d00430ba36053e414ebfa33.pdf.c

———. 2022b. *Myanmar Economic Monitor: Contending with Constraints.* Washington, DC: World Bank Group, January 2022. https://thedocs.worldbank.org/en/doc/c3299fac4f879379513b05eaf0e2b084-0070012022/original/World-Bank-Myanmar-Economic-Monitor-Jan-22.pdf

———. 2022c. *Myanmar Financial Sector Reforms.* World Bank Group, July 2022. https://documents1.worldbank.org/curated/en/099950007082234868/pdf/P17700209b1e6603e0822b0be869cb8882b.pdf

Xinhua. 2020. "Myanmar Burns Seized Narcotic Drugs Worth Over 839 Mln USD". 26 June 2020. http://www.xinhuanet.com/english/2020-06/26/c_139168819.htm3 (accessed 10 April 2024).

———. 2021. "Myanmar Chinese Chamber of Commerce Launches Vaccination Program". 25 August 2021. http://www.xinhuanet.com/english/asiapacific/2021-08/25/c_1310148514.htm (accessed 22 June 2022).

COMPARATIVE SYNTHESIS

Pandemic and Recovery in Cambodia, Laos and Myanmar

Jayant Menon

The experiences of Cambodia, Laos and Myanmar in managing the Covid-19 pandemic provide interesting insights and lessons, not just for the developing world but for any country trying to handle a major crisis under binding constraints. Cambodia, Laos and Myanmar are the newest and poorest members of the Association of Southeast Asian Nations (ASEAN). All three are transitional economies and are classified as least developed countries by the United Nations. In 2022, Laos had the highest gross domestic product (GDP) per capita (in current US dollars) among the three at US$2,088, followed by Cambodia (US$1,786) and Myanmar (US$1,096). The low level of income and the early stage of development in each of the three countries created their own challenges in dealing with the Covid-19 pandemic, but there were also a number of positive factors, both inherent and policy-related, that helped each deal with this major health and economic crisis. This essay surveys the key challenges they faced and how they dealt with them while examining how the advantages possessed by each of the three countries helped in the overall management of the pandemic. Drawing lessons can help governments to tackle the next crisis, health-related or otherwise.

As least developed countries, Cambodia, Laos and Myanmar were already struggling to address social and economic challenges to try and close a multi-dimensional development gap even before the pandemic arrived. When the pandemic struck in early 2020, they had to try and deal with it with severely constrained fiscal resources compared to other ASEAN countries. This meant that their fiscal stimulus programmes were limited and social safety nets incomplete and wanting. Figure 4A.1, panels A and B show that Laos and Myanmar were unable to implement any significant fiscal stimulus at the start of the pandemic when lockdowns were introduced. In per capita terms, spending on fiscal stimulus averaged only about US$1 in both countries. The situation in Cambodia was slightly better, with per capita spending averaging about US$13. This was a result of significant improvements in resource mobilization (particularly tax revenue collections) in recent years, but both the share of GDP and per capita spending were still below that in many other countries. The limited social safety nets affected the poor badly, especially those working in the informal sector, and limited fiscal space constrained the ability of governments to keep businesses afloat during the economic downturn.

Another manifestation of the limited fiscal resources was low government spending on healthcare, resulting in healthcare systems with some of the lowest capacities in Asia. For instance, during the pandemic, Cambodia had only about 0.7 hospital beds per 1,000 people, while Myanmar had 1.0 and Laos had 1.5 (Menon 2021). This compares poorly with an average of 4.7 for the countries of the Organization for Economic Co-operation and Development (OECD). The overall quality of healthcare also leaves significant room for improvement, and there is great variation in access to quality healthcare for urban versus rural populations.

These factors were a major limitation in managing the Covid-19 pandemic, requiring more stringent social distancing measures than in countries with more robust healthcare systems. The very low capacity of the healthcare systems was a key factor in the somewhat draconian response in all three countries to the initial and subsequent community outbreaks of the virus. Had there been more capacity in the healthcare systems, the governments would have had more breathing space to take a more nuanced and targeted approach to managing the outbreak. This would have reduced the toll on the economy and the loss of livelihoods.

These factors also bring into question the apparent trade-off between lives and livelihoods. Krueger (2020) and others argued that until

FIGURE 4A.1
Size of Stimulus Programmes in ASEAN

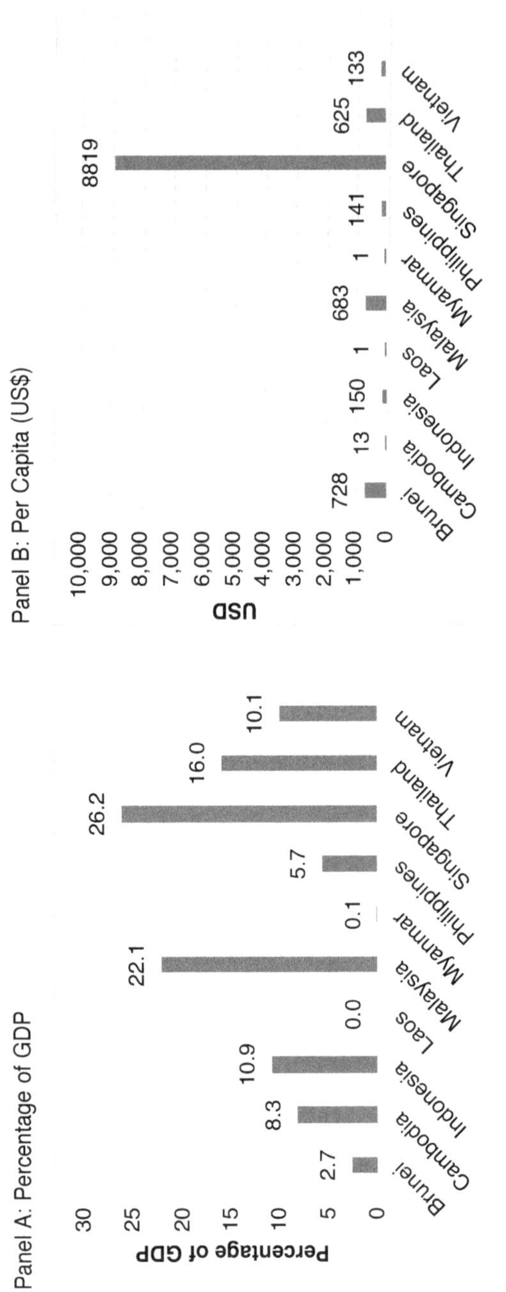

Source: Lee, Negara and Sambodo (2020).

community transmission of the virus was controlled, economic recovery would be uncertain and attempts at returning to pre-Covid-19 levels of normality might not be sustainable. This argument was used to justify lockdowns that attempted to control and curtail the spread of the virus and therefore save lives—even if they put jobs and livelihoods at risk. This discussion and debate were conducted in a developed country context where social safety nets were adequate and their coverage was quite broad.

The situation in developing countries, and least developed countries in particular, is very different, however. Not only are social safety nets weak, but many segments of society, such as informal workers and other marginalized groups, may not be covered at all. When fiscal resources are limited and safety nets wanting, lives or livelihoods are often one and the same for the poor and marginalized. Poor countries must consider the lives lost or shortened through livelihoods destroyed by policies aimed at preserving an ineffectual healthcare system with lives lost directly to the virus. During the pandemic in Cambodia, Laos and Myanmar, there was probably more that could have been done to preserve livelihoods. This is a lesson that should be heeded when dealing with future pandemics or health-related crises.

Different policy choices are available to achieve the desired balance between lives and livelihoods, or health and economy. That is, there are different combinations of restrictions on domestic and cross-border movement of people that can produce the desired economic and health outcomes. After the initial outbreak had subsided, most of the actions to support economic recovery in Cambodia, Laos and Myanmar, as well as the rest of Asia, focused on easing domestic restrictions on movement. Border restrictions are hardly featured in the calculations. But because borders remained mostly closed, the economic imperative required such extensive easing of domestic restrictions that health risks rose sharply with the new, more transmissible variants.

Because borders were not completely closed, however, the restrictions in place did not prevent the entry of the new, more contagious variants, and once they started circulating in the community, the relative value of border controls relative to domestic restrictions fell sharply. In other words, it was almost impossible to import new variants in sufficient quantities to match domestic transmission when the variant is highly transmissible and already circulating in the community. This suggests that shifting the focus from border to domestic restrictions, for any health-economy trade-off, would have been beneficial. Such a shift would have better addressed economic considerations, while also providing the best opportunity to contain the virus and avoid overwhelming inadequate healthcare systems.

Cambodia was the first country in the region to try to redress the imbalance between border and domestic mobility restrictions, unilaterally opening its borders on 1 November 2021. Apart from the country's high vaccination rate, its heavy reliance on tourism was a motivating factor. It took about another six months before most other Southeast Asian countries opened their borders. Laos and Myanmar only reopened in May and April 2022, respectively. The economic and social cost of the pandemic could have been significantly reduced had borders been opened sooner, without a commensurate increase in the health risk. Even though every crisis is different and needs to be individually examined, one clear lesson for the next pandemic is to avoid an over-reliance on cross-border mobility restrictions.

Despite these limitations, the news was not all bad. Cambodia, Laos and Myanmar have relatively young populations, and this was a major positive factor in minimizing the worst health effects of the pandemic. Had the demographic profile in these countries resembled that of the other ASEAN countries, which are ageing much more rapidly, the mortality rate would likely have been much higher given their weak healthcare systems.

The poor in these developing countries have been more exposed to viruses in the past, honing their immune systems to respond rapidly to new infections. Covid-19 was just one of several serious viruses that the poor in these countries have to deal with in their struggle for survival. However, malnutrition is still prevalent in these countries and can impair physical development and immune systems, which affects the capacity to respond effectively to infections. The net effect of these two opposing factors on immune systems can vary between and within countries, and even among those affected.

Although there have been dramatic changes in the structure of the economies of Cambodia, Laos and Myanmar over the past few decades, all three countries still have relatively large agricultural sectors. Table 4A.1

TABLE 4A.1
Sector Share of GDP and Employment, Selected Years

Country	*Sector*	*Share of GDP (%)*					*Share of Employment (%)*				
		1995	*2000*	*2005*	*2010*	*2018*	*1995*	*2000*	*2005*	*2010*	*2018*
Cambodia	Agriculture, hunting, forestry, fishing	51.4	37.8	32.4	36	23.5	79.0	73.5	62.0	57.3	33.7
	Industry	12.9	23	26.4	23.3	34.4	6.1	8.5	13.2	16.0	28.3
	Services	35.7	39.1	41.2	40.7	42.1	14.9	18.0	24.8	26.7	38.1
Laos	Agriculture, hunting, forestry, fishing	42.8	33.6	29.1	23.6	17.7	85.4	81.6	77.3	71.5	63.2
	Industry	15.7	24.1	26.2	30.9	35.5	3.5	4.5	6.0	8.3	11.6
	Services	41.5	42.2	44.7	45.5	46.8	11.1	13.8	16.7	20.2	25.1
Myanmar	Agriculture, hunting, forestry, fishing	60	57.2	46.7	36.9	26.3	66.6	61.5	57.1	53.5	49.7
	Industry	9.9	9.7	17.5	26.5	34.7	10.5	13.2	16.3	17.7	16.0
	Services	30.1	33.1	35.8	36.7	39	22.8	25.4	26.6	28.8	34.3

Source: UNCTADStat database at https://unctadstat.unctad.org/EN/ (accessed 14 October 2023).

presents GDP and employment shares of the major sectors prior to the pandemic. Just before the pandemic struck, agriculture provided employment for about one-third of the labour force in Cambodia, two-thirds in Laos and a half in Myanmar. Having a large and thriving agricultural sector provided an economic buffer during this crisis, as it did during the Asian financial and other crises.

Facing an undetermined period of unemployment as a result of the lockdowns, most informal and many formal workers in the urban manufacturing sector decided to return to their home provinces, temporarily reversing the long-term trend of rural-urban migration. The rural economy in general, and agriculture in particular, was less impacted by social distancing measures, as it requires less physical contact and comes with less workplace congestion than manufacturing in urban centres. The absence of adequate public social safety nets was another factor driving the reverse migration; people went to their private social safety nets, meaning their extended family and communities.

Finally, much has been said about the inequality in the distribution of vaccines globally, favouring rich countries over poorer ones. Cambodia provides a counter-example with the remarkable success of its vaccination programme. It achieved the highest vaccination rate in the region and was the first to vaccinate more than 85 per cent of its population, the rate required to achieve herd immunity. It was also one of the highest in the world at the time. This cannot simply be attributed to its close ties with China; China has similarly close relationships with Laos and Myanmar but in those two countries vaccination rates were some of the lowest in the region. Although adequate supplies of vaccines from China played a significant role, Cambodia deserves credit for enabling a rapid roll-out under challenging circumstances by managing the logistics efficiently. Furthermore, Cambodia was quick to recognize that its demographic profile necessitated extending vaccinations to younger age groups (five to twelve years old) if it was to reach herd immunity.

Although we should not ignore these factors that favoured Cambodia, Laos and Myanmar over their more developed neighbours, they could likely have been outweighed by the many financial and institutional constraints the countries faced. However, as outcomes varied across Cambodia, Laos and Myanmar, country-specific factors need to be carefully considered.

Each of the three countries also faced overlapping but different economic and social challenges, which were not directly related to the pandemic. Even before the pandemic struck, Cambodia was struggling to deal with the removal of trade preferences, which was affecting its exports of garments to its main industrialized markets. Laos was under severe pressure to try and curtail deteriorating macroeconomic conditions, with rising inflation and debt levels. Myanmar had a coup in the middle of its second wave of Covid-19 and had therefore to deal with two overlapping crises. Isolating the impact of the pandemic from these coincident developments is made more difficult by limitations with data.

Despite these challenges, the three chapters in this section provide a comprehensive analysis of how the three least developed countries of Southeast Asia managed the pandemic, trying to minimize both the direct and indirect costs, in terms of health and economy.

References

Krueger, Anne. 2020. "The Open Secret to Reopening the Economy". *Project Syndicate*, 23 July 2020. https://www.project-syndicate.org/commentary/covid19-virus-will-decide-when-economy-can-reopen-by-anne-krueger-2020-07

Lee, Cassey, Siwage Negara, and Maxensius Sambodo. 2020. "Southeast Asia Dodged the Worst of Covid-19, but the Economic Devastation May Last for Years". *South China Morning Post*, 30 September 2020. https://www.scmp.com/week-asia/opinion/article/3103645/southeast-asia-escaped-worst-covid-19-its-economic-effects-could

Menon, Jayant. 2021. "Cambodia Tests Living with COVID-19". *East Asia Forum,* 2 December 2021. https://eastasiaforum.org/2021/12/02/cambodia-tests-living-with-covid-19/

Theme 2

MANAGING AND MISMANAGING THE PANDEMIC

Indonesia, Philippines, Vietnam

5

INDONESIA'S COVID-19 MOBILITY RESTRICTIONS

Rationales and Consequences

Arief Ramayandi and Siwage Dharma Negara[1]

INTRODUCTION

Mobility restrictions, or lockdowns, are critical measures many economies used to respond to the Covid-19 outbreak. During the early stage of the pandemic, there was a common belief that an early and decisive decision to impose lockdowns was an appropriate policy response, given the uncertain nature of the coronavirus infection.

Countries including China, Italy, Australia and New Zealand imposed strict lockdown measures and rigid border controls when they recorded increased cases of infection. Nevertheless, for various reasons, primarily economic, not all economies implemented such strict lockdowns. Indonesia decided not to implement complete lockdown measures.

The Indonesian government decided that more relaxed and micro-scale restrictions on public activity were the preferred strategy for this populous archipelagic country. These relatively relaxed mobility restrictions provided some space for selected critical and essential activities (such as the health sector and local markets) to continue. At the same time, the government also tried to manage the spread of Covid-19 and provided social assistance and business support for those adversely affected by the mobility restrictions.

The effectiveness of halting people's day-to-day activities to save lives has been critically assessed (see Correia, Luck, and Verner 2020; Goolsbee and Syverson 2020; Bianchi, Bianchi, and Song 2020). These studies show the policy is economically and politically costly. Concerned about the economic and political repercussions, Indonesia did not implement a complete lockdown (Sparrow, Dartanto, and Hartwig 2020). As a result, the Indonesian economy only suffered a mild recession compared to those suffered by countries that enforced more stringent restrictions. In 2020, the Indonesian economy shrank by 2.07 per cent, the first recession since the 1997 Asian financial crisis.

This chapter explains the rationales behind Indonesia's decision to impose and ease its mobility restrictions. We attempt to answer three questions. First, what are the likely factors that determined lockdown decisions? Second, how effective were the lockdowns in controlling the pandemic? Finally, how did the lockdowns affect the economy?

COVID-19 TRENDS

By the end of 2022, Indonesia had reported more than 6.7 million Covid-19 cases and more than 160,000 Covid-19 deaths. During the Delta variant, which hit Indonesia in July 2021 and was more contagious and dangerous than the initial variant, the country experienced a significant increase in the infection rate. New daily infections topped 56,000 on 15 July 2021. This is far higher than the previous peak recorded in January 2021, which was around 13,000 new infections in one day. During the Delta period, fatalities due to Covid-19 increased significantly as the healthcare system could not cope with the rapid increase in cases. On 27 July 2021, there were more than 2,000 deaths. Only by October 2021 did Indonesia manage to significantly reduce the number of new cases to below 1,000 per day. Figure 5.1 shows the weekly Covid-19 cases and deaths in per million terms to facilitate comparisons across countries; the series in absolute terms is presented in Figure 5.9.[2]

FIGURE 5.1
Indonesia's Daily Infections and Deaths due to Covid-19, January 2020 to August 2023

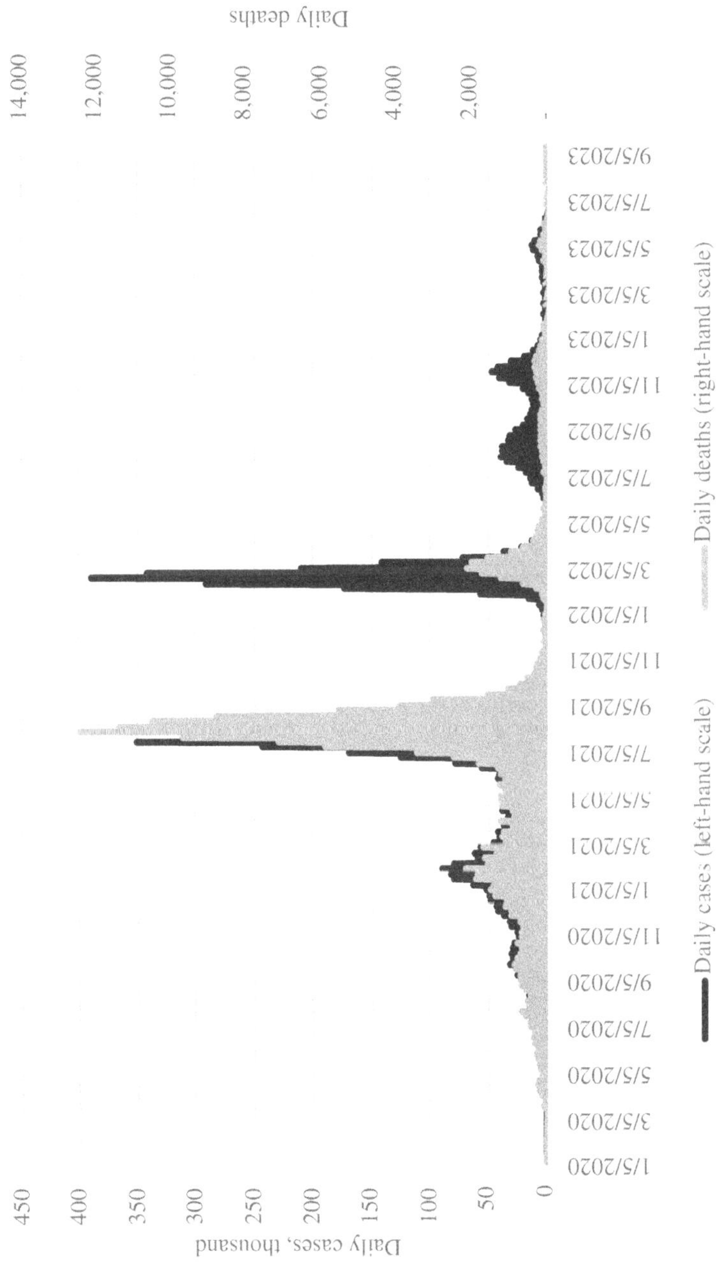

Source: Our World in Data, https://ourworldindata.org/explorers/coronavirus-data-explorer (accessed 21 May 2024).

Was this seemingly positive outcome in flattening the pandemic curve in 2021Q4 due to the mobility restrictions the government implemented? Or was it caused by other factors? Figure 5.1 shows that the declining trends in Covid-19 infections in the early months of 2021 were only temporary. As the country started to remove the restrictions in the fourth quarter of 2021, another new and more infectious variant, Omicron, hit the region. Daily infections increased to more than 64,000 by mid-February 2022, higher than the peak of daily infections during the Delta variant. Interestingly, fatalities did not rise as high as during the Delta wave. At the height of the third wave, Omicron, Indonesia experienced 300 to 400 deaths per day, much lower than the 1,000 to 2,000 deaths per day during the Delta wave. Progress in the vaccination programmes was a contributing factor; by the end of December 2021, Indonesia had reached almost 72 per cent of the population for the first dose and about 50 per cent for the second.[3] By the end of March 2022, the Omicron wave seemed to have subsided.

The number of Covid-19 cases in Indonesia was not equally distributed across provinces. Table 5.1 shows that most cases occurred in the two most populous islands, Java and Bali, which together contributed almost 70 per cent of the total infections in the country. Given the large number of cases in Java and Bali, the government focused its pandemic control measures there.

TABLE 5.1
Geographical Distribution of Covid-19 Cases

Provinces	*Confirmed Cases*[a]	*Share of Total Cases (%)*	*Population*	*Share of Population (%)*
Java and Bali	4,198,607	69.8	158,696,000	2.6
Sumatra	808,466	13.4	59,977,300	1.3
Kalimantan	454,555	7.6	17,052,200	2.7
Sulawesi	309,857	5.2	20,304,400	1.5
Nusa Tenggara	129,001	2.1	10,940,000	1.2
Maluku and Papua	112,332	1.9	8,802,900	1.3
Total	6,012,818	100	275,772,800	

Note: a. Confirmed cases as of 31 March 2022.
Sources: Coordinating Ministry for Economic Affairs; Statistics Indonesia (Badan Pusat Statistik).

MOBILITY RESTRICTIONS: INDONESIA'S TERMINOLOGY AND TIMELINE

Mobility restrictions were defined using various terms in Indonesia, depending on the timing and situation (see Figure 5.2). None of the restrictions were called a lockdown. In April 2020, at the start of the pandemic, Indonesia implemented large-scale social restrictions (Pembatasan Sosial Berskala Besar, or PSBB), which include working from home, online schooling and the closure of public facilities such as markets, shopping centres, terminals and theme parks (Figure 5.2). The national government also announced an international travel ban in April 2020, but the country did not enter into a total lockdown (Sparrow, Dartanto, and Hartwig 2020).[4] The PSBB were relaxed in June 2020 in preparation for the reopening of all economic activity. In January 2021, there

FIGURE 5.2
Mobility Restrictions in Indonesia

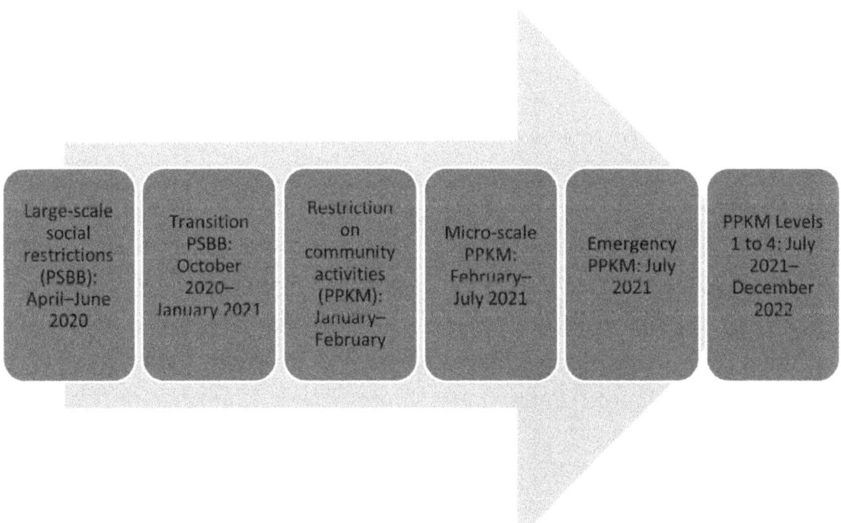

Note: The PSBB are the large-scale, top-down restrictions imposed by national government. Transitional PSBB are PSBB with gradual easing of restrictions. The micro PPKM are the smaller-scale, bottom-up restrictions imposed by subnational governments in coordination with national government. PPKM Levels 1 to 4 are restrictions defined by the level of virus transmission and the capacity of health services to respond.
Source: Republic of Indonesia (2022).

was a rapid increase of Covid-19 infections after the New Year holiday. Consequently, the government implemented restrictions on community activities (Pemberlakuan Pembatasan Kegiatan Masyarakat, or PPKM) through a centralized policy. Unlike the PSBB, in which every province can apply to the Minister of Health to implement the mobility restrictions they believe necessary (bottom-up approach), the PPKM allows the central government to assess and then instruct districts or municipalities to implement community restrictions (top-down approach).

The PPKM restrictions replaced the PSBB. They started in January 2021 and focused on seven provinces, Jakarta, West Java, Banten, Central Java, Yogyakarta, East Java and Bali. Travellers to Bali and Java were required to show rapid antigen and/or reverse transcription polymerase chain reaction (RT-PCR) tests. Businesses had to continue implementing a work-from-home arrangement for 75 per cent of their employees; the remainder could work in the office. In education, all learning continues online. In restaurants, dine-in was limited to 25 per cent of the establishment's capacity. Operating hours for shopping centres were limited and places of worship were only permitted to fill a maximum of 50 per cent of their capacity.

When the top-down PPKMs implemented by the central government in Java and Bali were judged to be ineffective in suppressing the spread of Covid-19, the government changed the policy to the micro PPKM. The micro PPKM required village and community leaders to actively manage and monitor the pandemic. The policy was implemented in select areas in Java and Bali. After the highly transmissible Delta variant hit the country in late June 2021, the government tightened the PPKM and renamed it an emergency micro PPKM in July 2021. Concern over the health and economic impacts of the Delta wave forced President Joko Widodo to appoint Luhut Binsar Pandjaitan, Coordinating Minister for Maritime Affairs and Investment, as coordinator for implementing the emergency micro PPKM for Java and Bali (Farisa and Rastika 2021). Although the government changed the name of the mobility restrictions, each new term essentially meant almost the same thing. Each restriction policy term differed only in its degree of tightness, such as the capacity level at which a business could operate; the operating hours of public facilities such as shopping malls, restaurants and mosques; and restrictions on residents' movements outside of an area.

From the beginning of the pandemic, the government's main concern was the economic implications of a full lockdown. This is reflected in the selection of the person in charge of coordinating the activity restrictions—the Coordinating Minister for Maritime Affairs and Investment instead of the Minister of Health. The central authorities believed that a total lockdown would be impractical and unsustainable given the population size, the significant size of the informal economy and the country's limited institutional and fiscal capacity. Indonesia instead chose to implement more relaxed mobility restrictions that allowed critical and essential business sectors to operate. The critical sectors are health; public safety and order; energy; logistics, transportation and distribution; food and beverages; fertilizers and petrochemicals; cement and building materials; national strategic projects; construction (public infrastructure) and basic utilities (electricity, water and waste management). The essential sectors included banking and financial institutions, the capital market, sectors related to information and communications technology, hotels and export-oriented industries.

The mobility restrictions began in April 2020 and were not fully or officially removed until end-2022 (see Appendix). The restrictions were evaluated every week or two and extended until the end of 2022. They were adjusted based on the evolution of daily infection cases and the capacity of the health system to respond.

The last change in mobility measures occurred on 21 July when levels 1 (safe) to 4 (unsafe) were added to the PPKM. The restrictions were essentially the same as previous restrictions, but this time the government used parameters such as the number of active cases and progress in vaccinations to categorize the status of a region from level 1 (green zone) to level 4 (red zone or emergency) (Figure 5.3).

On 21 July 2021, the government downgraded the PPKM level from 4 to 3 or 2 for several cities in Java. In August 2021, although the number of cases in the Java cities decreased, cities outside Java experienced spikes for several weeks. This led the government to implement different levels of PPKM outside Java. President Joko Widodo appointed the Coordinating Minister for Economic Affairs, Airlangga Hartarto, to coordinate the PPKM outside Java and Bali.

FIGURE 5.3
Different Levels of Restrictions on Community Activities (PPKM)

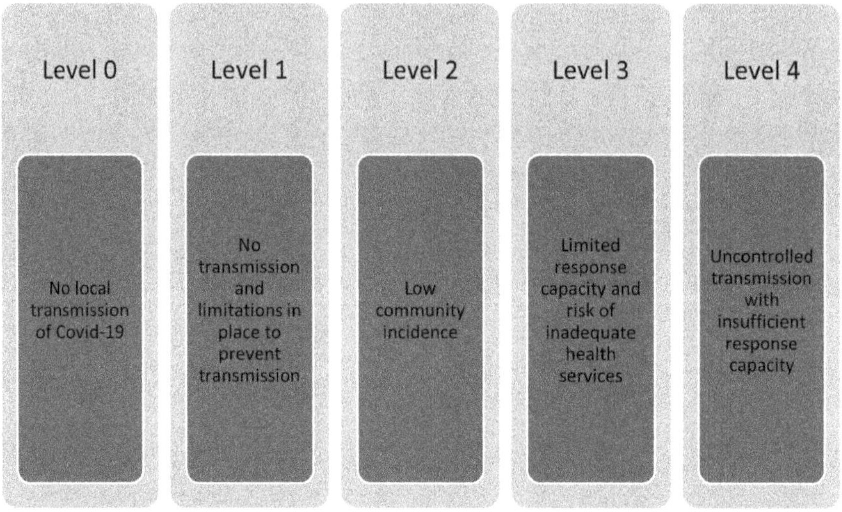

Source: Republic of Indonesia (2022).

Following a 21–27 September 2021 evaluation of the PPKM, the government decided to conduct a weekly evaluation of the PPKM policy and allowed retail activity and visits to recreation parks to resume gradually. Changes in the PPKM level were fluid from the end of 2021 to early 2022 as the Omicron variant spread. Varying levels of PPKM in different regions were imposed depending on the level of Covid-19 transmission and the adequacy of the health sector to respond (Figure 5.3).

In January 2022, the central government allowed schools and other educational institutions to restart limited face-to-face learning. All education units in areas at levels 1, 2 and 3 under a PPKM order were required to implement limited face-to-face learning. Regional governments were not able to prohibit limited face-to-face learning for areas that met the criteria, nor were they allowed to add more stringent rules. The guidelines for student capacity and duration of learning when limited face-to-face learning restarted were based on how many teachers and other staff were fully vaccinated in that particular education unit (Caesaria and Kasih 2022).

In mid-May 2022, the government started to relax flight rules for domestic and foreign travellers. Starting on 18 May, travellers who had proof they were vaccinated with at least two doses[5] were no longer required to take PCR and antigen tests for domestic and international flights (Simangunsong and Tashandra 2022).

CASE STUDIES: JAKARTA AND BALI

Given Indonesia's extensive decentralization, examining the regional variations in mobility restrictions and their implications is of interest. In Indonesia, regional governments played an active role in determining the timing and scope of the implementation of mobility restrictions. For instance, during the implementation of the PSBB restrictions, different regions imposed different degrees of restriction depending on the infection rates in their areas.

Arguably, large cities were more conducive environments for the virus to thrive (Sparrow, Dartanto, and Hartwig 2020). This was due not so much to population density but to their higher levels of mobility, connectivity and economic activity (Hsu 2020). To illustrate, we compare the impact of the mobility restrictions on health and economic outcomes in Jakarta and Bali, the two main gateways for foreign visitors.

Jakarta is an interesting case study for several reasons. The city is the financial and services centre of the country and is the barometer of its economy given its 17–18 per cent contribution to the national gross domestic product (GDP). Jakarta has a population of 10.7 million and has porous borders with the surrounding districts and municipalities (Bogor, Bekasi, Depok, Tangerang and Karawang). Millions of people commute in and out of the city daily, which makes it more prone to virus transmission.

Jakarta's governor, Anies Baswedan, continued to impose mobility restrictions when the national government eased restrictions for the whole country in June 2020 (see Appendix). The Jakarta restrictions were then tightened in response to the acceleration of infection cases in the city in August and September (Bramasta and Akbar 2020). These restrictions affected business activities in specific sectors, limited the number of employees in a workplace and reduced public transport volume. However, the restrictions contradicted national policy and drew criticism from central government officials who feared the economic repercussions (Sparrow, Dartanto, and Hartwig 2020, p. 295). Such tensions between the policy priorities of national and subnational jurisdictions are pervasive in Indonesia.

The mobility restrictions implemented in Jakarta caused the city's economy to contract by 1.6 per cent in 2020. Key sectors contracted during 2020's strict mobility restrictions. For example, accommodation and food and beverages contracted by 14.7 per cent, the manufacturing industry fell by 9.2 per cent and transportation and storage by 7.5 per cent (Table 5.2). Retail trade, the key employer for many workers in the informal sector, fell by 5 per cent in 2020. As restrictions were relaxed in 2021, most sectors recovered, and Jakarta's GDP grew by 5.3 per cent. It grew further by 9.4 per cent in 2022 as, in 2022Q2, Indonesia gradually relaxed its mobility restrictions and reopened its international borders to allow international visitors to enter.

Figure 5.4 shows that the implementation of mobility restrictions significantly reduced people's movements in Jakarta. Using Google mobility data, the implementation of the PSBB in April 2020 caused people's

TABLE 5.2
Jakarta's GDP Growth by Sector

	2019 (%)	*2020 (%)*	*2021 (%)*	*2022 (%)*
Manufacturing Industry	1.5	–9.2	13.6	9.5
Construction	4.9	–5.1	4.3	7.8
Wholesale and Retail Trade	10.1	–5.0	6.6	13.2
Transportation and Storage	11.0	–7.5	14.9	14.4
Accommodation, Food and Beverages	9.0	–14.7	10.4	13.0
Information and Communication	13.2	11.8	5.4	8.4
Financial and Insurance	10.8	5.0	3.8	8.9
Real Estate	7.0	4.2	2.7	4.1
Business Services	15.3	0.6	1.3	9.4
Public Administration	8.9	–4.5	–3.6	1.2
Education Services	5.7	3.3	1.0	1.9
Health and Social Work	9.1	22.1	7.9	12.0
Other Services	12.0	–3.4	–1.9	19.2
GDP	8.6	–1.6	5.3	9.4

Source: Statistics Indonesia (Badan Pusat Statistik).

FIGURE 5.4
Mobility Restrictions and Effects on Retail and Recreation in Jakarta

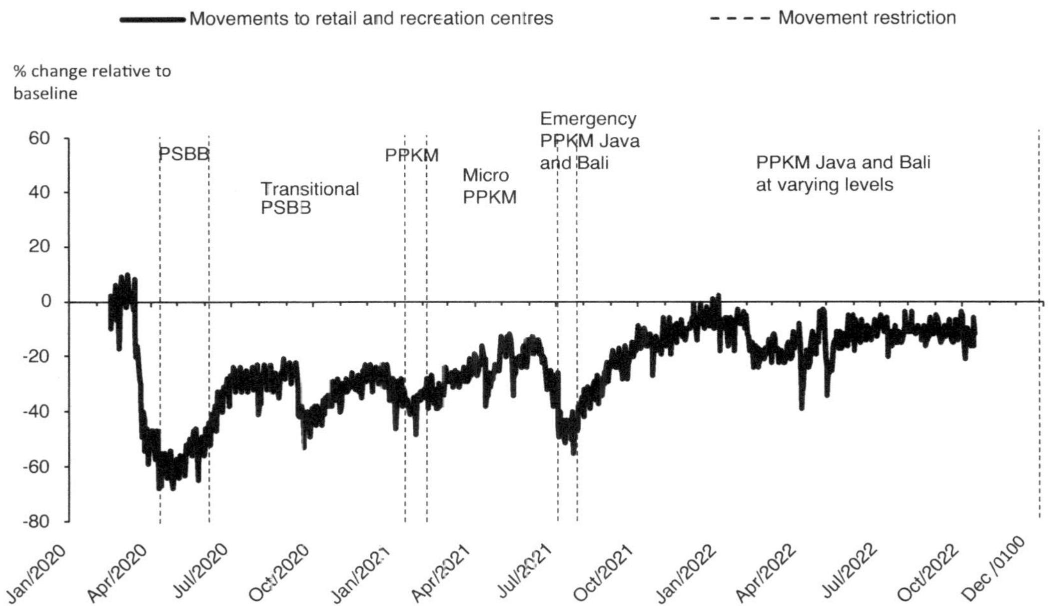

Note: The grids indicate the start of different episodes of the implemented mobility restrictions based on Figure 5.2 and detailed in the Appendix. The PSBB are the large-scale, top-down restrictions imposed by the national government. Transitional PSBB are PSBB with gradual easing of restrictions. The PPKM micro are the smaller-scale, bottom-up restrictions imposed by subnational governments in coordination with the national government.

Source: Google LLC. Community Mobility Reports, https://www.google.com/covid19/mobility/

movements to retail and recreation centres to drop by 60–70 per cent relative to a pre-pandemic baseline. Movements rebounded when restrictions were loosened, but in September 2020, when restrictions were tightened again, visits to retail and recreation centres again fell by 40–50 per cent below the baseline. Again, movements rebounded somewhat with a loosening of restrictions, but when they were tightened again in July 2021 due to the Delta variant, movements to retail and recreation centres dropped by around 40–50 per cent below the baseline. As of late 2022, visits to retail and recreation centres had not returned to the pre-pandemic level, partly due to a shift to online markets, which became the norm during the early stages of the pandemic.

The vast economic cost of the pandemic can be seen in the decline in the city's collection of tax revenue, which fell by 55 per cent to IDR22.5 trillion (US$1.6 billion) in 2020 versus pre-Covid-19 (Astutik 2020). Consequently, the Jakarta budget in 2020 declined by 47 per cent to IDR47.2 trillion (US$3.4 billion).

Bali is another interesting case study for several reasons. The island, also a province, has a population of 4.4 million, and is a prominent tourism centre and the barometer of the country's tourism sector recovery. In this context, the Indonesian government focused its efforts on a safe reopening of Bali, which could then also serve as a model for the reopening of other tourism destinations in the country.

Unlike Jakarta, which is diverse in terms of sectoral composition to growth, Bali's economy is highly dependent on tourism. Tourism contributes 60 per cent of Bali's GDP (Lazuardi 2021), which explains why Bali's economic growth plummeted to −11 per cent in 2020 when Indonesia closed its international borders in April of that year (Fauzan 2021). Two sectors, transport and accommodation, and food and beverages were the hardest hit, contracting by 36.8 per cent and 29.8 per cent respectively, as virtually no international tourists visited (Table 5.3). It was reported that 87.5 per cent of micro, small and medium-sized enterprises in Bali experienced negative impacts from the pandemic (Dhae 2021; BBC News Indonesia 2021). By August 2021, more than 49,000 people had lost their jobs and more than 593,000 experienced reductions in work hours (*Bisnis Bali* 2021). The only lifeline for the island's economy was the resumption of domestic tourism, which occurred when the international border was closed in April 2020, but this did not offset the losses caused by the absence of international tourists. There were efforts to reopen Bali for foreign visitors at the start of the fourth quarter of 2021, but these were slow and lacklustre. The prolonged closure of international borders in 2021 caused another economic contraction in Bali that year. Only when international tourism returned in May 2022 did the island economy regain its positive growth (Table 5.3).

Figure 5.5 shows that the border closures in Bali significantly reduced travel movements. The Google mobility data shows that the international border closure and the PSBB in April 2020 caused a 40–55 per cent decline in people's visits to retail and recreation centres, followed by a rebound. In January 2021, when restrictions were tightened due to the infection spike after the New Year holiday, movements again dropped 40–55 per cent relative to the pre-pandemic baseline. Then, in July 2021 this was repeated for a third time: restrictions were tightened due to the spread of the Delta variant.[6] Compared to Jakarta, activities in retail and recreation centres in Bali declined more drastically from 2020 to 2022 relative to their pre-pandemic level.

TABLE 5.3
Bali's GDP Growth by Sector

	2019 (%)	*2020 (%)*	*2021 (%)*	*2022 (%)*
Agriculture, Forestry and Fisheries	5.5	–0.1	2.8	3.5
Manufacturing Industry	8.4	–5.2	2.0	9.7
Construction	9.9	–1.7	2.5	8.1
Wholesale and Retail Trade	8.9	–6.1	0.2	11.0
Transportation and Storage	8.3	–36.8	–20.2	51.9
Accommodation, Food and Beverages	7.2	–29.8	–11.0	20.1
Information and Communication	8.6	6.5	4.1	1.3
Financial and Insurance	10.7	–5.1	1.6	18.6
Real Estate	7.9	1.4	1.6	5.9
Business Services	6.7	–2.1	–1.5	13.1
Public Administration	7.4	6.4	3.8	-0.1
Education Services	8.2	1.6	2.1	1.1
Health and Social Work	8.0	5.4	7.8	3.8
Other Services	10.4	–4.5	–0.8	14.1
GDP	7.8	–11.0	–1.7	11.2

Source: Statistics Indonesia (Badan Pusat Statistik).

FIGURE 5.5
Mobility Restrictions in Bali

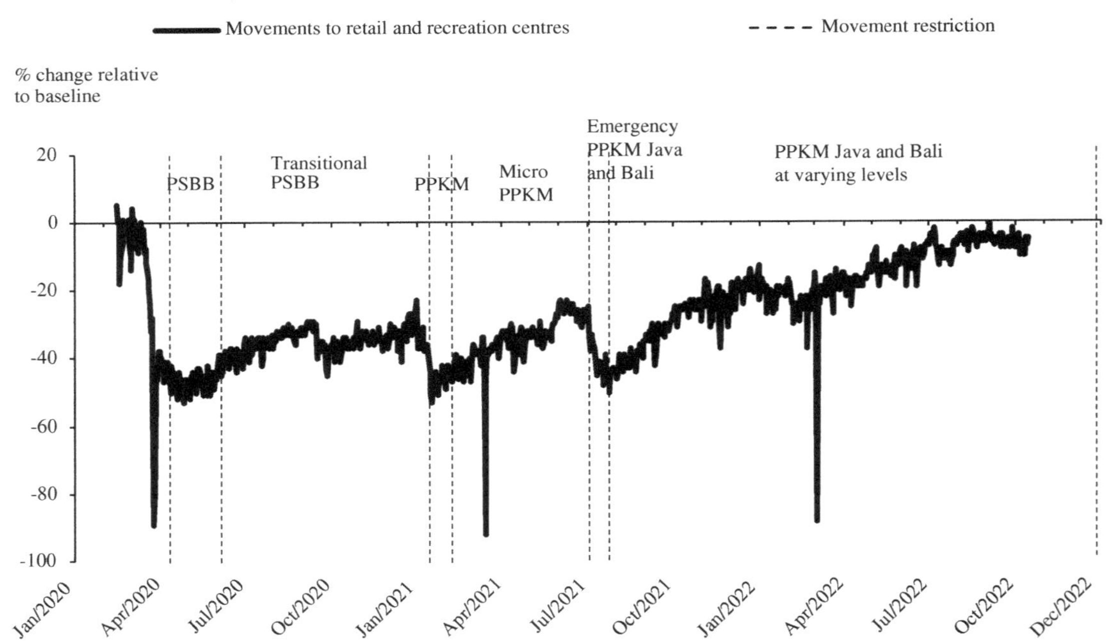

Note: The PSBB are the large-scale, top-down restrictions imposed by the national government. Transitional PSBB are PSBB with gradual easing of restrictions. The micro PPKM are the smaller-scale, bottom-up restrictions imposed by subnational governments in coordination with the national government.
Source: Google LLC. Community Mobility Reports, https://www.google.com/covid19/mobility/ (accessed 29 April 2023).

Jakarta led all other regions in Indonesia in terms of daily infections (see Figures 5.6 and 5.7 for Jakarta and selected regions). One possible explanation is that Jakarta is one of the main gateways to the country; in fact, the first case of Covid-19 was recorded in Jakarta. It should also be noted that while the populations of Sumatra, Sulawesi and Kalimantan are larger than that of Jakarta, the latter has conducted more testing and tracing[7] than other parts of the country, which naturally leads to a greater likelihood of finding positive cases.

FACTORS BEHIND THE MOBILITY RESTRICTIONS IN INDONESIA

The Covid-19 pandemic caught the world by surprise. It began drawing attention after the outbreak in Wuhan, China in December 2019 and its spread across countries, initiating a stream of travel restrictions across the globe in February and March 2020. People grappled with adjusting to a new reality where gatherings and physical interactions could invoke potentially deadly health hazards.

As the Indonesian government promotes tourism in the country, it responded rather late to the pandemic, still considering itself safe when it detected the first Covid-19 infection in early March 2020. The community mobility index outside residential areas briefly increased above its January 2020 level before dipping below its pre-pandemic level in mid-March after the total number of infections surpassed one hundred. The index bottomed out in April as the first PSBB, the large-scale social restriction, was implemented. Following that, different degrees and intensities of mobility restrictions were implemented across the country, depending on the Covid-19 situation. Fiscal and monetary policies were also implemented to mitigate the immediate impact on the economy (Rizvi, Juhro, and Narayan 2021; Nugroho and Syarief in this volume).

While it is well understood that political and economic implications are considered when initiating mobility restriction policies, they should not be the most influential factors. In Indonesia, the data suggest that, after a late start, all decisions to extend mobility restriction policies were related to the dynamics of daily infections and/or the total number of severe active cases,[8] which can be proxied by the number of patients in care units.

FIGURE 5.6
Mobility Restrictions and Covid-19 Infections in Jakarta and Bali

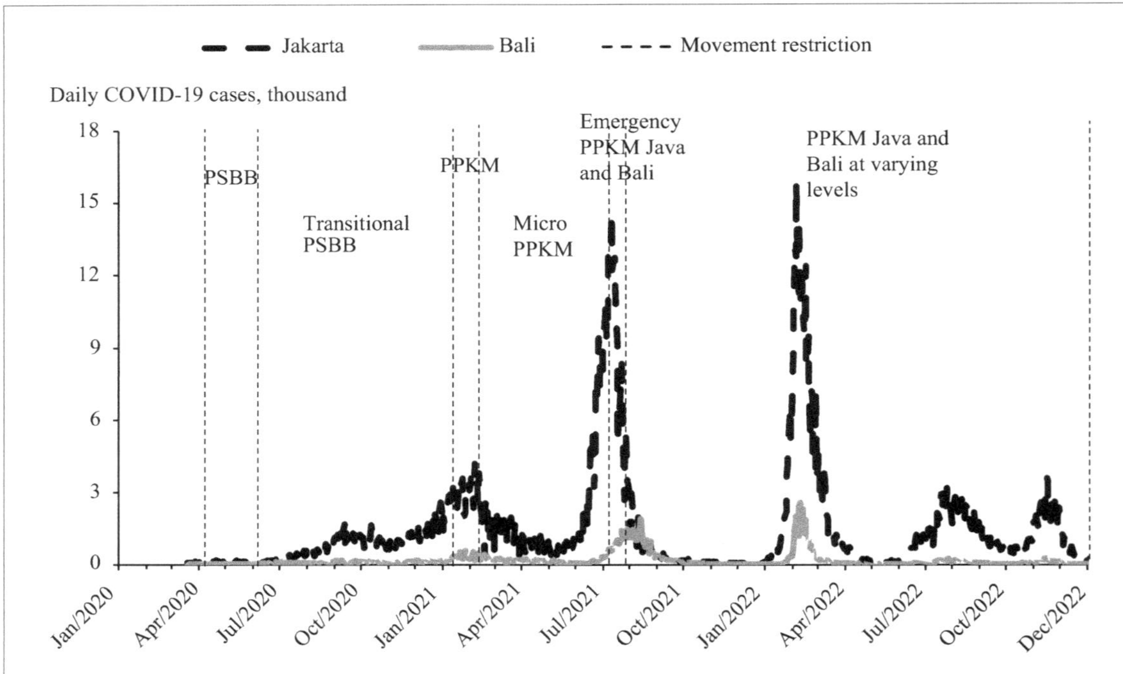

Note: The PSBB are the large-scale, top-down restrictions imposed by the national government. Transitional PSBB are PSBB with gradual easing of restrictions. The micro PPKM are the smaller-scale, bottom-up restrictions imposed by subnational governments in coordination with the national government.
Source: Peta Sebaran, https://covid19.go.id/peta-sebaran (accessed 29 April 2023).

FIGURE 5.7
Mobility Restrictions and Covid-19 Infections in Sumatra, Kalimantan and Sulawesi

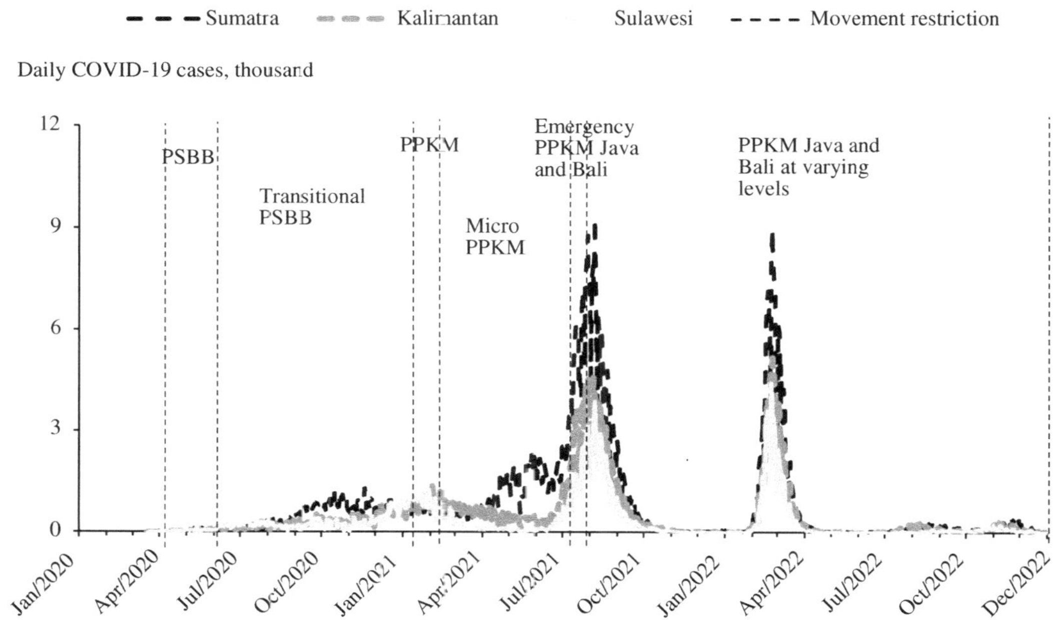

Note: The PSBB are the large-scale, top-down restrictions imposed by the national government. Transitional PSBB are PSBB with gradual easing of restrictions. The micro PPKM are the smaller-scale, bottom-up restrictions imposed by subnational governments in coordination with the national government.
Source: Peta Sebaran, https://covid19.go.id/peta-sebaran (accessed 29 April 2023).

Continuously increasing infection cases and hospitalizations prompted continuous renewals of mobility restriction orders in Indonesia, albeit with different degrees of stringency, which is discussed in the following section. Renewals of mobility restrictions extended to the implementation of the micro-scale PPKM from early February 2021 to the beginning of July 2021. Despite the declining number of daily new infection cases in this episode, health facilities remained under pressure given the high number of hospitalizations as the number of severe cases remained high (Figure 5.8).

Figures 5.8 and 5.9 also show that the number of new cases dictated the patterns observed in hospitalizations and the number of daily fatalities due to Covid-19. Both variables are positively correlated with the new daily cases, with a correlation coefficient of 91 per cent for hospitalizations and 65 per cent for daily fatalities. While the correlation between daily cases and hospitalizations was not much affected by the Omicron wave in early 2022 (Figure 5.8), the correlation between daily cases and fatalities dropped substantially during the Omicron wave (Figure 5.9)—the correlation coefficient between daily cases and deaths excluding the Omicron wave is 88 per cent. The drop in correlation is mainly attributable to the relatively large number of vaccinations, which significantly reduced the number of fatalities due to Covid-19 during the Omicron wave (Figure 5.9). Regardless, new daily cases consistently preceded the peaks of hospitalizations (by about a week) and daily fatalities (by about three weeks), and hence acted as a reliable leading indicator that was used as the main factor in implementing mobility restrictions.

EFFECTIVENESS OF THE RESTRICTIONS

The number of new daily and active Covid-19 cases also acted as the main determinant for people's mobility, which varied across places and time in Indonesia due to region-specific factors, seasonal factors and the stringency of government restrictions. Restricting people's mobility was often regarded as the most effective way to contain the spread of Covid-19, especially during the early part of the pandemic. Ridhwan et al. (2023) found that, to an extent, people did follow the restriction policies in Indonesia. People's mobility outside residential areas was higher in the months before

FIGURE 5.8
Daily Covid-19 Infections and Hospitalizations in Indonesia

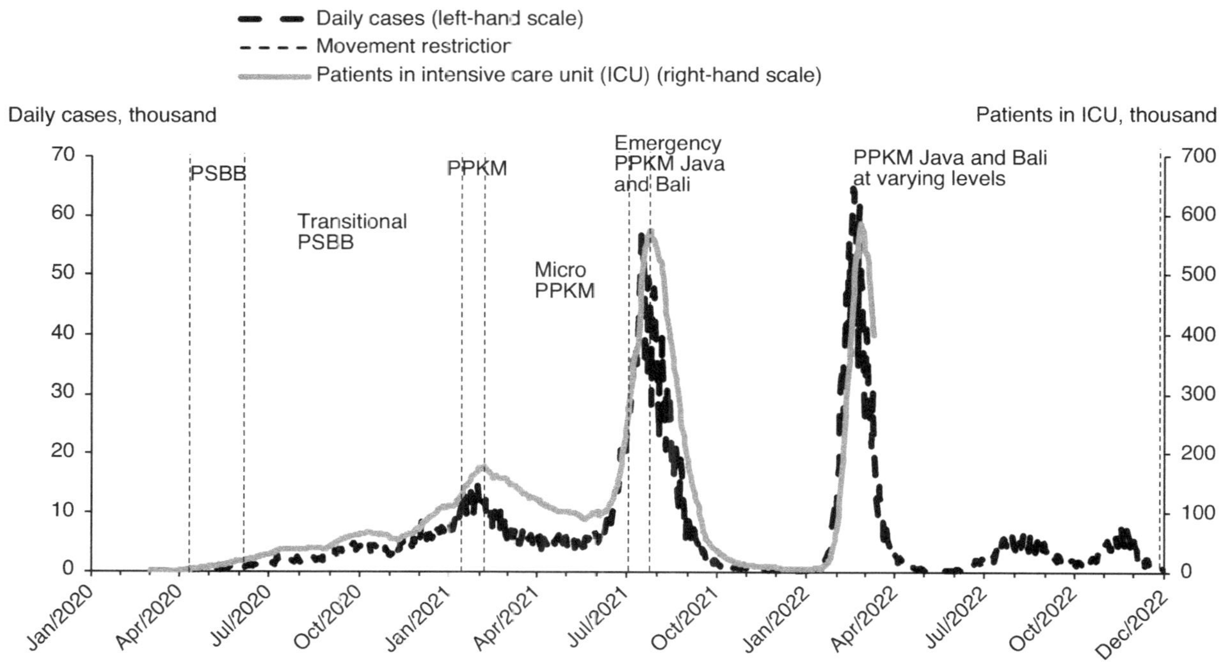

Note: Data on patients in ICU was discontinued in March 2022. The PSBB are the large-scale, top-down restrictions imposed by the national government. Transitional PSBB are PSBB with gradual easing of restrictions. The micro PPKM are the smaller-scale, bottom-up restrictions imposed by subnational governments in coordination with the national government.
Source: Our World in Data, https://ourworldindata.org/explorers/coronavirus-data-explorer (accessed 29 April 2023).

FIGURE 5.9
Daily Covid-19 Infections and Fatalities in Indonesia

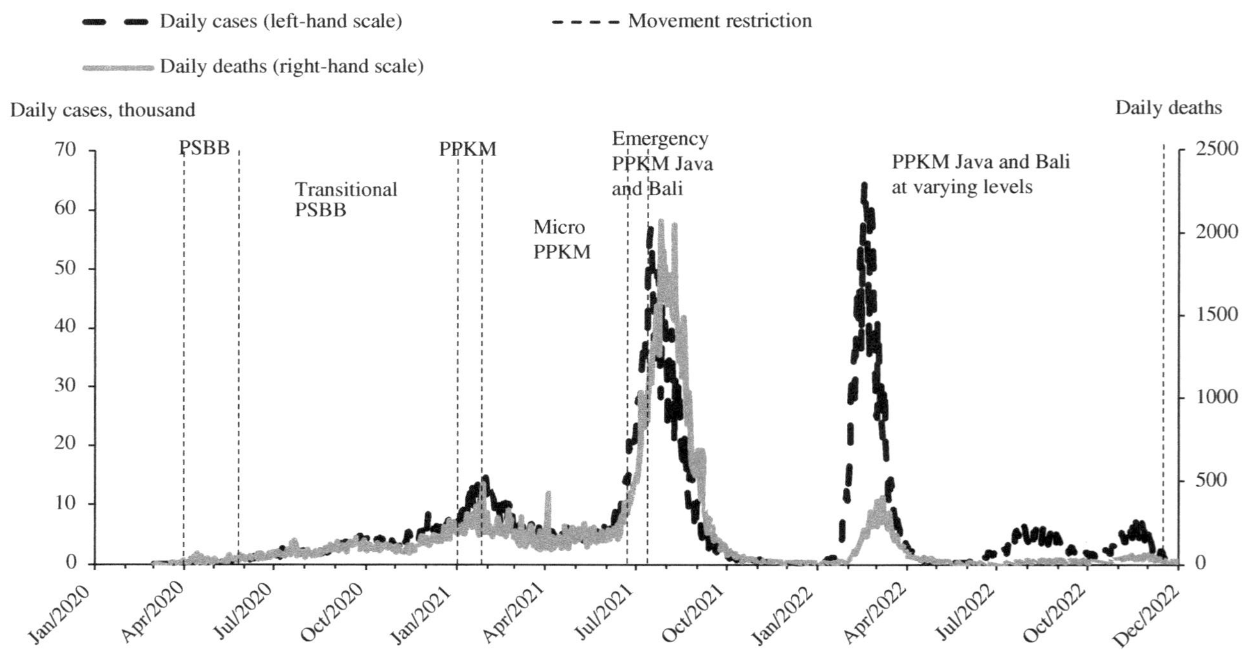

Note: The PSBB are the large-scale, top-down restrictions imposed by the national government. Transitional PSBB are PSBB with gradual easing of restrictions. The micro PPKM are the smaller-scale, bottom-up restrictions imposed by subnational governments in coordination with the national government.
Source: Our World in Data, https://ourworldindata.org/explorers/coronavirus-data-explorer (accessed 29 April 2023).

the implementation of mobility restrictions and they became more active again a month or two later.

The extent of mobility restrictions in Indonesia varied across regions, and they were not applied nationwide—some areas had no restrictions. Restrictions were predominantly used in Jakarta, which was the largest contributor to Covid-19 cases in the country. Ridhwan et al. (2023) noted that between February 2020 and February 2021, most periods of mobility restrictions were applied to less than 25 per cent of the regions in Indonesia. This is why people's mobility in Indonesia in July–December 2020 increased overall despite the continuing restriction policies, though with the proviso of Ridhwan et al. (2023) that in the areas where restrictions were implemented, they were quite effective. When applied to more regions, the restrictions reduce the average people's mobility nationwide, and vice versa.

Aside from public campaigns and restrictions on internal movements, no other measures of mobility restriction were applied nationwide in the country (Hale et al. 2020). Closing of schools and workplaces, for example, was applied nationwide at a very mild level—limited only to recommendations for closing—after the peak of the Delta wave in September 2021. The same nationwide treatment, with requirements to cancel public events, was also applied during the Omicron wave in early 2022. The variations in the restrictions applied across regions in Indonesia drove the changes in the stringency index (Figure 5.10).

Changing the stringency of the restrictions proved effective in containing people's movements outside their neighbourhoods, at least up to the peak of the second wave in February 2021. Figure 5.10 shows that as the authorities implemented measures to restrict movements in April 2020 in an attempt to contain the continued spread of Covid-19, people's mobility dropped by almost half compared to before the pandemic.

From April 2020, the measures were gradually eased. First, in May 2020, by changing the restriction on internal movements from a complete restriction to a recommendation to not travel across cities/regions, followed by the reopening of public transport. Further easings were introduced in June when selected workplaces and schools were partially reopened. Then, in August, international travel bans were eased for some regions of origin. Cumulatively, by late August these measures raised people's

FIGURE 5.10
Restriction Stringency Index and Average Mobility Outside Residential Areas

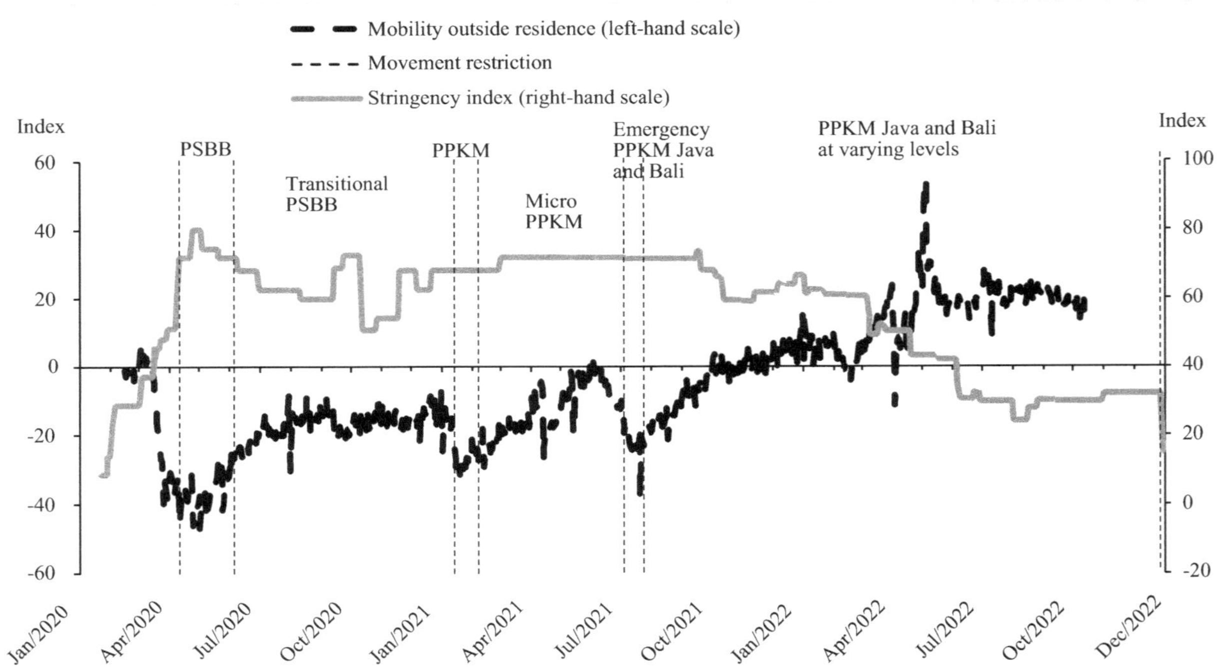

Note: Google mobility data is available only up to 15 October 2022. The PSBB are the large-scale, top-down restrictions imposed by the national government. Transitional PSBB are PSBB with gradual easing of restrictions. The micro PPKM are the smaller-scale, bottom-up restrictions imposed by subnational governments in coordination with the national government.
Source: Hale et al. (2020).

mobility rate to about 10 per cent below the pre-pandemic level from the low seen in April.

Accelerating Covid-19 infection cases in September 2020 prompted the authorities to retighten measures to restrict mobility, which again led to a fall in people's movements outside their residential areas. The correlation between the stringency index and mobility weakened somewhat from February 2021, however, after Covid-19 vaccination programmes took off in the country. There was even a brief episode when the stringency index seemed to correlate positively with mobility (October 2020 to January 2021), just before the Omicron wave hit the economy.

In summary, all these suggest that the mobility restriction policies were effective in helping to contain the exponential spread of Covid-19, especially with the alterations in stringency before the Covid-19 vaccination programme accelerated in May 2021. This effectiveness extends to containing the number of hospitalizations and fatalities. However, the correlation between the degree of restriction stringency and people's mobility seems to weaken after the government expedited the vaccination rate from May 2021 onwards. Aside from the role of vaccination, it is also worth noting that the growing variation of the stringency measures across provinces post-PSBB may have also contributed to weakening the correlation at the national level.

The increase in the share of the population vaccinated, from 10 per cent in May and June 2021 to over 30 per cent in October, helped Indonesia to shorten the length of the Delta wave. In less than three months, the number of daily infections fell from over 55,000 cases per day in August 2021 to around 1,500 cases per day in end-October/early November (Figure 5.11), and hospitalizations and deaths declined. However, new daily cases and hospitalizations once again surged during the Omicron wave in February and March 2022 (Figure 5.8), despite the continued increase in the share of people vaccinated. The vaccine was proven effective, however, in limiting fatalities due to Covid-19 as can be seen in the later part of Figure 5.9. This explains the jump in people's mobility to exceed its pre-pandemic level in late February 2022, even before the restrictions were eased. The effectiveness of the mobility restriction policies was enhanced tremendously by the rapid increase in vaccination, especially in reducing the rate of fatalities from Covid-19.

FIGURE 5.11
Daily Covid-19 Infections and Total Vaccination Doses

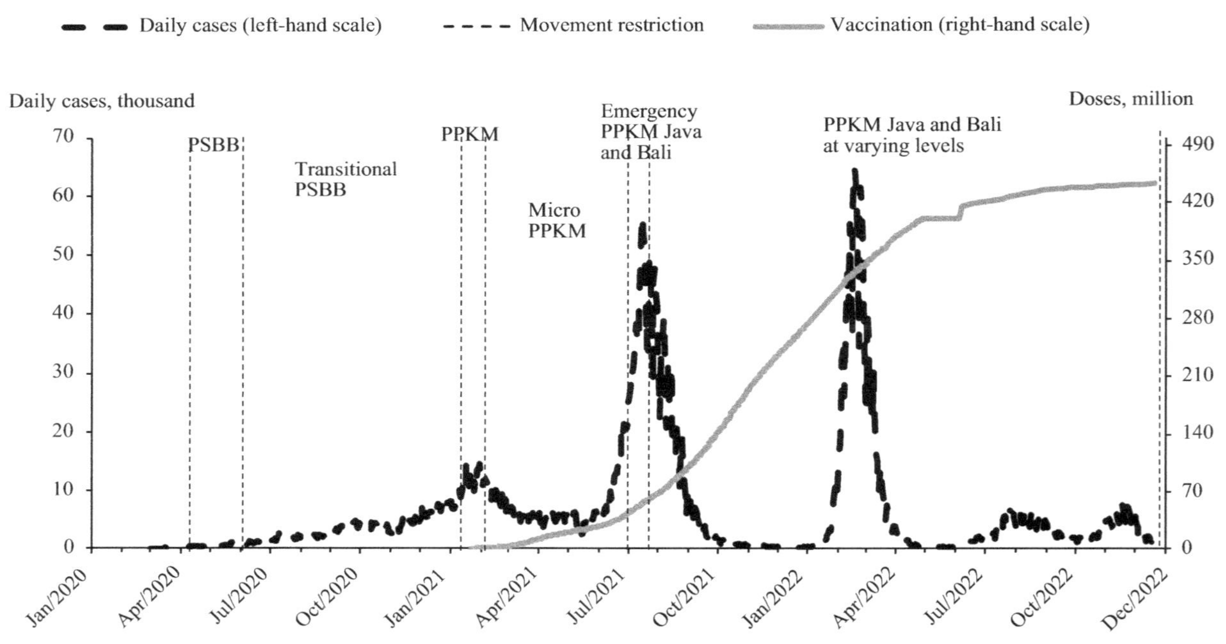

Note: The PSBB are the large-scale, top-down restrictions imposed by the national government. Transitional PSBB are PSBB with gradual easing of restrictions. The micro PPKM are the smaller-scale, bottom-up restrictions imposed by subnational governments in coordination with the national government.
Source: Our World in Data, https://ourworldindata.org/explorers/coronavirus-data-explorer (accessed 29 April 2023).

ECONOMIC IMPACTS OF MOBILITY RESTRICTIONS

Indonesia's GDP growth slowed to just below 3.0 per cent in the first quarter of 2020 as Covid-19 started to affect the economy. Following that, the country experienced a recession with four consecutive quarterly GDP declines: GDP was −5.3 per cent in the second quarter of 2021, −3.5 per cent in the third, −2.2 per cent in the fourth and −0.75 in the first quarter of 2021. The economy started to recover somewhat and grew 7.1 per cent in the second quarter of 2021. Since the fourth quarter of 2021, except for the hiccup of 3.5 per cent growth in the third quarter of 2021 due to the Delta variant, GDP growth has returned to an average of 5.0 per cent to 5.5 per cent—a solid growth rate, but insufficient to guarantee a quick recovery to the pre-pandemic path.

Due to data limitations, this section discusses the impact of Covid-19 mobility restriction policies on the economy through the lens of real economic activities and the financial markets. Real economic activities are represented by the manufacturing purchasing managers' index (PMI), which comes with a one-month lag and is available monthly. The financial markets are represented by market capitalization data from the Jakarta Stock Exchange, which shows the trading activity in the stock exchange and is available daily (Figure 5.12).

The pandemic and the restrictions on movement impinged on real economic activities, including those of manufacturing and other sectors. Domestic manufacturing activity, as represented by the manufacturing PMI, is negatively correlated with the degree of restriction and new daily infections. This is even true for the case of the Omicron wave in 2022 (Figure 5.13) when the average people's mobility had risen and exceeded its pre-pandemic level. This suggests that manufacturing activity is not immune to the re-emergence of new waves of Covid-19 cases even when fatalities are low and mobility remains relatively high.

The manufacturing PMI contracted sharply during the first phase of Covid-19 in Indonesia, March to July 2020. It plunged to below 30 in April 2020 after the first strict mobility restrictions were implemented, suggesting a deep contraction in manufacturing activity.[9] However, since the drop was offset by a drop in aggregate demand, inflation remained low during the period. The manufacturing sector worsened: the PMI continued

FIGURE 5.12
JSX Market Capitalization and Stringency Index

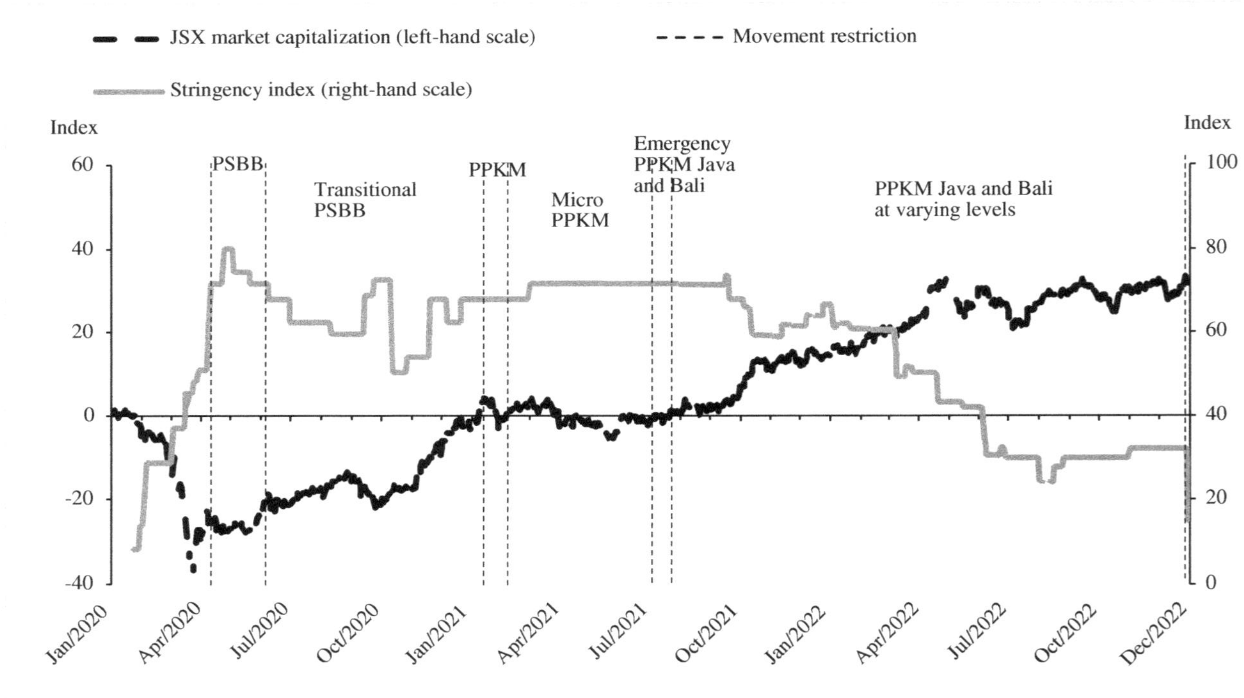

Note: The PSBB are the large-scale, top-down restrictions imposed by national government. Transitional PSBB are PSBB with gradual easing of restrictions. The micro PPKM are the smaller-scale, bottom-up restrictions imposed by subnational governments in coordination with national government.
Sources: CEIC; Hale et al. (2020).

FIGURE 5.13
Daily Covid-19 Infections and Manufacturing Purchasing Managers' Index

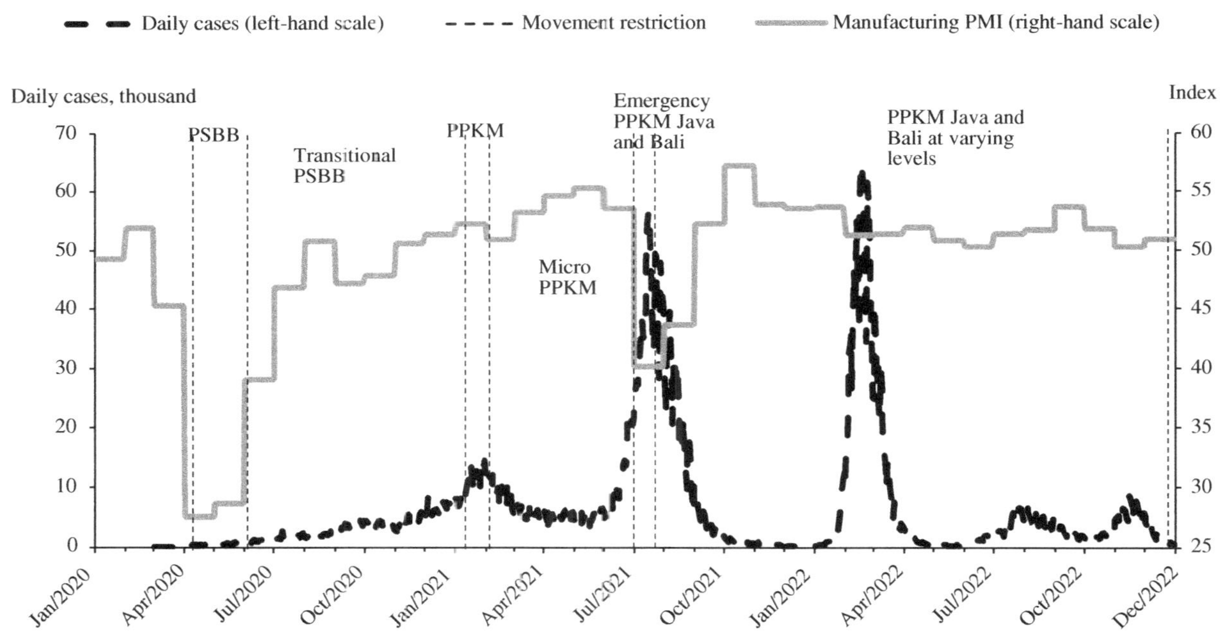

Note: The PSBB are the large-scale, top-down restrictions imposed by the national government. Transitional PSBB are PSBB with gradual easing of restrictions. The micro PPKM are the smaller-scale, bottom-up restrictions imposed by subnational governments in coordination with the national government.
Source: CEIC Data Company, Our World in Data, https://ourworldindata.org/explorers/coronavirus-data-explorer (accessed 29 April 2023).

to suggest month-on-month contractions in activity up to October 2020. After stagnating for several months, activity started to pick up slowly from March to June 2021, while new cases slowed (Figure 5.13). Before the improvements in activity could pick up sufficiently to compensate for the loss during the 2020 period of contraction, the Delta variant emerged. The PMI plunged to 40 in July 2021, indicating another large contraction in manufacturing activity which lasted into August. This pattern of weakening manufacturing activity was again repeated during the Omicron wave in early 2022. The dynamics of manufacturing activity after the Omicron wave were mainly dictated by economic factors as the spread of the Covid-19 virus became more contained, thanks to the increasing number of vaccinations administered.

Other real activity sectors also mirror the trend in manufacturing. Studies including Ridhwan et al. (2023) suggest that mobility restriction policies negatively and significantly affected household income. The current income index plunged significantly in April 2020 and continued to decrease. Only in November 2021 did the current income index regain a value over 100.[10] After seventeen months of continuous declines in income, household earnings in Indonesia started bottoming out in October 2021, albeit with income levels that were still far below the average earned prior to the pandemic (Figure 5.14) (Bank Indonesia 2022).

Turning to the financial sector, the effect of the pandemic on the stock market was mostly felt in 2020, during the first wave of the pandemic (Figure 5.14). By early 2021, the Jakarta stock exchange capitalization index had returned to its pre-pandemic level. It did not seem to be affected much by the 2021 Delta variant. Similarly, Omicron also did not seem to lower the capital market activity, as indicated by the high stock market capitalization index. Market confidence in the financial sector, represented by the rapid growth in stock market capitalization, returned after the Delta wave, boosted by looser restrictions on mobility and a rapid increase in Covid-19 vaccinations.

Observations on the economic impacts of mobility restrictions reveal a concerning implication of Covid-19 and its policy responses on potentially worsening inequality, at least in the medium run. While real economic activities continued to struggle with recurring Covid-19 waves, activities in the financial sector passed their pre-pandemic level. As financial

FIGURE 5.14
Daily Covid-19 Infections and the Current Income Index

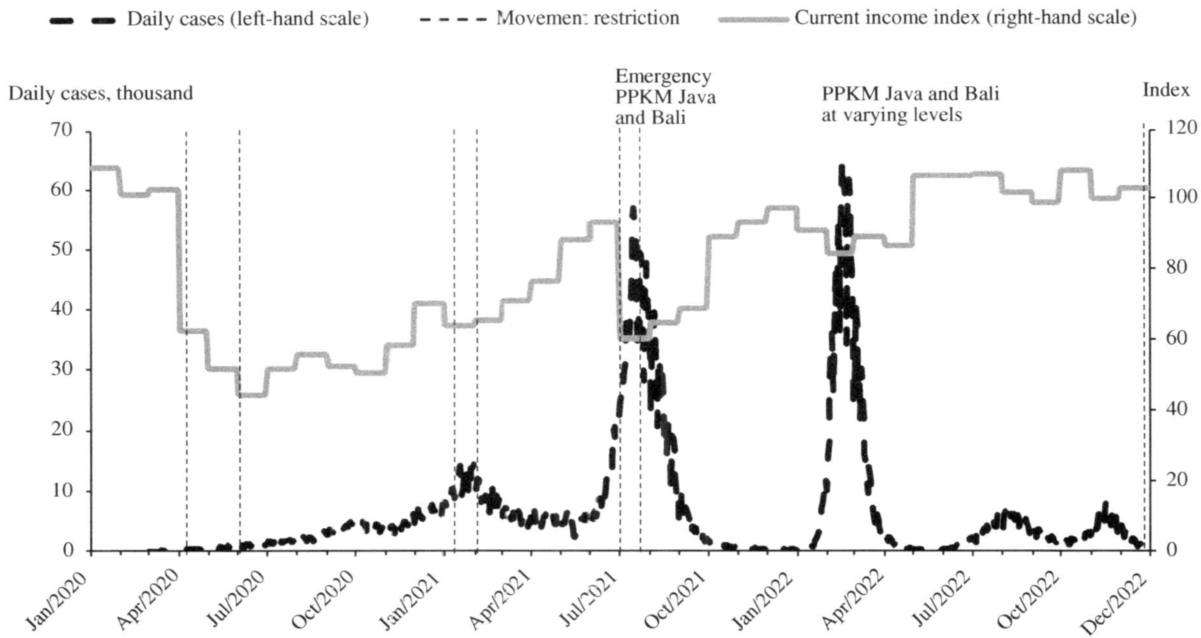

Note: The PSBB are the large-scale, top-down restrictions imposed by the national government. Transitional PSBB are PSBB with gradual easing of restrictions. The micro PPKM are the smaller-scale, bottom-up restrictions imposed by subnational governments in coordination with the national government.
Sources: Bank Indonesia (2022); Our World in Data, https://ourworldindata.org/explorers/coronavirus-data-explorer (accessed 29 April 2023).

development benefits the rich more than the poor, this may widen income inequality in the country. The breakdown of the current income index suggests that while the decline in income of households with monthly spending above IDR5 million (US$335) per month bottomed out from October 2021, this was not the case for those whose was less than IDR2 million (US$135) per month. The incomes of the latter group continued to decline before bottoming out in May 2022.

CONCLUSION

In the first year of the pandemic, mobility restrictions seemed to play a role in preventing the exponential spread of coronavirus and higher fatalities. Yet, over time, we observe that mobility restrictions became less effective. As national and subnational governments chose more relaxed rules at the micro level (districts/cities) rather than a strict lockdown policy at the national level, the focus of pandemic control moved to the vaccination programme. This shift in strategy was mainly driven by concern about the economic costs of a complete domestic lockdown. With more relaxed mobility restrictions, the expansion of the Covid-19 vaccination programme in mid-2021 became the game changer in controlling the pandemic. Our analysis indicates that, after the Delta wave, the effectiveness of the mobility restrictions became less clear due to the rapid increase in the vaccination rate. The latter is correlated with lower fatality rates from Covid-19.

Various political and economic considerations are involved in the decision to initiate mobility restrictions. Nevertheless, our analysis suggests that the decisions to prolong mobility restriction policies within Indonesia were associated with the dynamics of daily infections and/or the total number of severe cases. An increase in infections and hospitalization prompted the authorities to continue renewing mobility restrictions. The restrictions were implemented with different degrees of stringency, depending on the virus transmission level in an area and the ability of its health sector to respond.

By relaxing mobility restrictions and accelerating vaccinations, Indonesia avoided a prolonged recession. However, as of March 2022 pandemic impacts were quite different between the real and the financial sectors. The pandemic and its restrictions on mobility impinged on real economic activities, especially those in manufacturing and services. Our analysis shows that domestic manufacturing was negatively correlated with the degree of restriction and the dynamic of new infections. This suggests that manufacturing activity is highly sensitive to the re-emergence of new waves of Covid-19 that may lead to new mobility restrictions.

Interestingly, the impact of the pandemic on the financial sector was short-lived. The stock market was only adversely affected during the first wave of the pandemic in 2020. By early 2021, it had returned to its pre-pandemic level. It did not seem much affected by the Delta or Omicron variants—as indicated by the high stock market capitalization. This trend is not unique to Indonesia. Many stock markets in other economies also experienced a boom during the pandemic (Stewart 2021). These contrasting dynamics between the real and the financial sector might potentially worsen inequality in the post-pandemic era. Sluggish recovery in the real sector will adversely affect millions of wage earners, whose income level will, in turn, take a longer time to reach the pre-pandemic level. Meanwhile, capital owners will reap the benefits of the upwards movement of the financial market. While beyond the focus of this paper, this issue is worth further investigation.

APPENDIX

TABLE A5.1
Timeline of Indonesia's Mobility Restrictions

Suspension of all visits and transit by foreign nationals	• 2 April 2020
Large-scale social restrictions (PSBB)	• 10–23 April 2020 • 24 April–21 May 2020 • 22 May–4 June 2020
Transitional PSBB in Jakarta	• Transitional PSBB 1: 5 June–10 September 2020 • PSBB: 14 September–11 October 2020 (14–27 September, 27 September–11 October) • Transitional PSBB 2: 12 October 2020–11 January 2021 (extended every two weeks)
Emergency PPKM restrictions on public activity in Java and Bali	• 11–25 January 2021 • 26 January–8 February 2021
Micro PPKM	• 9–22 February 2021, 23 February–31 May 2021, 22 June 2021–5 July 2021
Emergency PPKM in Java and Bali	• 3–20 July 2021
PPKM levels 3 and 4 in Java and Bali	• 21–25 July 2021, 26 July–2 August 2021, 3–9 August 2021, 10–16 August 2021 • 17–23 August 2021 (including Sumatra, Kalimantan and Sulawesi)
PPKM level 3 (Java and Bali) and level 4 (other areas)	• 24–30 August 2021, 31 August–6 September 2021, 7–13 September 2021 • 14–20 September 2021 (level 4 only at six cities outside Java) • 21–27 September 2021 • 28 September 2021– October 2021 (government evaluated the policy weekly)
PPKM levels 1 and 2 in Java and Bali	• 3 October 2021: PPKM level 1 for Blitar, East Java (lowest level) • 23–30 October 2021: PPKM level 2 (Jakarta)

PPKM levels for Java and Bali and non-Java/Bali areas from end 2021 to 2022	• 1–15 November 2021: Jakarta restrictions reduced to level 1 • 29 November–13 December 2021: Jakarta restrictions increased to level 2 (due to Omicron variant) • 24 December 2021–2 January 2022: end of year restriction—level 3 applied nationwide (in and outside Java and Bali) • 3–17 January 2022: loosened to PPKM level 1 (in and outside Java and Bali), loosened to PPKM level 2 for Jakarta, Yogyakarta and the whole of Bali; extended three times • 8–14 February 2022: restrictions tightened to level 3 for Greater Jakarta, Bali and Yogyakarta (due to Omicron variant) • 15–21 February 2022: Bandung tightened from level 1 to level 3 • 21–28 February 2022: level 3 extended twice in Java and Bali • 7–14 March 2022: loosened from level 3 to level 2 in Greater Jakarta and Greater Surabaya (extended three times) • 24 May–6 June 2022: loosened from level 2 to level 1 in Greater Jakarta
Border reopens fully to international travellers	• 6 April 2022
PPKM is officially revoked in all regions of Indonesia	• 30 December 2022

Note: Levels 1 to 4 under PPKM indicate the severity of the pandemic situation in the region. The higher the level the greater the viral transmissions and the lower the healthcare capacity—hence tighter mobility restrictions.
Source: Official reports and media.

Notes

1. The views expressed here are entirely those of the authors and do not reflect the views and policies of the Asian Development Bank or any of the governments they represent. The authors thank Dennis Sorino for his excellent research assistance.
2. Data in this paragraph taken from Our World in Data, "Indonesia: Coronavirus Pandemic Country Profile" at https://ourworldindata.org/coronavirus/country/indonesia (accessed 12 March 2024).
3. The single dose Johnson & Johnson vaccine was also used in Indonesia; the government considered this as equivalent to the two-dose vaccines.
4. A total border closure, however, remained in place until August 2020. Subsequently, the international travel ban was eased somewhat, with travellers from some regions permitted to enter Indonesia. Full reopening of the border occurred on 6 April 2022.
5. Or the single dose Johnson & Johnson vaccine.
6. Figure 5.5 shows steep drops in Bali's mobility indicator in March 2020, 2021 and 2022. These drops were due to Bali's annual Nyepi public holiday, a day of seclusion.
7. Although contact tracing is an important element of managing infection outbreaks, it is a resource-intensive exercise for a populous country such as Indonesia. The use of a contact tracing application in the country was ineffective due to low use and weak enforcement (Fitriani, Handayani, and Hidayanto 2022). This led to use instead of a community-based surveillance mechanism (Haryono et al. 2022), which was less systematic and reliable.
8. Continuous and consistent data on the total number of active cases are difficult to compute since data on recoveries from Covid-19 are patchy and seem to have been discontinued in 2021. The data on patients in care units is the number of severe cases requiring hospitalization and, to some extent, demonstrates the degree of pressure on the health facility.
9. Values below 50 indicate contraction.
10. Values below 100 indicate that income is lower than the income earned six months previously.

References

Astutik, Yuni. 2020. "Dihantam Corona, Penerimaan Pajak DKI Jakarta Ambles 55%" [Hit by Corona, Jakarta tax revenue drops 55%]. *CNBC Indonesia*, 29 May 2020. https://www.cnbcindonesia.com/news/20200529172237-4-

161900/dihantam-corona-penerimaan-pajak-dki-jakarta-ambles-55 (accessed 13 November 2021).

Bank Indonesia. 2022. "Consumer Expectation Survey–May 2022". https://www.bi.go.id/en/publikasi/laporan/Pages/SK-Mei-2022.aspx

BBC News Indonesia. 2021. "PPKM Darurat Berdampak 'Masif' Pada Sektor Pariwisata, Asosiasi Minta Bantuan Dipercepat—'Mereka Perlu Makan'" [Emergency PPKM has 'massive' impact on tourism sector, association asks for aid to be accelerated—'They need to eat']. 6 July 2021. https://www.bbc.com/indonesia/indonesia-57723855 (accessed 13 November 2021).

Bianchi, Francesco, Giada Bianchi, and Dongho Song. 2020. "The Long-Term Impact of the Covid-19 Unemployment Shock on Life Expectancy and Mortality Rates". NBER Working Paper No. 28304, National Bureau of Economic Research, Cambridge, MA, December 2020, revised September 2021.

Bisnis Bali. 2021. "20,35 Persen Penduduk Usia Kerja di Bali Terdampak Covid-19" [20.35 percent of working-age population in Bali affected by Covid-19]. 7 November 2021. http://bisnisbali.com/2035-persen-penduduk-usia-kerja-di-bali-terdampak-covid-19/ (accessed 13 November 2021).

Bramasta, Dandy Bayu, and Jihad Akbar. 2020. "Perjalanan PSBB Transisi di Jakarta hingga Anies Tarik Rem Darurat" [Transitional PSBB journey in Jakarta until Anies pulls the emergency brake]. *Kompas*, 11 September 2020. https://www.kompas.com/tren/read/2020/09/11/190300865/perjalanan-psbb-transisi-di-jakarta-hingga-anies-tarik-rem-darurat-?page=all (accessed 13 November 2021).

Caesaria, Sandra Desi, and Ayunda Pininta Kasih. 2022. "Sekolah Tatap Muka Dimulai, Ini Daftar Aturan Lengkap 2022" [Face-to-face schooling begins, here is the complete list of rules for 2022]. *Kompas*, 3 January 2022. https://www.kompas.com/edu/read/2022/01/03/105145271/sekolah-tatap-muka-dimulai-ini-daftar-aturan-lengkap-2022?page=all (accessed 15 July 2022).

Correia, Sergio, Stephan Luck, and Emil Verner. 2020. "Pandemics Depress the Economy, Public Health Interventions Do Not: Evidence from the 1918 Flu". SSRN, 5 June. http://dx.doi.org/10.2139/ssrn.3561560

Dhae, Arnoldus. 2021. "Sebanyak 22,5% UMKM Bali tidak Terdampak Covid-19" [As many as 22.5% of Bali MSMEs were not affected by Covid-19]. *Media Indonesia*, 29 September 2021. https://mediaindonesia.com/nusantara/436431/sebanyak-225-umkm-bali-tidak-terdampak-covid-19 (accessed 15 July 2022).

Farisa, Fitria Chusna, and Icha Rastika. 2021. "Jokowi Tunjuk Luhut sebagai Koordinator PPKM Mikro Darurat untuk Jawa-Bali" [Jokowi appoints Luhut as emergency micro PPKM coordinator for Java–Bali]. *Kompas*, 29 June 2021. https://nasional.kompas.com/read/2021/06/29/22080051/jokowi-tunjuk-luhut-sebagai-koordinator-ppkm-mikro-darurat-untuk-jawa-bali?page=all (accessed 13 November 2021).

Fitriani, W.R., P.W. Handayani, and A.N. Hidayanto. 2022. "Challenges in Coronavirus Contact-Tracing Application Implementation in Indonesia: Users' Perspective". Paper presented at the 2022 International Conference on Information Management and Technology (ICIMTech), 11–12 August 2022, Semarang, Indonesia. https://ieeexplore.ieee.org/document/9915106

Fauzan, Herdanang Ahmad. 2021. "Ekonomi Bali Masih Rawan Minus Sampai Akhir Tahun 2021" [Bali's economy is still prone to negative impacts until the end of 2021]. *Bisnis.com*, 22 May 2021. https://ekonomi.bisnis.com/read/20210522/9/1396826/ekonomi-bali-masih-rawan-minus-sampai-akhir-tahun-2021 (accessed 13 November 2021).

Goolsbee, Austan, and Chad Syverson. 2020. "Fear, Lockdown, and Diversion: Comparing Drivers of Pandemic Economic Decline". NBER Working Paper No. 27432, National Bureau of Economic Research, Cambridge, MA, June 2020.

Hale, T., N. Angrist, E. Cameron-Blake, L. Hallas, B. Kira, S. Majumdar, A. Petherick, T. Phillips, H. Tatlow, and S. Webster. 2020. "Covid-19 Government Response Tracker". Blavatnik School of Government, University of Oxford. https://www.bsg.ox.ac.uk/research/covid-19-government-response-tracker

Haryono, M.A., A.P. Asih, L. Natoli, D. Ariyani, D. Handayani, N. Agrestryana, and A. Ardiyansyah. 2022. "Detection and Contact Tracing of Covid-19 in Indonesia through a Red Cross Community Based Surveillance System". *International Journal of Infectious Diseases* 116, Supplement: S35–S36. https://doi.org/10.1016/j.ijid.2021.12.085

Hsu, Jeremy. 2020. "Population Density Does Not Doom Cities to Pandemic Dangers". *Scientific American*, 16 September 2020. https://www.scientificamerican.com/article /population-density-does-not-doom-cities-to-pandemic-dangers/

Lazuardi, Adi. 2021. "Pandemi Pacu Bali Perkuat Sektor Pertanian dan Pendidikan" [The pandemic spurred Bali to strengthen the agricultural and education sectors]. Antara, 31 May 2021. https://www.antaranews.com/berita/2185274/pandemi-pacu-bali-perkuat-sektor-pertanian-dan-pendidikan (accessed 13 November 2021).

Nugroho, Yanuar, and Sofie Syarief. 2025. "To Be or Not To Be? Dilemmas of Covid-19 Policy Implementation and Coordination in Indonesia". In *Learning from Covid-19 in Southeast Asia: Restriction, Relief, Recovery*, edited by Lee Hwok Aun, Siwage Dharma Negara and Jayant Menon. Singapore: ISEAS – Yusof Ishak Institute.

Republic of Indonesia. 2022. "Strengthening Policy Synergy to Maintain Stability and Preserve Recovery Momentum amid Heightened Global Uncertainty and Increasing Inflation Pressure". Presentation by the Investor Relations Unit, Republic of Indonesia, November 2022. https://www.bi.go.id/en/iru/presentation/Documents/Republic%20of%20Indonesia%20Presentation%20Book%20-%20November%202022F.pdf

Ridhwan, Masagus M., Jahen F. Rezki, Asep Suryahadi, Arief Ramayandi, and Affandi Ismail. 2023. "The Impact of Covid-19 Lockdowns on Household Income, Consumption, and Expectations: Evidence from High-frequency Data in Indonesia". *Bulletin of Indonesian Economic Studies* 60, no. 1: 67–94. https://doi.org/10.1080/00074918.2023.2167930

Rizvi, S.A., S.M. Juhro, and P.K. Narayan. 2021. "Understanding Market Reaction to Covid-19 Monetary and Fiscal Stimulus in Major ASEAN Countries". *Bulletin of Monetary Economics and Banking* 24, no. 3: 313–34. https://doi.org/10.21098/bemp.v24i3.1690

Simangunsong, Wasti Samaria, and Nabilla Tashandra. 2022. "Pelaku Perjalanan Luar Negeri Sudah Tak Perlu Tes, Ini Syaratnya" [Overseas travellers no longer need a test, these are the conditions]. *Kompas*, 18 May 2022. https://travel.kompas.com/read/2022/05/18/180646927/pelaku-perjalanan-luar-negeri-sudah-tak-perlu-tes-ini-syaratnya?page=all (accessed 15 July 2022).

Sparrow, Robert, Teguh Dartanto, and Renate Hartwig. 2020. "Indonesia Under the New Normal: Challenges and the Way Ahead". *Bulletin of Indonesian Economic Studies* 56, no. 3: 269–99.

Stewart, Emily. 2021. "Why Stocks Soared while America Struggled". *Vox: Business and Finance*, 10 May 2021. https://www.vox.com/business-and-finance/22421417/stock-market-pandemic-economy (accessed 15 July 2022).

6

ECONOMICS OF LOCKDOWN

Balancing Health and the Economy in the Philippines

Ronald U. Mendoza and Sheena A. Valenzuela

INTRODUCTION

The Philippines is a Southeast Asian archipelagic country comprising 7,641 islands. With a population of almost 110 million, a growing middle class and increasing urbanization, it is one of the most dynamic economies in the world (World Bank 2022). The country's gross domestic product (GDP) grew steadily from 2012 to 2019 at an average of 6.5 per cent per year until the Covid-19 pandemic caused a contraction in the economy, resulting in negative GDP growth: −9.6 per cent in 2020 (World Bank 2021a). After the first Covid-19 case was confirmed on 30 January 2020 in the Philippines (a 38-year-old Chinese national), Covid-19 cases shot up to 450,000 confirmed infections and 8,800 deaths in 2020 and 2,800,000 confirmed infections and 49,000 deaths in 2021. At the time of writing this article, March 2023, the Philippines had registered more than 4 million cases and more than 66,000 deaths (WHO 2023).

Controlling the spread of Covid-19 involves effectively managing health risks, yet it presents a policy challenge as some disease control methods—

anchored around minimizing human contact and limiting the transmission of the disease—also create the conditions for a potentially severe economic downturn. This dilemma prompted policymakers to consider nuanced crisis relief and recovery plans to flatten the epidemiological curve without flattening the economy. Once Covid-19 was controlled, and a cost-efficient containment system was in place, hard lockdowns and mobility restrictions could be relaxed, allowing the economy to recover. Hence, countries that seemed to fare better in controlling the pandemic also minimized the economic damage they suffered due to comparatively shorter lockdown periods (McKinsey & Company 2020).

While the timing, length and severity of lockdowns are important factors in disease control, their success and effectiveness ultimately rests on resources, institutional capacity, the healthcare system and social protection. The Philippines was among the countries that implemented a relatively early lockdown, which was targeted and regional and began on 15 March 2020.[1] This was designed to help reduce the number of cases and deaths. However, the country failed to strengthen its weak healthcare system during its multiple lockdowns to prepare for reopening. The Philippines did not possess the necessary requirements of adequate Covid-19 testing, efficient contact tracing, sufficient facilities for treatment and rapid vaccinations. Moreover, the country also struggled to ensure the timely and adequate distribution of financial aid to affected families, exacerbating the economic and social impact of the pandemic. Without financial aid, some Filipinos were forced to work despite the high risk of infection. However, without social protection for the population, there was continuous pressure to reopen to allow businesses to operate. The country could not go into long lockdowns because it did not have sufficient resources to support households. Consequently, Covid-19 cases continued to rise, overwhelming hospitals and forcing yet another lockdown.

The Philippines experienced one of the world's longest periods of continuous lockdowns: over the twenty-two months from March 2020 to January 2022, the country had some form of restriction, albeit at varying levels. The Philippines also implemented some of the world's most stringent restrictions. According to a Covid-19 Stringency Index developed by the University of Oxford, the Philippines ranked 12th out of 185 countries in terms of strictness of government response to the pandemic (Oxford

Covid-19 Government Response Tracker (OxCGRT) and Blavatnik School of Government 2022). The index included response indicators such as school closures, workplace closures and travel bans. The Philippines also had the longest school closure in the world, which disrupted the education of 27 million students for twenty months (UNICEF 2021). From the start of the pandemic in March 2020 until January 2022, the Philippine government implemented hard lockdowns (meaning Enhanced Community Quarantine [ECQ], Modified Enhanced Community Quarantine [MECQ], Alert Level 4) in Metro Manila, Luzon and other high-risk areas six times, each with varying levels of strictness. However, despite the draconian measures, health outcomes did not improve—the Philippines could not flatten the curve but flattened its economy instead.

In this chapter, the authors examine the rationale, approaches and consequences of the Philippines pandemic management, examining the government's strategy, which focused on lockdowns. The authors discuss the governance challenge of pandemic response by outlining a theoretical framework for pandemic management and explain the Philippines' pandemic response and its impact. The authors provide a brief synthesis of key lessons learnt and conclude.

THEORETICAL FRAMEWORK FOR PANDEMIC CONTROL: BALANCING HEALTH AND THE ECONOMY

In pandemic response, there are several main and interlinked objectives. The first is to contain the spread of the virus, in this case, Covid-19, and flatten the epidemiological curve so that domestic health systems are not overwhelmed. A second objective is focused on a sustained and stable recovery, aspiring towards a V-shaped recovery rather than a W-shaped one. The latter implies the risk of relapse if the virus flares up again, triggering another round of demand- and supply-side shocks.

However, there were several main challenges as Covid-19 crisis relief efforts transitioned to crisis recovery. Policymakers grappled with the benefit-cost trade-offs between tempering the risk of Covid-19 contagion and mitigating the adverse economic impacts resulting from social distancing, quarantine and lockdowns. When exactly to open up was the subject of intense debate. On the one hand, reopening too soon could have risked a large upswing in infections; on the other hand, reopening too late could have caused a deeper than necessary economic contraction.

To help illustrate these points, Figure 6.1 juxtaposes the two curves of interest to a country's efforts to "flatten the epidemiological curve without flattening the economy". The first is the epidemiological curve illustrating the number of people infected with Covid-19. The goal is to flatten the curve by slowing the rate of infection so that the peak infection incidence (1a) is a manageable number that the country's health system can handle, as indicated by the horizontal grey line. Without interventions, the peak (1a) would surpass the healthcare system's capacity. With effective interventions, such as social distancing, travel restrictions, quarantines/ lockdowns, the peak infection incidence is reduced to (2b), which is smaller and more manageable.

However, these interventions designed to contain Covid-19 can result in a dramatic economic contraction. Hence, the second curve for policymakers to monitor is the economic curve represented by total GDP. Figure 6.1 roughly illustrates how policies designed to lower the peak incidence from 1a to 1b will also likely contract the economy. This contraction is illustrated by the drop in output from 2a to 2b. This period can be roughly described as the crisis response and relief stage when Covid-19 containment measures must be complemented by relief efforts for the disruptions caused by the lockdown.

In general, only when the incidence of new cases of Covid-19 starts to decline should the policies on lockdown and quarantine be relaxed. This is also when one expects the economy to begin to recover. This timeline is illustrated in Figure 6.1. Still, it is unclear to what extent the two—the relaxation of containment policies and the economic recovery—will coincide, given other factors, such as lingering demand-side chilling effects, where people are cautious in spending money, or complications due to the possible emergence of new variants. New variants can strain even well-functioning systems as scientists and medical experts continue to learn about their properties. Regarding the Delta and Omicron variants, for example, their greater infectiousness forced countries back into tighter lockdowns as containment measures were upgraded to deal with the new

FIGURE 6.1
Stages of Crisis Management Juxtaposed against Epidemiological and Economic Curves

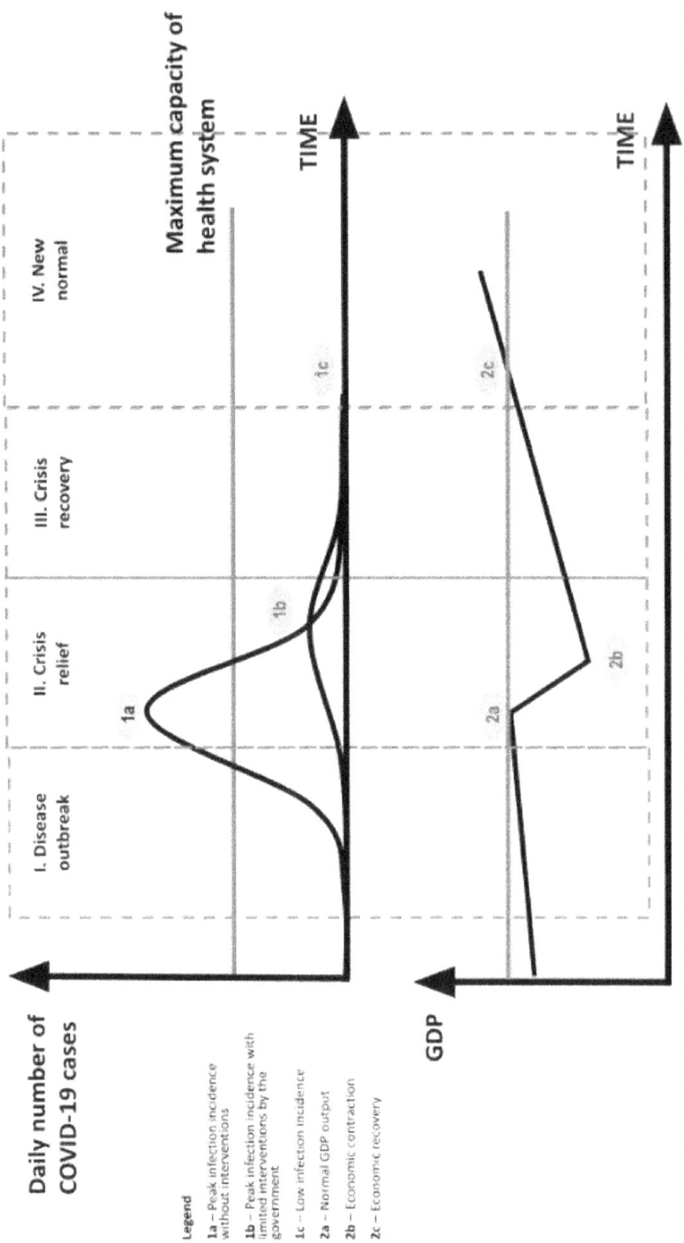

Sources: Based on Centers for Disease Control and Prevention (2007) and International Monetary Fund (2020).

variant.[2] Full output recovery occurs when the economic curve intersects the horizontal grey line in Figure 6.1 such that the total output implied by 2a is equal to 2c.

Figure 6.1 also illustrates the four possible stages of crisis management (disease/crisis outbreak, crisis relief, crisis recovery and the "new normal"). In practice, crisis management policies probably overlap across these different phases. However, it is helpful to illustrate them distinctly, to understand better how policy objectives evolve over the crisis period and the post-crisis situation (the new normal).

LOCKDOWN RATIONALE, APPROACHES AND CONSEQUENCES IN THE PHILIPPINES

Background

The Philippines comprises 81 provinces, 146 cities, 1,488 municipalities and 42,046 *barangays* (village-level government units) located in three major islands: Luzon, Visayas and Mindanao. Administratively, the country is subdivided into seventeen regions. Metro Manila is the metropolitan area where Manila, the capital, is located. With a population of 13.48 million in 2020 (Philippine Statistics Authority 2021b), Metro Manila is among the most densely populated areas in the world. Its regional GDP was 32.2 per cent of the national GDP in 2019, making it the largest regional contributor to the Philippine economy (Philippine Statistics Authority 2020b). Given Metro Manila's population density, the most stringent lockdowns were implemented in that region.

In response to the growing threat of Covid-19 (then called novel coronavirus), the Philippine government, through the Office of the President, reactivated the Inter-Agency Task Force for the Management of Emerging Infectious Diseases (IATF-EID) on 28 January 2020. The IATF-EID had been formed on 26 May 2014 to serve as a coordinating mechanism for the prevention of the spread of infectious diseases such as SARS, Middle East respiratory syndrome coronavirus, avian influenza and Ebola. However, it is only used on an ad hoc basis (i.e., when the administration identifies a threat) (Porcalla 2014). The task force, mandated to facilitate inter-sectoral collaboration on pandemic management, comprises members from different national government agencies. It is led by the Department of Health. While the IATF-EID formulates the policies, guidelines and strategies for pandemic response, the National Task Force Against Covid-19 is responsible for the implementation and execution of these policies. It was led by the Secretary of National Defense, and was formed on 24 March 2020 through IATF-EID Resolution No. 15 (IATF-EID 2020d). In April 2020, the national government also organized regional Covid-19 task forces to respond to localized issues and concerns.

The IATF-EID implemented four major types of lockdowns from March 2020 until November 2021. Ordered from strictest to least strict, they are ECQ, MECQ, General Community Quarantine (GCQ) and Modified General Community Quarantine (MGCQ). Table 6.1 summarizes the classifications.

In September 2021, the IATF-EID revised the classification into the Alert Level System with five tiers ranging from 5 to 1. This classification is based on the degree of case transmission and the rate of utilization of hospital beds and intensive care units and was implemented in November 2021. Table 6.2 summarizes the Alert Level System for Covid-19.

Timeline of Lockdowns

At the onset of a crisis such as the outbreak of a disease, countries usually have to deal with incomplete and unverified information, but, globally, policymakers have shown a proclivity towards downplaying the health risks posed by the Covid-19 crisis. It can be difficult for policymakers to discern whether a full-blown crisis will occur, or to what level a problem may develop. In the case of Covid-19, different countries responded to the threat with varying levels of urgency.

On 28 January 2020, a day after the WHO classified the risk of the global spread of Covid-19 as high, the Philippine government reactivated the IATF-EID through a resolution. The IATF-EID issued four recommendations: (1) the government should provide continuous support to Filipinos in China by providing health information and other support services, (2) the government should craft a comprehensive transportation and quarantine plan for Filipinos who returned voluntarily from Hubei province, where the outbreak began, (3) the government should implement a temporary

TABLE 6.1
Community Quarantine Classifications in the Philippines

Quarantine Level		*Date First Implemented (Implementation Dates Vary from Area to Area)*	*Description*
Enhanced Community Quarantine (ECQ)		17 March 2020	Total lockdown, including (1) restrictions on all forms of transportation, (2) cancellation of mass gatherings, (3) strict stay-at-home protocols, (4) nationwide school closure and (5) closure of non-essential businesses.
Modified Enhanced Community Quarantine (MECQ)		16 May 2020	Some restrictions lifted and limited outdoor exercise allowed, as well as small gatherings. Essential sectors, such as health, social services, food and utilities, were permitted a skeleton workforce, and inbound air travel was restricted to returning Filipinos.
General Community Quarantine (GCQ)	*Regular*	1 May 2020	Further restrictions lifted, allowing for public transport with safe distancing guidelines, a skeleton workforce for schools, select businesses allowed to operate at 50–100 per cent capacity, and shopping malls reopened.
	With heightened restrictions	15 May 2020	Allowed the operations of (1) lottery and horse racing with off-track betting stations, (2) non-contact sports, (3) personal care services at 30 per cent capacity, (4) outdoor tourist attractions at 30 per cent capacity, (5) hotels up to 100 per cent capacity (no age restrictions) and (6) indoor restaurant dining at 20 per cent capacity and outdoor dining at 50 per cent capacity.

continued on next page

TABLE 6.1 — cont'd

Quarantine Level		*Date First Implemented (Implementation Dates Vary from Area to Area)*	*Description*
	With some restrictions	16 June 2021	Allowed the operation of (1) gyms and fitness centres at 40 per cent capacity and indoor sports courts at 50 per cent capacity, (2) history museums at 40 per cent capacity, (3) meetings, conferences and exhibitions at 40 per cent capacity but 10 per cent capacity for social events, (4) personal care services at 50 per cent capacity, (5) outdoor tourist attractions at 50 per cent capacity and (6) indoor restaurant dining at 40 per cent capacity and outdoor dining at 50 per cent capacity.
	With heightened and additional restrictions	30 July 2021	Authorized persons permitted to travel nationally between one level of quarantine to another. People could receive authorization to leave home to access essential goods and services, to work in sectors permitted to operated and to be vaccinated.
Modified General Community Quarantine (MGCQ)		16 May 2020	Allowed full operation of government offices, public and private transportation, and maximum capacity for all businesses.

Sources: IATF-EID (2020a, 2020b, 2021b, 2021c).

TABLE 6.2
Covid-19 Alert Levels in the Philippines

Alert Level	*Virus Transmissions*	*Utilization Rate*	
		Hospital Beds	*Intensive Care Units*
5	Critical		
4	High (and increasing)	High	
3	High (and increasing)	Increasing	
2	Low (but increasing)	Increasing	
	Low (and decreasing)	Increasing	
	Low (and decreasing)	Low	
1	Low		

Source: IATF-EID (2021a).

restriction on issuing visas for non-Filipinos travelling from Hubei province and (4) the government should issue travel advisories discouraging non-essential travel of Filipinos to China (IATF-EID 2020a).

Several political personalities, including two mayors from the province of Cebu and a senator, called for a more proactive approach, namely an outright ban on Chinese tourists and all flights from China (Santos, R. 2020). Philippine President Rodrigo Duterte expressed reluctance to adopt this stronger approach, citing possible economic and diplomatic repercussions (Peralta 2020). The Secretary for the Department of Health, Francisco Duque, who also served as the chair of the IATF-EID, supported Duterte's statement and said China might question why the Philippines was not imposing the same restrictions on other countries (Peralta 2020).

The first reported case of Covid-19 in the Philippines was on 30 January 2020 (a 38-year-old Chinese national) which coincided with the WHO's declaration of Covid-19 as an international public health emergency. On 2 February 2020, President Duterte finally banned foreign travellers from China, Hong Kong and Macau (Jalea 2020). Nevertheless, he continued to publicly downplay the risks of the disease, noting in a press briefing on 3 February 2020: "Just like SARS, I assure you even without the vaccines it will just die a natural death" (translated from Filipino) (Geducos 2020).

Globally, the crisis response began with social distancing, travel restrictions and quarantine protocols, as well as many other policies adopted by individual countries with varying intensity. The Philippines' response was somewhat delayed (Quintos 2020), but this was the case for many other countries. On 7 March 2020, the Philippine Department of Health acknowledged the possibility of community transmission, as they could no longer associate some cases with a travel history (GMA News 2020).

After initially denying the gravity of Covid-19, and well over a month after the WHO declared it an international public health emergency, President Duterte eventually signed Proclamation 922 on 8 March 2020. This placed the entire Philippines in a state of public health emergency. By then, the Philippines had experienced ten reported cases, and many people suspected there were many more that went unreported due to a shortage of test kits.

On 11 March 2020, the WHO declared Covid-19 a global pandemic. Then, on 12 March 2020, President Duterte announced that Metro Manila would be placed into an ECQ from 15 March until 14 April 2020. The timeline of quarantine regimes and the number of daily cases is illustrated in Figure 6.2. On 16 March 2020, President Duterte extended this by declaring an ECQ covering the Luzon area. This was to be in place from 17 March 2020 to 14 April 2020. By 17 March 2020, there were already 187 Covid-19 cases in the Philippines (Galvez 2020).

As cases increased in other parts of the country, high-risk areas were also placed under ECQ. On 28 March 2020, Cebu was placed under ECQ, which was set to last until 28 April 2020. Davao City was also under ECQ starting from 2 April 2020. President Duterte later announced two extensions of the Metro Manila and Luzon ECQs: first extending them to the end of April 2020 (announced on 7 April 2020) and later to 15 May 2020 (announced on 24 April 2020).

In late April, Duterte also announced the extension of the ECQ in all high-risk areas (Calabarzon, Cebu, Davao, Central Luzon and Metro Manila), while the ECQ was relaxed to a GCQ in areas with zero reported Covid-19 infections (Casas 2020).

On 12 May 2020, the national government announced that community quarantine measures would be completely lifted, with the first lifting on

FIGURE 6.2
Community Quarantine during the Covid-19 Pandemic, Metro Manila

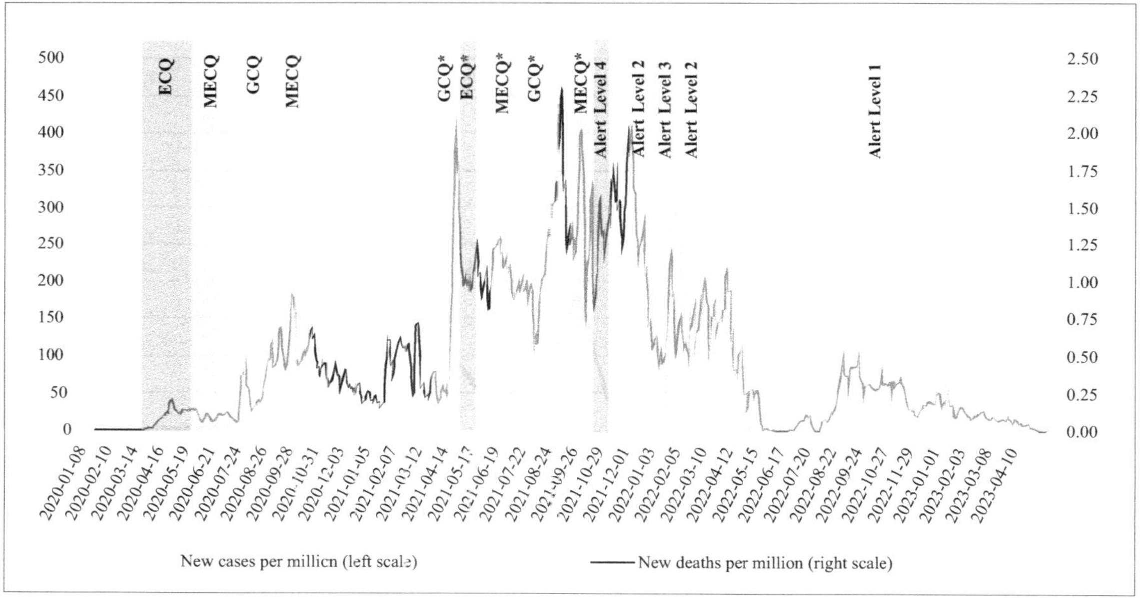

Notes: ECQ: Enhanced Community Quarantine; MECQ: Modified Enhanced Community Quarantine; GCQ: General Community Quarantine; Alert Level 4: virus transmissions are high and increasing, while the utilization rate of hospital beds and intensive care units is high; Alert Level 3: virus transmissions are high and increasing, while the utilization rate of hospital beds and intensive care units is increasing; Alert Level 2: virus transmissions are low but increasing, while the utilization rate of hospital beds and intensive care units is increasing OR virus transmissions are low and decreasing, while the utilization rate of hospital beds and intensive care units is increasing OR virus transmissions are low and decreasing, while the utilization rate of hospital beds and intensive care units is low; Alert Level 1: virus transmissions are low and the utilization rate of hospital beds and intensive care units is low.

Sources: Based on data from ourworldindata.org, Saavedra (2020), Palicte (2020), Sunstar Manila (2020), Baclig (2021b), GMA News (2022), Rappler (2022, 2023) and Relativo (2023).

16 May 2020 in forty-one low-risk provinces and eleven low-risk cities. However, due to appeals from executives within local government units (LGU), provincial- and city-level units, an MGCQ was imposed instead.

Emerging studies on lockdowns during this period found empirical evidence of the effectiveness of these in controlling contagion. For instance, researchers analysing big data on mobility in the Chinese city of Wuhan concluded that the lockdown reduced cases by 65 per cent in Chinese cities outside Hubei province and 53 per cent in sixteen cities within Hubei province (Fang, Wang, and Yang 2020). On the other hand, it also quickly became clear that the cure could be worse than the disease if the lockdown generated an economic contraction, with social and economic costs mounting over time. Based on a survey of over 100,000 respondents in the United States, for example, Coibion, Gorodnichenko, and Weber (2020) found evidence that the lockdown caused income and wealth losses and increased unemployment.

Starting June 2020, the IATF-EID lifted the ECQ in Metro Manila and two other major regions, while the rest of the country was placed under an MGCQ. The easing of restrictions was aimed at restarting economic activity. Workers from selected industries were allowed to leave their homes to go to work, but restrictions on public transportation were not lifted. However, Covid-19 cases and deaths soon started rising again that same month, June 2020, and through July 2020, prompting medical associations to appeal for the imposition of an ECQ in Metro Manila and neighbouring provinces for 1–15 August 2020 (Cordero 2020; Romero and Regalado 2020). The government went ahead and imposed the second form of hard lockdown (MECQ) in the country, illustrated on Figure 6.2. During this time, the government introduced the Coordinated Operations to Defeat Epidemic protocol, which aimed to operationalize a "government-enabled approach, local government-led, people-centred response, with health taking the primacy in the approach" (National Task Force Against COVID-19 2020).

In September 2020 the ECQ was lifted and a GCQ was imposed again. There were no lockdowns for six months until April 2021, when cases peaked at almost 8,000 daily. Then, three months later, the fourth lockdown (fourteen days) was imposed in August 2021. The fifth was in September 2021 (fourteen), and the sixth and final lockdown (fifteen days) was in January 2022, when the country recorded the highest number of daily cases at 17,000. This was due to the Omicron variant.

In summary, the Philippines implemented hard lockdowns, meaning ECQs, MECQs and Alert Level 4 six times: (1) March 2020, (2) August 2020, (3) April 2021, (4) August 2021, (5) September 2021 and (6) January 2022. Whenever the threat of a surge in cases appeared, the government implemented a lockdown. It relaxed the restrictions a few days later to let the economy recover a little. The lockdowns covered entire regions instead of focusing on areas with high cases. The government only started adopting a granular approach to lockdowns in November 2021.

Why Weren't the Lockdowns Effective?

The Philippines failed to develop a more cost-efficient containment strategy, so it was forced back into draconian and comprehensive lockdowns six times to temper each surge in Covid-19. The domestic economic environment flip-flopped several times between closed and slightly more open, and yet crisis managers never achieved full economic openness nor a total flattening of the Covid-19 curve. This resulted in one of the longest lockdowns in the world along with fragile results in tempering Covid-19 cases. Despite stringent measures for the pandemic, why was the Philippines unsuccessful in its lockdowns?

Lack of Resources and Weak Institutions

When the ECQ was implemented in March 2020, it quickly became apparent that the Philippines lacked the resources immediately necessary for crisis relief, so legislators rushed the Bayanihan to Heal as One Act (Figure 6.3). It was proposed on 23 March 2020 and signed into law on 24 March 2020 (Republic Act 11469). Its implementing rules were published on 1 April 2020 (*Official Gazette* 2020a), but bureaucratic delays affected part of the roll-out that month. The law allowed the executive branch of government to reallocate PHP200 billion (approximately US$4 billion) to Covid-19 relief and response.

On 11 September 2020, the Philippine government enacted a second Covid-19 response package amounting to PHP165.5 billion (approximately

FIGURE 6.3
Social Protection Funding under the Bayanihan to Heal as One Act

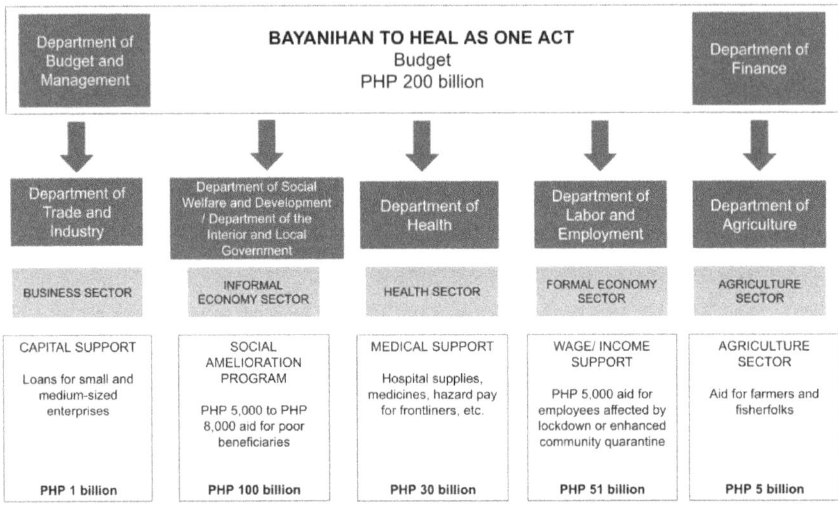

Note: The remaining budget was allocated to the construction of quarantine facilities and the purchase of vehicles for health workers (PHP3 billion), repatriation of overseas Filipinos (PHP1 billion) and other programmes under the IATF-EID (PHP40 billion).
Source: Official Gazette of the Philippines (2020a).

US$3.3 billion) through the Bayanihan to Heal as One Act (Official Gazette 2020b). The law provided additional funding for Covid-19 response measures and economic stimulus programmes for economic recovery, among others.

Although these Covid-19 response packages were in place, there were issues on sufficiency, implementation and transparency. First, due to limited resources, the government could not provide aid to all those who needed it; hence they had to choose who should receive it. This created opportunities for politicians to take advantage of their influence to make sure their own supporters received aid, while others were left out (Magno and Teehankee 2022). The Department of Interior and Local Government received numerous complaints in early May that some local officials were prioritizing their relatives and political allies in the distribution of cash handouts, though others tried to distribute the funds to a large set of families in the area (Cabrera 2020). The politicization of pandemic aid distribution reflects the deeper problem of patronage politics, which has long hindered effective governance and service delivery in the Philippines (Magno and Teehankee 2022).

Second, there were delays in the distribution and use of the pandemic budget due to bureaucratic inefficiency. The agencies in charge of pandemic response were understaffed and under-resourced, causing delays and confusion in distribution. This inefficiency created openings for corruption and political patronage (De Vera 2021).

Lastly, mismanagement of funds for pandemic response further strained the country's weak and fragmented health system. From the beginning of the pandemic to August 2021, more than 40 per cent of nurses in private hospitals had resigned due to extreme physical and mental stress, low wages and unpaid pandemic-related benefits (Alibudbud 2022). In October 2021, healthcare workers demanded the resignation of the Health Secretary amid allegations of corruption in the procurement of medical supplies (Baclig 2021a).

The long-standing issues of weak state capacity and scarce resources led to more problems that hindered effective pandemic management in the Philippines. These are detailed in the subsequent subsections.

Inadequate Social Transfers

The Philippines implemented hard lockdowns (ECQ, MECQ, Alert level 4) six times in total. Despite the long periods of severe mobility restrictions, the government only gave two months' worth of cash transfers to low-income households: upwards of PHP5,000 or US$98 per person with a maximum of PHP8,000 or US$158 per family. Two months after the first lockdown, only around 71 per cent of the 18 million household beneficiaries had received payment and PHP70 billion had been disbursed to families.

A survey on family expenditure and income shows that the median monthly family income in the Philippines was PHP23,692 in 2018 (Philippine Statistics Authority 2019). In comparison, the cash transfers were low and insufficient and forced people to leave their homes to seek work despite the mobility restrictions (Santos, A.P. 2020). If the government does not give enough cash aid to the most vulnerable sectors of the population, it will be difficult for them to adhere to quarantine protocols.

Lack of Investment in the Public Healthcare System

The healthcare system in the Philippines is characterized by a mix of public and private healthcare providers, with services delivered by various levels of government and fragmented financing (Dayrit et al. 2018). Public and privately managed health systems were designed to complement each other. However, due to the inability of the government to regulate the expanding private sector, out-of-pocket health expenses paid by patients themselves continue to increase—more than 50 per cent of total health spending in 2018 was paid for by patients, rather than by the government or insurance (Dayrit et al. 2018). The country has a ratio of ten hospital beds and six physicians per 10,000 people, and only 2,335 critical care beds in total, which are unevenly distributed nationwide (World Bank 2019a, 2019b; Phua et al. 2020). The public health system has suffered decades of underinvestment, with health spending reaching only 3–4 per cent of GDP from 1995 to 2010. It faces workforce shortages, insufficient capacity and inadequate funding. Given this, it is unsurprising that the Philippines was poorly prepared to deal with Covid-19, as public health experts reported (Amit, Pepito, and Dayrit 2021).

The chronic underinvestment manifested in the weak test, trace, treat and vaccinate system. The lack of sufficient Covid-19 testing during the early stage of the pandemic made it difficult to identify and isolate infected individuals, leading to a higher number of cases and an overwhelmed healthcare system.

Insufficient Covid-19 Testing

Testing is part of the backbone of effective pandemic management. It is the window that provides a clear picture of the spread of Covid-19—who is infected by the virus and how many are dying from it. Without testing, there is no data (Hasell 2020). Without data, there is no way to predict the scale of the infections and the resources that the health system and citizens need. Epidemiologists and public health experts claimed at the start of the pandemic that mass testing—conducting millions of tests per country per week—was the most practical way out of the Covid-19 crisis (Guglielmi 2020; Ricciardi, Verme, and Serajuddin 2020). However, for a developing economy like the Philippines, scaling up testing require a lot of new resources—equipment, laboratory facilities and personnel.

Consequently, there were extensive debates on the extent to which the Philippines needed to test. Some advocated for mass testing (Saludes 2020; Torres-Tupas 2020; Romero et al. 2020), but the government turned down these calls, saying that "it is not yet needed" (Gita-Carlos 2020) and "indiscriminate mass testing of asymptomatic individuals is neither feasible nor practical" (Crismundo 2021). Instead, the government pursued a risk-based testing strategy, prioritizing health workers and patients with critical symptoms.

On a seven-day rolling average, about 30,000 to 40,000 tests were conducted daily in the Philippines in 2020 and 2021 (Our World in Data 2021) (Figure 6.4).

To understand if a country is testing sufficiently is to ask: what share of the tests confirm a case? What is the positivity rate? The Philippine daily positive rate reached peaks of around 27.5 per cent in September 2021 and 46.11 per cent in January 2022 (see Figure 6.5). The WHO has recommended a positive rate below 10 per cent as representative of adequate testing, but below 3 per cent is a better general benchmark (WHO 2020; Dowdy and D'Souza 2020).

Testing was supposed to make the test, trace, treat and contain strategy cost-efficient and effective. However, the Philippines was not able to prioritize testing. Detailed and disaggregated data are needed to inform urgent policy decisions and contain a possible risk of a surge in Covid-19 cases. The disaggregated data shows the areas in which Covid-19 cases are surging; that is the only area that needs to be locked down. However, the response was one-size-fits-all and everyone was locked down. Evidence-based pandemic response was a challenge, but its implementation proved crucial to recovery.

Worsening Contact Tracing

Contact tracing complements testing; it allows the health authorities to identify persons who may have contracted the virus upon contact with a Covid-positive patient and implement measures, such as isolation, to prevent further spread. In March 2021, a year after the pandemic began,

FIGURE 6.4
Daily Covid-19 Tests per Thousand People in the Philippines, 2020–22

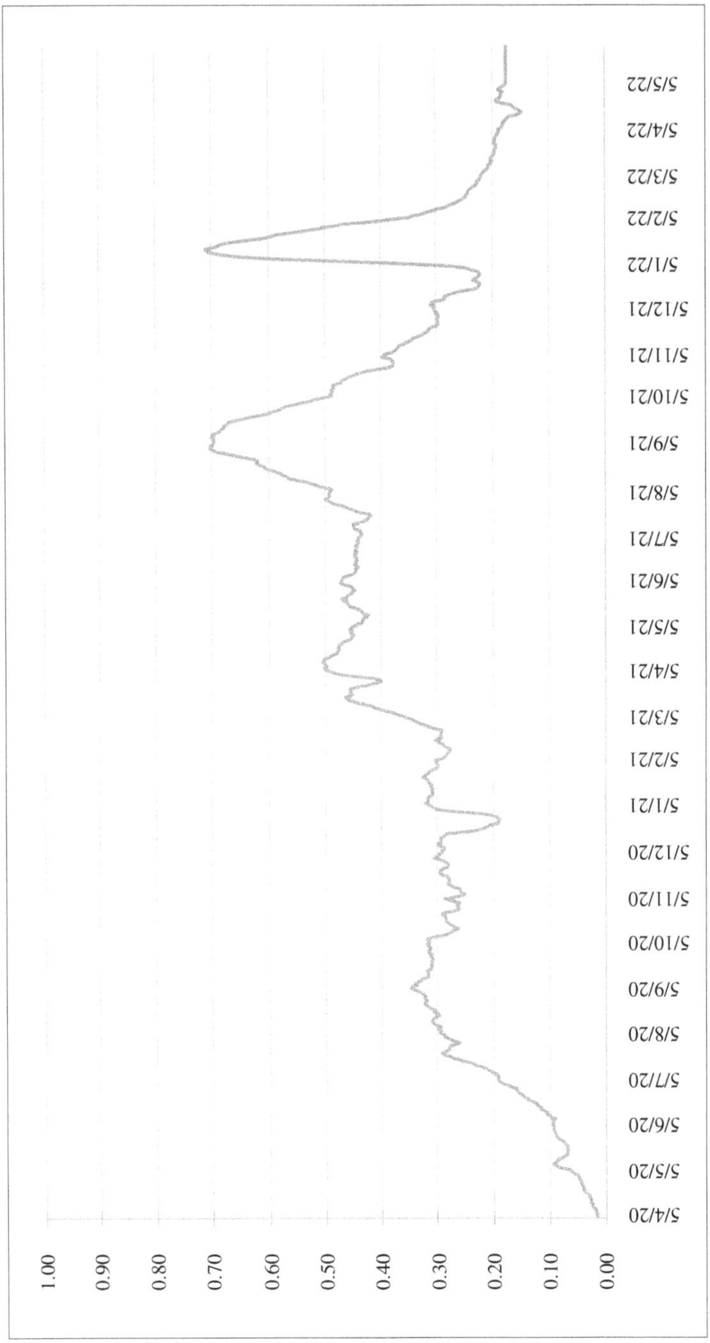

Source: ourworldindata.org.

FIGURE 6.5
Positive Share of Covid-19 Tests
Daily Positive Rate, Given as a Rolling Seven-Day Average (April 2020 to May 2022)

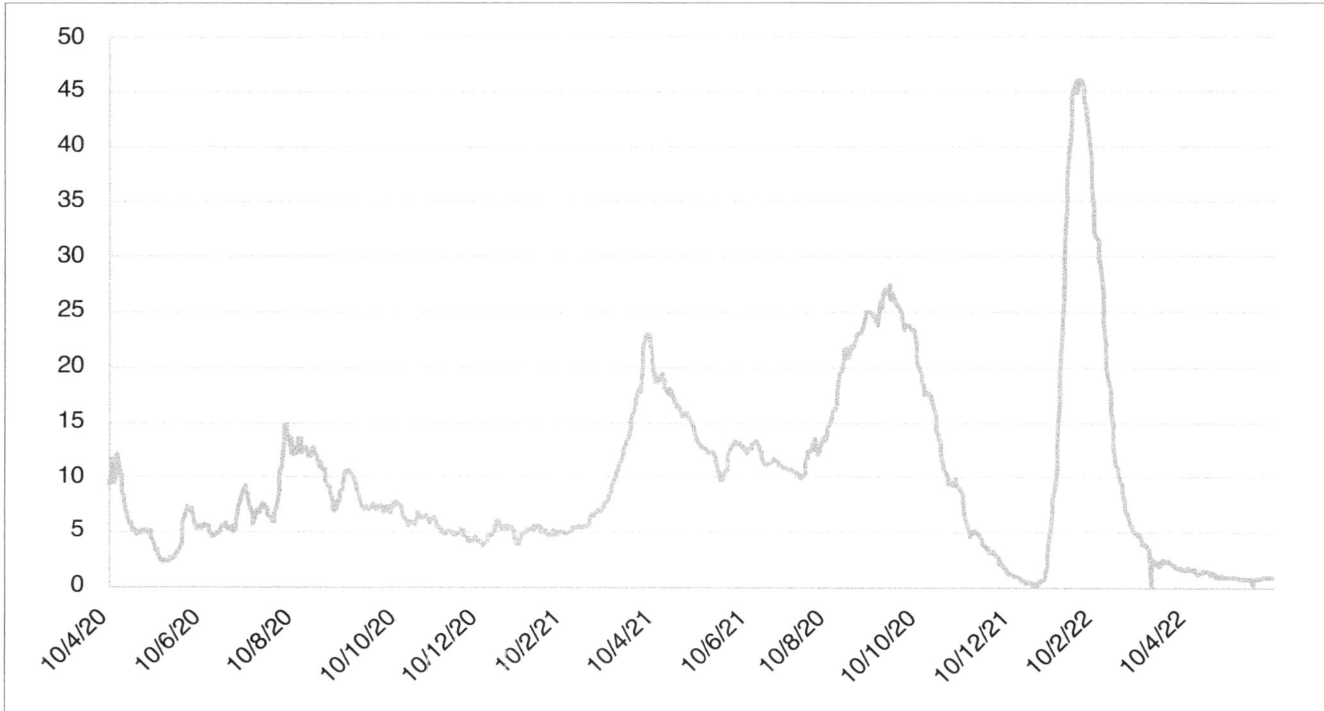

Source: ourworldindata.org.

the Philippine contact tracing chief lamented that in many areas of the country, contact tracing did not go beyond the household of a Covid-19 case (Talabong 2021). He also said that for every Covid-19 case the country was only tracing three close contacts, far from the standard ratio of one to fifteen.

One reason for the country's inefficient contact tracing, which worsened in 2021, was the lack of a uniform data collection tool among LGUs. Although the national government introduced contact tracing platforms such as Covid KAYA, Kontra Covid Bot and Stay Safe, they were ineffective and were not fully used. Some LGUs and private sector establishments introduced their own contact tracing apps, but they were not integrated with each other and with the central government and therefore cannot provide accurate data. Moreover, the contact tracing system was beset with challenges, including the lack of trained staff, issues in encoding data and the lack of capacity of the LGUs (Talabong 2021). Contact tracing was the weakest link of pandemic management in the Philippines.

Slow, Delayed and Inequitable Vaccinations

While some countries started vaccinating in December 2020, the Philippines began vaccinating health workers only in March 2021, with a seven-day average of 5,000 doses administered (Figure 6.6). There were delays at the start, and progress was slow due to supply issues. Vaccinations peaked from 29 November 2021 to 7 December 2022 with 12.48 million vaccines administered—due to a massive vaccination drive by the national government—but then slowed again.

The Philippines was a laggard in mass vaccination in Southeast Asia, administering only 137 vaccine doses per 100 people, compared to Singapore's 259 doses per 100 people in May 2022 (Our World in Data 2022). The government's target for vaccination coverage was 70 per cent in 2021; this was increased to 90 per cent in early 2022. However, as of May 2022, only 58 per cent of people were fully vaccinated. In addition to the slow vaccination progress, vaccine coverage was unequal across regions (Table 6.3). More than 98 per cent of the target population were vaccinated in Metro Manila as of May 2022, but only 16.47 per cent in Bangsamoro Autonomous Region in Muslim Mindanao.

FIGURE 6.6

Covid-19 Vaccine Doses Administered in the Philippines

Seven-Day Rolling Average (March 2021 to May 2022)

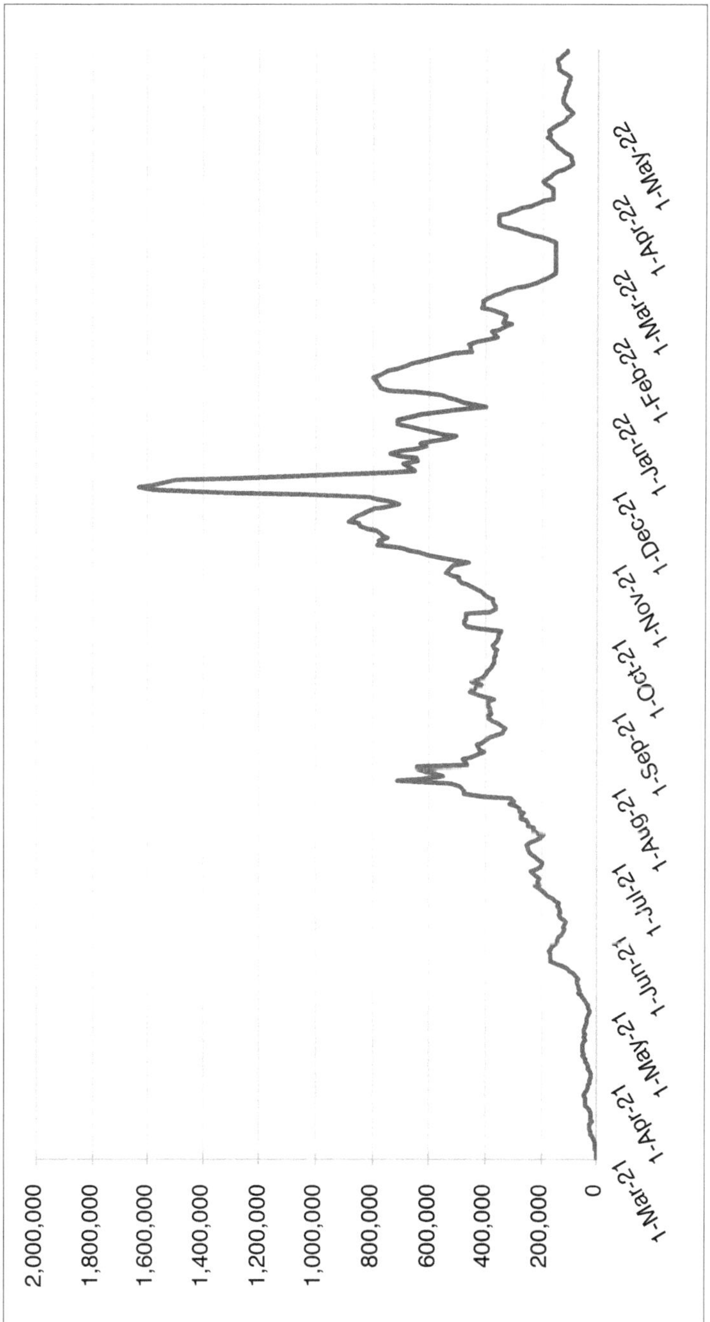

Source: Department of Health (2021).

TABLE 6.3
Regional Distribution of Fully Vaccinated Individuals in the Philippines, May 2022

Region	*Target*	*Fully Vaccinated (%)*	*Total Cases*	*Poverty Rate (2018) (%)*
Metro Manila	9,776,356	98.20	1,173,324	1
Cordillera Administrative Region	1,275,903	66.66	119,155	3
Central Luzon	8,759,693	62.42	361,947	5
Ilocos Region	3,719,256	60.94	133,701	7
Cagayan Valley	2,585,565	59.77	162,331	12
Cavite, Laguna, Batangas, Rizal, Quezon	11,452,775	59.09	655,951	5
Davao Region	3,759,878	55.04	140,619	14
Western Visayas	5,579,386	49.19	194,894	12
Eastern Visayas	3,362,637	45.56	64,405	24
Northern Mindanao	3,552,194	45.49	106,153	17
Mindoro Occidental, Mindoro Oriental, Marinduque, Romblon and Palawan	2,248,548	44.35	44,176	10
Agusan del Norte, Agusan del Sur, Surigao del Norte, Surigao del Sur and the Province of Dinagat Islands	1,947,553	42.98	61,955	24
Central Visayas	5,638,340	42.22	193,214	13
Zamboanga Peninsula	2,666,678	41.65	66,040	25
Bicol Region	4,335,047	40.26	65,747	20
South Cotabato, Cotabato, Sultan Kudarat, Sarangani, General Santos	3,490,115	37.24	75,858	22
Bangsamoro Autonomous Region in Muslim Mindanao	2,989,135	16.47	25,853	54
Returning Overseas Filipinos			39,239	
Unknown			3,360	
Total PH	77,139,059	58.06	3,687,922	12

Sources: Fully vaccinated percentage and target population taken from Department of Health (2022b) as of 18 May 2022; number of cases taken from Department of Health Covid19 Tracker (Department of Health 2022a) as of 22 May 2022; poverty rate from Philippine Statistics Authority (2021a).

An additional gap in vaccination coverage is that poorer regions had lesser access to vaccines. Inequitable distribution of vaccines creates significant problems in pandemic management (Bayati et al. 2022). The slow pace of vaccine roll-out in poorer regions meant that some deaths occurred that could have been avoided (Duroseau, Kipshidze, and Limaye 2023). When supply was no longer a hurdle, vaccine hesitancy and logistical issues hampered vaccination progress.

A survey by the World Bank conducted in 2021 revealed vaccine acceptance in the Philippines was 41 per cent; this was very low compared to Indonesia's 70 per cent, Malaysia's 80 per cent, Vietnam's 83 per cent and Laos's 85 per cent (World Bank 2021b). The findings showed that the main reasons for vaccine hesitancy were the "lack of information about vaccines, misinformation about their efficacy or side effects, mistrust, and underestimation of benefits compared to overestimation of risks and costs of vaccination (World Bank 2021b). There were also instances when people would refuse Sinovac vaccines, which comprised the majority of the country's stocks in 2021, and preferred to wait for other brands such as Pfizer (Alfonso et al. 2021). The mistrust of vaccines overall resulted from a 2018 controversy related to the dengue vaccine, which caused a crisis of confidence in public health authorities (Dayrit, Mendoza, and Valenzuela 2020).

Logistical issues, including difficulties in transportation and access, lack of adequate storage capacity and lack of staff, also affected the pace of vaccination. Tomacruz (2022) described the situation:

> In geographically isolated areas, the lack of personnel means health workers play the role of vaccinator, manager, and coordinator, to name just a few. Jory Allorde, a rural health worker serving in Barangay Dikapinisan, a coastal village of 2,500 people in San Luis, Aurora, told us there were more than enough doses to vaccinate all willing people in his community. However, arranging a two- to three-hour boat ride into town, gathering additional health personnel, ensuring stable power supply, and facilitating documentation with *barangay* officials, regional offices, and community members took up more time than actually getting doses into people's arms. These were tasks Allorde had to manage all by himself.

To resolve logistical issues, the government deployed mobile vaccination clinics to reach underserved and remote communities (Abad 2022).

Socio-economic Consequences of On-Again, Off-Again Lockdowns

Due to the pandemic, the country encountered one of the deepest economic contractions since 1985, when political instability and an external debt crisis took their toll, posting a year-on-year contraction of 17 per cent in the second quarter of 2020 (Figure 6.7).

The consequences of pandemic mismanagement in the Philippines are most evident in the temporary and permanent closures of businesses and loss of income and jobs, school drop-out rates and increased hunger and poverty.

Before the pandemic, there were 957,620 business enterprises in the Philippines, with 99.51 per cent categorized as micro, small and medium-sized enterprises (MSMEs) (Department of Trade and Industry 2020). These MSMEs created 5,380,815 jobs, or 62.66 per cent of the country's total employment, while large enterprises created 3,206,011 jobs or 37.34 per cent (Department of Trade and Industry 2020). The on-again, off-again lockdowns implemented by the government severely affected the operations of these businesses and their employees. The Department of Trade and Industry reported that 26 per cent of all businesses had to close in 2020 (Crismundo 2020), and even after the easing of restrictions in November 2021, 10 per cent remained closed (Business World 2021). Over 7.2 million workers were unemployed in 2020, resulting in a record-high unemployment rate of 17.6 per cent compared to only 5.1 per cent in 2019 (Philippine Statistics Authority 2020b). With the loss of income, an additional 4.2 million families experienced hunger in May 2020 (CNN Philippines 2020), and 3.1 million families remained hungry in the first quarter of 2022 (Sarao 2022).

The National Economic Development Authority (NEDA) reported that the Philippines lost US$86 billion in economic output in 2020 and that the pandemic and the lockdowns would cost the country PHP41.4 trillion over the following forty years (*Rappler* 2021). This is due to reduced consumption and investment, reduced productivity because of untimely

FIGURE 6.7
Philippines GDP (at Constant 2018 Prices)
Year-on-Year Growth Rates (in per cent), 2019Q1 to 2022Q1

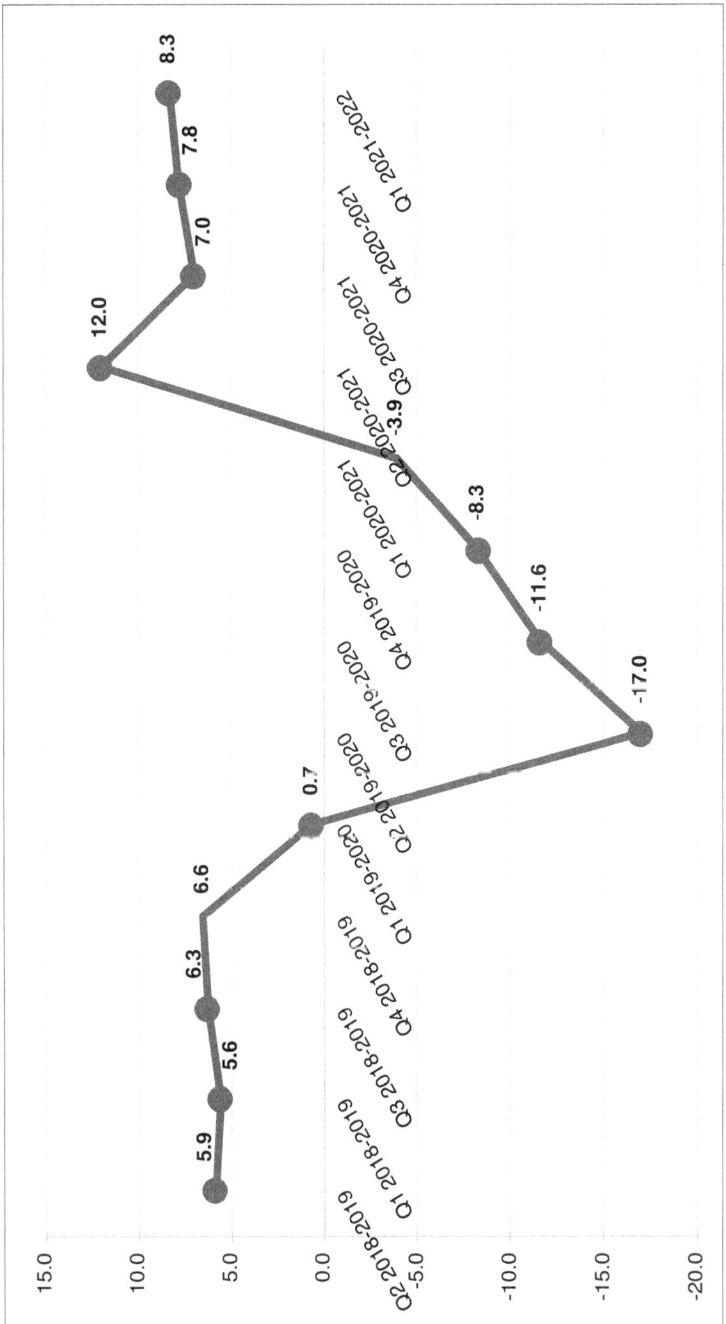

Source: Philippine Statistics Authority (2022).

deaths and sickness, and loss of future wages based on the impact of lower-quality education during online and distance learning.

While some children and young people were able to transition to online education, millions did not have the resources to do so—further widening the digital divide. Around one-fifth of Filipino elementary and high school students or more than 5 million children did not enrol for the academic year 2020/21 (Gamboa 2021).

There is a growing concern over a "lost generation" whose human capital may have suffered from the crisis; some may permanently fall through the cracks of the social safety net. These are the long-term risks and consequences of the Covid-19 pandemic, and it is likely Covid-19 will impose deep and long-term human development costs on the Philippines and exacerbate inequality (NEDA 2021; World Bank 2023).

Lessons Learnt

Among the main lessons learnt from pandemic management include how to transition from total lockdowns to granular lockdowns; the crucial role of LGUs, the private sector and civil society groups in crisis response and recovery; the importance of healthcare and social protection systems for the most vulnerable populations and, ultimately, the need for institutional and governance reforms.

Graduating from Total Lockdowns to Granular Lockdowns

After eighteen months of implementing the strategy of community quarantine levels, the Philippine government finally introduced its Alert Level System that simplified the guidelines for quarantine and started the transition to localized lockdowns (Table 6.2). Under this new system, only areas tagged as Covid-19 hotspots were to be placed into lockdown, allowing businesses and other activities (but not schools) in areas outside the hotspots to continue to operate. Lockdowns moved from regional level to localized to a group of houses in a street or a subdivision. Although delayed, the transition to granular lockdowns allowed the government to control Covid-19 cases while ensuring that the rest of the economy functioned normally.

Crucial Role of LGUs, Private Sector and Civil Society Groups in Crisis Response

While the national response to the pandemic had many shortcomings, the Covid-19 crisis also demonstrated the capacity and agility of LGUs, the private sector and civil society groups in implementing innovative solutions and mobilizing resources. Within days of the ECQ in March 2020, the private sector, civil society and church groups, followed later by local and central governments, pushed for various crisis response and relief efforts. The relative agility of civil society, the private sector, local governments and central government (in that order) appears to be a pattern in crisis relief efforts in the Philippines. Private sector groups adjusted their operations to the ECQ period, with some continuing to pay fully their employees and suppliers, while others adapted work arrangements so that some staff could work from home.

Nevertheless, around 40 per cent of the country's 45 million labour force are in the informal economy, with little access to social protection and insurance (International Labour Organization n.d.). Hence, at least 16 million workers and their families immediately needed support to supplement their incomes during the Covid-19 crisis. Civil society and church groups mobilized donations of food and other items for lockdown-affected poor and low-income communities in April 2020. Many small and large donors, both individuals and companies, mobilized domestic production capacity to manufacture personal protective equipment due to an apparent lack of equipment for health sector front liners in public and private sector hospitals. Some of the country's largest firms and conglomerates mobilized to support poor and low-income communities, displaced workers and medical frontliners, collectively providing several billion pesos of crisis relief and support by early April 2020 (Philippine Disaster Resilience Foundation 2020). These initiatives included direct cash transfer programmes like Project Ugnayan, organized by several large Philippine corporations, and the Philippine Disaster Relief Foundation (Philippine Disaster Resilience Foundation 2020). Project Ugnayan sought to transfer food vouchers worth PHP1,000 to each of almost 8 million Filipinos in crisis-affected communities in Metro Manila (Philippine Disaster Resilience Foundation 2020). The Bayan Bayanihan partnership brought together the Asian Development Bank, the Department of Social Welfare and Development, the Philippine Army, Philippine Chamber of Commerce and Industry and the Philippine Disaster Resilience Foundation (Asian Development Bank 2020b). It was a bridging programme to provide quick emergency food relief to about 55,000 of the most vulnerable households in Metro Manila.

Among the most notable initiatives of some LGUs in increasing vaccination were opening more vaccination sites in partnership with the private sector and providing incentives to encourage people to be vaccinated. For instance, the LGU of Quezon City, the largest city in the country, partnered with malls to set up vaccination sites (Quezon City Local Government 2021). Some LGUs and establishments also provided incentives such as discounts for food products (*Inquirer* 2021; Sunnexdesk 2021). These efforts by local government, the private sector and civil society groups not only supplemented the national government's shortcomings but also showed the significance of social cohesion during crises.

Importance of Healthcare and Social Protection

The global pandemic also re-emphasized the importance of inclusive social safety nets and a robust domestic healthcare system. These are vital not only for assisting citizens face financial hardships after spending significant amounts on healthcare, but are essential for all individuals, regardless of their health expenditure. Moreover, they are pivotal in anchoring or reinforcing most countries' resilience strategies, particularly against health shocks like Covid-19. In countries with weak healthcare systems, such as the Philippines, contagion control becomes more complex and is often delayed, allowing the health crisis to fester and generate higher social and economic costs (Gilbert et al. 2020; Chalkido and Krubiner 2020). The landmark Philippine Universal Health Care Law was only passed in February 2019, but it could create an appetite for healthcare reform in the country. The Philippines has an opportunity for collective action to drive greater investment in health, improved social protection and more equitable health coverage and access in the new normal.

CONCLUSION

Covid-19 exposed the weaknesses in the Philippines' healthcare and social protection systems—notably, inequality in coverage and access. This inequality is prevalent across different dimensions—rural areas lack facilities, financial constraints limit access for low-income groups and marginalized communities often lack health insurance. Furthermore, these disparities have been shown to exacerbate the social costs of the crisis. The case of the Philippines provides important lessons in pandemic management. It emphasizes how important it is to build resilient and inclusive health systems so that a pandemic response is more effective and containment carried out faster. Lockdowns are only effective if they buy more time to strengthen health and test, trace and treat systems. If a country is unable to graduate to more efficient containment strategies, it is stuck with on-again, off-again lockdowns, which severely damages the economy and the lives of the people.

The Philippines' healthcare system could be further strengthened through innovations and reforms. For instance, information and communications technology and innovative telemedicine apps could be used to share and manage information and conduct appointments in collaboration with central and local governments and across public and private hospitals, testing centres and other healthcare facilities.

Before a crisis, the Philippines could set up emergency coordination mechanisms to rapidly rearrange and realign the national and local health systems so that they can cope with surges in cases. These could be anchored on solid public-private partnerships, which are part of the government's strategy to achieve universal healthcare coverage and service delivery. Policymakers could also develop the institutions and skills that would strengthen resilience against future health shocks. Reforms and investments could help make healthcare more affordable by minimizing what patients must pay themselves, particularly in the case of poor and low-income citizens, and by more effectively managing costs through inclusive social insurance and an efficient balance of public and private sectors in healthcare provision (Hartigan-Go, Mendoza, and Ong 2020).

In summary, both the literature and emerging experiences from the Covid-19 pandemic suggest that stronger, more inclusive healthcare and social protection systems are essential for building resilience. Unsurprisingly, those same countries tend to have deep wells of social capital and public trust in the crisis responses of the state, which in turn makes the crisis response more effective.

Notes

1. In the Philippines, the terms "community quarantine" and "lockdown" were used interchangeably, but the difference lay in implementation and scope. Community quarantines refers to a range of measures to control disease within specific communities, while lockdowns were focused on more stringent measures aimed at restricting movement and activities on a larger scale.
2. Nevertheless, gradually over the course of the pandemic, the metric for lockdown measures shifted from number of infections to healthcare capacity. This is due to the recognition that lockdowns are implemented not merely to reduce cases but also to ensure that the healthcare system can cope.

References

Abad, Michelle. 2022. "PH to Shift Focus of Vaccine Drive to Mobile, House-To-House Jabs". *Rappler*, 22 February 2022. www.rappler.com/nation/philippines-to-shift-focus-covid-19-vaccine-drive-mobile-house-to-house-jabs/ (accessed 4 April 2024).

Alfonso, Cenon, Manuel Dayrit, Ronald Mendoza, and Madeline Ong. 2021. "From Dengvaxia to Sinovac: Vaccine Hesitancy in the Philippines". *The Diplomat*, 8 March 2021. https://thediplomat.com/2021/03/from-dengvaxia-to-sinovac-vaccine-hesitancy-in-the-philippines/ (accessed 4 April 2024).

Alibudbud, Rowalt. 2022. "When the 'Heroes' 'Don't Feel Cared for': The Migration and Resignation of Philippine Nurses amidst the Covid-19 Pandemic". *Journal of Global Health*, May. https://jogh.org/2022/jogh-12-03011#R3

Amit, Arianna Maever, Veincent Christian Pepito, and Manuel Dayrit. 2021. "Early Response to Covid-19 in the Philippines". *Western Pacific Surveillance and Response Journal* 12, no. 1: 56–60. https://doi.org/10.5365/wpsar.2020.11.1.014

Baclig, Cristina Eloisa. 2021a. "Doctors Come out of Their Shells, Demand End to Corruption, Incompetence in Covid Handling". *Inquirer*, 12 October

2021. https://newsinfo.inquirer.net/1500925/doctors-come-out-of-their-shells-demand-end-to-corruption-incompetence-in-covid-handling (accessed 4 April 2024).

———. 2021b. "Timeline: One Year of Covid-19 in the Philippines". *Inquirer*, 12 March 2021, newsinfo.inquirer.net/1406004/timeline-one-year-of-covid-19-in-the-philippines (accessed 14 May 2024).

Bayati, Mohsen, Rayehe Noroozi, Mohadeseh Ghanbari-Jahromi, and Faride Sadat Jalali. 2022. "Inequality in the Distribution of Covid-19 Vaccine: A Systematic Review". *International Journal for Equity in Health* 21, 122. https://doi.org/10.1186/s12939-022-01729-x

Business World. 2021. "DTI Estimates 10% of Businesses in Metro Manila Remain Closed". 25 November 2021. https://www.bworldonline.com/economy/2021/11/25/413065/dti-estimates-10-of-businesses-in-metro-manila-remain-closed / (accessed 4 April 2024).

Cabrera, Romina. 2020. "DILG Receives Thousands of SAP Complaints vs Barangay Officials". *Philstar*, 4 May 2020. https://www.philstar.com/headlines/2020/05/04/2011645/dilg-receives-thousands-sap-complaints-vs-barangay-officials (accessed 4 April 2024).

Casas, Willie. 2020. "ECQ Extension in NCR Eyed". *Manila Standard*, 5 May 2020. https://manilastandard.net/mobile/article/323022 (accessed 4 April 2024).

Centers for Disease Control and Prevention. 2007. "Interim Pre-pandemic Planning Guidance: Community Strategy for Pandemic Influenza Mitigation in the United States: Early, Targeted, Layered Use of Nonpharmaceutical Interventions". February. https://stacks.cdc.gov/view/cdc/11425

Chalkido, K., and C. Krubiner. 2020. "What Covid-19 Should Teach Us about Smart Health Spending in Developing Countries". Center for Global Development, 5 March 2020. https://www.cgdev.org/blog/what-covid-19-should-teach-us-about-smart-health-spending-developing-countries (accessed 4 April 2024).

CNN Philippines. 2020. "SWS Survey Reveals 4.2 Million Families Suffered Involuntary Hunger amid Covid-19 Pandemic". 22 May 2020. https://www.cnnphilippines.com/news/2020/5/22/sws-survey-four-million-families-involuntary-hunger-covid-pandemic.html/ (accessed 4 April 2024).

Coibion, O., Yuriy Gorodnichenko, and Michael Weber. 2020. "The Cost of Covid-19 Crisis: Lockdowns, Macroeconomic Expectations, and Consumer Spending". NBER Working Paper Series No. 27141. National Bureau of Economic Research, Cambridge, MA, May 2020. https://doi.org/10.3386/w27141

Cordero, Ted. 2020. "Medical Groups Call for 'Time Out', Want NCR Reverted to ECQ". *GMA News Online*, 1 August 2020. https://www.gmanetwork.com/

news/topstories/nation/749428/medical-groups-call-for-time-out-want-ncr-reverted-to-ecq/story/ (accessed 4 April 2024).
Crismundo, Kris. 2020. "26% of Businesses Closed Operations in June: DTI Survey". Philippine News Agency, 16 July 2020. https://www.pna.gov.ph/articles/1109217 (accessed 4 April 2024).
———. 2021. "NTF Exec Explains Why Gov't Can't Do Mass Testing". Philippine News Agency, 6 April 2021. https://www.pna.gov.ph/articles/1135922 (accessed 4 April 2024).
Dayrit, Manuel M., Liezel Lagrada, Oscar Picazo, Melahi Pons, and Mario Villaverde. 2018. *The Philippines Health System Review*. Health Systems in Transition 8, no. 2, edited by Walaiporn Patcharanarumol, Viroj Tangcharoensathien and Asia Pacific Observatory on Health Systems and Policies. World Health Organization, Regional Office for South-East Asia. https://apps.who.int/iris/handle/10665/274579
———, Ronald U. Mendoza, and Sheena A. Valenzuela. 2020. "The Importance of Effective Risk Communication and Transparency: Lessons from the Dengue Vaccine Controversy in the Philippines". *Journal of Public Health Policy* 41, no. 3: 252–67. https://doi.org/10.1057/s41271-020-00232-3
De Vera, Ben. 2021. "P 169-B Covid Funds Unspent Due to Red Tape". *Inquirer*, 2 July 2021. https://newsinfo.inquirer.net/1454392/p-169-b-covid-funds-unspent-due-to-red-tape (accessed 4 April 2024).
Department of Health. 2020. "DOH Updates on Collaboration with Healthcare Workers, Deployment of C.O.D.E Protocol". 6 August 2020. https://doh.gov.ph/press-release/DOH-UPDATES-ON-COLLABORATION-WITH-HEALTHCARE-WORKERS-DEPLOYMENT-OF-C-O-D-E-PROTOCOL
———. 2022a. "Covid-19 Tracker: Philippines". https://public.tableau.com/views/COVID-19CasesandDeathsinthePhilippines_15866705872710/Home?:embed=y&:showVizHome=no&:host_url=https%3A%2F%2Fpublic.tableau.com%2F&:embed_code_version=3&:tabs=no&:toolbar=yes&:animate_transition=yes&:display_static_image=no (accessed 4 April 2024).
———. 2022b. "Covid-19 Vaccination Dashboard". https://app.powerbi.com/view?r=eyJrIjoiMzliZTBjZWQtNjcwYi00YmM3LWFjYjktZDNjYWRjNDdiMmJmIiwidCI6IjM3ZDFjZmJmLTM1NTMtNDc5ZS1iOGM0LTVhZDdkNjNkNDM4MyIsImMiOjEwfQ%3D%3D (accessed 4 April 2024).
Department of Trade and Industry. 2020. "Defining Philippine Micro, Small and Medium Enterprises (MSMEs)". Department of Trade and Industry. https://dtiwebfiles.s3.ap-southeast-1.amazonaws.com/BSMED/MSME+2020+Sta

tistics/2020+Philippine+MSME+Statistics+in+Brief.pdf (accessed 4 April 2024).

Dowdy, David, and Gypsyamber D'Souza. 2020. "COVID-19 Testing: Understanding the "Percent Positive". Johns Hopkins Bloomberg School of Public Health,10 August 2020. https://publichealth.jhu.edu/2020/covid-19-testing-understanding-the-percent-positive (accessed 26 March 2024).

Duroseau, Brenice, Nodar Kipshidze, and Rupali Jayant Limaye. 2023."The Impact of Delayed Access to COVID-19 Vaccines in Low- and Lower-Middle-Income Countries". *Frontiers in Public Health* 10 (12 January 2023). https://doi.org/10.3389/fpubh.2022.1087138

Fang, Hanming, Long Wang, and Yang Yang. 2020. "Human Mobility Restrictions and the Spread of the Novel Coronavirus (2019-NCoV) in China". NBER Working Paper No. 26906, National Bureau of Economic Research, National Bureau of Economic Research, Cambridge, MA, March 2020. https://www.nber.org/papers/w26906

Galvez, Daphne. 2020. "DOH Records 45 New Cases of COVID-19; Total Now at 187". *Inquirer*, March 2020. newsinfo.inquirer.net/1243684/breaking-doh-record-45-new-cases-of-covid-19-total-now-at-187 (accessed 14 May 2024).

Gamboa, Rey. 2021. "Dropouts Left Behind in the Pandemic". *Philstar*, 29 June 2021. https://www.philstar.com/business/2021/06/29/2108717/dropouts-left-behind-pandemic (accessed 4 April 2024).

Geducos, Argyll. 2020. "'Everything Is Well': Duterte Downplays nCoV Threat". Manila Bulletin. 3 April 2024. https://mb.com.ph/2020/02/03/everything-is-well-duterte-downplays-ncov-threat/ (accessed 4 April 2024).

Gilbert, Marius, Giulia Pullano, Francesco Pinotti, Eugenio Valdano, Chiara Poletto, Pierre-Yves Boëlle, Eric D'Ortenzio, et al. 2020. "Preparedness and Vulnerability of African Countries against Importations of Covid-19: A Modelling Study". *The Lancet* 395, no. 10227: 871–77. https://doi.org/10.1016/S0140-6736(20)30411-6

Gita-Carlos, Ruth Abbey. 2020. "No Need for Covid-19 Mass Testing yet: DOH". Philippine News Agency, 20 March 2020. https://www.pna.gov.ph/articles/1097298 (accessed 4 April 2024).

GMA News. 2020. "DOH: Philippines Now Has Sustained Covid-19 Community Transmission". 17 March 2020. https://www.gmanetwork.com/news/news/nation/730026/doh-philippines-now-has-sustained-covid-19-community-transmission/story/

———. 2022. "6 Provinces Placed under Alert Level 3 Starting Jan. 28, 2022". 27 January 2022. www.gmanetwork.com/news/topstories/regions/819814/6-

provinces-placed-under-alert-level-3-starting-jan-28-2022/story/ (accessed 14 May 2024).

Guglielmi, Giorgia. 2020. "The Explosion of New Coronavirus Tests That Could Help to End the Pandemic". *Nature* 583, no. 7817: 506–9. https://doi.org/10.1038/d41586-020-02140-8

Hartigan-Go, Kenneth, Ronald U. Mendoza, and Madeline Ong. 2020. "Financing Public-Private Partnership in Health for Inclusive Recovery from Covid-19 and Stronger Resilience to Future Health Shocks". SSRN, 11 May 2020. https://papers.ssrn.com/sol3/papers.cfm?abstract_id=3597287

Hasell, Joe. 2020. "The Our World in Data Covid-19 Testing Dataset Has Been Published in the Academic Journal, *Nature*". *Our World in Data* (blog). 9 October 2020. https://ourworldindata.org/our-world-in-data-covid-19-testing-dataset-published-by-nature (accessed 4 April 2024).

IATF-EID (Inter-Agency Task Force for the Management of Emerging Infectious Diseases). 2020a. "Omnibus Guidelines on the Implementation of Community Quarantine in the Philippines". *Official Gazette*, Republic of the Philippines, 5 May 2020. https://www.officialgazette.gov.ph/downloads/2020/05may/20200429-Omnibus-Guidelines-on-the-Implementation-of-Community-Quarantine-in-the-Philippines.pdf

———. 2020b. "Omnibus Guidelines on the Implementation of Community Quarantine in the Philippines with Amendments as of June 3, 2020". *Official Gazette*, Republic of the Philippines, 3 June 2020. https://www.officialgazette.gov.ph/downloads/2020/06jun/20200603-omnibus-guidelines-on-the-implementation-of-community-quarantine-in-the-philippines.pdf

———. 2020c. "Recommendations for the Management of Novel Coronavirus Situation". Resolution No. 1, Series of 2020, *Official Gazette*, Office of the Secretary, Republic of the Philippines Department of Health, 28 January 2020. https://www.officialgazette.gov.ph/downloads/2020/01jan/20200128-IATF-RESOLUTION-NO-1-RRD.pdf

———. 2020d. "Resolutions Relative to the Management of the Coronavirus Disease 2019 (COVID-19) Situation". Resolution No. 15, Series of 2020, *Official Gazette*, Republic of the Philippines, 25 March 2020. https://www.officialgazette.gov.ph/downloads/2020/05may/20200324-IATF-RESO-15.pdf

———. 2021a. "Guidelines on the Pilot Implementation of Alert Levels System for COVID-19 Response in the National Capital Region". *Official Gazette*, Republic of the Philippines, 13 September 2021. https://www.officialgazette.gov.ph/downloads/2021/09sep/20210913-Certified-Guidelines-for-Pilot-Areas.pdf

———. 2021b. "Omnibus Guidelines on the Implementation of Community Quarantine in the Philippines with Amendments as of August 19, 2021". *Official Gazette*, Republic of the Philippines, 19 August 2021. https://www.officialgazette.gov.ph/downloads/2021/05may/20210520-OMNIBUS-RRD.pdf

———. 2021c. "Omnibus Guidelines on the Implementation of Community Quarantine in the Philippines with Amendments as of May 20, 2021". *Official Gazette*, Republic of the Philippines, 20 May 2021. https://www.officialgazette.gov.ph/downloads/2021/05may/20210520-OMNIBUS-RRD.pdf

Inquirer. 2021. "188 Restaurants to Offer Exclusive Deals for Vaccinated Filipinos through Smart Bakuna Benefits". 16 June 2021. globalnation.inquirer.net/197054/188-restaurants-to-offer-exclusive-deals-for-vaccinated-filipinos-through-smart-bakuna-benefits (accessed 27 March 2024).

International Labour Organization. n.d. "Informal Economy in the Philippines". https://www.ilo.org/manila/areasofwork/informal-economy/lang--en/index.htm (accessed 4 April 2024).

International Monetary Fund. 2020. *World Economic Outlook, April 2020: The Great Lockdown*. https://www.imf.org/en/Publications/WEO/Issues/2020/04/14/weo-april-2020

Jalea, Glee. 2020. "CAB Clarifies: Duterte's NCoV Ban Still Allows Flights from Mainland China, Hong Kong, Macau". *CNN Philippines*, 9 February 2020. https://www.cnnphilippines.com/news/2020/2/9/Duterte-travel-ban-still-allows-China-flights.html (accessed 4 April 2024).

Macusi, Edison D., Stefenie Katrin V. Siblos, Martha Elena Betancourt, Erna S. Macusi, Michael N. Calderon, Michael Jeriel I. Bersaldo, and Larry N. Digal. 2022. "Impacts of Covid-19 on the Catch of Small-Scale Fishers and Their Families Due to Restriction Policies in Davao Gulf, Philippines". *Frontiers in Marine Science* 8 (January): 770543. https://doi.org/10.3389/fmars.2021.770543

Magno, Francisco A., and Julio C. Teehankee. 2022. "Pandemic Politics in the Philippines: An Introduction from the Special Issue Editors". *Philippine Political Science Journal* 43, no. 2: 107–22. https://doi.org/10.1163/2165025x-12340047

McKinsey & Company. 2020. "COVID-19: Saving Thousands of Lives and Trillions in Livelihoods". 17 August 2020. https://www.mckinsey.com/industries/healthcare/our-insights/covid-19-saving-thousands-of-lives-and-trillions-in-livelihoods (accessed 4 April 2024).

National Task Force Against COVID-19. 2020. *National Action Plan Against COVID-19: Phase III*. https://ndrrmc.gov.ph/attachments/article/4148/

National-Action-Plan-against-COVID19-Phase-III.pdf (accessed 14 May 2024).

Official Gazette. 2020a. "Implementing Rules and Regulations of Section 4(Aa) of Republic Act No. 11469, Otherwise Known as the 'Bayanihan to Heal As One Act.'" Philippines: Republic of the Philippines. https://www.officialgazette.gov.ph/2020/04/01/implementing-rules-and-regulations-of-section-4aa-of-republic-act-no-11469-otherwise-known-as-the-bayanihan-to-heal-as-one-act/

———. 2020b. "Republic Act No. 11494, An Act Providing for Covid-19 Response and Recovery Interventions and Providing Mechanisms to Accelerate the Recovery and Bolster the Resiliency of the Philippine Economy, Providing Funds Therefor and For Other Purposes". Republic of the Philippines. https://www.officialgazette.gov.ph/downloads/2020/09sep/20200911-RA-11494-RRD.pdf

Our World in Data. 2021. "Our Checklist for COVID-19 Testing Data". University of Oxford. https://ourworldindata.org/coronavirus-testing#our-checklist-for-covid-19-testing-data (accessed 4 April 2024).

———. 2022. "Philippines: Coronavirus Pandemic Country Profile". University of Oxford. https://ourworldindata.org/coronavirus/country/Philippines (accessed 4 April 2024).

Oxford Covid-19 Government Response Tracker (OxCGRT) and Blavatnik School of Government. 2022. "COVID-19: Stringency Index". 1 December 2022. https://ourworldindata.org/explorers/coronavirus-data-explorer?uniformYAxis=0&country=USA~ITA~CAN~DEU~GBR~FRA&hideControls=true&Interval=7-day+rolling+average&Relative+to+Population=true&Color+by+test+positivity=false&Metric=Stringency+index (accessed 4 April 2024).

Palicte, Che. 2020. "Davao City to Implement Enhanced Community Quarantine". Philippine News Agency, 3 April 2020. www.pna.gov.ph/articles/1098762 (accessed 14 May 2024).

Peralta, Janine. 2020. "Duterte Not Keen on Banning Travel to China amid Coronavirus Scare". *CNN Philippines*, 29 January 2020. http://www.cnnphilippines.com/news/2020/1/29/duterte-on-china-travel-ban.html (accessed 4 April 2024).

Philippine Disaster Resilience Foundation. 2020. "Business Groups Raise 1.5 Billion to Help Metro's Urban Poor under 'Project Ugnayan' Initiative". 22 March 2020. https://mbc.com.ph/2020/03/23/business-groups-raise-1-5-billion-to-help-metros-urban-poor-under-project-ugnayan-initiative/ (accessed 4 April 2024).

Philippine Statistics Authority. 2019. "Annual Family Income is Estimated at

PhP 313 Thousand, on Average, In 2018. Family Income and Expenditure Survey. https://psa.gov.ph/statistics/income-expenditure/fies/node/144731 (accessed 4 April 2024).

———. 2020a. "Employment Situation in April 2020". https://psa.gov.ph/content/employment-situation-april-2020 (accessed 4 April 2024).

———. 2020b. "Highlights on the Economic Performance of Regional Economies for 2019". https://psa.gov.ph/statistics/grdp/highlights/node/163414#ncr (accessed 4 April 2024).

———. 2021a. "2021 Official Full Year Poverty Statistics". https://econgress.gov.ph/wp-content/uploads/publications/FF2022-51%20Regional%20Poverty%20Statistics%20Update.pdf (accessed 14 May 2024).

———. 2021b. "Highlights of the National Capital Region (NCR) Population 2020 Census of Population and Housing (2020 CPH)". https://psa.gov.ph/content/highlights-national-capital-region-ncr-population-2020-census-population-and-housing-2020 (accessed 4 April 2024).

———. 2022. "GDP Posts an 8.3 Percent Growth in the First Quarter of 2022". News release, 12 May 2022. https://psa.gov.ph/content/gdp-posts-83-percent-growth-first-quarter-2022#:~:text=The%20Philippine%20Gross%20Domestic%20Product,the%20first%20quarter%20of%202022

Phua, Jason, Mohammad Omar Faruq, Atul P. Kulkarni, Ike Sri Redjeki, Khamsay Detleuxay, Naranpurev Mendsaikhan, Kyi Kyi Sann, et al. 2020. "Critical Care Bed Capacity in Asian Countries and Regions". *Critical Care Medicine* 48, no. 5: 654–62. https://doi.org/10.1097/CCM.0000000000004222

Porcalla, Delon. 2014. "Task Force on Emerging Infectious Diseases Formed". *Philstar*, 3 June 2014. https://www.philstar.com/headlines/2014/06/03/1330458/task-force-emerging-infectious-diseases-formed (accessed 4 April 2024).

Quezon City Local Government. 2021. "Private Sector Partners with QC for Vaccine Rollout". News release, 13 April 2021. https://quezoncity.gov.ph/private-sector-partners-with-qc-for-vaccine-rollout/ (accessed 4 April 2024).

Quintos, Paul. 2020. "The Philippines' COVID-19 Response: Symptoms of Deeper Malaise in the Philippine Health System". Policy Paper, University of the Philippines National College of Public Administration and Governance, June 2020. https://ncpag.upd.edu.ph/wp-content/uploads/covid19response.pdf (accessed 4 April 2024).

Rappler. 2021. "Covid-19 Pandemic to Cost Php 41.4 T For The Next 40 Years—NEDA". 25 September 2021. https://www.rappler.com/business/neda-estimate-cost-covid-19-pandemic-long-term-september-2021/ (accessed 4 April 2024).

———. 2022. "COVID-19 Pandemic: Latest Situation in the Philippines—August

2022". 20 August 2022. www.rappler.com/nation/covid-19-pandemic-latest-situation-philippines-august-2022/ (accessed 14 May 2024).

———. 2023. "COVID-19 Pandemic: Latest Situation in the Philippines—November to December 2022". 12 January 2023, www.rappler.com/nation/covid-19-pandemic-latest-situation-philippines-november-december-2022/ (accessed 14 May 2024).

Relativo, James. 2023. "Marcos Finally Lifts COVID-19 State of Public Emergency. What Happens Next?". *Philstar*, 22 July 2023. www.philstar.com/headlines/2023/07/22/2282996/marcos-finally-lifts-covid-19-state-public-emergency-what-happens-next (accessed 14 May 2024).

Ricciardi, Vinny, Paolo Verme, and Umar Serajuddin. 2020. "Covid-19: Testing for All or Testing for Some? A Town's Key Lesson in Testing Everyone for Coronavirus". World Bank Blogs, 29 April 2020. https://blogs.worldbank.org/opendata/covid-19-testing-all-or-testing-some-towns-key-lesson-testing-everyone-coronavirus (accessed 4 April 2024).

Romero, Alexis, and Edith Regalado. 2020. "Timeout: Metro Manila back to MECQ August 4 to 18". *Philstar Global*, 3 August 2020. https://www.philstar.com/headlines/2020/08/03/2032522/timeout-metro-manila-back-mecq-august-4-18 (accessed 4 April 2024).

———, Janvic Mateo, Shiela Crisostomo, and Vince Nonato. 2020. "Ateneo Paper: Millions of Covid-19 Cases May Have Been Undetected; Mass Testing Urged; 'Lockdowns Not Sustainable Strategy'". *One News*, 19 August 2020. https://www.onenews.ph/articles/ateneo-paper-millions-of-covid-19-cases-may-have-been-undetected-mass-testing-urged-lockdowns-not-sustainable-strategy (accessed 4 April 2024).

Saavedra, John Rey. 2020. "Guv Imposes Enhanced Community Quarantine in Cebu". Philippine News Agency, 26 March 2020. www.pna.gov.ph/articles/1097844 (accessed 14 May 2024).

Saludes, Mark. 2020. "Philippine Churches Back Calls for Mass Testing of Covid-19". *LiCAS News*, 26 March 2020. https://www.licas.news/2020/03/26/philippine-churches-back-calls-for-mass-testing-of-covid-19/ (accessed 4 April 2024).

Santos, Ana P. 2020. "Poverty Punished as Philippines Gets Tough in Virus Pandemic". *Al Jazeera*, 13 April 2020. https://www.aljazeera.com/news/2020/4/13/poverty-punished-as-philippines-gets-tough-in-virus-pandemic (accessed 14 May 2024).

Santos, Rudy. 2020. "'No Order to Ban Chinese from Philippines'". *Philippine Star*, 29 January 2020. https://www.philstar.com/headlines/2020/01/29/1988673/no-order-ban-chinese-philippines (accessed 4 April 2024).

Sarao, Zacarian. 2022. "3.1 Million Filipino Families Experienced Hunger in Q1 of 2022—SWS". *Inquirer*, 7 June 2022. https://newsinfo.inquirer.net/1607293/3-1m-filipinos-experienced-hunger-in-q1-of-2022-sws-survey-shows (accessed 4 April 2024).

Sunnexdesk. 2021. "Incentives Might Promote Vaccine Confidence, DOH Agrees". SunStar Publishing Inc, 29 May 2021. www.sunstar.com.ph/manila/local-news/incentives-might-promote-vaccine-confidence-doh-agrees (accessed 27 March 2024).

SunStar Manila. "Timeline: Covid-19 in the Philippines". SunStar Publishing Inc. 12 May 2020. www.sunstar.com.ph/manila/local-news/timeline-covid-19-in-the-philippines (accessed 14 May 2024).

Talabong, Rambo. 2021. "Magalong: Contact Tracing Is Worsening in PH". *Rappler*, 30 March 2021. https://www.rappler.com/nation/magalong-says-covid-19-contract-tracing-worsening/ (accessed 4 April 2024).

Tomacruz, Sofia. 2022. "What Prevents Swift Covid-19 Vaccine Deliveries to Philippines' Provinces?". *Rappler*, 1 February 2022. https://www.rappler.com/newsbreak/investigative/what-prevents-swift-deliveries-provinces-analysis-philippines-covid-19-vaccination-drive-2022-part-2/ (accessed 4 April 2024).

Torres-Tupas, Tetch. 2020. "SC Asked to Compel Gov't to Do 'Proactive' Mass Testing, Tell Truth on Virus Fight". *Inquirer*, 3 July 2020. https://newsinfo.inquirer.net/1301319/sc-asked-to-compel-govt-to-do-proactive-mass-testing-tell-truth-on-virus-fight (accessed 4 April 2024).

UNICEF (United Nations Children's Fund). 2021. "Schools Still Closed for Nearly 77 Million Students 18 Months into Pandemic—UNICEF". News release, 15 September 2021. https://www.unicef.org/press-releases/schools-still-closed-nearly-77-million-students-18-months-pandemic-unicef

World Bank. 2019a. "Hospital Beds (per 1,000 People)—Philippines". 2019. https://data.worldbank.org/indicator/SH.MED.BEDS.ZS?end=2019&locations=PH&start=1960&view=chart (accessed 3 April 2024).

———. 2019b. "Physicians (per 1,000 People)—Philippines". 2019. https://data.worldbank.org/indicator/SH.MED.PHYS.ZS?locations=PH (accessed 4 April 2024).

———. 2021a. "GDP Growth (Annual %)—Philippines". 2021. https://data.worldbank.org/indicator/NY.GDP.MKTP.KD.ZG?locations=PH (accessed 3 April 2024).

———. 2021b. *Reducing Vaccine Hesitancy in the Philippines: Findings from a Survey Experiment*. World Bank. https://thedocs.worldbank.org/en/doc/9b206c064482a4fbb880ee23d6081d52-0070062021/original/Vaccine-Hesitancy-World-Bank-Policy-Note-September-2021.pdf

———. 2022. "The World Bank in the Philippines". World Bank. 1 March 2022. https://www.worldbank.org/en/country/philippines/overview (accessed 4 April 2024).

———. 2023. "COVID-19's Devastating Impact on Human Capital—World Bank Expert Answers". Video blog, 6 March 2023. World Bank Group. www.worldbank.org/en/news/video/2023/02/24/human-capital-children-young-covid19-pandemic-expert-answers (accessed 4 April 2024).

WHO (World Health Organization). 2020. *Public Health Criteria to Adjust Public Health and Social Measures in the Context of COVID-19: Annex to Considerations in Adjusting Public Health and Social Measures in the Context of COVID-19*. 12 May 2020. https://iris.who.int/bitstream/handle/10665/332073/WHO-2019-nCoV-Adjusting_PH_measures-Criteria-2020.1-eng.pdf

———. 2023. "Philippines". WHO Health Emergency Dashboard. https://data.who.int/dashboards/covid19/cases?m49=608&n=c (accessed 4 April 2024).

7

VIETNAM'S PANDEMIC PASSAGE

From "Zero Covid" to Flexible Adaptation

Nguyen Thu Huong

INTRODUCTION

The Covid-19 pandemic, one of the most serious health crises in human history, spread rapidly across the globe since the end of 2019. As Covid-19 spread and the death toll mounted, governments faced the hard reality that saving lives entailed severely limiting or strictly monitoring social contact, with most opting to impose mobility restrictions and economic shutdowns that came at high economic cost. Strategies adopted by governments around the world did, however, range from no intervention at all to strict measures imposed on the population, such as lockdowns (Zibaseresht 2020).

One year into the pandemic, Vietnam emerged as one of the few countries that had largely succeeded in controlling the outbreak, while others, including more advanced and developed nations, witnessed an out-of-control spread of the virus, causing hundreds, even thousands, of deaths every day. However, the emergence of the Delta variant in 2021 put into question the entire system of rigorous contact tracing and other preventive mechanisms, which had until then enabled the country to perform well. In 2021, Vietnam hit its hardest days since the beginning of the pandemic, with the daily infection rate swelling to the thousands and the death toll rising. In end-August 2021, after several lockdowns and closures of most activities, Prime Minister Pham Minh Chinh announced that the country could not rely indefinitely on these measures and quarantines. Instead, it would switch to a strategy of living safely with the virus.

Vietnam's Covid-19 experience thus followed two distinct phases. For the first year and a half of the pandemic, the country adopted strict measures and a zero-Covid strategy. Thereafter, the government declared that people would have to learn how to live with the virus instead of avoiding it and incurring high economic costs. Vietnam's second phase was a move to a strategy of flexible adaptation in dealing with the pandemic. The country moved into this second phase later than some other countries, but it marked the end of an era of severe restrictions and a shift towards more flexible and adaptive measures that allowed daily life and business to return to normal. This chapter provides an account of Vietnam's Covid-19 coping strategy and its policy interventions and outcomes.

Vietnam's initial success is attributable to a combination of many factors, with a centralized policy system playing a key role. From January 2020 through April 2021, when the Delta variant caused a fourth wave of infection in Vietnam, the country recorded less than 4,000 cases, a large proportion of which were imported. It also recorded only thirty-five deaths related to Covid-19 over that period. The early response to the pandemic can be summarized as mass mobilization of the government at all levels and the healthcare system, combined with a successful communication campaign focused on public information and education. Although the government started with a national lockdown in April 2020, it quickly adapted to more targeted lockdowns coupled with extensive contact tracing and containment and prevention measures. This was the only national lockdown. The availability of tracing applications developed in response to previous flu epidemics, and their repurposing for Covid-19, facilitated the process. This permitted business activities to resume across the country through most of 2020 and early 2021, until the arrival of the Delta variant.

More transmissible strains of the virus emerged that were more difficult to detect, isolate and keep up with; this presented a serious challenge to the system of rigorous contact tracing and other mechanisms put in place from the onset of the pandemic. Beginning in May 2021, new infections grew exponentially, and Vietnam found itself, like most countries, struggling to cope with the spread of the virus. Cumulative Covid-19 cases spiked, from about 20,000 in early July 2021 to over 400,000 by end-August 2021. While Vietnam recorded just 100 Covid-19 deaths from January 2020 to early July 2021, by end-August 2021 that count had exceeded 10,000 (Our World in Data n.d.). Prolonged mobility restrictions were enforced, which caused economic hardship. However, with vaccine supply substantially secured, Vietnam's Prime Minister was able to announce on 29 August 2021 that the country might be facing a protracted battle and could not rely on indefinite closures and quarantines. That marked the start of a shift in strategy towards an accelerated vaccination campaign as the means for living safely with the virus and gradually phasing out restrictions.

COUNTRY CONTEXT

Vietnam is the fifth-largest economy in Southeast Asia, with a gross domestic product (GDP) of approximately US$369 billion in 2021 and a population of 99 million (Thuy 2022). It has grown quickly and transformed from a poor post-war country to a lower-middle-income nation. The *Doi Moi* reforms initiated in the mid-1980s, coupled with favourable global trends, enabled the country to achieve rapid economic growth, thus propelling it from poor to lower-middle-class status. The International Monetary Fund forecasts that, by 2025, Vietnam will have become the third-largest economy in Southeast Asia with a GDP of US$571.12 billion, surpassing the Philippines and Singapore (Thuy 2022).

Before 2020, Vietnam's economy was growing impressively at about 7 per cent. It was exceeding its target rate and had become one of the world's fastest-growing economies since first opening up to foreign trade and investment more than three decades ago. Its success has been largely attributed to its ability to attract and capitalize on foreign direct investment, which has helped create a large number of jobs, boost the state budget, foster economic and administrative restructuring and improve competitiveness. In the last several decades, the Vietnamese government has attempted to boost international economic integration through many free trade agreements and communities, such as the World Trade Organization, the Comprehensive and Progressive Agreement for Trans-Pacific Partnership, the EU-Vietnam free trade agreement and the UK-Vietnam free trade agreement. This has led to significant year-on-year increases in foreign direct investment.

With the intensification and diversification of global supply chains, Vietnam became a top destination for investment in manufacturing due to its strategic location, logistical strengths in shipping and trade facilitation, and competitive labour and production costs. Prior to the pandemic, total foreign investment reached US$38.02 billion for 2019 (up to 20 December 2019), a 7.2 per cent increase from the same period in 2018 (Ministry of Planning and Investment 2020). This has been supported by the strategy of major international firms to relocate out of China where labour costs were growing. It is also supported by the "China + 1" strategy of multinationals, whereby they diversify their investment beyond China. Compared to some other Southeast Asian countries, Vietnam enjoys the advantage of long coastlines, making it an appealing destination for seaborne trade, land transport links to other countries and proximity to China. This has resulted in the development of international airports, seaports and rail links facilitating production flow and transportation. These transport links are close to major cities. In 2020, the manufacturing and processing sector continued to lead the country's foreign direct investment, accounting for 58.2 per cent of the total. However, facing the pandemic, Vietnam found itself in a more vulnerable position than others, due to its concentration of manufacturing and high-contact services around the two megacities, Hanoi and Ho Chi Minh City. These factors may partly explain the aggressive strategy pursued by the government.

OVERVIEW OF THE PANDEMIC: FOUR WAVES

As China announced that it had found a novel and dangerous virus, Vietnam, which shares a 1,281 km border with China and enormous trade volumes, promptly prepared for cross-border infections. Vietnam registered its first case of Covid-19 on 23 January 2020 when the world was still assessing the emerging virus.[1] Throughout 2020, Vietnam was on high alert. It experienced two Covid-19 waves in 2020, the first of which involved a national lockdown, while the second was centred on Da Nang city and triggered a city lockdown (Table 7.1). The government contained the virus so that the number of cases and deaths were minimized. The third wave, in the first quarter of 2021, involved targeted lockdowns, which continued to avert deaths from Covid-19. However, the fourth wave, which began around May 2021, caused a spike in cases and deaths, most acutely from August to September 2021 (Figure 7.1).

In 2020, the lockdowns and Covid-19 regulations restricted economic activity, with negative consequences for household income. Although Vietnam did not technically experience a recession in 2020 due to Covid-19, the effects were severe enough to halt, and in some cases reverse, the preceding years' rapid income and wage growth for workers and households. Real household income per capita measured using the Vietnam Household Living Standard Surveys of 2020 declined by 5 per cent compared to 2019 (World Bank 2021, Chapter 2). Vietnam experienced job losses, lower incomes, lower business turnover and business closures, in addition to substantial slowdowns in economic growth and activity. The adverse impacts of Covid-19 affected households across the entire welfare distribution.

Fourth Wave: From Star Performer To Below Average

Vietnam entered a fourth wave of infection on 27 April 2021 due to the emergence of the highly contagious Delta variant. It proved the most complicated wave to handle and inflicted the most fatalities. The Delta variant challenged Vietnam's previously effective response to the pandemic, spreading in hospitals, with many becoming critically ill due to pre-existing conditions, and also in local communities and large manufacturing regions. Thousands of cases in selected communities put a massive burden on the entire system, including healthcare and contact tracing. The mechanisms put in place during previous waves, including contact tracing, high levels of vigilance (wearing masks, washing hands, keeping a safe distance) and localized lockdowns, ceased to work during the Delta variant.

During the first three waves, Vietnam registered a cumulative 3,000 cases, but in the twelve months from May 2021 onwards, Vietnam detected 10.7 million cases, which resulted in 43,000 deaths, corresponding to a fatality rate of about 0.4 per cent (General Department of Preventive

TABLE 7.1
Four Waves of Infection in Vietnam

Wave	*Date*	*Cases*	*Deaths*	*Lockdown Scale*
1	23 January 2020 to 24 July 2020	415 (106 domestic, 309 imported)	0	First commune lockdown in February. National lockdown in April.
2	25 July 2020 to 27 January 2021	1,136 (554 domestic, 582 imported)	35	Lockdown in Da Nang city.
3	28 January 2021 to 26 April 2021	1,301 (910 domestic, 391 imported)	0	Targeted lockdowns in selected areas.
4	27 April 2021 to 31 December 2021	1,728,405 (1,725,518 domestic, 2,887 imported)	32,394 (1.9% of total cases)	Targeted lockdowns in selected cities, provinces and districts.

Sources: Based on news updates from the Ministry of Health.

FIGURE 7.1
Vietnam: Covid-19 New Cases and Deaths (per Million), January 2020 to April 2023

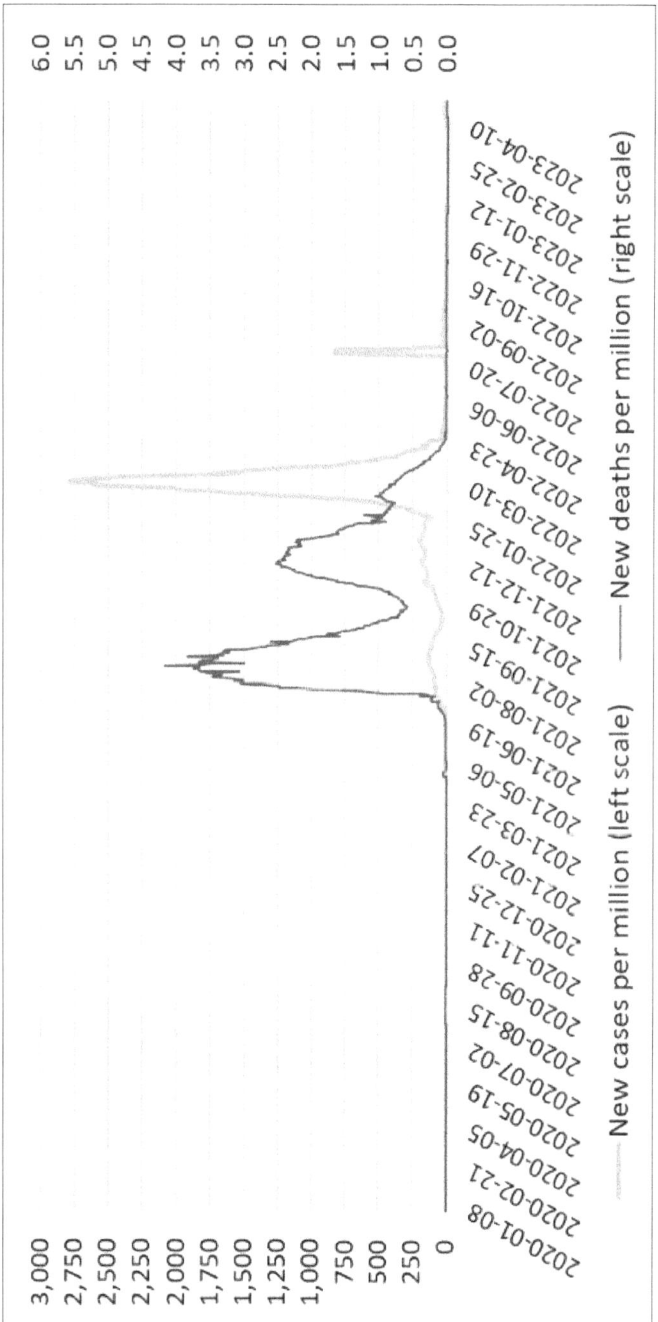

Source: ourworldindata.org.

Medicine 2022). People were shocked to find themselves in a situation little different to that of any other country, whereas only a few months previously they had felt lucky to be enjoying relative normalcy—which was almost nowhere else to be found. The most restrictive and unprecedented measures, including targeted lockdown and mobility restrictions (both road and air), were enforced in the second half of 2021 in locations where the virus was spreading quickly and causing high rates of fatalities—the south of the country, Ho Chi Minh City and surroundings, and provinces with a high concentration of manufacturing companies. This was in addition to prolonged closures of businesses and factories, in an attempt to slow down the exponential spread of community cases in those parts of the country.

From July 2021, nineteen cities and provinces in the south,[2] the country's key economic region, were placed in lockdown under social distancing orders supervised and monitored by provincial governments but accountable to the Prime Minister's office (Government of Vietnam 2021a). This was a tough decision as it would affect the economic activities and social welfare of millions of people, but it was regarded as crucial given the limited supply of Covid-19 vaccines at the time and the ongoing zero-Covid policy.

The spread of the Delta variant disrupted the national economy and forced millions of domestic migrant workers living in the country's major economic centres to return home. Provinces reported that as of mid-December 2021, some 2.2 million labourers had returned home, mainly from Hanoi (447,100), Ho Chi Minh City (524,000), other southern cities and provinces (594,000) and other localities (676,000) (*Vietnamplus* 2022).

Disruption of goods and services delivery networks resulted in a surge in transportation costs, which compounded supply chain problems. The most economically precarious segments of the population—migrant workers in urban areas and the urban poor—even suffered food insecurity despite Vietnam being a food surplus country. By end-August 2021, military forces were deployed to help with the transportation of essential food to each household in Ho Chi Minh City (Thanh Niên 2021). Inequalities in capacity to weather the crisis were apparent. Poor households, already earning low income and with minimal savings, could least afford income loss, and their hardships were compounded by a concurrent rise in the cost of living and difficulties in self-isolating. That Vietnam's confirmed cases and deaths were concentrated in economically lagging areas that were densely populated areas with poor, unskilled people only further aggravated the situation. The thousands of new cases that emerged each day exceeded the city's capacity to handle the pandemic and brought the healthcare system to the brink of collapse (Huong Le Thu 2021).

The city of Ho Chi Minh, Vietnam's largest in terms of area, population and economic power, was hit the hardest. Its population of 9 million, particularly the informal workers and immigrants to the city, struggled in the face of the increased restrictions. Although half a million or so returned to their non-urban homes, the vast majority remained in the city. People were required to stay at home and some essential services were halted, but their crowded lodging conditions and the nature of their work made it impossible for many to stay home and cease earning income.[3] Millions of workers subsisting on the income provided by precarious, informal jobs suffered a loss of earnings and had no savings to draw on. In Ho Chi Minh City, rapidly rising cases and deaths forced authorities to restrict mobility inside the city, but in other cities, the delivery of goods and services was allowed to continue.

The slow vaccine roll-out and rampant transmission of the new virus mutations complicated the government's dual target of controlling the pandemic while continuing to grow economically. At this point, on 29 August 2021, Prime Minister Pham Minh Chinh announced the strategic change from closures and quarantines to an acceleration of the vaccination campaign in order to live safely with the virus.

GOVERNMENT RESPONSE TO THE PANDEMIC

Vietnam's pursuit of a zero-Covid strategy while keeping the economy largely operational was enabled by aggressive contact tracing, social distancing and targeted lockdowns, although the country could not avoid adverse socio-economic impacts. The severity of the fourth wave triggered more widespread restrictions and an acceleration of the vaccination programme. This section takes a deeper dive into Vietnam's specific Covid-19 responses.

Pandemic Preparedness

The author adopts the definition of pandemic preparedness offered by the Organization for Economic Co-operation and Development (OECD 2015): it is "governments' ability to anticipate a pandemic before it materializes and prepare for a global public health emergency, by developing the right knowledge and capacities".

The government of Vietnam took the news of the coronavirus outbreak in China very seriously and reacted quickly. Its proximity to China made Vietnam much more vulnerable to transmission. Immediately after China's announcement, Vietnam went on high alert, closely monitoring the situation while kickstarting a series of preventive protocols. Its previous experience with highly contagious diseases such as SARS in 2003 and Middle East respiratory syndrome, first identified in 2012, helped it to respond quickly.

As early as 3 January 2020, even before China's first casualty and its announcement of the outbreak, Vietnam's Ministry of Health issued a directive on implementing quarantine procedures at the Vietnam-China border (La et al. 2020). On 10 January 2020, the Public Health Emergency Operation Center under the Ministry of Health followed up with a meeting to evaluate the situation and suggest preventive and treatment measures.

To contain the virus, in January 2020 the Ministry of Health activated procedures and guidelines for hospitals to follow in the event of a pandemic. Across health facilities, patients were screened based on respiratory symptoms and body temperature. Specifically, on 23 January 2020, Prime Minister Nguyen Xuan Phuc issued Official Telegram 121/ CD-TTg on preventing acute respiratory infections caused by new strains of coronavirus. The dispatch clearly identified the virus as a dangerous, acute infectious disease caused by a mutated coronavirus, for which there was no specific treatment or vaccine. The Ministry of Health would strictly control people entering the country. If suspected cases were detected, they were to be quarantined and managed promptly (Government Office 2020). On 19 February 2020, the Ministry of Health issued guidelines on the prevention and control of Covid-19 in all healthcare facilities. This included comprehensive guidance to hospitals on screening, admission and isolation of confirmed or suspected Covid-19 cases, among others.

In the two months from 23 January 2020, when the first case of Covid-19 was detected in Vietnam, there were 239 confirmed cases and zero deaths (Ministry of Health n.d.).

A national steering committee was created to coordinate strategies and measures against Covid-19 at all levels of government, from central to provincial and lower authorities. Risk anticipation was key; the steering committee prepared for various scenarios. Bold measures were quickly introduced, including school closures and travel restrictions, as early as the end of January 2020.

Crisis Communication

Vietnam conducted an effective communications campaign to disseminate information and facilitate public compliance. These efforts were deployed as soon as China announced the new virus, to inform the public on the danger of the virus and the roll-out of preventive measures and government policies. The government communicated directly with citizens via channels such as mobile phone messaging, social media (e.g., Facebook, Zalo, YouTube), national television and radio channels, and online and offline newspapers. The government used slogans extensively and creatively and these were regularly updated alongside changes in government policies. The government even provided funding to remix a popular song refitted with lyrics teaching Covid-19 prevention. The song, *Ghen Co Vy*, soon became a hit nationwide and also became widely known on international social media (CBS News 2020).

The government's rapid and direct communication through a variety of channels helped it inform the population in real time, which strengthened confidence in the pandemic strategy (Nguyen and Ho 2020). Information about the virus and the number of cases, placed in domestic and international contexts, were timely, frequently updated and easily accessible, with the Ministry of Health's official website as the definitive source. Clear and widespread messaging facilitated public compliance with social distancing policies and other restrictions that in turn helped the country to navigate the first waves of infections (Lahiff, Pham, and Nguyen 2022).

Starting from the second half of 2021, a communications campaign on the importance and benefits of vaccination was launched to support the accelerated vaccination strategy. It was also a period where control of misinformation on social media was intensified due to inaccurate information circulating online that was causing distrust in vaccines. The communications may have contributed to a reduction in vaccine hesitancy or vaccine preference that was initially present: as soon as doses were more widely available in Vietnam, vaccinations took off. The government used the tagline, "the best vaccine is the one you get the soonest".

Decisive Measures

The first significant demonstration of aggressive pandemic management was the decision to lock down a whole commune of 10,000 people, Son Loi, situated in the northern province of Vinh Phuc, for just over two weeks. The decision was taken following just a few confirmed cases, but it affected the lives of 10,000 people. Only six cases were confirmed in the commune, but the isolation and quarantine measures sent out a clear message from central and provincial governments that they would not let the virus spread out of control.

The National Steering Committee for Covid-19 Prevention and Control, headed by the Prime Minister, met every two days to assess the situation and take action. It assumed responsibility for issuing recommendations and instructions to the subnational government on implementing Covid-19 measures.

Extensive and Rigorous Contract Tracing

Contact tracing and quarantine are key to the containment of any pandemic (Zibaseresht 2020). Vietnam was quick to devise an extensive system of contact tracing and to operationalize applications nationwide (Figure 7.2). It updated these regularly to reflect changes in Vietnam's pandemic situation. Bluezone was the first domestic application for determining whether a person had come into contact with a person infected with Covid-19. It was launched by the government in April 2020 (Chau 2020). Vietnam's contact tracing strategy was comprehensive, being based on tracing degrees of contact from F0 (the infected person) through F1 (those who had close contact with F0 or were suspected of being infected) and F2 (close contact with F1), all the way to F5.[4]

FIGURE 7.2
Extensive Third-Degree Contact Tracing in Vietnam

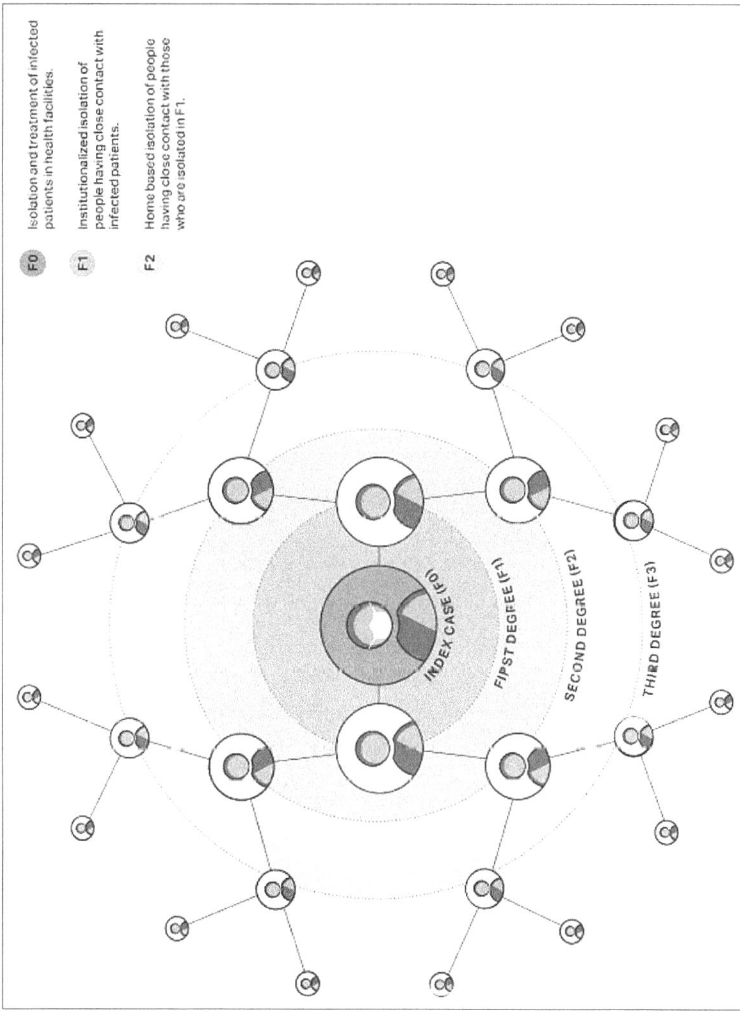

Source: Vietnam's Ministry of Health.

There is a small window of time in which to track and quarantine contacts before they become infectious. The incubation period between contact with the virus and the start of symptoms is on average five days (CDC 2021). Infectiousness begins two days before the onset of symptoms, leaving about three days from contact with a case to the transmissible stage (He et al. 2020). It is critical to move fast, mobilize the contract tracing apparatus, locate people affected and initiate quarantine protocols.

One noteworthy aspect of Vietnam's approach is that it identified and quarantined suspected cases based on their epidemiological risk of infection (if they had contact with a confirmed case or travelled to a Covid-19 affected country), not whether they exhibited symptoms (Pollack et al. 2021). The high proportion of confirmed cases that never developed symptoms (43 per cent) suggests that this approach may have been a key contributor to limiting community transmission early on in the pandemic (La et al. 2020).

When the first cluster of infections appeared in Son Loi commune, Binh Xuyen district, Vinh Phuc province in February 2020, after a group of workers returned from a company training visit to Wuhan, strict quarantine measures were put in place for just over two weeks. In addition to quarantine and contact tracing, additional preventive measures were also deployed including large-scale health monitoring and sterilization of all vehicles entering and exiting the commune. All suspected cases were sent to central quarantine centres,[5] while those who came into contact with them were quarantined at home. The remaining local residents were recommended not to leave the commune without urgent cause. This was the first large-scale lockdown outside China (Van Duan 2020).

Mobility Restrictions, Closures and Gatherings

School closures and travel restrictions were introduced nationwide as early as the end of January 2020 in an attempt to halt the spread of the virus. International inbound flights and domestic flights were limited during certain periods to slow the arrival of new cases from abroad and limit the spread domestically. Senior leadership, excluding the Prime Minister, was held directly accountable for any negligence resulting in the spread of the virus in their area of responsibility. In March 2020, Vietnam suspended the granting of visas for foreigners wanting to enter the country and shortly afterwards suspended all entry for foreigners. Only planes repatriating Vietnamese citizens were permitted to enter, and all passengers were sent into quarantine, which was predominantly state-run but with a few government-authorized private facilities.

On 31 March 2020, Prime Minister Pham Minh Chinh issued Directive No. 16/CT-TTg on the implementation of urgent measures to prevent and control the Covid-19 pandemic. The directive mandated strict social distancing throughout the country for fifteen days, from 1 April 2020 through 15 April 2020. It also prohibited any close contact between different families, neighbourhoods/villages, communes, districts and provinces, mandated closures of non-essential businesses and restaurants, banned public gatherings and severely limited transportation services. The fifteen-day period was the only national lockdown in Vietnam; the government learnt from it and improved its decisions on lockdowns and other restrictive measures (Nguyen and Nguyen 2020). Subsequently, only targeted lockdowns were implemented, to a varying degree depending on the outbreak (Table 7.2).

Vietnam adopted a stricter approach in schools, which remained closed nationwide for most of the two academic years, during which education moved online (see Table 7.3 for timeline). Despite the negative implications, the policy proceeded under the premise that it was better to avoid interaction between children, which would have brought a risk of contagion to households at a time when there was no available vaccine or specific treatment. The decision to keep schools closed, though difficult, was sustained for a long period in line with the government's strategy of widespread and strict social distancing to contain Covid-19. Schools in Vietnam typically have large numbers of pupils per class and had limited facilities even before the pandemic. A decision to reopen schools would have jeopardized the efforts to contain the virus. The Prime Minister emphasized that children's learning had to continue even though schools were closed (Government of Vietnam 2020). The Ministry of Education and Training, together with education authorities at provincial and local levels, and in close cooperation with school headteachers, was able to implement online learning in a relatively short period of time. In 2022, school reopening was postponed on several occasions due to a surge

TABLE 7.2
Targeted Lockdowns in 2020

Region	*Date*	*Population Affected*	*Details*
Son Loi commune (Vinh Phuc province)	13 February 2020 to 4 March 2020	10,000	Sixteen cases of Covid-19 in the country, with six in Son Loi.[a]
Truc Bach street (Hanoi)	6 to 20 March 2020	190	The first confirmed case of the second wave lived on this street; sixty-six households were included in the lockdown.[b]
Phan Thiet (Binh Thuan province)	13 March 2020 to 3 April 2020	150	Lockdown of two streets (Hoang Van Thu and Ngo Sy Lien) around the home of a confirmed case; twenty-nine households affected.
Van Lam 3 village (Phuoc Nam commune, Thuan Nam district, Ninh Thuan province)	17 March 2020 to 14 April 2020	5,000	Two Covid-19 infections led to total lockdown in this area. Movement restrictions were put in place for all residents and all sixteen entrances to the village were closed off and monitored.
Thua Loi village (Ben Tre province)	23 March 2020 to 20 April 2020	1,600	Isolation measures enforced on 480 households after a resident was infected with the virus.
Bach Mai Hospital (Hanoi)	28 March 2020 to 11 April 2020	4,000–5,000	Locked down after forty-five people connected to the hospital tested positive for Covid-19. More than 15,000 people who had been associated with the hospital were tested for the virus, and 40,000 people who had come in contact with the hospital sometime before the lockdown were tracked down.
Ha Loi village (Me Linh district, Hanoi province)	7 April 2020 to 6 May 2020	10,000	Village sealed off (these were the last known community cases, apart from Ha Giang patient 268).
Dong Van district (Ha Giang province)	22 to 23 April 2020	7,600	Lockdown put in place before test results for suspected cases were received. Lockdown lifted after one day when test results came back negative.

Sources: [a] *Vietnamnet* (2020a); [b] *Vietnamnet* (2020b); Pollack et al. (2021).

TABLE 7.3
School Closures from 2020 to 2022

30 January 2020 to 4 May 2020	Schools closed on New Year holiday, then extended until end of March 2020, then national lockdown until April 16 2020.
4 May 2020 to end-May 2020	Schools reopened.
June 2020 to August 2020	Schools closed for summer holidays.
September 2020 to 27 April 2021	Schools reopened.
1 May 2021 to 30 April 2022	Schools closed for pandemic and summer holidays, then again for pandemic.
End-April 2022 to end-May 2022	Schools reopened for the last semester and final examinations.
End-May 2022	Schools closed for summer holidays.

Sources: Based on documents from the Ministry of Education and Training and other government offices.

in the number of cases across the country from February 2022. They finally reopened in April 2022. During the period that schools remained closed, though the country moved to a more flexible adaptation to the pandemic, social distancing requirements under the directives and other legal documents on anti-pandemic measures still applied, and the power over which measures to apply was assigned to the Ministry of Health. It made its decisions based on the number of community infections, the vaccination rate and treatment capacity. Children gathering at schools was considered high risk since it involved indoor activities for large groups of unvaccinated participants.

Public Spending and Support for Businesses and Households

From the beginning, the government set out an ambitious dual objective of both containing the virus and supporting economic development. Restrictions and lockdowns, however, hindered economic activity and diminished state revenues, while spending on health and disease control significantly increased. The cost of financing the Covid-19 response was a heavy burden on both central and local budgets and social health insurance. According to a government report by the Ministry of Finance presented to the National Assembly, as of 24 September 2020, nearly VND18 trillion from the state budget had been spent on pandemic prevention and supporting those affected (Ministry of Finance 2020). Table 7.4 summarizes the funding of Covid-19 responses.

During the pandemic, Vietnam's central bank, the State Bank of Vietnam, required all commercial banks to offer solutions to support businesses, including extending loans, adjusting loan terms, providing exemption from or reducing loan fees and reducing interest rates. As a result, Vietnam was among the countries of the Association of Southeast Asian Nations with the largest interest rate reduction. Financial institutions, having access to low-cost capital from the State Bank of Vietnam, expanded credit by lending on more attractive terms. The banking industry announced a policy of supporting interest rates of 2 per cent per year for two years (2022 and 2023), through commercial loans to businesses, cooperatives and household businesses.

State interventions to help people and businesses were introduced following the national lockdown in April 2020. In addition to reducing

TABLE 7.4
Source of Funding for Covid-19 Prevention and Treatment

Expenditure Item	*Source of Funds*
Overall national response plan	Central and local budgets, other local funds, social health insurance
Quarantine	Central budget, local budget, other local funds
Testing	Social health insurance
Treatment for Covid-19	Social health insurance for Vietnamese patients; own funds or own health insurance for foreign patients
Cost of treatment for other existing/ chronic conditions of Covid-19 patients	Social health insurance covers 80 per cent and the central budget covers 20 per cent co-payment for Vietnamese patients; own funds or own health insurance for foreign patients

Sources: Department of Planning and Finance, Ministry of Health; Health Insurance Department, Ministry of Health.

taxes and bills for electricity and water, the government also introduced cash support. In 2020, it provided a relief package of VND62 billion, the largest ever issued by the Vietnamese government. It was designed to provide additional support to those who were already beneficiaries of state social support and those whose income had been significantly reduced by the pandemic, who had lost their jobs, were unemployed or had fallen beneath a minimum standard of living. The second vulnerable group receiving assistance included workers, business households and enterprises that were negatively affected by the pandemic. However, the programme encountered implementation difficulties. Many adversely affected workers, most of whom were occupied in the informal sector, were unable to provide the documents that would enable them to receive the support.

Relief packages designed for formal firms were different to those offered to households. They were primarily in the form of deferments and credits and were available for a longer period of time, beginning from end-2020. These programmes also experienced challenges in their early stages of implementation, which began in end-2020. However, government agencies appear to have learnt from experience and improved implementation over time.

In 2020, the Vietnamese government passed a US$2.6 billion financial support package. This targeted six categories of individuals and businesses, including poor and near-poor households, furloughed workers or those who were put on leave without pay, and household businesses (Anh Minh 2020). In 2021, the government implemented a second relief package, this time worth US$1.13 billion, with twelve groups of policies to support affected workers. According to the Viet Nam Social Security, nearly 3.1 million workers benefited from the two packages.

Vietnam's Covid-19 impacts and responses are encapsulated in Table 7.5 and Figure 7.3. The country was one of very few that averted an economic recession in 2020, though it did experience negative effects in various socio-economic outcomes not captured in these variables, notably household income. However, its numerous policy interventions, represented at the macro level by the increase in state expenditure and reduction in interest rates, helped mitigate the slowdown, moderated the rise in unemployment and sustained the growth in foreign direct investment.

TABLE 7.5
Key Macro Indicators in Vietnam, 2022

GDP growth	*+8.02%*
Sector growth	
Agriculture/forestry/fisheries	+3.36%
Industry/construction	+7.78%
Services	+9.99%
State budget revenue (year-on-year growth)	+13.8%
State budget expenditure (year-on-year growth)	+8.1% (VND1.562 billion)
Baseline interest rate	4.5%
Unemployment among those of working age	2.21%
Total foreign direct investment	US$27.7 billion (+13.5%)
Consumer price index (year-on-year)	3.15%
Trade turnover	US$730 billion

Sources: General Statistics Office; State Bank of Vietnam

Vaccination—Lagging, but Quickly Catching Up

Vietnam took early action to contain Covid-19 and managed many health risks well. However, it was behind on vaccinations amid rising cases during the fourth wave of infections from 27 April 2021 to 31 December 2021. By May 2021, only 0.02 per cent of the population was fully vaccinated far below averages in developing countries in Southeast Asia and worldwide (World Bank 2021, Chapter 4). Globally, about half a billion people had been fully vaccinated by May 2021, roughly 6 per cent of the population. Vietnam, however, was struggling to secure an adequate supply of vaccines, in part due to a global shortage but also as a consequence of the government's procurement rules, which made accessing vaccines complex. Government expenditure was high given the significant costs of Covid-19 contact tracing, the quarantine system and healthcare, and budgets were tight. According to the World Health Organization (WHO) and the Vietnamese government, on 1 April 2021, Vietnam received its first shipment of 811,200 Covid-19 vaccine doses; these were shipped via COVAX, the Covid-19 Vaccine Global Access facility, with support from the WHO, United Nations Children's Fund (UNICEF), GAVI, the Vaccine Alliance and the Coalition for Epidemic

FIGURE 7.3
GDP Growth: Vietnam and Selected Countries

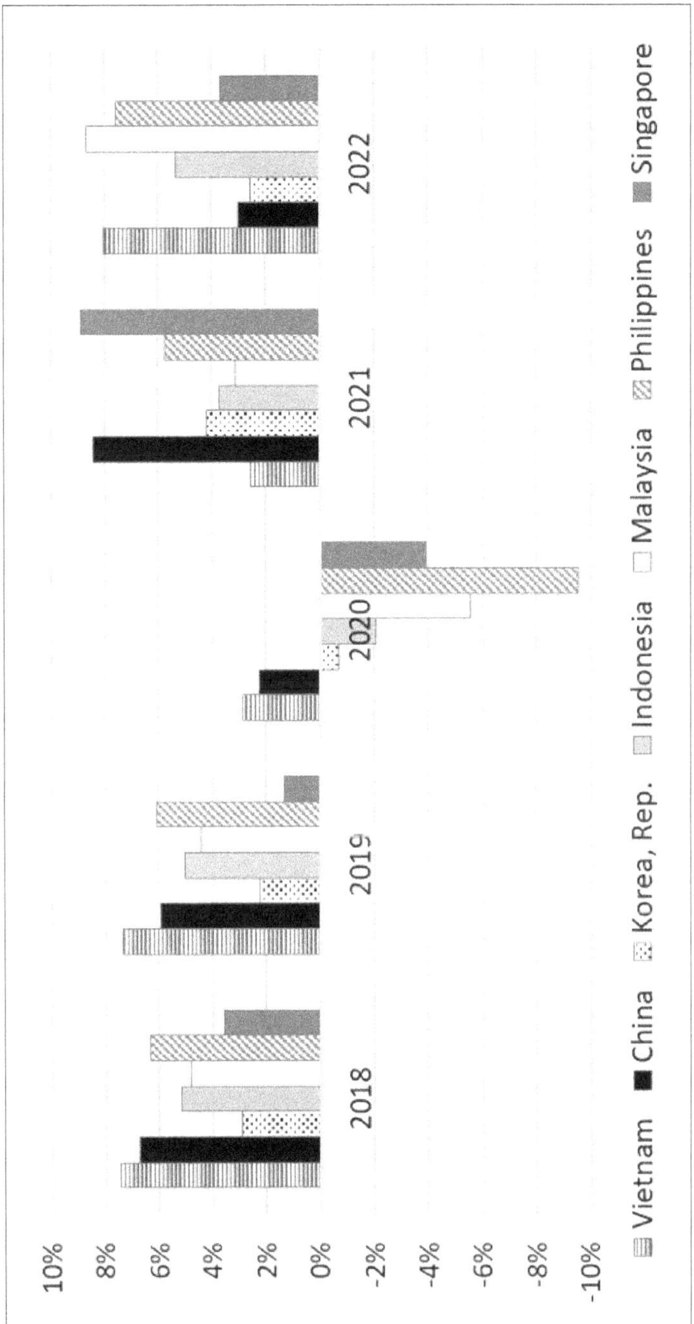

Source: World Bank's World Development Indicators (accessed 30 June 2023).

Preparedness Innovations. An additional shipment of 3,364,800 doses arrived end-May. These figures illustrate the limited quantities of vaccine secured for Vietnam. The government used multiple channels and strategies to ensure vaccine supply; COVAX was a game changer in the early days, from May 2021, as it subsidized the vaccines, but Vietnam also employed vaccine diplomacy and was given vaccines and medical equipment by international donors.

In June 2021, along with the shifting strategy from containment to vaccination, the country launched the Vietnam Fund for Vaccination and Prevention of Coronavirus Disease, a public fund to secure 120 million vaccine doses by the end of the year. The government fund was tasked with "the activities of purchasing, importing, researching and producing vaccines in the country and using Covid-19 vaccines for people". It received generous contributions from Vietnamese citizens at home and abroad, and domestic and foreign companies. South Korea, Japan and Taiwan were also among major donors, with many foreign manufacturers and companies operating in Vietnam coming from those three nations. The fund had secured US$390 million by 30 June 2022 from more than 646,442 organizations and individuals.

Among the vaccines approved by the Vietnamese Ministry of Health, the most popular were the Oxford/AstraZeneca product, Pfizer–BioNTech, Moderna and Sinopharm BIBP (Table 7.6). As of 30 June 2022, a total of 232,430,000 doses had been administered in Vietnam.[6]

TABLE 7.6
Vaccines Approved by Vietnam's Ministry of Health

Vaccine	*Manufacturer*	*Country of Origin*
Comirnaty	Pfizer/BioNTech	United States, Germany
Spikevax	Moderna	United States
Vaxzevria	Oxford/AstraZeneca	United Kingdom, Sweden
Sputnik V	Gamaleya	Russia
Ad26.COV2.S	Janssen (Johnson & Johnson)	United States
Covilo	Sinopharm	China
Covaxin	Bharat Biotech	India
Abdala	Center for Genetic Engineering and Biotechnology	Cuba

Source: Author.

Vaccinations in Vietnam began on 8 March 2021 but the roll-out was significantly slower than other countries in the region before taking off in July 2021. As of mid-August 2021, only 1 per cent of the population had been fully vaccinated (with two shots), and 7.7 per cent with just one dose. The government targeted completing vaccinations for 70 per cent of the population by mid-2022. Despite a late start, Vietnam outperformed many countries in vaccinating the majority of the population. As of 11 June 2022, Vietnam had administered more than 223 million vaccine doses, with the basic coverage in people aged twelve years and older approximately 100 per cent.

CONCLUSION

For the first eighteen months of the pandemic, the Vietnamese government pursued an ambitious strategy of zero infection, deploying a rigorous system of contact tracing once an individual was identified as positive (F0). Highly restrictive measures were employed, most notably compulsory quarantine in government-run or -approved facilities, though as Vietnam gained experience, quarantine at home was approved.

These measures enabled Vietnam to successfully contain the spread of Covid-19, but came at a significant cost to the economy. In 2020, the first year of the pandemic, Vietnam was able to limit the number of deaths (35 in 2020) and also to record positive GDP growth of 2.9 per cent. A study conducted in twenty-three countries in May 2020 found that Vietnamese respondents reported the second-highest level of satisfaction after China with their government's Covid-19 response; 77 per cent of those surveyed in Vietnam rated the government response positively (Gilchrist 2020).

The success, however, lasted for only eighteen months, until the emergence of the Delta variant, which marked the fourth wave of the Covid-19 pandemic in Vietnam. In this phase, the country was hit hard with rising cases and deaths at a level on par with the global averages. However, extensive contact tracing and quarantine systems, lockdowns, social distancing and accelerated vaccinations helped Vietnam to gradually return to normal. These measures to contain the spread of the virus were complemented by measures to build economic recovery while also safely adapting to the situation for the short and long terms. The government's announcement at end-August 2021, that Vietnam perhaps faced a protracted battle and could not rely indefinitely on closures and quarantines, marked a major change in strategy, a change in mentality and a move towards an accelerated vaccination campaign and phasing out of restrictions.

Vietnam was not alone in its vaccine shortage. Indeed, Vietnam's case exemplifies the difficulties of combating the pandemic with limited resources, a situation that was exacerbated by institutional rigidities, most notably the government procurement regulations. Strong governance can help control the spread, but for long-term recovery, government resources that can be made available quickly are critical for securing vaccines. In its vaccination campaign, Vietnam, like most developing countries, lagged behind developed countries, which were able to secure vaccines earlier and moved more quickly into advanced phases of immunization.

On 11 October 2021, Resolution 128/NQ-CP of 2021 of the Government on Temporary Regulations on Safe and Flexible Adaptation and Effective Control of the Covid-19 Epidemic paved the way for Vietnam to transition to a new normal (Government of Vietnam 2021b). In March 2022, international flights were resumed, boosting tourism (Government Office 2022). On 15 May 2022, Vietnam dropped all Covid-19 testing requirements for international arrivals after a decrease in cases, aligned with its strategy of opening up. High-contact services recovered strongly, thanks in large part to a significant increase in spending by Vietnam's rapidly growing middle class, who had saved during the two years of the pandemic. In May 2021, Vietnam and the Philippines logged their best performances in the Nikkei's Covid-19 Recovery Index, a monthly ranking of countries and regions on infection management, vaccine roll-outs and social mobility, as both countries managed to ease restrictions while keeping infections low.

According to the General Statistics Office of Vietnam (2022), the country ended the first quarter of 2022 with a GDP growth of 5.03 per cent. In the second quarter of 2022, Vietnam performed even better, with a growth of 7.72 per cent year-on-year, and higher than the growth for the same quarter in each year from 2011 to 2021. The outlook for the country remains promising, with Vietnam maintaining its image as a safe, attractive and promising destination for foreign investors. Policymaking based on responsiveness, pragmatism and adaptability, which helped steer the country through the pandemic, will continue to serve Vietnam well.

Notes

1. The World Health Organization declared the Covid-19 outbreak a public health emergency of international concern on 30 January 2020, and a pandemic on 11 March 2020.
2. The impacted provinces and cities include: Ho Chi Minh city, Binh Duong, Dong Nai, Can Tho, Binh Phuoc, Tay Ninh, Ba Ria – Vung Tau, Tien Giang, Long An, Vinh Long, Dong Thap, Ben Tre, Hau Giang, An Giang, Bac Lieu, Soc Trang, Tra Vinh, Ca Mau, and Kien Giang.
3. Prior to Covid-19, these workers tended to rent only a place to sleep for when they were not working. It was therefore common to find many people sharing a room. During the pandemic, the concentration of people at home made it extremely difficult to respect social distancing requirements.
4. The contact tracing proceeded as follows (Pollack et al. 2021):
    - Once a patient with Covid-19 was identified (F0), local public health officials, with support from health professionals, security officers, the military and other civil servants worked with the patient to identify who they might have been in contact with and infected in the preceding fourteen days.
    - All close contacts (F1), defined as people who had been within approximately two metres of or had prolonged contact of thirty minutes or more with a confirmed Covid-19 case, were identified and tested for the virus.
    - If F1s tested positive for the virus, they were placed in isolation at a hospital. All Covid-19 patients in Vietnam were hospitalized at no cost to the patient, regardless of symptoms.
    - If F1s did not test positive, they were quarantined at a government-run quarantine centre for fourteen days.
    - Close contacts of the previously identified close contacts (F2s) were required to self-isolate at home for fourteen days.
    - Likewise, F3s are those who came into close contact with F2s, F4s are those who came into close contact with F3s and F5s are those who came into close contact with F4s.
5. During the pandemic, military and health facilities and schools were turned into central quarantine centres to host suspected cases (those who had come into contact with confirmed cases).
6. Covid-19 Vaccination Tracker at https://covidvax.live/location/vnm

References

Anh Minh. 2020. "Vietnam Approves $2.6 Billion Support Package for Covid-19 Crisis Victims". *VnExpress International*. 10 April 2020. https://e.vnexpress.net/news/business/economy/vietnam-approves-2-6-billion-support-package-for-covid-19-crisis-victims-4082541.html (accessed 30 June 2023).

CBS News. 2020. "Catchy PSA about Coronavirus Turns into Viral TikTok Challenge about Washing Your Hands". https://www.cbsnews.com/news/coronavirus-prevention-vietnam-song-ghen-co-vy-tik-tok-challenge-about-washing-hands-quang-dang-john-oliver/ (accessed 30 June 2023).

CDC (Centers for Disease Control and Prevention). 2021. "Symptoms of COVID-19". Updated 15 March 2024. https://www.cdc.gov/coronavirus/2019-ncov/symptoms-testing/symptoms.html (accessed 30 June 2023).

Chau, An. 2020. "Vietnam Develops Coronavirus Contact Tracing App". *VnExpress*, 21 April 2020. https://e.vnexpress.net/news/news/vietnam-develops-coronavirus-contact-tracing-app-4087702.html (accessed 30 June 2023).

General Department of Preventive Medicine. 2022. *Covid-19 Update Newsletter June 30, 2022*. https://vncdc.gov.vn/ban-tin-cap- nhat-covid-19-ngay-3062022-nd16977.html (accessed 30 June 2023).

General Statistics Office. 2022. Report on Socio-economic Situation in Q4 and 2022. https://www.gso.gov.vn/du-lieu-va-so-lieu-thong-ke/2022/12/bao-cao-tinh-hinh-kinh-te-xa-hoi-quy-iv-va-nam-2022/ (accessed 30 June 2023).

Gilchrist, Karen. 2020. "China Gets Top Score as Citizens Rank Their Governments' Response to the Coronavirus Outbreak". *CNBC News*, 6 May 2020. https://www.cnbc.com/2020/05/07 /coronavirus-china-vietnam-uae-top-list-as-citizens-rank-government-response.html (accessed 30 June 2023).

Government Office. 2020. "Imprint of the 2020 Guidance and Administration Documents". Notice of Prime Minister's Opinion, 3 January 2021. https://vpcp.chinhphu.vn/dau-an-van-ban-chi-dao-dieu-hanh-nam-2020-11525325.htm (accessed 30 June 2023).

———. 2022. "Official Dispatch No. 1606/VPCP-QHQT on Resumption of Immigration Services of Vietnam". 15 March 2022. https://lawnet.vn/en/cv/Official-Dispatch-1606-VPCP-QHQT-2022-Resumption-of-immigration-services-of-Vietnam-7BDF9.html (accessed 30 June 2023).

Government of Vietnam. 2020. "Conclusion of Prime Minister Nguyen Xuan Phuc after the Government Meeting on Covid-19 Control Measures". Notice No. 164/TB-VPCP, Government Office, 23 April 2020. https://lawnet.vn/en/vb/Notice-164-TB-VPCP-2020-conclusion-of-the-Prime-Minister-Covid-19-control-measures-6BAC9.html

———. 2021a. "Official Dispatch No. 969/TTg-KGVX dated 17 July 2021 on Implementing Social Distancing to Prevent and Control Epidemics in Some Localities". https://vanban.chinhphu.vn/default.aspx?pageid=27160&docid=203676 (accessed 30 June 2023).

———. 2021b. "Resolution 128/NQ-CP of 2021 of the Government on Temporary Regulations on Safe and Flexible Adaptation and Effective Control of the Covid-19 Epidemic". 11 October 2021. https://thuvienphapluat.vn/van-ban/the-thao-y-te/Nghi-quyet-128-NQ-CP-2021-Quy-dinh-tam-thoi-thich-ung-an-toan-linh-hoat-dich-COVID19-490931.aspx (accessed 30 June 2023).

He, Xi., Eric. H.Y. Lau, Peng Wu, Xilong Deng, Jian Wang, Xinxin Hao, Yiu Chung Lau, et al. 2020. "Temporal Dynamics in Viral Shedding and Transmissibility of COVID-19". *Nature Medicine* 26: 672–75. https://doi.org/10.1038/s41591-020-0869-5

Huong Le Thu. 2021. "Delta Variant Outbreak Challenges Vietnam's Covid-19 Response Strategy". Brookings Institute, 11 August 2021. https://www.brookings.edu/articles/delta-variant-outbreak-challenges-vietnams-covid-19-response-strategy/ (accessed 30 June 2023).

IMF (International Monetary Fund). 2021. "Vietnam: 2020 Article IV Consultation–Press Release; Staff Report; and Statement by the Executive Director for Vietnam". IMF Country Report No. 21/42, 1 March 2021. https://www.imf.org/en/Publications/CR/Issues/2021/02/24/Vietnam-2020-Article-IV-Consultation-Press-Release-Staff-Report-and-Statement-by-the-50121 (accessed 30 June 2023).

La, Viet-Phuong, Thanh-Hang Pham, Manh-Toan Ho, Minh-Hoang Nguyen, Khanh-Linh P. Nguyen, Thu-Trang Vuong, Hong-Kong T. Nguyen, et al. 2020. "Policy Response, Social Media and Science Journalism for the Sustainability of the Public Health System amid the COVID-19 Outbreak: The Vietnam Lessons". *Sustainability* 12, no. 7: 2,931. https://doi.org/10.3390/su12072931 (accessed 30 June 2023).

Lahiff, Edward, Pham Quang Minh, and Nguyễn Trọng Chính. 2022. "Vietnam's Response to the Covid-19 Pandemic". In *Covid-19, the Global South and the Pandemic's Development Impact*, edited by Gerard McCann, Nita Mishra and Padraig Carmody, pp. 181–96. Bristol, United Kingdom: Bristol University Press.

Ministry of Finance. 2020. "Chi ngân sách gần 18 nghìn tỷ đồng cho công tác phòng chống Covid-19" [Budget spending of nearly VND18 trillion for Covid-19 prevention]. https://mof.gov.vn/webcenter/portal/btcvn/pages_r/l/tin-bo-tai-chinh?dDocName=MOFUCM183497 (accessed 30 June 2023).

Ministry of Health. n.d. "Information Portal of the Ministry of Health about the

Covid-19 Respiratory Disease Outbreak". https://ncov.moh.gov.vn/ (accessed 30 June 2022).

Ministry of Planning and Investment. 2020. Foreign Investment Department, Foreign Investment Electronic Information page. "Situation of Foreign Investment Attraction in 2019". 7 January 2020. https://fia.mpi.gov.vn/Detail/CatID/f3cb5873-74b1-4a47-a57c-a491e0be4051/NewsID/944d566b-fb6f-457d-a025-de823c02785f (accessed 30 June 2023).

Nguyen, Hong Kong, and Tung Manh Ho. 2020. "Vietnam's COVID-19 Strategy: Mobilizing Public Compliance Via Accurate and Credible Communications.". *ISEAS Perspective*, no. 2020/69. 25 June 2020. https://www.iseas.edu.sg/wp-content/uploads/2020/05/ISEAS_Perspective_2020_69.pdf (accessed 30 June 2023).

Nguyen Quynh, and Nguyen Dieu Tu Uyen. 2020. "Vietnam Orders 15-day Nationwide Isolation From April 1". Bloomberg, 31 March 2020. https://www.bloomberg.com/news/articles/2020-03-31/vietnam-orders-15-day-nationwide-isolation-from-april-1#xj4y7vzkg (accessed 30 June 2023).

OECD (Organization for Economic Co-operation and Development). 2015. *The Changing Face of Strategic Crisis Management.* OECD Reviews of Risk Management Policies. Paris: OECD Publishing. https://doi.org/10.1787/9789264249127-en

Our World in Data. n.d. "Cumulative Confirmed COVID-19 Cases and Deaths, Vietnam". https://ourworldindata.org/grapher/cumulative-deaths-and-cases-covid-19?tab=chart&country=~VNM (accessed 30 June 2023).

Pham, Quang Thai, Maia A. Rabaa, Duong Huy Loung, Dang Quang Tan, Tran Dai Quang, Ha-Linh Quach, Ngoc-Anh Hoang Thi, et al. 2021. "The First 100 Days of SARS-CoV-2 Control in Vietnam". *Clinical Infectious Diseases* 72, no. 9: e334–e342. https://doi.org/10.1093/cid/ciaa1130

Pollack, Todd, Guy Thwaites, Maia Rabaa, Marc Choisy, Rogier van Doorn, Le Van Tan, Duong Huy Luong, et al. 2021. "Emerging Covid-19 Success Story: Vietnam's Commitment to Containment". Our World in Data, 5 March 2021. https://ourworldindata.org/covid-exemplar-vietnam (accessed 30 June 2023).

Thanh Niên. 2021. "'Ai ở đâu, ở yên đó': Lực lượng quân đội đồng loạt xuất quân hỗ trợ người dân chống dịch Covid-19" ['Whoever is there, stay there': Military forces simultaneously deploy to support people fighting the Covid-19 epidemic"]. https://thanhnien.vn/ai-o-dau-o-yen-do-luc-luong-quan-doi-dong-loat-xuat-quan-ho-tro-nguoi-dan-chong-dich-covid-19-1851103781.htm (accessed 30 June 2023).

Thuy Dung. 2022. "Viet Nam to Become Third Largest Economy in Southeast

Asia by 2025: IMF". *Socialist Republic of Viet Nam Government News,* 11 July 2022. https://en.baochinhphu.vn/viet-nam-to-become-third-largest-economy-in-southeast-asia-by-2025-imf-111220611102129165.htm (accessed 30 June 2023).

Van Duan. 2020. "In the 'Epidemic Centre' Son Loi, before G Lifted the Blockade and Quarantine". *Người lao động*, 3 March, 2020. https://nld.com.vn/thoi-su/vao-tam-dich-son-loi-truoc-gio-g-do-bo-lenh-phong-toa-cach-ly-20200303172344818.htm (accessed 30 June 2023).

Vietnamnet. 2020a. "Lockdown on COVID-19 Cluster in Vinh Phuc Lifted". 4 March 2020. https://vietnamnet.vn/en/lockdown-on-covid-19-cluster-in-vinh-phuc-lifted-621366.html (accessed 30 June 2023).

———. 2020b. "Lockdown on Hanoi's Covid-19-Hit Area Lifted". 22 March 2020. https://vietnamnet.vn/en/lockdown-on-hanois-covid-19-hit-area-lifted-626115.html (accessed 30 June 2023).

Vietnamplus. 2022. "Government's Pandemic Fight Efforts Pay Off". 5 September 2022. https://special.vietnamplus.vn/2022/05/09/en-governments-pandemic-fight/ (accessed 30 June 2023).

World Bank. 2021. *A Year Deferred: Early Experiences and Lessons from Covid-19 in Vietnam (English)*. Washington, DC: World Bank Group. http://documents.worldbank.org/curated/en/826921633442977133/A-Year-Deferred-Early-Experiences-and-Lessons-from-Covid-19-in-Vietnam

Zibaseresht, Ramin. 2020. "How to Respond to the Ongoing Pandemic Outbreak of the Coronavirus Disease (Covid-19)". *European Journal of Biomedical and Pharmaceutical Sciences* 7, no. 6: 1–6.

COMPARATIVE SYNTHESIS

Lockdown Rationales, Approaches and Consequences, Based on the Experience of Indonesia, the Philippines and Vietnam

Jayant Menon

Indonesia, the Philippines and Vietnam, the three most populous countries in the Association of Southeast Asian Nations (ASEAN), account for almost 500 million people or three-quarters of the bloc's total population. Despite this, the three countries account for disproportionally less of the region's gross domestic product (GDP), less than two-thirds, reflecting the fact that they are home to the majority of the region's poor and near-poor. In terms of the level of economic and social development, Indonesia, the Philippines and Vietnam sit between ASEAN's least developed countries—Cambodia, Laos and Myanmar—and its richer upper-middle-income and high-income countries. However, they share many of the challenges and constraints faced by Cambodia, Laos and Myanmar in managing the pandemic, albeit perhaps in less severe and constraining ways. That is, like Cambodia, Laos and Myanmar they had to manage the pandemic with limited government resources and a weak healthcare system with limited and unequal access. They also had to deal with inadequate logistical and other infrastructure that affected the management of mobility restrictions and the distribution of financial assistance and vaccines.

Although Indonesia, the Philippines and Vietnam share many economic and social characteristics, each employed a different approach to managing the pandemic at its various stages. Not surprisingly, therefore, each experienced varying degrees of success in managing health and economic impacts. The chapter authors for each country have examined the different approaches taken, the reasons behind the approach and the consequences on health and economic outcomes, drawing lessons for the management of future pandemics.

LOCKDOWN, CONTAINMENT, VACCINATION

The Philippines responded to the initial outbreak by trying to impose one of the world's longest and most stringent general lockdowns. As noted by the chapter authors, the Philippines ranked 12th out of 185 countries in terms of stringency of measures based on a widely cited index developed by the University of Oxford (Oxford Covid-19 Government Response Tracker and Blavatnik School of Government 2022). This resulted in the largest fall in GDP in 2020 among ASEAN countries, with the economy contracting by almost 10 per cent. Despite the draconian response, the Philippines could not contain community transmission or have much of an impact on flattening the infection curve. There are a number of reasons for this, which we will consider.

In contrast to the Philippines, the authors of the Indonesia chapter in this section highlight how the country resisted a general lockdown, focusing instead on a host of less stringent social distancing measures. As a result, it experienced one of the smallest reductions in GDP in 2020 among ASEAN countries; the economy contracted by only about 2 per cent. Given this approach, it is perhaps unsurprising that Indonesia could not contain transmission to any significant degree and it experienced an outbreak similar to that in the Philippines.

Vietnam responded to the initial outbreak with a national lockdown but moved quickly to more targeted and time-bound measures. For instance, its second outbreak in July 2020 involved social distancing measures only in the city of Da Nang. This approach allowed Vietnam to get through the pandemic without suffering a recession—the only country in ASEAN to do so. In fact, the economy expanded by almost 3 per cent in 2020. While both Indonesia and the Philippines could not avoid major outbreaks, Vietnam was much more successful in doing so and stood out in the region for its success in containing the initial outbreak, which occurred in the second quarter of 2020. It was the only ASEAN country that managed to get through the first outbreak without recording a single fatality. The Vietnam chapter authors attribute part of the country's success to its centralized planning system; this aided in the implementation of the original lockdown and the targeted measures subsequently, enabling greater oversight and monitoring.

When the Delta strain emerged in 2021, it changed almost everything by producing the worst outbreaks throughout the region. The high transmissibility of this virulent strain brought into question the efficacy of the protocols that had worked with the initial outbreak, such as vigilant testing and tracing, and threatened to overwhelm healthcare systems. Vietnam succumbed early, Indonesia replaced India as the epicentre for a period, and the Philippines was late but eventually went through the inevitable spikes seen elsewhere. All three countries struggled to contain the spread of this highly transmissible variant while trying to revive their economies after more than a year of containment measures. All three also struggled to ramp up their vaccination drives and faced different supply (access to vaccines), demand (vaccine hesitancy) and other constraints, including logistical difficulties. While access to an adequate supply of vaccines was a problem in all three countries, vaccine hesitancy appeared to be the highest in the Philippines. When supply eventually caught up with demand, Vietnam faced fewer logistical challenges in the roll-out, probably due to its centralized planning system, compared to the Philippines and Indonesia.

BALANCING PRIORITIES, HELPING THE POOR, MANAGING BORDER CLOSURES

What lessons can be drawn from the experience of these three countries to avoid repeating mistakes when the next pandemic hits?

The first is similar to a lesson learnt from Cambodia, Laos and Myanmar, because it is closely linked to the level of economic development: it is that the apparent trade-off between lives and livelihoods, or health and economy, may not exist at the same degree or operate in the same way in developing countries as it might in developed ones. There are important differences between developing and developed countries, exemplified by the experiences of Indonesia, the Philippines and Vietnam, that need to be considered in designing policies that aim to minimize overall harm in the balancing act between health and economy. For the poor who live hand to mouth and who still number in the millions in Indonesia, the Philippines and Vietnam, the deprivation of livelihoods through stringent and prolonged lockdowns can often lead to a shortening or even loss of life when public social safety nets are weak or missing.

This was clearly evident in the experience of Indonesia as compared to the Philippines in dealing with the initial outbreak. While both countries suffered massive outbreaks, Indonesia was able to minimize the overall harm from the pandemic and avoid a deep recession by resisting a prolonged general lockdown. The Philippines could not, and the harm from the massive economic contraction probably rivalled that emanating from the virus itself. Although it attempted to impose a hard, general lockdown, it could not do so for several reasons.

Not only were social safety nets weak in these countries, but many segments of society, such as informal workers and other marginalized groups, were not covered at all. The homeless, for instance, are intrinsically mobile populations and cannot be locked down unless special facilities are provided for them and their basic needs are catered for. The poor who have shelter but do not have access to basic facilities such as running water may be forced to breach lockdowns simply to survive. Similarly, informal workers such as scavengers or unrecorded migrant workers (more prevalent in Vietnam than in Indonesia or the Philippines) who are not covered by public social safety nets would rather bear the consequences of breaching lockdown measures than risk starving to death. The predicament of the poor was captured succinctly in a sign outside a major scavenger community at the Payatas rubbish dump in the Philippines: it read "Feed us, or free us!".

These conditions and circumstances were prevalent in all three countries. They explain why the stringent and prolonged lockdown in the Philippines was limited in its ability to contain the community spread of the virus but not in inducing the deep economic recession the country endured. In this regard, it is important that the lockdowns are implemented in a way that is cognizant of local conditions and on-the-ground realities, which appeared to occur to a greater extent in Indonesia and Vietnam than in the Philippines.

When fiscal resources are limited and social safety nets are wanting, lives or livelihoods are often one and the same among the poor and the marginalized. Poor countries must consider the lives lost or shortened when livelihoods are destroyed by policies aimed at preserving an ineffectual healthcare system with lives lost directly to the virus. It would seem that Indonesia and Vietnam took greater notice of these realities in designing their pandemic response than did the Philippines. Nevertheless, all three countries, and other developing countries with large populations of poor, could probably have done more to preserve lives indirectly by safeguarding livelihoods, rather than trying to preserve lives directly through lockdowns, which had limited success in containing community spread.

The second lesson is that once a health/economy trade-off is struck, there are various ways in which the desired health and economic outcomes can be reached. In particular, there are various combinations of restrictions affecting mobility *within* and *across* national borders that can be used to minimize harm to health and the economy. While border control measures were the first policy response to the outbreak of the pandemic, they were also the last restrictions to be removed. Throughout the pandemic and through the various waves or outbreaks with the emergence of new variants, border controls were periodically tightened through country-specific travel bans and sometimes almost complete border closures. Even when domestic mobility restrictions were eased following a reduction in the rate of community transmissions, border control measures remained largely intact. That is, the gap between domestic mobility restrictions and international border controls increased consistently throughout the pandemic, irrespective of health or economic conditions.

In hindsight, it is clear that prolonged border closures weakened economic recovery by cutting off connectivity while providing a false sense of security since they did not prevent the entry of new variants. Even countries like Australia and New Zealand, which almost completely closed their borders and enjoyed the advantage of relative isolation, could not keep out the new variants. The fact that the new variants were becoming more transmissible meant that the value of border restrictions also started to fall relative to their cost to the economy. That is, once a highly transmissible variant is present in the local community, its spread will be determined mainly by the efficacy of domestic protocols, rather than border measures that aim to limit their importation. This reality seemed to have escaped the calculation of policymakers in most countries, including Indonesia, the Philippines and Vietnam.

The prolonged border closures in Indonesia, the Philippines and Vietnam had a devastating impact on their tourism sectors, as well as on the employment of low- and medium-skilled workers who are not easily moved or redeployed. It also had a bigger impact on the broader economy than suggested by the share of the tourism sector in GDP because of relatively large multiplier effects. In each country, there was a regional dimension in which the cost was concentrated; specific islands were badly affected, such as Bali in Indonesia, Boracay in the Philippines and Phu Quoc in Vietnam. Attempts to offset the loss in revenue by encouraging domestic tourism were largely unsuccessful, as the numbers and spending power of local tourists were low relative to international ones. It also failed to safeguard health since testing and quarantine protocols were mainly directed at international border crossings rather than domestic travel. Thus, the economic outcome would have been better with little or no increase in health risks if international borders had been opened earlier.

CONCLUSION

The experience of Indonesia, the Philippines and Vietnam, as documented by the chapter authors in this section, suggests that prolonged, general lockdowns cannot serve the desired objective of containing community spread if the poor cannot be adequately compensated to stay at home and/or if monitoring and oversight are weak. In this context, there is a real possibility that the loss of livelihoods from lockdowns resulted in as much harm, meaning shortening or loss of lives, as that which would have been attributable directly to increased infection rates had lockdowns been avoided. Developed country notions of the lives versus livelihoods trade-off do not always apply to developing countries that have limited resources and large populations of poor. Any pandemic response that must balance health and economy needs to consider on-the-ground realities in its design.

Once the balance between health and economy is struck, however, the combination of domestic versus border mobility restrictions needs to be carefully considered and reviewed periodically. While closing borders to guard against a new and unknown virus may have been justified at the start, the fact that border controls were the last barriers to be removed despite mounting evidence of their inability to prevent the entry of new strains was curious, to say the least. The experiences of Indonesia, the Philippines and Vietnam, as well as Cambodia, Laos, Myanmar and many others, suggest an enduring bias against the border that hurt the economy without a compensating improvement in health outcomes. This bias needs to be overcome before the next pandemic hits if we are to learn from mistakes and more successfully implement a harm minimization strategy in the future.

References

Oxford Covid-19 Government Response Tracker and Blavatnik School of Government. 2022. "Relationship between Number of COVID-19 Cases and Government Response". 1 December 2022. https://covidtracker.bsg.ox.ac.uk/stringency-map

Theme 3

POLICY COORDINATION
Horizontal and Vertical Dimensions: Indonesia, Malaysia, Thailand

8

TO BE OR NOT TO BE? Dilemmas of Covid-19 Policy Implementation and Coordination in Indonesia

Yanuar Nugroho and Sofie Syarief

INTRODUCTION

On 30 December 2022, President Joko Widodo, popularly known as Jokowi, declared an end to Indonesia's restrictions on community activities (PPKM). The wearing of masks, which had not been required for small-group outdoor activities since May 2022, was still encouraged for group indoor activities or in large crowds. The government urged the public to continue with vaccinations and waived Covid-19 testing requirements for fully vaccinated domestic and foreign travellers. The lifting of the restrictions followed the decline in infections and the government's earlier mass serology test, which took place in November and December 2021 and was publicized in March 2022. The test showed that nine out of ten Indonesians already had Covid-19 antibodies, while the infection rate had declined through 2022 as people increasingly completed their vaccination regimes. Indonesia also averted new waves of infection in the wake of the Eid-ul Fitr holiday travels in May 2022. The President's message at end-2022 marked a watershed in the country's Covid-19 journey, which had begun with his 2 March 2020 acknowledgement that the pandemic had become a top priority.

This three-year path may have concluded with the health crisis under control, but we can trace a long and fluid journey to that point. Despite the pandemic's malignancy and the seemingly simple "recipe" to control it, the fight to curb it became a highly dynamic arena of interactions between government policymakers, health practitioners, businesses, civil society organizations, media and scientists. During the pandemic, these interactions often became highly politicized. Despite knowing that the virus was spreading and understanding some of the effects on health and the economy early on, the government downplayed the dangers and seemed to prioritize protecting the economy over saving lives, even if it officially and publicly claimed otherwise. The dilemma between economy and life was reflected in the early policies and approaches to fighting the pandemic, which was incoherent and ambiguous, with occasional denialist and anti-science tendencies. The approach was complicated by structural factors, especially ambiguities inherent in the country's decentralization. The eventual priority placed on the economy can be observed in the lack of vigour and coordination in the implementation of mobility restrictions, contact tracing, case finding and vaccination, as well as the distribution of social protection and strengthening of the health system. Inadequacies in government policy implementation and coordination arguably derived from "cognitive dissonance" (Nugroho and Syarief 2021), which was worsened by severely self-serving political interests.

As the pandemic worsened in mid- to late 2020, many criticized the government's downplaying of infection and prioritizing the economy; this created tension between the government and the public, and among the public themselves. Unfortunately, the government and its supporters (meaning political parties and actors, but not necessarily the bureaucracy), instead of urgently improving policy coordination and implementation (Nugroho and Negara 2020a), often responded unfavourably, sometimes mobilizing to persecute critics online. This in turn created more criticism—not of the pandemic response, but of how the government treated its own citizens. There were also groups and parties that deliberately took political advantage of the situation and used the government's stuttering pandemic response as an opportunity for politicization.

This pattern of politicization persisted until the second wave, the Delta variant, which hit Indonesia so severely that both government and opposition were compelled to set aside their political agendas. Indeed, over the course of the pandemic, the government's policies seemed to gradually improve and become more adaptive; it began adjusting and recalibrating its response to the changing circumstances and the accumulation of knowledge on the virus and its behaviour. Arguably, the major shift began when the surge of the Delta variant in 2021 wreaked unimaginable havoc on Indonesia's health system. The system was overwhelmed by the mounting deaths and the sight of patients overflowing from hospital corridors was horrific. Since 2022, Indonesia had geared up to enter the endemic phase, which was officially announced by the government on 21 June. From then on, nationwide Covid-19 cases have been low, due in part to better coordination between authorities and the vaccination programme. There were no new waves of Delta-variant cases. Indonesia was even praised by the international community for its pandemic response (*Tempo* 2021).

This chapter offers a reflection on the government's response to the challenges and dilemmas of the pandemic from a policy perspective, particularly in the early and severe stages. We discuss the shortcomings in vertical coordination, notably the lack of central government decisiveness and leadership and the lack of effective devolution to subnational governments, which resulted in some conflicts between governments at different levels. We also delve into problems of horizontal coordination, due to lack of clarity of roles, notably some overlapping of ministerial responsibilities and the marginalization of the Minister of Health. These problems were compounded by poor communication and excessive military involvement in implementing health protocols. This chapter discusses how Indonesia could have coordinated and implemented policy responses more effectively and offers lessons for better handling of early pandemic dilemmas.

COVID-19 IMPACTS AND TURNING POINTS

The Covid-19 pandemic hit Indonesia harder than many Asian countries. While its vast population translated into a large number of cases and fatalities, the country also recorded a staggeringly high Covid-19 severity, meaning the percentage of people who needed hospitalization. By end-May 2022 (the cut-off date for the data used in this chapter), the total cumulative cases numbered 6,054,973 with 5,895,423 recoveries (97.4 per cent) and 156,591 deaths (2.6 per cent).[1] The period with the highest casualties was during the second wave when the Delta variant peaked in mid-2021, although vaccinations had already started in January 2021. Over the Delta period, the highest number of new daily cases was recorded on 15 July 2021 with 56,757 and the highest number of deaths was 2,069 on 27 July 2021 (Ministry of Health 2022c). Moreover, Indonesia's Covid-19 positive test rate was consistently around 20 per cent—sharply exceeding the 5 per cent level recommended by the World Health Organization (WHO). This made it a community transmission country (WHO 2020)—and it was so practically from the beginning of the pandemic until the Delta wave subsided in September 2021, at which the country finally saw its positive test rate descend below 5 per cent. Several months after the second wave, concern developed over the spread of the Omicron variant. First detected on 27 November 2021, Omicron peaked in January and February 2022. During this third wave, new cases peaked at 118,914 on 24 February 2022, the highest daily figure since the first coronavirus case was detected in Indonesia on 2 March 2020. At that point in time, Indonesia had the highest number of cases in Southeast Asia. From mid-March 2022 the number of cases decreased.

In terms of impacts, the pandemic almost paralysed the country, reflected in the worsening of key macroeconomic indicators: gross domestic product (GDP) growth, poverty, inequality and unemployment. The formal sector collapsed and the informal sector suffered badly although it managed to survive and help other sectors survive too. In contrast to the 1998 monetary crisis, which hit the middle-upper class harder than the lower class, the pandemic hit hard what has long been the shock-breaker in the Indonesian economy: the informal sector, especially micro and small enterprises. Many micro and small enterprises were bankrupted, and the economy contracted (Nugroho and Negara 2020b) as they make up 95 per cent of all businesses in the country.

The multidimensional impact on the economy also worsened the Jokowi administration's performance significantly. By the end of 2020,

FIGURE 8.1
Cumulative Covid-19 Cases and Deaths in Indonesia to May 2022

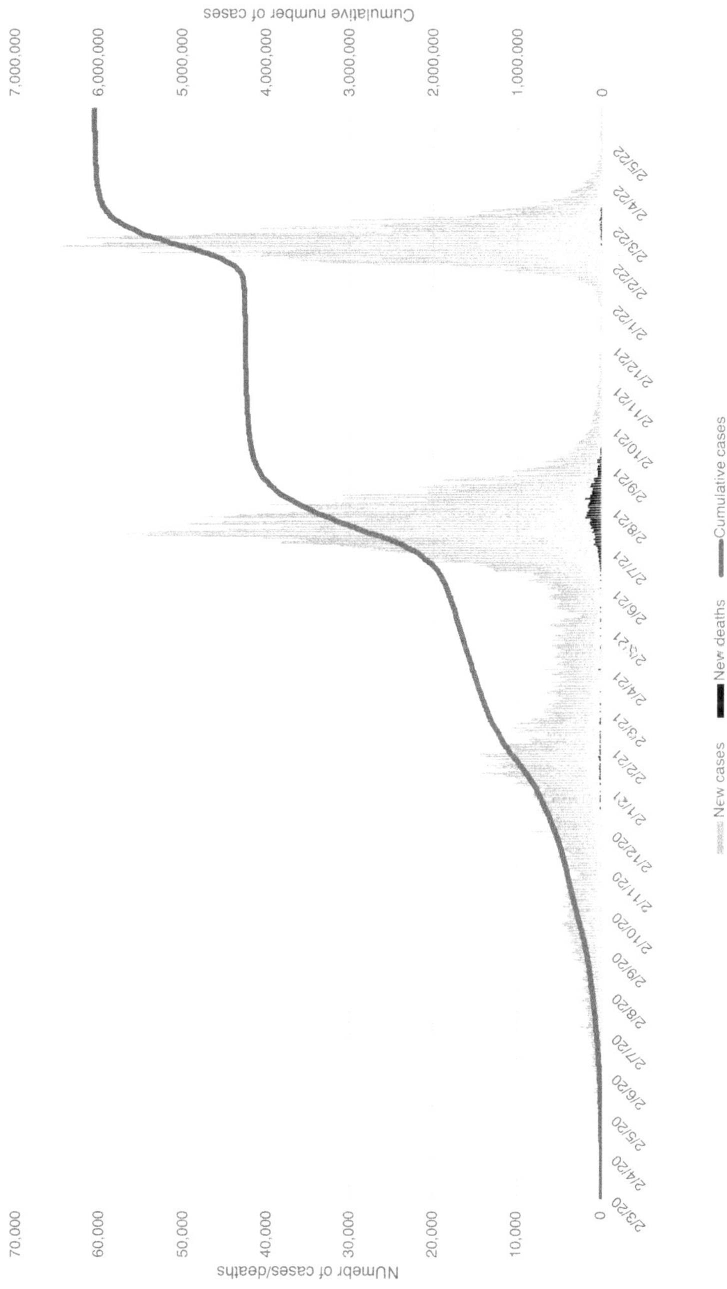

Source: Based on data from www.Covid19.go.id.

Indonesia's economic growth had contracted to minus 2.07 per cent, the unemployment rate had soared to 7.07 per cent and the poverty rate regressed back to double digits at 10.19 per cent (ADB 2021, pp. 2–3). Those macroeconomic indicators subsequently improved; from December 2021 Indonesia saw improvements in economic growth, inflation, poverty, unemployment and inequality (Table 8.1). Even at the regional level, the Indonesian economy's growth of 3.69 per cent in 2021 was higher than that of Malaysia for the same year (3.1 per cent), Vietnam (2.6 per cent) and Thailand (1.6 per cent). However, such achievements are insufficient if Indonesia wants to get back on track to reach its goal of being the fourth- or fifth-largest world economy by 2045 and to fully recover from the pandemic-driven recession. Growth was targeted for 5.2 per cent for 2022, in real terms and controlling for inflation (Media Indonesia 2022), and economic recovery became the focus of the Indonesian government agenda.

The government obviously worked hard but could not focus on containing the pandemic due to its concern about the economy. Its attempts to curb the pandemic through policies and institutional arrangements were often cancelled out by other policies which prioritized economy over health.

TABLE 8.1
Indonesia's Macroeconomic Indicators Before and During Covid-19

Item	*2018*	*2019*	*2020*	*2021*		*2022*
				Projection	*Actual*	*Projection*
GDP Growth (%)	5.2	5.0	–2.07	3.5–4.0	3.69	5.2
Inflation (%)	3.13	2.72	1.68	3.00	1.87	3.0
Unemployment (%)	5.3	5.3	7.07	5.9–6.5 (2021)	6.49 (9M)	5.5–6.3
Poverty Rate (%)	9.66	9.22	10.19	9.2–9.7 (2021)	9.71 (9M)	8.5–9.0
Gini Index	0.389	0.382	0.381	0.377–0.382 (2021)	0.381 (9M)	0.376–0.378
Human Development Index	71.39	71.92	71.94	72.69	72.29	73.41–73.46

Source: Ministry of Finance; Ministry of National Development Planning; Statistics Indonesia.

The economy began to recover only in the second quarter of 2021 after a period of contraction from the second quarter of 2020 until the end of the first quarter of 2021. The government's economic stimulus and social assistance packages also contributed to the economic recovery.

Government policies for pandemic handling, particularly its mobility restrictions, health protocol and vaccination, are summarized and depicted in the following section.

The first case of Covid-19 was reported in Indonesia on 2 March 2020. A government spokesperson was appointed on 3 March 2020 to coordinate public communications of the government's policy to strengthen public health services to contain the virus and minimize the economic impact of the pandemic. On 13 March 2020, the government established the Covid-19 Response Acceleration Task Force,[2] and on 31 March 2020 it declared Covid-19 a public health emergency, imposed stringent social restrictions[3] and issued several fiscal policies to contain the pandemic and mitigate its impact on the economy.[4] On 20 July 2021, the government set up an inter-ministerial committee to handle the pandemic and recover the national economy (known as Komite Percepatan Penanganan Covid-19 dan Pemulihan Ekonomi Nasional or KPCPEN) (Figure 8.2).[5] For overall pandemic handling and economic recovery, the government allocated US$46.7 billion (1.19 per cent of GDP) in 2020. Of this amount, only 80 per cent was disbursed. In 2021, this allocation increased by 2.68 per cent to US$47.9 billion and disbursement increased to 87.77 per cent (ADB 2022, p. 9).

Several measures were implemented to, as argued by the government, strike a balance between containing the pandemic and protecting the economy. These measures included large-scale restrictions on social activity, mask-wearing and hygiene campaigns, reallocation of state budget for pandemic response and distribution of social assistance. But the spread of Covid-19 was worrying. While it took 8.5 months from March 2020 to the end of November 2020 to reach 500,000 cases, it took only 2 months from end-November 2020 to end-January 2021 for that number to double (Figure 8.1). The pandemic curve did not show signs of flattening, and in the second quarter of 2021 the second wave, the Delta variant, hit severely. Vaccinations started in January 2021, but uptake was not fast enough to prevent the deadly Delta variant from spreading quickly, although it is

FIGURE 8.2
Daily Cases and Related Measures and Policies, March to December 2020

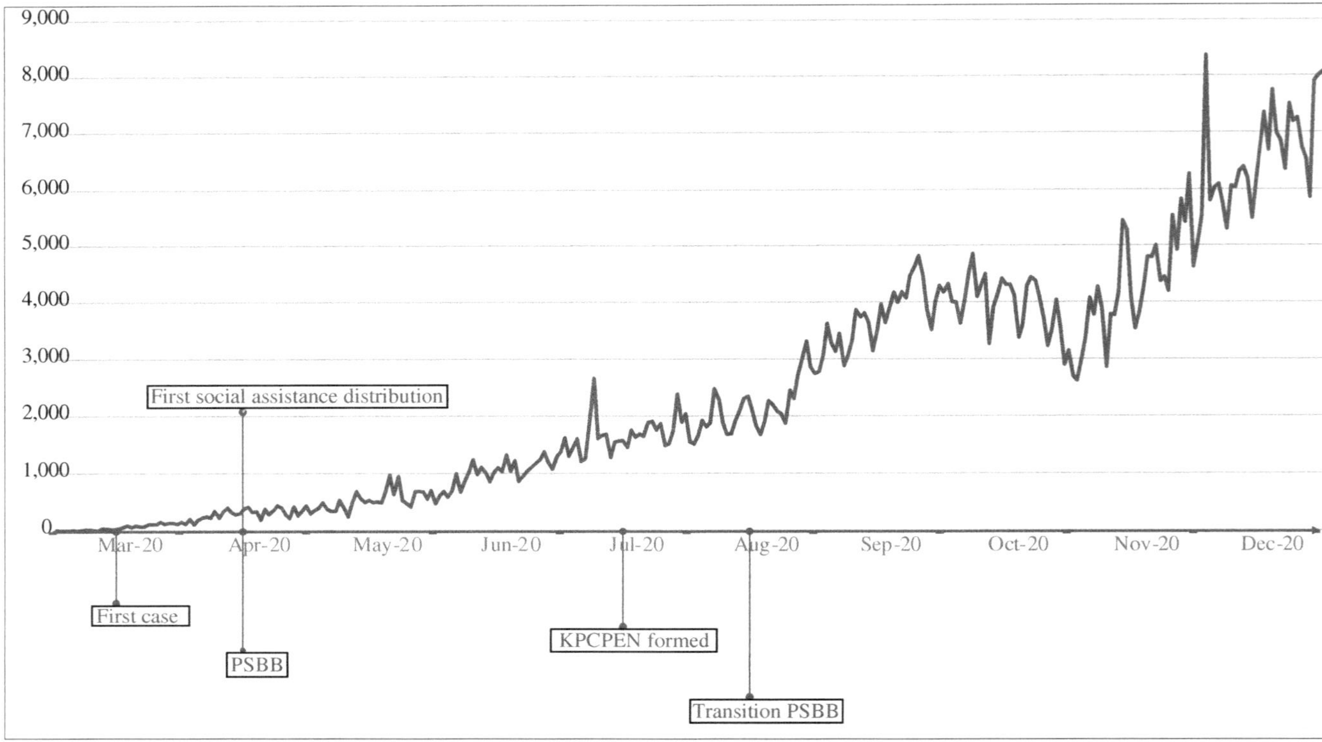

Notes: PSBB: *pembatasan sosial berskala besar* (large-scale social restrictions); KPCPEN: Komite Percepatan Penanganan Covid-19 dan Pemulihan Ekonomi Nasional (Committee for Acceleration of Covid-19 Response and National Economic Recovery).
Source: Based on media reports and data from www.covid19.go.id.

believed that vaccinations helped reduce the fatality rate (Watson et al. 2022) (Figure 8.3).

The game-changers in 2021 were vaccination and economic revitalization. In this respect, the government devised two broad strategies, the National Covid-19 Vaccination Program and incentives to boost production, consumption and investment. The roll-out of vaccinations began on 13 January 2021 and the programme was divided into four phases. The first two phases were initially planned for January to April 2021, prioritizing medical workers, public service employees and the elderly. The third and fourth phases of the vaccination programme were anticipated to take place from April 2021 to March 2022, targeting individuals living in high-risk areas (e.g., dense urban communities, traditional markets) and the remaining citizens. To obtain herd immunity, Indonesia needed to vaccinate around 181.5 million people (70 per cent of the population). Six months into the programme, the government revised the vaccination targets, perhaps realizing the inaccuracies of the initial data, particularly as relating to the vulnerable.

Table 8.2 details the vaccination plan, targets and realization. The booster shot for Covid-19 vaccine, which had started on 23 July 2021 focusing only on healthcare workers, was provided free of charge to the public from 12 January 2022 for those aged 18 years and above six months or more after they had received their second shot. According to the Ministry of Health, priority was given to the elderly and immunocompromised individuals. Sinovac, AstraZeneca, Moderna, Pfizer and Zifivax were used for the booster shots.

In addition to the national vaccination programme, the government also allowed a paid vaccination scheme (Vaksinasi Gotong Royong*).* The scheme, proposed by the Indonesia Chamber of Commerce, officially started on 18 May 2021. It was mandated to use different vaccines—Sinopharm and Cansino—than those used in the national vaccination programme. In this scheme, companies would bear the vaccination cost for employees and their families and other related individuals. The vaccination cost to companies participating in the scheme was set at IDR188,984 (US$13.03) per person. It aimed to vaccinate 7.5 million people. By 31 December 2021 (after seven months of implementation), 1,298,516 people had received the first dose and 1,222,423 people also a second. The scheme had minimal

FIGURE 8.3
Daily Cases and Related Measures and Policies, January to December 2021

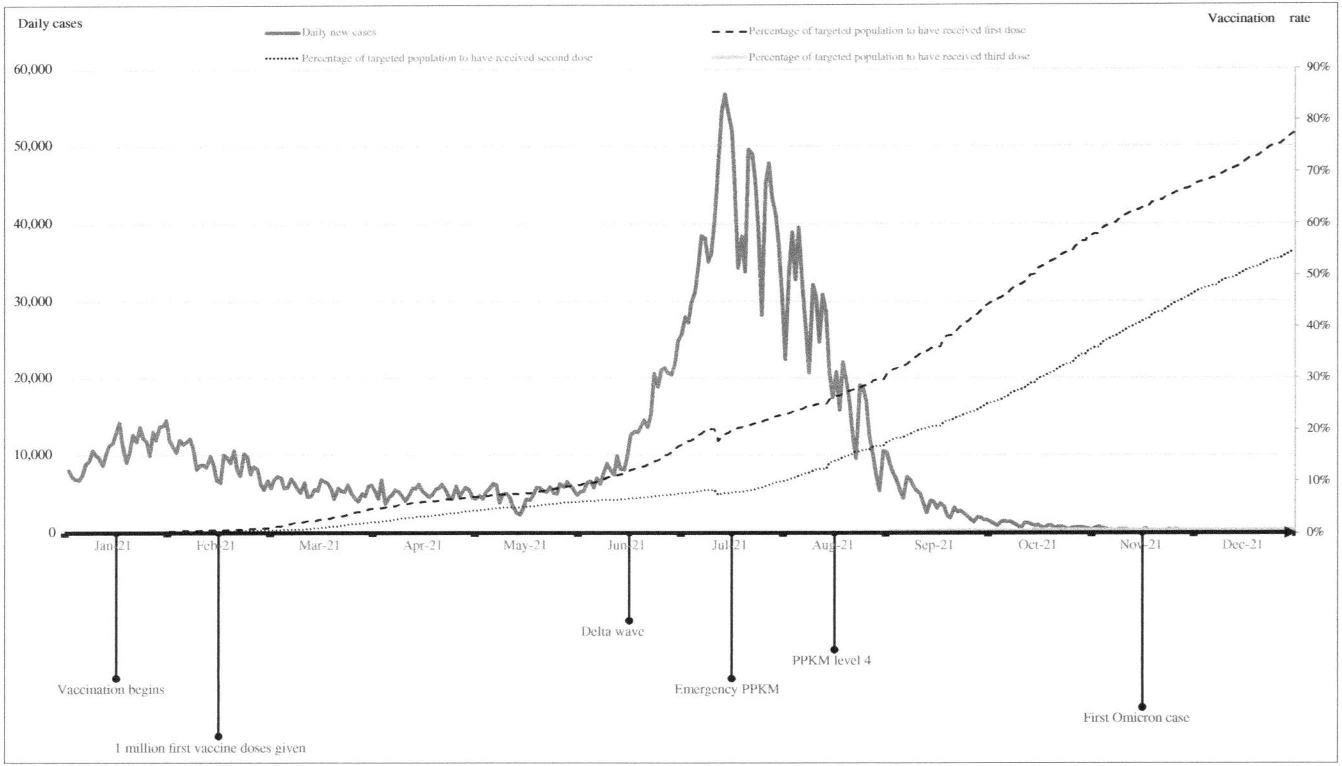

Note: PPKM: *pemberlakukan pembatasan kegiatan masyarakat* (enforcement of restrictions on community activities)
Source: Based on media reports and data from www.covid19.go.id.

TABLE 8.2
Indonesia's Covid-19 Vaccination Programme

Phase	*Groups*	*Targeted Population (Target Set January 2021)*	*Revised Targeted Population (Revised July 2021)*	*Realization*[f]			
				First Dose	*Second Dose*	*Third Dose*	*Fourth Dose*
1	Medical workers	1,300 000	1,468,764	2,049,738	2,012,115	1,810,104	824,350
2	Public service employees	17,400 000	17,327,167	18,305,772	17,079,142	9,738,732	0
	Elderly (> 63 years old)	21,500 000	21,553,118	18,320,332	15,221,773	7,244,681	413,295
3	Vulnerable citizens (living in high-risk areas)	63,900 000	141,211,181[b]	117,103,576	99,628,231	48,210,624	0
4	Other citizens (assessed based on age and vaccine availability vaccine)	77,400 000					
	Age 12–17 years old		26,705,490[c]	25,534,321	22,328,989	1,507,480	–
	Age 6–11 years old		26,400,300[d]	21,709,786	17,627,858	1,712	–
	TOTAL	181,500,000[a]	208,265,720[e]	203,023,525	173,898,108	68,513,333	1,237,645

Notes:

a. Number of individuals targeted to receive two doses of vaccine. (Indonesia did not use the one-dose Johnson & Johnson vaccine in its vaccination programme.)
b. The category "other citizens" or "general public" originally targeted for vaccination in phase four was moved to the revised phase three.
c. Revision was announced on 13 July 2021.
d. Targeted population in the 6–11 age group was based on the BPS 2020 national population census.
e. Targeted population in the 6–11 age group is not included in the total target of vaccinated individuals.
f. Data as per 24 January 2023.

Source: Ministry of Health (24 January 2023)

take-up. It was reported that approximately 28,000 corporations had enlisted in the scheme by mid-June 2021, targeting 10.5 million individuals (Waseso 2021). However, by 21 October, only 1,838 corporations had carried out vaccinations, administering 3.6 million doses, and 3.9 million vaccine doses were still available.[6] Further, approaching the vaccines' expiration in 2023, in November 2022 there were still 3.2 million doses left, and these were taken over by the Ministry of Health to avoid losses (Bio Farma 2023).

In the period January to May 2022, despite the third wave of Omicron at the beginning of the year, the situation improved substantially. The economy had slowly but steadily recovered, as indicated by GDP growth—2.07 per cent for 2020 to 3.69 per cent for the first nine months of 2021. The Ministry of Finance projected growth for 2022 at 5.2 per cent, and actual growth was 5.31 per cent (Table 8.1).

Indonesia began 2022 with restrictions on public activities (PPKM) at level 3 (level 4 being the strictest). Despite the country recording its highest-ever daily cases at the end of February 2022, in early March the government dropped the requirement that domestic travellers (on all forms of transport) take polymerase chain reaction (PCR) and antigen tests (Figure 8.4). In May 2022, President Jokowi announced that Indonesia had transitioned from pandemic to endemic after the WHO pronounced that the pandemic had ended. For Indonesia, this culminated in the cessation of all Covid-19 restrictions in December 2022.

Reflecting on the handling of the pandemic from March 2020 to May 2022, while the situation improved significantly over time, Indonesia experienced a grave period from the beginning and through the second wave, the Delta variant, which accounted for the bulk of Covid-19 deaths. It is important therefore to draw lessons on how the government responded to the pandemic from the policy perspective, particularly policy coordination, implementation and communication.

POLICY COORDINATION: THEORY, STRUCTURE AND COVID-19 OUTCOMES

Theoretical Foundations and Indonesian Context

To help us understand the nature of public policy, particularly in the context of Indonesia during the pandemic, we propose Thomas Dye's best-known,

FIGURE 8.4
Daily Cases and Related Measures and Policies, January to May 2022

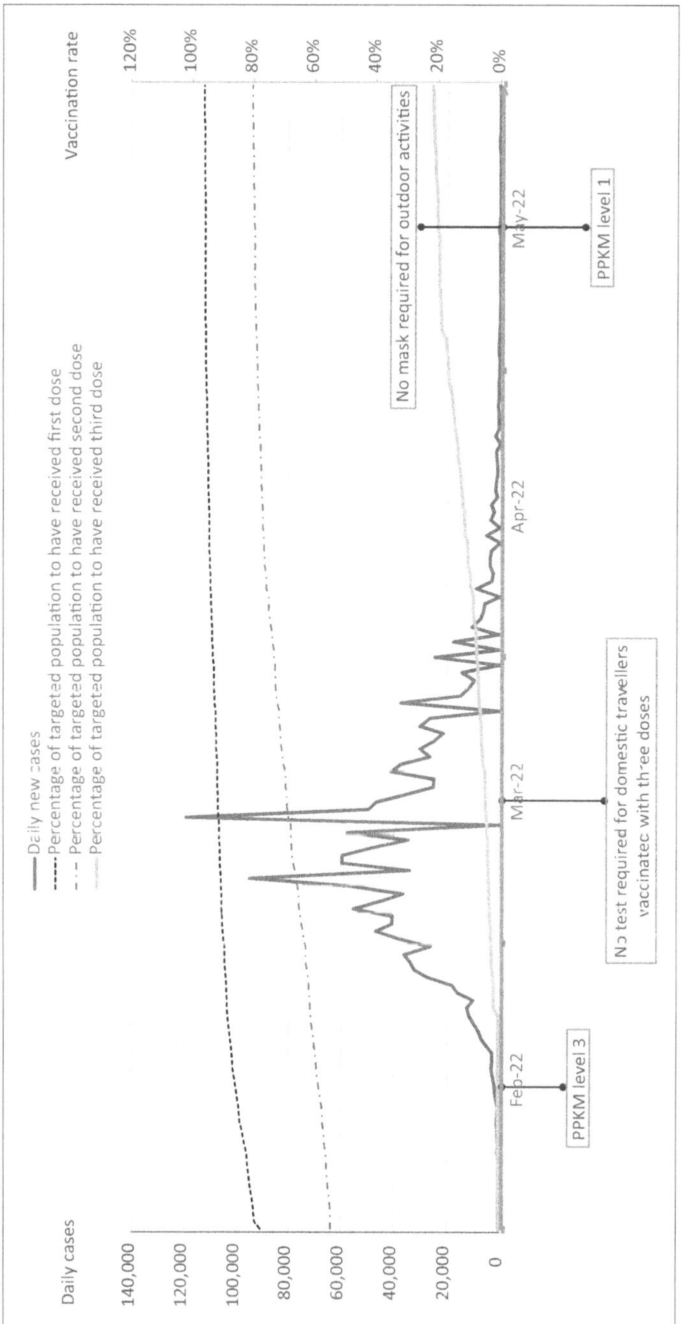

Note: PPKM: restrictions on public activities.
Source: Based on data from covid19.go.id.

concise definition: public policy is "anything a government chooses to do or not to do" (1972, p. 2). Therefore, policy is a course of government action or inaction in response to public, real-world problems. According to Clark (1982), public policy can also be seen from the perspectives of "goal attainment" and "power configuration". In Clark's view, public policies are steps taken by the government to solve problems, make decisions, allocate resources and implement policies—things that are expected of them by their constituents.

Events of major public concern, such as acts of terror, financial crises, major natural disasters or the Covid-19 pandemic, provide a good way to examine the above. As policy is not made in a vacuum, it is important to examine how policy decisions are made, in whose interest and by which actors, as well as the process, agents and outcomes of policy implementation.

There are four main factors that inform the policymaking process: the political environment, the economic environment, the social and cultural environment, and the administrative environment. This might be better formulated, according to Lasswell (1936), as "who gets what, when and how". Public policy can also be seen from two perspectives: (1) as a set of inter-related decisions by a political actor or group of actors whose power can be exercised to achieve them (Jerkins 1978), and (2), as proposals, programmes, major decisions or refusals to make certain decisions (Sharkansky 1978)—recognizing also government inaction as policy.

While evidence-based policymaking is a widely expressed principle, it is much harder to put into practice. Evidence and knowledge reside in the intellectual domain, while policy is made in the political space—and these two realms are often distant if not entirely disconnected. It is very rare that knowledge and evidence genuinely inform or shed light on policy. Instead, they are often used after the event to provide legitimacy. This perspective, while rather gloomy, is illustrated by the example of Indonesia's lack of transparency even on something as unambiguous as the death count, whereby some subnational governments downplayed the number of Covid-19 deaths, playing with the definition set by the WHO, and achieved lowered or under-reported death counts. There was also an unexplained discrepancy in data on deaths reported by subnational and national governments, with the national government reporting 19,000 fewer deaths than subnational governments.[7] This, clearly, seriously compromises policymaking processes.

One further major concern relates to the nature of policy and the government's capacity to coordinate, implement and communicate it. Policy—whether government action or inaction—invariably pertains to a range of socio-economic issues of consequence in public life. The complexity of real-world problems and the inability of the government to solve them on its own posed two intertwined challenges in Indonesia. First, the government's limited capacity compels prioritization, but priorities keep changing; this creates or contributes to many dilemmas the government faces during crises. The second challenge, seeking to mitigate these dilemmas, involves shifting policymaking towards greater use of evidence in policy design, implementation and communication.

Since the reforms of 1998, Indonesia's government has become more decentralized. Subnational governments—whose leaders are directly elected by citizens—deliver most public services. The central government (ministries) sets policies, provides funds and occasionally oversees and assesses subnational offices that administer key services including education, health and social protection. This system of devolution strains central-subnational relations. Central government appears feeble, with only three instruments at its disposal for controlling the latter: fiscal instruments, determining civil service formations and general powers, such as annulment of local regulations. And, in some spheres, governance involves both politics and regulations, meaning that policymaking is not always straightforward and can be influenced by factors other than ideology. National and local political divides have hampered central–subnational policy coordination. Leadership, communication and policy direction are key to removing the political blockage.

After two decades, decentralization in Indonesia has managed to achieve some of what it promised in delivering public services. Yet, disparities and gaps remain: some local governments have been more effective than others, but many, especially those outside Java, have failed to provide public services that meet local demand. Despite institutional failures and corruption, local governments are often able to construct good regulatory frameworks, accountability procedures and effective local institutions for local public administration and public services. Yet, political economy and "sectoral ego", working in silos, make it difficult for the national government to coordinate policy across ministries and with subnational governments (Nugroho and Sujarwoto 2021).

Coordination during Covid-19

Fundamental problems in both horizontal and vertical coordination hindered, if not sabotaged, Indonesia from attaining the best possible outcome in pandemic response. In addition, the government's lack of political resolve to curb the pandemic and prioritize public health and safety over economic considerations contributed to the magnitude of the crisis; it appears this prioritization was rooted in political interests (Nugroho and Syarief 2021) and low state capacity (Nugroho and Negara 2020b; Nugroho and Sujarwoto 2021).

HORIZONTAL COORDINATION

One of the main problems with Indonesia's handling of the second wave of the pandemic—roughly from June to September 2021—lies in two fundamental decisions made by President Widodo. First was his single-minded focus on economic development (Aspinall 2022). Rather than saving lives, the overall strategy of Jokowi's administration in battling Covid-19 was more oriented towards protecting the economy (*Jakarta Post* 2021). His policies throughout the pandemic heavily favoured the economy, rather than tackling the problem of containing Covid-19. This tendency was apparent in his early press conferences, which were typically brief with little explanation of the virus. Instead, he publicized details of the handouts the government had given to citizens affected by the economic downturn.

The second issue in Indonesia's handling of the second wave was the President's reluctance to take command and handle the pandemic himself. Instead, many other figures stepped into roles beyond their official responsibilities, which created confusion within the chain of command. Jokowi's reluctance, along with the orientation towards economic relief, lead to an odd sequence in pandemic response.

Initially, in the first five months after the President announced Indonesia's first case, the pandemic response was coordinated under the

Covid-19 task force, which was led by General (Ret.) Doni Monardo, the Head of the National Disaster Mitigation Agency. However, as the government started to feel the harsh economic impact of the pandemic, which prompted it to begin planning the new normal prematurely, just a few months into the pandemic, the new normal, the KPCPEN was established, led by the Minister for Coordinating Economic Affairs Airlangga Hartarto (Ministry of Finance n.d.). The Covid-19 task force was dissolved and its functions merged into the KPCPEN, confirming the President's economic priority over health.

Luhut Panjaitan, Coordinating Maritime Affairs and Investment Minister and President Widodo's right-hand-man (Erdianto 2017) stepped in during the second wave when deaths began to rise sharply, and the President was allegedly dissatisfied with Hartarto's handling of the pandemic (BBC News Indonesia 2020c). During that time, the government started to impose emergency mobility restrictions (PPKM) to replace the earlier and more lax PSBB (large-scale social restrictions). The division of labour started: Panjaitan coordinated the PPKM for Java and Bali, while Hartarto coordinated all other islands while retaining his post as chief of KPCPEN. However, in reality, Panjaitan was in charge of the larger chunk of the pandemic handling, especially on vaccine procurement, the vaccination programme and the levels of restrictions that were put in place, with the rationale that Java and Bali were the epicentre of Covid-19 nationally. Also significant, in this sequence of events, is that there was no single circumstance in which the Minister of Health was given the final say.

In the view of the authors, the refusal to decisively acknowledge that the pandemic was a health crisis—and that it should be treated as one—and the blurry chain of command created confusion in horizontal coordination within the administration and reduced the effectiveness of vertical coordination.

VERTICAL COORDINATION

Among many problems Indonesia faces in vertical coordination between national and subnational governments, which affected pandemic handling, one of the most notable is its concept of regional autonomy—it is half-hearted, if not ambiguous. Regional autonomy is now based on Law

23/2014 on Local Government; the regulations have undergone several major amendments from the original regulation, Law 22/1999.

The law, however, does not provide a genuine division of authority (Rasyid 2004). Instead it allows local government authority to be bypassed by central government but also gives both parties power to pass the buck or veto the other's policy where their powers overlap. Confusion arises from the central government's failure to deal with many old laws and regulations that are no longer in accordance with the new autonomy law (Samadhi 2015). They have neither been revoked nor aligned with the autonomy law. Former Jakarta Governor Basuki Tjahaja Purnama puts it as, "(the) head is being freed (while the) tail is being held" (Rahadian 2015). However, many subnational governments also do not have the capacity to manage their own powers and responsibilities, including in healthcare (Nugroho and Sujarwoto 2021; Kristiansen and Santoso 2006).

This lack of clear division of authority between central and subnational government creates continuous discoordination and, during the pandemic, did so particularly in mobility restrictions. At times, political actors took advantage of this situation for their own political gain, including to preserve their popularity with the public. Mietzner offers an example of how this discoordination damaged the effort to contain the pandemic: two political rivals, President Jokowi and Jakarta Governor Anies Baswedan, opted for "diametrically opposed approaches to fighting the outbreak" (2020, p. 236). Given the vagueness of the regional autonomy law, the President could block the Jakarta Governor's policies, but the Governor could find ways to uphold them and question the strategy of the central government. Both were seen as sabotaging each other's pandemic policies (Sulaiman 2020) in the absence of a clear division of authority. This problem subsided in relation to Covid-19 as the pandemic waned, but, for as long as the current vertical coordination regulations remain in place, the potential remains for conflicting action by national versus subnational leaders.

POLICY IMPLEMENTATION AND COMMUNICATION

State Capacity and Vested Interest

Successful policy outcome is determined by at least three factors: (1) translating political aspirations via the policymaking process throughout the bureaucratic structure, (2) executing the policy using the machinery of government and (3) communicating the substance of the policy to the wider public and bureaucracy alike. These all are dependent on the state's capacity, which is commonly understood as its ability to implement a range of policies and deliver development outputs and outcomes (Nugroho and Sujarwoto 2021, p. 299). For the purpose of this chapter, expanding on the works of Tilly (1985), Berwick and Christia (2018) and Herbst (1990), we offer a broader working definition of state capacity: the ability of the government to make and deliver policies and regulations, create institutions, ensure plans are executed, set up accountability mechanisms and mobilize resources to support development.

State capacity in Indonesia, particularly relating to its regulatory and institutional framework, is worryingly weak and was not effective in addressing the risk of Covid-19 to lives and livelihoods. Nor could it prevent lasting damage to the public health system and the longer-term impact on the country's economy and social fabric. The problem is further complicated by political interventions within the bureaucracy, which serves various political interests. As a result, not only did the pandemic spiral out of control and the economy halt but public trust in the government was eroded.

The root of this problem is fundamental: what drives policy is the politics behind it, which, in Indonesia, is mainly self-interest, instead of ideology and collective interests, as we argued earlier (Nugroho, Kenawas, and Syarief 2021). In making decisions in response to the pandemic, the government arguably did not always act in the collective interest, meaning preventing infections and deaths in the best possible way. Arguably, the elite, the oligarchs, dominate the economy (Gilens and Page 2014), and this has created the self-serving nature of Indonesian politics. This clouded deliberations over Covid-19 measures—and even created a number of dilemmas—as several political actors came to discuss, or negotiate, policy (Nugroho and Syarief 2021). We argue that it is this self-serving interest that is the main cause of Indonesia's poor policymaking processes and hampers communication, implementation and coordination—both vertically (between central and subnational governments) and horizontally (among and between ministries and agencies).

To summarize, the pandemic response highlighted two important issues: first, Indonesia's problematic decentralization and second, its low state capacity, worsened by self-serving politics, which severely damaged the policymaking process and implementation. When it comes to problematic coordination and implementation of policy at the subnational level, often the excuse—or explanation—given is simplified as "*otonomi setengah hati*" or half-hearted autonomy. When the same happens across ministries and agencies, the most-used pretext is "*pejabat tidak kompeten*" or incompetent officials. These are perpetuated because they effectively mask incompetence and/or low state capacity (Figure 8.5).

Within the vertical dimension, however, the Covid-19 pandemic exposed a much deeper problem regarding Indonesia's regional autonomy. On the surface, subnational autonomy theoretically enables better responses to crises as local governments are more knowledgeable about their regions and the strengths and weaknesses regarding virus transmission. Subnational governments should, after careful coordination with the central government, be able to tackle their problems according to local

FIGURE 8.5
What Drives Policy in Indonesia?

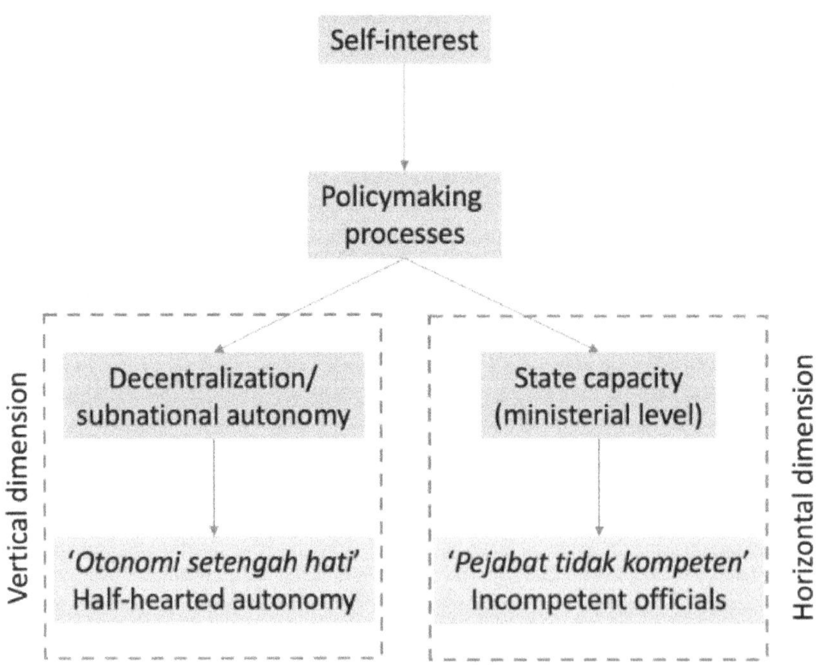

Source: Authors.

needs. However, in addition to the possibility of national and subnational governments either passing the buck or vetoing each other's policies, at least two further issues are at play. First, as the central government did not provide effective Covid-19 leadership, subnational governments were unable to deliver meaningful localized policies. An important case, which arguably helped set the tone for further local policies, was when the regent of Tegal, a city in Central Java, was reprimanded for imposing a local lockdown four weeks into the pandemic and unintentionally disrupting rice distribution (*Tempo* 2020). Rather than exercising meaningful coordination, the central government decided that from then on subnational governments were to obtain written permission before imposing social restrictions (CNN Indonesia 2020a), thereby discouraging region-specific pandemic response policies. Second, a lack of regional resources, especially health-related, significantly affected regional pandemic policies and hindered many subnational governments in their efforts to implement an adequate response. Gaps were apparent between regions in testing capacity and the availability of healthcare, as well as in vaccine distribution and vaccination rate (*Detik* 2020a; Conversation 2021; CNN Indonesia 2021b).

Arguably there was no political will to implement the Health Quarantine Law (UU No. 6/2018 Kekarantinaan Kesehatan); this would have required the government to provide widespread support to people when imposing quarantine. The government avoided using the words "quarantine" or "lockdown", instead using alternative terms, such as restrictions on public activity. Many suspect this was an attempt to avoid the obligation to provide universal social support. Not only did this avoidance hinder the optimum pandemic response by the bureaucracy, but it was also one of the main reasons for low public compliance. People in the informal sector particularly could not comply because they needed to go out to work. This created injustice; the Health Quarantine Law was only used to punish those deemed to be violating activity restrictions (Nugroho 2021; Nugroho and Syarief 2021).

In summary, there was no clear vision and no clear division of labour in the pandemic response between the central and subnational governments and across ministries and state agencies—except for the difference in roles of Luhut Panjaitan and Airlangga Hartarto as explained previously. This explains the overlaps and inconsistencies between policies, which gave mixed messages to the public and bureaucracy. This had serious political implications, bringing into question the competency of the government in managing the crisis and also undermining public trust, which further complicated efforts to control the pandemic.

Policy Communication

Policy communication is important during a pandemic—when people take in, process and act on information in a different way to normal times (Covello et al. 2001; Glik 2007). This different processing affects risk communication, which is how risk perception is built in the public. Risk communication is also an integral part of emergency response by government agencies and subnational governments. Effective risk communication also allows authorities and experts "to listen to and address people's concerns and needs so that the advice they provide is relevant, trusted, and acceptable" (WHO 2018). Ideally, messages should be simple, consistent and accurate, come from credible sources and be released in a timely manner (CDC 2019). A government should provide trustworthy and relevant information during the pandemic to inform people about risk, create behaviour change and encourage participation in decision-making about emergency measures (Lohiniva et al. 2020).[8]

The Indonesian government's inability to effectively communicate those pandemic policies that it was able to put in place indicated something more fundamental: the government's own initial lack of understanding regarding the transmission of Covid-19 virus and the absence of a comprehensive and coherent risk communication strategy. Prime examples are inconsistencies in the mask-wearing mandate and the decision of the government, in the early days of the pandemic, to only suggest to people that they limit travel, rather than requiring them to do so.

Indonesia made it mandatory for citizens to wear face masks outside their homes on 5 April 2020, with a stern warning from the government's Covid-19 spokesperson in May 2020 that face masks should cover the nose and mouth, and that exposing the nose while wearing a mask—or worse, leaving the mask hanging on the chin—was equivalent to not wearing one at all (*Detik* 2020b). These statements were followed by the issuance of Presidential Instruction (Inpres) No. 6/2020 on 4 August 2020, which ordered nationwide enforcement of Covid-19 protocols and made violations subject to legal sanctions. However, these measures were not followed by cues to show the government's own comprehensive understanding of why one should cover the face properly. From time to time, President Jokowi himself failed to exhibit an understanding of how masks were supposed to be worn. On many occasions, he was seen lowering his mask so that it only covered his chin, rather than his nose and mouth.

The lack of comprehension of the transmission of the virus was made worse by the fact that there was no orchestrated effort to produce coherent public messaging until immediately before the peak of the second—and deadliest—wave of the pandemic, caused by the Delta variant. Government officials made conflicting statements about transmission, often causing confusion, and hindering the effectiveness of their own limited risk and policy communication. While Covid-19 cases started to rise significantly by the end of June 2021, both the President and Vice President offered contrasting statements only five days apart: President Widodo appealed to the public to stay at home and only venture out for urgent tasks (23 June 2021), while Vice President Amin encouraged Indonesians to travel for holidays to the exotic Raja Ampat, Papua (28 June 2021). The conflicting statements sparked mockery on social media and prompted the public to question whether there was any coherency in government communications.

Failure to communicate policy and how it was to be implemented and coordinated during the crisis undermined public trust towards authorities from whom the public should have been able to expect reliable information. The lack of trust also extended to political actors and elites able to influence policymaking. Arguably, it is this failure in policy implementation, coordination and communication, early and consistently, that contributed to views in the general public that the Indonesian government was slow and ineffective in responding to the Covid-19 crisis (Nugroho and Negara 2020b).

POLICY DILEMMAS AND TURNING POINTS

Managing any development policies during a pandemic is highly challenging, particularly when dealing with difficult dilemmas and trade-offs. Despite the argument that the root cause of these dilemmas is the inconsistencies and self-serving nature of those in government with power, it is useful however to learn from how the government addressed the dilemmas and did improve its policies over time. This was particularly the case after the deadly Delta variant when the government was forced to alter its approach and orchestrate a more coherent policy formulation process and coordination.

One main important policy is the Covid Response and National Economic Recovery (Penanganan Covid dan Pemulihan Ekonomi Nasional or PC-PEN) programme. Through this programme, the government actively attempted to limit the impacts of the pandemic, particularly on the poor and the informal sector (including micro, small and medium-sized enterprises [MSMEs]), and to recover the economy. For example, the government provided a large amount of social assistance from the beginning of the pandemic (ADB 2022).[9] The efforts were provided via the pre-existing Family Hope Program (PKH), non-cash food assistance and social cash transfers, among others. These social assistance programmes helped more than 40 million recipient households or more than 75 million individuals. The government also created more than 5 million jobs and activated the economy from the beginning of 2021. It helped 250,000 house buyers (Cabinet Secretariat 2021), 15,000 Islamic boarding schools and more than 200,000 madrasahs (Ministry of Religious Affairs 2020). It also provided incentives to operate to hotels, restaurants and public transport operators. In addition, subnational governments received economic support through a subnational financing facility. The government also supported the informal sector by aiding more than forty million MSMEs, including 15 million micro and ultra-micro businesses (CNN Indonesia 2020b). It provided an interest subsidy to more than 27 million MSMEs and enterprise income tax relief benefited more than 300,000 MSMEs. Further, the government gave individual tax relief to 500,000 taxpayers as incentives to invest in their businesses. Final income tax relief also helped more than 150,000 taxpayers.[10] The government also made deductions on business income tax for about 70,000 company taxpayers, while 15,000 taxpayers were exempt from import tax and 2,400 taxpayers benefited from income tax restitution. Through this programme, the government actively attempted to limit the impacts of the pandemic, particularly on the poor and informal sector (including MSMEs), and to recover the economy because they could not afford to face further economic decline (Nugroho and Syarief 2021).

In the health sector, in addition to strengthening primary healthcare services, the government initiated programmes to fight the pandemic. It covered medical expenses for more than 300,000 Covid-19 patients and bonuses for more than 1 million medical workers. It provided compensation to the families of more than 200 medical workers who died due to the virus and paid the health insurance subsidies for more than 55 million beneficiaries. Besides setting up Covid-19 task forces (in March and July 2020), and pushing vaccination, the government also prioritized the development of a nationally produced vaccine, which is being used for non-mandatory, on-demand booster jabs. The efforts in combination seem to have contributed to the eventual containment of the pandemic.

Indonesia's Covid-19 situation distinctly improved as the first half of 2022 progressed. In May 2022, there were 8,177 new cases, down 75.9 per cent compared to April 2022 (33,978), which was already significantly lower than March (448,370) and February (1,211,078). The number of deaths in May was 334, down 71.4 per cent compared to April (1,168). The average positivity rate in testing has decreased to 0.43 per cent in May from 1.39 per cent in April. A first dose of the vaccine had been administered to 200.27 million or 96.2 per cent of the targeted population by end-May, while 167.4 million or 80.4 per cent of the targeted population had received a second dose. The booster jab, however, had reached only 45.7 million or 21.9 per cent of the target. As of end-May 2022, 16 per cent more people had returned to offices as compared with January 2022, activity in retail and recreation had risen by 11 per cent, and footfall in markets and shops selling daily necessities by 31 per cent.

Yet, what seems to appear as smooth sailing in balancing health and economy in the latter chapters of Indonesia's pandemic response should not mask the turbulence of the earlier period. As explained, this stemmed from the self-serving nature of those with power in the government. In Indonesia, it is this combination of this self-serving nature and the weak state capacity (including in policy coordination and implementation), that created impediments in responding to the pandemic dilemmas. This in turn contributed to the difficult circumstances the country encountered. We highlight four of the many dilemmas faced by the government.

First—and Key—Dilemma: Economy or Health?

As argued elsewhere in this chapter, at the beginning of the pandemic, government policies favoured economic interest over health. In addition, the government was seen to possess little sense that the country faced a crisis—which angered the President himself (Nugroho 2020). Indeed, the worry that the pandemic, which hit the world economy hard, would also knock back Indonesia became the very reason the government tended to prioritize economy over health when facing this difficult choice. For example, in March 2020, after the President announced the first cases, the government then allocated IDR298.5 billion to promote tourism, particularly to international tourists, given that the tourism sector had already been hit hard. It even budgeted IDR72 billion to recruit influencers (Halim and Galih 2020). However, at the same time that this policy was issued by the Coordinating Ministry for Economic Affairs, many other countries were closing their borders.

Second Dilemma: To Lock Down or Not?

The government's attempts to curb Covid-19 infection by restricting mobility through many levels of PPKM and PSBB/large-scale social restriction were suboptimal and even controversial (BBC News Indonesia 2021b). Furthermore, the implementation of many restrictions on movements, particularly the emergency restrictions policy (PPKM Darurat), was inconsistent and lacked coordination among ministries and agencies and between central and subnational governments. As the authors argue in another commentary (Nugroho and Syarief 2021), the root of the problem was that the emergency restriction was carried out regionally through "community activity restrictions" (PPKM). This term is not used in the Health Quarantine Law (UU No. 6/2018 Kekarantinaan Kesehatan), which only acknowledges regional quarantine and large-scale social restrictions. The use of the alternative term meant the government could avoid providing social support to people affected that would otherwise have been required by law.

As argued earlier in this chapter, the government opted for restrictions on community activities (PPKM), which are implemented at the village level, rather than imposing a broader regional quarantine, because the use of the latter term would have obliged it to provide food for both humans and livestock in the quarantined areas. The implementation of the PPKM policy became more problematic when the terms used kept changing and even different localities used different names—confusing the public. Since April 2020, the government has used seven different terms: PSBB, Transition PSBB, PPKM Java-Bali, Micro PPKM, Emergency PPKM, Level 3 PPKM and Level 4 PPKM. Only three months into the pandemic, in June 2020, the government announced the "new normal", cancelling the PSBB. This was heavily criticized (Arif 2020) because it gave the false illusion that the pandemic was over, which was clearly not the case. Further, there was serious inconsistency: after the PPKM policy was implemented, social mobility remained high—people violated the rules, such as related to dining in or wearing a mask. Mobility of the public in Jakarta, West Java and Banten provinces was extremely high: many people crossed road barriers and heavy traffic jams continued across Jakarta. As a result, the number of infections rose (*Koran Tempo* 2021).

Third Dilemma: Maintaining Democracy While Containing the Pandemic

Tensions between democratic space and freedoms and pandemic restrictions had to be negotiated. The dilemma between preserving democracy and responding to the pandemic was rooted in the government's preference for "procedural democracy" rather than "substantive democracy", which was clearly restricted. This was particularly concerning when the government attempted to shut down criticism of its pandemic response. The Government Regulation in Lieu of Law (Perpu) No. 1/2020 on State Financial Policy and the Stability of the Financial System was used by the government as emergency legislation, but it also allowed it to misuse laws and limit and deny citizens their rights, and was unnecessary and excessive.[11]

At the same time, instead of taking control and leading proper policy communication, with participation from the public, the government repressed criticisms of many of the contradictions in pandemic handling—leading to real concern about the end of democracy. For example, in May 2021 an emergency Covid-19 hospital, Wisma Atlet, fired health workers who demanded payment of the bonuses they were entitled to for their pandemic work (Taher 2021). Another quoted example is the repression, including through arrest, intimidation and denial of attorney, of people protesting against the Omnibus Bill on Job Creation in October 2020 (BBC News Indonesia 2020b).

However, perhaps to show that democracy continued, the government insisted on running simultaneous subnational elections to elect 279 subnational leaders on 9 December 2020 with a budget of IDR5.2 trillion (US$370 million), despite considerable objections. It transpired that the elections created new infection clusters in many areas, especially in Java (BBC News Indonesia 2020d). The clusters formed from the beginning of the election process and advanced during it, meaning through the declaration and registration of candidates, campaigns and voting (BBC News Indonesia 2020d). On 12 September 2020, 63 out of 1,470 candidates for subnational governments tested positive for Covid-19 (Pikiran Rakyat 2020).

Fourth Dilemma: Military or Civilian Enforcement of Health Protocols?

The seemingly excessive involvement of the military and police in the overall Covid-19 response resulted in public criticism (BBC News Indonesia 2020a). According to the structure of the Covid-19 Task Force as stipulated in Presidential Decree No. 7/2020 and its revision as Presidential Decree No. 9/2020, the government assigned the military and police to take central roles of control during the pandemic response period. The military operated in three areas: medical, security and general support. The government handed more responsibility to the military than to the health authority, but they proved ineffective in implementing health protocols. For example, from July 2020 to April 2021 there were 1,096 reports of health protocol disobedience and breaches of curfew, despite the deployment of troops by the Chief of the Armed Forces to enforce them. There were also cases of physical violence against those protesting various issues and physical sanctions imposed on violators of health protocols (Lapor Covid-19 n.d.-a). However, in punishing people, the authorities themselves breached regulations, for example, by not adhering to social distancing in police stations.

The turning points that finally enabled the government to announce a transition from pandemic to endemic were vaccinations; the government's success in dealing with the third wave, Omicron, due to the vaccination campaign; and economic recovery. Some would also add to this list the result of the government's serology survey (Ministry of Health 2022a). As the proportion of targeted people in Indonesia who were fully vaccinated was nearing 80 per cent by the end of the first quarter of 2022, the government and the public had more confidence in facing the pandemic. The public also understood that although vaccination might not prevent infection, it could help reduce severity and casualties (Arlinta 2021).

After Statistics Indonesia announced in March 2022 that economic growth in 2021 had recovered to 3.69 per cent (compared to –2.07 per cent in 2020)—and other macroeconomic indicators had also improved—the government became more confident in its ability to control the pandemic (Ministry of Health 2022b; Coordinating Minister for Economic Affairs 2022). Indonesia was even applauded as one of the most successful countries in curbing the pandemic (World Bank 2022; Yanwardhana 2023). Development organizations, including multilateral development banks, praised the government's adaptive policy as key to the economic recovery (World Bank 2022). Further, the result of the government's serology test, also in March 2022, confirming that nine out of ten people already had Covid-19 antibodies, boosted confidence—as did the fact that there was no further wave after the long Eid holiday in early May 2022. The government carried out three serology surveys: in December 2021, March 2022 and July 2022. These showed an increase in the population with antibodies from 87.8 per cent in December 2021 to 98.5 per cent in July 2022.

POLICY EFFICACY

As the key dilemmas revolve around balancing health and economy, we also look into these when analysing, discussing and reflecting on policy efficacies.

Public Health and Pandemic Containment

At the end of the Delta wave, Indonesia was praised by the WHO and World Bank for its success in curbing the pandemic (*Tempo* 2021). As the Delta wave ended, the number of cases fell sharply—from more than 55,000 per day during the peak of Delta infection to around 2,000 per day at the end of September 2021. Over the same period, fatalities dropped from 2,000 per day to approximately 120 per day. Indonesia's swift actions in obtaining, distributing and administering the vaccine were also ranked among the best of the low- and middle-income countries (Febriady, Ali, and Purnamasari 2021; Antara 2022), significantly changing the trajectory of the pandemic. By June 2022, 80 per cent of the targeted population were fully vaccinated and 22 per cent had been given a booster shot. This was not a small feat.

The concerted effort to boost vaccinations may stem from the fact that the government did not have much choice: it had no other option than to use the vaccine as its main, if not single, policy. Rather than being the continuation of a large, comprehensive pandemic response, vaccination became the preeminent weapon to fight the pandemic, since previous measures, such as mobility restrictions and the test and trace system, had not contained it (Jaffrey 2021; Nugroho and Syarief 2021).

The vaccination programme was, by design, greatly increased during the peak Delta wave, just as the numbers of cases and deaths started to rise. There was a shift in the vaccination strategy and major public and private institutions were mobilized to push vaccine procurement and inoculation, including the police and army—a controversial move justified by the government as the most effective approach, as described previously (Rochmyaningsih 2022). The vaccination campaign also enlisted popular public figures to promote the safety and efficacy of the Covid-19 vaccine (Antara 2021). These factors massively boosted the campaign. In rural areas, prizes were used to entice the public to come to their local health facilities to be vaccinated (Sood 2021). Moreover, as the public saw the cases and deaths increase due to the Delta variant in July and August 2021, interest in vaccination soared (Murtisari 2021). The ultimate push for the vaccination programme was when the government decided to restrict the activities of the unvaccinated, especially in major cities (Rizal and Kurniawan 2021).

However, vaccination alone could not curb the exponential increase in infections and deaths, which was overwhelming health facilities in many parts of the country. Emergency restrictions (PPKM Darurat) were finally imposed in 3 July 2021, along with a more extensive public campaign on health protocols. The emergency restrictions, which included a ban on dine-in services at restaurants and mandated workers in non-essential sectors to work from home, were initially enacted across Java and Bali and were set to end on 20 July 2021 to coincide with the Eid-ul Adha holiday, but extended until 25 July 2021. The policy was later expanded to fifteen regions outside the two islands, which had experienced surges in new infections and also met other criteria (Paramaditha 2021).

The dire situation brought about by the Delta variant brought a realization within the government: it needed a comprehensive approach to curb the pandemic; a policy focused only on vaccination would not protect the lives and well-being of citizens. This shift in pandemic response was later apparent during the Omicron wave, in which Indonesia opted for a more comprehensive approach to facing the new variant.

While several elements of pandemic response were on the right track during the Delta variant (despite stagnation in booster vaccinations), the government still owes the people a larger and more fundamental debt: transparency in data on key pandemic indicators, especially the number of cases and deaths. As with all other national data, one would expect the government to use a multi-tiered process to tally the figures from the subdistrict level upwards. However, during Covid-19 there was no standardized procedure to tally the daily data.

More often than not, data at all levels of government—cities/regencies, provinces, national—showed discrepancies. Civil organizations such as Lapor Covid-19 and Kawal Covid-19[12] provided data comparisons that showed inconsistencies between subnational and national numbers, including 19,000 fewer deaths reported by central government versus local and regional governments during the Delta wave. To this day, the government has yet to show where and how the data errors occurred. As Covid-19 is no longer seen as a threat, especially after the country established the endemic status of the virus on 29 June 2023, it is unlikely that the government will try to calculate the real number of infections and mortality, let alone perform an audit. However, the WHO has given a figure for Indonesia's excess deaths seven times the government's number (Dewi 2022).

Economic Recovery

If vaccination was the game-changer in pandemic response, countercyclical and flexible fiscal policy is the game-changer in economic recovery.

Flexible fiscal policy gave the government room in 2020–22 to exceed the budget deficit cap of 3 per cent, although it had to observe that cap from 2023 onwards. Further, the government was also allowed to readjust and reallocate budget items in the state budget in order to mitigate the impact of the pandemic. What was needed was an anticipative and responsive budget, and though it may have begun as a policy experiment—which is common in times of crises—the government ultimately realized that its policies had indeed to be adaptable. While health policy was solely aimed at curbing the pandemic, other policies also had to have the same goal—even those for recovering the economy. If there is no confidence in pandemic handling, the economy will not move, whether or not there are sufficient incentives.

Entering 2021, the government started to implement an adaptive fiscal policy. Countercyclical policies such as tax breaks for corporations, MSMEs and individuals were extensively enacted. These helped stimulate demand and production and resulted in multiplier effects that contributed to economic recovery. Hence, although Indonesia experienced a pandemic-induced recession in mid-2020, it recovered in 2021, partly thanks to this policy. For example, the removal of VAT from car purchases resulted in a significant increase in car sales in 2021—as much as 66 per cent growth between January and November 2021 (Priyanto 2022). The policy significantly impacted not only the demand side, but also the supply side, and boosted job creation (Pratama and Rezki 2022). There were also significant multiplier effects on supporting sectors such as the metal and rubber industries and financial services (ibid.). The government views Indonesia's automotive sector as a strategic sector with high value-added and a high level of technological and innovation adoption. The informal sector and MSMEs also benefited from support programmes, particularly subsidies of loan interest, financial support for MSMEs and street vendors, payment of guarantee fees for MSMEs and corporations and exemption of costs related to debt and credit restructuring.

The flexible fiscal policy, which allowed the government to reallocate budget, helped ease the impact of the pandemic as it enabled the government to react swiftly to the effects of the virus, for example by increasing social assistance when infections surged. Further, social assistance programmes safeguarded the economy and livelihoods as they helped consumption—

which is key to the economy. The assistance programmes benefited many recipients: families and households, students, Covid-19 patients and particularly the poor and most affected.

The government's adaptive policy played a key role in mitigating the impact of the pandemic and promoting economic recovery. As the pandemic transitioned to an endemic state, the government needed to move towards budget consolidation or regularization, while also keeping its flexible approach to policymaking. In particular, its newfound ability to make policy adaptive and flexible reflects its enhanced capacity to deal with challenging and changing circumstances with a significant impact on citizens.

LESSONS FOR THE FUTURE

With the benefit of hindsight, the Indonesian government now understands that the pandemic was much more serious than generally believed, and we highlight lessons learnt. First, self-interest should never cloud judgements on overcoming a crisis. Governments operate within the realm of realpolitik, but must govern in a way that serves the people; commitment towards the overall public well-being should be paramount. Many crises will challenge the government to bridge the gap between public and political interests; this can only be achieved with solid leadership, a quality that is needed in facing other crises, such as climate change.

The second lesson is the importance of improving the state's capacity to mitigate current and anticipate future crises. The government needs to build its capability to prepare and operationalize a coherent, science- and evidence-based framework for mitigating future pandemics while continuing to deliver development as it learns. This means it needs the capacity to create a regulatory framework and must set up the institutional arrangements, create an accountability mechanism, implement plans and mobilize resources. The adaptive fiscal policy was a valuable lesson: the government finally let itself deviate from business as usual and built its capacity for agility. This capacity needs to be built across governmental agencies and institutions at the central and subnational levels.

The state's capacity also has an impact on the quality of the relationships of citizens with their government. The capacity of the government to coordinate across government agencies and institutions and with non-state actors (civil society, business and academia, among others) determines how effective the government can be in fighting a pandemic and protecting citizens. For that, the overall state capacity of the government has to be improved and strengthened so that the government does not depend on just one or two members of the Cabinet. In addition, and perhaps more significantly, Indonesia needs to reflect on its choices when implementing regional autonomy. There are indeed some issues that are governed centrally (e.g., fiscal, military, foreign policy), but there are also many more that fall within subnational authority (such as the provision of public services). This division of responsibility must be clear and adhered to. Half-hearted regional autonomy will most likely only create unnecessary, and perhaps dangerous, tensions during crises.

Finally, as with many aspects of public policy, the government's actions and inactions in addressing dilemmas during the Covid-19 pandemic takes us to the ultimate lesson for the future: the paradox of preparation and how preventative measures can seem like a waste of time both before and after the fact, and that the only way to get ahead of the exponential infection curve is to take action that at the time may seem like overreaction (Leuven Institute for the Future 2021).

Notes

1. Data from "Peta Sebaran", https://covid19.go.id/peta-sebaran
2. Presidential Decree No. 7/2020.
3. Government Regulation No. 21/2020.
4. Among others, Government Regulation in Lieu of Law No. 1/2020 on State Financial Policy and Maintaining Financial System Stability to Mitigate the Covid-19 Pandemic and/or Other Threats to the National Economy and/or Financial System Stability (31 March 2020); Government Regulation No. 23/2020 on the National Economic Recovery (Pemulihan Ekonomi Nasional or PEN) Program (9 May 2020); and Presidential Regulation No. 72/2020 (24 June 2020). Government Regulation in Lieu of Law No. 1/2020 was then enacted as Law No. 2/2020 (16 May 2020).
5. Presidential Regulation No. 82/2020 on the Committee for Handling Covid-19 and the PEN.
6. Data collection questionnaire for Mutual Cooperation Vaccination Program by Indonesian Chamber of Commerce: https://vaksin.kadin.id/#!/kuesioner

7. For example, during the Delta wave there were discrepancies between deaths compiled by local and regional governments versus the central government. The central government recorded at least 19,000 fewer deaths than local and regional governments combined. See Lapor Covid-19 (n.d.-b), CNN Indonesia (2021a) and BBC News Indonesia (2021a).
8. Here, accurate information from the government and political elites can lead to rapid behavioural change (Green et al. 2020), which is paramount in the effort to save lives.
9. Unless otherwise stated, all data in this paragraph is taken from ADB (2022).
10. In Indonesia, income tax is applied to any income received by a taxpayer. Final income tax refers to the total amount of tax that has to be paid after all incomes are accounted for (one taxpayer can have multiple income sources).
11. The title in full: Government Regulation in Lieu of Law No. 1 Year 2020 on State Financial Policy and the Stability of Financial System for Covid-19 Pandemic Handling and/or in order to Address Threats that Endanger National Economy and/or the Stability of Financial System (Perpu No 1/2020 tentang Kebijakan Keuangan Negara dan Stabilitas Sistem Keuangan Untuk Penanganan Pandemi Covid-19 dan/atau Dalam Rangka Menghadapi Ancaman Yang Membahayakan Perekonomian Nasional dan/atau Stabilitas Sistem Keuangan).
12. "Lapor Covid-19", https://laporcovid19.org/; "Kawal Covid-19", https://kawalcovid19.id/

References

ADB (Asian Development Bank). 2021. "Indonesia: COVID-19 Active Response and Expenditure Support Program Monitoring Report (January–May 2021)". Asian Development Bank, August 2021. https://www.adb.org/projects/documents/ino-54139-001-dpta-1

———. 2022. "Indonesia: COVID-19 Active Response and Expenditure Support Program Monitoring Report (June–December 2021)". Asian Development Bank, March 2022. https://www.adb.org/projects/documents/ino-54139-001-dpta-2

Antara. 2021. "Vaksinasi Masif Diharapkan Kurangi Angka Kematian Akibat Covid-19" [Massive vaccination expected to reduce death rate due to Covid-19]. *Medcom.id*, 31 July 2021. https://www.medcom.id/nasional/peristiwa/Gbmoo9xK-vaksinasi-masif-diharapkan-kurangi-angka-kematian-akibat-covid-19

———. 2022. "Role of Vaccinations after Two Years of Pandemic in Indonesia".

2 March 2022. https://en.antaranews.com/news/217893/role-of-vaccinations-after-two-years-of-pandemic-in-indonesia (accessed 28 July 2022).

Arif, Ahmad. 2020. "Oxymoron 'Normal Baru'" [The oxymoron of the 'new normal']. *Kompas*, 3 June 2020. https://www.kompas.id/baca/ilmiah-populer/2020/06/03/oxymoron-normal-baru

Arlinta, Deonisia. 2021. "Vaksinasi Bukan Peluru Perak Pengendalian Pandemi" [Vaccination is not a silver bullet in pandemic control]. *Kompas*, 2 September 2021. https://www.kompas.id/baca/ilmu-pengetahuan-teknologi/2021/09/02/rencana-jangka-panjang-penanganan-covid-19-perlu-disiapkan (accessed 28 July 2022).

BBC News Indonesia. 2020a. "'New Normal': Pelibatan Tentara Justru Menciptakan 'Abnormalitas', Pemerintah Beralasan Demi 'Mendisiplinkan' Warga" ["New normal": Involvement of the army actually creates "abnormalities", the government argues to "discipline" citizens]. 29 May 2020. https://www.bbc.com/indonesia/indonesia-52834296 (accessed 28 July 2022).

———. 2020b. "Omnibus Law: Demo Tolak UU Cipta Kerja di 18 Provinsi Diwarnai Kekerasan, YLBHI: 'Polisi Melakukan Pelanggaran'" [Omnibus Law: Demonstrations against the Job Creation Law in 18 provinces were marred by violence, Indonesian Legal Aid Institute: "Police committed violations"]. 9 October 2020. https://www.bbc.com/indonesia/indonesia-54469444 (accessed 28 July 2022).

———. 2020c. "Penanganan Covid-19 Indonesia dan Luhut Panjaitan: 'Saya Manajer Yang Baik, Saya Dibantu Para Epidemiolog Yang Berkualitas'" [Indonesia's handling of Covid-19 and Luhut Panjaitan: "I am a good manager; I am assisted by qualified epidemiologists]. 18 September 2020. https://www.bbc.com/indonesia/indonesia-54206332 (accessed 28 July 2022).

———. 2020d. "Pilkada: Klaster Virus Corona Merebak Setelah Pemilihan Kepala Daerah, Ahli Sebut 'Akibat Penelusuran Kontak Yang Lemah'" [Regional elections: Coronavirus clusters spread after regional head elections, experts say 'due to weak contact tracing']. 18 December 2020. https://www.bbc.com/indonesia/indonesia-55321183 (accessed 28 July 2022).

———. 2021a. "Angka Kematian Covid-19: Beda Data Pemerintah Pusat dan Daerah Capai 19.000 Kasus, 'Hijau di Luar Merah di Dalam'" [Covid-19 death rate: difference between central and regional government data reaches 19,000 cases, 'green on the outside, red on the inside']. 28 July 2021. https://www.bbc.com/indonesia/indonesia-57971840 (accessed 28 July 2022).

———. 2021b. "Lonjakan Covid-19 dan Desakan Lockdown: Mengapa Pemerintah Pertahankan Pembatasan Skala Mikro?" [Covid-19 surge and lockdown calls:

Why is the government maintaining micro-scale restrictions?]. 22 June 2021. https://www.bbc.com/indonesia/indonesia-57550056 (accessed 28 July 2022).

Berwick, Elissa, and Fotini Christia. 2018. "State Capacity Redux: Integrating Classical and Experimental Contributions to an Enduring Debate". *Annual Review of Political Science* 21: 71–91.

Bio Farma. 2023. "Bio Farma Telah Distribusikan Seluruh Vaksin Gotong Royong" [Bio Farma has distributed all 'gotong royong' vaccines]. 8 December 2023. https://www.biofarma.co.id/id/announcement/detail/-bio-farma-telah-distribusikan-seluruh-vaksin-gotong-royong (accessed 28 July 2022).

Cabinet Secretariat. 2021. "Tahun 2021, Target Bantuan Subsidi Perumahan Sebanyak 222.876 Unit" [In 2021, the target for housing subsidy assistance is 222,876 units]. 25 January 2021.https://setkab.go.id/tahun-2021-target-bantuan-subsidi-perumahan-sebanyak-222-876-unit/

CDC (Centers for Disease Control and Prevention). 2019. *Crisis and Emergency Risk Communication (CERC): Psychology of a Crisis*. Atlanta: Center for Disease Control (CDC). https://emergency.cdc.gov/cerc/ppt/CERC_Psychology_of_a_Crisis.pdf

Clark, Robert P. 1982. *Power and Policy in the Third World*. Santa Barbara, New York: John Wiley and Co.

CNN Indonesia. 2015. "Otonomi Daerah Setengah Hati dari Pemerintah Pusat" [Half-hearted regional autonomy from the central government]. 27 April 2015. https://www.cnnindonesia.com/nasional/20150427102846-20-49421/otonomi-daerah-setengah-hati-dari-pemerintah-pusat (accessed 28 July 2022).

———. 2020a. "Jejak Kota Tegal Lawan Corona: Lantang Lockdown Hingga PSBB" [Tegal City's steps against corona: strict lockdown to large-scale social restrictions]. https://www.cnnindonesia.com/nasional/20200514134104-20-503332/jejak-kota-tegal-lawan-corona-lantang-lockdown-hingga-psbb (accessed 28 July 2022).

———. 2020b. "Penerima Bantuan Modal Kerja Bakal Ditambah Jadi 15 Juta UMKM" [Recipients of working capital assistance will be increased to 15 Million MSMEs]. CNN Indonesia, 28 August 2020. https://www.cnnindonesia.com/ekonomi/20200828163013-532-540404/penerima-bantuan-modal-kerja-bakal-ditambah-jadi-15-juta-umkm

———. 2021a. "IDI Jatim soal Data Nol Kematian Covid-19: Coba Lihat Kuburan" [East Java's Indonesian Medical Association regarding Covid-19 zero death data: Try looking at graves]. 23 July 2021. https://www.cnnindonesia.com/nasional/20210723110456-20-671205/idi-jatim-soal-data-nol-kematian-covid-19-coba-lihat-kuburan (accessed 28 July 2022).

———. 2021b. "Menkes Akui Distribusi Vaksin Terhambat Jalur Logistik Dingin" [Minister of Health admits vaccine distribution is hampered by cold logistics]. 12 January 2021. https://www.cnnindonesia.com/nasional/20210112134421-20-592627/menkes-akui-distribusi-vaksin-terhambat-jalur-logistik-dingin

Conversation. 2021. "Discrepancies in Facilities and Services among Hospitals in Indonesia Increase Covid-19 Risks among Health Workers". 17 June 2021. https://theconversation.com/discrepancies-in-facilities-and-services-among-hospitals-in-indonesia-increase-covid-19-risks-among-health-workers-157336 (accessed 28 July 2022).

Coordinating Minister for Economic Affairs. 2022. "Peningkatan Sinergi antar Kementerian Mendorong Pertumbuhan Ekonomi yang Berkelanjutan" [Improvement in inter-ministerial synergy enables sustainable economic growth]. News release, 10 March 2022. https://www.ekon.go.id/publikasi/detail/3906/peningkatan-sinergi-antar-kementerian-mendorong-pertumbuhan-ekonomi-yang-berkelanjutan (accessed 28 July 2022).

Covello, V., R. Peters, J. Wojtecki, and R. Hyde. 2001. "Risk Communication, the West Nile Virus Epidemic, and Bioterrorism: Responding to the Communication Challenges Posed by the Intentional or Unintentional Release of a Pathogen in an Urban Setting". *Urban Health* 78, no 2: 382–91.

Detik. 2020a. "Jokowi Soroti Ketimpangan Tes Corona: DKI 324 Ribu, Jatim Masih 184 Ribu" [Jokowi highlights inequality in corona testing: DKI 324 Thousand, East Java Still 184 Thousand]. 14 September 2020. https://news.detik.com/berita/d-5172296/jokowi-soroti-ketimpangan-tes-corona-dki-324-ribu-jatim-masih-184-ribu (accessed 28 July 2022).

———. 2020b. "Pemerintah: Tak Tutup Hidung Sama Saja Tak Pakai Masker, Berisiko Kena Corona" [Government: Not covering your nose is the same as not wearing a mask, risk of getting corona]. 21 May 2020. https://news.detik.com/berita/d-5023216/pemerintah-tak-tutup-hidung-sama-saja-tak-pakai-masker-berisiko-kena-corona

Dewi, Intan Rakhmayanti. 2022. "WHO: Kematian Akibat Covid RI Lebih Tinggi dari Laporan Resmi" [WHO: Indonesia's Covid deaths higher than official reports]. *CNBC Indonesia*, 7 May 2022. https://www.cnbcindonesia.com/tech/20220507112126-37-337084/who-kematian-akibat-covid-ri-lebih-tinggi-dari-laporan-resmi

Dye, Thomas R. 1972. *Understanding Public Policy*. Englewood Cliffs: Prentice-Hall.

Jakarta Post, 2021. "They Did Not Have to Die". 3 July 2021. https://www.

thejakartapost.com/academia/2021/07/02/they-did-not-have-to-die.html (accessed 28 July 2022).

Erdianto, Kristian. 2017. "Luhut Menolak Disebut Menteri Super 'Tangan Kanan' Jokowi" [Luhut refuses to be called Jokowi's 'right hand' super minister]. *Kompas*, 25 July 2017. https://nasional.kompas.com/read/2017/07/25/10224701/luhut-menolak-disebut-menteri-super-tangan-kanan-jokowi

Febriady, Ade, Rabia Ali, and Ririn Salwa Purnamasari. 2021. "Rollout of the Covid-19 Vaccination Campaign in Indonesia: Progress to Date, Emerging Challenges, and Priority Actions in Coming Months". Observer Research Foundation, 19 August 2021. https://www.orfonline.org/expert-speak/rollout-of-the-Covid-19-vaccination-campaign-in-indonesia/

Gilens, Martin, and Benjamin I. Page. 2014. "Testing Theories of American Politics: Elites, Interest Groups, and Average Citizens". *Perspectives on Politics* 12, no. 3: 564–81.

Glik, D. 2007. "Risk Communication for Public Health Emergencies". *Annual Review of Public Health* 28: 33–54.

Green, J., J. Edgerton, D. Naftel, K. Shoub and S.J. Cranmer. 2020. "Elusive Consensus: Polarization in Elite Communication on the cOVID-19 pandemic". *Science Advances* 6: eabc2717.

Halim, Devina, and Bayu Galih. 2020. "Rp72 Miliar untuk Influencer dalam Atasi Dampak Virus Corona, Pengamat: Mau Diapain?" [IDR72 billion for influencers to overcome the impact of the coronavirus, observer: What do you want to do?]. *Kompas*, 2 March 2020. https://nasional.kompas.com/read/2020/03/02/10323441/rp-72-miliar-untuk-influencer-dalam-atasi-dampak-virus-corona-pengamat-mau?page=all (accessed 28 July 2022).

Herbst, Jeffrey. 1990. "War and the State in Africa". *International Security* 14, no. 4: 117–39.

Jaffrey, Sana. 2021. "How the Global Vaccine Divide Is Fueling Indonesia's Coronavirus Catastrophe". Carnegie Endowment for International Peace, 5 August 2021. https://carnegieendowment.org/2021/08/05/how-global-vaccine-divide-is-fueling-indonesia-s-coronavirus-catastrophe-pub-85107

Jenkins, W. 1978. *Policy Analysis: A Political and Organization Perspective*. London: Martin Robertson.

Koran Tempo. 2021. "Sempoyongan Redam Pergerakan: Evaluasi PPKM Darurat, Mobilitas Warga Masih Tinggi" [In limbo controlling mobility: Emergency PPKM evaluation, public mobility remains high]. 19 July 2021. https://koran.

tempo.co/read/berita-utama/466446/evaluasi-ppkm-darurat-mobilitas-warga-masih-tinggi (accessed 28 July 2022).

Kristiansen, Stein, and Purwo Santoso. 2006. "Surviving Decentralisation? Impacts of Regional Autonomy on Health Service Provision in Indonesia". *Health Policy* 77, no. 3: 247–59.

Lapor Covid-19. N.d.-a). "Kekuasaan dan Militer Dalam Merespon Pandemi: Bukti dari Lapangan" [Military authority during pandemic response: evidence from the field]. https://laporcovid19.org/post/kekuasaan-dan-militer-dalam-merespon-pandemi-bukti-dari-lapangan

———. N.d.-b). "Lebih dari 19.000 Kematian Belum Tercatat" [More than 19,000 deaths have not been recorded]. https://laporcovid19.org/post/lebih-dari-19-000-kematian-belum-tercatat

Lasswell, H. 1936. *Politics: Who Gets What, When, and How?* New York: Whittlesey House.

Leuven Institute for the Future. 2021. *Introducing Pandemic Preparedness Goals.* Leuven Institute for the Future; KU Leuven, Institute of Tropical Medicine Antwerp; and Vrije Universiteit Brussel, 25 June 2021. https://rega.kuleuven.be/if/pandemicpreparedness/pandemic-preparedness-goals-en

Lohiniva, Anna-Leena, Jusi Sane, Katja Sibenberg, Taneli Puumalainen, and Mika Salminen. 2020. "Understanding Coronavirus Disease (COVID-19) Risk Perceptions among the Public to Enhance Risk Communication Efforts: A Practical Approach for Outbreaks". *Eurosurveillance* 25, no. 13: pii=2000317.

Media Indonesia. 2022. "Keberhasilan Transisi Pandemi ke Endemi Dorong Akselerasi Perekonomian" [Successful transition from pandemic to endemic encourages economic acceleration]. 21 March 2022. https://mediaindonesia.com/ekonomi/479709/keberhasilan-transisi-pandemi-ke-endemi-dorong-akselerasi-perekonomian (accessed 28 July 2022).

Mietzner, Marcus. 2020. "Populist Anti-Scientism, Religious Polarisation, and Institutionalised Corruption: How Indonesia's Democratic Decline Shaped Its COVID-19 Response". *Journal of Current Southeast Asian Affairs* 39, no. 2: 227–49.

Ministry of Finance. n.d. "Respon Kebijakan Penanganan Covid-19 di Indonesia".

Ministry of Health. 2022a. "Hasil Sero Survey: 86,6% Penduduk Indonesia Memiliki Antibodi terhadap COVID-19" [Serology survey results: 86.6% of the Indonesian population has antibodies to COVID-19]. News release, 18 March 2022. https://sehatnegeriku.kemkes.go.id/baca/rilis-media/penelitian-dan-pengembangan-kesehatan/20220318/3139545/hasil-sero-survey-866-penduduk-indonesia-memiliki-antibodi-terhadap-covid-19/

———. 2022b. "Kasus Konfirmasi Turun, Pemerintah Terus Perkuat Upaya Pencegahan" [Confirmed cases decrease, government continues to strengthen prevention efforts]. 13 February 2022. https://sehatnegeriku.kemkes.go.id/baca/rilis-media/20220213/0439309/kasus-konfirmasi-turun-pemerintah-terus-perkuat-upaya-pencegahan/

———. 2022c. "Kasus Melonjak Melebihi Delta, Namun Keterisian RS Terjaga" [Cases soar above Delta, but hospital occupancy is maintained]. 19 February 2022. https://sehatnegeriku.kemkes.go.id/baca/rilis-media/20220219/0539355/kasus-melonjak-melebihi-delta-namun-keterisian-rs-terjaga/

Ministry of Religious Affairs. 2020. "Tahap II, 1 Triliun Bantuan Pesantren di masa Covid Segera Cair" [Phase II, IDR 1 trillion in Islamic boarding school assistance during Covid disbursed immediately]. 3 October 2020. https://kemenag.go.id/nasional/tahap-ii-1-triliun-bantuan-pesantren-di-masa-covid-segera-cair-onjhyc

Murtisari, Mardella Savitri. 2021. "Viral Cara Kreatif Warga Saat Antre Vaksinasi Covid-19, Titip Sandal Hingga Mengular" [Residents' creative way of queuing for Covid-19 vaccinations goes viral: Leave a sandal in the queue]. *Liputan6*, 1 September 2021, https://hot.liputan6.com/read/4646853/viral-cara-kreatif-warga-saat-antre-vaksinasi-covid-19-titip-sandal-hingga-mengular (accessed 28 July 2022).

Nugroho, Yanuar. 2020. "Joko's Fire and Fury: A Chance to Reform the Cabinet?". *Fulcrum*, 21 June 2020. https://fulcrum.sg/jokos-fire-and-fury-a-chance-to-reform-the-cabinet/

———. 2021. "To Lockdown or Not? Indonesia's Dilemma in Handling the Covid-19 Second Wave". *Fulcrum*, 30 June 2021. https://fulcrum.sg/to-lockdown-or-not-indonesias-dilemma-in-handling-the-covid-19-second-wave/

———, and Siwage Dharma Negara. 2020a. "Urgent Need to Strengthen State Capacity: Learning from Indonesia's COVID-19 Crisis". *ISEAS Perspective,* no. 2020/66, 19 June 2020. https://www.iseas.edu.sg/articles-commentaries/iseas-perspective/2020-66-urgent-need-to-strengthen-state-capacity-learning-from-indonesias-covid-19-crisis-by-yanuar-nugroho-and-siwage-dharma-n-egara/

———, and Siwage Dharma Negara. 2020b. "COVID-19's Impact on Micro, Small, & Medium Enterprises and Tourism in Indonesia". *ISEAS Perspective*, no. 2020/124, 26 October 2020. https://www.iseas.edu.sg/articles-commentaries/iseas-perspective/2020-124-covid-19s-impact-on-micro-small-medium-enterprises-and-tourism-in-indonesia-by-yanuar-nugroho-and-siwage-dharma-negara/

———, and Sofie S. Syarief. 2021. "Grave Failures in Policy and Communication in Indonesia during the Covid-19 Pandemic". *ISEAS Perspective*, No. 2021/113, 25 August 2021. https://www.iseas.edu.sg/articles-commentaries/iseas-perspective/2021-113-grave-failures-in-policy-and-communication-in-indonesia-during-the-Covid-19-pandemic-by-yanuar-nugroho-and-sofie-shinta-syarief/

———, and Sujarwoto. 2021. "Institutions, Outputs and Outcomes: Two Decades of Decentralization and State Capacity in Indonesia". *Journal of Southeast Asian Economies* 38, no. 3: 296–319.

———, Yoes C. Kenawas, and Sofie S. Syarief. 2021. "How the 2020 Pilkada Reflected Major Structural Flaws in Indonesian Politics". *ISEAS Perspective*, no. 2021/5, 25 January 2021. https://www.iseas.edu.sg/articles-commentaries/iseas-perspective/iseas-perspective-2021-5-how-the-2020-pilkada-reflected-major-structural-flaws-in-indonesian-politics-by-yanuar-nugroho-yoes-c-kenawas-and-sofie-s-syarief/

Paramaditha, Andjarsari. 2021. "PPKM Darurat Necessary for Sustainable Recovery in Indonesia". *Jakarta Post*, 6 July 2021. https://www.thejakartapost.com/news/2021/07/06/ppkm-darurat-necessary-for-sustainable-recovery-in-indonesia.html (accessed 28 July 2022).

Pikiran Rakyat. 2020. "63 Calon Kepala Daerah Positif Covid-19, KPU Sebut Penyebaran Berasal dari Aktivitas Kampanye" [63 regional head candidates positive for Covid-19, Election Commission says the spread came from campaign activities]. 13 September 2020, https://www.pikiran-rakyat.com/nasional/pr-01740259/63-calon-kepala-daerah-positif-covid-19-kpu-sebut-penyebaran-berasal-dari-aktivitas-kampanye (accessed 28 July 2022).

Pratama, R.A., and J.F. Rezki. 2022. "Bagaimana Dampak Kebijakan Insentif PPnBM Ditanggung Pemerintah Terhadap Kinerja Industri Kendaraan Bermotor? Bukti Dari Indonesia" [What are the impacts of the policy on income tax relief on the performance of the automotive industry? Evidence from Indonesia]. *Jurnal Pajak Indonesia* [Indonesian Tax Journal] 6, no. 1. https://doi.org/10.31092/jpi.v6i1.1582

Priyanto, Wawan. 2022. "Penjualan Mobil 2021 Naik 66,7 Persen, Dekati 900 Ribu Unit" [Car sales increase in 2021 by 66.7 percent, approaching 900 thousand units]. *Tempo*, 13 January 2022. https://otomotif.tempo.co/read/1549679/penjualan-mobil-2021-naik-667-persen-dekati-900-ribu-unit (accessed 28 July 2022).

Rahadian, Lalu. 2015. "Otonomi Daerah Setengah Hati dari Pemerintah Pusat" [Half-hearted regional autonomy from the central government]. *CNN Indonesia*, 27 April 2015. https://www.cnnindonesia.com/

nasional/20150427102846-20-49421/otonomi-daerah-setengah-hati-dari-pemerintah-pusat (accessed 28 July 2022).

Rasyid, Muhammad R. 2004. "The Policy of Decentralization in Indonesia". In *Reforming Intergovernmental Fiscal Relations and the Rebuilding of Indonesia*, edited by James Alm, Jorge Martinez-Vasquez, and Sri M. Indrawati. Cheltenham: Edward Elgar Publishing.

Rizal, Jawahir Gustav, and Rendika Ferri Kurniawan. 2021. "Jadi Syarat Aktivitas, Ini Cara Download Sertifikat Vaksin via PeduliLindungi" [Required for activities, here's how to download vaccine certificate via the PeduliLindungi app]. *Kompas*, 11 August 2021. https://www.kompas.com/tren/read/2021/08/11/133000465/jadi-syarat-aktivitas-ini-cara-download-sertifikat-vaksin-via (accessed 28 July 2022).

Rochmyaningsih, Dyna. 2022. "How Indonesia Got Vaccinated". *Gavi*, 2 June 2022. https://www.gavi.org/vaccineswork/how-indonesia-got-vaccinated (accessed 28 July 2022).

Samadhi, Willy Purna. 2015. "Desentralisasi Setengah Hati: Berpindahnya 'Sentralisme' Ke Daerah" [Half-hearted decentralization: The move of "centralism" to the locals]. Indonesian Centre for Democracy and Human Rights. https://www.neliti.com/publications/411/desentralisasi-setengah-hati-berpindahnya-sentralisme-ke-daerah (accessed 28 July 2022).

Sharkansky, I. 1978. *Public Administration: Policy Making in Government Agencies*. Chicago: Rand McNally College Publishing Co.

Sood, Amy. 2021. "Indonesian Officials Give Away Live Chickens to Residents Willing to Get Vaccinated". *CNN*, 17 June 2021. https://edition.cnn.com/2021/06/17/asia/indonesia-town-chickens-vaccinated-intl-hnk-scli/index.html (accessed 28 July 2022).

Sulaiman, Yohanes. 2020. "Indonesia's Politicisation of the Virus Is Stopping Effective Response". *Southeast Asia Globe*, 10 April 2020. https://southeastasiaglobe.com/indonesia-Covid-19-response/ (accessed 28 July 2022).

Taher, Andrian Pratama. 2021. "Ketika Nakes Dipecat Usai Protes Insentif yang Telat & Dipotong" [When health workers fired after protesting late & reduced incentives]. *Tirto*, 12 May 2021. https://tirto.id/ketika-nakes-dipecat-usai-protes-insentif-yang-telat-dipotong-gfS6 (accessed 28 July 2022).

Tempo. 2020. "Tegal Covid-19 Lockdown, Mayor: No Reprimands from Central Govt". Tempo.co, 3 April 2020. https://en.tempo.co/read/1327582/tegal-covid-19-lockdown-mayor-no-reprimands-from-central-govt

———. 2021. "Indonesia Earns Praise from WHO, WB for Curbing COVID-19 Cases". Tempo.co, 29 September 2021. https://en.tempo.co/read/1511549/

indonesia-earns-praise-from-who-wb-for-curbing-covid-19-cases (accessed 28 July 2022).

Tilly, Charles. 1985. "War Making and State Making as Organized Crime". In *Bringing the State Back In*, edited by Peter B. Evans, Dietrich Rueschemeyer, and Theda Skocpol. Cambridge: Cambridge University Press.

Waseso, Ratih. 2021. "Antusias tinggi, sudah 28.000 perusahaan mendaftar vaksinasi gotong royong". [High enthusiasm: 28,000 companies have registered for mutual cooperation vaccination]. *Kontan*, 17 June 2021. https://newssetup.kontan.co.id/news/antusias-tinggi-sudah-28000-perusahaan-mendaftar-vaksinasi-gotong-royong (accessed 28 July 2022).

Watson, O.J., G. Barnsley, J. Toor, A.B. Hogan, P. Winskill, and A.C. Ghani. 2022. "Global Impact of the First Year of COVID-19 Vaccination: A Mathematical Modelling Study". *The Lancet Infectious Diseases* 22, no. 9: 1,293–302. https://www.thelancet.com/journals/laninf/article/PIIS1473-3099(22)00320-6/fulltext

WHO (World Health Organization). 2018. *Communicating Risk in Public Health Emergencies: A WHO Guideline for Emergency Risk Communication (ERC) Policy and Practice*. Geneva: World Health Organization. https://www.who.int/publications/i/item/9789241550208

———. 2020. *WHO Situation Report No. 84*. https://www.who.int/docs/default-source/coronaviruse/situation-reports/20200413-sitrep-84-covid-19.pdf

World Bank. 2022. "Indonesia's Economy Sees Rebound in 2022 Following Post-Covid Reopening". News release, 15 December 2022. https://www.worldbank.org/en/news/press-release/2022/12/15/indonesia-s-economy-sees-rebound-in-2022-following-post-covid-reopening

Yanwardhana, Emir. 2023. "Top! Penanganan Darurat Covid RI Dipuji 2 Lembaga Besar Dunia". [Good! RI's Covid emergency handling praised by 2 major world institutions]. *CNBC Indonesia*, 20 March 2023. https://www.cnbcindonesia.com/news/20230320094505-4-423083/top-penanganan-darurat-covid-ri-dipuji-2-lembaga-besar-dunia (accessed 28 July 2022).

9

CONFLICT AND COOPERATION
Covid-19 Policy Coordination in Malaysia

Tricia Yeoh

INTRODUCTION

The Covid-19 pandemic took Malaysia by surprise, as it did most other countries. The first wave of cases came about as the country faced a political crisis, which led to a rapid change of government at the federal level in early March 2020 when the Pakatan Harapan administration fell. The newly formed Perikatan Nasional coalition—comprising Parti Pribumi Bersatu Malaysia (Bersatu), Parti Islam Se-Malaysia (PAS) and the United Malays National Organization (UMNO)—took over. It is important to note that the Perikatan Nasional government took over with only a slim majority of 113 parliamentary seats out of 222. In July 2021, UMNO officially withdrew its support from the Perikatan Nasional government, leading to political and policy uncertainty and instability.

Between 2020 and 2022, there was also a second change in the top leadership position, when in August 2021 the Prime Minister was replaced with another member of the same coalition—but from a different party—and the Cabinet was reshuffled significantly. Consequently, Malaysia had three different health ministers in as many years and it was amid high levels of political instability that the pandemic took hold in several increasingly devastating waves.

Following the March 2020 federal government change, four states—Kedah, Perak, Malacca and Johor—also changed government. Then, in September 2020, Sabah held a state election due to political defections from the ruling coalition, leading to a fifth change in state government. Three other state elections took place in 2021 and 2022 (in Malacca, Sarawak and Johor), and although the incumbent coalitions retained power, the Chief Minister of Johor was replaced. Such rapid political changes over a short period of time would be expected to and did disrupt policy coordination at the state level.

The policy coordination required to handle a national health crisis tested the robustness of the institutions and leadership. Indeed, Malaysia needed efficient horizontal and vertical coordination to facilitate effective pandemic management. Instead, changes in the individuals helming federal government agencies crucial to this coordination within health and socio-economic spheres meant interrupted administration.

Although Malaysia is a constitutional federation, law- and policymaking has been historically highly centralized (Hutchinson 2014; Ostwald 2017). During the pandemic and the political crisis between 2020 and 2022, the federal government continued this centralized approach and adopted top-down approaches to managing Covid-19 through federal laws and regulations. In several cases, federal-state relations became fractious when disagreements arose, particularly when the federal government did not conduct meaningful prior consultation with the states.

Given this backdrop of turbulent political and administrative instability in Malaysia, how did policy coordination unfold? How did the federal government coordinate itself across ministries and agencies, in gathering and sharing data? How did the central health and economic authorities make decisions and coordinate with each other? How coordinated were responses to unemployment and labour-related issues of job protection and migrant workers? Further, how did the federal and state governments cooperate, especially given the oppositional nature of several states? Was there a devolution of decision-making regarding lockdowns and social assistance? Did conflict arise and how was this resolved? This chapter aims to analyse the efficacy of horizontal and vertical policy coordination in Malaysia's management of Covid-19 from 2020 to 2022.

BACKGROUND: AN OVERVIEW OF COVID-19 IN MALAYSIA

The first Malaysian case of Covid-19 was confirmed on 4 February 2020, after a Malaysian returned from Singapore (Elengoe 2020). Thus began the first wave of Covid-19 cases, which ended fairly quickly with only twenty-two cases and no deaths. The second wave of infections broke out soon after, in late February 2020, and grew rapidly in the following three weeks.

After being sworn in as the new Prime Minister on 1 March 2020, Muhyiddin Yassin publicly banned mass gatherings on 13 March. The federal National Security Council mobilized a national response with technical guidance from the Ministry of Health (Kyaw et al. 2023). Up to the end of this second wave, which concluded at the end of September 2020, 10,167 people tested positive (*Malaysiakini* 2020). National testing capacity increased from 1,000 tests per day in January 2020 to over 38,000 tests per day in September 2020; selected government hospitals were converted into full or partial Covid-19 hospitals, and training institutes and nursing dormitories, among others, were converted into quarantine centres (Ministry of Health 2020).

The third wave of Covid-19 infections started from late September to early October 2020, following the return of politicians to Peninsular Malaysia from Sabah, East Malaysia, where they had held election campaigns in the lead-up to the 26 September 2020 state election (Yeoh 2021). Escalating exponentially from an average of 400 new daily cases in early October to 2,525 new cases on 31 December 2020,[1] the Covid-19 situation was further exacerbated by the fact that state borders were open throughout December, and many Malaysians travelled across the country for the end-of-year holidays. The Malaysian government's relaxed measures may also be attributed to pressure from players within the tourism industry and, more generally, to economic pressure (lockdown coordination is covered later in this chapter). This wave eased in February 2021.

After about a four-week lull, a fourth wave hit Malaysia, in part due to the considerable movement of individuals during the Ramadan and Hari Raya period, which encouraged the spread (Code Blue 2021). This fourth wave, the result of the Delta variant, rose steadily in June 2021 and peaked on 26 August 2021 with 24,599 new daily cases. It was during this period that public hospitals struggled to cope with the increase in caseload, with medical personnel anonymously citing insufficient facilities and poor conditions (*New Straits Times* 2021a).

As seen in Figure 9.1, in January 2022, the number of daily new infections averaged 3,000, but a fifth wave arose rapidly from February to April, peaking on 5 March 2022 at 33,406 new cases. Where the fourth wave had been more lethal given that most individuals were not yet vaccinated, this fifth wave, the result of the Omicron variant, was more infectious but produced less severe symptoms. As of 18 April 2024, 37,349 Malaysians had died due to contracting Covid-19 or related complications. Between 2020 and 2022, Malaysia experienced more than 5 million cases.

INSTITUTIONAL FRAMEWORK

Constitutional and Legal Framework of the Three Levels of Government

Article 1 of the 1957 Federal Constitution of Malaysia describes the country as a federation of thirteen states and three territories. However, state powers have gradually eroded, as a result of expanded central powers within the federal government. That process began when local council elections were abolished in 1965 and, over the following decades, other institutional mechanisms were introduced that further strengthened the federal government's hold over states.

On the surface, there appears to be a clear demarcation of powers between the federal and state governments. The Ninth Schedule of the Federal Constitution recognizes the semi-autonomous nature of states, which have some "constitutionally entrenched division of powers in the legislative, executive, judicial and financial fields" (Shad 2019, p. 74). In practice, however, there was ample scope for the solidification of a powerful central government. For example, Article 71(3) allows the federal government to amend a state constitution if there is non-compliance by

FIGURE 9.1
Confirmed Covid-19 New Cases and New Deaths, Daily (per Million), January 2020 to May 2023

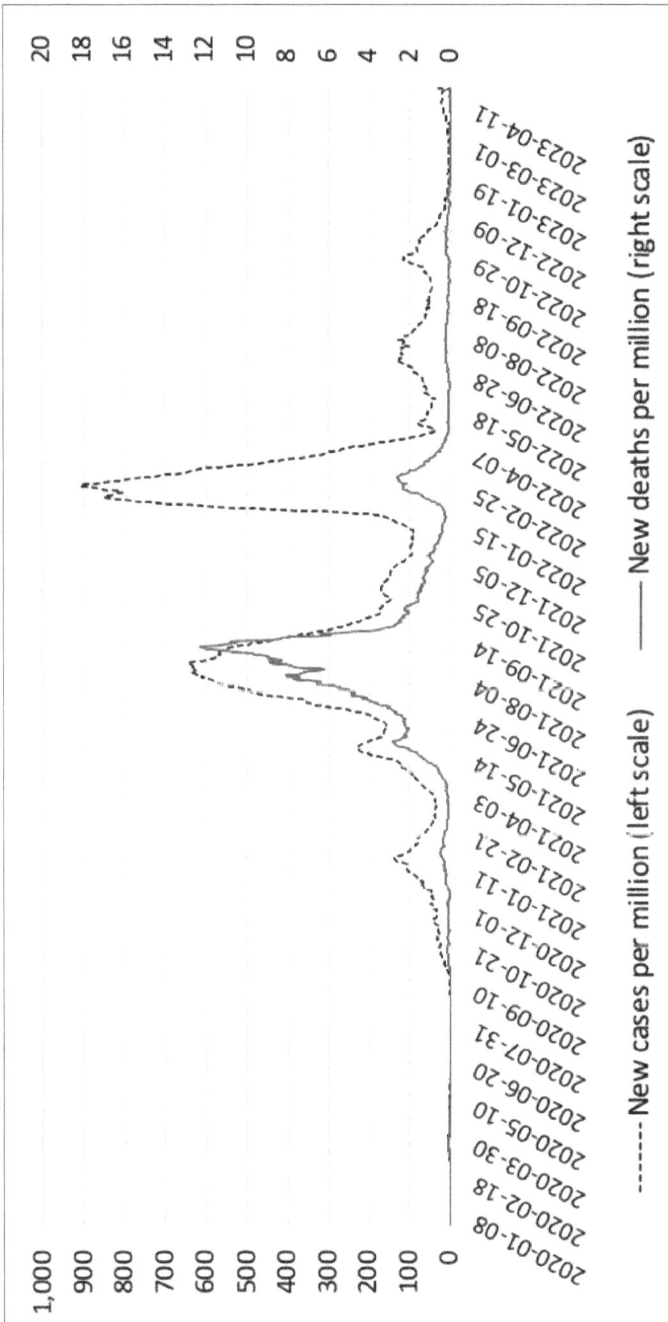

Source: ourworldindata.org.

a state with the Federal Constitution. Article 75 provides that federal law prevails when any state law is inconsistent with the former, while Article 76 allows the federal government to make laws pertaining to state matters if it promotes the uniformity of laws between federal and state governments, or if it is requested to do so by a state making a request for itself. Article 76A permits parliament to delegate its powers to the states, whether collectively or individually. Article 81 of the Federal Constitution states that the executive authority of every state is to be exercised in compliance with federal law, and should not impede or prejudice the exercise of the federal government's authority.

The Federal Constitution recognizes three levels of government: federal, state and local. Article 150 of the Federal Constitution provides authority to the King to proclaim emergency measures (the King acts upon the advice of the Prime Minister). The federal government can also use emergency provisions to suspend states' rights under the same article. The Ninth Schedule, which spells out the jurisdiction of the federal and state governments, includes "public health, sanitation and prevention of infectious diseases" in the Concurrent List, which contains items over which federal and state governments share control. However, "medicine and health" fall under the Federal List, meaning the federal government has ultimate control over the funding and administration of the Ministry of Health, state health departments, and public hospitals and community clinics throughout the country (Table A9.1). Local governments, although also empowered for public health and disease prevention functions, in practice work closely with state governments and often merely operationalize policies as directed by the state government (Yeoh 2022).

Despite the highly centralized nature of Malaysia's federation, in which the central government controls most policy matters leaving less substantive areas to the states, state governments do have some policy autonomy (over land, religion, local councils and raw water). More importantly, however, there have historically existed political tensions whenever state governments have been controlled by opposition parties, where the latter have in some cases attempted to push boundaries of their policy jurisdiction, or where there were conflicting decisions, especially over items in the Concurrent List (where decision-making is shared). Tensions have also occurred when the federal government has attempted to destabilize opposition state governments by a range of means, including withholding development funds. Some of these tensions arose again during the pandemic.

Governing Laws and Regulations

While federal and state governments have joint jurisdiction over public health, the 1988 Prevention and Control of Infectious Diseases Act (the law used to enforce Malaysia's movement control orders [MCOs]) is a federal law, and it sets out the authorities that are permitted to act during an outbreak and under what circumstances. Malaysia also has regulations and orders on the prevention and control of infectious diseases, which spell out what is permitted under an MCO. These were enforced from 2020 onwards. Further, a related regulation, the 2020 Prevention and Control of Infectious Diseases (Declaration of Infected Local Areas) Order, defined all states and all three federal territories in Malaysia as "infected areas". This became a point of legal contention when the federal government chose to open the economy more quickly, whereas states wanted to retain stricter lockdown measures.

Malaysia's National Security Act 2016 provides a legal basis for the establishment of the National Security Council. It also defines areas classed as "security areas" that can have restrictive conditions imposed on them and the special powers by which the Security Forces may act. Other related laws and policies that were significant in the Covid-19 response included the Ministry of Health Disaster Management Plan and the Malaysia Strategy for Emerging Diseases and Public Health Emergencies (MySED) II Workplan (2017–2021) (Ministry of Health 2020), both of which fall under the purview of the federal government. The Declaration of Quarantine Stations (No. 2) 2020 listed 409 institutions as potential quarantine stations, though in the end not all were used.

The government also had to introduce legislation to enable a Covid-related financial stimulus package; this was the Temporary Measures for Government Financing Act 2020 (Coronavirus Disease 2019), which provided MYR45 billion for twenty-nine stimulus programmes. The Act was later amended to raise the ceiling of the Covid-19 fund to MYR65 billion. As well as funding the stimulus package, it also provided funds for aid and future vaccine procurement. The Act also temporarily raised the statutory debt limit from 55 per cent to 60 per cent of gross domestic product (GDP) until the end of 2022; this self-imposed limit is a crucial measure of fiscal discipline. The government increased the limit further to 65 per cent of GDP in October 2021 to balance funding needs, taking into account the increase in the Covid-19 fund ceiling and funding needed to implement the Twelfth Malaysia Plan. Many academics and think-tanks have cautioned against continually raising it, stating that a higher debt would reduce the country's ability to handle emergencies and its development opportunities, and would also lead to negative effects on the domestic financial system (Focus Malaysia 2022).

In January 2021, the federal government passed the Emergency (Essential Powers) Ordinance 2021 and declared a national emergency, which meant that no election could take place. This therefore secured the position of the then governments (at both federal and state levels). The national emergency was put into place to tackle Covid-19, but it provided unfettered powers to the federal government without corresponding institutional checks and balances, since parliament and state legislative assemblies were suspended. Between February and April 2021, a further series of emergency-related ordinances were also passed into law: among these, the key ordinances made it illegal to distribute misinformation (Emergency [Essential Powers] [No. 2] Ordinance 2021), allowed Chief Ministers of states to withdraw state funds for whatever expense they deemed necessary during the emergency (Emergency [Essential Powers] [Amendment] Ordinance 2021) and allowed the federal government to withdraw funds from the National Trust Fund (Kumpulan Wang Amanah Negara [KWAN]) for vaccination procurement and related expenses.

Although the emergency status was justified by the federal government on the basis of the pandemic, in reality, there was widespread criticism that it was implemented to ensure that the general election would be postponed in order to secure the Perikatan Nasional government's position—given its razor-thin majority. In June 2021, following public pressure that parliament be allowed to resume, the Malaysian King called on the Prime Minister to reconvene parliament as soon as possible. This led to a series of unprecedented public disputes with the Palace regarding the revocation of the emergency status (Kumar 2021).

Main Government Bodies and Their Responsibilities

Multiple government bodies were given responsibilities for the extensive amount of work involved in managing the national pandemic. From healthcare and vaccinations to security and economic matters, the following sections outline the key government bodies in charge of three distinct areas: movement control, standard operating procedures (SOPs) and the economy; public health and vaccinations; and budgets and stimulus packages.

Movement Control, SOPs and the Economy

Table 9.1 sets out the main ministries and committees responsible for movement control, SOPs and the economy during Covid-19.

The first government body tasked with the responsibility of overseeing the pandemic was the National Action Council, which monitors national development. It is chaired by the Prime Minister and its members consist of the members of the federal Cabinet. The first meeting of the National Action Council, at which Covid-19 mitigation plans were discussed, excluded the heads of state governments controlled by the opposition coalition. The federal government later reversed this and invited all state government leaders to subsequent meetings. The National Security Council, also chaired by the Prime Minister, was appointed to lead in formulating SOPs in response to Covid-19. The National Security Council's Telegram account was one of two channels from which the public could obtain daily updates regarding Covid-19.

The National Recovery Council was set up in July 2021. In October 2021, after the government signed a historic memorandum with the opposition coalition Pakatan Harapan, four Pakatan Harapan Members of Parliament from different political parties were invited to join the National Recovery Council (*Malay Mail* 2021).[2] Representatives from the private sector and NGOs were also appointed to the National Recovery Council, whose task was to ensure the smooth implementation of the National Recovery Plan. The SOP Expert Panel set up by the National Recovery Council was responsible for formulating a new set of SOPs as the nation moved towards recovery.

The police force was deployed to help ensure public adherence to SOPs, among other tasks. On the night before the first MCO was implemented,

TABLE 9.1
Main Ministries and Committees Responsible for Movement Control, SOPs and Economy During Covid-19

Ministry/Agency	*Functions/Responsibilities*	*Remarks*
National Security Council	Formulate SOPs in response to Covid-19.	Chaired by the Prime Minister. Executive members include Deputy Prime Minister, Director General of the National Security Council, Minister of Defence, Minister of Home Affairs, Minister of Communications and Multimedia, Chief Secretary to Government, Chief of Defence Forces and Inspector General of Police.
National Recovery Council	Ensure smooth implementation of the National Recovery Plan.	Chaired by the Prime Minister. Jointly administers agencies under Ministry of Finance and under the Economic Stimulus Implementation and Coordination Unit Between National Agencies (LAKSANA). Administered the National Recovery Plan, while the Ministry of Finance was the coordinator of the plan. Also set up National Recovery Council SOP Expert Panel.
Ministry of International Trade and Industry (MITI)	Defines the list of essential services and businesses allowed to operate.	MITI was tasked to approve businesses allowed to operate throughout MCO periods. Businesses were certified with an MITI letter.
Police Force, under the Home Ministry	Ensure public adherence to SOPs, maintain roadblocks, approve cross-state travel on case-by-case basis.	N.A.+
Malaysian Armed Forces	Tasked to help the police to implement movement control orders (MCOs).	Based on Section 5 of the Prevention and Control of Infectious Diseases Act 1988 authorizes the Minister to confer power on any agency to enforce the law.

Sources: National Security Council (n.d.); Ministry of Finance (2021); MITI (2021); Prevention and Control of Infectious Diseases Act 1988; Bernama (2020b).

there were extremely long queues at numerous police stations across the country, as citizens applied for approval to travel out of town. Such scenes were observed from 2020 to 2022 prior to each MCO. The Malaysian armed forces were also tasked to help the police in implementing the MCOs. Both law enforcement agencies report to the Ministry of Home Affairs.

During the pandemic, it was the Ministry of International Trade and Industry (MITI) that was most aggressive in calling for the MCOs to ease, as businesses started to feel the effects of an economic shutdown. State governments generally took a position of greater caution. It was MITI's responsibility to define essential services, thereby determining which businesses were allowed to operate during the MCOs. MITI would also, subject to application, provide approval letters to permit these companies to operate, but that would prove complicated to administer.

Public Health and Vaccinations

Table 9.2 delineates the main ministries and committees responsible for delivering Covid-19 public health and vaccination services during the pandemic.

The Special Committee for Ensuring Access to Covid-19 Vaccine Supply (JKJAV) was a unique committee jointly chaired by the Minister of Health and the Minister of Science, Technology and Innovation. It was responsible for planning, implementing and monitoring the national vaccination programme. The Covid-19 Immunisation Task Force was established in January 2021.

It was largely believed that this unique joint coordination between the two ministries was because the Minister of Health was not as capable of delivering on this nationwide exercise as the more competent Minister of MOSTI, Khairy Jamaluddin of UMNO. MOSTI led the coordination, in consultation with the Ministry of Health, up to the time of change in political leadership. When the Prime Minister stepped down in August 2021 and the Cabinet was reshuffled, Khairy was appointed Minister of Health. From then on, vaccinations were managed primarily by the Ministry of Health, and without the involvement of MOSTI.

While at MOSTI, Khairy led the process of commissioning and approving the use of the national mobile contact tracing application

TABLE 9.2
Main Ministries and Committees Responsible for Covid-19 Public Health and Vaccinations

Ministry/Agency	*Functions/Responsibilities*	*Remarks*
National Crisis Preparedness and Response Centre	Monitor the development of Covid-19 and oversee medical response and preparedness for outbreak.	Placed under the Surveillance Section of the Disease Control Division, Ministry of Health Malaysia.
Special Committee for Ensuring Access to Covid-19 Vaccine Supply	Plan, implement and monitor the national vaccination programme.	Co-chaired by Ministry of Health and Ministry of Science, Technology and Innovation.
Covid-19 Immunisation Task Force	Support the implementation of the national vaccination programme.	Established on 20 January 2021. Placed under the Special Committee for Ensuring Access to Covid-19 Vaccine Supply, led by the Ministry of Science, Technology and Innovation.
Greater Klang Valley Task Force	Assist Ministry of Health in Covid-19 measures in Greater Klang Valley, particularly in oxygen tank supply and corpse management.	Established by the Malaysian Army on 6 August 2021 at the height of the fourth wave. Consisted of 1,000 members.
Ministry of Science, Technology and Innovation (MOSTI)	Jointly coordinate national vaccination programme, develop local vaccine production.	Minister of MOSTI is also the Coordinating Minister for the national vaccination programme.
Ministry of Health	Prepare guidelines for health providers and hospitals, provide Covid-19-related information to the public.	Focus on matters related to health services.

Sources: My Government (2020); Ministry of Foreign Affairs (2021); MOSTI (2021); National Security Council (2021); Ministry of Health (2020).

MySejahtera. It used individualized QR codes, and it was mandatory for Malaysians and non-Malaysian residents to use it to check in at locations. The application was also used for vaccination purposes; Malaysians and residents registered for vaccinations and made appointments within the app itself.

Although the MySejahtera application was generally well-received, concerns were expressed regarding the data privacy of app users. The legal requirement for all residents of the country to use the application when entering all types of premises was believed by some to be unnecessary. In March 2022, it was revealed that the company contracted by the Malaysian government to develop MySejahtera had done so with no payment from the government. Without payment and a clear contractual agreement with the company, this meant that it was unclear as to whether the app developer owned the rights to user data. This revelation sparked confusion and concerns about the lack of transparency regarding the ownership of the app and, more importantly, the protection of the private data of more than 38 million users nationwide.[3] Then Minister of Health Khairy Jamaluddin, however, later stated that the data and information acquired from the use of MySejahtera was fully owned by the government (*The Sun* 2022).

Budgets and Stimulus Packages

Table 9.3 details the different ministries and government agencies or committees responsible for the government's pandemic-related budgets and stimulus packages.

The Ministry of Finance was the main ministry in charge of allocating the necessary fiscal resources for the series of economic stimulus packages provided in 2020 and 2021. Chiefly, it set up LAKSANA (the Economic Stimulus Implementation and Coordination Unit Between National Agencies) on 16 March 2020[4] to monitor the disbursement of Covid-19 stimulus packages, with the dual objectives of tracking and monitoring these through weekly reports (document and video format) and ensuring the stimulus packages were delivered.

Malaysia's central bank, Bank Negara Malaysia, was responsible for several measures to address the impacts of Covid-19. First, it established a fund for small and medium-sized enterprises (SMEs), with available

TABLE 9.3
Main Ministries and Committees Responsible for Budgets and Stimulus Packages during Covid-19

Ministry/Agency	*Functions/Responsibilities*	*Remarks*
Ministry of Finance	Allocate fiscal resources for economic stimulus packages.	On 16 March 2020, set up LAKSANA (Economic Stimulus Implementation and Coordination Unit Between National Agencies) to monitor the disbursement of Covid-19 stimulus packages. Objectives of LAKSANA: • Tracking and monitoring the disbursement of Covid-19 stimulus packages through weekly reports (document and video format); • Ensuring economic stimulus packages were delivered to and benefit all levels of society.
Bank Negara Malaysia	Establish funds to assist targeted sectors. Regulate banks offering loan repayment moratoriums to their users.	Established a fund for small and medium-sized enterprises with facilities targeting different sectors. Regulating loan repayment assistance.
Employees Provident Fund	Administer account holders' withdrawals from their own Employees Provident Fund accounts.	Launched three schemes, i-Lestari, i-Sinar and i-Citra.
Individual State Governments	Allocate fiscal resources for individual state economic stimulus packages.	State governments took initiative to inject additional funds to aid frontliners, households from the bottom 40 per cent of household income (known in Malaysia as B40 households) and provide rental waivers on government-owned property, among others.

Sources: Bernama (2020a); Bank Negara Malaysia (2022); Employees Provident Fund (2021); Welsh (2020).

funds as of September 2021 of MYR11.2 billion. Among the facilities were the Targeted Relief and Recovery Facility, High Tech and Green Facility, SME Automation and Digitalisation Facility, Agrofood Facility, Business Recapitalisation Facility, Low Carbon Transition Facility, Micro Enterprises Facility, All Economic Sectors Facility and PENJANA Tourism Financing.

Bank Negara Malaysia was also responsible for regulating loan repayment assistance. Borrowers would have to contact their respective banks to arrange for loan repayment aid. The loan repayment moratoriums, for example, would be facilitated by individual banks, but Bank Negara Malaysia had oversight over the process—and also had valuable data regarding the impact of the loan moratorium on the overall economy. Bank Negara Malaysia also had a financial management and resilience programme to assist vulnerable borrowers who experienced cash flow difficulties during the pandemic. Further, other assistance packages included seed capital for micro-entrepreneurs (iTEKAD), protection for the bottom 40 per cent of households (Perlindungan Tenang), and initiating an assistance programme enabling insurance providers to support policyholders adversely affected by Covid-19 (Bank Negara Malaysia 2022). The emphasis for Bank Negara Malaysia was to assist SMEs that were badly impacted by the pandemic.

The Employees Provident Fund (EPF), a retirement fund to which employees must contribute monthly from their salary, was depended upon heavily throughout the Covid-19 period. The federal government approved, controversially, a scheme allowing individuals to withdraw from their accounts in several rounds starting from March 2020. The first scheme, called i-Lestari, allowed account holders to withdraw up to MYR500 per month for twelve months. The second and third schemes, i-Sinar and i-Citra, allowed contributors to access their retirement fund account (Account 1), which had previously been reserved for use after retirement. Finally, a one-off scheme permitting individuals to withdraw MYR10,000 from their EPF account was announced in April 2022.[5] A total of MYR145.4 billion was withdrawn by members under the four withdrawal schemes in 2020 and 2021 (*The Edge Malaysia* 2024). The criticisms against these schemes centre on the concerns that Malaysians will have depleted their funds by the time they retire and will not have the means to support themselves in their old age.

POLICY COORDINATION

The policy coordination section of this chapter is categorized into four areas, namely information and communication; lockdown implementation; distribution of economic aid; and vaccination roll-out. More emphasis will be given to lockdown implementation and vaccinations, as another chapter in this volume covers the distribution of economic aid.

Information and Communication

In Malaysia, public communication regarding the pandemic was conducted primarily by the federal government, and was coordinated across ministries chiefly via the Ministry of Health, the National Security Council and MOSTI (the latter was more actively involved in informing the public about the vaccination roll-out, as discussed later in this chapter). While initially sketchy and inconsistent, the daily press conferences led by the Ministry of Health (and later jointly with the National Security Council) were helpful in providing regular data to Malaysians. This data was also communicated via the MySejahtera app. There was less coordination when it involved providing consistent information from federal to state governments. State governments took a more proactive approach to inform their constituents about the local situation and share relevant information. This way, information dissemination was decentralized.

The Ministry of Health was the primary actor in providing information to the public. Its Director General, Noor Hishamuddin Abdullah, took over its daily press conferences after the Minister of Health Adham Baba stated in March 2020 in a widely shared television interview that drinking warm water would prevent Covid-19 infection (*The Star* 2020a). Before he was appointed Prime Minister, Senior Minister Ismail Sabri (Security Cluster) gave regular press briefings on SOPs that the public and industries were expected to comply with, as well as MCO enforcement. It was only from May 2021 onwards that there were joint press conferences by the Ministry of Health Director General and the Defence Minister, indicating that there was some level of improved coordination between the two ministries.

In addition, public communication was carried out using government platforms including websites, social media and messaging applications. As mentioned earlier, the National Security Council was extremely active on its Telegram channel, sharing daily Covid-19 case numbers. The Ministry of Health did the same through the Telegram channel of the National Crisis Preparedness and Response Centre. However, the information disseminated was typically already incorporated into an infographic, as opposed to being granular data that could be downloaded. The national contact tracing app MySejahtera was also used as a communication platform. Updates were uploaded daily—this included information on the numbers of new cases and hospitalization rates—and users were reminded to maintain their hygiene practices and continue social distancing.

In May 2021, Khairy Jamaluddin, who was then still MOSTI Minister, rolled out rather haphazardly a system called the Hotspots Identification for Dynamic Engagement (HIDE) system. This was meant to be an early warning system to identify potentially risky locations. While such a system had indeed been called for, there had been no engagement with the public or representatives of industry and corporations prior to the announcement on 4 May 2021 that it would be implemented. The system was designed to enable "pre-emptive intervention and appropriate action to be taken by the authorities, owners of premises and the public" (Bernama 2021). However, just four days later, on 8 May 2021, the Prime Minister was reported saying that 152 premises listed under the HIDE system would be ordered to close for three days effective immediately, including major shopping malls (*Free Malaysia Today* 2021c). This prompted several shopping malls and retail advocate groups to issue a joint statement, stating that they were being unfairly penalized as they were complying with national SOPs.

After Khairy Jamaluddin was appointed Minister of Health, data was reported in a more disaggregated format. Under his tenure it was captured in a new website called "Covid Now", launched in September 2021.[6] Prior to the existence of this website, the public could only view such detailed historical data on a range of Covid-related themes from a popular media website, *Malaysiakini*'s Covid Tracker,[7] which, due to a lack of funding, stopped tracking cases in the same month Covid Now was launched.

Apart from the national-level mobile application MySejahtera, several state governments also developed their own contact tracing applications. These included Penang (PGCare), Selangor (SELangkah), Sabah (Sabah Trace), Sarawak (CovidTrace and Qmunity), Terengganu (Masuk.la) and Johor (Jejak Johor) (Welsh 2020). Penang and Sarawak provided particularly regular updates to their constituents, and Penang also opened twenty-four-hour hotlines and its own Covid-19 website (Welsh 2020). State governments took the opportunity to provide increased public communication at the state level, which was necessary given that public health conditions differed drastically from state to state.

However, in October 2020, Dr Dzulkefly Ahmad (former Minister of Health under the Pakatan Harapan administration) who was appointed by the Selangor state government as Chair of the Selangor Task Force for Covid-19 (STFC) took the federal government to task for being unwilling to share data, which he claimed had previously occurred through close cooperation between the Ministry of Health, National Security Council and the Selangor state government's own operation centres. According to him, the Ministry of Health had stopped sharing data with Selangor state, and the latter's calls for data integration, which would have allowed greater coordination in pandemic management, had fallen on deaf ears (Dzulkefly 2020). Selangor had opened access to its own application SELangkah to all Ministry of Health personnel in Selangor and Kuala Lumpur.

Lockdown Implementation

The government implemented an MCO, which was announced on 16 March 2020 and began on 18 March 2020. It was tightened soon after as the number of cases rose steadily. Under the MCO, only industries falling into a strictly defined list of essential goods and services were permitted to operate, and even those would have to apply and receive approval from the MITI. Schools were also closed nationwide simultaneously, and consequently school shutdowns and reopenings took place throughout the year. Cross-state travel was allowed only with police approval, and individuals were not allowed to travel more than 10 kilometres from their residence. These rules were gradually loosened under the subsequent Conditional MCO (CMCO) from 4 to 12 May 2020, as the number of daily new infections and the risk to health fell.

The coordination of the various MCOs was poorly managed, with little learning taken from them. On 15 March 2020, one day before the first MCO announcement, the Minister of Health stated that the government would meet the next day to introduce further measures on Covid-19, which caused people to start panic-buying groceries; supermarkets were extremely crowded as a result. Prime Minister Muhyiddin's announcement the following day, 16 March 2020, stating that the public should expect a big news announcement that night exacerbated the panic.

Throughout the pandemic, some of the announcements themselves were also vague enough to lead to confusion. For example, after the first MCO announcement, it was unclear whether Malaysians with Singaporean work permits would be allowed to cross Malaysian borders to enter Singapore. That they would be able to do so was only confirmed at 12:40 p.m. on 17 March 2020 by the Immigration Director General. However, due to the confirmation delay, there was a massive exodus of Malaysians to Singapore on the night of 16 March 2020, causing congestion at the borders, with some Malaysians even physically running across the causeway. Second, a Frequently Asked Questions (FAQs) document was issued relatively late by the National Security Council, on the afternoon of 17 March, and three different versions were issued with some inconsistencies. The first version said the Malay marriage (*nikah*) ceremony was advised against, whereas the final version said it was banned. Similarly, the first version said all public and private university students were to return to their hometowns, whereas the third version said they could stay on campus. However, this had already sparked an exodus of students to their hometowns in other states. A day later, students were again asked to return to their hometowns. Finally, the Inspector General of Police announced that all interstate travellers needed to notify their nearest police station, leading to long queues at police stations, but rescinded this requirement several hours later. During those early weeks, these policy flip-flops caused tension and confusion to people already unsure about what Covid-19 entailed.

Most ministries did not release their own set of FAQs until 22 March 2020, and then made multiple changes made to them. The FAQs published by the Ministry of Home Affairs on its website did not tally with those it posted on its Telegram channel, which added to the confusion.

The lockdown implementation itself was inconsistent, in that the government was heavily criticized for applying the rules differently to different categories of people. By the end of 2020, five people who breached quarantine orders had been charged in court and were convicted, with three of them fined a combined MYR13,000 and two more fined a combined MYR20,000 and given prison sentences (Yahoo News 2020). Senior government officials, however, were treated differently. For example, Khairuddin Aman Razali, Minister of Plantation Industries and Commodities, was fined only MYR1,000 for failing to observe quarantine SOPs after a trip to Turkey in August 2020 (*South China Morning Post* 2020). Many high-profile individuals were also publicly seen to be disregarding rules.[8] Finally, a new federal gazette issued in February 2021 allowed ministers returning from official visits to undergo a shortened quarantine period, three days instead of the standard ten days, again causing public outcry.

The government eventually rolled out several versions of the MCO. After the first four MCOs (MCO 1.0) in the period from 18 March 2020 to 3 May 2020, a Conditional MCO (CMCO) was implemented from 4 May 2020 to 9 June 2020. Under the CMCO, the only restrictions were that there would be no interstate travel and no social gatherings. This was followed by a Recovery MCO (RMCO) from 10 June 2020 to 31 March 2021. Under the RMCO, social gatherings were allowed but not interstate travel. However, from 13 January 2021 to 31 May 2021, some individual states switched between MCO (MCO 2.0 from 13 to 26 January 2021), CMCO, RMCO, Enhanced MCO (EMCO) and semi-EMCO, depending on their situation. Under the EMCO, residents were required to stay at home after 8:00 p.m. and most factories were shut, whereas under the semi-EMCO, authorities could force Covid-19 testing on residents and people would be allowed to move in and out of the area—a district or residential neighbourhood, not a state—with a valid reason. A full MCO (MCO 3.0) was once again implemented nationwide from 1 June 2021 to 28 June 2021, and Malaysia was placed under a new National Recovery Plan from 15 June 2021 to 31 December 2021.

Industries Allowed to Operate

A large part of the coordination had to do with the government determining which industries were essential services and were allowed to operate. The MITI was tasked with this role, but difficulties arose. Defining what constituted "essential" was complicated. Some industries that were not deemed essential, such as manufacturers of packaging materials, were critical in the supply of parts or components to essential industries, and their closure caused supply chain disruptions, shortages and supply shortages of the final products (Ferlito and Perone 2020). Further, some sectors that were initially classified as essential were later deemed non-essential. On 6 April, the government reversed its decision on alcohol production and halted production at Heineken and Carlsberg, which had previously been permitted to operate on a limited basis.[9] The flip-flop was clearly a response to religious voices within the coalition, who had questioned whether alcohol production was really essential, and was clearly an example of poor decision-making.

Companies were required to submit applications to operate online, but the MITI website received more than 100,000 requests and crashed within several hours on 13 April 2020, the day it was launched. The website was eventually restored, but the website crash recurred each time the government imposed a new lockdown. Some companies reported never receiving responses to their applications, or receiving approvals only close to the end of the MCO period in question. They were then required to apply anew for the next MCO, but responses were again tardy, leading to an economic slowdown since businesses could not legally operate.

Logistics and transport operators were only allowed to provide services to manufacturers that had received MITI permission to operate. This caused tremendous confusion since the logistics and transport operators then had to provide documentation to show that they were working with approved manufacturers. Following that, on 19 March 2020, in addition to the requirement to obtain permission to operate, MITI stated that manufacturers could only operate at 50 per cent capacity. While this was based on public health concerns, it caused massive supply problems for key sectors within the industry, such as manufacturers of disposable gloves and food supply, which were producing goods that were in increasing demand during the pandemic. In the public transport sector, including trains and buses, operations continued normally, but passenger volumes decreased significantly during the lockdowns; for example, rail ridership in 2020 was significantly lower compared to 2019 (Rahmat and Khoo 2022).

A new requirement was announced for food supply, e-commerce and personal care companies to obtain a certificate to operate from the Ministry of Domestic Trade and Consumer Affairs. This was not quickly communicated to companies. It was only on 24 March 2020, more than a week after the announcement, that a task force was formed, comprising MITI, the Ministry of Domestic Trade and Consumer Affairs and the Ministry of Agriculture, to handle food supply chain issues.[10] By this time, companies were confused and had also been unable to obtain an official response to requests for clarification.

As part of phase three of the MCO (MCO 3.0 from 1 June 2021 to 28 June 2021), additional businesses were allowed to operate, including barber shops, hair salons, opticians, launderette and car wash centres. However, it later turned out that this only applied to businesses within areas with no reported Covid-19 cases (green zones). Then Senior Minister Ismail Sabri stated that the original announcement by MITI to allow businesses to operate as part of the MCO 3.0 was not final, as it was still to be decided. The Director-General of the Health Ministry also stated that the government should have consulted the health authorities before publicizing the list. Eventually, the government announced that barber shops, hair salons and opticians were not allowed to reopen, contrary to previous notices (*The Star* 2020b).

Reopening of the Economy

On 1 May 2020, the federal government abruptly announced that it would ease the MCO, giving only three days' notice. From 4 May 2020, Malaysia would operate under a Conditional Movement Control Order (CMCO). Six state governments (Kedah, Sabah, Pahang, Penang, Kelantan and Sarawak) immediately said they would not follow this, and three (Selangor, Perak and Negeri Sembilan) said they would not fully comply.

The states believed that the reopening of all sectors and industries was too abrupt and argued that buffer time was needed to allow state governments and companies to adopt new SOPs to ensure hygiene and public health. Interestingly, four of these nine states were politically aligned with the federal government; prior to Covid-19, federally aligned states would typically have adhered to instructions from the centre without protest.

Many of the states' Chief Ministers felt they should have been properly consulted beforehand; they said they would be the ones implementing the decisions and the federal government should have assessed the situation in each state and their capacity before making a decision (The Malaysian Reserve 2020). The federal government responded with a statement saying that companies might sue state governments if they refused to reopen (*Malaysiakini* 2020). However, the Penang state government said it was prepared to face legal challenges from industry if that was the consequence for protecting its people from the pandemic. A CMCO was thus implemented nationwide on 4 May 2020, followed by a Recovery Movement Control Order (RMCO) on 10 June the same year. The nine state governments gradually and eventually did reopen their economies.

Some experts cited Article 81 of the Federal Constitution to argue that states must adhere to federal laws, including the 1988 Prevention and Control of Infectious Diseases Act, since all had in 1989 agreed to promulgate a uniform law to prevent and control infectious diseases in Malaysia (NUS Law 2020). There is, however, an alternative, and equally compelling, expert view that states have the right to defy a federal government law because "public health, sanitation, and prevention of infectious diseases" are on the Concurrent List, the list of joint responsibility (*The Sun* 2020). This view is also bolstered by the provisions of the Local Government Act, which gives state governments through local councils certain powers to regulate and enforce quarantine, as well as preserve public health and prevent the outbreak and spread of diseases (Yeoh 2020). Since all laws must adhere to the Federal Constitution, both federal and state governments are to jointly decide on items listed in the Concurrent List and the voices of both levels of government are to be given equal weight.

The constitution is vague on how joint decisions are to be made; it has never been clear whether state legislative assemblies need to vote on a matter of joint interest—and further, pass state-level legislation to that end—or whether consultation is all that is required. Although the federal government's decision was eventually adhered to by all states over a period of time, and the states never in reality actively challenged the federal government, this was an interesting case study on whether the states could exercise their joint rights over public health.

The number of confirmed cases in Malaysia reached a cumulative 113,010 by the end of December 2020 (*The Edge Malaysia* 2020). The government resorted to announcing a CMCO in Sabah, Selangor, Kuala

Lumpur and Putrajaya commencing 7 October 2020. It was initially to be in place for two weeks, but this was later extended to January 2021.

However, this decision was not well-received by the Selangor state government, which claimed that the federal government had not consulted it beforehand. The Selangor Chief Minister was surprised by the decision to implement a CMCO as the Covid-19 situation was worrying only in four districts within the state (*Free Malaysia Today* 2020). A few days prior to the October announcement, the federal government had announced a CMCO for Klang, a district in Selangor that was more severely affected by Covid-19, without consulting the state government (*Malay Mail* 2020). It was only after the state government expressed dismay at not having been consulted that the National Security Council met with the Selangor Chief Minister. The latter then announced that the National Security Council would provide the details of the CMCO requirements to be imposed within Klang, and that the state government would work with all agencies accordingly to ensure these were complied with.

Sabah, Penang and Selangor were the only state governments that expressed disappointment over a lack of consultation, including over the federal government's decision to reopen the economy in May 2020, and later when it unilaterally implemented the CMCO in Selangor. These public expressions were led by the opposition coalitions that controlled the states. In short, the political coalitions that were not aligned with the centre made their views publicly and vehemently known. By the time the October 2020 CMCO was announced, the Sabah state government had already changed hands from an opposition-aligned coalition to one that was supportive and aligned with the ruling coalition at the centre.

In July 2021, most parts of Selangor were announced to be under EMCO between 3 to 16 July. Restrictions were tightest under an EMCO: no one was allowed to leave their home, all businesses were shut down, all roads to the areas under the EMCO were closed, a medical base was to be established within the area and food supplies were to be provided. Several Selangor parliamentarians opposed the EMCO, while the Selangor Chief Minister stated that insufficient notice had been given and that the views of its state Covid-19 task force had not been taken into consideration. He also stated that 80 per cent of infection clusters in the state came from factories, which the MITI had the authority to close these but had not done so (*Free Malaysia Today* 2021b). An opposing view is that the local governments could have closed the factories because the Local Government Act 1976 grants them the power to preserve public health and prevent the outbreak and spread of diseases, as well as the authority to issue operating licences and regulate premises' opening hours. Local governments, which are constitutionally under the purview of state governments, may therefore have had the authority to override MITI letters, meaning that states could supersede federal authority. This, however, was never tested.

Management of the MCOs was extremely centralized, as they were governed by federal laws and regulations. Decisions to implement movement control orders were largely made by the National Security Council and announced by the Home Ministry. State governments were not meaningfully consulted when it came to decisions about implementing and ending lockdowns. This often resulted in confusion as state governments were not informed beforehand and attempted to oppose these, but in vain. Ultimately, lockdown implementation did not offer any new opportunities for state or local governments to participate in the decision-making process.

Distribution of Economic Aid

The government provided an array of economic stimulus packages totalling US$68.7 billion in the initial outlay on 27 March 2020 (PENJANA Short-Term Economic Recovery Plan). This included a six-month loan repayment moratorium and wage subsidies. Low-wage earners were already vulnerable; a large proportion of those living in low-cost flats work as informal labourers such as petty traders and tailors and lack the social security that formal workers enjoy (Muzafar and Kunasekaran 2020).

Since many of the poorest households did not have the facilities to work from home, not going to work would have meant a significant loss of income (ibid.). The number of poor households increased from 405,400 in 2019 to 639,800 in 2020, and a report from the Department of Statistics Malaysia (2021) showed the incidence of absolute poverty increased from 5.6 per cent in 2019 to 8.4 per cent in 2020. Kelantan recorded the most significant increase in poverty, 8.8 per cent, followed by Terengganu; both are east coast states in Peninsular Malaysia. Data on household income and poverty is centralized under the federal government's Department of

Statistics, while the eKasih system, which tracks household poverty levels nationwide, is a separate database meant to serve six ministries. However, the data on poor households is not shared with state governments.

The 2021 budget, passed by Parliament in November 2020, also contained an array of offerings, including tax relief measures, cash aid programmes, an extension of existing wage subsidy programmes and other handouts aimed at assisting the economy.

On 24 March 2020, Bank Negara Malaysia announced a moratorium on repayments of mortgages and hire purchase loans, and also offered the option to convert credit card balances to term loans. Initially this was greeted positively, but upon closer inspection, it was found that interest would still accumulate. This led to a public uproar (*New Straits Times* 2020a), and Bank Negara Malaysia released an FAQ document the following day.

Although Malaysia has a robust public healthcare system with universal access, private citizens and communities contributed to the control and prevention of the virus spread. A "whole of government, whole of society" approach was adopted to respond to the crisis (Ministry of Health 2020). Communities rallied together under a *#kitajagakita* tagline (we all take care of each other), which is also the name of a Covid-19 website set up to connect non-governmental organizations (NGOs) with communities in need, raise funds and provide food, goods and services. The approach meant that all members of society ought to contribute to preventing the spread of Covid-19.

Some fundamental problems in Malaysia included a shortage of medical equipment. In an online survey conducted by a group of Malaysian doctors, of the respondents working in Ministry of Health hospitals, 77 per cent said they had experienced shortages of personal protective equipment (PPE), while 58 per cent had resorted to using DIY protective clothing (Boo 2020). To counter these shortcomings throughout the MCO period, private citizens gave money and made PPE.

Despite the shortage of goods and health- and aid-related services, the government banned NGOs from distributing food to communities on 28 March 2020. However, several days later, on 30 March 2020, the government named twelve NGOs that were allowed to distribute food, but only until the end of 31 March. On that day, another new list was released that qualified what NGOs should do if they wanted to distribute aid, including getting the Malaysian Volunteers Department (RELA) and the Army to accompany them. This resulted in confusion and in many communities not receiving food aid. The Malaysian Welfare Department, which was supposed to coordinate this, in fact, had closed its offices throughout this period. Some NGOs stated that they had received direct messages from the Welfare Department asking them for food, presumably for onward supply to citizens in need. On 1 April 2020, the Women and Family Ministry softened its stance, allowing NGOs to distribute food and essential items to the homeless and needy without having to be on a registered list.

Individual state governments also provided funds to aid frontliners, households from the bottom 40 per cent of household income (B40 households) and provided rental waivers on government housing. They complemented the federal government's social assistance packages by reallocating budget to further aid affected communities. The two largest budgets for Covid-19 assistance packages were provided by the East Malaysia states of Sarawak and Sabah, followed by the highly developed states of Selangor and Penang (both of which are opposition-controlled). Other states that provided funds to assist communities included Perak, Pahang, Kelantan, Negeri Sembilan, Johor, Terengganu, Malacca and Perlis. Among the assistance provided was cash aid to medical frontliners, rent relief and food aid (Welsh 2020).

Vaccinations

The Special Committee for Ensuring Access to Covid-19 Vaccine Supply was a joint committee between MOSTI and the Ministry of Health, but there was a significant delay in procuring vaccines. It was only in late 2020 that there were reports that the government was close to purchasing vaccines, but there was suspicion of tension between the two ministries. As of August 2021, the federal government had procured 87.9 million vaccine doses of Pfizer-BioNTech, Sinovac, AstraZeneca (through the global COVID-19 Vaccines Global Access [COVAX] facility), CanSino and Sputnik V (Ngio 2021).

Eventually, it was the MOSTI Minister (at that time, Khairy Jamaluddin) who coordinated the National Immunization Programme. The public perception of the Minister of Health had plummeted, resulting in MOSTI being given a more significant role in the vaccination roll-out. In fact, when Khairy was appointed Minister of Health in August 2021 in the change in federal administration, he continued to lead the national vaccination roll-out. By early 2021, it was possible for the priority groups (the elderly and those with serious health conditions) to register through the MySejahtera application for vaccination.

Local Muslims initially expressed concerns about the vaccinations not being halal, but these fears were eventually allayed after several key individuals stated publicly that the vaccine was safe. A special meeting of the National Council for Malaysian Islamic Affairs was convened on 3 December 2020 to determine whether the vaccine could be administered to Muslims; subsequently, the mufti of Perlis state, Mohd Asri Zainul Abidin, said that "even if there is an ingredient which is not permissible, the chemical transformation will make it clean and halal" (Hassan 2020).

Rumours also initially circulated about blood clots as a potential side effect of the AstraZeneca vaccination, which resulted in thousands within the elderly target group rejecting the vaccine. Khairy Jamaluddin activated an opt-in facility, which allowed people of any age to choose to be inoculated with the AstraZeneca vaccine. This proved extremely successful in nudging the public to sign up for vaccinations, as those individuals shared vaccination photos and stories on social media and with their friends and families. More people began registering for their vaccinations, allaying fears of lethal side effects.

In July 2021, Malaysia's daily Covid-19 vaccine doses administered peaked at more than 500,000. By June 2022, 71.2 million doses had been given, with 27.3 million Malaysians fully vaccinated, representing 84.2 per cent of the population. This is represented in Figure 9.2, which shows the daily Covid-19 vaccinations in Malaysia between February 2021 and December 2022.

The Public-Private Partnership Covid-19 Industry Immunization Programme (PIKAS) was launched in June 2021 to accelerate vaccinations among the public, focusing on the workforce. Companies, particularly in the manufacturing sector, would be able to apply to PIKAS for faster vaccinations for their employees. These would be free but required approval from the Covid-19 Immunization Task Force, MOSTI and MITI. By the end

FIGURE 9.2
Daily Covid-19 Vaccinations in Malaysia, February 2021 to December 2022

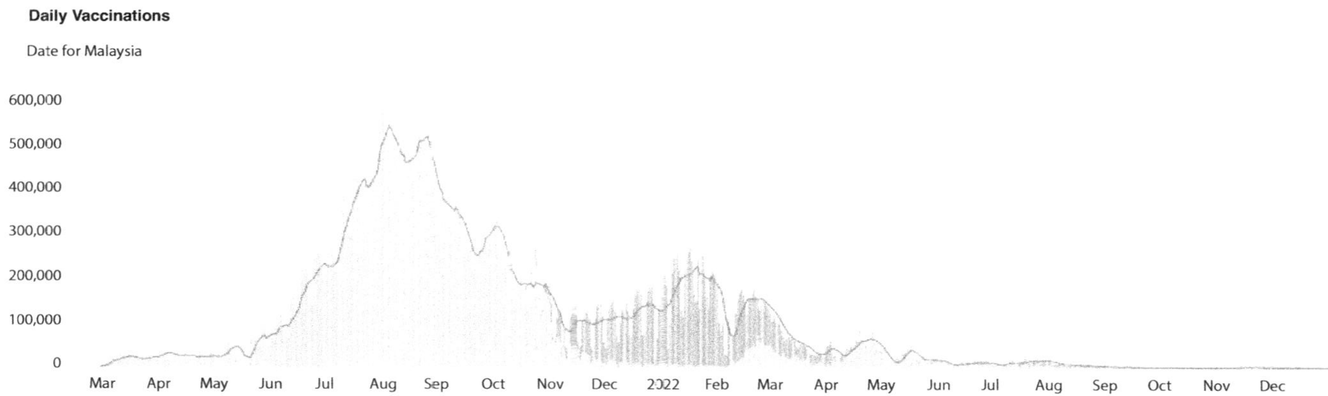

Source: Kementerian Kesihatan Malaysia NOW (KKMNOW), Ministry of Health and the Department of Statistics Malaysia.

of July 2021, 17,053 companies with 1.3 million workers had registered for the programme, while 298,306 workers had received their first dose and 28,596 also a second (MIDA 2021).

Two other programmes were also initiated for specific sectors from January 2022, namely the Agrofood Industry Vaccination Programme (AiVAC), implemented by the Ministry of Agriculture and Food Industries (*New Straits Times* 2021c), and the Retail Industry Vaccination Programme (RiVAC), led by the Ministry of Domestic Trade and Consumer Affairs. The latter expedited vaccination for customer-facing staff in the retail sector. It started operations in the Klang Valley with centres in five major shopping malls, and then spread to other states. The goal for RiVAC was to enable the retail sector to reopen and fully operate earlier than other sectors, as planned for under the National Recovery Plan (*The Malaysian Reserve* 2021c).

Then, in November 2021, a Vaccination Centre Outreach Programme was launched, which replaced the three industry-focused immunization programmes (PIKAS, AiVAC and RiVAC). Under this new programme, companies or associations could request private medical practitioners and health NGOs to conduct vaccinations for their employees or members. The practitioners and NGOs were required to be registered with ProtectHealth Corporation Sdn Bhd, a company fully owned by and reporting to the Ministry of Health. The government would bear the costs of the vaccine, and ProtectHealth would pay the private medical practitioner or the health NGO for each vaccination given.

This was an interesting collaboration with the private sector. ProtectHealth had been appointed by the Ministry of Health several months earlier in May 2021 to facilitate the participation of private medical practitioners and NGOs in the National Covid-19 Immunisation Programme, with the aim of accelerating and expanding vaccination access nationwide. Its role included developing proprietary software to connect all private medical practitioners for registration, management, training materials, reporting and other functions, as well as monitoring vaccination activities, investigating incident reports, training, performing audits and providing assistance at vaccination centres throughout the country (Anas 2021). ProtectHealth stated that as of 9 January 2022, it had contributed 49.5 per cent of the total vaccinations given in Malaysia, equivalent to

29.35 million doses, as well as 72.1 per cent of the total booster dose vaccinations, equivalent to 5.63 million doses (Anas 2021).

The opposition-led state government of Penang tried to capitalize on the race to vaccinate. In May 2021, the state's Chief Minister Chow Kon Yeow claimed that the Ministry of Health had failed to approve the use of 2 million Sinovac vaccine doses given by a private firm from China (*Free Malaysia Today* 2021a). However, in an immediate response, National Covid-19 Immunization Programme coordinating minister Khairy Jamaluddin said the offer had been made by a non-existent company (*The Malaysian Reserve* 2021b). Chow then stated that Penang would use its own funds to procure additional vaccines directly from vaccine suppliers or manufacturers. However, Penang eventually cancelled its plans, instead relying solely on the federal government (*New Straits Times* 2021b).

Similarly, another opposition state government, Selangor, pushed to procure vaccines directly and bypass the federal government vaccination scheme (through the National Immunization Programme and via MySejahtera). It negotiated directly with Pharmaniaga, a Malaysian pharmaceutical company linked to the government, to buy Sinovac vaccines, and an initial supply of 80,000 doses was then bought and made available. Like Penang, opposition-led Selangor had a political interest in demonstrating that they were proactive, were providing valuable services to their constituents and were able to compete with the federal government. Selangor launched its SelVAX programme, to be rolled out under its state-owned company SelCare, and by the end of 2021, more than 30,000 had received their booster doses under this programme (*Berita Harian* 2021).

As infections resulting from the Delta variant, the fourth wave of Covid-19, peaked in July and August 2021, the federal government believed that greater efforts were needed to hasten the speed of vaccinations, especially within the Klang Valley, as cases were concentrated there. At the end of July 2021, the Klang Valley—comprising Selangor, Kuala Lumpur and Putrajaya—was contributing 58.1 per cent of new daily cases. Given the high population density within this area, the Klang Valley also recorded the highest number of hospitalizations in the country.

Hospitals within the Klang Valley were overwhelmed, with healthcare staff working around the clock and hospitals running out of beds and medical equipment (*The Malaysian Reserve* 2021a). An initiative run by two NGOs, IDEAS Community Projects and Projek Bangsa Malaysia, raised more than MYR1 million to buy hospital equipment for Klang Valley hospitals. Efforts to raise funds and supply medical equipment, however, faced hostility as the Selangor health department issued a letter banning hospitals from officially requesting aid from external parties. This was, apparently, in order to prevent the Malaysian public from having a bad impression of the public healthcare system.

As a result of the Covid-19 surge in the Klang Valley, Operation Surge Capacity was launched in July 2021 to ensure every adult resident of Selangor and Kuala Lumpur received at least one dose of vaccine by August of the same year. Under the scheme, the daily vaccination capacity for Selangor and Kuala Lumpur was increased. Ong Kian Ming, a Member of Parliament from the Democratic Action Party, was appointed to coordinate between the Selangor state government, MITI, the Ministry of Health and the Covid-19 Immunisation Task Force. This was an interesting appointment, as it capitalized on Ong's previous experience as Deputy Minister at MITI, as well as his affiliation with the Pakatan Harapan coalition, which was in opposition at the federal level but in power in Selangor. Such coordination efforts required trust and cordial relationships across the different levels of government and political coalitions, which is something that Ong was able to achieve given his previous roles.

DISCUSSION

The preceding sections have detailed aspects of Malaysia's Covid-19 coordination at horizontal and vertical levels, specifically within the areas of information and communication; lockdown implementation; distribution of economic aid; and vaccinations. This section synthesizes those narratives and analyses key factors that shaped coordination in Malaysia over the pandemic period.

Leadership within the federal government was particularly weak as Covid-19 hit. While the Pakatan Harapan administration had laid out some initial Covid-19 plans, the intense waves of the pandemic came about just as the new Perikatan Nasional government was inducted in early March 2020. As a new government, with relatively new Cabinet ministers, there was very little time to coalesce; the new leaders had to hit the ground running.

Health Minister Adham Baba appeared particularly ill-equipped to manage the public health crisis. Amid the fallout from the false information Baba gave about how to prevent Covid-19 infection, the Director General of the Ministry of Health, Noor Hisham Abdullah, rose to prominence and, through his daily press conferences, built up a reputation as a strong leader among a public that was hungry for information. Khairy Jamaluddin was one of the Perikatan Nasional leaders who demonstrated strong leadership as Minister of MOSTI, and then later on as Minister of Health, given his ability to steer the nationwide immunization programme so successfully. Azmin Ali as Minister of MITI also had the opportunity to lead the reopening of the economy well, but given the problems of giving businesses permission to operate, he did not emerge from the Covid-19 crisis with a positive reputation (*Sinar Harian* 2021).

The fact that Covid-19 took place simultaneously with political change affected the way in which policies were implemented, especially at the state level. Continual political contestations between the Perikatan Nasional-led federal government and opposition-led state governments, in which politicians switching parties led to the fall of the state governments of Johor, Malacca, Perak and Kedah (the Pakatan Harapan opposition coalition continued to hold Selangor, Penang and Negeri Sembilan), fuelled the underlying tensions between them. This was evidenced by the way lockdowns were implemented, as well as how the states of Selangor and Penang attempted—successfully in the case of Selangor—to emerge with their own vaccination plans.

However, despite public disagreements as to how lockdowns were rolled out (or eased), ultimately there was very little that state governments could do to stop the federal government from enforcing central decisions. This is because enforcement agencies, including the police and armed forces, fall under the jurisdiction of the federal government, and state governments, even with local governments under their purview, would not have been able to strongly oppose these. The declaration of a national emergency, for example, was something that the state governments had to eventually accept, given that the Federal Constitution is clear in determining the federal government's power in this matter.

Malaysia's highly centralized federalism was prominently displayed throughout the Covid-19 period. Economic policymaking, the distribution of economic aid and the formation of LAKSANA to monitor disbursement were highly centralized. However, Sri Murniati, Rode, and Low (2023) found that some of the information reported by LAKSANA on the disbursement of the Covid-19 stimulus packages was not reflective of the actual aid provided, but largely comprised *expected* savings, discounts or financial injections from government-linked entities or private sources. The government contributed only about half to the total MYR530 billion of economic stimulus packages, and the vast bulk of the other half was made up of the estimated value of the loan repayment moratorium programmes, which were not direct aid per se—and involved the private sector through private banks, not the public sector.

Nevertheless, aid did reach intended targets, with 16.79 per cent of the total amount of direct expenditure comprising targeted measures for vulnerable groups (Sri Murniati, Rode, and Low 2023). In addition, of the MYR162.5 billion set aside for businesses, the largest allocation of MYR6.5 billion to small-scale construction was for small to medium-sized Malay and Indigenous contractors, demonstrating the priority focus of the government. LAKSANA reporting had further gaps, including a failure to disclose an estimated fiscal impact for all programmes in the stimulus packages, a failure to identify clearly the source of funding for these programmes, inconsistencies in the type of information reported and more than half of programmes not reported on (ibid.).[11]

Covid-19 put to the test Malaysia's institutions and state capacity. The Ministry of Health eventually demonstrated that it had the capacity to deal with the Covid-19 crisis—but only just. As the crisis deepened, hundreds of contract doctors went on strike to demand fairer treatment; only 789 out of 23,077 contract physicians had received permanent placements, though they were crucial front liners in the fight against Covid-19; 60 per cent of medical workers in the country's healthcare system are contractors with no job security (AP News 2021).

Several state governments did attempt to create their own Covid-19 management, namely Sarawak, Selangor and Penang. In both East Malaysian states, Sabah and Sarawak, which have more autonomy than states in Peninsular Malaysia, this was an opportunity to stand their ground, especially on issues related to immigration—both Sabah and Sarawak imposed their own immigration regulations during the pandemic.

Economic aid and stimulus packages, contact tracing applications, a limited vaccination programme in Selangor and the creation of state Covid-19 task forces, however, were the only areas in which state governments could realistically act to manage the pandemic. Although public health and sanitation fall under the Concurrent List of the Constitution, in reality the fact that medicine and health is placed under the federal government prevailed—hospitals, health clinics and medical facilities are administered by the Ministry of Health and their corresponding state and district health offices throughout the country.

CONCLUSION

Covid-19 caught all countries off guard—they had to grapple with a new and unknown virus, and the resulting public health crisis. Over a period of three years, countries had to strike a difficult and delicate balance between maintaining an open economy and limiting the transmission of Covid-19. Public health concerns and the economy were often pitted against each other with disagreements over which took precedence of primary importance.

While the economy continues to recover, many lessons can be learnt from Malaysia's management of the public health crisis. Both conflict and cooperation took place, between ministries and between federal and state governments.

The first lesson is that public healthcare systems must be prepared for a sudden health crisis. Although this coronavirus was new, Malaysia, as other countries, has had to deal with previous health crises such as SARS. Financial allocations must therefore be sufficient in ensuring state capacity in both hardware (equipment, hospital facilities) and software (coordinating hospitals' equipment needs with procurement at the Ministry of Health, as well as resolving outstanding matters with regards to medical workers).

Although Malaysia's public health sector and other supporting services (including those involved in the National Security Council, National Recovery Council, MITI and MOSTI) demonstrated resilience and dedication over the Covid-19 period, the institutions failed to ensure the right support was provided. At the peak of the pandemic in July and August 2021, public health workers spoke anonymously to Projek Bangsa Malaysia, a local NGO (in a video that went viral) to publicize the lack of physical and emotional support provided by the Ministry of Health (Projek Bangsa Malaysia 2021). Many public health workers were experiencing severe mental and emotional challenges given the long hours and lack of available human resources. As stated above, doctors and hospital personnel were discouraged from sharing their specific equipment needs for fear that this would reflect poorly on the Ministry of Health's inability to provide them. Although Covid-19 has now passed, public health institutions in Malaysia have not reformed themselves, and have not corrected many of the flaws or failures that emerged during the pandemic. This is unfortunate, given the acute problems that continue to plague the public health administration—which could potentially be of great concern should there be another public health crisis that reaches Malaysia.

Second, early and fast coordination between ministries at the federal level is imperative to ensure effective outcomes within the public health services, as well as efficient implementation of SOPs. In Malaysia, such coordination did eventually come about, but it took several months for the government to put into motion a proper system. In the intervening months, during which SOPs were revamped multiple times, inconsistent rules were announced and regulations reversed, businesses were left with little to no recourse. At the highest levels, the purpose of establishing a National Action Council and a National Recovery Council was therefore to ensure better consistency in the approach to Covid-19. However, apart from coordinated press conferences, the resultant SOPs were often in disarray. It was only after the National Recovery Council finally implemented a new set of SOPs, consolidating the earlier iterations such that they were not written in fine detail for every different sector, that industries had an easier time obtaining the information they needed.

Third, the twin crises of political turbulence and the Covid-19 pandemic embedded centralization trends even further. Several states did use the pandemic as an opportunity to push for a greater role in decision-making, but with limited success in creating autonomy. Malaysia's legal and policy systems did not prevent states from activating some of their own response mechanisms and the federal government did not intervene, possibly having considered that these responses would result in net positive outcomes (Yeoh 2021). However, ultimately, both structurally (in terms of laws and institutions) and politically (decisions over resource allocation, both horizontally and vertically downward), the centre still wields the most power. This was demonstrated during the Covid-19 pandemic.

Nevertheless, "public health and sanitation" are listed within the Concurrent List of Malaysia's Federal Constitution, meaning this is an issue in which federal and state governments are both constitutionally authorized to act. Thus, Covid-19 gave the country an opportunity to revisit the policy domains of each level of government during which some contestations occurred, with some state governments pushing their boundaries. It should be pointed out, however, that it was only the well-resourced and politically motivated states that purchased their own vaccinations; among these were Selangor and Penang, which are both controlled by the opposition Pakatan Harapan coalition.

If healthcare administration is decentralized to state and local governments, this could conceivably allow for better coordination—and resolve some of the coordination complications pointed out in this chapter. The principle of subsidiarity holds that a central authority should have a subsidiary function, performing only those tasks that cannot be performed at a more local level—this is something Malaysia could certainly explore. For example, the implementation of SOPs surrounding any future pandemic could be decentralized to state governments (and local governments by default), as could the administration of local healthcare clinics. Malaysia could also empower doctors and other healthcare workers at the state level to contribute to policymaking as they are the most familiar with the issues and challenges on the ground. However, to do this, a holistic national discourse needs to take place, including discussion over the devolution of finance and administration. Policy decentralization without commensurate financial and administrative autonomy could be disastrous. In the short term, without having to take large steps towards decentralization, small steps can be taken to ensure better vertical coordination, especially in conducting consultations and incorporating feedback into decision-making processes.

The Covid-19 pandemic has passed and countries must now reflect on their pandemic experiences and identify how they can improve their policy coordination and implementation, for the sake of their communities. Malaysia is no exception.

APPENDIX

TABLE A9.1
Division of Responsibilities between Federal and State Governments

Federal List	*Concurrent List*[a]	*State List*[b]
External affairs	Social welfare	Islamic law and Malay customs
Defence	Scholarships	Land matters
Internal security	Protection of wild animals and wild birds and national parks	Agriculture and forestry
Civil and criminal law and procedure and the administration of justice	Animal husbandry	Local government
Federal citizenship and naturalization	Town and country planning	Other services[c]
Machinery of government	Vagrancy and itinerant hawkers	State works and water[d]
Finance	Public health and sanitation	Machinery of the state government
Trade, commerce and industry	Drainage and irrigation	State holidays
Shipping, navigation and fisheries	Rehabilitation of mining land and land with erosion	Creation of offences related to state matters
Communications and transport	Fire safety measures	Inquiries for state purposes
Federal works and power	Culture and sports	Indemnity in respect to state matters
Surveys, inquiries and research	Housing	Turtles and riverine fishing
Education	Water supplies and services	Libraries, museums, ancient and historical monuments and records and archaeological sites and remains
Medicine and health	Preservation of heritage	
Labour and social security		
Welfare of Indigenous Peoples		
Professional occupations		
Holidays other than state holidays		
Unincorporated societies		
Control of agricultural pests		

Newspapers, publications, publishers, printing and printing presses
Censorship
Theatres, cinemas, films (subject to State List)
Cooperative societies
Tourism

Note:

a. Supplement to Concurrent List for the states of Sabah and Sarawak: personal law relating to marriage, divorce, guardianship, maintenance, adoption, legitimacy, family law, gifts or succession and testate or intestate deaths; adulteration of foodstuffs and other goods; shipping under 15 registered tons; maritime and estuarine fishing and fisheries; the production, distribution and supply of water power and of electricity generated by water power; agricultural and forestry research; control of agricultural pests and prevention of plant diseases; charities and charitable trusts and institutions in the state, theatres, cinemas, cinematograph films, places of public amusement; and elections to the State Assembly held during the period of indirect elections;

b. Supplement to State List for the states of Sabah and Sarawak: native law and custom; incorporation of authorities and other bodies set up by state law; ports and harbours (other than those declared to come under federal jurisdiction); regulation of traffic by water in ports and harbours or on rivers wholly within the state, except traffic in federal ports or harbours; foreshores; cadastral land surveys. In Sabah: the Sabah Railway and, subject to the Federal List, water supplies and services; [c] Boarding houses and lodging houses; burial and cremation grounds; pounds and cattle trespass; markets and fairs; and licensing of theatres, cinemas and places of public amusement; [d] Includes rivers and canals, excludes water supplies and services; control of silt and riparian rights.

Source: Federal Constitution, Ninth Schedule.

Notes

1. Cases continued to climb steadily to daily averages of between 3,000 and 4,000 new cases at the end of January 2021.
2. The four opposition parliamentarians are Wong Chen (Parti Keadilan Rakyat), Chong Chieng Jen (DAP), Dzulkefly Ahmad (Amanah) and Bernard Dompok (United Progressive Kinabalu Organization) (*Malay Mail* 2021).
3. Khairy, as Minister of Health, stated that all data and information obtained through the app remained the property of the Malaysian government. The company that initially developed MySejahtera in March 2020 was KPISoft Malaysia, which later changed its name to Entomo Malaysia Sdn Bhd. It entered into an agreement with MySJ, a special vehicle for the commercialization of the app. There was a government plan to sell MySejahtera to a private firm via a direct tender (*Edge Malaysia* 2022). However, to date, there is no further information regarding this sale.
4. While Minister of Finance Tengku Zafrul stated that no consultants were paid by the Ministry (*New Straits Times* 2020b), several sources stated that LAKSANA was in fact staffed with external consultants, primarily from private consulting firm Ernst & Young (EY) and a few from CIMB. Tengku Zafrul was formerly group chief executive officer of CIMB (Focus Malaysia 2020).
5. The board of the EPF was resistant to the multiple withdrawals, but the government pushed it through nonetheless.
6. https://covidnow.moh.gov.my/
7. https://newslab.malaysiakini.com/covid-19/en
8. For example, former Prime Minister Najib Razak was issued two MYR1,500 fines for failing to record his temperature and failing to register his entry to a restaurant, while the owner of the restaurant was fined MYR10,000 for not enforcing the rules. Malaysian television host Neelofa's wedding in March 2020 saw hundreds of guests flouting rules on social distancing and wearing masks (Chin 2021).
9. It is unclear which other alcohol companies were affected.
10. No further information is available on how issues relating to e-commerce and personal care companies were handled.
11. Former Prime Minister Muhyiddin Yassin and several Bersatu colleagues have been charged with alleged corruption, abuse of power and money laundering in the implementation of a programme named "Jana Wibawa" (translated loosely as "to generate authority"). The programme was introduced as a Covid-19 stimulus initiative to help Malay and indigenous contractors (*Free Malaysia Today* 2023). The case is ongoing.

References

Anas, Alam Faizli. 2021. "Turning Crisis Into Opportunity". *CodeBlue*, 24 December 2021. https://codeblue.galencentre.org/2021/12/24/turning-crisis-into-opportunity-anas-alam-faizli/ (accessed 8 July 2022).

AP News. 2021. "Malaysian Contract Doctors Walk Out to Seek Fairer Treatment". 26 July 2021. https://apnews.com/article/health-coronavirus-pandemic-malaysia-b609f64bb66e08e14cb40571196c4037 (accessed 9 July 2022).

Bank Negara Malaysia. 2022. "Measures to Address Covid-19 Impact". https://www.bnm.gov.my/covid19#:~:text=Measures%20include%20deferment%20on%20life,contributions%2C%20and%20expedited%20claims%20processing (accessed 9 July 2022).

Berita Harian. 2021. "Lebih 30,000 Rakyat Selangor Daftar Program SelVAX Booster" [More than 30,000 Selangor residents register for the SelVAX Booster programme]. 16 December 2021. https://www.bharian.com.my/berita/wilayah/2021/12/899635/lebih-30000-rakyat-selangor-daftar-program-selvax-booster (accessed 8 July 2022).

Bernama. 2020a. "LAKSANA Also Monitors Implementation of Budget 2021 Initiatives". 24 November 2020.

———. 2020b. "Military to Help Police Enforce Movement Control Order—Chief of Defence Force". 20 March 2020. https://www.astroawani.com/berita-malaysia/military-help-police-enforce-movement-control-order-chief-defence-force-234498 (accessed 28 May 2024).

———. 2021. "Premises Listed under 'HIDE' Not COVID-19 Clusters". 8 May 2021. https://www.bernama.com/en/general/news_covid-19.php?id=1960039 (accessed 18 April 2024).

Boo, Su-Lyn. 2020. "Poll Reveals Almost Half of Private, Public Health Workers Don't Feel Safe". *CodeBlue*. 8 May 2020. https://codeblue.galencentre.org/2020/05/08/poll-reveals-almost-half-of-private-public-health-workers-dont-feel-safe/ (accessed 28 May 2024).

Chin, James. 2021. "Commentary: Najib Razak's Fine and a Tale of Double Standards in Malaysia". *Channel NewsAsia*, 8 May 2021. https://www.channelnewsasia.com/commentary/covid-19-najib-fined-sop-breaking-malaysia-double-standards-1381066 (accessed 8 July 2022).

Code Blue. 2021. "Beware the Fifth Wave of Covid-19–Dr Amar-Singh HSS". 25 June 2021. https://codeblue.galencentre.org/2021/06/25/beware-the-fifth-wave-of-covid-19-dr-amar-singh-hss/ (accessed 13 February 2023).

Department of Statistics Malaysia. 2021. "Household Income Estimates and Incidence of Poverty Report, Malaysia, 2020". 6 August 2021. https://www.dosm.gov.my/v1/index.php?r=column/cthemeByCat&cat=493&bul_id=VTN

HRkdiZkFzenBNd1Y1dmg2UUlrZz09&menu_id=amVoWU54UTl0a21NWmdhMjFMMWcyZz09 (accessed 8 July 2022).

Dzulkefly, Ahmad. 2020. "MP Speaks: Data Sharing Key to Combating Covid-19". *Malaysiakini*, 20 October 2020. https://www.malaysiakini.com/news/547265 (accessed 22 April 2024).

Edge Malaysia, The . 2020. "Malaysia Closes 2020 with New Daily High of 2,525 Covid-19 Cases, About Half from Selangor". 31 December 2020. https://theedgemalaysia.com/article/malaysia-posts-record-high-new-covid19-cases-totalling-2525-including-1205-selangor-eight (accessed 22 April 2024).

———. 2022. "Ideas: MySejahtera Episode Poses Questions about Data Privacy". 27 April 2022. https://www.theedgemarkets.com/article/ideas-mysejahtera-episode-poses-questions-about-data-privacy (accessed 9 July 2022).

———. 2024. "EPF Assets Under Management Back on the Rise, Annual Contributions Exceed RM100 Bil Mark". 3 March 2024. https://theedgemalaysia.com/node/703203 (accessed 18 April 2024).

Elengoe, Asita. 2020. "COVID-19 Outbreak in Malaysia". *Osong Public Health and Research Perspectives* 11, no. 3: 93–100.

Employees Provident Fund. 2021. "EPF Committed to Help Members Rebuild Savings and Secure Retirement Future". 28 December 2021. https://www.kwsp.gov.my/w/epf-committed-to-help-members-rebuild-savings-and-secure-retirement-future (accessed 28 May 2024).

Ferlito, Carmelo, and Gaetano Perone. 2020, "Covid-19 and the MCO: An Exit Strategy for Malaysia". IDEAS Brief Ideas No. 20, The Institute for Democracy and Economic Affairs, Kuala Lumpur, April. https://www.ideas.org.my/publications-item/brief-ideas-no-20-covid-19-and-the-mco-an-exit-strategy-for-malaysia/ (accessed 1 September 2023).

Focus Malaysia. 2020. "Stimulus Implementation Agency Staffed with External Consultants, Say Sources". 30 April 2020. https://focusmalaysia.my/stimulus-implementation-agency-staffed-with-external-consultants-say-sources/ (accessed 1 September 2023).

———. 2022. "As M'sia Inches towards Debt Ceiling, Don't Increase Debt-to-GDP". 27 July 2022. https://focusmalaysia.my/as-msia-inches-towards-debt-ceiling-dont-increase-debt-to-gdp/ (accessed 13 February 2023).

Free Malaysia Today. 2020. "Selangor MB 'Surprised' after Statewide CMCO". 12 October 2020. https://www.freemalaysiatoday.com/category/nation/2020/10/12/selangor-mb-surprised-over-statewide-cmco/ (accessed 26 May 2024).

———. 2021a. "Penang Gets 2 Million Sinovac Doses but Putrajaya Says No".

18 May 2021. https://www.freemalaysiatoday.com/category/nation/2021/05/18/penang-gets-2-million-sinovac-doses-but-putrajaya-says-no/ (accessed 22 April 2024).

———. 2021b. "Selangor MPs Slam 'Clueless' Knee-Jerk EMCO". 1 July 2021. https://www.freemalaysiatoday.com/category/nation/2021/07/01/selangor-mps-slam-clueless-knee-jerk-emco/ (accessed 7 July 2022).

———. 2021c. "Why Focus on Malls and Not Factories, Govt Asked". 9 May 2021. https://www.freemalaysiatoday.com/category/nation/2021/05/09/why-focus-on-malls-and-not-factories-govt-asked/ (accessed 18 April 2024).

———. 2023. "MACC Hunts 'Main Planner' of Graft Case Linked to Jana Wibawa Probe". 12 March 2023. https://www.freemalaysiatoday.com/category/nation/2023/03/12/macc-on-hunt-for-main-planner-behind-jana-wibawa-scandal/ (accessed 1 September 2023).

Hassan, Hazlin. 2020. "Malaysia Says Halal Issue Won't Affect Covid-19 Vaccine Roll-Out amid Concerns among Muslims". *Straits Times*, 10 December 2020. https://www.straitstimes.com/asia/se-asia/halal-issue-will-not-impede-malaysias-vaccine-roll-out-says-health-chief-amid-muslim (accessed 1 September 2023).

Hutchinson, Francis E. 2014. "Malaysia's Federal System: Overt and Covert Centralisation". *Journal of Contemporary Asia* 44, no. 3: 422–42.

Kumar, P. Prem. 2021. "Malaysian King Slams Muhyiddin's Sudden COVID Emergency Reversal". *Nikkei Asia*, 29 July 2021. https://asia.nikkei.com/Politics/Malaysia-in-transition/Malaysian-king-slams-Muhyiddin-s-sudden-COVID-emergency-reversal (accessed 18 April 2024).

Kyaw, S.W., W.Y.K. Khine, J.M. Lim, P.H.M. Neo, R.K.J.T. Tan, and S.E. Ong. 2023. "Malaysia, Myanmar and Singapore: Common Threads, Divergences, and Lessons Learned in Responding to the COVID-19 Pandemic". In *COVID-19 in the Commonwealth*, edited by D. McDougall and S. E. Ong. Oxford: Routledge.

Malay Mail. 2020. "Selangor Exco: More Than One Klang Area but Govt's CMCO Notice Failed to Specify Which Affected". 8 October 2020. https://www.malaymail.com/news/malaysia/2020/10/08/selangor-exco-more-than-one-klang-area-but-govts-cmco-notice-failed-to-spec/1910746 (accessed 28 May 2024).

———. 2021. "Four Pakatan MPs Formally Join National Recovery Council Today". 15 October 2021. https://www.malaymail.com/news/malaysia/2021/10/15/four-pakatan-mps-formally-join-national-recovery-council-today/2013619 (accessed 6 May 2022).

Malaysiakini. 2020. "Azmin Warns of Possible Legal Action if State Gov'ts

Refuse to Reopen Economies". 4 May 2020. https://www.malaysiakini.com/news/524074 (accessed 22 April 2024).

Malaysian Reserve, The. 2020. "Federal, State Govts Have Jurisdiction on CMCO". 6 May 2020. https://themalaysianreserve.com/2020/05/06/federal-state-govts-have-jurisdiction-on-cmco/ (accessed 22 April 2024).

———. 2021a. "Malaysia's Healthcare at the Brink of Collapse as Cases Remain High". 8 July 2021. https://themalaysianreserve.com/2021/07/08/malaysias-healthcare-at-the-brink-of-collapse-as-cases-remain-high/ (accessed 9 July 2022).

———. 2021b. "Sinovac Vaccine Offer to Penang a Scam: Khairy". 19 May 2021. https://themalaysianreserve.com/2021/05/19/sinovac-vaccine-offer-to-penang-a-scam-khairy/ (accessed 22 April 2024).

———. 2021c. "Vaccination for Retailers to Expand to Johor and Penang Soon". 28 July 2021. https://themalaysianreserve.com/2021/07/28/vaccination-for-retailers-to-expand-to-johor-and-penang-soon/ (accessed 8 July 2022).

MIDA (Malaysian Investment Development Authority). 2021. "17,053 Companies Have Registered under PIKAS". 25 July 2021. https://www.mida.gov.my/mida-news/17053-companies-have-registered-under-pikas/ (accessed 8 July 2022).

Ministry of Finance. 2021. "National Recovery Plan Council to Replace Special Committee". News Release, 16 July 2021. https://www.mof.gov.my/portal/en/news/press-citations/national-recovery-plan-council-to-replace-special-committee

Ministry of Foreign Affairs. 2021. "The Special Committee for Ensuring Access to COVID-19 Vaccine Supply (JKJAV)". https://www.kln.gov.my/web/chl_santiago/news-from-mission/-/blogs/the-special-committee-for-ensuring-access-to-covid-19-vaccine-supply-jkjav- (accessed 28 May 2024).

Ministry of Health. 2020. "Covid-19 Malaysia". https://covid-19.moh.gov.my/ (accessed 28 May 2024).

MITI (Ministry of International Trade and Industry). 2021. "Economic Sectors in the Essential Services Allowed to Operate Throughout the Period of Movement Control Order (MCO) in Pulau Pinang, Selangor, Wilayah Persekutuan (Kuala Lumpur, Putrajaya, Labuan), Melaka, Johor and Sabah". News Release, 12 January 2021. https://www.miti.gov.my/redir/pkp/media-release-en.html (accessed 28 May 2024).

MOSTI (Ministry of Science, Technology and Innovation). 2021. "COVID-19 Immunisation Task Force (CITF)". https://www.mosti.gov.my/en/citf/ (accessed 28 May 2024).

Muzafar, Puteri M.M., and Theebalakshmi Kunasekaran. 2020. "The Impact of Covid-19 on the Urban Poor: Three Major Threats—Money, Food and Living Conditions". 27 March 2020. Kuala Lumpur: Khazanah Research Institute.

My Government. 2020. "New Digital Normal (Post-Covid)". https://www.malaysia.gov.my/portal/content/30953 (accessed 28 May 2024).

National Security Council. n.d. https://www.mkn.gov.my/ (accessed 28 May 2024).

———. 2021. "Pasukan 'Greater Klang Valley Task Force' Mula Beroperasi". 12 August 2021. https://www.mkn.gov.my/web/ms/2021/08/12/pasukan-greater-klang-valley-task-force-mula-beroperasi/ (accessed 28 May 2024).

New Straits Times. 2020a. "Bank Negara, Banks Face Backlash over Alleged Moratorium U-turn". 1 May 2020. https://www.nst.com.my/business/2020/05/589031/bank-negara-banks-face-backlash-over-alleged-moratorium-u-turn (accessed 1 September 2023).

———. 2020b. "No External Consultants in Laksana: Tengku Zafrul". 1 May 2020. https://www.nst.com.my/business/2020/05/589035/no-external-consultants-laksana-tengku-zafrul (accessed 1 September 2023).

———. 2021a. "Hospital Operating beyond Its Capacity". 22 May 2021. https://www.nst.com.my/news/nation/2021/05/692120/hospital-operating-beyond-its-capacity (accessed 18 April 2024).

———. 2021b. "Penang Cancels Plans to Secure Own Covid-19 Vaccines". 7 June 2021. https://www.nst.com.my/news/nation/2021/06/696618/penang-cancels-plan-secure-own-covid-19-vaccines-nsttv (accessed 22 April 2024).

———. 2021c. "Ronald: Vaccination for Agrofood Industry to Be Implemented Soon". 6 August 2021. https://www.nst.com.my/news/nation/2021/08/715702/ronald-vaccination-agrofood-industry-be-implemented-soon (accessed 8 July 2022).

Ngio, Hua Yi. 2021. "With Vaccine Shortages, Malaysia Covid-19 Vaccinations Slow as Epidemic Grows". *CodeBlue*, 25 August 2021. https://codeblue.galencentre.org/2021/08/25/with-vaccine-shortages-malaysia-covid-19-vaccinations-slow-as-epidemic-grows/ (accessed 7 July 2022).

NUS Law. 2020. "Liberalization Woes Tension in the Federal–State Relationship in Malaysia". Singapore: National University of Singapore Faculty of Law.

Ostwald, Kai. 2017. "Federalism without Decentralization: Power Consolidation in Malaysia". *Journal of Southeast Asian Economies* 34, no. 3: 488–506.

Prevention and Control of Infectious Diseases Act 1988. Putrajaya: Government of Malaysia.

Projek Bangsa Malaysia. 2021. "Frontliners Reveal Truth about the Covid-19 Crisis in Klang Valley Hospitals". 12 July 2021. https://www.facebook.com/

watch/?ref=search&v=2394529767357997&external_log_id=400d9b1f-3713-41af-996d-9aa86e46463e&q=projek%20bangsa%20malaysia%20hospital%20emergency%20fund (accessed 1 September 2023).

ProtectHealth Sdn Bhd. 2022. "In-Situ Booster Dose Outreach Programmes for Companies, Associations and Communities". 10 January 2022. https://protecthealth.com.my/in-situ-booster-dose-outreach-programmes-for-companies-associations-and-communities/ (accessed 9 July 2022).

Rahmat, Lyshaida, and Hooi Ling Khoo. 2022. "An Analysis Study of Covid-19 Pandemic Impact on Transport System". E3S Web of Conferences 347, 01015, ICCEE 2022. https://www.e3s-conferences.org/articles/e3sconf/abs/2022/14/e3sconf_iccee2022_01015/e3sconf_iccee2022_01015.html (accessed 1 September 2023).

Shad Saleem Faruqi. 2019. *Our Constitution*. Subang Jaya: Thomson Reuters Asia.

Sinar Harian. 2021. "Azmin Sangkal Kerajaan Gagal Tangani Covid-19" [Azmin denies that the government has failed to manage Covid-10]. 18 June 2021. https://www.sinarharian.com.my/article/144942/khas/covid-19/azmin-sangkal-kerajaan-gagal-tangani-covid-19 (accessed 22 April 2024).

South China Morning Post. 2020. "In Malaysia, Questions over Minister's Small Fine for Coronavirus Quarantine Breach". 22 August 2020. https://www.scmp.com/week-asia/politics/article/3098451/malaysia-questions-over-ministers-small-fine-coronavirus (accessed 22 April 2024).

Sri Murniati Yusuf, Alissa Rode, and Zhen Ting Low. 2023, "PANTAU LAKSANA: Assessing Malaysia's Transparency and Accountability Initiatives in Implementing Emergency Fiscal Responses". IDEAS Policy Ideas No. 77. The Institute for Democracy and Economic Affairs, Kuala Lumpur, February.

Star, The . 2020a. "Health Minister's 'Warm Water Method' to Kill Coronavirus Questioned". 20 March 2020. https://www.thestar.com.my/news/nation/2020/03/20/health-minister039s-039warm-water-method039-to-kill-coronavirus-questioned (accessed 1 July 2022).

———. 2020b. "No Go for Hairdressers, Opticians and Ramadan Bazaars". 14 April 2020. https://www.thestar.com.my/news/nation/2020/04/14/no-go-for-hairdressers-opticians-and-ramadan-bazaars (accessed 7 July 2022).

Sun, The . 2020. "Can State Governments Choose to Defy CMCO?". 5 May 2020. https://thesun.my/local_news/can-state-governments-choose-to-defy-cmco-BA2376434 (accessed 22 April 2024).

———. 2022. "MySJ Data Fully Owned by Govt of Malaysia: Khairy". 31 March 2022. https://thesun.my/local_news/mysj-data-fully-owned-by-govt-of-malaysia-khairy-AB9021435 (accessed 18 April 2024).

Welsh, Bridget. 2020. "The Unsung Role of State Govt's in Battling Covid".

Malaysiakini, 3 July 2020. https://www.malaysiakini.com/columns/532836 (accessed 7 July 2022).

Yahoo News. 2020. "Minister: No 'Antara Dua Darjat' over Covid-19 SOPs; Five Charged in Court for Breaching Quarantine". 24 November 2020. https://malaysia.news.yahoo.com/minister-no-antara-dua-darjat-221427510.html (accessed 8 July 2022).

Yeoh, Tricia. 2020. "Federal-State Friction amid Malaysia's Dual Political and Pandemic Plight". *New Mandala*, August 2020. https://www.newmandala.org/federal-state-friction-amid-malaysias-dual-political-and-pandemic-plight/ (accessed 1 September 2023).

———. 2021. "Federalism and the Covid-19 Crisis: Trends, Tensions, and Testing Innovations in Malaysia". In *Federalism and the Response to Covid-19: A Comparative Analysis,* edited by R. Chattopadhyay, F. Knüpling, D. Chebenova, L. Whittington and P. Gonzalez. London: Routledge.

———. 2022. "Opposition Subnational Strongholds in Dominant Party Authoritarian Regimes (DPARs): The Pakatan Coalition in Selangor and Penang from 2008 to 2018". PhD dissertation, University of Nottingham Malaysia.

10

THE DRAMA OF VACCINE POLITICS

Covid-19 Inoculation Distribution in Thailand

Punchada Sirivunnabood

INTRODUCTION

In early 2020, Thailand was remarkably successful in containing the spread of the Covid-19 pandemic, controlling the number of total cases and deaths more effectively than other members of the Association of Southeast Asian Nations (ASEAN) (Poum 2021). The Centre for Covid-19 Situation Administration (CCSA), a new unit set up by the government to manage the pandemic, started out well but performed inconsistently over time, with critical roles in deliberation, expert consultation and decision-making undermined by vested interests. In mid-2020, Thailand had only one domestically transmitted case, averting a second wave of the Covid-19 pandemic. In 2021, however, the administration of General Prayut Chan-ocha failed to effectively manage the country's third Covid-19 outbreak, the Delta variant, which hit severely in April 2021 (BBC News 2020). The third wave originated at entertainment venues in Bangkok and then spread rapidly across the country when people travelled during the

Songkran festival. In May 2021, new infections lingered at around 2,000 to 3,000 cases daily, with no improvement until September (Worldometer 2023). Thousands of people died from the Delta variant. This triggered public concern about whether the country would have adequate access to the Covid-19 vaccines, which would allow a return to normal life.

Governments arguably bear the responsibility for vaccinating all residents. The Thai government, however, mismanaged the beginning of the vaccine roll-out in early 2021 (Punchada 2021a). This was primarily a result of infighting among the government organizations responsible for managing Thailand's pandemic response and power struggles between coalition parties who wanted to control vaccine procurement and distribution. The coalition parties believed controlling vaccine procurement and distribution would secure their political fortunes ahead of the next general election, which was eventually held in May 2023. Conflicts within government organs and between coalition parties not only led to the initial failure of vaccine delivery, but also caused the release of confusing public information at both central and local levels of administration.

Thailand began its vaccine roll-out—approximately 1.7 million doses—in June 2021 (BBC Thai 2021). AstraZeneca and Sinovac were the two major inoculations in use during the initial period of the campaign. The government secured approximately 117,000 imported AstraZeneca shots from the United Kingdom, with another 61 million doses locally produced by royal-owned company Siam BioScience.[1] The country also imported 6 million doses of Sinovac— also known as CoronaVac—from China, including 500,000 jabs donated by the Chinese government. Sinovac then became the key to Thailand's nationwide vaccination operation. The Thai government distributed more than 30 million Sinovac jabs from February 2021 through to the end of the year, beginning with two doses allocated to each frontline healthcare worker, to each resident of areas with severe disease clusters and to each resident of Phuket, the famous holiday island that the government hoped to reopen for tourists in July 2021. Later in 2021, the government also permitted further vaccines to be distributed: Johnson & Johnson, Moderna and Pfizer.

During the spread of the Delta variant, however, the Bangkok-based Siriraj Institute of Clinical Research revealed that China's Sinovac vaccine produced a lesser immune response than vaccination combinations that included an mRNA-based injection (*Matter* 2021; Jitsiree 2021). In response to this study and to demands from frontline medical workers for the mRNA-based vaccine, the Ministry of Public Health adopted a new vaccination strategy, combining China's Sinovac with the Western-developed mRNA-based vaccines. Then Thailand ceased buying Sinovac Covid-19 vaccines when its supply was exhausted (Chayut and Panarat 2021). Thailand was the first country to mix the Chinese and Western mRNA-based jabs to increase immune protection. Anyone who received a first and/or second dose of Sinovac was encouraged to have an additional dose of AstraZeneca or any other mRNA-based vaccine. This combination vaccination campaign caused public confusion, partly due to ambiguous information and a poor communication strategy from the central government and the Centre for Covid-19 Situation Administration (CCSA).

Vague and rapidly changing policy announcements by the CCSA confused the public: there was confusion on where to register for the vaccine, how it would be distributed—which provinces or demographic groups would get the vaccine first—and how local governments would facilitate vaccine delivery to remote areas. The unclear government policy was also partly a result of infighting between coalition parties. Ministers responsible for vaccine distribution were from different political parties, and they attempted to secure vaccines to further their own political interests, leading to mismanagement and delays.

This chapter explores how Thailand's high centralization of power constrained the roles of local government in managing the pandemic, and how the authority of the CCSA was undermined by vested interests. Coordination of vaccine distribution, in particular, was skewed by the involvement of political parties and their efforts to exploit the process to boost their popularity for the 2023 election.

BACKGROUND: GOVERNMENT RESPONSE TO THE COVID-19 CRISIS IN THAILAND

In January 2020, Anutin Charnvirakul, Deputy Prime Minister and Minister of Public Health, announced that Covid-19 was considered a regular cold rather than a more serious disease. He claimed that the government was equipped to handle it and that the Thai people should not be worried

(ThaiPBS Online 2021b). Soon after, in late January, approximately ten doctors were reportedly infected with Covid-19 (ibid.). Anutin publicly blamed the doctors for not avoiding the disease; he further claimed that doctors should set an example to the public on how to remain healthy. He even suggested punishing doctors who became infected with the coronavirus (ThaiPBS Online 2020). Thailand's first wave of Covid-19 began in March 2020, sparked by Thai boxing events and nightclubs in Bangkok; the virus spread to sixty-eight of the country's seventy-seven provinces, including Bangkok (*Bangkokbiz* 2020). The government responded rapidly with strong public health and social measures on 26 March 2020. It announced further measures in April 2020 including curfews, mandatory lockdown for all residents and a fourteen-day compulsory quarantine for incoming international travellers. Thailand's strong health policy arguably contained the effects of the first wave to a relatively low 3,017 cases and 56 deaths (1.9 per cent). On 13 May 2020, Thailand recorded zero locally transmitted Covid-19 cases and the country continued that way for at least 200 consecutive days (*Thaipublica* 2020).

After seven months of lockdown from April to October 2020, many Thais believed they would go back to the same pattern of life as before the pandemic. However, a series of illegal activities triggered a second outbreak of Covid-19 in November 2020. Only a couple of weeks before the New Year 2021 celebration, the number of new Covid-19 cases in Thailand skyrocketed, breaking a single-day record on 20 December 2020. This caused the authorities to issue urgent control measures, especially in the city of Samut Sakhon, whose central shrimp market was the epicentre of the new outbreak.

New cases were also increasingly detected among Myanmarese migrant workers in Thailand as authorities conducted more tests at their dormitories. As of mid-January 2021, cases linked to the central shrimp market in Samut Sakhon had been reported in fifty-three provinces, with particularly close attention being paid to parts of Bangkok and provinces neighbouring the city. Provinces were categorized into four colour-coded tiers, green, blue, yellow and red, and during the second wave of Covid-19, a total lockdown was implemented in the red zone of Samut Sakhon province and another four provinces, namely Chantaburi, Chonburi, Ranong and Trat. Although there were more cases during the second wave, approximately 20,000 in 2.5 months (18 December 2020 to 27 February 2021)—seven times more than the 3,042 of the first wave—the government effectively controlled the spread of the pandemic. By the last week of February 2021, the number of new daily cases had decreased to less than one hundred, suggesting that the spread of Covid-19 was being successfully controlled by the government's policy decisions and implementing agencies (Nattadhanai et al. 2021).

In April 2021, Thailand's third Covid-19 wave arrived a few days before the Songkran holidays. The contagion originated at entertainment venues in Bangkok and spread nationwide as millions of people travelled for the holidays. This threatened plans to restart tourism and decimated an already fragile economy. In May 2021, several new clusters were found in Bangkok's pubs, bars, local markets and migrant worker sites (dormitories and workplaces). New infections hovered at around 2,000 to 3,000 cases a day with no improvement for six months. Figure 10.1 shows the steep rise in cases and fatalities in August to September, with deaths exceeding 1,000 per month at the peak of the crisis. With the high rate of deaths and the escalating number of cases, many Thais questioned the government's management of the pandemic and delays in the vaccination roll-out, which they perceived as slow, disorderly and inequitable (Wee 2021). Many critics said the government had not done enough with regards to vaccinations—it had not procured sufficient vaccines and had not distributed them quickly enough—or in support of people whose businesses had been destroyed by the pandemic (Punchada 2021a).

From the beginning of 2022, after 53 million people, or 77.3 per cent of the population, had received Covid-19 vaccines, the situation improved. The Thai government stated that people should learn to live with Covid-19 instead of resorting to drastic measures like lockdowns, weeks-long quarantines and tough controls on travel and tourism (BBC News 2021c). On 1 April 2022, the CCSA removed Covid-19 from the list of diseases for which people were eligible for free treatment under the Universal Coverage for Emergency Patients scheme. From then on, only patients with severe Covid-19 symptoms were permitted to use the scheme. The government also lifted the requirement that fully vaccinated tourists take a reverse transcription polymerase chain reaction (RT-PCR) test before entering the country and on arrival. The government also allowed

FIGURE 10.1
Thailand: Covid-19 Cases and Deaths, January 2020 to April 2023

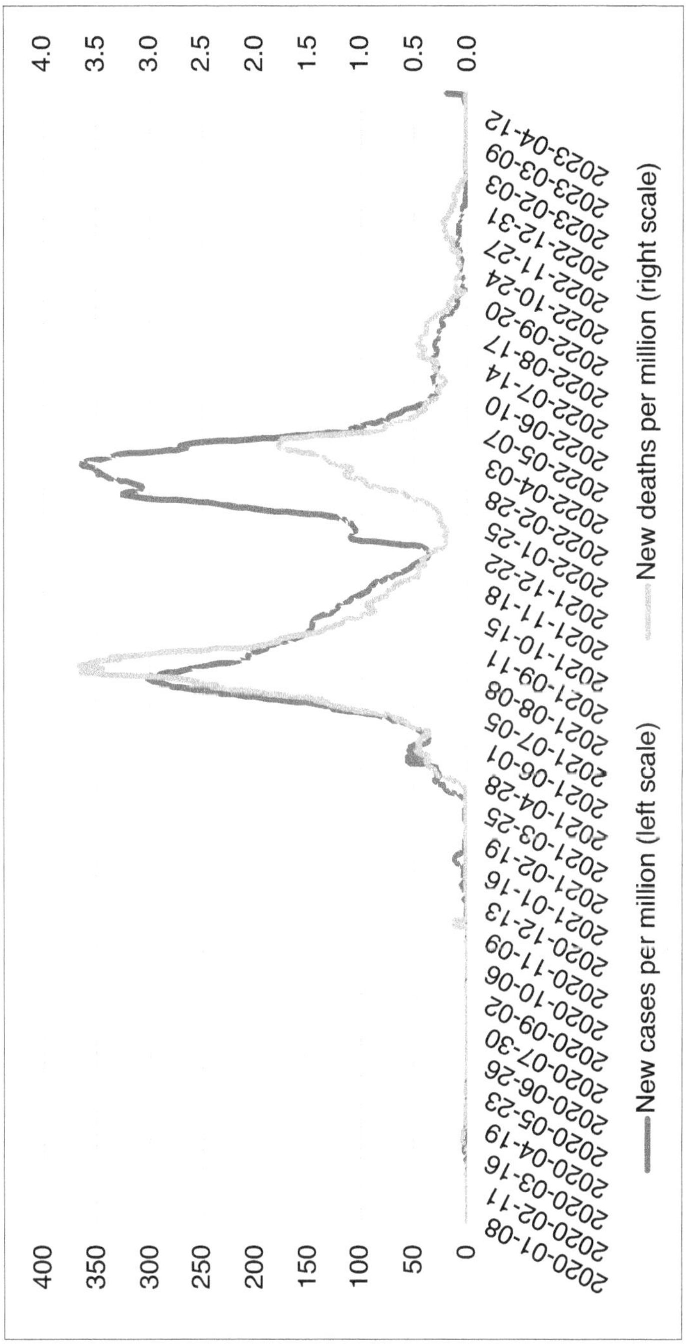

Source: ourworldindata.org.

all schools in Thailand to resume onsite classes. The Covid-19 situation in Thailand was gradually improving in mid-2022. With people returning to pre-pandemic lifestyles, the CCSA shut down permanently at the end of September 2022.

Covid-19 was part of life in Thailand from 2020 to 2023. The Thai government tried to manage the crisis by centralizing its power in the Prime Minister as the head of the CCSA. This allowed the Prime Minister and bureaucrats to control policies related to Covid-19 relief. However, the CCSA's structure and the infighting among ministries in the coalition government obstructed the process of resolving the pandemic and particularly in rolling out the vaccines.

DECENTRALIZATION AND EFFECTIVE CENTRALIZATION

It is useful to understand Thailand's history of de facto centralized power alongside formal local autonomy, in particular to provide context for observing the country's vertical power relations and coordination in response to Covid-19. After the coup in 1932, the Constitutional Revolution abolished absolute monarchy and introduced democracy. The leader of the 1932 revolution and former Minister of Interior, Pridi Bhanomyong, introduced the Thesaban Act (Municipal Administration Act) of 1933, which later led to the formation of municipality administration in thirty-five areas across the country. Local government was formally instituted in 1933, and Thailand gradually progressed in its decentralization. Five categories of local authority were institutionalized. The basic organ of local authority in urban areas is called a *thesaban* or municipality. The second type is the *sukhaphiban* or sanitary districts in semi-urban areas. The third are the provincial administrative organizations, which have authority at the provincial level. These three types of local authorities played a role in the rural areas. The other two categories of local authority are the Bangkok Metropolitan Administration for Bangkok, the capital of Thailand, and the City of Pattaya, a tourist destination, established during the mid-1970s (iLaw 2022).

Although decentralization began after the 1932 revolution, the powers of local governments were substantially constrained. They were controlled by government officers appointed by the central government instead of being empowered by local elections. Riggs (1966) calls this model of power struggle a "bureaucratic polity" in which bureaucrats, instead of elected local representatives, have the power to allocate and distribute resources to local people and rural areas (Anek 1992; Arghiros 2001; Supasawad 2010). This vertical relationship between the central and local governments limits the role of local government, especially in remote provinces.

Thailand's 1997 Charter, the revised Thai Constitution, and its concomitant political reforms marked a turning point in decentralization. They included a major reform of the local authority system and the decentralization process in the 1997 Charter. The 1997 Charter, in section 78, defined decentralization as a basic national policy. By the end of 1999, several laws relating to the development of local government had been revised and better implemented. The objectives of the legislative revisions included blocking the direct control of the central government, particularly the Ministry of Interior, in local authority management, and promoting local autonomy.

Although Thailand has promoted decentralization and local autonomy for more than twenty years, the governmental power structure continues to be concentrated in Bangkok. Elected local governments still have limited control over their areas. Central government ministries appoint delegates to represent their offices at the provincial and district levels and there is no coordination between central and local governments in territorial administration. Rather, a vertical extension of the ministries reaches out from Bangkok into Thailand's peripheries. The central authority thus appoints its officers to run the local government in order to deliver public services to local residents (Nelson 2002; Anek 2000).

This vertical power wielded by the centre limits the authorities and capacities of local governments to create and manage policy related to development in their areas, including in education, environmental management and public health. As detailed in this chapter, during the Covid-19 crisis, the local government did not have legal authority over many critical aspects of pandemic response.

Policies related to Covid-19 control, including vaccine purchases and allocations, were determined by the central government. When local governments, such as in Nonthaburi and Khon Kaen, expressed interest in procuring vaccines for their residents at the beginning of the roll-out, the central government did not permit it. The Ministry of the Interior asserted that "only the central government has the power to buy vaccines and manage the initial phase of the vaccination drive" (*Khaosod English* 2021). During the Covid-19 crisis, the local government did not have the legal authority to issue any policy to control the spread of the virus in their areas. The power to control vaccines was in the hands of the central government, ministries and political parties.

CENTRE FOR COVID-19 SITUATION ADMINISTRATION

Pandemic management necessitated some degree of centralized data gathering, consultation and decision-making, mainly in the horizontal dimension among different authorities and jurisdictions. On 24 March 2020, the government declared that a state of emergency would begin two days later. On 25 March 2020, Prime Minister and Defence Minister General Prayut Chan-o-cha set up the Centre for Covid-19 Situation Administration (CCSA) under the Order of the Prime Minister Decree (No. 5/2020). The move consolidated his power in Covid-19 crisis management; prior to the CCSA the power was in the hands of multiple ministers. The CCSA became the government vehicle to manage the Covid-19 pandemic (Cabinet Resolution 2020). Government House became the command centre and the operating authorities were shifted away from ministers to senior bureaucrats in numerous ministries. Cabinet members and the Prime Minister had direct authority over all government bodies and policies related to Covid-19 management. As the CCSA Chair, Prime Minister General Prayut Chan-o-cha instructed all relevant government departments to work together and report directly to the CCSA.

According to the Order of the Prime Minister (No. 6/2020), the CCSA was responsible for forming policy to control the Covid-19 crisis, managing vaccine imports and distribution and communicating with the public regarding government policy towards the pandemic. The CCSA was restructured twice in mid-2020 to ensure its effectiveness (iLaw 2021b). In December 2020, the Order of the Prime Minister No. 39/2020 restructured the CCSA once again. Under this new structure, the Prime Minister appointed the Permanent Secretary General from each of several ministries, instead of the ministers, to head the CCSA's subunits, each of which was responsible for an operation centre (Figure 10.2) This order was implemented primarily to control the power of other ministers and give authority to the Prime Minister. This centralization of decision-making in the Prime Minister allowed the government to respond promptly to the rapidly changing Covid-19 situation. The CCSA's committee members were mostly technocrats from the ministries and had more expertise on

FIGURE 10.2
Organizational Structure of the Centre for Covid-19 Situation Administration

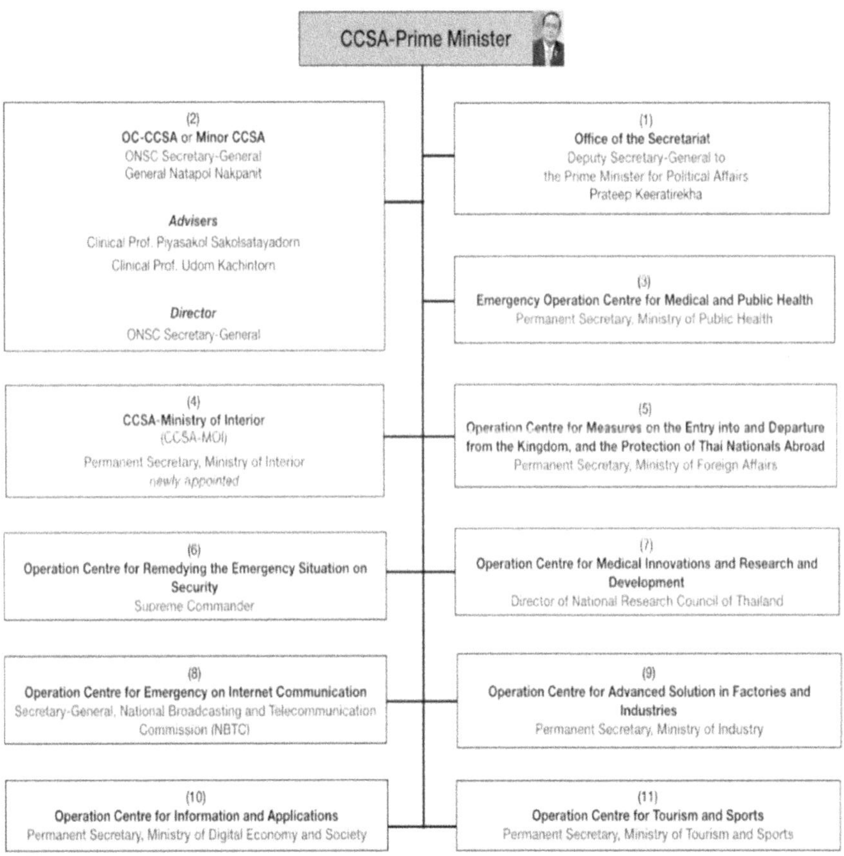

Note: OC: Operation Center; CCSA: Centre for Covid-19 Situation Administration.
Source: Order of the Prime Minister No. 39/2020, No. 22/2021; iLaw (2021b).

the disease and other matters related to Covid-19 than elected politicians. They provided in-depth information to the government before it made and implemented Covid-19 prevention policies. Figure 10.2 shows the structure of the CCSA as indicated in the Order of the Prime Minister No. 39/2020 and No. 22/2021.

In order to enhance the government's capacity to deal with the Covid-19 pandemic, the Prime Minister also formed an operations centre for the CCSA. It was headed by Dr Piyasakol Sakolsatayadorn, the Secretary General of the Office of the National Security Council and the 2015 Minister of Public Health during the military junta government. He was supported by prominent technocrats.

The operations centre was a subunit of the CCSA, but played a significant role in forming and recommending policies for the CCSA's consideration and approval. These included policies on travel control, festival restrictions, school reopenings, economic recovery management, vaccine procurement and distribution, and inoculation. The CCSA, chaired by the Prime Minister, approved policies related to Covid-19 management to be implemented across the country. All provincial and other authorities were required by law to follow the CCSA's guidelines on managing Covid-19 and the vaccine programme in their province (Secretariat of the Cabinet 2021).

VACCINE DISTRIBUTION AND ITS COMPLEXITY

The AstraZeneca and Sinovac vaccines were the first vaccines in use at the beginning of the Thai government's nationwide vaccination campaign in 2021. The public, however, doubted the efficacy of the Sinovac vaccine and were concerned about the lack of transparency over the procurement deal between the Thai and Chinese governments. The junta government, which took power in the 2014 military coup, had a difficult diplomatic relationship with the West (Pavin 2018) and became a closer ally of China (Tita 2021a; Strangio 2021). When the more contagious and deadly Delta variant emerged in mid-2021, however, the government switched to a mix-and-match vaccine policy to better protect people (Pravit 2021). The first dose of Sinovac was mixed with a second dose from AstraZeneca and then the government announced in October 2021 that it would not purchase any further Sinovac. From October 2021 onwards Western-developed vaccines completely replaced Chinese jabs.

In Thailand, the vaccination programme was undermined by complicated bureaucracy, which resulted in public confusion on vaccine distribution and delayed vaccine delivery, particularly to rural areas. Vaccine procurement and distribution were controlled by the central government, through the CCSA. According to the National Vaccine Security Act B.E. 2561, the National Vaccine Institute and the Department of Disease Control under the Ministry of Public Health are responsible for purchasing vaccines. The government was criticized for monopolizing vaccine imports and preventing private hospitals from buying and selling jabs. In response, the Prime Minister set up a committee for the private purchase of the vaccines headed by Dr Piyasakol Sakolsatayadorn, an adviser to the operations centre of the CCSA. Together with the Ministry of Public Health, the Government Pharmaceutical Organization, the Food and Drug Administration and the Private Hospital Association Thailand, the CCSA decided to import alternatives to AstraZeneca and Sinovac, including Moderna and Pfizer (iLaw 2021a). Although the government allowed private firms to buy alternative vaccines, the buying, selling and inspecting processes were controlled by the central government and the CCSA.

All imported vaccines needed approval from several bureaucratic levels, ranging from the Food and Drug Administration to the Department of Disease Control. The Department of Disease Control decided on the vaccine quota for each province or other government organ before delivering them. Figure 10.3 shows the vaccine inspection and distribution process from the central government to local communities.

After inspecting for quality and quantity, the CCSA gave permission for vaccine use to vulnerable groups to prevent severe symptoms and fatalities: these groups included people aged sixty and over, pregnant women and people at risk of chronic disease or death. The distribution of the vaccines was based on the seriousness of the Covid-19 infection in the area and the number of vulnerable groups, including families with children and the number of elderly in each province. During the period of vaccine shortage, from late 2020 until the beginning of 2021, many healthcare workers and media criticized the government's complex inspection process as an obstacle to rapid vaccine allocation to local communities (BBC

FIGURE 10.3
Vaccine Inspection and Distribution Process

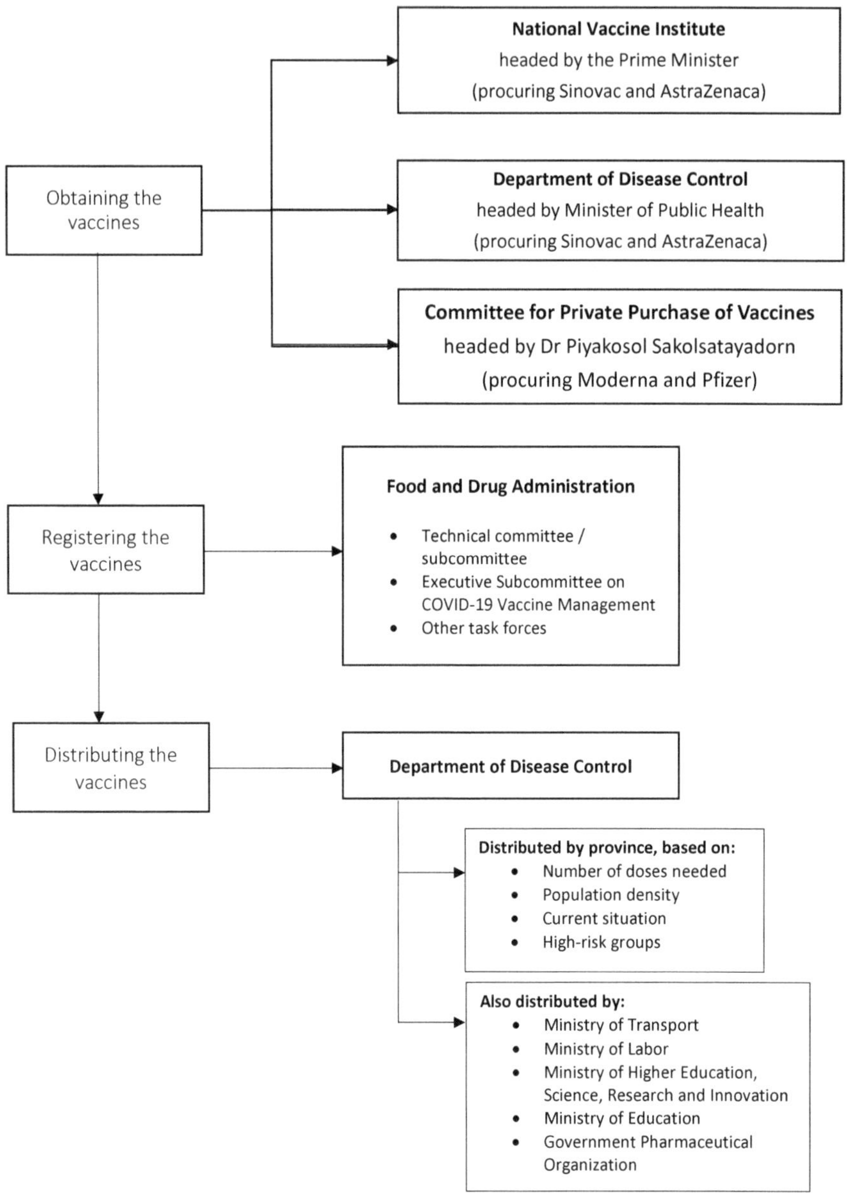

Source: Developed from BBC (2021).

News 2021b). Some also complained that the vaccine allocation criteria prioritized certain provinces and ministries rather than the crisis areas. Critics stressed that the areas with more severe outbreaks, such as Chiang Mai and Samut Prakan, should be prioritized.

Due to the shortage of vaccines during the early phase of the roll-out, many different elements of government, including political parties and provincial and local governments, competed to secure doses. The opponents of the government criticized the Minister of Public Health, Anutin Charnvirakul, for his failure to procure sufficient vaccines, believing this was his responsibility (BBC News 2021c). However, his authority to buy and distribute Covid-19 vaccines had been moved to an ad hoc committee of the CCSA. Anutin's political party, Bhumjaithai, stated correctly that the power to purchase and distribute vaccines had been taken from them when the Prime Minister Prayut, the CCSA Chairman, set up an ad hoc panel for vaccine purchases and delivery (*Bangkok Post* 2021b). Thus, Anutin could not be blamed for the vaccine shortage or mismanagement. Conflict over vaccine management continued to grow, as parties appeared to be concerned with obtaining more vaccines to boost their political capital for the upcoming elections (Punchada 2021b; Tita 2021b).

COMMUNICATION MATTERS

Thailand's pandemic management was beset by confusing messages concerning the availability of vaccines, the location of inoculation sites and other significant information around Covid-19 and the jabs. This situation widely frustrated the public (TDRI 2021a). In the first quarter of 2021, for instance, the CCSA revised its vaccine distribution policy four times, changing the process by which people could register for a vaccine and switching between walk-in vaccination and registering ahead of an appointment, rescheduling people's vaccination dates without giving notice and altering the online process for registering for the vaccine. The plan was for the general public to register for vaccines in early May 2021, with inoculations to begin later in the month. In practice, however, many registration and vaccination dates were postponed without clear notification (*Thairath Online* 2021).

The central government created five mobile apps through which people could register for the vaccination and find Covid-19 updates, while some provinces also created their own (BBC News 2021a). The Mor Prom app, meaning Doctor's Ready, was Thailand's first Covid-19 app and it was designed by the Ministry of Public Health. It allowed residents to access vaccination services, including making an appointment for vaccination and viewing their vaccine record, and also contained updated information concerning the Covid-19 situation. The app also included a feature to monitor any vaccine side effects. The app, however, crashed on the day of its launch as an overwhelming number of users attempted to access it (Newton 2021).

Due to a three-month instability of the Mor Prom app, other provinces, including Bangkok and Nonthaburi, launched their own vaccination apps for residents. The Bangkok Metropolitan Administration launched the Thai Ruam Jai registration app for Bangkok's citizens to make vaccine appointments. Government authorities in Nonthaburi province introduced the Non's Prom (Nonthaburi's Ready) app to allow people to book a vaccination appointment. Aside from these two provinces, other provinces such as Phuket, Chiang Mai and Samut Sakhon, also launched their own online apps to facilitate vaccinations for their populations.

While apps initiated by provinces did assist people in receiving their inoculations faster than the central government app, the multiple apps caused confusion in the system. Many people who registered for a jab with the Mor Prom app also registered with other apps, hoping to obtain an earlier appointment. The system was overwhelmed and many people were prevented from securing an appointment.

Aside from apps for vaccine appointments, the government also introduced other apps related to the Covid-19 pandemic, including Thai Chana to track entry and exit to all public venues via QR codes, Mor Chana to track the locations where Covid-19 was found, and Thai Safe Thai, a tool helping people to evaluate their health before the returned to the workplace (Wichiranon 2021). Unlike other countries that developed a single application for Covid-19, such as Singapore's TraceTogether application, in Thailand confusion was created by the use of multiple apps. This indicates coordination failures among government agencies and it resulted in the mismanagement of vaccine distribution and communications.

VACCINE DISTRIBUTION: COORDINATION AND COMPETITION

Covid-19 vaccine distribution in Thailand was centralized and managed by the CCSA and the Ministry of Public Health. During the early period of vaccine roll-out, high demand for vaccinations across the country caused intense competition between government agencies and ministries and among political parties to secure vaccines for their constituents. According to the CCSA's vaccine allocation plan, as shown in Figure 10.3, vaccines were to be distributed based on an area's population density, its Covid-19 status, the number of people in vulnerable groups and the number of frontline medical workers. Many provinces, particularly those located in the border areas such as Kanchanaburi and Chiang Rai, which neighbour Myanmar, were not satisfied with the government's vaccine allocation plan. They received insufficient vaccines to protect their residents from infections that were brought in with migrant workers or other foreign travellers (*Khaosod* 2021). Provinces dependent on tourism, other than Phuket, also complained that their vaccine quotas were too small, and insufficient to protect their citizens (Amarin 2021). This led to strong criticism of the authorities, particularly the Ministry of Public Health and Anutin Charnvirakul, Minister of Public Health from the Bhumjaithai Party, who was responsible for the vaccination programme. The Thailand Development Research Institute (TDRI), a Bangkok-based think-tank, argued that the failures of the vaccination programme were a result of the government's underestimation of the Covid-19 situation, the complicated vaccine procurement and import process and the lack of cooperation among the government ministries responsible for vaccine delivery (TDRI 2021b).

While many provinces received insufficient Covid-19 jabs, politically connected provinces such as Buriram, controlled by the Bhumjaithai Party, received more vaccines than others at the beginning of the vaccine roll-out. Table 10.1 compares the number of vaccines provided to major provinces during the early period of inoculation roll-out in 2021.

In August 2021, large provinces such as Chiang Mai, Khonkaen and Nakhon Ratchasima received a smaller number of first doses than Buriram, which was controlled by the politically connected Bhumjaithai Party (excluding Phuket, which had received its first vaccines earlier) (*MGR*

TABLE 10.1
Vaccine Distribution in August 2021

Province	*Number of Doses Received*
Buriram	Approximately 600,000, sufficient for one dose for 26.5 per cent of the provincial population
Chiang Mai	503,038 doses, sufficient for one dose for 21 per cent of the provincial population
Khonkaen	300,653 doses, sufficient for one dose for 12.3 per cent of the provincial population
Nakhon Ratchasima	651,000 doses, sufficient for one dose for 17 per cent of the provincial population
Phuket	781,963 doses, sufficient for one dose for 76.31 per cent of the provincial population

Source: Developed from data in the Mor Prom/Doctor's Ready app (accessed August 2021) and the Department of Disease Control (accessed August 2021).

Online 2021b; Parpart 2021). The Ministry of Public Health intended that the vaccines should first be given to provinces with higher levels of Covid-19 cases, such as Bangkok, and the tourism provinces for which the government planned an early reopening. Many politicians from opposition parties, including a party-list MP from the Move Forward Party, raised questions about the larger number of vaccines allocated to Buriram. As of June 2021, Buriram had received more jabs than other provinces even though it was not a major tourist destination and had fewer Covid-19 cases than others (TDRI 2021; Isra News 2021).

The roll-out was also criticized because vaccines were provided first to some VIPs instead of healthcare workers and vulnerable groups. In many provinces, the vaccines were reportedly distributed first to well-connected people (Prachatai 2021). Some were VIPs closely linked to members of a hospital board. Others were politicians from the ruling government party or provincial-level bureaucrats (*Nation Thailand* 2021). While the vaccination campaign was postponed in many places due to vaccine scarcity and delayed deliveries, these VIPs, who did not have underlying health problems, received their jabs before others (Panumet 2021). This patronage practice emerged throughout Thailand during the process of vaccine distribution.

The vaccine shortage and favouritism in vaccine allocation resulted in conflict (TDRI 2021a). The competition to secure vaccines caused conflict between ministries controlled by different political parties and also caused serious disputes between the central and local governments. For example, a conflict between Minister of Public Health Anutin and Aswin Kwanmuang, the governor of Bangkok (appointed by Prime Minister Prayut Chan-ocha in 2014) echoed the conflict on the insufficiency of inoculation allocations between the Ministry of Public Health and provincial authorities.

Aswin, the governor of Bangkok, planned to run for the position again in 2022. Likewise, Deputy Prime Minister and Minister of Public Health Anutin wanted to win in the 2023 national elections. Clashes between the Bangkok governor's office and the Ministry of Public Health over the Bangkok vaccine quota and how to deal with Covid-19 caused information confusion among residents and undermined the capital's recovery (*Standard* 2021). While the Bangkok governor preferred to focus on providing vaccinations at outbreak sites, the Ministry of Public Health wanted to distribute vaccines to all areas equally across Bangkok (Punchada 2021b). Bangkok also requested additional doses in order to prepare the capital for the reopening, but the Ministry of Public Health refused, claiming it had to follow the national distribution policy.

A disagreement on vaccination policy between the Ministry of Public Health and the CCSA also led to confusion. Mr Anutin backed a walk-in vaccination policy in certain spots to reduce infection numbers and decrease the rate of fatalities. But the Prayut-led CCSA overturned the walk-in policy and advocated for advance registration. This would ensure vaccine centres had sufficient doses for attendees (ThaiPBS Online 2021). Unhappy with General Prayut's decision, Mr Anutin and another minister from the Bhumjaithai Party, Minister of Transport Saksayam Chidchob, set up a walk-in vaccination centre at Bang Sue Grand Station in Bangkok (*MGR Online* 2021a). This constituted an act of defiance against the Prime Minister.

Bang Sue Grand Station in Bangkok was the only walk-in Covid-19 vaccination site in early 2021. Minister of Transport Saksayam Chidchob opened the station to distribute vaccines to public transport workers, including bus, taxi and motorcycle taxi drivers. Later, due to the vaccine scarcity, many people from Bangkok's neighbouring provinces, including

Phechaburi, Suphan Buri and Ratchaburi, flocked to the station to obtain the jab. Large queues of people waiting for vaccination may have increased the spread of Covid-19 infection in the area the government speculated at the time (*MGR Online* 2021a). In August 2021, the CCSA ceased the walk-in service at the railway station and people who wanted to be inoculated had to register online and in advance.

The crowds packing into Bang Sue Grand Station in Bangkok is a clear illustration of the mismanagement of Covid-19 vaccine supplies; it indicated a serious shortage of vaccines across the nation. The author of this chapter interviewed people queuing for the vaccine at the station and found they could not access vaccines in their own provinces.[2] They were under sixty years old and did not have chronic medical conditions (considered high-risk for Covid-19), but wanted to be vaccinated as quickly as possible. They came to the centre of vaccine distribution at Bang Sue Central Station hoping to be vaccinated via the walk-in system.

The scarcity of the vaccine induced corruption and fraudulent registrations. Some people faked their age in the registration system to cut the queue; once they arrived for their appointments, however, their actual age appeared in the system and they were rejected (Fronde 2021). It was reported that some staff who worked at the main vaccine distribution centre sold vaccination appointments at Bang Sue Grand Station in Bangkok at THB400–1,200 each (*Bangkok Post* 2021a). This alleged fraudulence delayed vaccinations for vulnerable people.

Although local governments and private hospitals wanted to help and proposed securing their own vaccines, they were hampered by the Ministry of Public Health. According to the 2018 National Vaccine Security Act B.E. 2561 or C.E. 2018, the purchase and allocation of vaccines are the responsibility of the central government or the CCSA (Thanyapon 2021). The Act also states that local authorities are required to follow the central government's vaccine distribution plan. Anutin stated that "vaccines that were approved for emergency use can only be sold to the government" (*Khaosod* 2021). As a result, local authorities could not secure their own vaccine supply, even though the roll-out of the national vaccination drive was progressing slowly—caused in part in 2021 by a vaccine shortage, which resulted in public anxiety. The CCSA continued to control the vaccine roll-out across the country. However, the vaccine situation improved in late 2021 when the government was able to procure more vaccines and set up more vaccination centres.

During the early period of vaccine roll-out in 2021, Thailand progressed very slowly, with inoculation campaigns ineffective and poorly implemented. The vaccine crisis was caused by the central government's mishandling of vaccine policy, a failure to secure options beyond the AstraZeneca and Sinovac vaccines and the infighting for vaccines among authorities keen to boost their political popularity ahead of the 2023 election. The government usurped the powers of all authorities to control vaccine procurement and allocation. This worsened the uneven distribution of vaccines, which particularly affected people in rural areas.

In 2022, the vaccine situation eased: more vaccines arrived in late 2021, and this also brought a halt to the fighting between the CCSA and other government bodies over supply. In addition to Sinovac, the use of which ceased from October 2021 when purchases ran out, and AstraZeneca, the Thai government also purchased approximately 30 million doses of the mRNA-based Pfizer vaccine, which arrived in Bangkok in late 2021 (TDRI 2021a). Further, in November 2021, the first Moderna shipment of 1.4 million doses arrived and more vaccines from a variety of suppliers came in the first quarter of 2022 (*Bangkokbiz* 2021a). The Moderna vaccine was first distributed only to private hospitals that were permitted to offer vaccinations after going through a quality inspection process. The government also received vaccine donations from its dialogue partners, including the United States and France. In response to the emergence of the Omicron variant, Bangkok's Bang Sue Grand station again offered a walk-in vaccination service, this time with a wider choice of vaccines (ThaiPBS Online 2022). Both Thais and foreigners were permitted to use the service, and they were able to choose their vaccine. With a large number of vaccine doses in hand, Thailand was able to pursue a mass nationwide vaccination in 2022. Figure 10.4 shows the increasing number of inoculations from late 2021 to early 2022.

Bangkok and other provinces set up their own vaccine centres across areas under their purview. The Bangkok Metropolitan Administration and local authorities urged residents to ensure they had obtained two jabs and a booster dose before the Songkran festival in mid-April 2022, when people would travel to see family. Bangkok opened six walk-in vaccination

FIGURE 10.4
Vaccinations in Thailand, September 2021 to April 2022

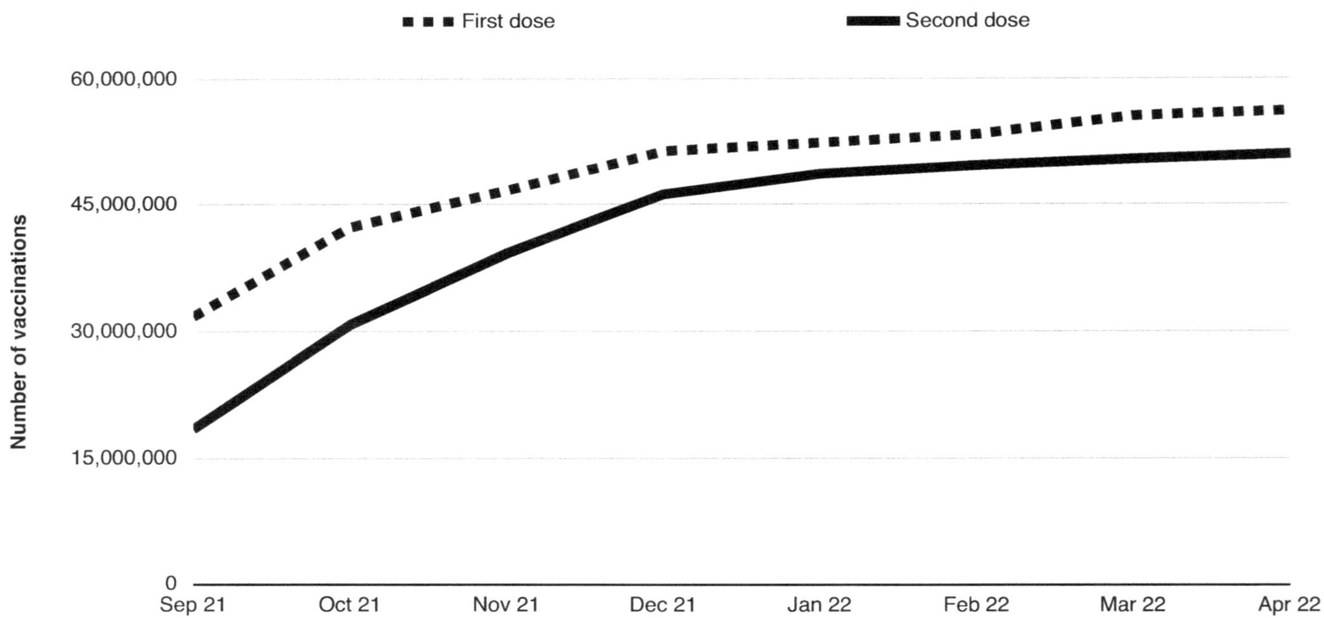

Note: By February 2022, 76.6 per cent (53,282,587) of Thailand's population had received a first dose and 71.3 per cent (49,582,984) had also received a second. Two months later, the percentage of Thai citizens who had received a first dose had increased to 80.54 per cent (56,018,378), while 73.26 per cent (50,955,417), had also received a second.
Source: Department of Disease Control (n.d.).

facilities in addition to the station site. As of April 2022, approximately 80.54 per cent of Thailand's population of 56 million had received a first shot and 73.26 per cent a second, while more than 30 per cent had received a third (Department of Disease Control n.d. and 2022).

During the spread of the Omicron variant in early 2022, the government urged people to obtain a booster shot. In contrast to the situation of 2021, by early 2022 more vaccines were available. However, some people refused a third (*Thairath Online* 2022). This was due to the lack of information on the importance of a booster dose. Figure 10.5 shows the number of booster doses given since the start of the Omicron variant in late 2021 to April 2022.

Medical doctors and frontline workers were concerned that the Omicron variant would spready quickly as people did not want to obtain booster jabs (*Bangkokbiz* 2021b), not realizing that they would help to protect from future infections and help the country return to normality. Although the number of new cases declined after the Songkran festival at the end of April 2022, the risk of Covid-19 remained high.

CONCLUSION

In March 2022, Thailand planned to move from pandemic to endemic from July 2022, allowing people to return to normal life. Under the endemic policy, there were no requirements for Covid-19 testing, and tourists no longer needed to register with the Thailand Pass before entering the country. Wearing masks was no longer compulsory in public, except for those infected with Covid-19. But some medical workers were still concerned about the country's readiness to enter the endemic state. They worried about the emergence of new, easily transmissible variants; while some endemic diseases can disappear, others can cause unexpected outbreaks. Thus, Thai medical workers continued to caution the government and residents to protect themselves from Covid-19 infection by maintaining as many prevention strategies as possible, including good hand hygiene, consistently and correctly wearing a high-quality mask, keeping away, when possible, from those infected with Covid-19 and continuing to obtain booster jabs.

The CCSA played a crucial role in formulating Covid-19 policies, including on vaccination, economic recovery, mobility restrictions,

FIGURE 10.5
Booster Doses from September 2021 to April 2022

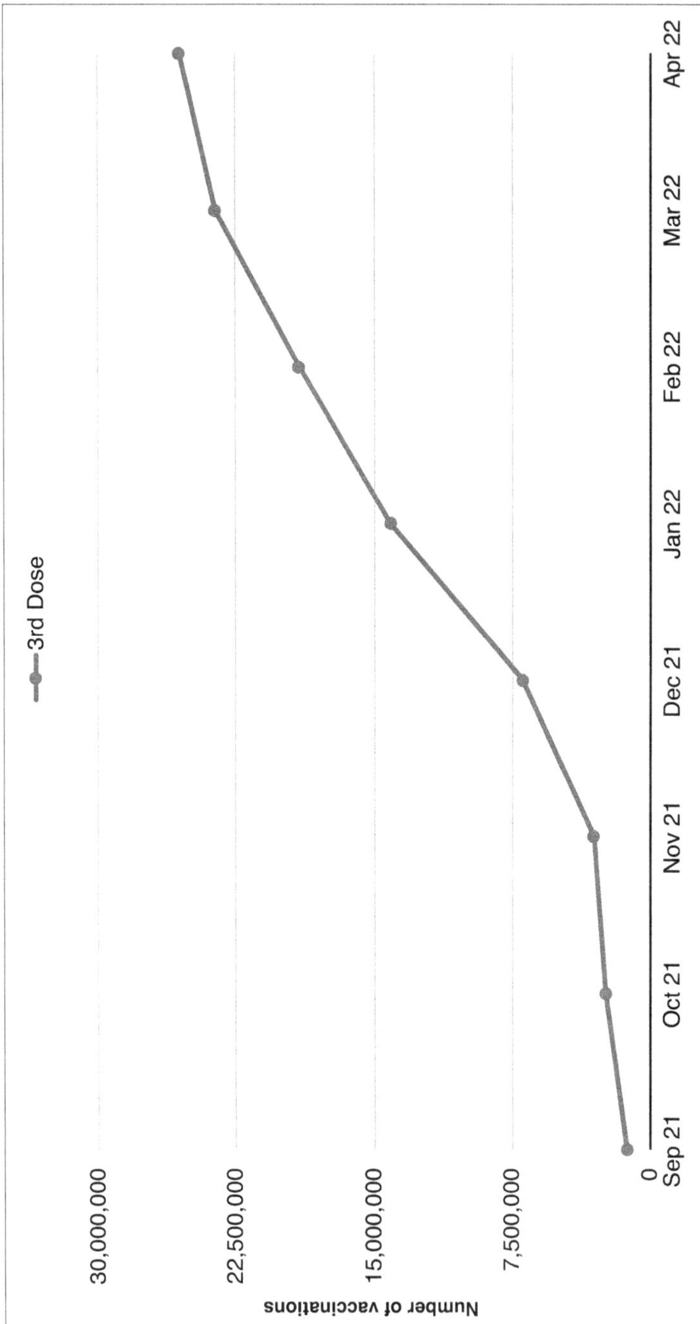

Source: Department of Disease Control (n.d.)

reopening of schools and businesses, and providing information to the public about the Covid-19 situation. Although the provincial governments had some jurisdiction over the scope and timeline of some policy matters, such as mobility restrictions and mask-wearing, the central government exercised overriding authority over health and had strong powers to control local government. The centralization of pandemic policy gave the central government and its coalition partners policy advantages, including promoting economic recovery, opening schools and businesses and controlling vaccine procurement and distribution to Thai citizens.

Cooperation across government agencies at the national level, however, was hampered by infighting within the government coalition. Ministers obstructed policy implementation, particularly vaccine procurement and roll-out. They appeared to be more concerned with dispensing vaccines to boost their political capital ahead of the elections. The absence of coordination among different government agencies at the national level caused multiple problems including inefficiency in vaccine delivery and miscommunications about Covid-19. The impact of these issues was especially strong in rural areas and included confusion regarding vaccine registration and Thailand's reopening.

The CCSA's vertical management of policies was weakened by a lack of horizontal coordination among different government ministries and institutions, which delayed Thailand's opening relative to its ASEAN neighbours. After the mid-2022 closure of the CCSA and transfer of power to the provincial governments to handle Covid-19, the situation improved. When policy decisions began to be made at the local level, conflicts among political parties over Covid-19 policy disappeared. Local governments better understood the needs and characteristics of their provinces, were better able to gather information regarding the on-the-ground situation, and were more effective in implementing policies than the central government or the CCSA.

Notes

1. AstraZeneca worked with the royal-owned company Siam BioScience to produce and distribute vaccines across Southeast Asia.
2. Author's interviews with five people who received a vaccine at Bang Sue Grand Station in December 2021. Interview transcripts on file with author.

References

Amarin. 2021. "Chao Pattaya Voy Roe Cheet Vaccine Sud Thay Walk In Te Har Daicheet Bai Sam" [Pattaya residents queue for vaccination: discouraged, walked in at 5 a.m. and got the injection at 3 p.m.]. 21 May 2021. https://www.amarintv.com/news/detail/80948 (accessed 18 April 2022).

Anek Laothamatas. 1992. *Business Associations and the New Political Economy of Thailand: From Bureaucratic Polity to Liberal Corporatism*. Boulder, CO: Westview Press.

———. 2000. *Wisaithat Kanpokkhrong Thongthin Lae Phaen Kankrachaiamnat* [Vision of local government and decentralization plan]. Krungthep: Mitimai.

Arghiros, Daniel. 2001. *Democracy, Development and Decentralisation in Provincial Thailand.* Richmond, Surrey: Curzon Press.

Bangkokbiz. 2020. "Phupui Covid 19 Nai Thai Patu Jak 4 Pub Nai Krungthep Lae Sanam Mui Pre Pai 9 Changwat" [Covid-19 patients in Thailand erupted from 4 pubs in famous Bangkok areas and boxing stadiums; spread to 9 provinces]. 20 March 2020. https://www.bangkokbiznews.com/social/871604 (accessed 22 December 2023).

———. 2021a. "Vaccine Moderna Ongkorn Pesat Confirm Thueng Thai Eak 1.4 Lan Dose Pray Duean Ni" [Moderna vaccine: Government Pharmaceutical Organization confirms another 1.4 million doses will arrive in Thailand at the end of this month]. 13 November 2021. https://www.bangkokbiznews.com/news/971615 (accessed 20 April 2022).

———. 2021b. "Tham Mai Sai Phan Omicron Prea Kracha Pai Yang Ruad Reu Nai Lai Prathet" [Why is the Covid Omicron spreading so quickly in many countries?]. 30 November 2021. https://www.bangkokbiznews.com/social/974823.

Bangkok Post. 2021a. "11 Nabbed for Bang Sue Jab System Fraud". 30 July 2021. https://www.bangkokpost.com/thailand/general/2156895/11-nabbed-for-bang-sue-jab-system-fraud (accessed 28 April 2022).

———. 2021b. "Enough Is Enough". 24 July 2021. https://www.bangkokpost.com/thailand/politics/2154007/enough-is-enough (accessed 18 April 2022).

BBC News. 2021a. "Covid-19 jak Thai chana su Moh chana; app chuea damg jak ratthaban tob joat pong kan rok dai pheang dai" [Covid-19 from Thai Chana to Mor Chana: can applications created by the government respond to the Covid-19 crisis or not?]. 24 January 2021. https://www.bbc.com/thai/thailand-55784607 (accessed 26 April 2022).

———. 2021b. " Covid 19: Jak Thang Ma Tua Diew Thung Vaccine Tem Khem Sarup 9 Hetkarn Vaccine Nai Rop Pi 2564". [Covid-19: From betting on a single horse to an armful of vaccines. Summary of 9 notable COVID vaccine events in 2021]. 28 December 2021. https://www.bbc.com/thai/thailand-59807039 (accessed 26 April 2022).

———. 2021c. "Pued prathet nayok yam 'tong yuk ab Covid hai dai" [Open the country; the prime minister stressed we have to live with Covid]. 20 October 2021. https://www.bbc.com/thai/thailand-58968273 (accessed 27 April 2022).

BBC Thai. 2021. "Covid-19: puead phaen rat Chadha vaccine tua nai ma muearai krai chadai cheet gorn" [Covid-19: Revealing the government's plan to procure which vaccine: When will it come? Who will get the shot first?]. 25 May 2021. https://www.bbc.com/thai/thailand-57243640 (accessed 26 April 2022).

Cabinet Resolution. 2020. "Khamsang Ti. 76/2563 Chattang Suan Borihand Sathanakarn Kan Prea Rabat Khong Rok Tid Chuea Virus Corona 2019 (Covid 2019) [Order of the Prime Minister No. 76/2020 regarding the establishment of the Centre for COVID-19 Situation Administration (CCSA). 12 March 2020. https://www.opm.go.th/opmportal/multimedia/phoobeas/covid-19/nr2563/76-2563.pdf.

Chayut Setboonsarng, and Panarat Thepgumpanat. 2021. "Thailand to Cease Sinovac Vaccine Use When Stocks End This Month". Reuters, 18 October 2021. https://www.reuters.com/world/asia-pacific/thailand-cease-sinovac-vaccine-use-when-stocks-end-this-month-2021-10-18/ (accessed 10 April 2022).

Department of Disease Control. n.d. "Satanakarn Kan Cheed Vaccine Covid 19 Prajamwan" [Daily report on Covid-19 vaccinations]. https://ddc.moph.go.th/vaccine-covid19/diaryReport (accessed 20 April 2022).

———. 2022. "Raingan Kwam Kawna Kan Hai Borikan Cheed Vaccine Covid 19 Prajam Wan Tee 27 Maysayon 2565" [Daily progress report of Covid-19 vaccination services as of 27 April 2022]. 27 April 2022. https://ddc.moph.go.th/uploads/files/2489020220427032142.jpg (accessed 27 April 2022).

Fronde, Neill. 2021. "People Fake Age to Get Appointment at Elderly Vaccination Centre". *The Thaiger*, 17 July 2021. https://thethaiger.com/coronavirus/people-fake-age-to-get-appointment-at-elderly-vaccination-centre (accessed 28 April 2022).

iLaw. 2021a. "Jadsue Vaccine Covid-19 Krai Tong Rabpidchaub?" [Procurement of Covid-19 vaccines: Who is responsible?]. 17 August 2021. https://ilaw.or.th/node/5944 (accessed 11 April 2022).

———. 2021b. "'Sor-Bor-Kor' Kue Arai? Puet Krongsang Lae Raichue Bukkon Buenglang" [What is the "CCSA"? Disclosing the structure and a list of the persons behind the scenes]. 9 July 2021. https://ilaw.or.th/node/5908 (accessed 11 April 2022).

———. 2022. "Lueak tang thongthin: rujak Pattaya aongkorn thongthin rup baeb phiset hang te song" [Local elections: get to know Pattaya, the second special local government organization]. 24 April 2022. https://www.ilaw.or.th/articles/5163 (accessed 11 April 2022).

Isra News. 2021. "TDRI Kai Kamthob Chanai 'Buri Ram' Dairab Kan Jadsan Vaccine Lamdub Tonton Kong Pratet" [TDRI answered why Buri Ram was among the first to receive vaccines in the country]. 15 July 2021. https://www.isranews.org/article/isranews-article/100504-tdri-3.html (accessed 20 April 2022).

Jitsiree Thongnoi. 2021. "Coronavirus: Thai Doctors Want Pfizer Vaccines Amid Doubts over Sinovac's Efficacy against Delta Variant". *South China Morning Post*, 13 July 2021. https://www.scmp.com/week-asia/health-environment/article/3140979/coronavirus-thai-doctors-want-pfizer-vaccines-amid (accessed 10 April 2022).

Khaosod. 2021. "Po.Tho. Hor Kanka Kan Aud Ratthaban La Cha Mai Tan Kan Che Chata Kanchanaburi Tong Ched Vaccine Reing Duan". [President of the Thai Chamber of Commerce in Kanchanaburi: the government is too slow; Kanchanaburi must urgently be vaccinated]. 26 May 2021. https://www.khaosod.co.th/around-thailand/news_6419919 (accessed 9 April 2022).

Khaosod English. 2021. "Local Gov't, Private Hospitals Blocked from Starting Vaccine Drive". 10 February 2021. https://www.khaosodenglish.com/news/crimecourtscalamity/2021/02/10/local-govt-private-hospitals-blocked-from-starting-vaccine-drive/ (accessed 24 April 2022).

Matter. 2021. "Soonwijai Clinic Siriraj Puey Sinovac 2 Kem Pongkan Delta Maidai Tae Ta Kratoon Kem 3 Duay AZ Ja Dai Poom Soong Kwa Cheed Pfizer 2Kem" [Siriraj clinical research centre disclosed that the second dose of Sinovac cannot prevent Delta, and a booster dose of AZ will provide higher immunity than two doses of Pfizer]. 20 August 2021. https://thematter.co/brief/152833/152833 (accessed 8 April 2022).

MGR Online. 2021a. " Kai Pritsana 'Oasis Vaccine Bangsue' Jud Duead Te Tam Hai Asawin Yakyub Thing" [Solving the mystery of Bang Sue vaccine oasis; the boiling point that made Asawin want to dissolve it]. 31 July 2021. https://mgronline.com/daily/detail/9640000074777 (accessed 20 April 2022).

———. 2021b. " 'Somchai' Chee 'Buri Ram' Mueng Na Yoo Dai Vaccine Andab Hok Kong Pratet Saeng Na Khorat-Udon-Khon Kaen" [Somchai says Buri Ram is a nice place to live, ranking sixth in the country for vaccines, ahead of Khorat, Udon Thani and Khon Kaen]. 24 May 2021. https://mgronline.com/onlinesection/detail/9640000049826 (accessed 19 April 2022).

Nation Thailand. 2021. "No VIP List for Pfizer Shots Insists State Hospital". 16 August 2021. https://www.nationthailand.com/in-focus/40004735 (accessed 22 April 2022).

Nattadhanai Rajatanavin, Titiporn Tuangratananon, Rapeepong Suphanchaimat and Viroj Tangcharoensathien. 2021. "Responding to the Covid-19 Second Wave in Thailand by Diversifying and Adapting Lessons from the First Wave". *BMJ Global Health*, no. 6: e006178.

Nelson, Michael H. 2002. "Thailand: Problems with Decentralisation?". In *Thailand's New Politics: KPI Yearbook 2001*, edited by Michael H. Nelson, pp. 219–81. Nonthaburi and Bangkok: King Prajadhipok's Institute and White Lotus Press.

Newton, Tim. 2021. "Mor Prom App Crashes Yesterday as People Rush to Register for Vaccine Roll Out". *The Thaiger*, 2 May 2021. https://thethaiger.com/news/national/mor-prom-app-crashes-yesterday-as-people-rush-to-register-for-vaccine-roll-out (accessed 25 April 2022).

Panumet Tanraksa. 2021. "PM Denies 'VIP Vaccine' Claim". *Bangkok Post*, 3 March 2021. https://www.bangkokpost.com/thailand/general/2077271/pm-denies-vip-vaccine-claim (accessed 22 April 2022).

Parpart, Erich. 2021. "Opinion: Why is Buriram Getting More Vaccines than Other Provinces?". *Thai Enquirer*, 16 July 2021. https://www.thaienquirer.com/29919/opinion-why-is-buriram-getting-more-vaccines-than-other-provinces/ (accessed 20 April 2022).

Pavin Chachavalpongpun. 2018. "Thailand's Post-coup Foreign Policy". East Asia Forum, 30 October 2018. https://www.eastasiaforum.org/2018/10/30/thailands-post-coup-foreign-policy/ (accessed 27 April 2022).

Poum Tangkitvanich. 2021. "The Paradox ofThailand's Success in Controlling Covid-19". *Asian Economic Papers* 20, no. 1: 175–199.

Prachatai. 2021. "Reports of VIPs Jumping the Covid-19 Vaccine Queue". 16 June 2021. https://prachatai.com/english/node/9298 (accessed 21 April 2022).

Pravit Rojanaphruk. 2021. "Sinovac: The 'Slandered Vaccine' for Thailand". *Khaosod English*, 11 September 2021. https://www.khaosodenglish.com/opinion/2021/09/11/sinovac-the-slandered-vaccine-for-thailand/ (accessed 13 April 2022).

Punchada Sirivunnabood. 2021a. "Thailand's Second Covid-19 Outbreak: Corruption and Its Consequences". *ISEAS Commentaries*, 2021/16, 20 January

2021. https://www.iseas.edu.sg/media/commentaries/thailands-second-covid-19-outbreak-corruption-and-its-consequences/ (accessed 2 February 2023).

———. 2021b. "Thailand's Third Pandemic Wave: Felled by Infighting". *Fulcrum*, 10 June 2021. https://fulcrum.sg/thailands-third-pandemic-wave-felled-by-infighting/ (accessed 8 April 2022).

Riggs, Fred W. 1966. *Thailand: The Modernization of Bureaucratic Polity*, Honolulu: East-West Center Press.

Secretariat of the Cabinet. 2021. "Prakad Soon Borihan Satanakarn Kan Prae Rabad Kong Roktidcheu Virus Corona 2019 (Covid-19) Rueng Naewtang Kan Borihan Jadkan Vaccine Pongkan Rok Covid-19" [Announcement of the Centre for Covid-19 Situation Administration on Covid-19 vaccine management]. *Royal Thai Government Gazette* 138, no. 123 D: 17–18. http://www.ratchakitcha.soc.go.th/DATA/PDF/2564/E/123/T_0017.PDF (accessed 12 April 2022).

Standard. 2021. "Anutin Tou Clear Asawin Pom Vaccine Laew Chee Hak Kued Panha Vaccine Tong Harue Kan Maichai Post Hai Pai Tam Ratthamontri" [Anutin called Asawin to clarify the vaccine issue, noting that if a vaccine problem occurs, a discussion is needed, not a post to a minister]. 14 June 2021. https://thestandard.co/anutin-phone-in-with-asawin-on-vaccine-issue/ (accessed 23 April 2022).

Strangio, Sebastian. 2021. "Thailand to Cease Using Sinovac Vaccines After Supplies Are Exhausted". *The Diplomat*, 20 October 2021. https://thediplomat.com/2021/10/thailand-to-cease-using-sinovac-vaccines-after-supplies-are-exhausted/ (accessed 13 April 2022).

Supasawad Chardchawarn. 2010. "Local Governance in Thailand: The Politics of Decentralisation and the Roles of Bureaucrats, Politicians, and the People". V.R.F. Series no. 459. Japan: Institute of Developing Economies, Japan External Trade Organization.

TDRI (Thailand Development Research Institute). 2021a. "Kho sanue nae kan jad ha vaccine lae kan krajae vaccine Covid-19" [Recommendations for procurement and distribution of Covid-19 vaccines]. 19 July 2021. https://tdri.or.th/2021/07/procurement-and-distribution-of-covid-19-vaccines/ (accessed 21 April 2022).

ThaiPBS Online. 2020. "Anutin Khaotod pom tamni hmor seajai nai sing ti seesan phid". ["Anutin" apologizes for blaming the doctor; regrets what was not communicated clearly]. 26 March 2020. https://www.thaipbs.or.th/news/content/290288.

———. 2021a. "Drama 'Covid Krajok' khong 'Anutin' Suanthang Kho Kankha

Chao Lok" [Anutin's shoddy Covid drama counters the world's concerns]. 18 December 2021. https://www.thaipbs.or.th/news/content/310801.

———. 2022. "Free Walk-In COVID-19 Vaccinations at Bang Sue Station Vaccination Centre". 5 June 2022. https://www.thaipbsworld.com/free-walk-in-covid-19-vaccinations-at-bang-sue-station-vaccination-centre/

TDRI. 2021b. "Pramuen Polngan Klang Term Ratthaban Prayut 2: Kan Kaubkum Kan Rabad Kong Covid-19 Lae Kan Borihan Jadkan Vaccine" [Assessing the mid-term performance of the second Prayut administration: Covid-19 pandemic control and vaccine management]. 11 July 2021. https://tdri.or.th/2021/07/report-2years-prayut-cabinet2/?fbclid=IwAR3JP5xha0YZnEJe2oaSNVNZ9D2ECYAUZogSvlB6n65T-zimgGGrtw2Iahs (accessed 21 April 2022).

Thaipublica. 2020. "Nayok phorjai lek titchua Covid 19 rai mai pen suao wan rak" [The Prime Minister is satisfied with the number of people infected with Covid-19. Zero new cases for the first time]. 13 May 2020. https://thaipublica.org/2020/05/prime-minister-on-zero-infection/ (accessed 19 April 2022).

Thairath Online. 2021. "Suek Ching Vaccine Jau Tang Kao" [The battle for vaccines is about to begin]. 26 May 2021. https://www.thairath.co.th/news/politic/2101002 (accessed 19 April 2022).

———. 2022. "Cheed Kon Ruem Chincha Muen Cheed Vaccine Kem 3 Aaj Tong Ting Bang Suan Tee Mon Ayu" [People becoming unconcerned and ignoring a third vaccination. Some expired vaccines may be disposed of]. 24 March 2022. https://www.thairath.co.th/news/local/south/2349602 (accessed 27 April 2022).

Thanyapon Buathong. 2021. "Cheed Vaccine: Kwam Mai Naenon Kong Vaccine Covid Jak Rattaban Plag Tongtin Din Sue Vaccine Eng" [Vaccination: uncertainty about Covid vaccines from the government pushing local communities to buy their own vaccines]. *BBC News*, 31 May 2021. https://www.bbc.com/thai/thailand-57305291 (accessed 24 April 2022).

Tita Sanglee. 2021a. "Sinovac or Not: Thai Vaccine Politics". *Fulcrum*, 31 May 2021. https://fulcrum.sg/sinovac-or-not-thai-vaccine-politics/ (accessed 12 April 2022).

———. 2021b. "Thailand's Reopening Confusion: Another Reflection of Government Disunity". *The Diplomat*, 30 September 2021. https://thediplomat.com/2021/09/thailands-reopening-confusion-another-reflection-of-government-disunity/ (accessed 12 April 2022).

Wee Phuanpersuk. 2021. "Khon Thai Roira 60.39 Bok Phakrat Lomlaew Nai Kan Borihan Jatkar Covid lae Roira 70.49 Prom Ti Cha Chet Vaccine Doi Lueak Cha Cheet Vaccine Pfizer Mak Tee Dud. [60.39 per cent of Thais say the government sector has failed in administering the vaccine, and 70.49 per cent are ready to get vaccinated. They chose to get the Pfizer vaccine if possible]. Center for Agricultural Economic Research and Forecasting, 14 May 2021. https://maejopoll.mju.ac.th/poll.aspx?id=1134 (accessed 27 April 2022).

Wichiranon Thongthep. 2021. “Covid-19: Jak “Thai Chana“ Soo ‘Mor Chana’ App Chuedang Jak Fang Rat Tob Jote Pongkan Rok Dai Piengdai” [Covid-19: From “Thai Chana” to “Mor Chana”. How effective are these famous government apps in disease prevention?]. *BBC News*, 24 January 2021. https://www.bbc.com/thai/thailand-55784607 (accessed 24 April 2022).

COMPARATIVE SYNTHESIS

Horizontal and Vertical Policy Coordination and Efficacy—Indonesia, Malaysia and Thailand

Siwage Dharma Negara

Policy coordination is vital if Covid-19 mitigation measures are to effectively control the spread of the virus and minimize the adverse impacts. Good coordination ensures a unified and comprehensive approach, reduces misperceptions among the public about government Covid-19 policy and optimizes resource allocation. In the early stages of the Covid-19 pandemic, many countries faced significant challenges in coordinating policies to effectively address the crisis.

Governments implemented a range of measures to control the outbreak, including travel restrictions, border controls and the establishment of quarantine facilities. They also implemented various public health measures such as social distancing, the closure of non-essential businesses and the enforcement of mask-wearing.

Many governments faced challenges when balancing the two policy objectives of maintaining an open economy and limiting the transmission of Covid-19. Often, public health and economic needs were pitted against each other in a debate over which should take precedence. In reality, both are equally important (Yeoh, Ch 9 in this volume).

The Covid-19 crisis taught us that good coordination needs strong leadership supported by reliable and timely data and information.

Nevertheless, the pandemic shows how capacity and capability are often lacking across governmental agencies and institutions, at both the central and subnational levels.

The three chapters in this section reflect on how the governments of Indonesia, Malaysia and Thailand coped with coordination failures during the crisis. Each country initially struggled to implement proper policy measures. In the three country studies, different authorities and jurisdictions implemented conflicting or contradictory policies, leading to confusion and uncertainty among the public. Nevertheless, after several policy changes and as more information and data became available, policy coordination improved. This bolstered the efficacy of the pandemic responses. This essay focuses on three elements of effective coordination.

POLITICAL STABILITY AND ORGANIZATIONAL COHERENCE

One crucial factor that affects policy efficacy is political system stability. Indonesia, Malaysia and Thailand have different political systems. Indonesia is a democratic country with a decentralized system of governance. The regional governments have more power, augmenting the influence of the regional context in national decision-making. Malaysia is a federal state with a parliamentary democracy and a constitutional monarchy. Nevertheless, decision-making power, especially concerning the pandemic, was highly centralized at the federal level as emphasized in Yeoh's chapter in this volume. Meanwhile, Thailand is a constitutional monarchy with a democratic form of government. Thailand had adopted a more decentralized governance, but after the military took over from the civilian government the power became more concentrated in Bangkok.

In Malaysia, political contestation and changes in the top leadership made Covid-19 policy coordination more difficult. As a result of political instability, Malaysia struggled to form strong leadership in the federal government when the pandemic hit the nation (Yeoh, this volume).

In Thailand, party political interests led to mismanagement and delays in implementing critical policies, especially in vaccination distribution (Punchada, this volume). During the early part of the Covid-19 outbreak, in 2020, the crisis response was hampered by a lack of coordination among different ministries controlled by different political parties in the coalition government.

Indonesia seemed more politically stable than Malaysia or Thailand, but politics and a silo and competitive mentality made it difficult for the national government to coordinate policy across ministries. Moreover, its complex decentralized system of governance complicated its Covid-19 policy responses. The central and subnational governments often created conflicting policies, including on mobility restrictions and data management (Nugroho and Syarief, this volume).

Given the need to improve coordination and effective delivery of programmes related to Covid-19 response, the government in each of the three countries created an ad hoc national task force to coordinate pandemic mitigation measures. The three countries implemented a highly centralized form of Covid-19 control.

Indonesia set up an inter-ministerial committee to handle the pandemic and recover the national economy (Komite Percepatan Penanganan Covid-19 dan Pemulihan Ekonomi Nasional, or the KPCPEN). Malaysia set up the National Security Council to lead in formulating standard operating procedures in response to Covid-19. Meanwhile, Thailand set up the Centre for Covid-19 Situation Administration (CCSA) to manage health data, the vaccine roll-out and mobility restrictions and to provide information to the public concerning the pandemic.

ADAPTABILITY AND FLEXIBILITY

The pandemic also taught us that crisis mitigation policy needs to be adaptable and flexible. Throughout the pandemic, governments adapted policies as information about the virus and its impact on people became clearer. At the same time, both coordination among policies and programme implementation improved gradually.

In Malaysia, Indonesia and Thailand, it took several months for the respective governments to establish a proper system for crisis response and management. In the intervening months, standard operating procedures were adjusted multiple times, inconsistent rules were announced and regulations were reversed. This left people and businesses confused and with little to no information and assistance. That situation was understandable, as new information about the virus and its effects was only gradually emerging.

Another lesson from the crisis is that Covid-19 mitigation measures require significant resources—medical supplies, personnel and financial support. This means budget flexibility is needed so that funds can be reallocated and mobilized quickly. Then, after securing the budget, there is a need for a coordinated policy for effective resource distribution. Policymakers must ensure that areas and communities with the most significant outbreaks receive timely support.

The three case studies show how national and subnational governments must adjust and reallocate budgets and deviate from business as usual. In this, there were variations in capacity and capability across governmental agencies and institutions, both at the central and subnational levels. Indonesia's half-hearted regional autonomy created unnecessary tensions during the crisis; for example, it pitted the Jakarta and national governments against each other, with each vetoing the other's policy where their authorities overlapped, creating continuous discoordination, particularly in mobility restrictions (Nugroho and Syarief, this volume).

DATA-DRIVEN AND APPROPRIATELY DECENTRALIZED IMPLEMENTATION

The coordination challenge was worsened by poor data quality and governance. Effective mitigation measures depend on accurate and timely data about metrics including infection rates and hospitalizations. As with all other national data, the Indonesian government tallied the national count on Covid-19 cases and deaths from subdistrict level upwards. However, there seemed to be no standardized procedure for how the daily data were tallied. Additionally, there were concerns about the transparency of data reporting and the accuracy of testing and case numbers. As a result, data at all levels of government—cities/regencies, provinces and national—showed discrepancies. Moreover, data sharing between different entities was sometimes difficult, inhibiting robust analysis and effective decision-making.

Likewise, Malaysia experienced coordination and data-sharing issues between the federal and state governments. The different levels of government sometimes disagreed or took different approaches, affecting the overall coordination and effectiveness of the pandemic response.

At the state government level, the effectiveness of pandemic management varied from state to state in Malaysia. In both East Malaysian states, Sabah and Sarawak, which have more autonomy than the states of Peninsular Malaysia, the pandemic created an opportunity to stand their ground against the federal government, especially on issues related to immigration. Nonetheless, the capacity of state healthcare systems and resources varied across Malaysia, affecting their ability to respond effectively. Some state governments, such as Sarawak, Selangor and Penang, were better equipped and ready to develop their own Covid-19 management.

Thailand experienced challenges in ensuring consistent implementation and coordination between different provinces and districts due to the decentralized nature of the Thai government. This was worsened by political capture, especially concerning vaccine roll-out. However, policy efficacy seemed to improve after the CCSA was shut down in September 2022, with power to handle Covid-19 having been transferred to the local governments in mid-2022. Transferring policy decisions to the local level minimized conflicts among political parties over Covid-19 policy. Local governments knew better the needs of their provinces and were better at gathering information on the ground. Therefore, they were more effective in implementing policies than the central government or the CCSA.

CONCLUSION

Covid-19 allowed many countries to revisit the policy domains of each level of government, during which some contestations occurred, with subnational governments pushing their boundaries. Eventually, both structurally in terms of laws and institutions and/or politically in terms of decisions over resource allocation, the centre exercised the most power (Yeoh, this volume).

The capacity of the government to create and execute coordination mechanisms across public agencies and institutions and with non-state actors, including civil society, determined how efficient and effective the government was able to be in fighting the pandemic. For each of the three countries studied, Indonesia, Malaysia and Thailand, we see that state capacity must be strengthened to minimize dependency on the power and capabilities of just one or two Cabinet members.

Finally, the Covid-19 pandemic has shown that effective mitigation requires a comprehensive approach that involves public health, economic recovery, data governance, policy communications and social protection. In facing future pandemics, countries must invest in building their capability to prepare a coherent, science- and evidence-based decision-making framework to mitigate adverse impacts. This means the capacity to create a sufficient regulatory framework, set up the necessary institutional arrangements, create and implement an accountability mechanism and mobilize resources. Such capacity and capabilities must be built across governmental agencies and institutions at the central and subnational levels.

Theme 4

ECONOMIC RELIEF AND STIMULUS
Malaysia, Singapore, Thailand

11

A STORY OF TOO LITTLE, TOO LATE

Malaysia's Covid-19 Economic Stimulus Packages

Melati Nungsari

INTRODUCTION

When history looks back at the Covid-19 pandemic, it will perhaps recall "social distancing" as one of the most important phrases to enter humankind's lexicon. At a time when countries were urging their residents to physically distance themselves from each other, the Internet and social media came to the fore as channels to gain information about the virus and its devastating effects on the economy and healthcare. Citizen sentiments as expressed on social media can predict support (or not) for national policies and happenings in the world (Neri et al. 2012). Thus, it is useful to recall the public discourse during this time as a proxy, imperfect as it may be, for the impact of government policies.

At the beginning of the Covid-19 pandemic and the first lockdown in Malaysia, people rallied together on social media in support of each other and healthcare professionals. Hashtags such as #KitaJagaKita (we take care of each other), #DudukRumah (stay home) and #StayHome went viral, with citizens urging solidarity against an invisible enemy—the SARS-CoV-2 virus (Lee 2023). The #KitaJagaKita movement was then co-opted by the government to build support for its policies surrounding movement restrictions and lockdowns. This led to a public backlash in which the hashtag #RakyatJagaRakyat (citizens take care of citizens) went viral in the face of weakening economic opportunities and increasing unemployment (Abdul Halim 2021). In July 2021, as the country entered another round of lockdowns and many peoples' savings were running short, the hashtag #BenderaPutih (White Flag Movement) went viral, with citizens urging those who needed financial support or food supplies to display white flags on their balconies or homes (BBC 2021). This movement, driven by civil society (primarily individuals), was effective in getting aid to those who needed it. For example, more than twenty households in a fishing village in Kedah found help after putting white flags on their doors (Wang 2021). Tech entrepreneurs in Malaysia—such as Reza Razali, the founder of Terato Tech—also rose to the occasion, creating a web-based platform to connect those who needed aid to those who wanted to donate. The platform featured tens of thousands of requests for help mere weeks after launching; it lives on until today at kitajaga.co, having morphed into an instrument used by the Malaysian Ministry of Finance to disseminate pricing data for specific controlled goods to the public (*Malaysiakini* 2023).

The White Flag Movement, though effective, was damning for the government at the time—the Perikatan Nasional coalition, led by Muhyiddin Yassin. It was a clear signal that the public was suffering and that the aid being given was insufficient. As argued by Lee (2023), the movement could be seen as a form of delegitimization of the Perikatan Nasional government, stemming from growing discontent with repeated lockdowns and heavy restrictions on movement and economic activity. This chapter argues, using secondary data, that Malaysia paid a heavy economic price for the way in which its pandemic restrictions were managed. Despite restrictions, more than 30,000 individuals in Malaysia died, and aid provided to communities from 2020 to 2022 came too slowly and in insufficient amounts. Recent academic evidence from countries with available microdata support this hypothesis—for example, McDevitt and Sojourner (2023) found that "(welfare) account holders are willing to pay

$11.17 per day for faster access to their (assistance) funds", highlighting the need for speed in granting assistance.

BACKGROUND ON MALAYSIA'S EXPERIENCE WITH COVID-19

Like many other tropical countries, Malaysia had a significant amount of experience dealing with infectious diseases prior to the Covid-19 pandemic—these included dengue, Nipah, tuberculosis and leptospirosis. Malaysia is even sometimes referred to as an "epicentre for emerging and re-emerging infectious diseases" (Kit 2002). Consequently, Malaysia designed its public health and public hospital infrastructure with the threat of infectious diseases in mind. For example, though varying heavily between neighbourhoods of different densities, with a significant gap in the provision of services between urban and rural areas, all citizens are typically able to obtain primary care through government-operated health clinics spread across the country (Hazrin et al. 2013). However, Malaysia's health expenditure was only 3.8 per cent of its gross domestic product (GDP) in 2019, significantly below the world average of 9.83 per cent but similar to its regional neighbours, such as Singapore (4 per cent) and Thailand (3.8 per cent) (World Bank 2023). The pandemic was also interspersed with protests from doctors working with the Ministry of Health on contract—coordinated through a movement called "Hartal Doktor Kontrak" (Contract Doctors' Strike)—with demands including equal and fair treatment and benefits, as well as job security for all doctors and other healthcare workers (*CodeBlue* 2021). A brain drain of healthcare workers to richer nations such as Singapore, the United Kingdom and Australia was a problem even before the pandemic, but increased during it, causing further strain on the national healthcare system (*Straits Times* 2022).

Malaysia therefore entered the pandemic with knowledge on dealing with infectious diseases but with an overburdened (though functional) public healthcare system, a combination that could have swung the fate of the nation in either direction in the face of the highly transmissible SARS-CoV-2 virus. Mortality rates, a contentious statistic but one that is well monitored in Malaysia, showed that the country fared well at the start of the pandemic with a 5.5 per cent reduction in all-cause mortality to 23.7 per cent in 2020, but this trend reversed in 2021 (Jayaraj et al. 2023).

Malaysia recorded its first Covid-19 case on 25 January 2020—a Chinese traveller arriving in Johor, at the southernmost tip of Peninsular Malaysia, from Singapore (Reuters 2020). The outbreak caused by this first case was contained in a few weeks after the discovery of the initial case. However, a large cluster of travellers from abroad who attended a religious event in Sri Petaling, Malaysia in the second half of February 2020 caused a larger, harder-to-trace disease cluster, which emerged on 26 February 2020 (Hashim et al. 2021). A strict nationwide lockdown—in Malaysia these were known as movement control orders—was imposed from 18 March 2020 to help reduce the spread of the virus. This was in line with similar policies enacted regionally and globally. In Malaysia's case, the movement control order meant that all schools, workplaces and nonessential economic sectors were closed. Public transportation was shut down, gatherings beyond the household were banned and residents were ordered to stay home to help prevent transmission. Figure 11.1 presents the trend of detected Covid-19 in Malaysia. The first wave in February and March 2020 is barely visible next to the subsequent, more lethal waves. This includes the Delta variant of late September 2021, which contributed to most of Malaysia's deaths throughout the pandemic.

Malaysia's first movement control order set the tone for a period of instability for all economic sectors in the country as it was the first of many heavy restrictions imposed by the government to combat the virus. Figure 11.2 presents a comparison of the stringency of restrictions in Malaysia, Thailand and Singapore. This Stringency Index was created by researchers at the University of Oxford under the Oxford Covid-19 Government Response Tracker. It aggregates twenty-three indicators, such as school closures and travel restrictions, in order to compare the strictness of lockdown-style policies across countries.

Lockdowns and restrictions on business and economic activities remained one of Malaysia's biggest weapons against the virus throughout 2020 and 2021, even as the country ramped up vaccination. In July 2023 almost 90 per cent of the targeted population was fully vaccinated and roughly 50 per cent had also received a first booster jab, according to the national Covid-19 dashboard, KKMNow. This happened despite the fact

FIGURE 11.1
Daily New Confirmed Covid-19 Cases

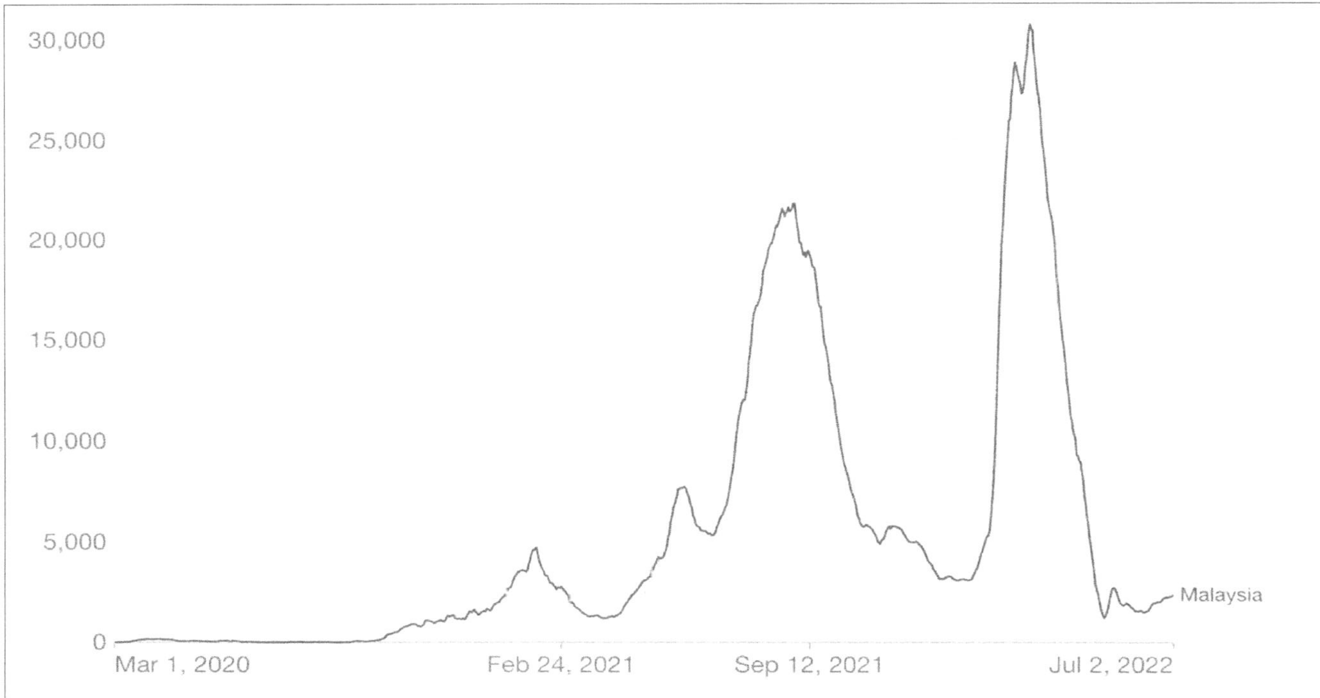

Notes: 7-day rolling average. Due to limited testing, the number of confirmed cases is lower than the true number of infections.
Source: Johns Hopkins University CSSE Covid-19 Data.

FIGURE 11.2
Covid-19: Stringency Index

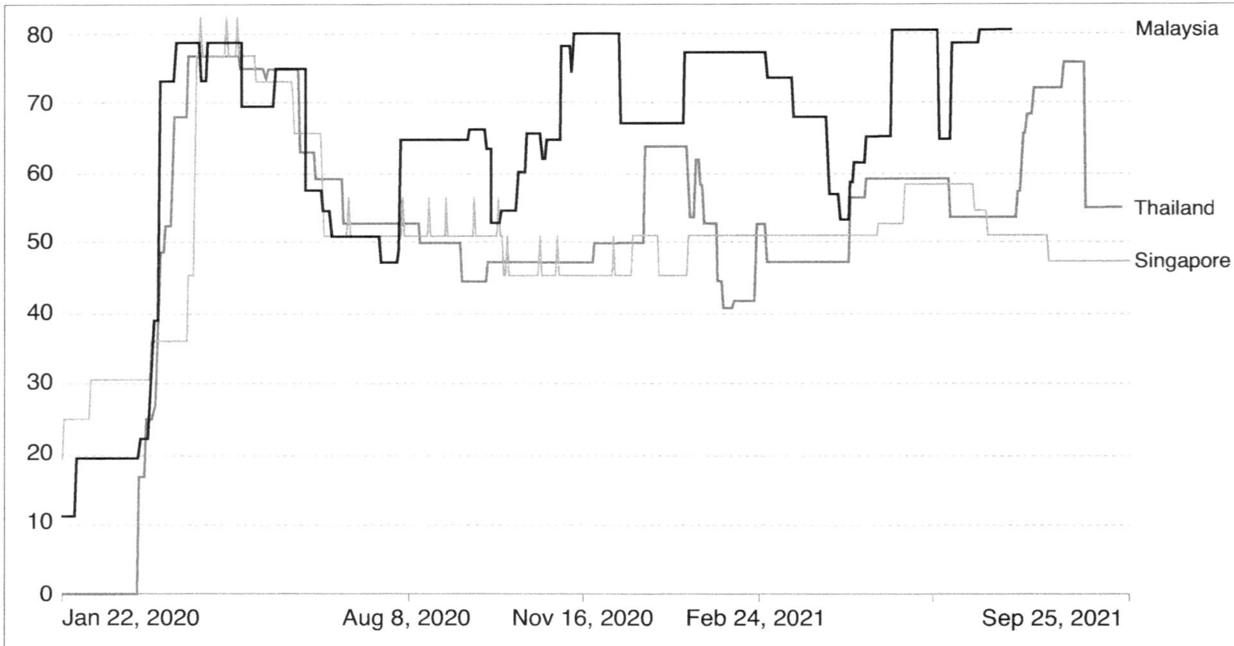

Notes: This is a composite measure based on nine response indicators including school closures, workplace closures and travel bans, rescaled to a value from 0 to 100 (100 = strictest). If policies vary at the subnational level, the index is shown as the response level of the strictest subregion.
Source: Oxford Covid-19 Government Response Tracker, Blavatnik School of Government, University of Oxford—Last updated 28 September 2021, 09:12 (London time).
OurWorldInData.org/coronavirus – CC BY

that lockdowns stopped being effective against the more lethal and more transmissible Delta variant and caused most of the deaths in Malaysia. Additionally, these measures harmed economic activity, growth and, consequently, resilience. For example, the authors of a large-scale study conducted in Chile, a country of similar size and per-capita income to Malaysia, found that lockdowns were associated with a 10–15 per cent drop in local economic activity, a rate twice that of municipalities that were not under lockdown, and that a "3 to 4 month lockdown had a similar effect on economic activity [as] a year of the 2009 great recession" (Asahi et al. 2021). Lockdowns also contributed to increasing mental illness globally, and this affected vulnerable and minority groups significantly more than the privileged (Le and Nguyen 2021). Similar to Thailand and Singapore, Malaysia varied its Covid-19 restrictions during the pandemic, loosening restrictions when the situation improved and tightening to prevent outbreaks. However, Malaysia's restrictions were comparatively highly stringent for most of 2020 and 2021 (see Figure 11.2). This meant, among many other issues, that (1) business continuity and planning was an issue for the private sector and (2) economic activity decreased and caused loss or reduction in livelihoods for a significant portion of the population. Furthermore, significant deficiencies in policy coordination and messaging caused confusion, increased the public's frustration with the restrictions and also decreased their willingness to comply, causing them to become less effective (see Yeoh, Ch 9 this volume).

Political turmoil also featured heavily in Malaysia's pandemic experience. The Pakatan Harapan government, which came to power in the 2018 general elections, fell on 24 February 2020, just a few weeks before the first movement control order was announced. The fall of the government coincided roughly with the Sri Petaling religious event. Pakatan Harapan was replaced by Perikatan Nasional, a coalition consisting of Barisan Nasional and Barisan Nasional-aligned political parties, such as Bersatu and Parti Islam Se-Malaysia (PAS). Perikatan Nasional lasted until 21 August 2021, at which point it was replaced by a new government consisting mainly of political players from Perikatan Nasional, but with changes to the Prime Minister and Deputy Prime Minister and in the Cabinet. The general elections in November 2022 resulted in yet another new government, a unity government comprising members of Pakatan

Harapan, Barisan Nasional and three other Malaysian Borneo political parties under the helm of Anwar Ibrahim, former Deputy Prime Minister in the 2018 Pakatan Harapan government.

The construct of political instability has been well studied. Jong-A-Pin (2009) states that political instability has four dimensions: politically motivated violence, mass civil protest, instability within the political regime and instability of the political regime itself. Malaysia undoubtedly suffers from the last two dimensions as infighting within parties of the ruling coalition has been very common since 2018 when the coalition government began, and increasingly so since the start of the pandemic. The infighting, in turn, has caused multiple changes in the federal government. Giving a sense of the frequency of this change, Malaysia was ruled by the same political parties from 1957 till 2018 but then went through three governments in two years from 2020 to 2022. Jong-A-Pin (2009) also showed that the instability of a political regime can have a "robust and significant negative effect on economic growth", which occurred in Malaysia, as shown in this chapter.

The constant changes of government caused three major issues. First, for most of 2020 and 2021, important legislation was neither debated nor passed, with Covid-19 given as the reason, as well as the national emergency. The emergency was declared by the King of Malaysia on 12 January 2021 and was in place until 1 August 2021. For example, in July 2021, a special parliamentary sitting was suspended after the detection of Covid-19 infections among Members of Parliament and staff (Reuters 2021). The national emergency also allowed for sweeping ordinances to be enacted nationwide. These included The Emergency (Essential Powers) No. 2 Ordinance 2021, enacted in March 2021, which was intended to suppress rumours and misinformation surrounding the Covid-19 pandemic. However, critics and activists pointed out that this ordinance could also be used to suppress the freedom of speech of individuals who opposed the government (Koya 2021). Important actions such as raising the debt ceiling early in the pandemic, around the middle of 2020, could not be achieved, and were instead carried out more than a year later, in October 2021. The government's ability to react to the pandemic through fiscal policy was constrained at exactly the time it was most needed.

Second, the lack of political stability, caused by the infighting and government changes, meant that the government had trouble enacting policies that could help reduce the spread of the virus without having to resort to sweeping, nationwide lockdowns. The alternative of stringent monitoring, contact tracing and localized mobility restrictions required high degrees of coordination, responsiveness and efficiency—and Malaysia's government could not muster these in its politically fractious state. Indeed, political instability directly contributed to the spread of Covid-19. A failed power grab in Sabah in late 2020 destabilized the state government and triggered elections. Due to the importance of maintaining political power in Sabah, a large number of politicians from Peninsular Malaysia travelled to Sabah, which was experiencing a large-scale Covid-19 outbreak. However, they were not advised to quarantine or test before returning to Peninsular Malaysia. Lim et al. (2021) showed that 70 per cent of the Covid-19 cases in Sabah's first major wave were directly attributable to the elections, as were 64.4 per cent of the Covid-19 cases in the rest of Malaysia, including the Klang Valley. Due to the large number of cases following the Sabah elections, then Prime Minister Muhyiddin Yassin was forced to announce yet another movement control order in early January 2021, as there were concerns that the public healthcare system would not cope. Figure 11.3 shows the daily new confirmed Covid-19 cases in the country.

Emphatically, the political uncertainty hampered the government's ability to make the hard yet necessary choices surrounding Covid-19 restrictions. These included alternatives to sweeping, nationwide lockdowns such as expanded, easily accessible and free testing, particularly for vulnerable groups—who were grossly underprovided with health services all along—and targeted lockdowns for specific areas, which were only enacted for brief periods in 2020 to 2022. These targeted lockdowns, called enhanced movement control orders, and targeted business closures lasted only for brief periods and were never widely used. Furthermore, as the vaccination drive ramped up in the country in the period from June to August 2021, the government also decided to increase the number and frequency of immigration raids (Human Rights Watch 2021). This meant some migrants and other vulnerable individuals did not seek help when they were sick, and many were too afraid of arrest to go to the large government-run centres for vaccinations (*Al Jazeera* 2021).

FIGURE 11.3
Daily New Confirmed Covid-19 Cases

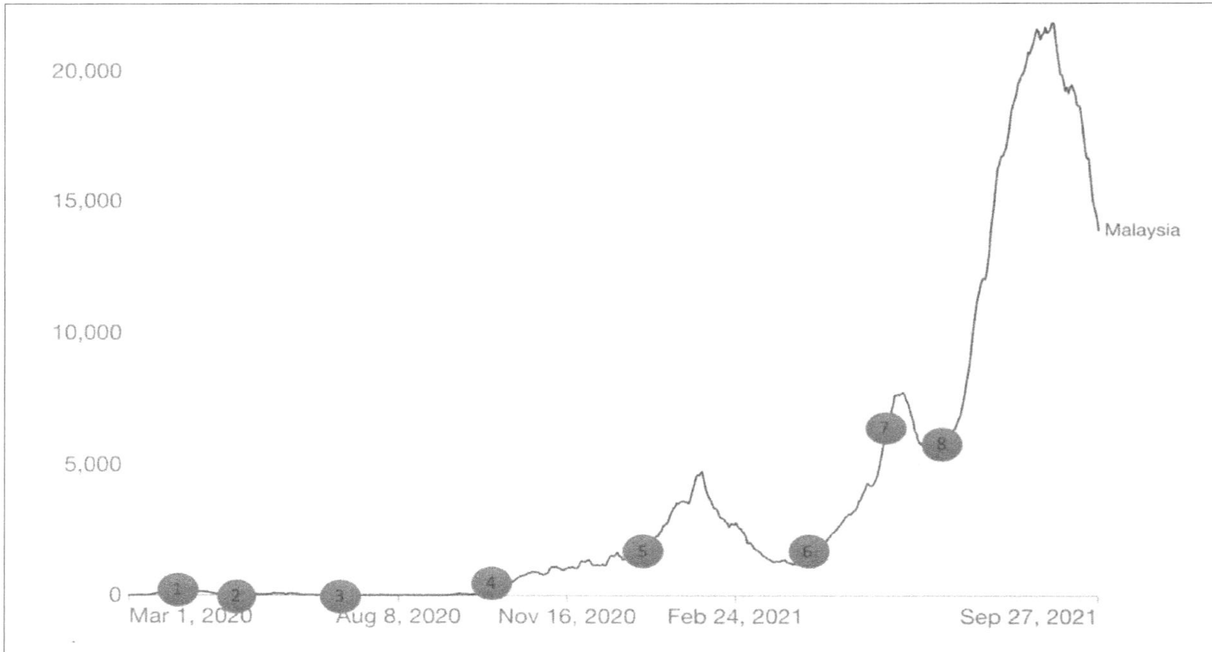

Notes: Shown is the rolling 7-day average. The number of confirmed cases is lower than the number of actual cases; the main reason for that is limited testing.
Source: Johns Hopkins University CSSE Covid-19 Data.

OVERVIEW OF FEDERAL STIMULUS PACKAGES

All the Malaysian Covid-19 stimulus packages were announced during the time of the Perikatan Nasional government, which was in power from March 2020 to August 2021. It created eight stimulus packages valued at a total of MYR530 billion (approximately US$127 billion). Only about 16 per cent of these were direct fiscal injections into the economy (MYR83 billion or approximately US$20 billion). The timing and size of each of the eight packages can be seen in Figure 11.4. Some packages were targeted at particular populations. For example, PENJANA, under the Ministry of Human Resources, offered foreign manufacturing companies a zero per cent tax rate for a decade if they relocated their operations to Malaysia. The rate was contingent on a company bringing investments in fixed assets of between MYR300 million (US$70 million) and MYR500 million (US$116 million) (Medina 2021). PRIHATIN PLUS, the second stimulus package, was targeted at small and medium-sized enterprises (SMEs), which constitute about 97 per cent of the total number of businesses in Malaysia (Lim Wai Yin 2023) and was held under the portfolio of the Ministry of Finance. Among others, it offered an income tax rebate of up to MYR20,000 per year for three years for SMEs established between 1 July 2020 and 31 December 2021 (*Edge Markets* 2020).

Aside from direct fiscal injections in the form of cash handouts, the majority of assistance given through the stimulus packages included employment-related measures such as the creation and expansion of a wage subsidy programme, a reduction of the foreign worker levy for all companies in the country, a halt on repayments of loans and financing agreements (under PRIHATIN and PEMULIH), increased access to credit and grants for micro, small and medium-sized enterprises, and allowing Malaysians with retirement money saved in the national private retirement fund, the Employees Provident Fund (EPF), to withdraw funds. This latter move was controversial, as it caused a wave of early withdrawals and 81 per cent of members are now expected to retire in poverty (*Focus Malaysia* 2023). The EPF withdrawals occurred in stages and through three different programmes in 2020 and 2021, i-SINAR, i-LESTARI and i-CITRA, and a fourth in 2022. Each of these had its own requirements for withdrawal—such as having been laid off recently by an employer—

FIGURE 11.4
Covid-19 Stimulus Packages

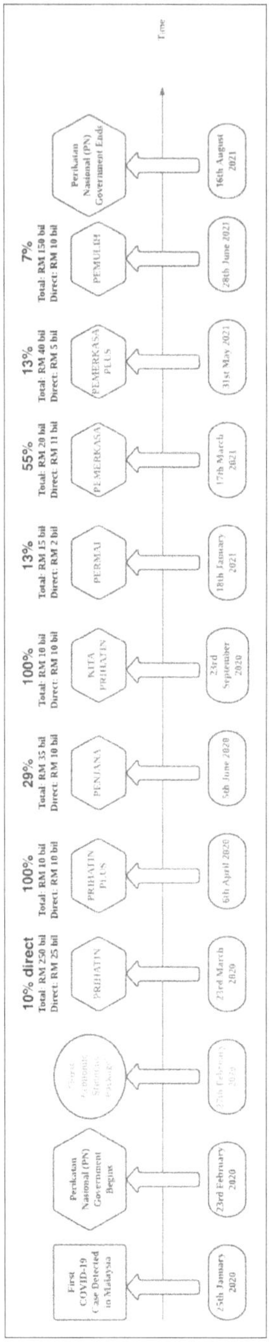

Source: Author's compilation.

and were limited to a fixed amount, subject to the level of savings in the account. The fourth scheme was announced on 1 April 2022; members were allowed to withdraw a maximum amount of MYR10,000 (with MYR50 minimum) and were allowed to fully deplete their savings in Account 2, an account that allows for pre-retirement withdrawals in emergencies such as health crises, and then withdraw from their Account 1 savings. The EPF estimated that MYR100.9 billion was withdrawn by 7.3 million members between April 2020 and February 2022; this does not include the last tranche of payments that was allowed in April 2022 (Yeap 2022). Given that the Department of Statistics Malaysia estimated in 2023Q2 that the Malaysian workforce consists of about 16.3 million people, the amount of EPF withdrawals is worrying, signalling mass liquidity issues among households, as approximately half of the formal workforce have accounts with and save with the EPF.

It is important to note that aside from federal stimulus packages, states also extended their own assistance to residents. For example, as of September 2021, the state of Sabah had spent MYR324 million (approximately US$71 million) on pandemic-related aid and projects, such as a fund to bring home students from Sabah stranded in Peninsular Malaysia and six-month rental exemptions for tenants of public housing (Chan 2021). Many states gave discounts or exemptions on rental payments for public premises to businesses and reductions in business licensing fees. The state of Sarawak spent MYR151 million in the first five months of 2021 solely on Covid-19 responses such as quarantine allowance and food aid (*Dayak Daily* 2021). At the start of the pandemic, the state government of Penang launched the Penang Relief Package, comprising sixteen initiatives targeting various sectors of society. The Penang Relief Package was valued at MYR75 million (approximately US$16.5 million).

IMPLEMENTATION OF THE STIMULUS PACKAGES

Aid in any form is only useful if it is able to reach the intended recipients. During the pandemic, given the physical restrictions imposed on many Malaysian subpopulations in the country, it became difficult to make sure that those who most needed aid from the government actually received it. Conventional wisdom dictates that direct cash transfers can be useful in a variety of settings, and are very effective at producing short-term outcomes such as improving dietary diversity and improving the use of health services (Bastagli et al. 2016). That said, many individuals could not leave their homes to access banking services in order to obtain cash; additionally, access to food for those in rural areas or for those under enhanced lockdowns who were confined to their homes became an issue (Nungsari et al. 2022b). Malaysia, similar to other developing countries, is also vulnerable to the problem of elite capture, whereby a public good or public resources are monopolized by an elite few to the detriment of society. Thus, concerns of whether or not the aid given in the stimulus packages actually reaches beneficiaries are very valid.

Nungsari et al. (2022a), for example, documented difficulties experienced by individuals trying to access aid from the federal government. This section highlights three of those challenges. First, Malaysians without documentation to prove their nationality experienced significant difficulties in accessing aid. The following is a quote from a non-governmental organization (NGO) worker describing their experience trying to get aid to the community they work with during the first movement control order in 2020:

> During the MCO [movement control order], a few of us went around to check on people who actually needed help. We thought the government initiatives were very good and encouraging. But those people who are getting this kind of benefits are only Malaysians who have citizenship. So, our focus at that time was actually to help the people who do not have citizenship. People who are not even looked at by any of these government agencies. Many of them are daily workers and they don't have wages per month. So, the employer doesn't pay them if they don't work. But during the period also they couldn't work and a lot of them can't really afford to pay for food and things like that. So, we saw a lot of these kinds of situation; we saw a lot of these families who are actually having this kind of difficulty (Nungsari et al. 2022b).

The second challenge was that communities in rural areas, which included many indigenous populations in Peninsular Malaysia and Malaysia Borneo, were not able to access aid. The following are two quotes from distinct individuals documenting this fact:

> (Quote 1) You know the government cash aid programme—they give you MYR200 in cash aid, right? So, a lot of indigenous people, they didn't manage to get it ... They need to pay for things like for the kids' school and all that ... [but] because they don't stay in a place where there's any [Internet] reception so they missed the date to register.

> (Quote 2) If you remember, the government came up with an aid programme of about MYR500–1,000, which was a very good programme, very helpful, but many indigenous people were not registered ... because they don't pay income taxes or they don't work, and so on. So, we moved from food distribution to registration [so that they can qualify for cash aid]. The government was giving about 1,000 [ringgit] to one family and we were giving out at most 3,000 [ringgit] per village ... The problem is that they are entitled to it but they're not getting it because of all this bureaucracy (Nungsari et al. 2022b).

Most informal and undocumented populations in Malaysia, including indigenous people, live in rural areas. The bureaucracy mentioned in the second quote is a reference to the amount of paperwork that needed to be filed by recipients in order to access certain aid. For example, some programmes targeted at micro-entrepreneurs required the business to be legally registered with the Companies Commission of Malaysia and to have been operating for a certain amount of time already (Lim 2023). This meant that young individuals who fell out of formal employment and started their own small businesses at the start of the pandemic or in their first year did not qualify to apply for most of the aid.

Nungsari et al. (2022b) also documented other issues in rural areas that affected whether or not the stimulus packages reached intended beneficiaries, with unclear government policies and non-cooperation between agencies reported as being a key issue. For example, during lockdowns multiple permissions were needed to cross districts; aid disbursement was also contingent on these approvals. Putting a large burden on documentation on populations to access aid was also reported, with difficulties in completing paperwork more severe in areas with spotty or no internet connection and access.

Third, the reliance of the federal government on partnering with local or state-specific NGOs sometimes caused more difficulties than benefits. Members of indigenous communities in Peninsular Malaysia said NGOs who received funding from the federal government sometimes cared more about social media appearances and public relations than doing the actual work (Nungsari et al. 2022b). The indigenous population in Malaysia, especially those of Peninsular Malaysia, have suffered for decades as a result of a variety of factors. These include land disputes, statelessness, lack of citizenship and forced religious conversion by the state (Winzeler 1997; Lemière 2013). All these factors have led to heightened vulnerability for this community, which NGOs have traditionally assisted with. An indigenous person explained their experience as a beneficiary:

> Some [people] are building NGOs, or they're running NGOs, just to do the charity, or just to do the welfare. And mostly just want this to do a one-off programme. There are many popular NGOs; they will have artists, and singers as ambassadors … they will go to the field and they will sell it in their Facebook posts or other social media posts, more on sentiment, more on the sad story of the beneficiaries … The last time I saw this was during the earlier lockdown. There was one female actor who came from Peninsular Malaysia. She distributed the food but in front of the [stateless] people who were begging for food … So then netizens will say "pity them, they have no food". But if you distribute it properly, if you tell them early, they will come in groups according to the time that we gave. We educate them to follow instructions and also to be patient in taking food packs, because they are not animals that we just give food [to] right away. The way some NGOs do this is that they sell stories of marginalized communities, of beneficiaries [not] being [genuine], sentiments, sad stories, without uplifting their capabilities … The other point is they didn't highlight the real issue of why [they] are not getting help from the government or other things (Nungsari et al. 2022b).[1]

IMPACT OF THE STIMULUS PACKAGES: WERE THEY ENOUGH?

A study conducted by the author of this chapter in April 2020, immediately after the PRIHATIN stimulus package was released, found that at that time a substantial minority of M40 respondents (i.e., individuals occupying the middle 40 per cent of the national income distribution) and nearly half of B40 respondents (i.e., individuals occupying the bottom 40 per cent of the national income distribution) reported negative cash flow due to the crisis. Most households suffered a drop in income in April, resulting in negative cash flow in order to sustain expenditures. Cash transfers and public relief packages mitigated this negative cash flow for most respondents (Flanders, Nungsari, and Chuah 2020). Among the minority who had negative cash flow, most had enough savings to survive for more than three months, but a small minority were likely to run out of money in the next few months, especially among the B40 group. The main policy recommendation from this study was to increase cash transfers to lower-income individuals, meaning families making MYR4,000 or less per month and single individuals making MYR2,000 or less per month, since these targeted transfers were significantly more effective than transfers to households in higher income groups.

The findings of the April 2020 study foreshadowed the significant national economic losses and suffering that occurred over the next year or so, especially given that the cash transfer programme was not expanded in any meaningful way. According to the Department of Statistics Malaysia (2021), the median household income fell by more than 11 per cent in 2020; in the same year, the economy contracted by 5.6 per cent. Some 20 per cent of households who earned more than MYR4,840 a month in 2019 earned less than that per month in 2020. The number of poor households rose by more than 50 per cent from 405,400 households in 2019 to 639,800 households in 2020. The incidence of absolute poverty increased from 5.5 per cent to 8.4 per cent in a single year. Median monthly household salaries fell by almost 16 per cent from MYR2,442 in 2019 to MYR2,062 in 2020. In September 2021, the World Bank revised Malaysia's GDP growth down to 3.3 per cent in 2021 from the 4.5 per cent prediction made in June 2021, partly due to restrictions on businesses and economic activity that were still in place (*The Star* 2021).

Furthermore, the adverse effects of the first movement control order were clearly reflected in the unemployment rates and GDP in the first few months of the pandemic. Unemployment rose 60.6 per cent between February and May 2020, from 3.3 per cent to 5.3 per cent. The country's GDP shrank 5.6 per cent in 2020, its worst performance since the 1998 Asian financial crisis.

Lee and Zhang (2021) state that Malaysia's stimulus packages prioritized more experienced workers and very few measures targeted young workers and fresh graduates. Specifically, young people in Malaysia suffered significantly in terms of wages and income, and experienced a severe decline in human capital investment due to interrupted schooling. Malaysian youth unemployment was 10.5 per cent in 2019, but it had risen to 13.7 per cent in June 2021. Graduate unemployment also rose to 4.4 per cent in 2020 against 3.9 per cent in 2019, highlighting worries about job-skills mismatches and quality concerns with graduates. The country's unemployment rate, as of 2022Q1, remained high at 4.1 per cent. Skill-related underemployment of graduates remains enormous at 1.81 million persons; this means graduates are placed in jobs that do not require their qualifications (i.e., jobs in semi-skilled and low-skilled occupations). One in four people in the Malaysian workforce was self-employed in 2020, a year that was also hit hard by pandemic restrictions. And although unemployment was declining at the end of 2021, it was still higher than before the pandemic. Another major concern with the end-2021 economic situation was inflationary pressures and supply chain issues pushing food prices up, increasing vulnerabilities for households. However, more pressing for Malaysia was the fact that "normal times" policymaking—such as price controls on certain goods including chicken and cooking oil—might have been limited in its efficacy in the face of multiple negative supply shocks, such as the war in Europe and rising energy prices. In 2022, many households were still reeling from the effects of multiple lockdowns in 2020 and 2021, and the inability to afford food exacerbated these concerns.

It should also be said that the Malaysian Ministry of Finance had prioritized minimizing inclusion errors from their federal stimulus packages instead of granting a broader net of support and potentially subsidizing subpopulations that did not need it. This narrative can be summarized through the following quote by the Malaysian Minister of Finance, Tengku Zafrul Aziz, in the eighty-third report from the Ministry of Finance on the Economic Stimulus Implementation and Coordination Unit Between National Agencies (LAKSANA). The reports contain updates on Covid-19 programmes and the support they provide to citizens (Ministry of Finance 2022):

> [Translated from Bahasa Malaysia] So, targeted subsidies are something we need to focus on. For example, RON95 petrol subsidies are enjoyed by everyone, whether or not you are B40 or T20 [individual occupying the top 20 per cent of the national income distribution]. Research carried out by the Khazanah Research Institute in 2014 found that 80 per cent of subsidies are actually received by high-income individuals. Imagine if these subsidies could be executed in a targeted manner—they would be used to uplift poor people and micro-businesses, or channelled to other initiatives to support citizens' socioeconomic development.

In the following subsections, we analyse the wage subsidy programme, which was a key focus of multiple federal stimulus packages throughout the pandemic, structural labour market issues related to skill-related underemployment that was present prior to and exacerbated by Covid-19, schooling disruptions and the potential long-term economic impacts, and the impact of skills-based training programmes that were a part of the federal stimulus packages.

Wage Subsidy Programmes and Unemployment

The Malaysian government provided five wage subsidy programmes in federal stimulus packages.[2] For each Malaysian citizen employee earning MYR4,000 or less, the government gave employers up to MYR1,200 a month for a maximum of six months. This was to help employers retain workers. The Ministry of Finance reported that MYR20.2 billion was disbursed through the wage subsidy programme to 357,468 employers to retain 2,952,064 local workers under this scheme (Ministry of Finance 2022). Other wage subsidy programmes targeted specific sectors affected by the pandemic. For example, Program Subsidi Upah 3.0 targeted services related to tourism.

It is impossible to observe the counterfactual to the wage subsidy programme—to measure how employment would have been affected in the absence of the programme. That said, the main economic indicator for the success of the five programmes is unemployment rates throughout the pandemic, particularly at the beginning of 2022, when the country started relaxing all restrictions on all economic sectors. According to the Department of Statistics Malaysia, Malaysia entered the pandemic in February 2020 with a labour force of 15.86 million. Throughout the pandemic, the labour force increased, reaching 16.44 million in March 2022. A rough calculation would imply that a range of 2.95 million workers out of 16.44 million to 2.95 million workers out of 15.86 million would have been (positively) impacted by the wage subsidy programme—a percentage of about 17.9 per cent to 18.6 per cent.

Unemployment rates in Malaysia remained high throughout the pandemic. The country entered the pandemic with unemployment of 3.3 per cent in February 2020, rising to 5.3 per cent in May 2020. Unemployment stayed mostly above 4.5 per cent until April 2022, when it dropped to 3.9 per cent, the lowest since the first wave of Covid-19 (Chong 2022). The wage subsidy programme was fairly wide in its impact, reaching almost one in five workers in Malaysia. Nonetheless, there are logical grounds to argue that it should have been expanded to further avert unemployment throughout the pandemic. Expansion could have taken the form of a higher wage threshold in order to include more employees, or a higher subsidy per worker. Further research, with access to the wage subsidy data, will be needed to inform that policy choice.

Skill-Related Underemployment and Structural Labour Market Problems

A key observation on the Malaysian labour market is that the incidence of skill-related underemployment within the economy, defined as the employment of graduates in low- and medium-skilled jobs, was high even before the pandemic. Between the first quarter of 2017 and the fourth quarter of 2019, an average of 32.7 per cent of total employed persons, roughly 1.4 million individuals, experienced skill-related underemployment. This meant that diploma or degree holders were working in jobs not requiring tertiary-level qualifications. In the third quarter of 2020, skill-related underemployment rose to 36.8 per cent of total employed persons. This indicator remained persistently high throughout the pandemic; in the first quarter of 2022, 36.9 per cent of individuals experienced skill-related underemployment. As the country struggles to remain competitive internationally, attract foreign investment, retain talent and create high-skilled jobs, this remains a structural problem that has a long history in the economy but remains unresolved.

Skill-related underemployment was not explicitly addressed through any of the stimulus packages. It is likely to remain unaddressed for the foreseeable future as it requires structural changes that take time to implement and execute. The programmes and aid distributed through the federal stimulus packages were meant as short-term measures and were not intended to address much-needed reforms to the economy. While the focus on short-term protection is understandable, the pandemic also provided impetus for retraining and for promoting and financially supporting online training programmes. Future crisis responses can certainly build on lessons from Malaysia's Covid-19 experience and from ongoing deficiencies in the training system.

The federal stimulus packages did provide for training programmes, but questions can be raised about their design and targeting. Notably, the Professional Training and Education for Growing Entrepreneurs (PROTEGÉ) programme gave participants business training to help them professionalize their small businesses. The Ready-To-Work programme gave more than 9,000 university graduates professional training and placements with government-linked companies (Ministry of Finance 2022). Since the returns to any sort of human capital training typically take a significant amount of time to be realized, the full effects cannot yet be evaluated. However, one may query whether these programmes address the acute problems with accessing economic opportunities, and whether participation might even constitute a waste of time—training may not help in improving their economic outcomes (Nungsari et al. 2022b).

Due to the lack of data measuring the impact of these training programmes, an assessment of whether or not they constituted fruitful spending through the federal stimulus programmes cannot be made. However, given the long-term outlook needed when assessing whether there were meaningful effects of human capital development programmes, expanding the wage subsidy programme to protect individuals from losing their jobs might objectively have been a better policy response for the already-employed, rather than spending money on training in programmes with unproven impacts. The Malaysian government has always spent significant amounts of its higher education budget on entrepreneurship education and training programmes, and at least nineteen universities nationwide offer such programmes (Kamaruddin et al. 2017). This is despite the fact that systematic reviews of the academic literature have undermined the belief that entrepreneurship education produces entrepreneurship (Rideout and Gray 2013).

Schooling Disruptions and Future Economic Woes

The significant length of Malaysia's school closures and disruptions also raises red flags for possible worsening economic outcomes for the workforce. For example, schools in Klang Valley were shut for most of 2020. The first closure was from the middle of March 2020 until the middle of July 2020. This was followed by a brief reopening until the middle of October, when they closed again until March 2021 (Loganathan et al. 2021). In fact, school closures were so long in Malaysia that the Malaysian Ministry of Education decided to move the start of the school year from January to the middle of March—a move that was still in place as of 2023 (*Free Malaysia Today* 2022).

Although evidence is still being gathered, economists have started to explore the long-term impacts of school closures on economic outcomes by looking at past pandemics. Ager et al. (2020) studied the 1918–19 influenza pandemic and found that school closures had no effects on adult educational attainment, wage income, non-wage income and hours worked in 1940 (i.e., more than a decade later). However, they caution against interpreting these results in the context of Covid-19, stating that the 1918–19 influenza pandemic was very different (and possibly more favourable), because:

1. American schools were closed in 1918 for many fewer days on average compared to American rates in 2020—and far fewer than in Malaysia;
2. The 1918 virus was deadlier than Covid-19 to adolescents and children, which meant that absenteeism was high even in schools that were kept open;
3. The lack of effective remote learning platforms in 1918 may have

created a socio-economic levelling effect in that all families, rich or poor, were affected.

Using data from 174 countries, the World Bank found that the present value of lifetime earnings lost for a typical student was between US$6,680 and US$32,397 (Azevedo et al. 2021). Globally, this would mean that a "school shutdown of 5 months could generate learning losses that have a present value of $10 trillion" (Azevedo et al. 2021, p. 32). For a point of comparison, Malaysia had significantly more than five months of learning disruptions. The authors also point out that this disruption in schooling could set back the goal of reducing global poverty. Finally, Malaysia is an upper-middle-income country, and its schoolchildren are more vulnerable compared to their peers in richer countries where social safety nets are more extensive and more effectively prevent disadvantaged students from falling through the cracks (Psacharopoulos et al. 2020). Malaysia generally fares better than lower-middle-income countries in terms of mitigating the rich-poor schooling gap, but children from poorer backgrounds remain more susceptible to learning disruptions and economic losses and may face compounded effects from the long school closure and online learning.[3]

Lack of Support for Tourism

Malaysian youth have long pursued hospitality as a degree option, with annual student enrolment in hospitality institutions more than doubling from 1999 to 2001 (Zahari 2004). Just prior to the pandemic, in 2019, tourism contributed MYR102.3 billion (approximately US$22.5 billion) to the national GDP. This plummeted to MYR28.4 billion in 2020 and MYR13.1 billion in 2021 (Statista 2022). Though many hotels across the country qualified for and did apply for government assistance through the various stimulus packages, industry players remained uncertain of the industry outlook and requested increased, targeted financial assistance from the state (Hanafiah et al. 2021).

The fact that China remained closed to the world until early 2023 exacerbated the problem caused by the lack of aid for the tourism industry.

From 2012 until the start of the Covid-19 pandemic, China had been one of the highest tourist-generating countries for Malaysia (Puah, Huan, and Thien 2018). Malaysia only welcomed 3 million visitors in 2022; this was an increase from 2021, but is a mere 12 per cent of 2019 arrivals. Malaysia also trailed its neighbours Indonesia and Thailand in spurring a recovery in the sector (Ferrarese 2023). There has been an alarming lack of introspection on the part of the Malaysian government as to why tourism had yet to bounce back at the beginning of 2022.

CONCLUSION

Though most economies experienced contractions and higher unemployment during the pandemic, this chapter argues that a significant portion of Malaysia's economic trauma was caused by the policymaking of an ineffective government. It therefore seems unlikely that policymaking will be able to resolve the self-inflicted problems. Nonetheless, the Malaysian economy grew by 8.7 per cent in 2022, surpassing pre-Covid levels, and expanded by a further 5.6 per cent in the first quarter of 2023—comparable to regional growth such as in Indonesia (5.0 per cent), China (4.5 per cent) and Vietnam (3.3 per cent) (Ministry of Finance 2023). Short-term economic statistics seem to indicate that recovery is happening, though employment is recovering more slowly.

The pandemic exposed a number of deep structural problems in Malaysia that have yet to be corrected by policymaking. This includes, for example, a depleted national healthcare service, a severe brain drain in high-skilled jobs such as specialized healthcare and professional services, issues associated with undocumented individuals hindered by cumbersome aid applications and large amounts of informality in the economy. Further, there are a number of additional long-term issues that are very troubling. First, Malaysian schoolchildren were out of physical classrooms for the majority of 2020 and 2021, which may translate to longer-term negative economic outcomes. Second, there are concerns surrounding the ability of individuals to retire, particularly older individuals who significantly drew from their EPF savings. Third, labour shortages in the country and a reliance on increasingly reluctant neighbours for cheap labour will continue to harm the Malaysian economy.

One of the few benefits that the pandemic brought was nationwide digitalization and an increase in demand for services provided through digital platforms. The Malaysian Investment Development Authority reported in late 2021 that the pandemic had accelerated business digitalization by three to four years (Bernama 2021). Though none of the stimulus packages addressed digitalization specifically, it was born out of the need to stay home. Plugging more businesses into the digital space and getting the workforce used to working digitally could potentially be a door to the high-value jobs that Malaysia has long searched for, as it seeks to move upwards from the upper-middle-income bracket. A significant amount of policymaking and, most importantly, political will, will be needed if the economy is to become more productive along these lines. It remains to be seen when the country will see such leadership.

Notes

1. The beneficiary added: "It is easier for NGOs to do one-off programmes, compared to thinking about one programme that can sustain the community … So I can say they are unethical, because they just come and go. They post sentiments about beneficiaries without highlighting the real issues … that they are stateless or undocumented, they cannot get education. The people who don't live here don't have a proper idea. We don't get the picture. So that's how I think it leads to the judgemental and prejudice parts. Do we Malaysians not take it as an issue that the government has to be responsible for?"
2. The federal stimulus packages were PRIHATIN, KITA PRIHATIN, PERMAI, PEMERKASA and PEMERKASA PLUS.
3. This is true even assuming very conservative assumptions, that closures only last four months and that teaching quality while learning online is unaffected.

References

Abdul Halim, Khadeejah. 2021. "#BenderaPutih Is a Depressing Display of Government Incompetence". *Malaysiakini*, 1 July 2021. https://www.malaysiakini.com/columns/581206 (accessed 9 August 2023).

Ager, Philipp, Katherine Eriksson, Ezra Karger, Peter Nencka, and Melissa A. Thomasson. 2020. "School Closures During the 1918 Flu Pandemic". NBER Working Paper No. 28246, National Bureau of Economic Research,

Cambridge, MA. https://www.nber.org/system/files/working_papers/w28246/w28246.pdf

Al Jazeera. 2021. "Fear of Arrest Among Undocumented Risks Malaysia Vaccine Push". 6 August 2021. https://www.aljazeera.com/news/2021/8/6/mixed-messaging-in-malaysia-leaves-migrants (accessed 11 August 2023).

Asahi, K., E.A. Undurraga, R. Valdés, and R. Wagner. 2021. "The Effect of Covid-19 on the Economy: Evidence from an Early Adopter of Localized Lockdowns". *Journal of Global Health* 11: 05002. https://doi.org/10.7189/jogh.10.05002

Azevedo, J.P., A. Hasan, D. Goldemberg, K. Geven, and S.A. Iqbal. 2021. "Simulating the Potential Impacts of Covid-19 School Closures on Schooling and Learning Outcomes: A Set of Global Estimates". *World Bank Research Observer* 36, no. 1: 1–40.

Bastagli, F., J. Hagen-Zanker, L. Harman, V. Barca, G. Sturge, T. Schmidt, and L. Pellerano. 2016. *Cash Transfers: What Does the Evidence Say? A Rigorous Review of Programme Impact and the Role of Design and Implementation Features*. London: Overseas Development Institute. https://cdn.odi.org/media/documents/11316.pdf

BBC. 2021. "Malaysians in Covid Lockdown Fly White Flags to Ask for Help". 5 July 2021. https://www.bbc.co.uk/news/world-asia-57717214 (accessed 9 August 2023).

Bernama. 2021. "Digitalisation During the Pandemic: A Force for Organisational Change and Talent Development". 19 January 2021. https://www.bernama.com/en/news.php?id=1923473 (accessed 4 October 2023).

Chan, J. 2021. "Sabah Spent RM324m on Covid-19 Related Aid, Says Governor". *Yahoo News*, 21 September 2021. https://malaysia.news.yahoo.com/sabah-spent-rm324m-covid-19-060538537.html?guccounter=1 (accessed 4 October 2023).

Chong, Jin Hun. 2022. "DoSM: Malaysia's Unemployment Rate Dips below 4% for the First Time since Covid Onset". *The Edge Malaysia*, 9 June 2022. https://theedgemalaysia.com/article/dosm-malaysias-unemployment-rate-dips-below-4-first-time-covid19-outbreak (accessed 4 October 2023).

CodeBlue. 2021. "'Code Black' Protest Launched Ahead of Contract Doctors' Strike". 28 June 2021. https://codeblue.galencentre.org/2021/06/28/code-black-protest-launched-ahead-of-contract-doctors-strike/ (accessed 9 August 2023).

Dayak Daily. 2021. "RM151 Mil Spent This Year on Sarawak's Covid-19 Response". 19 May 2021. https://dayakdaily.com/cm-rm151-mil-spent-this-year-on-sarawaks-covid-19-response/ (accessed 4 October 2023).

Department of Statistics Malaysia. 2021. "Household Income Estimates and Incidence of Poverty Report, Malaysia". 6 August 2021. https://v1.dosm.gov.my/v1/index.php?r=column/cthemeByCat&cat=493&bul_id=VTNHRkdiZkFzenBNd1Y1dmg2UUlrZz09&menu_id=amVoWU54UTl0a21NWmdhMjFMMWcyZz09

Edge Markets, The. 2020. "PM Muhyiddin's Full Speech (April 6) on Malaysia's Prihatin SME+ Economic Stimulus Package announcement". 6 April 2020. https://theedgemalaysia.com/article/pm-muhyiddins-full-speech-april-6-malaysias-prihatin-sme-economic-stimulus-package (accessed 9 August 2023).

Ferrarese, Marco. 2023. "Malaysia's Tourism Recovery Flops as Thailand, Indonesia Cash In". *Al Jazeera*, 16 January 2023. https://www.aljazeera.com/economy/2023/1/16/malaysia-tourism-recovery-lags-thailand-indonesia-vietnam (accessed 4 October 2023).

Flanders, S., M. Nungsari, and H.Y. Chuah. 2020. "The Covid-19 Hardship Survey: An Evaluation of the Prihatin Rakyat Economic Stimulus Package". Asia School of Business Discussion Paper Series (2020). Asia School of Business, Kuala Lumpur.

Focus Malaysia. 2023. "Report: 81% EPF Members Cannot Live above Poverty Level on Retirement". 11 April 2023. https://focusmalaysia.my/report-81-epf-members-cannot-live-above-poverty-level-upon-retirement/#:~:text=Report%3A%2081%25%20EPF%20members%20cannot%20live%20above%20poverty%20level%20upon%20retirement,-By%20Bernie%20Yeo&text=PRIME%20Minister%20Datuk%20Seri%20Anwar,poverty%20line%20after%20they%20retire (accessed 28 May 2024).

Free Malaysia Today. 2022. "New School Year to Start on March 19, March 20". 10 December 2022. https://www.freemalaysiatoday.com/category/nation/2022/12/10/new-school-year-to-start-on-march-19-march-20/ (accessed 4 October 2023).

Hanafiah, Mohd Hafiz, Ann Selvaranee Balasingam, Vikneswaran Nair, Mohd Raziff Jamaluddin, and Mohd Salehuddin Mohd Zahari. 2021. "Implications of Covid-19 on Tourism Businesses in Malaysia: Evidence from a Preliminary Industry Survey". *Asia-Pacific Journal of Innovation in Hospitality and Tourism* 10, no. 1: 81–94.

Hashim, J.H., M.A. Adman, Z. Hashim, M.F. Mohd Radi, and S.C. Kwan. 2021. "Covid-19 Epidemic in Malaysia: Epidemic Progression, Challenges, and Response". *Frontiers in Public Health* 9: 560592.

Hazrin, H., Y. Fadhli, A. Tahir, J. Safurah, M. Kamaliah, and M. Noraini. 2013. "Spatial Patterns of Health Clinic in Malaysia". *Health* 5, no. 12: 2104–9. https://doi.org/10.4236/health.2013.512287

Human Rights Watch. 2021. "Malaysia: Raids on Migrants Hinder Vaccine Access". 12 June 2021. https://www.hrw.org/news/2021/06/30/malaysia-raids-migrants-hinder-vaccine-access (accessed 11 August 2023).

Jayaraj, Vivek Jason, Diane Woei-Quan Chong, Kim-Sui Wan, Noran Naqiah Hairi, Nirmala Bhoo-Pathy, Sanjay Rampal, and Chiu-Wan Ng. 2023. "Estimating Excess Mortalities due to the Covid-19 Pandemic in Malaysia between January 2020 and September 2021". *Scientific Reports* 13: 86. https://doi.org/10.1038/s41598-022-26927-z

Jong-A-Pin, R. 2009. "On the Measurement of Political Instability and its Impact on Economic Growth". *European Journal of Political Economy* 25, no. 1: 15–29.

Kamaruddin, Kamarulzaman, Che Anuar Che Abdullah, Mohd Noor Idris, and Mohd Nasrun Mohd Nawi. 2017. "Teachers' Level of ICT Integration in Teaching and Learning: A Survey in Malaysian Private Preschool". Conference Paper in *AIP Conference Proceedings* 1891: 020075.

Kit, L.S. 2002. "Emerging and Re-emerging Diseases in Malaysia". *Asia Pacific Journal of Public Health* 14, no. 1: 6–8. https://doi.org/10.1177/101053950201400103

Koya, Z. 2021. "MCMC Promises Fair Probes, but Doubts Persist". *The Star*, 13 March 2021. https://www.thestar.com.my/news/nation/2021/03/13/mcmc-promises-fair-probes-but-doubts-persist (accessed 9 August 2023).

Le, K., and M. Nguyen. 2021. "The Psychological Consequences of Covid-19 Lockdowns". *International Review of Applied Economics* 35, no. 2: 147–63.

Lee, Charity. 2023. "#KitaJagaKita: (De)legitimising the Government During the 2020 Movement Control Order". In *Discursive Approaches to Politics in Malaysia: Legitimising Governance*, edited by Kumaran Rajandran and Charity Lee, pp. 229–49. Singapore: Springer Nature Singapore.

Lee, H.A., and K. Zhang. 2021. "The Covid-19 Recession: Rough Times for Young Malaysians". *ISEAS Perspective*, no. 2021/116, 3 September 2021.

Lemière, Sophie. 2013. "Conversion and Controversy: Reshaping the Boundaries of Malaysian Pluralism". In *Proselytizing and the Limits of Religious Pluralism in Contemporary Asia*, edited by Juliana Finucane and R. Michael Feener, pp. 41–64. Singapore: Springer Singapore.

Lim, J. 2023. "14 Economic Stimulus Packages for Malaysian SMEs (Updated)". *Foundingbird*, 17 March 2023. https://foundingbird.com/my/blog/economic-stimulus-packages-for-smes-covid-19-pandemic (accessed 4 October 2023).

Lim Wai Yin. 2023. "Enabling SMEs to Be a Catalyst to Advance Malaysia

Forward". *The Star*, 9 February 2023. https://www.thestar.com.my/business/business-news/2023/02/09/enabling-smes-to-be-a-catalyst-to-advance-malaysia-forward (accessed 7 June 2024).

Lim, J.T., K. Maung, S.T. Tan, S.E. Ong, J.M. Lim, J.R. Koo, H. Sun, M. Park, K.W. Tan, J. Yoong, and A.R. Cook. 2021. "Estimating Direct and Spill-Over Impacts of Political Elections on Covid-19 Transmission Using Synthetic Control Methods". *PLoS Computational Biology* 17, no. 5: e1008959.

Loganathan, Tharani, Zhie X. Chan, Fikri Hassan, Watinee Kunpeuk, Rapeepong Suphanchaimat, Huso Yi, and Hazreen Abdul Majid. 2021. "Education for Non-citizen Children in Malaysia during the Covid-19 Pandemic: A Qualitative Study". *PLoS One* 16, no. 12: e0259546.

Malaysiakini. 2023. "Price Data at Your Fingertips with 'KitaJaga' Application". 27 March 2023. https://www.malaysiakini.com/news/660177 (accessed 9 August 2023).

McDevitt, Ryan C., and Aaron Sojourner. 2023. "The Need for Speed: Demand, Regulation, and Welfare on the Margin of Alternative Financial Services". *Review of Economics and Statistics*. https://doi.org/10.1162/rest_a_01308

Medina, A.F. 2021. "How Malaysia's PERMAI Stimulus Package Benefits Businesses". 9 February 2021. Dezan Shira & Associates. https://www.aseanbriefing.com/news/how-malaysias-permai-stimulus-package-benefits-businesses/ (assessed 11 August 2023).

Ministry of Finance. 2023. "Economic Achieves Growth of 5.6% in First Quarter 2023". News release, 12 May 2023. https://www.mof.gov.my/portal/en/news/press-release/economy-achieves-growth-of-5-6-in-first-quarter-2023#%20:~:text=The%20Malaysian%20economy%20expanded%20by,of%204.0%25%20to%205.0%25 (accessed 4 October 2023).

Ministry of Finance. 2022. "LAKSANA Reports". https://www.mof.gov.my/portal/ms/arkib3/laporan-laksana

Neri, Federico, Carlo Aliprandi, Federico Capeci and Montserrat Cuadros. 2012. "Sentiment Analysis on Social Media". In *2012 IEEE/ACM International Conference on Advances in Social Networks Analysis and Mining*, pp. 919–26. IEEE. https://www.researchgate.net/publication/230758119_Sentiment_Analysis_on_Social_Media

Nungsari Melati, Chuah Hui Yin, Nicole Fong, and Veena Pillai. 2022a. "Understanding the Impact of the Covid-19 Outbreak on Vulnerable Populations in Malaysia through an Ethical Lens: A Study of Non-state Actors Involved in Aid Distribution". *Wellcome Open Research* 6: 263. https://doi.org/10.12688/wellcomeopenres.17239.2

———, Denise Ni Shi Wong, Chin Jia Wei, Ngu Kirjane, Chee Shu Yee, Samuel

Flanders, and Phoon Yong Shian. 2022b. "Perceptions of Entrepreneurship and Online Learning During the Coronavirus-2019 (Covid-19) Pandemic". *Entrepreneurship Education and Pedagogy* 6, no. 4: 665–95. https://doi.org/10.1177/25151274221104706

Psacharopoulos, G., V. Collis, H.A. Patrinos, and E. Vegas. 2020. "Lost Wages: The Covid-19 Cost of School Closures". IZA Discussion Paper No. 13641, IZA Institute of Labor Economics, Bonn, Germany, August 2020.

Puah, Chin-Hong, Suk-Hie Huan, and Fung-Thai Thien. 2018. "Determinants of Chinese Demand for Tourism in Malaysia". *Business and Economic Horizons* 14, no. 3: 501–12.

Reuters. 2020. "Malaysia Confirms First Cases of the Coronavirus Infection". 25 January 2020. https://www.reuters.com/article/china-health597malaysia/malaysia-confirms-first-cases-of-coronavirus-infection-idUSL4N29U03A (accessed 9 August 2023).

———. 2021. "Malaysia Suspends Parliament Session Citing Risk of COVID Infection". 31 July 2021. https://www.reuters.com/world/asia-pacific/malaysia-suspends-parliament-session-citing-risk-covid-infection-2021-07-31/ (accessed 9 August 2023).

Rideout, Elaine C., and Denis O. Gray. 2013. "Does Entrepreneurship Education Really Work? A Review and Methodological Critique of the Empirical Literature on the Effects of University-Based Entrepreneurship Education". *Journal of Small Business Management* 51, no. 3: 329–51.

Star, The. 2021. "World Bank Revises Malaysia's Economic Growth Forecast to 3.3% in 2021". 28 September 2021. https://www.thestar.com.my/business/business-news/2021/09/28/world-bank-revises-malaysia039s-economic-growth-forecast-to-33-in-2021 (accessed 7 June 2024).

Statista. 2022. "Travel, Tourism & Hospitality: Gross Domestic Product Direct Contribution from Tourism in Malaysia from 2012 to 2021". October 2022. https://www.statista.com/statistics/1126334/malaysia-gdp-direct-contribution-tourism/ (accessed 4 October 2023).

Straits Times. 2022. "Malaysia Faces Brain Drain in Every Skilled Sector, Officials Say". 24 December 2022. https://www.straitstimes.com/asia/se-asia/malaysia-faces-brain-drain-in-every-skilled-sector-officials-say (accessed 9 August 2023).

Wang, Yimin. 2021. "More Than 20 White Flags Were Raised in the Fishing Village, and Supplies from the Volunteer Fire Brigade Were Quickly Delivered". *China Press*, 30 June 2021. https://www.chinapress.com.my/?p=2572182 (accessed 4 October 2023).

Winzeler, Robert L., ed. 1997. *Indigenous Peoples and the State: Politics, Land,*

and Ethnicity in the Malayan Peninsula and Borneo. New Haven: Yale University Southeast Asia Studies.

World Bank. 2023. Global Health Expenditure Database. "Current Health Expenditure (% of GDP)". https://data.worldbank.org/indicator/SH.XPD.CHEX.GD.ZS (accessed 7 April 2023).

Yeap, C. 2022. "The Bad and Ugly Side of Allowing More EPF Account 1 Withdrawals". *The Edge Malaysia*, 28 March 2022. https://theedgemalaysia.com/article/bad-and-ugly-side-allowing-more-epf-account-1-withdrawals (accessed 4 October 2023).

Zahari, Mohd S. 2004. "A Study of Factors Moderating Malaysian Hospitality Students Selection of Tertiary Education Institutions, Programme and Subsequent Career Intentions". PhD dissertation, Lincoln University.

12

SINGAPORE
Support for Households and Businesses During the Pandemic

W.L. Terence Ho

INTRODUCTION

The Covid-19 pandemic has taken a significant toll on many countries, both in terms of lives lost and economic disruption through the impact on jobs, incomes and livelihoods.

In the long battle against Covid-19, the Singapore government prioritized the protection of both lives and livelihoods. Singapore's approach at the outset of the pandemic was to control the spread of the virus so as to minimize deaths and prevent the healthcare system from being overwhelmed. Concurrently, substantial financial support was provided to keep businesses and households afloat.

Singapore's experience of SARS in 2003 and the global financial crisis of 2008–9 informed its approach to dealing with Covid-19 and the economic fallout. Task forces comprising government ministers and civil servants were quickly set up to coordinate policies, both for infection control and management of the economy. State assistance covered jobs, citizens, households and businesses. The assistance was a buffer against job and income losses, designed to mitigate the impact of the pandemic on the economy and labour market. To finance this exceptional support, the Singapore government enacted five budgets in 2020 and drew on the nation's Past Reserves[1] for the first time since the global financial crisis.

Subsequently, with Covid-19 becoming endemic, it became necessary to open up the economy in phases, accepting a rise in infections while seeking to minimize deaths and serious illness. Singapore's reopening was aided by the efficient roll-out of its vaccine and booster programme, as the more transmissible Delta and Omicron strains of the virus made a zero-Covid policy untenable for a country heavily dependent on global connectivity.

Singapore emerged from the pandemic with a relatively low mortality rate (below 0.1 per cent as of end-2022, compared with the global average of about 1 per cent).[2] It also significantly mitigated the fallout of the pandemic on the economy and labour market. However, the longer-term impact of the pandemic in areas such as inequality and foreign workforce policies will require sustained attention.

COVID-19 CONTEXT AND OVERALL ECONOMIC IMPACT

As of December 2022, Singapore had recorded more than 2.2 million Covid-19 cases since the start of the pandemic. The aggregate death toll from Covid-19 complications stood at 1,711, representing a fatality rate of 0.08 per cent, one of the lowest in the world. Eighty-two per cent of Singapore's eligible population (aged five years and above) had received minimum protection (at least three or four doses, depending on the vaccine) under the national vaccination programme, with 92 per cent receiving at least one dose (Prime Minister's Office 2023).

TRAJECTORY OF THE OUTBREAK

The daily number of Covid-19 infections from the onset of the pandemic to early 2023 is shown in Figure 12.1.

FIGURE 12.1
New Daily Covid-19 Cases and Daily Deaths in Singapore

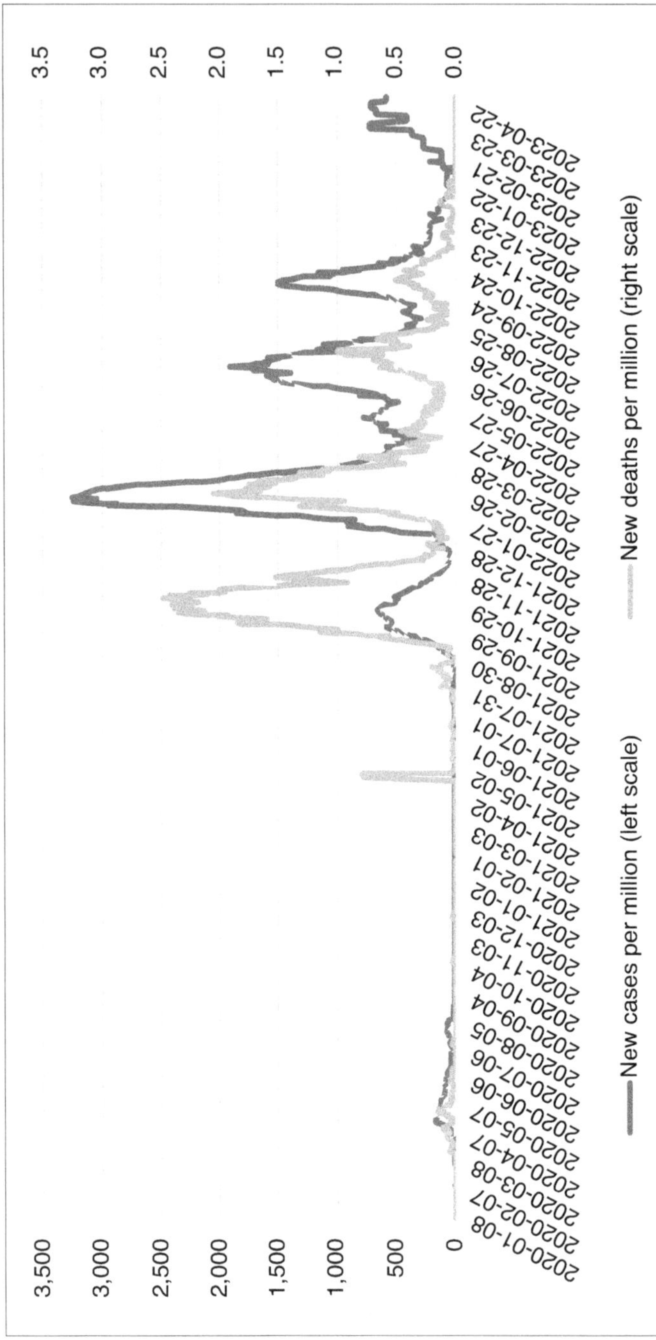

Source: ourworldindata.org.

Singapore's first case, a Chinese national who entered Singapore after travelling to Wuhan, China, was confirmed on 23 January 2020, not long after the outbreak in Wuhan was first reported. Local transmission of the virus accelerated in February and March 2020, along with imported cases. This prompted a progressive closure of international borders to travellers, beginning with people from the countries most affected by the virus. Singapore residents and work pass holders returning from affected countries abroad were subject to quarantine or stay-home orders.

In response to the first wave of infections, which included cases where a connection could not be established through contact tracing, the government announced a "circuit breaker", a nationwide partial lockdown, on 3 April 2020. It was initially intended to run from 7 April to 4 May but was extended to 1 June 2020. During this period, workplaces and shops deemed non-essential were closed, and dining at food and beverage establishments was prohibited. Social gatherings in homes and public places were banned and schools implemented home-based learning from 7 April 2020.

The circuit breaker was followed by a phased reopening. The government imposed measures such as limits on group sizes in public areas, caps on unique visitors to households and capacity limits at places of worship. Mask-wearing outdoors and in indoor public places was imposed from 14 April 2020. With the Covid-19 outbreak in foreign worker dormitories under control by September 2020, overall case numbers came down by the end of the year. Singapore's vaccination programme, which began towards the end of 2020, picked up speed in 2021.

However, hope for a quick and conclusive victory over Covid-19 in 2021 did not materialize. Recurring outbreaks, driven by the more infectious Delta variant, kept economies worldwide in stop-start mode. Even economies that had previously brought the disease under control, such as Taiwan and New Zealand, were forced to revert to more stringent safe-distancing measures as cases resurged. Singapore was no exception, also experiencing recurrent outbreaks despite strict safe-distancing measures, frequent testing and speedy contact tracing.

The first road bump following the start of the vaccination programme was experienced in May 2021, with a rash of imported Covid-19 cases sparking off a modest community spread. Once again, the government tightened safe-distancing measures, and Singapore entered a "Phase 2 heightened alert" from 16 May to 13 June 2021. The government restricted the size of groups meeting in public and limited household visitors to two persons a day, with dining at restaurants suspended.

In July 2021 Singapore experienced a larger rise in locally transmitted cases, centred around karaoke establishments and the Jurong Fishery Port, from where infections spread to wet markets throughout Singapore. This led to a reimposition of heightened alert measures in July 2021, not long after the government had signalled its intent to transition towards treating Covid-19 as endemic. These tighter measures were intended to buy Singapore time as it ramped up the national vaccination drive, with a view to protecting vulnerable seniors who had yet to receive their jabs. By August 2021, 80 per cent of the population had been fully vaccinated, making Singapore one of the world's most vaccinated countries (Deutsche Welle 2021).

In September 2021, Covid-19 cases began to rise exponentially in Singapore as the more transmissible Delta variant took root. Cases had subsided by December 2021, but this was followed by an even higher infection peak from February to March 2022 arising from the Omicron variant, which was even more transmissible than Delta but triggered milder symptoms. With the vast majority of the population fully vaccinated and most having received a third shot, a booster, Covid-19 measures could finally be unwound as the wave of infections subsided in April 2022. The lifting of restrictions began on 26 April 2022.

ECONOMIC AND LABOUR MARKET IMPACT

Singapore's economy suffered a sharp downturn in 2020 but recovered steadily over the following two years; the effects felt in the labour market were relatively moderate, considering the magnitude of the economic shock. Due to the virus, in 2020 Singapore experienced its deepest-ever recession, with real gross domestic product (GDP) contracting by 3.9 per cent.[3] The 11.8 per cent year-on-year decline in the second quarter of 2020, during the circuit breaker, was Singapore's largest quarterly economic contraction on record (Figure 12.2). The Singapore economy recovered

FIGURE 12.2
Singapore's Quarterly Real GDP Growth Rate (Year-on-Year)

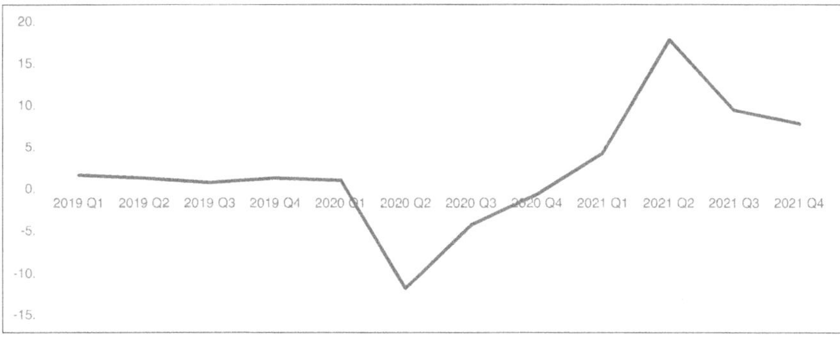

Source: Singapore Department of Statistics.

strongly in 2021, growing by 9.7 per cent in real terms, although sectors such as aviation and tourism remained weak. Real economic growth was 3.8 per cent in 2022.

The resident unemployment rate—unemployment of citizens and permanent residents—which had spiked in 2020, had recovered to pre-pandemic levels by the end of 2021 (Figure 12.3). The number of quarterly retrenchments had already returned to baseline levels—by the beginning of 2021 (Figure 12.4). The labour force participation rate even rose from 68.0 per cent in 2019 to 68.1 per cent in 2020 and 70.5 per cent in 2021.

Median gross monthly income from work for full-time employed residents grew by 3.2 per cent in nominal terms in 2021 after declining by 0.6 per cent in 2020. The real change in median monthly household income from work for resident households rebounded by 4.0 per cent in 2021, after contracting by 2.8 per cent in 2020.

POLICY RESPONSE: COVID-19 SUPPORT MEASURES

Saving Jobs for Locals

The Singapore government's economic contingency plans are frequently reviewed by the Ministry of Trade and Industry and other economic and

FIGURE 12.3
Singapore's Quarterly Resident Unemployment Rate (Seasonally Adjusted) and Hours Worked

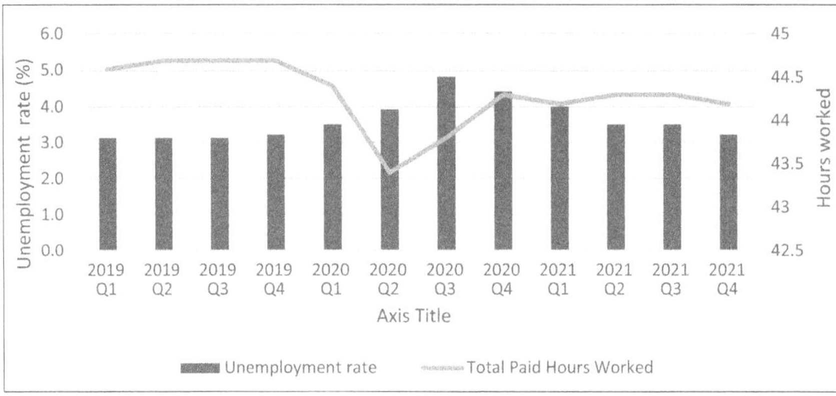

Source: Singapore Department of Statistics.

FIGURE 12.4
Retrenchments

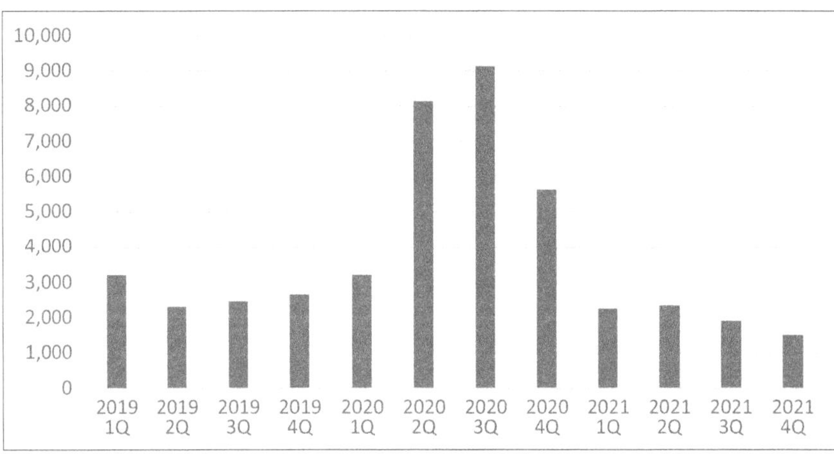

Source: Singapore Department of Statistics.

central planning agencies and are ready to be activated at short notice. Following SARS in 2003 and the global financial crisis in 2008–9, inter-ministerial teams have kept the contingency plans continually updated.

The centrepiece of Singapore's response to the global financial crisis was the Jobs Credit Scheme. This was credited with averting a major spike in unemployment at the height of the crisis (Hui and Toh 2014). The scheme, which provided employers with a wage subsidy of 12 per cent for every Singapore citizen or permanent resident they kept on their books, might even have been too effective. By shielding less-productive firms from market forces, it may have left the economy operating below its potential. But as the Covid-19 pandemic started to bite, this wage subsidy approach, reincarnated as the Jobs Support Scheme, once again became the preferred response.

Singapore introduced the Jobs Support Scheme in its first 2020 budget, called the Unity Budget, on 18 February. Support under the scheme was set at 8 per cent of gross monthly wages. Concurrently, the pre-existing Wage Credit Scheme, which co-funded wage *increases* given by firms to Singapore citizens and permanent residents, was enhanced with a higher government contribution and support cap.

As the Covid-19 outbreak gathered pace globally, it became evident that a much larger intervention would be needed to save businesses and jobs. Many countries across the developed world rushed to implement job protection schemes. Singapore introduced a supplementary budget, the Resilience Budget, on 26 March 2020. Support under the Jobs Support Scheme was increased to 25 per cent, 50 per cent or 75 per cent of gross monthly wages, depending on the sector, and the qualifying income ceiling was raised from S$3,600 to S$4,600, approximately the median wage in Singapore.

For ease and speed of implementation, support for firms under the Jobs Support Scheme was based on sector rather than revenue or profit loss. This avoided penalizing firms that were better able to respond to the pandemic and adapt to the changing market conditions. Firms (regardless of size) in the most badly affected sectors (aviation and tourism) received support at 75 per cent of wages, those moderately affected (food services) were given 50 per cent support and firms in the remaining sectors 25 per cent of wages. In recognition of the general disruption to business caused by the circuit breaker, support was, however, set at 75 per cent for all firms for April and May 2020. The Jobs Support Scheme was extended to March 2021 and subsequently to December 2021. However, support was reduced across the board in stages from September 2020, January 2021 and March 2021. Sectors that were faring well, such as information and communications technology (ICT) and biomedical, received no support after December 2020.

In 2021 the Jobs Support Scheme was stepped up again to help businesses affected by a tightening of pandemic-response measures. Wage support had been reduced to 30 per cent for many sectors, including food and beverage, but was raised again to 50 per cent from 16 May to 11 July 2021 for sectors required to suspend their activities, including food and beverage, gyms and performing arts. It was raised to 30 per cent for other significantly affected sectors such as retail, cinemas and personal care services. Support was raised again to 60 per cent and 40 per cent for the respective groups from 22 July to 18 August 2021. In total, more than S$28.1 billion was disbursed through the Jobs Support Scheme from February 2020 to March 2022 (Inland Revenue Authority of Singapore and Enterprise Singapore 2022).

The pandemic affected firms very differently, even those in the same sector and tier of the Jobs Support Scheme. Most businesses experienced some income loss; revenue for some, such as those catering to tourists, dropped to nearly zero (Ong 2022). However, others, such as supermarkets and other food stores, were unaffected or even saw their earnings grow (*Today Online* 2020). The pressing circumstances did not allow the government to make a careful assessment of each firm's specific situation. The priority at the outset of the pandemic, especially in view of the circuit breaker restrictions, was to put firms in suspended animation, avoiding an indiscriminate cull that would have condemned even viable businesses.[4]

Wage adjustment—cutting wages to save jobs, rather than cutting jobs to save on wages—was another vital move to keep Singaporeans employed during the crisis. In March 2020, the Ministry of Manpower convened the National Wages Council, a tripartite advisory body comprising government, employers and union representatives. It was tasked with providing guidance to firms on cutting wages in a responsible way and provided a first set of recommendations that month. With the Covid-19 situation rapidly evolving, the National Wages Council was reconvened in August 2020 and released supplementary recommendations in October. Observing wage restraint and demonstrating solidarity with other Singaporeans whose incomes had been affected by the pandemic, the public sector announced that most public servants would not receive an annual variable bonus, although the thirteenth-month bonus[5] would still be paid (Public Service Division 2020).

Supporting the Self-Employed

The self-employed fell outside the ambit of the Jobs Support Scheme. The Resilience Budget (the second budget of 2020) attempted to address this gap with the Self-Employed Training Support Scheme, funding training of up to S$7.50 an hour (later increased to S$10 an hour) in programmes approved under the SkillsFuture Series[6] or certain sector-specific training programmes. The National Trades Union Congress (NTUC) stepped in with a top-up for union members who attended training. The government then introduced the Self-Employed Persons Income Relief Scheme, giving S$9,000 (spread over nine months) to self-employed Singaporeans of less means and without family support.

Simplicity and generosity in administering these support measures were the order of the day. People who had previously declared self-employment income to the Inland Revenue Authority of Singapore (IRAS) or Central Provident Fund (CPF) Board were automatically included in the scheme. Those who had not previously made income declarations to the IRAS or CPF Board had to apply, and those who narrowly missed any of the eligibility criteria and were facing financial difficulty could appeal. The Self-Employed Persons Income Relief Scheme was extended in the April 2020 Solidarity Budget (the third budget of 2020) as the needs of the self-employed became clearer. This time, it automatically included self-employed people who also drew a salary (not more than S$2,300 a month) from employment. In response to an appeal from the public for more flexibility in the eligibility criteria, the annual property value threshold was also raised, allowing some self-employed people living in condominiums and other private properties to be eligible for support. In total, about S$1.8 billion was disbursed to about 200,000 beneficiaries through the Self-Employed Persons Income Relief Scheme (Ministry of Social and Family Development 2021).

Helping Employers with Foreign Worker Upkeep

The government's priority was to help locals, but foreigners were not neglected. Many employers were unable to repatriate their foreign workers due to border closures or lack of flights and had to provide for the workers' upkeep. With the rapid spread of Covid-19 infection in foreign worker dormitories, many workers were confined to their residences and unable to work and were understandably anxious about their livelihoods and circumstances. Even if workers could be repatriated, firms would need to keep a core group with whom to resume operations when conditions allowed: otherwise viable firms could go under, leading to job losses for locals and foreigners alike.

To help employers meet their obligations to their foreign workers, the government announced that foreign worker levies (a fee paid to the government by employers of foreign workers on certain types of work permits) due in April 2020 would be waived for employers of people holding work permits and S-Passes.[7] Employers also received a further S$750 rebate per worker for levies previously paid.

The rebate was extended for another month, on condition that employers made a commitment to use the money to support their foreign employees. This recognized that while companies that reduced their local employees' salaries or put them on no-pay leave would receive correspondingly lower payouts in subsequent tranches under the Jobs Support Scheme, there was no similar mechanism for the foreign worker levy rebate. Employers were reminded to treat all workers fairly and responsibly, regardless of nationality.

A third round of levy waivers and rebates was announced in the May 2020 Fortitude Budget, the fourth budget of 2020, for firms that were still unable to restart operations after the circuit breaker. It also applied to all firms in the construction, marine shipyard and process sectors, whose operations had been badly disrupted by the dormitory outbreaks. These sector-specific levies were reduced from October 2020 onwards. Firms in these sectors continued to receive a S$90 rebate per worker until December 2021, to ease the adjustment to more stringent Covid-19 measures.

The government balanced fiscal prudence and speed when implementing support measures. It targeted support at affected firms to limit spending and ensure it was efficient, while also providing support expediently and minimizing administrative burden. While these measures to support companies' upkeep of foreign workers were meant to help them through the difficult pandemic period, the prevailing policy stance remained: firms relying heavily on foreign workers should review their workforce strategy and grow their pipeline of local workers for sustainability and resilience in the medium to long term.

Keeping Businesses Going

Besides employment support, the government also increased financing support for businesses, as it had done during the global financial crisis. This was to avert insolvencies arising from short-term cash flow difficulties caused by Covid-19. The maximum loan amount offered by financial institutions under the Small and Medium Enterprise (SME) Working Capital Loan scheme (part of the Enterprise Financing Scheme) was increased to S$1 million, while the government's risk share was raised to 90 per cent.

A one-year Temporary Bridging Loan Programme allowed businesses to borrow up to S$5 million from financial institutions with interest capped at 5 per cent and the government bearing 90 per cent of the risk. The application deadline was to have been in March 2021 but it was extended by six months, albeit with a lower maximum loan amount and a lower risk share for the government. Banks and financial institutions making new loans under the Working Capital Loan scheme and Temporary Bridging Loan Programme could apply to the Monetary Authority of Singapore (MAS) for low-cost funding through the MAS Singapore Dollar (SGD) Facility, thus further lowering interest rates charged.

The Enterprise Financing Scheme Trade Loan Programme and Loan Insurance Scheme were likewise enhanced to provide more support for SMEs facing financing difficulties. These enterprises could opt to defer principal payments on their secured term loans till the end of 2020. Laws were passed to provide businesses and individuals temporary relief from legal action for inability to perform certain contracts and to increase the thresholds for bankruptcy and insolvency for financially distressed individuals and businesses. The relief was given for six months from 20 April to 19 October 2020. Also passed was a bill that provided temporary relief from onerous contractual terms such as excessive interest for late payments.

On the government's part, it deferred income tax payments and committed not to raise government fees and charges for all services for a year from April 2020. Property tax rebates were given for non-residential properties and landlords of non-residential properties were required to pass the rebate on in full to tenants. The government also gave rental waivers of two to five months to food stall owners and commercial tenants in public properties. SME tenants of private properties received two weeks' rental relief in cash grants from the government, and landlords were required to match this. To help businesses affected by the tightened Covid-19 response in 2021, credit support measures were extended and the government also provided a fresh round of rental relief for commercial tenants.

Besides the wage, cash flow and rental support given to all firms, special support packages were rolled out for the most affected sectors, which included aviation, tourism, land transport, maritime and arts and culture (Table 12.1).

Supporting Households

The general uncertainty at the outset of the outbreak called for a time-tested budgetary measure—cash handouts to citizens and households. With employment at risk and income loss widespread, cash handouts provided help and assurance to households in financial difficulty, while giving a much-needed lift to consumption and aggregate demand. Such measures were based on the principle that everyone would receive something, but the less well-off would receive more. This would balance the intent to foster solidarity with more targeted support for those in greater need.

The Care and Support Package, introduced in the February 2020 Unity Budget, gave every adult Singaporean S$100 to S$300 (depending on income and property ownership) in one-off support. Parents of Singaporean children aged twenty and under received an additional S$100. Seniors received a further S$100 in cash. The package also included grocery vouchers and household rebates.[8]

By the March 2020 Resilience Budget, the worsening situation prompted a tripling of support under the Care and Support Package to

TABLE 12.1
Sectoral Support Packages

Sector	*Key Measures*
Aviation	• Cost relief from government for airlines, ground handlers, cargo agents and airport tenants, with the aim of maintaining a minimum level of air connectivity. • Temporary redeployment of aviation sector workers to other sectors.
Tourism	• Support for training of industry professionals to ensure pipeline of events and products. • S$320 million provided in tourism credits to citizens to stimulate domestic tourism.
Land Transport	• S$95 million package for transport operators, including relief for taxi and private hire car drivers and waiver of operator licence fees. • Road tax rebate and waiver of parking fees for private bus operators.
Maritime	• Concessions given on port dues for cruise ships and ferries • Rebates given on certain port fees
Arts, Culture	• S$55 million provided to safeguard jobs, develop capabilities and step up digitalization.
Built Environment	• Government paid a share of costs associated with new safety measures when construction activity resumed.

Source: Singapore Government Agency (2020); Ministry of Finance (2020); Tay (2020).

a range of S$300 to S$900 per adult. The Workfare Special Payment, a one-off payment to low-wage workers announced in the Unity Budget, was increased to S$3,000. The Solidarity Budget of April 2020 added a further one-off cash handout of S$300 to all citizens which, together with the earlier announced payment, amounted to a minimum of S$600 for every adult citizen (called the Solidarity Payment). Each permanent resident and holder of a Long-Term Visit Pass-Plus received a minimum of S$300. A utilities rebate of S$100 was also given to all households, in recognition that consumption of utilities had risen with more people staying home, especially during the circuit breaker.

The main individual and business support measures announced in each of the 2020 budgets are summarized in Table 12.2.

TABLE 12.2
Singapore's Main Covid-19 Support Measures and Cost

	Main Support Measures for Individuals/ Households	*Main Support Measures for Employers*	*Cost of Support Measures*
Unity Budget (18 February 2020)	• Care and Support Package (cash payments, Workfare Special Payment, grocery vouchers, voucher for the goods and services tax, rebate on service charge for those in public housing)	• Stabilization and Support Package (Jobs Support Scheme support at 8 per cent of wages, enhanced Wage Credit Scheme, corporate tax rebate).	S$6.4 billion
Resilience Budget (26 March 2020)	• Enhanced Care and Support Package (tripled cash payouts, increased Workfare Special Payment) • Temporary Relief Fund, Covid Support Grant • SGUnited jobs and traineeships • Self-Employed Person Income Relief Scheme	• Increase in Jobs Support Scheme support of 25 per cent to 75 per cent depending on sector. • Sectoral support packages for aviation, tourism, land transport and arts and culture. • Enhanced property tax rebate, rental waivers, financing (cash flow) support.	S$48.4 billion, including S$17 billion drawn on reserves
Solidarity Budget (6 April 2020)	• Expanded eligibility criteria for Self-Employed Person Income Relief Scheme • Topped up cash payout, making a S$600 Solidarity Payment for all citizens	• 75 per cent Jobs Support Scheme support for all sectors in April and May. • Foreign worker levy waiver and rebate. • Enhanced financing support.	S$5.1 billion, including S$4 billion drawn on reserves
Fortitude Budget (26 May 2020)	• Solidarity Utilities Credit • SGUnited Jobs and Skills Package to include mid-career traineeships, skills programmes and hiring incentives	• Extended Jobs Support Scheme. • Extended foreign worker levy waiver and rebate for firms unable to resume operations.	S$33 billion, including S$31 billion drawn on reserves

		• Deferred increase in contributions to the Central Provident Fund for older workers. • Expanded rental relief for SMEs and government tenants. • Digital resilience bonus.	
Ministerial Statement (17 August 2020)	• Extended Covid Support Grant • Widened eligibility for Workfare Special Payment	• Extended and stepped down Jobs Support Scheme, depending on sector. • Further support for aviation and tourism.	No additional outlay (S$8 billion from budget savings elsewhere)
Total Sum			S$92.9 billion, of which S$52 billion was approved to be drawn from reserves[a]

Notes: a. Eventually, a total of S$40 billion from the reserves was used for Covid-19 measures from FY2020 to FY2022.
Source: Author's compilation.

Another suite of measures was needed to help individuals and households that had run into financial difficulty due to the pandemic. This was because the existing Community Care (ComCare) schemes, which provided financial support to needy families but were subject to rigorous means testing, would not be able to handle the anticipated surge in demand. The Temporary Relief Fund was introduced in April 2020 as an interim assistance scheme for lower- to middle-income locals who had lost their jobs or suffered substantial income loss.

In May 2020, the Temporary Relief Fund was superseded by the Covid-19 Support Grant, which provided income support for up to three months to those who had lost their jobs, were on involuntary no-pay leave for at least three months or had suffered income loss of at least 30 per cent. From January 2021, the Covid-19 Support Grant and the Self-Employed Persons Income Relief Scheme were replaced by the Covid-19 Recovery Grant, which provided support for both employees and the self-employed who had been placed on involuntary no-pay leave or suffered significant income loss. Compared with the Covid-19 Support Grant and the Self-Employed Persons Income Relief Scheme, financial support under the Covid-19 Recovery Grant was lower. Also, the eligibility criteria were tightened to target support to those who needed it most. Applicants were required to show that they were actively seeking job or training opportunities or, in the case of the self-employed, that they had reached out to potential clients.

When Covid-19 safe-distancing measures were tightened in May and July 2021, the Covid-19 Recovery Grant–Temporary was introduced. It was given to workers who had lost their jobs or experienced significant income losses for at least a month due to the tighter measures. Monthly payouts were similar to that of the Covid-19 Recovery Grant, but there were no job search and training requirements. Support for specific groups of workers including food stall owners and drivers was also disbursed through the Market and Hawker Centre Relief Fund and the Covid-19 Driver Relief Fund. The Covid-19 Recovery Grant was extended to the end of 2022 to continue providing support to those who are affected by the Covid-19 pandemic.

A summary of the criteria and support provided under the Temporary Relief Fund, Covid-19 Support Grant, Covid-19 Recovery Grant and Covid-19 Recovery Grant–Temporary is given in Table 12.3.

Securing Jobs and Other Opportunities for Locals

Even with the Jobs Support Scheme in place, unemployment and retrenchments rose in 2020. The economic contraction was more severe than during the global financial crisis or SARS. Still, opportunities remained. Covid-19 swab testing, temperature taking, the surge in hospital admissions and the need for safe-distancing/safe management ambassadors created short-term job opportunities. Meanwhile, hiring in the ICT sector continued to be strong, with the pandemic accelerating digitalization. Recruitment for longer-term needs, such as in the publicly funded healthcare and early childhood education sectors, was also brought forward.

Matching workers who had suffered job or income losses with these opportunities was a priority. Initially, short-term job opportunities were given the "SGUnited Jobs" branding, under the broader SGUnited scheme.[9] Public sector agencies Workforce Singapore and SkillsFuture Singapore organized virtual careers fairs to match workers with immediate vacancies. The Public Service Division, in charge of human resources for the Singapore Public Service, worked directly with companies to redeploy affected staff. For instance, airline crew were redeployed as patient care coordinators in hospitals and nursing homes, or as safe-distancing ambassadors in transport hubs.

However, the government feared there would not be enough jobs to go around. Fresh graduates from universities, polytechnics and the Institute of Technical Education were entering a challenging job market. Research shows that entering the workforce in a recession can have a long-lasting impact on earnings (Kahn 2010; Oreopoulos, Wachter, and Heisz 2012). There was a need to create new opportunities for fresh graduates, as well as displaced mid-career workers.

This motivated the government to develop the SGUnited Jobs and Skills Package, unveiled in the May 2020 Fortitude Budget. The package aimed to create close to 100,000 opportunities for local workers within a year;

TABLE 12.3
Covid-19 Relief Schemes

	Temporary Relief Fund	*Covid-19 Support Grant*	*Covid-19 Recovery Grant*	*Covid-19 Recovery Grant–Temporary*
Period	April 2020	May to December 2020	January 2021 onwards	May to August 2021
Beneficiaries	Employees (Singaporean citizens and permanent residents) aged 16 and above.	Employees (Singaporean citizens and permanent residents) aged sixteen and above. (The self-employed received assistance under the Self-Employed Persons Income Relief Scheme instead.)	Employees and the self-employed (Singaporean citizens and permanent residents) aged twenty-one and above.	Employees, the self-employed (Singaporean citizens and permanent residents) aged twenty-one and above.
Income / property thresholds	Household income no more than S$10,000 (or S$3,100 per household member).	Household income no more than S$10,000 (or S$3,100 per household member). Property annual value no more than S$21,000.	Household income no more than S$7,800 (or SGD2,800 per household member). Property annual value no more than S$21,000.	Household income no more than S$7,800 (or S$2,800 per household member). Property annual value no more than S$21,000.
Amount of support and conditions for job loss and involuntary no-pay leave	One-off S$500 in April 2020 for those who lost jobs; and for those placed on involuntary no-pay leave for at least three consecutive months.	Up to S$800 a month for three months for anyone who lost a job or was placed on involuntary no-pay leave for at least three months.	Up to S$700 a month for three months for workers retrenched or placed on involuntary no-pay leave for at least three months.	Up to S$700 for workers placed on involuntary no-pay leave for at least one month due to tightened Covid-19 safety measures.

Amount of support and conditions for significant income loss	One-off S$500 in April 2020 for income loss of 30 per cent or more.	Up to S$500 a month for three months for income loss of 30 per cent or more for at least three consecutive months.	Up to S$500 a month for three months for income loss (overall loss of 50 per cent or more) for at least three consecutive months.	Up to S$500 for income loss of 50 per cent or more for at least one month due to tightened Covid-19 safety measures.
Job/training requirement	No.	Yes, need to agree to participate.	Yes, proof required of job search or training in two months prior to application.	No.

Source: Author's compilation.

this was to comprise 40,000 jobs, 25,000 traineeships and 30,000 skills training opportunities. A National Jobs Council, made up of government, unions and business leaders, was established to oversee its design and implementation.

Under this programme, government and companies co-funded traineeship allowances for fresh graduates and mid-career workers. The SGUnited Traineeship Programme was for new graduates of publicly funded universities, polytechnics and the Institute of Technical Education. It aimed to equip them with industry experience so they would gain a foothold in the job market during the economic recovery. The government paid for 80 per cent of their training for up to six months.

The SGUnited Mid-Career Pathways Programme was an equivalent programme of between four and six months for mid-career individuals. It aimed to help them widen their professional networks and gain industry-relevant skills and experience. Training allowances were higher than those for fresh graduates to reflect the greater work experience. A subsidy of 80 per cent was provided for workers under forty and 90 per cent for those aged forty and above. To further increase opportunities for mid-career workers, the SGUnited Mid-Career Pathways Programme also offered a scheme whereby participants could acquire industry-relevant skills by training with leading companies.

Finally, the SGUnited Skills Programme offered workers of all ages training courses to help them acquire in-demand skills, such as digital marketing, especially in sectors with many opportunities. These courses were designed in partnership with industry and delivered by continuing education and training centres, including tertiary education institutions. Their modular format allowed flexibility and early exit without penalty upon finding a job. Participants received a monthly training allowance of S$1,200 and assistance with their job search.

By the end of 2020, nearly 76,000 locals had been placed in jobs or training opportunities through the SGUnited Jobs and Skills Package (Heng 2021a). As of end-October 2021, more than 166,300 jobs and skills opportunities had been taken up, including 122,300 job placements, with more than seven in ten being long-term jobs (Ministry of Finance 2022).

Pivoting to Job Creation and the Future Economy

With the economy improving towards the end of 2020, the challenge was to pivot support for jobs and households to something more fiscally sustainable and in line with medium-term economic priorities, such as business restructuring and digitalization. The aviation and hospitality sectors were expected to remain weak for some time, notwithstanding progress on vaccine development and roll-out. The acceleration of remote working and digital commerce meant that some lost jobs would never return. Hence, suspended animation had to give way to helping businesses and citizens take up new opportunities in areas with strong growth potential.

To spur job recruitment, the Jobs Growth Incentive was introduced on 1 September 2020, for firms expanding their local workforce over the next six months. Under this scheme, companies received 25 per cent wage support for up to twelve months for new local hires aged below forty, and 50 per cent wage support for up to eighteen months for new local hires aged forty and above. Some 130,000 new local hires, nearly half of whom were mature workers aged forty or above, had benefited from this scheme within three months of its implementation (Ministry of Manpower 2021b).

Budget 2021 reflected the government's intent to equip businesses and workers for the future while engineering a soft landing for the Singapore economy. Of the S$11 billion Covid-19 Resilience Package announced, S$700 million was set aside to extend the Jobs Support Scheme for targeted sectors until September 2021, while S$5.2 billion went towards extending the Jobs Growth Incentive.[10] At the same time, the government stepped up financing support for high-growth enterprises, as well as co-funding technology adoption and digitalization for SMEs. The government also unveiled an Enterprise Sustainability Programme to help Singapore businesses build sustainability capabilities and capture opportunities for growth in the burgeoning green economy.

OUTCOMES AND IMPLICATIONS

Size and Impact of Support Measures

In the financial year 2020, S$83.5 billion was set aside to deal with the pandemic: S$73.5 billion for workers and businesses and S$10 billion for social and household support (Heng 2021b). The overall budget deficit for the financial year 2020 amounted to S$51.6 billion, or 10.5 per cent of GDP, the largest deficit in Singapore's history. Compared with other countries, Singapore's Covid-19 fiscal spending as a proportion of GDP was relatively high, similar to that of the United States (Figure 12.5).

These measures helped to mitigate the impact of Covid-19 on the labour market and economy. Government estimates based on macroeconomic modelling suggest that the budget support measures in 2020 and 2021, along with accommodative monetary policy, had a significant positive impact on GDP and unemployment. The fiscal and monetary policy measures prevented the economy from contracting by a further 6.6 percentage points in 2020 and by 0.8 percentage points in 2021 (Figure 12.6). They also reduced the resident unemployment rate by an estimated 2.0 percentage points in 2020 and 4.0 percentage points in 2021 (Ministry of Finance 2022).

FIGURE 12.5
Fiscal Spending on Covid-19 Support (Excluding Liquidity Support) as a Percentage of GDP

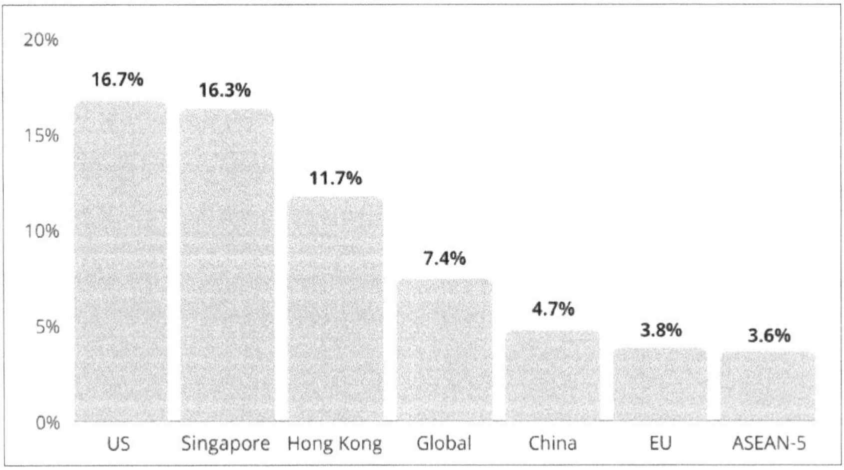

Note: The ASEAN-5 comprises Indonesia, Malaysia, Thailand, the Philippines and Vietnam. It is weighted by each country's share of Singapore's non-oil domestic exports. Figures are on a calendar-year basis, except for Hong Kong and Singapore. The fiscal responses exclude liquidity support such as loans and guarantees.
Source: Figure reproduced from Ministry of Finance (2021).

FIGURE 12.6
Real GDP Growth and Projected Growth Without Fiscal and Monetary Support

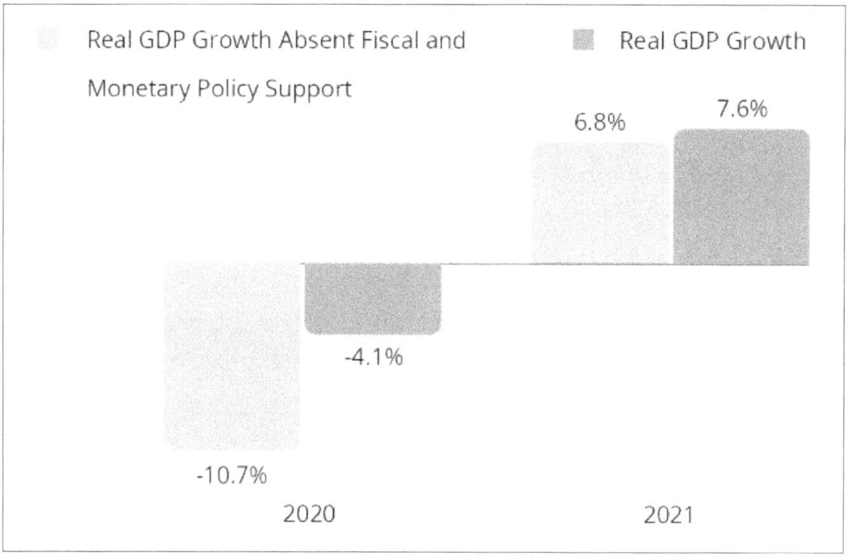

Source: Figure reproduced from Ministry of Finance (2021).

In the financial year 2020, the President granted approval for the government to draw S$52 billion from the Past Reserves; this is the nation's "rainy day" fund and it is used only in times of utmost need. This was significantly more than the S$4.9 billion approved in 2009 during the global financial crisis. Of this amount, S$36 billion was used in the 2020 and 2021 financial years, with a further estimated S$3.1 billion spent in the 2022 financial year.

While Singapore was able to tap into accumulated reserves (built up from past budget surpluses) to finance Covid-19 support measures, there was also an impetus to rebuild public finances given the considerable sums spent. Prior to Covid-19, the government had already announced in 2018 that the goods and services tax would be raised from 7 per cent to 9 per cent some time between 2021 and 2025 to fund growing public expenditure, particularly on healthcare as the population ages. This is estimated to bring in additional revenues of about S$3.5 billion a year when fully implemented (Goh 2022).

Business Formation and Cessation

The impact of Covid-19 on businesses varied significantly by sector, but was in aggregate milder than initially feared. Overall business formation did not decline, although business cessation did see a pronounced uptick (Figure 12.7).

Financing support also cushioned the blow for firms and financial institutions. The non-performing loans of commercial banks rose slightly from 2 per cent before the pandemic, peaking at 2.71 per cent in the third quarter of 2020, before gradually declining (Figure 12.8).

From March 2020 to December 2021, the government, through financing schemes, supported more than 27,000 enterprises in accessing loans worth more than S$24.7 billion, substantially higher than in 2019 (Figure 12.9).

Results from a study by the Ministry of Trade and Industry on the Temporary Bridging Loan Programme indicated that it helped to alleviate financial distress across firms of all sizes and supported employment in firms with fifty or fewer employees (Ministry of Finance 2022). In particular, an additional loan of the average size given under the Temporary Bridging

FIGURE 12.7
Business Formation and Cessation

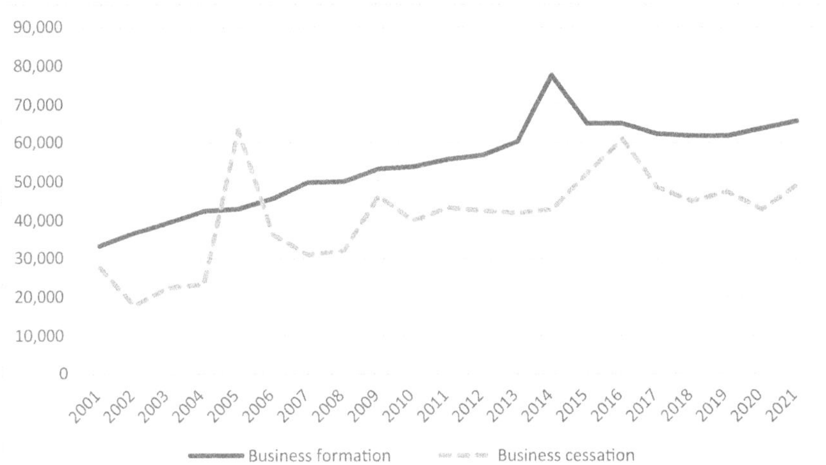

Source: Singapore Accounting and Corporate Regulatory Authority.

FIGURE 12.8
Non-performing Loan Rate of Commercial Banks

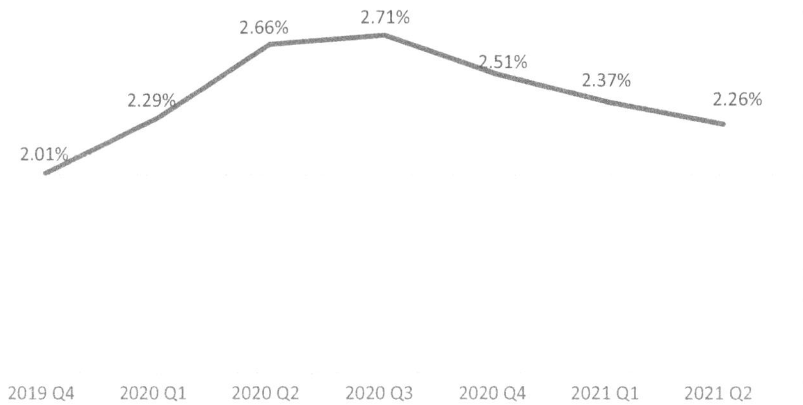

Note: Figures are for end of period.
Source: Figure reproduced from Ministry of Finance (2022).

FIGURE 12.9
Value of Approved Loans (S$ billion)

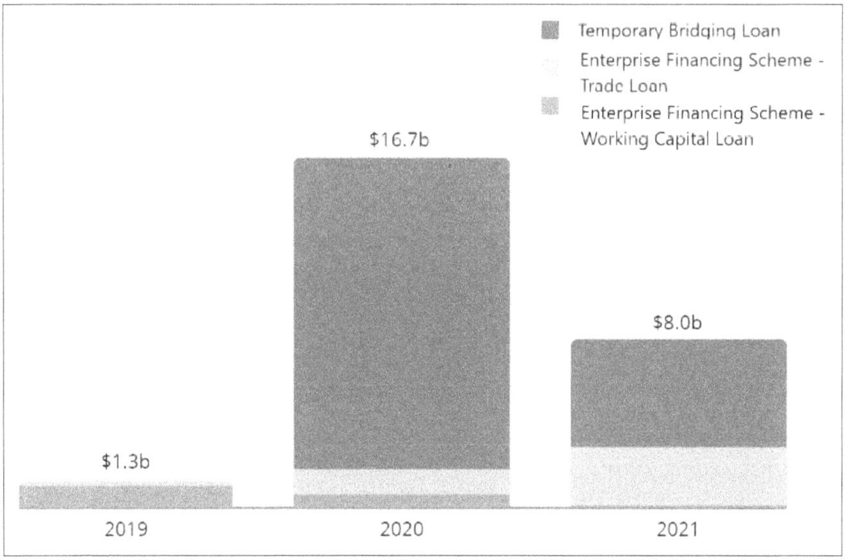

Source: Figure reproduced from Ministry of Finance (2022).

Loan Programme reduced the probability of firm financial distress (i.e., the probability of a firm missing its payment obligations) by 0.05 percentage points and had a positive impact on firms' total employment of 0.26 per cent on average.

Income and Unemployment Support

The exceptional income and unemployment support provided by the government during the Covid-19 pandemic was timely and impactful: S$225 million was disbursed to some 450,000 beneficiaries through the Temporary Relief Fund, while a further S$215 million was distributed to approximately 98,000 beneficiaries through the Covid-19 Support Grant.

Some challenges were encountered in administering these schemes, which were intended to provide quick support without onerous application procedures. Verifying employment status and income was difficult during the circuit breaker, as it was difficult to contact employers or firms' human resource departments. As with all such schemes, the government had to be alert to fraud and managed to uncover several such cases (Channel NewsAsia 2022).

It is necessary to shore up precautionary and retirement savings, especially for self-employed workers who are susceptible to income and job disruptions and may not have built up adequate savings in the Central Provident Fund.[11] The government has accepted the recommendation of an Advisory Committee on Platform Workers that online platform companies and workers must both contribute to the Fund. This will be compulsory for platform workers aged below thirty in the first year of implementation, while older workers may opt in to the full contribution regime.

There is also a need to help individuals and households through periods of unemployment. While a quick return to employment is preferred, this may not always be possible during heightened economic and job market volatility. The government has accepted the recommendation of a task force comprising the NTUC and Singapore National Employers Federation to provide supplementary income relief for the involuntarily unemployed, so that they can take their time to retrain for a job with good prospects rather than have to accept the first offer that arises. Unlike unemployment insurance schemes that rely on contributions from employers and workers, the government will bear the cost of the income support.

Jobs and Employability

Labour market data show that Singapore substantially mitigated job and income losses during the pandemic. While the resident unemployment rate climbed to 4.7 per cent in the third quarter of 2020, it fell short of the peak during the global financial crisis (Figure 12.10). By the fourth quarter of 2020, resident unemployment had fallen to 4.4 per cent. The number of retrenchments came to more than 26,000 in 2020, but the rate of retrenchment (12.8 per thousand employees) was below that of previous recessionary highs in 2003 and 2009 (Table 12.4). Resident employment, which contracted in the first half of 2020, turned around in the third and fourth quarters and had recovered to pre-pandemic levels by the end of the year.

A joint study by the Ministry of Finance and Ministry of Manpower estimated that a 10 percentage point increase in the effective Jobs Support Scheme wage subsidy[12] led to a net increase of 0.44 and 0.13 in local jobs saved per firm per month for firms in Tier 1 and Tier 2 sectors respectively

FIGURE 12.10
Quarterly Resident Unemployment Rate (Seasonally Adjusted)

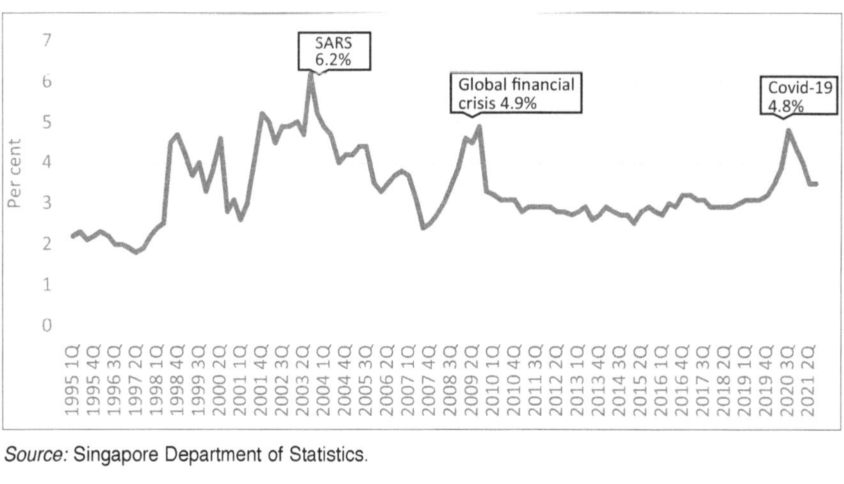

Source: Singapore Department of Statistics.

TABLE 12.4
Retrenchment Rate

Year	*Incidence of Retrenchment (Per Thousand Employees)*
1998: Asian financial crisis	32.7
2001: Dot-com bust	26.3
2003: SARS	16.7
2009: Global financial crisis	14.2
2020: Covid-19	12.8

Source: Ministry of Manpower.

(Ministry of Finance 2022).[13] This suggests that the Jobs Support Scheme preserved around 165,000 local jobs in 2020. Local wages were found to have increased by between 1.7 per cent and 5.3 per cent for every 10 percentage point increase in the effective Jobs Support Scheme wage subsidy. These results suggest that the impact of the pandemic on local workers would have been significantly worse without the Jobs Support Scheme.

A study by government economists on phase one of the Jobs Growth Incentive scheme (September 2020 to February 2021) found that it incentivized the hiring of an additional 47,000 local workers, including 27,300 workers aged forty and above (Ministry of Finance 2022). This increased the proportion of hired workers over forty. The average wages of new hires also improved. The Jobs Growth Incentive supported the hiring of vulnerable jobseekers, in particular: nearly half of the hires supported by the Jobs Growth Incentive were previously not in employment (whether unemployed or outside the labour force), and close to 30 per cent had been out of employment for more than six months.

Traineeships under the SGUnited Jobs and Skills Package played a role alongside the Jobs Growth Incentive in securing opportunities for fresh graduates and mature workers, in particular. The six-month post-programme employment outcomes for each of the SGUnited schemes are shown in Figure 12.11. More than 80 per cent of participants in the SGUnited Traineeship (SGUT) and SGUnited Mid-Career Pathways Programme-Company Attachment (SGUP-CA) found employment. Further, 52 per cent of SGUP-Company Training (SGUP-CT) trainees found employment,

FIGURE 12.11
Six-Month Post-Programme Employment Status

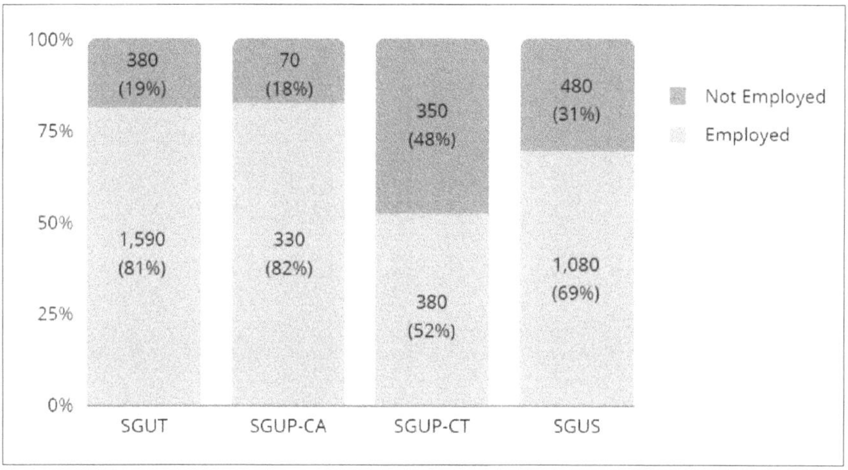

Notes: SGUT= SGUnited Traineeship Programme; SGUP-CA=SGUnited Mid-Career Pathways Programme-Company Attachment; SGUP-CT=SGUP-Company Training; SGUS=SGUnited Skills Programme.
Source: Figure reproduced from Ministry of Finance (2022).

as did 69 per cent of SGUnited Skills Programme (SGUS) trainees found employment respectively.

Overall employment, once traineeships are included, held up well for university and polytechnic graduates in 2020 versus 2019, although there was a slight decline in the employment of graduates from the Institute of Technical Education (ITE) in 2020 (Figure 12.12). However, the proportion of those in full-time, permanent employment declined for each group.

Among university, polytechnic and ITE graduates who found full-time, permanent employment, the median salaries in 2020 remained comparable to those of 2019 (Table 12.5), suggesting no overall decline in job quality for this group of fresh graduates.

Older workers aged over fifty and mature workers aged over forty are among those particularly vulnerable to retrenchment. They also find it more difficult to re-enter employment after being retrenched. This is the reason they received higher wage support under the Jobs Growth Incentive and the SGUnited Mid-Career Pathways Programme.

FIGURE 12.12
Graduate Employment Outcomes

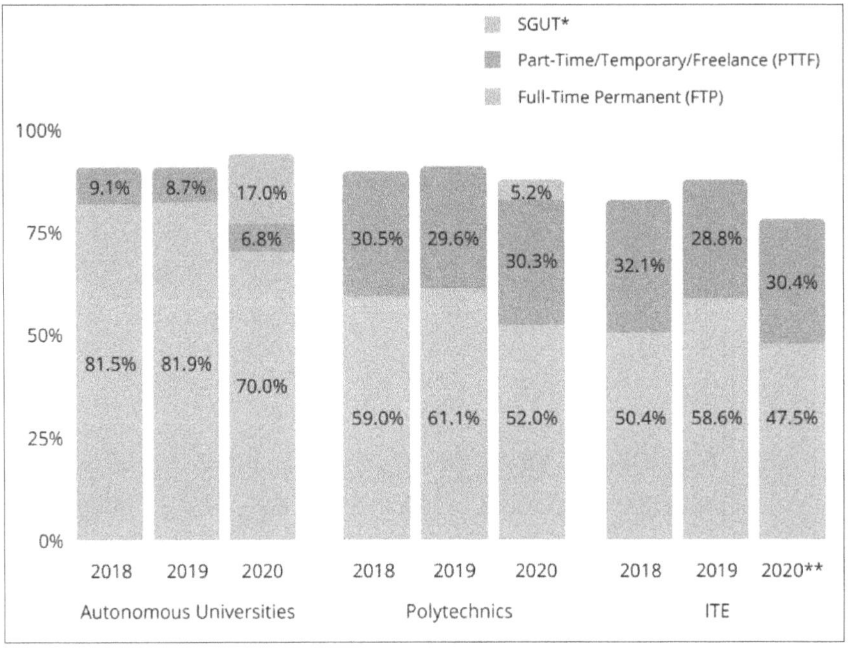

Source: Ministry of Finance (2022).

TABLE 12.5
Median Salaries of New Graduates in Full-Time, Permanent Employment

	Universities	*Polytechnics*	*ITE (Fresh)*	*ITE (Post-National Service)*
2018	S$3,500	S$2,350	S$1,700	S$2,200
2019	S$3,600	S$2,400	S$1,700	S$2,050
2020	S$3,700	S$2,400	S$1,720	S$2,200

Source: Ministry of Manpower.

The training provided under the SGUP-CT and the SGUS schemes has become a permanent feature of Singapore's training and placement ecosystem with the launch of a new SkillsFuture Career Transition Programme in April 2022. This is intended to strengthen support for mid-career workers, particularly those in their forties and fifties, through training, skills advisory, industry exposure and employment facilitation with government support. It is a "train and place" programme, and it will complement the Career Conversion Programmes offered by the Workforce Singapore Agency, which are mostly "place and train" (whereby a company first hires a worker before training commences). Through the programme, training in promising sectors will be scaled up.

ADDRESSING INEQUALITY

Addressing inequality has become a more urgent priority, given the impact of the Covid-19 pandemic on income and wealth distribution and its implications for social mobility. The fallout of the virus on jobs and incomes was highly uneven, with the impact on workers mirroring the impact on companies. Companies and workers heavily dependent on cross-border tourism and travel were worst affected, along with those providing in-person services or whose work required workers to be on site.

Data from the Ministry of Manpower's Comprehensive Labour Force Survey in June 2020 showed that lower-wage workers who were neither professional, managerial, executive nor technician (non-PMET) bore the brunt of income and job losses at the onset of the pandemic (Ministry of Manpower 2020).

Real median gross monthly income from work declined by 0.4 per cent between June 2019 and June 2020, compared with a 4.6 per cent decline for income in the twentieth percentile. The PMET unemployment rate rose by 0.6 percentage points to 3.5 per cent in June 2020 versus June 2019, while the non-PMET unemployment rate rose 1.7 percentage points to 6.4 per cent over the same period. This corroborates the results of a study by DBS bank, which found that lower-income earners (those earning S$2,999 and below per month), and those with less in savings, formed the bulk of bank customers whose incomes had declined substantially (Seah et al. 2020). While income inequality as measured by the household income Gini coefficient after taxes and transfers fell to a new low in 2020 due to sizeable government transfers (Figure 12.13),[14] inequality, particularly wealth inequality, remains a pressing concern.

The pandemic was accompanied by a surge in asset prices globally, spurred by unprecedented fiscal and monetary stimulus, particularly in the

FIGURE 12.13
Singapore's Resident Household Income Gini Coefficient

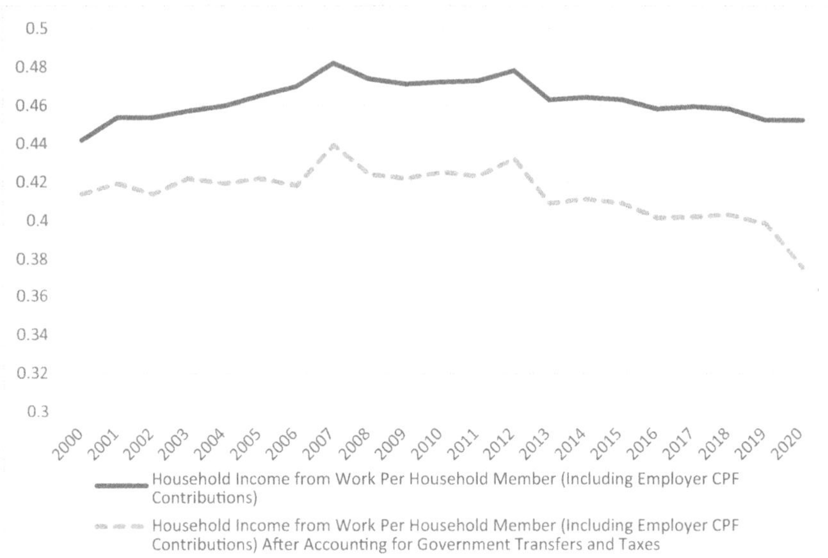

Source: Singapore Department of Statistics.

United States. This depressed interest rates and sent property and equity prices soaring. In the fourth quarter of 2020, Singapore's private residential property price index breached its previous all-time high (Figure 12.14), while the HDB Resale Price Index reached a new high in the third quarter of 2021 (Figure 12.15).[15]

The government recognized the need to uplift lower-income workers and households and commissioned a tripartite working group to develop proposals to improve their long-term prospects. This would build on the Workfare scheme and the Progressive Wage Model to boost incomes and provide for career progression by enhancing skills.[16]

At the National Day rally in August 2021, Prime Minister Lee Hsien Loong announced that the government would accept the tripartite workgroup's recommendation to extend the Progressive Wage Model to more sectors and occupations. It also implemented a requirement that all firms hiring foreign workers pay their local workers at least S$1,400 per month, a figure that can be revised upwards. With these measures, the

FIGURE 12.14
Private Residential Property Price Index

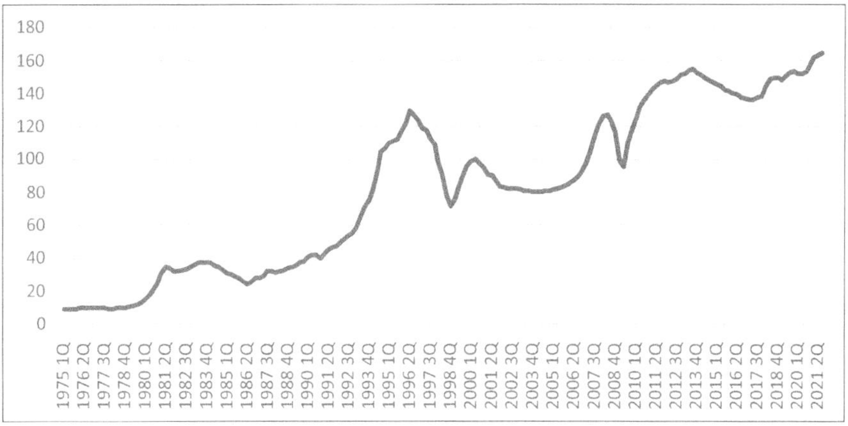

Source: Urban Redevelopment Board.

FIGURE 12.15
HDB Resale Price Index

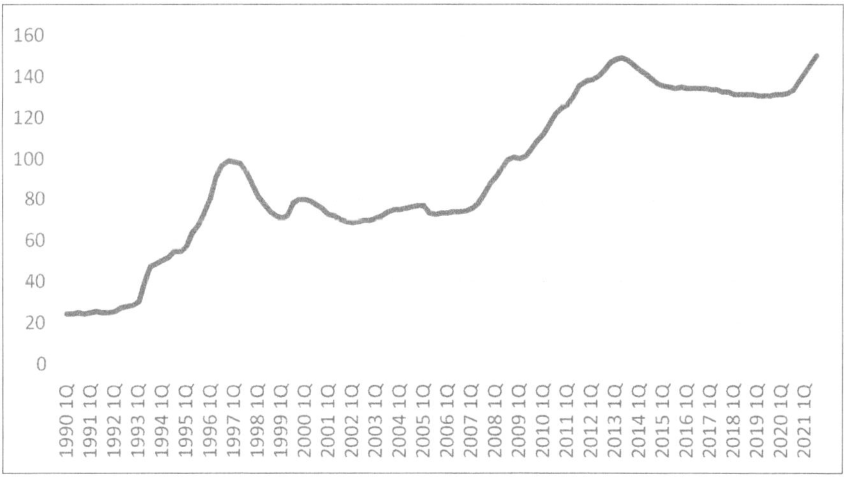

Source: Housing and Development Board.

Progressive Wage Model would cover more than eight in ten lower-wage workers (i.e. those in the bottom 20 per cent of the wage distribution). A new Progressive Wage Mark (an accreditation scheme that recognizes firms that pay progressive wages to lower-wage workers) was introduced to encourage the remaining firms to adopt the Progressive Wage Model, which would allow them to bid for government contracts.

In concept, wages under the Progressive Wage Model would rise in tandem with skills and productivity. In practice, however, there are limits to productivity gains in domestic services sectors such as cleaning and waste management. While higher productivity may partly offset business costs and better service may increase consumer willingness to pay, the higher wage cost would have to be shared between businesses and consumers, with the government providing transitional support. Hence, it will take broad societal consensus to grow wages sustainably through the Progressive Wage Model. To this end, it is hoped that greater public awareness of the important role played by cleaners and other frontline service workers during the Covid-19 crisis may bolster support for initiatives that benefit lower-income workers.

As announced in 2021 and elaborated on in Budget 2022, the Workfare Income Supplement, a wage supplement, was enhanced to provide greater support for lower-income workers. The eligibility criteria have been relaxed to enable more workers, including workers aged thirty to thirty-four, to benefit from the scheme.

In the lead up to Budget 2022, there was speculation as to whether Singapore would introduce new wealth taxes or reinstate the estate duty payable on death, which was abolished in 2008. The government opted instead to work within the existing framework of taxes on residential properties and luxury cars, given the practical difficulty of fairly assessing a person's net wealth, as well as the mobility of other forms of wealth across borders.

Residential property taxes were made more progressive, with the top 7 per cent in value of owner-occupied properties and all non-owner-occupied properties affected. This is estimated to be netting additional tax revenues of S$380 million more a year (Wong 2022). Concurrently, marginal personal income taxes were raised for those earning more than S$500,000 a year. This increase in personal income taxes for the top 1.2 per cent of wage earners was expected to raise about S$170 million in additional revenues each year (Wong 2022), a small amount compared with total personal income tax revenue of S$14.2 billion in the 2021 financial year.

IMPACT ON SINGAPORE'S OPENNESS AND GLOBAL CITY STATUS

While Singapore did well in insulating the population from Covid-19, some questioned how long the nation could afford to maintain strict immigration and social distancing measures (Power and Sim 2021). On reaching high vaccination rates, countries such as the United States and United Kingdom rolled back Covid-19 measures and allowed their economies to reopen. Meanwhile, reports surfaced that foreign professional workers were becoming frustrated with the difficulty of obtaining entry permits to Singapore, as well as the strict quarantine requirements on arrival in Singapore (Aravindan and Chen 2021). The periodic tightening of Covid-19 measures in 2021 also added uncertainty for businesses and constrained the recovery of domestic economic activity.

In August 2021, the authorities announced a four-stage reopening plan to reach the end goal of becoming a Covid-resilient nation. This would entail learning to live with Covid-19 as an endemic disease, allowing the economy and society to settle into a new normal. In his National Day message, Prime Minister Lee Hsien Loong referred to the "difficult balance" between protecting lives and livelihoods (Lee 2021). Health Minister Ong Ye Kung warned that Singaporeans would have to be "psychologically prepared" for infections, serious illnesses and deaths to rise as Singapore opened up, though the government would strive to minimize the incidence of serious illness (Lai 2021). The trade-off between lives and livelihoods would be mitigated by "public health measures, social discipline and financial support for families, workers and businesses," said the Prime Minister.

The Delta and Omicron infection waves in November 2021 and March 2022 respectively set back the timeframe for opening up; the government announced that Covid-19 safe management measures would be rolled back when the Omicron wave subsided. From 31 March 2022, all fully vaccinated people were permitted to enter Singapore without quarantining or having to book flights designated only for those who had been vaccinated, as had previously been the case. Further, for the fully vaccinated there was no longer a need for prior entry approval and there were no more quotas on the number of daily arrivals. From 26 April 2022, travellers entering

Singapore were not required to take a Covid-19 test before departure or on arrival.

Foreign Worker Inflow and Policy

The number of foreign workers in Singapore fell by some 230,000 between December 2019 and December 2021, with declines across all pass types (Figure 12.16).[17] This was due to border closures and limits on the entry or return of foreign workers, given capacity constraints in quarantine facilities.

The disease outbreak in foreign worker dormitories in 2020 also highlighted foreign worker housing and safety, with updated designs and more stringent safety and liveability standards for new foreign worker dormitories mandated since September 2021 (Ministry of Manpower 2021a).

With the gradual reopening of borders, the number of work permit holders (basic-skilled workers) increased modestly from 848,200 at end-2020 to 849,700 at end-2021. However, the number of S Pass (mid-skilled) and Employment Pass holders (higher-skilled workers) continued to decline. The tight labour market in 2022 triggered strong demand for foreign workers to fill vacancies and alleviate staffing shortages across various sectors.

FIGURE 12.16
Number of Foreign Workers by Work Pass Type

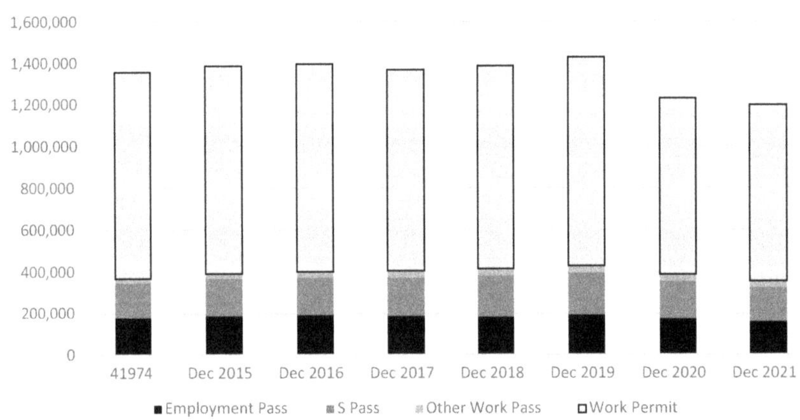

Source: Ministry of Manpower.

However, in order to manage reliance on foreign workers and to give firms sufficient impetus to build a local workforce, the government has taken steps to tighten the inflow of foreign workers and to improve complementarity between the local and foreign workforce. Policy measures adopted in Budget 2022 included raising the qualifying salaries to taken on higher and mid-skilled foreign workers under the Employment Pass and S Pass respectively. A points-based system has been introduced for Employment Pass applications which takes into account not just the worker's salary and qualifications, but also the employer's workforce diversity and its efforts to support local employment. Foreign worker levies paid by companies have also been raised for workers employed on an S Pass, and quotas for the number of Work Permits permitted to companies in the construction and process sectors have been lowered.

CONCLUSION

The Covid-19 pandemic has been the crisis of a generation. Beyond fiscal support, tackling the pandemic has required adroit policy navigation to protect both lives and livelihoods. It has also demanded a whole-of-society effort to minimize infections and limit the economic fallout from the disease. Following the government's release of a White Paper reviewing its Covid-19 response in March 2023, Deputy Prime Minister Lawrence Wong announced that a dedicated centre for public health would be set up, along with a planning team to prepare Singapore for the next pandemic (Prime Minister's Office 2023).

Covid-19 has had far-reaching ramifications for the economy and society in various dimensions, accelerating digitalization and altering our vision of the future of work. The pandemic required more businesses to adopt e-commerce and more local stores and food stalls to accept e-payments. This has positioned the economy well for the future, although the risks such as cybersecurity threats and scams must be addressed—this work has begun. Working from home has gained currency, with the public sector and many private sector firms allowing staff to work remotely several days a week, even beyond the pandemic. The increased prevalence of remote working has led to demand for more home space and larger properties. This will in turn affect the demand for commercial and private property.

Besides economic efficiency, public policy will have to increasingly take cognizance of resilience and equity as it anticipates future pandemics and other social and economic dislocations. This means the government must create resource buffers and redundancies, including dual-use infrastructure, and stockpile essential supplies. In social policy, Singapore needs greater protection for workers, and financial assurance for citizens, against the vicissitudes of economic and labour market cycles, along with measures to stem inequality and sustain social mobility.

Notes

1. Net assets accumulated during previous terms of government, which are protected under the Singapore Constitution.
2. Data from the Singapore Ministry of Health (accessed 31 December 2022) and the World Health Organization Coronavirus dashboard, cited in the Singapore government's *White Paper on Singapore's Response to Covid-19* (Prime Minister's Office 2023).
3. The previous largest economic contraction occurred during the Asian financial crisis in 1998, when real GDP declined by 2.2 per cent.
4. The business community joined a groundswell of civic solidarity prompted by the pandemic. The Ministry of Finance reported in June 2020 that more than 130 companies had returned a total of S$97 million in Jobs Support Scheme payments for April and May, while over 250 companies had pledged to decline future payments. Other companies donated their Jobs Support Scheme payments to charitable causes. Firms also joined with Singaporeans from all walks of life in making donations in cash or kind to support the needy and vulnerable or in showing appreciation for frontline workers in the Covid-19 fight.
5. It is a common practice in Singapore for employers to pay staff a bonus of one month's salary (informally called the thirteenth-month bonus) at the end of the year.
6. The SkillsFuture Series is a list of short, industry-relevant training programmes. It focuses on emerging skills in four economic growth areas: digital economy, green economy, the care sector and industry 4.0.
7. The work permit and S-Pass are foreign work passes for basic skilled and mid-skilled workers respectively.
8. Grocery vouchers were disbursed to citizens living in one- or two-room public housing. Those in public housing were also given additional utilities

rebates, on top of the S$100 rebate given to all Singaporeans. Those in public housing also received rebates on their service charges of between 1.5 to 3.5 months.

9. SGUnited is an initiative to foster resilience and solidarity among Singaporeans through volunteerism and community action. It was set up in response to the Covid-19 pandemic.
10. The Jobs Growth Incentive was extended by seven months to September 2021 in Budget 2021, and was subsequently further extended to cover hiring up to September 2022.
11. The Central Provident Fund is a mandatory savings scheme for employees, both Singapore citizens and permanent residents. It funds retirement, healthcare and housing.
12. The effective Jobs Support Scheme subsidy refers to the subsidy as a share of total local wages paid by the firm.
13. Tier 1 sectors are aerospace, aviation, tourism and the built environment. Tier 2 sectors are arts and entertainment, food services, land transport, marine and offshore, and retail.
14. This was the lowest since the government began tracking the Gini coefficient in 2000, though it fell to another new low in 2023.
15. About 80 per cent of Singapore households live in public housing, known as Housing and Development Board (HDB) flats. New flats are sold by the HDB to residents, who may then resell them after a minimum period of occupation.
16. The Progressive Wage Model is a mandatory wage structure that specifies wage floors and ladders in specific sectors and occupations with the aim of raising the wages and productivity of lower-income workers.
17. Foreign work passes comprise the Employment Pass for foreign professionals, managers and executives, the S Pass for mid-skilled workers, the Work Permit for basic-skilled workers and other work passes such as the Training Employment Pass and Training Work Permit.

References

Aravindan, Aradhana, and Chen Lin. 2021. "Expats Wait Anxiously as Singapore Weighs COVID-19 Reopening". Reuters, 5 August 2021. https://www.reuters.com/world/asia-pacific/expats-wait-anxiously-singapore-weighs-covid-19-reopening-2021-08-05/ (accessed 25 May 2024).

Channel NewsAsia. 2022. "11 People Charged over Defrauding Jobs Support Scheme, 2 Other COVID-19 Government Grants". 5 May 2022. https://

www.channelnewsasia.com/singapore/11-charged-fraud-jobs-support-scheme-covid-19-police-2665626 (accessed 25 May 2024).

Deutsche Welle. 2021. "Coronavirus Digest: Singapore Is Now the Most-Vaccinated Country". 29 August 2021. https://www.dw.com/en/coronavirus-digest-singapore-is-now-the-most-vaccinated-country/a-59016931 (accessed 25 May 2024).

Goh Yan Han. 2022. "Budget 2022: Singapore to Raise GST from 7% to 9% in Two Stages in 2023 and 2024". *Straits Times*, 21 February 2022. https://www.straitstimes.com/singapore/budget-2022-singapore-to-raise-gst-from-7-to-9-in-two-stages-in-2023-and-2024 (accessed 25 May 2024).

Heng Swee Keat. 2021a. "Budget 2021: Emerging Stronger Together". Ministry of Finance. https://www.mof.gov.sg/docs/librariesprovider3/budget2021/download/pdf/fy2021_budget_statement.pdf.

———. 2021b. "Utilisation Rates of Funds Set Aside to Help Families, Workers and Businesses during COVID-19 Pandemic". Written Reply to Parliamentary Question by Ms Foo Mee Har, 1 February 2021. https://www.mof.gov.sg/news-publications/parliamentary-replies/utilisation-rates-of-funds-set-aside-to-help-families-workers-and-businesses-during-covid-19-pandemic

Hui, Weng Tat, and Ruby Toh. 2014. *Growth with Equity in Singapore: Challenges and Prospects*. Conditions of Work and Employment Series, No. 48. Geneva: International Labour Office. https://webapps.ilo.org/wcmsp5/groups/public/---ed_protect/---protrav/---travail/documents/publication/wcms_244819.pdf

Inland Revenue Authority of Singapore and Enterprise Singapore. 2022. "More than $28.1 Billion Disbursed under Jobs Support Scheme since February 2020". News release, 29 March 2022. https://www.enterprisesg.gov.sg/-/media/esg/files/media-centre/media-releases/2022/march/mr01922_more-than-281-billion-disbursed-under-jobs-support-scheme29-mar-2022.pdf

Kahn, Lisa. 2010. "The Long-Term Labor Market Consequences of Graduating from College in a Bad Economy". *Labour Economics* 17, no. 2: 303–16.

Lai, Linette. 2021. "Singapore Must Be Prepared for More Covid-19 Infections, Deaths with Reopening: Ong Ye Kung". *Straits Times*, 2 September 2021. https://www.straitstimes.com/singapore/health/singapore-must-be-prepared-for-more-covid-19-infections-deaths-with-reopening (accessed 25 May 2024).

Lee, Hsien Loong. 2021. "National Day Message 2021". Prime Minister's Office Singapore, 8 August 2021. https://www.pmo.gov.sg/Newsroom/National-Day-Message-2021

Ministry of Finance. 2020. "Our Resilience Budget: Support Workers. Stabilise Businesses. Build Resilience". Version of 7 April 2020, 7 p.m. https://

www.mof.gov.sg/docs/librariesprovider3/budget2020/summary/fy2020_supplementary_audience_centric_infographic.pdf (accessed 25 May 2024).

———. 2021. "An Interim Assessment of the Impact of Key Covid-19 Budget Measures". Occasional Paper, February 2021. https://www.mof.gov.sg/docs/default-source/default-document-library/news-and-publications/featured-reports/interim-assessment---covid-19-budget-measures-(final).pdf

———. 2022. "Assessment of the Impact of Key Covid-19 Budget Measures". Ministry of Finance Occasional Paper, 17 February 2022. https://www.mof.gov.sg/docs/default-source/default-document-library/news-and-publications/featured-reports/assessment-of-the-impact-of-key-covid19-budget-measures-final.pdf?sfvrsn=ed7a98eb_2

Ministry of Manpower. 2020. *Labour Force in Singapore 2020: Impact of COVID-19 on the Labour Market.* Manpower Research and Statistics Department, Ministry of Manpower. https://stats.mom.gov.sg/iMAS_PdfLibrary/mrsd_2020LabourfForce.pdf

———. 2021a. "Improved Standards for New Migrant Worker Dormitories to Strengthen Public Health Resilience and Enhance Liveability". News release, 17 September 2021. https://www.mom.gov.sg/newsroom/press-releases/2021/0917-improved-standards-for-new-migrant-worker-dormitories

———. 2021b. "Jobs Situation Report 20th Edition". News release, 31 March 2021. https://www.mom.gov.sg/newsroom/press-releases/2021/0331-jobs-situation-report-20th-edition

Ministry of Social and Family Development. 2021. "Covid-19 Recovery Grant Extended until 31 Dec 2022 to Provide Further Support". News release, 21 December 2021. https://www.msf.gov.sg/media-room/Pages/Covid-19-RECOVERY-GRANT-EXTENDED-UNTIL-31-DEC-2022-TO-PROVIDE-FURTHER-SUPPORT.aspx

Ong, Justin Guang-Xi. 2022. "The Big Read: Fancy Spending Weeks on a Tropical Island? Singapore Aims to Shed 'Stopover' Tag Amid Tourism Market Shifts". Channel NewsAsia, 25 April 2022. https://www.channelnewsasia.com/singapore/big-read-singapore-aims-shed-stopover-tag-amid-tourism-market-shifts-2642741(accessed 25 May 2024).

Oreopoulos, Philip, Till von Wachter, and Andrew Heisz. 2012. "The Short- and Long-Term Career Effects of Graduating in a Recession". *American Economic Journal: Applied Economics* 4, no. 1: 1–29.

Power, John, and Dewey Sim. 2021. "Should Hong Kong and Singapore Relent from Tight Covid-19 Rules to Retain Foreign Talent?". *South China Morning Post*, 20 June 2021. https://www.scmp.com/week-asia/economics/

article/3137905/should-hong-kong-and-singapore-act-appease-expats-chafing-tight (accessed 25 May 2024).

Prime Minister's Office. 2023. *White Paper on Singapore's Response to Covid-19: Lessons for the Next Pandemic*. 8 March 2023. https://www.gov.sg/docs/default-source/media/gov/covid-19-white-paper/publication/white_paper_on_singapore_response_to_covid19_130323.pdf?sfvrsn=c33ec046_1

Public Service Division. 2020. "Civil Service Year-End Payments 2020". 27 November 2020. https://www.psd.gov.sg/newsroom/media-releases/civil-service-year-end-payments-2020/.

Seah, Irvin, Yeo Kee San, Lim Rui Wen, Lorna Tan, Yong Woon Bing, and Chung Wei Le. 2020. *Same Storm, Different Boat: Impact of Covid-19 on Financial Wellness in Singapore*. DBS Asian Insights Sector Briefing 89. https://www.scribd.com/document/644172857/DBS-200818-insights-sg-financial-wellness-pdf.

Singapore Government Agency. 2020. "Solidarity Budget 2020: Further Support for Businesses through the Circuit Breaker Period". 6 April 2020. https://www.gov.sg/article/solidarity-budget-2020-further-support-for-businesses-through-the-circuit-breaker-period (accessed 25 May 2024).

Tay, Tiffany Fumiko. 2020. "Singaporeans to Get $320 Million in Tourism Vouchers to Boost Sector". *Straits Times*, 19 August 2020. https://www.straitstimes.com/singapore/singaporeans-to-get-320-million-in-tourism-vouchers-to-boost-sector-says-heng-swee-keat (accessed 25 May 2024).

Today Online. 2020. "Sheng Siong's Q1 Profit Up Nearly 50% on Back of 'Elevated' Covid-19 Demand; Staff to Get Additional Month of Salary". 29 April 2020. https://www.todayonline.com/singapore/sheng-siongs-q1-profit-nearly-50-back-elevated-covid-19-demand-staff-get-additional-month (accessed 25 May 2024).

Wong, Lawrence. 2022. "Budget 2022 Speech". Ministry of Finance. https://www.mof.gov.sg/docs/librariesprovider3/budget2022/download/pdf/fy2022_budget_statement.pdf

13

ECONOMIC RELIEF AND STIMULUS

Evidence from Thailand

Archanun Kohpaiboon, Juthathip Jongwanich
and Mayoon Boonyarat

INTRODUCTION

The Covid-19 pandemic was, first and foremost, a human tragedy. Most countries prioritized public health and launched various measures—chiefly lockdowns, social distancing and workplace closures—to reduce the spread of the virus. These policies resulted in unprecedented economic impacts on individuals and businesses: access to essential services, food and livelihoods was disrupted, economic activity slowed, firms defaulted and jobs were lost.

Countries also responded with decisive economic policies to cushion the short-term human costs of the downturn induced by the pandemic response. Global fiscal support of US$14 trillion contributed to saving lives and livelihoods and mitigated the effects of the pandemic on consumption and output. Fiscal response, nonetheless, varied greatly across countries, from 2 per cent of gross domestic production (GDP) in Egypt to 46 per cent in Italy (World Bank 2022b). Combined with the economic contraction that caused lower revenues, such support led to a rise in national deficits and public debt. Government budget deficits for 2020 were projected at 13.3 per cent for advanced economies, 10.3 per cent for emerging market and middle-income economies and 5.7 per cent for low-income developing countries (ibid.). Global public debt soared to an estimated 98 per cent of GDP at the end of 2020, compared with 84 per cent in 2019 (Gaspar et al. 2021; World Bank 2022b). Despite the decisive economic policy responses, together with a massive amount of fiscal stimulus, the world experienced the largest global economic crisis in more than a century (World Bank 2022b).

A wide range of policy measures were introduced to confront the short-term impacts of the pandemic. These included direct income support programmes, temporary debt relief (i.e., debt moratoriums for households and businesses, regulatory forbearance for banks) and tax breaks for firms and individuals. These measures were introduced differently across countries, depending on the availability of resources and the specific nature of risks each country faced. In the context of developing countries, implementing these measures was in some cases challenging as social safety net schemes are nascent. Further, developing-country governments also often lack basic information that would allow them to identify and reach the vulnerable and those eligible for support during a crisis, thereby hindering policy efforts. As a result, the magnitude of fiscal resources spent by a country during the crisis might not be a reliable indicator of the impact of Covid-19 on its economy.

The exceptional circumstances of Covid-19 underscore the need for country case studies to analyse government responses to the crisis, challenges that emerged in implementing these measures and policy lessons to be applied in the next crisis. So far, country-specific analysis remains sparse (OECD 2021; Subramaniam et al. 2021). Against this backdrop, this chapter aims to reveal how the Thai government responded to the pandemic, with an emphasis on economic relief and stimuli.

The chapter begins with an overview of the four waves of Covid-19 in Thailand and the government responses for containing infection. This is followed by an overview and discussion of the economic relief and stimulus measures implemented.

COVID-19 SITUATION, BORDER CONTROLS AND MOBILITY RESTRICTIONS

Thailand was the first country affected by Covid-19 after China: it is a popular destination for Chinese tourists. Thailand's first confirmed Covid-19 case was reported on 13 January 2020. At the end of June 2022, there were around 2,000 new cases per day and the cumulative number of infected cases had reached 4.5 million, ranking Thailand twenty-sixth in the world.[1]

Up to June 2022, Thailand had experienced four waves of Covid-19: 15 March 2020 to 30 April 2020; 15 December 2020 to 15 March 2021; April 2021 to December 2021; and January 2022 onwards (Figure 13.1). The government did not declare an end to the fourth wave but at the end of May 2022 stopped reporting positive Covid-19 cases and began to report only cases requiring hospitalization (*Bangkok Post* 2022b). The most severe wave was the third—April 2021 to December 2021—during which new daily cases peaked at 23,418 cases on 13 August 2021. New daily cases remained above 5,000 until December 2021, resulting in more than 20,000 cumulative deaths. This represented two-thirds of total deaths over the four waves (Figure 13.2). Even though the increase in infected cases in the fourth wave was higher than in the third, the fourth was dominated by the Omicron variant which was less severe than the Delta variant of the third wave.

Like other countries, Thailand imposed border controls and social distancing measures to suppress viral transmission. The former was managed with a conservative stance, whereas the latter was imposed pragmatically to ensure businesses could remain in operation.

When new cases surged in early March 2020, border control was promptly imposed, taking effect from 19 March 2020. Thailand did well in containing Covid-19 infection from April 2020 to November 2020 but reopened its border in a slow and laborious manner. Reopening schemes were associated with strict procedures that continued to constrain the entry of foreign visitors.[2] The first attempt to reopen the border was on 8 December 2020. People from fifty-six countries could apply for a standard thirty-day visa, which could be extended to forty-five days, or could apply for a Special Tourist Visa. All tourists were required to have a negative Covid-19 test result within seventy-two hours before their arrival, take a

FIGURE 13.1
New Daily Covid-19 Cases from 15 March 2020 to 30 June 2022

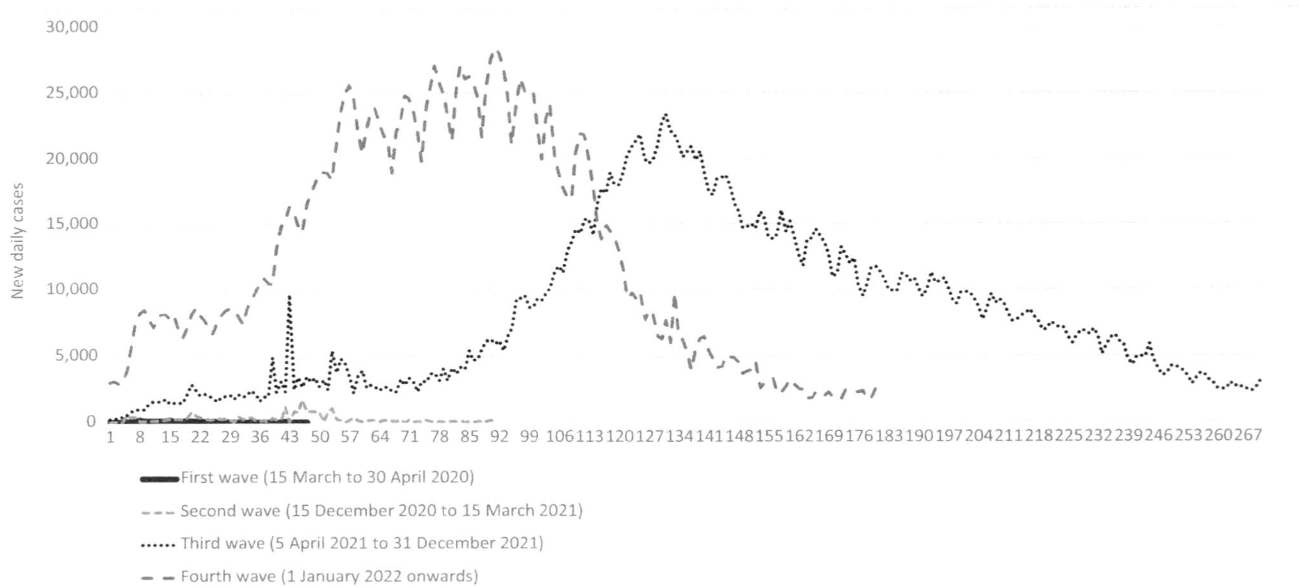

Source: Based on data from the World Health Organization at https://covid19.who.int/data (accessed 30 June 2022).

FIGURE 13.2
Cumulative Deaths Caused by Covid-19 from April 2021 to June 2022

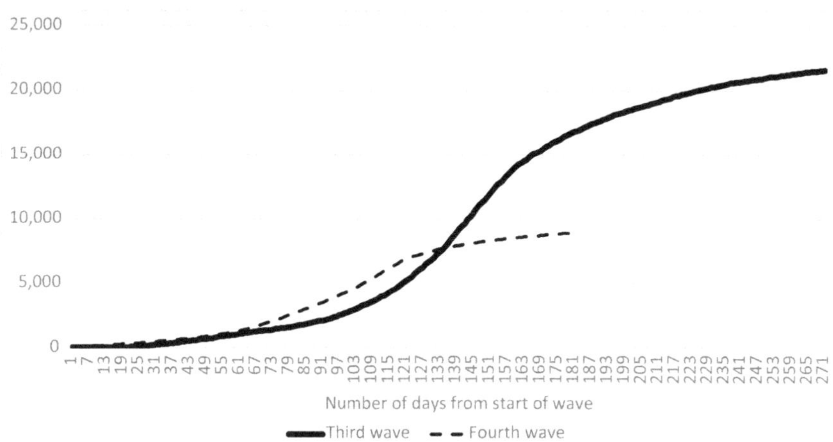

Source: Based on data from the World Health Organization at https://covid19.who.int/data (accessed 30 June 2022).

second test on landing in Thailand and quarantine for fourteen days on arrival. If visitors tested positive in their arrival test, they were required to quarantine for fourteen days in a state hospital. Such procedures were not practical for temporary visitors or those on short trips, meaning that the border was still de facto closed.

In July 2021, a pragmatic reopening scheme began for selected tourist destinations. It began with the Phuket sandbox scheme, which allowed vaccinated international travellers[3] to visit Phuket without quarantining on arrival. International arrivals had to have tested negative for the virus upon arrival. If they went on to other destinations in Thailand, they needed to spend at least fourteen nights in Phuket before leaving. The travellers were also required to download an app allowing their location to be traced. It was essentially a field experiment before a wider reopening—if there were no noticeable surges in COVID-19-infected cases in Phuket.

After fifteen days a similar scheme was launched in five other tourist destinations: Surat Thani province (with the tourist destinations of Samui Island, Pha Ngan Island and Tao Island) on 15 July 2021; Krabi province (with Phi Phi Island) on 30 July 2021; Chonburi province (Pattaya), Prachuap Khiri Khan province (Hua Hin) on 1 October 2021 and Perchaburi province (Cha-am) on 1 October 2021.[4] The schemes applied elsewhere in Thailand were different in terms of the required quarantine period.[5] Five provinces—Bangkok, Chonburi, Chiang Mai, Prachuap Khiri Khan (Hua Hin) and Phetchaburi—were forced to delay reopening from 1 October 2021 to 1 November 2021 because their vaccination rate was too low, whereas the others reopened on 1 October 2021.

Even though the partial reopening of some provinces with tourist destinations did not fulfil the target of 100,000 international arrivals,[6] it revitalized the country's tourism sector (*Bangkok Post* 2022a). Such experiments also made a strong case for the government to continue gradually reopening the border. Eventually, by 11 May 2022, fully vaccinated international visitors entering Thailand were no longer required to quarantine in a hotel and take a reverse transcription polymerase chain reaction (RT-PCR) Covid-19 test upon arrival, and other requirements were also eased, such as the amount of health insurance cover, which was reduced from US$20,000 to US$10,000 (*Bangkok Post* 2022c).

The government was fully aware of the adverse economic impact of nationwide lockdowns as a social distancing measure, so these were used as a last resort to combat the spread of the virus. The first nationwide lockdown was for the entire month of April 2020 to combat the first wave. The full national lockdown, including a curfew from 10:00 p.m. to 4:00 a.m., and a further stay-home policy were introduced (Nattadhanai et al. 2021; OECD 2020b). As illustrated by Google mobility data, there was a significant reduction in people's movements in April 2020 to major transit coach and railway stations (60 per cent) and workplaces (30 per cent), and a moderate increase in people staying in their residential areas (20 per cent) (Nattadhanai et al. 2021, Figure 4). When the number of daily cases dropped sufficiently, lockdown measures were eased, and cases and deaths were closely monitored.[7]

Experience from the management of the first wave of the pandemic, during which the national lockdown induced steep economic hardship, led the government to impose only a partial lockdown during the second wave: it locked down only Samut Sakhon province, the epicentre of this outbreak. This measure worked well in containing local contagion as the virus spread in the second wave was relatively short and was concentrated around Samut Sakhon.

When the third wave arrived, the government was slow to impose a nationwide lockdown even when new cases started to surge in mid-April 2021. A nationwide lockdown was imposed on 28 June 2021. In early August the government began to gradually unwind the lockdown (Directive No. 30 published on 1 August 2021). During this third wave, provinces were categorized into three zones according to the number of new cases: (1) maximum and strictly controlled areas/dark-red zone (twenty-nine provinces); (2) strictly controlled areas/red zone (thirty-seven provinces) and (3) controlled areas/orange zone (eleven provinces).

In dark-red zone provinces (defined as new daily cases continuing to rise), the night-time curfew (9:00 p.m. to 4:00 a.m.) remained unchanged. People were asked to go out only if necessary, for example, to shop for food and medical supplies, to visit the doctor or to receive a vaccine. In red zone provinces, restaurants and eateries were allowed to offer dine-in services until 11:00 p.m., but alcohol was prohibited. In orange zone areas, the controls were eased further.

From 1 August 2021, controls on local movement were further relaxed, although there was another wave of the virus spread, the fourth wave from January 2022. New Year festivities (31 December/1 January), as well as traditional New Year (Songkran) in April, were allowed. At the end of June 2022, controls on local movements were abolished following a reduction in new cases and hospitalizations, with 52.9 million people or 89 per cent of the population having received two vaccine doses (WHO 2022). Outdoor mask-wearing was made voluntary, although people were advised to continue wearing a face mask in crowded places such as public transport, markets and concert venues, or if they had certain health conditions.

Social distancing was supplemented with an ad hoc contact tracing scheme to identify those who had been in contact with Covid-19 patients. This scheme was well-managed and effective in the first two waves due to the longstanding strength of the public health system and was run by more than 1,000 nurses and officers, including epidemiologists (WHO 2020). The staff were stationed at provincial health offices and district hospitals and were networked with subdistrict health centres. In Bangkok, the scheme's staff were linked to the Department of Disease Control and the Bangkok Metropolitan Administration. At the subdistrict level, more than 1 million village health volunteers and staff from subdistrict health centres supported the contact tracing scheme (WHO 2020). Village health volunteers helped to assess people's risk of exposure to infection and liaised with the subdistrict health centres. The cost of lab testing and treatment was fully subsidized by the government in all cases, regardless of nationality. This ensured that tracing and testing measures were effective in combatting the contagion in the first and second waves, especially in rural areas where understanding of the virus may have been lower (Nattadhanai et al. 2021).

However, during the third wave, when cases were higher, the contact tracing scheme was inadequate. The World Health Organization (WHO 2020) highlighted Thailand's limited fiscal resources, stating that this prevented the country from having an overarching national infection prevention and control programme. Most healthcare facilities conducted activities using their own limited resources (WHO 2020, p. 7). This constrained the country's capability to combat a large surge in infections, as experienced during the third wave.

The government also enhanced laboratory capacity, scaling up PCR analysis capacity from 80 certified laboratories in April 2020 to 230 in October 2020 (154 public and 76 private laboratories), covering most of Thailand. It also installed intensive care units and stockpiled personal protective equipment and medicines. This was to enhance healthcare capacity for Covid-19 and to combat any future infectious diseases.

ECONOMIC RELIEF AND STIMULUS

Measures to prevent the spread of the virus slowed economic activity, and unemployment in Thailand doubled from 1.1 per cent in the first quarter of 2020 to 1.9 per cent in the third quarter of 2020. In the first quarter of 2023, the unemployment rate had returned to the pre-pandemic level.[8]

Like other countries, the Thai government swiftly launched measures to cushion the effects of the pandemic, beginning in March 2020. From an accounting standpoint, it implemented two broad categories of fiscal policy responses: *above-the-line* measures (involving government deficit spending or borrowing) and *liquidity support* (Gaspar et al. 2021). The former refers to increases in government expenditure and tax deductions that directly impact economic activity via fiscal multipliers, all of which are reflected in the fiscal balance (IMF 2020, Box 1). The latter encompasses equity injections, loans, asset purchase or debt assumptions and contingent liabilities (guarantees and quasi-fiscal operations). Figure 13.3 illustrates how fiscal resources and financial sector interventions were deployed around the world to combat the adverse economic effects of the Covid-19 crisis.

The total value of the policy measures the Thai government launched between January 2020 and September 2021 was THB2.5 trillion or 14.2 per cent of the 2019 GDP. Some of these measures, while budgeted for the full year 2022, did not operate beyond June 2022 or were repurposed more generally for cost of living and other social assistance.[9] Above-the-line measures totalled THB1.8 trillion, equivalent to 10.6 per cent of the 2019 GDP, whereas liquidity support amounted to THB0.67 trillion or 3.9 per

FIGURE 13.3
Covid-19 Responses: Fiscal Measures in Selected Countries (Percentage of 2020 GDP)

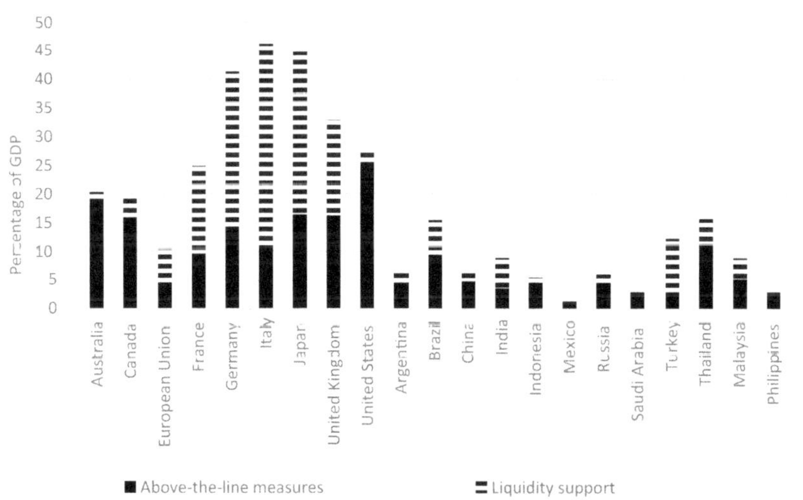

Note: The average figures for above-the-line measures provided by advanced and emerging market economies were 12.9 per cent and 4.3 per cent, respectively. Average figures for liquidity measures were 14.8 per cent and 3.3 per cent for advanced and emerging market economies, respectively. The numbers are based on official estimates covering cumulative spending in 2020 and the first five months of 2021.

Source: Based on data from the IMF Database of Fiscal Policy Responses to Covid-19, available at https://www.imf.org/en/Topics/imf-and-covid19/Fiscal-Policies-Database-in-Response-to-Covid-19 (accessed 30 June 2022).

cent of the 2019 GDP.[10] To finance these measures, Thailand borrowed THB1.5 trillion, THB1 trillion in 2020 and THB0.5 trillion in May 2021. Thailand's fiscal policy responses were far larger than the standard in emerging market economies. This is particularly true of above-the-line measures, where the size of Thailand's fiscal measures was more or less in line with the average of advanced economies (Figure 13.3).

Such a magnitude of fiscal measures by Thailand seems sensible for at least two reasons. First, by middle-income-country standards, Thailand's informal sector is a sizeable share of total employment. In 2018, informal workers accounted for 63.2 per cent of Thailand's employed population (Figure 13.4). This is relatively large compared to middle-income and urbanizing economies, in which the labour in the subsistence agricultural sector in rural areas is relatively small. However, Thailand's large informal economy is largely driven by rural-urban migration, often to engage in petty trade or work for microenterprises trading at business hubs or tourism spots in and around Bangkok. These businesses tend to rely on social interaction, such that their workers are likely to be adversely affected by measures preventing the virus from spreading. More importantly, they were not, and still are not, protected by Thailand's social safety nets. The country's Covid-19 relief measures are needed to fill these gaps.

Second, sizeable fiscal measures were advisable given the importance of tourism to the Thai economy. Tourism accounted for nearly 20 per cent of total exports pre-pandemic (i.e., 2018–19) and was also the sector most adversely affected by Covid-19 restrictions (Figure 13.5). Social distancing and border closures imposed in many countries to suppress the infection caused sudden stops of international arrivals.

Generally, all the packages can be broadly divided into two main categories and their respective components: (1) direct fiscal measures, comprising economic relief and cash transfers, economic stimulus and co-payment and sector-targeted schemes and (2) indirect fiscal measures, comprising liquidity support and other assistance.

Direct Fiscal Measures

Economic Relief and Cash Transfers

The main measure of economic relief was cash handouts, known in Thai

FIGURE 13.4
Informal Employment and Per Capita Income

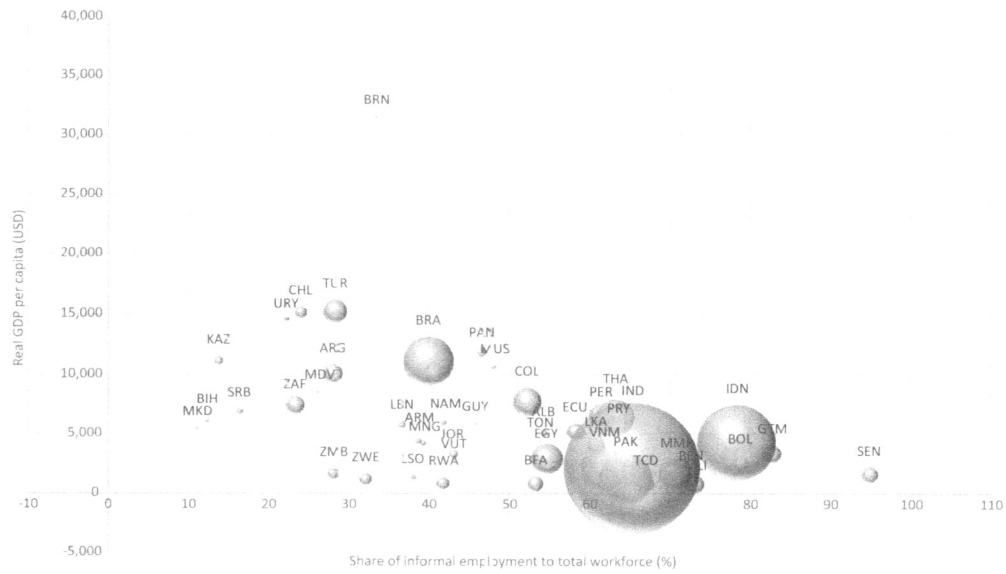

Note: Bubble size indicates number of workers in the informal sector. ALB: Albania; ARG: Argentina; ARM: Armenia; BEN: Benin; BFA: Burkina Faso; BIH: Bosnia and Herzegovina; BOL: Bolivia; BRA: Brazil; BRN: Brunei Darussalam; CHL: Chile; COL: Colombia; ECU: Ecuador; EGY: Egypt, Arab Rep.; GTM: Guatemala; GUY: Guyana; IDN: Indonesia; IND: India; JOR: Jordan; KAZ: Kazakhstan; LBN: Lebanon; LKA: Sri Lanka; LSO: Lesotho; MDV: Maldives; MKD: North Macedonia; MLI: Mali; MMR: Myanmar; MNG: Mongolia; MUS: Mauritius; NAM: Namibia; PAK: Pakistan; PAN: Panama; PER: Peru; PRY: Paraguay; RWA: Rwanda; SEN: Senegal; SRB: Serbia; TCD: Chad; THA: Thailand; TON: Tonga; TUR: Turkey; URY: Uruguay; VNM: Vietnam; VUT: Vanuatu; ZAF: South Africa; ZMB: Zambia; ZWE: Zimbabwe.

Sources: Data on real GDP per capita and workforce are from the World Bank's World Development Indicators database https://databank.worldbank.org/source/world-development-indicators (accessed 15 June 2022). Data on informal workers are from the International Labour Organization at https://ilostat.ilo.org/data/# (accessed 15 June 2022).

FIGURE 13.5
International Tourism as a Percentage of Total Exports, 2018–19

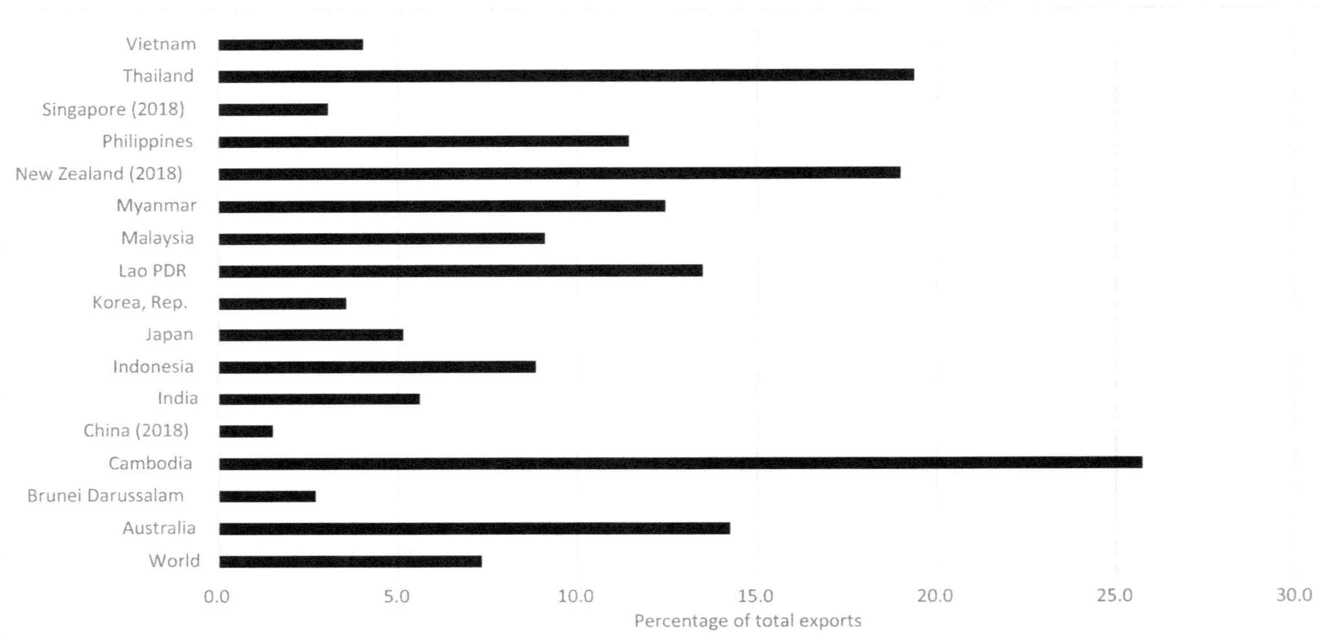

Source: Based on data from the World Bank's World Development Indicators database https://databank.worldbank.org/source/world-development-indicators (accessed 15 June 2022).

as "Rao Mai Thing Kan", meaning "no one left behind". This scheme, operating from April to June 2020, was introduced after the first and only national lockdown was imposed (during the first wave). It offered THB5,000 a month, or 75 per cent of the minimum wage, for each person working in the informal sector, including temporary workers, contract workers and the self-employed (NNT 2020).[11] It aimed to supplement income and discourage workers from leaving the capital and possibly spreading the virus. The total budget was initially set at THB45 billion to cover 3 million workers.

The main problem with this scheme was that the government underestimated the number of affected workers. By 1 April 2020, nearly 20 million people had registered for the scheme, far higher than the targeted 3 million (Yuda 2020). Together with poor communication on how to receive the money, this underestimation ignited public frustration. As a consequence, at the end of April, the Cabinet approved an extension to the scheme to cover 16 million people in total (NNT 2020).[12]

A similar scheme was implemented for 10 million farmers from May to July 2020. The total budget for cash handouts to farmers was THB390 billion, accounting for 22 per cent of all above-the-line measures. Also, some 6.78 million infants, seniors and disabled people were each provided with THB1,000 a month for three months, while 1.16 million people holding the state welfare card were given extra financial assistance on top of their monthly living allowances.

Company workers are protected under the Social Security System. Workers furloughed because of Covid-19 were eligible to receive 62 per cent of their daily wages for up to ninety days. Thailand's Social Security System has a wage ceiling of THB15,000 a month and hence the maximum amount offered per worker was THB9,300 a month. Employers were required to confirm that the business had closed due to Covid-19, and this led to some delays in receiving benefits (World Bank 2022a). By 29 May 2022, 1.4 million salaried employees, representing approximately 8 per cent of the 15.9 million enrolled in Thailand's Social Security System, had made claims on their unemployment insurance; 1.29 million claims were approved. It is worth noting that this funding comes from the Social Security Fund, to which employers and employees contribute—it is not government funding.

The second round of cash handouts was offered from January and June 2021. The government addressed problems and shortcomings experienced in the first round. In particular, this time the scheme covered almost all vulnerable people and made use of e-wallets to control how money was spent. The interventions began with the Rao Chana scheme (meaning "we win"), introduced on 29 January 2021. It offered e-money of THB3,500 per month for February and March 2021, which had to be spent by 31 May 2021. E-money was for buying necessities (foods, beverages and other services) from registered shops. Rao Chana covered 30 million individuals, including vulnerable people who were not eligible for any other social safety net scheme, and the poor.[13] Notably, 14 million holders of the state welfare card were also eligible for the second cash handout; they received up to THB2,800 (*Bangkok Post* 2021b).

Two programmes supplemented Rao Chana. The first, Rao Rak Kan (meaning "we love each other"), assisted firms in keeping their operations and jobs. First, company employees under section 33 of the Social Security System were targeted, covering 9 million employees. Each employee was offered THB4,000 in total, receiving THB1,000 a week from 22 March 2021 to 12 April 2021. The second programme targeted self-employed workers or freelancers who contributed to the Social Security Fund (sections 39 and 40)—an estimated 3.5 million workers. Each was offered THB3,500 a month in February and March 2021. Those who had not registered with the Social Security Office could do so to qualify for it. The total budget of Rao Chana, Rao Rak Kan and the scheme targeting the self-employed and freelancers was THB232 billion, representing 12.8 per cent of above-the-line measures (World Bank 2021).

Shortly after the onset of the third wave, the government extended the third round of cash handouts. Under Rao Chana, an additional THB2,000 was offered, split into two and transferred to each employee in the weeks of 21 and 28 May. A further THB2,000 was offered to each employee under section 33 (Rao Rak Kan). By the end of June, the total budget for the third round was THB273.5 billion, and it had covered 27.2 million people. The third wave of the pandemic began in April 2021, and, as the number of new cases was still continuing to increase in July 2021, the government launched the fourth round of cash handouts on 6 July 2021 (World Bank 2021). This was offered only to certain areas and economic activities, based on infection rates. Out of twenty-nine provinces in the dark-red zone, only ten were eligible.[14]

Under the third round, Rao Rak Kan provided employees with an additional THB2,500 a month for two months, while the self-employed and freelancers were entitled to THB5,000 each. In addition, companies with employees not covered by the Social Security Scheme had to register them by July 2021. Companies received support for their employees (THB3,000 for each employee but not more than 200 employees) and for their owners. The transfer was made in August 2021. The packages were slightly modified in August 2021 because only 40.5 per cent of the total budget was used. The modification included an extension to the registration deadline, and this time covered all twenty-nine provinces in the dark-red zone (Cabinet Resolution, 9 August 2021).

Despite the surge of the fourth wave, strict control of local movement was not imposed, and no further cash handouts were given. Table 13.1 presents the summary of cash handouts in the first three waves of Covid-19 infections.

Economic Stimulus

The government also launched the stimulus package in the hope of creating more demand to cushion the negative economic shock of the Covid-19 crisis. In line with standard Keynesian measures, this direct government expenditure recognized that mobility restrictions and commercial shutdown had constrained the capacity for private investment or financial incentives to spur economic recovery.

Initially, the stimulus package was set at THB358 billion, or 60 per cent of the total Covid-19 budget of THB600 billion (covering the stimulus package, economic relief and healthcare expenses). The stimulus package was implemented slowly, whereas the other two components were spent urgently to combat the virus spread. Some budget for the stimulus package was reallocated to economic relief and healthcare. By September 2021, the share of the stimulus package in the total Covid-19 budget had fallen to 22.7 per cent.

At the end of May 2021, the government borrowed an additional THB0.5 trillion as the Covid-19 crisis continued.[15] Of this, THB170 billion was allocated to the stimulus package, returning its total budget to

TABLE 13.1
Cash Handout Schemes from April 2020 to September 2021

	Company Employees (8.1 million Workers)	*Freelancers and Self-employed (3.5 million Workers)*	*Those Not in Social Security System (33 million Workers)*
First wave of Covid-19: (15 March 2020 to 30 April 2020)			
Amount	Maximum THB9,300 a month	THB5,000 a month	THB5,000 a month
Duration	Three months	Three months	Three months
Conditions	Business closure declared by the government	Approved by government	Approved by government
Start of Assistance	Standard procedure	May 2020	May 2020
Second wave (15 December 2020 to 15 March 2021)			
Amount	THB1,000 a week	THB3,500 a month	THB3,500 a month
Duration	Four weeks	Two months	Two months
Conditions	Company remains operating and employees working	n.a.	n.a.
Start of Assistance	March 2021	February 2021	February 2021
Third wave (April 2021 to December 2021)			
Amount	Two rounds of handouts: THB1,000 a week; THB2,500 a month	THB5,000	THB1,000 a week
Duration	Two weeks; two months	One month	Two weeks
Conditions	None	None	n.a.
Start of Assistance	21, 28 May 2021; August and September 2021	September 2021	21 May 2021

Source: Cabinet resolutions (various dates).

around THB358 billion. The rest financed healthcare measures (especially acquiring Covid-19 vaccines) and economic relief.

The government used the budget for the economic stimulus package slowly. Figure 13.6 presents the budget utilization rate (the share of approved to total planned budget). It increased from 35.7 per cent in January 2021 to 38.9 per cent in May 2021. It then surged to 98 per cent in June 2021 due to the budget reallocation and returned to its previous trend in July. The utilization rate reached 48 per cent in November 2021 and 70 per cent in June 2022.

Public funds for economic stimulus were directed at various objectives, such as promoting a coffee farming project (THB0.9 million) and small and medium-sized enterprises (SMEs) in Nonthaburi province (THB1 million), and strengthening the production capacity of mulberries (THB3 million). Despite high local content, they were small and it was hard to stimulate aggregate demand countrywide. They were also slowly implemented. Hence, the efficacy of cushioning the negative economic shock induced by Covid-19 was limited.

Co-paying and Targeted Measures

Another set of policy measures involved co-payment by recipients and targeting of beneficiaries by sector or function, as distinct from general assistance. Some partial subsidies were offered in which the recipients had to co-pay to be eligible for the support, and among these, notable interventions were specific to tourism and domestic consumption.

The first measure was for buying necessities. It was known as the half-half programme: the government paid 50 per cent of the cost of food, drink and general goods purchases in a subsidy worth up to THB150 per person per day.[16] Phase 1 of this subsidy was implemented from 23 October 2020 to 31 December 2020 with a ceiling of THB3,000. The scheme was extended three times: phase 2 ran from 1 January 2021 to 31 March 2021, phase 3 from 1 July 2021 to 31 December 2021 and phase 4 from 1 February 2022 to 30 April 2022. The ceiling varied across phases, increasing to THB3,500 in phase 2, then dropping to THB1,500 and THB1,200 in phases 3 and 4, respectively. Phases 1 to 3 involved around 1.5 million beneficiaries and resulted in THB223.9 billion in spending, 48 per cent of which was the government subsidy. The government

FIGURE 13.6
Covid-19 Response: Economic Stimulus from May 2020 to June 2022

Panel A: First Round of Borrowing, THB1 trillion (Emergency Decree Issued in 2020)

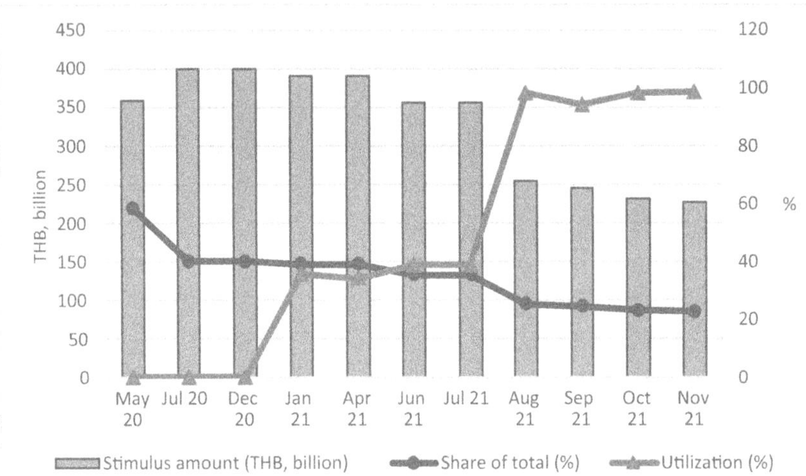

Panel B: Second Round of Borrowing, THB0.5 trillion (Emergency Decree Issued in 2021)

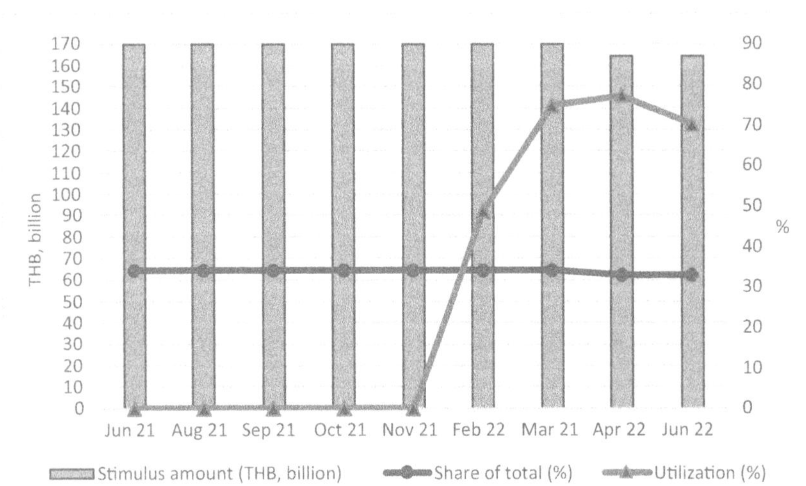

Source: Cabinet resolutions (various dates).

TABLE 13.2
Dual Purpose Measures

Schemes	*Duration*	*Total value*	*Purposes*
Half–half	Phase 1: 1 23 October 2020 to 31 December 2020 Phase 2: 1 January 2021 to 31 March 2021; Phase 3: 1 July 2021 to 31 December 2021; Phase 4: 1 February 2022 to 30 April 2022	Phase 1: THB3,500 per person (THB150 per day); Phase 2: THB3,500 per person (THB150 per day); Phase 3: THB3,000 per person (THB150 per day) from 1 July 2021 to 30 September 2021, and THB1,500 per person from 1 October 2021 to 31 December 2021; Phase 4: THB1,200 per person (THB100 per day)	Food and necessities
Tourism stimulus	Phase 1: 15 July 2020 to 31 October 2020 (extended to 30 April 2021); Phase 2[a]: May 2021 to 31 July 2021; Phase 3: 1 October 2021 to 31 January 2022; Phase 4: initially February 2022 to June 2022, but delayed to 1 July 2022 to 30 October 2022	THB600–900 e-vouchers for food and other hotel services THB3,000 per night for up to five nights 40 per cent subsidy on ticket prices	Domestic travel
Shopping	Phase 1: 23 October to 31 December 2020; Phase 2: 4 June 2021 to 28 February 2022	Tax deduction to a maximum of THB30,000 (Phase 1) 10–15 per cent cashback in the form of e-vouchers with THB60,000 maximum	Spending

Note: a. This phase was not officially referred to as phase two. Nonetheless, the next round of the programme was referred to as phase 3, hence the use of the term phase 2 in this chapter.
Source: Cabinet resolutions (various dates).

launched phase 4 on seeing how much money had been spent in the first three phases. The subsidy was given as e-money and transferred into a government e-money application, Pao Tang.

The second targeted measure was to promote domestic travel for Thai citizens and permanent residents through the Rao Tiew Duay Kan scheme, meaning "we travel together") (Table 13.3).[17] The government subsidized hotel accommodation at 40 per cent of normal room rates, with a ceiling of THB3,000 per night for up to five nights. Tourists were responsible for paying the remaining 60 per cent. Subsidies for other services were also available, including food, which was capped at THB600–900[18] per room per night, and air travel. For air travel, the government offered a refund of 40 per cent of the normal ticket price, up to a maximum of THB3,000 per person (increased from THB1,000 and THB2,000 in the first few months of the scheme), for up to two million seats. Similar to the first package, it was transferred in e-money.[19] This scheme did fairly well; THB20.6 billion was claimed in its first three phases from July 2020 to 28 February 2022. The take-up in phase 4 (February 2022 to June 2022) was rather low; only THB2.9 billion out of a budgeted THB9 billion was spent, for reasons that are difficult to pinpoint. However, the programme was extended beyond June 2022, and likely performed better due to the decline in daily Covid-19 infections.

Two additional schemes were introduced in May 2021 to boost consumer spending. One was entitled "the more you spend, the more you get" (Ying Chai Ying Dai), which ran from June to December 2021.[20] Cashback e-vouchers were offered to domestic spenders between July 2021 and September 2021. Participants received cashback in their e-wallets at a rate of 10–15 per cent of spending, with a maximum limit of THB10,000 per person. The e-voucher was available from August 2021 to December 2021 (Table 13.3).

Second, the Shop and Payback programme (Shop Dee Mee Khuen) offered a tax deduction for individual taxpayers of up to THB30,000 when purchasing goods or services. The government used the scheme to promote domestic shopping between 23 October and 31 December 2021. It aimed to help deplete high inventory levels of goods, but also to boost sales volumes and increase liquidity for various businesses. In addition, the increased spending would help the retail sector to recover. By 29 December 2021,

TABLE 13.3
Thailand's Measures for Easing Liquidity Constraints

Relief and Recovery Packages	*Billion THB (Per Cent of 2020 GDP)*	*Duration*	*Target*	*Loan Cap*	*Remark*
Soft loans to financial institutions offered by the Government Savings Bank (GSB)	150 (0.89%)	10 March 2020 to December 2020	Enterprises	THB150 million for existing customers; THB50 million for new customers	0.01% interest rate charged by the GSB to financial institutions; financial institutions charged businesses 2% interest rate for two years
Soft loans offered by Social Security Office to promote employment	30 (0.18%)	Three years (starting from 10 March 2020)	Enterprises	THB5, 10 and 15 million for small (50 or fewer workers), medium-sized (51–200) and large (more than 200 workers) enterprises	n.a.
Bank of Thailand Decree to provide soft loans to SMEs via commercial banks and specialized financial institutions	500 (3.0%)	19 April 2020 to 18 April 2021	Enterprises		THB138.2 billion out of THB500 billion used by 12 April 2021. The remaining funds were reallocated to a new soft loan scheme worth THB250 billion and a debt restructuring programme (also known as asset warehousing) in April 2021
Postponement of principal payments, reduction in interest and extension to repayment period for debtors affected by Covid-19	n.a.	10 March 2020 to October 2020, but extended to December 2021	Individuals	n.a.	By 21 June 2021, THB3.46 trillion in credit lines supported

continued on next page

TABLE 13.3 — *cont'd*

Relief and Recovery Packages	*Billion THB (Per Cent of 2020 GDP)*	*Duration*	*Target*	*Loan Cap*	*Remark*
Loans for freelancers/self-employed/informal workers offered by the GSB and Bank for Agriculture and Agricultural Cooperatives	40 (0.24%)	Initially 23 March 2020 to 30 December 2020, extended to 30 June 2021	Individuals	THB10,000 per person (0.1% monthly interest rate); 6 months grace period with no interest, 2.5 years duration	50% credit guarantee by the government; THB17,328.46 and THB8,797 million lent on 18 January 2021 by the GSB and Bank for Agriculture and Agricultural Cooperatives respectively; on 15 February 2021 interest-free period extended from six to twelve months; loan duration from 2.5 years to 3 years
Special credit facilities for employees with collateral offered by the GSB	20 (0.12%)	23 March 2020 to December 2020	Individuals	THB10,000 per person (0.35% monthly interest rate); maximum three years; six months interest free	Credit guarantee 30%
Soft loans made by GSB to the Office of the Government Pawnshop for low-income groups	2 (0.01%)	Two years starting from 23 March 2020	Individuals	0.125% monthly interest; maximum two years	GSB charged 0.1% interest rate to Office of the Government Pawnshop; the government subsidized 2.4%
Soft loans to support SMEs offered by SME Development Bank	10 (0.06%)	Initially 23 March 2020 to 30 December 2020, extended to 30 June 2021 and then 30 December 2021	Enterprises	Less than THB3 million; 3% interest rate for the first two years, loan duration of five years	Collateral required; THB3,250 million used by 14 June 2021

Loans to support SMEs in the tourism business offered by the GSB	10 (0.06%)	15 February 2021 to 30 June 2021, extended to 30 December 2021	SMEs in tourism	THB10 and 50 million for individuals and enterprises, respectively; 0.1%, 0.99% and 5.99% annual interest rates for the first, second and third years, respectively	Fixed asset required; THB2,400 million utilized by 4 January 2021 and THB7,253 million utilized by 14 June 2021; in June 2021, relaxing collateral requirements (low-quality assets could be used, for example, land without commercial potential)
Loans to support SMEs in tourism-related business offered by the GSB	5 (0.03%)	Initially 18 August 2020 to 30 December 2020; extended three times, first to 30 June 2021, then to 30 December 2021 and finally to 30 September 2022	SMEs in tourism	THB0.5 million per individual, have been in business for at least two years; 3.99% annual interest rate	Personal collateral; THB1.1 billion used by 14 June 2021; conditions eased in June 2021, when loan duration was extended from five to seven years and interest-free period from one to two years; Only THB1.1 billion and THB1.7 billion utilized, accounting for 22% and 34% of total budget respectively by 29 June and 29 November 2021
Fight with Covid-19 Loan offered through the GSB and Bank for Agriculture and Agricultural Cooperatives	20 (0.12%)	5 May 2021 to 31 December 2021; extended to 30 September 2022	SMEs	0.35% monthly interest rate; maximum loan duration of three years	30% credit guarantee by the government; THB8.2 billion approved by in November 2021; THB0.3 billion approved by Bank for Agriculture and Agricultural Cooperatives on 30 December 2021

Source: Cabinet resolutions (various dates).

91,952 participants had spent THB3.8 billion (Ministry of Finance 2021). This was far from the revised target of 1.4 million participants. The official report about the performance of Shop Dee Mee Khuen has not yet been published, but the available information suggests it has underperformed, similar to Ying Chai Ying Dai.

Indirect Fiscal Measures

Liquidity Support

Liquidity support, principally to help firms with credit lines and debt relief, complemented the above-the-line measures. The first soft loan package was launched on 10 March 2021 through the state-owned Government Savings Bank (GSB) (Cabinet Resolution, 10 March 2020). In this measure, the GSB offered 0.01 per cent interest rate to financial institutions, which could then lend to businesses at a 2 per cent interest rate for two years. The credit limit was THB20 million per account. The GSB was urged to make the loans within March 2020. The Bank of Thailand set a THB7.5 billion budget ceiling of subsidies to the GSB for any foregone interest income. As it was launched at the onset of Covid-19 when the crisis was not expected to last as long as it did and the first lockdown had not yet been imposed, the perceived risk and uncertainty were low. The soft loan was quickly and fully utilized even though there was no sharing of default risk. There were subsequent liquidity supports as summarized in Table 13.3. All were injected through existing financial institutions, including the GSB, and the Bank for Agriculture and Agricultural Cooperatives. This allowed the new liquidity to be injected without delay. Another advantage of using the existing financial institutions is their ability to use the information they already possess about their customers to minimize opportunistic behaviour and potential fraudulent claims, thus helping to ensure that the special low-interest credit went to those legitimately needing it. At the same time, a limitation of the scheme was the exclusion of companies that were not clients of those banks.

Thailand's liquidity support was accompanied by a much more limited credit guarantee than provided in similar programmes in developed countries.[21] A clear example is the largest soft loan scheme provided by the Bank of Thailand, worth THB0.5 trillion in April 2020, which addressed this credit guarantee shortcoming (Bank of Thailand 2020). The compensation offered to financial institutions for losses was limited to 60–70 per cent (Bank of Thailand 2020). The guarantee was smaller than those of similar schemes in Singapore, Malaysia and OECD countries, which guaranteed in the range of 80 per cent to 90 per cent (Archanun et al. 2021; OECD 2020). As a consequence, financial institutions in Thailand tended to rely on their usual practice of seeking collateral and prioritizing existing good clients when extending this soft loan, which in the end was hardly used.

The Bank of Thailand made minor changes to the scheme in October 2020, for example, allowing companies listed on Thailand's Market for Alternative Investment to apply for loans (*Bangkok Post* 2020), but the guarantee level was not addressed. A further THB19.2 billion was lent from October 2020 to March 2021 (Bank of Thailand 2021b). However, the overall take-up was modest. By 12 April 2021, only THB138.2 billion out of the earmarked THB500 billion had been lent to 77,787 borrowers.[22]

Subsequently, a new soft loan scheme was introduced in April 2021, as the original soft loan target of THB500 billion was underused and the number of new infections continued to grow daily (the third wave). From the previous scheme, THB0.35 trillion remained; this was split into two—a new soft loan scheme worth THB250 billion and a debt restructuring programme (asset warehousing). The provision of soft loans in this round did address the credit guarantee problem, the shortcoming of the previous scheme. It used the Thai Credit Guarantee Corporation mechanisms (TCG)[23] to set credit ceilings and allowed firms without credit lines with any financial institution as of 28 February 2021 to participate (*Bangkok Post* 2021a; Bank of Thailand 2021a). By 27 June 2022, 131,637 borrowers had been approved for THB318,469 billion worth of loans.[24] The budget for the new soft loan scheme was THB250 billion, so the reported loan disbursement likely covers both the first and second schemes. Hence, the additional lending in the second scheme, from April 2021 to June 2022, would be THB180.3 billion. For both schemes combined, the figure had increased from THB102.6 billion as of 13 September 2021.[25]

The debt restructuring or asset warehousing programme was a standardized programme for adversely affected borrowers whose businesses required a prolonged recovery period. Companies were protected from losing their loan collateral, enabling them to formulate new business models and rescue plans. The programme gave companies priority on repurchasing their collateral at the agreed transfer price plus an additional cost of 1 per cent per annum (for the period the bank held the asset) and incurred asset maintenance costs and other fees. Businesses whose assets were transferred to their lender were permitted to lease their assets to continue business operations; and the rents received by financial institutions were to be deducted from the repurchase price. The scheme shielded businesses from having to sell collateral at low prices and helped them continue operating through the recovery. The Bank of Thailand supported the programme by providing low-cost funding to financial institutions equivalent to the price of the transferred asset (as agreed by the financial institution and the borrower). At the same time, public agencies provided exemptions or reductions on taxes or other fees, such as those levied on asset transfers during transfer and repurchase. The measures were designed to use the limited resources of both public and private sectors to yield the greatest impact. Nonetheless, the programme utilization was quite low. By 27 June 2022, only 356 firms had applied to the programme, representing THB49 billion in funds.[26]

Despite being highly relevant, the size of firms was overlooked by policymakers. The targets of the liquidity support were SMEs under the assumption that large firms were capable of surviving by themselves. In fact, this assumption was not always true in the context of the Covid-19 crisis, where the economic impact was largely driven by the sudden stoppage of economic activity. The tourism industry illustrates this issue: all enterprises were affected badly, regardless of size. In addition, the definition of SMEs was arbitrary and applied too rigidly, which excluded borderline firms (Archanun et al. 2021).

Other Indirect Measures

A few other indirect economic relief measures are worth mentioning, each of which was implemented with time limits. These include reduction of certain taxes and fees (including property tax, and housing transfer and mortgage fees), refund of household water and electricity meter deposits in the first wave, reduction of water bills and electricity during the lockdown, reduction of social security contributions (to 4 per cent for employees, and 1 per cent for freelancers and the self-employed) from March to May

2020, and a four-month extension on the deadline for submitting social security forms and for remitting social security contributions.

IMPLICATIONS FOR ECONOMIC RECOVERY

Even though the fiscal resources Thailand spent to combat the Covid-19 crisis were comparable to developed countries, their effect on the economy was limited (Figure 13.7). In particular, Thailand's year-on-year GDP growth dropped from 1.3 per cent in 2019Q4 to −12.2 per cent in 2020Q2 (Figure 13.7). This compares to 2020Q2 GDP declines in Malaysia (−17.2 per cent), the Philippines (−16.9 per cent) and Singapore (−13.3 per cent). However, Thailand's economic recovery took longer than those of its counterparts in the Association of Southeast Asian Nations (ASEAN). By 2022Q2, Thailand's year-on-year GDP growth was 2.2 per cent, the worst performance among all ASEAN members (Figure 13.7).

The nature of fiscal resources Thailand spent to combat the crisis partly explains the slow recovery. Two fundamentals of the Thai economy—the sizeable informal sector and the importance of tourism—explain the size of the GDP contraction as well as the slow recovery. The implementation of the relief and stimulus measures also impacted on the slow recovery, given the much larger size of fiscal resources spent (Figure 13.3). With regard to cash handout schemes, the amounts became smaller with each successive Covid-19 wave, although the effects from prolonged closure were becoming increasingly severe, especially for the informally employed and the tourism sector. In general, relief and stimulus arrived too slowly for the most vulnerable people.

The second and third cash handout programmes came with a half-half co-payment scheme. It helped people buy necessities for living to a certain extent, but did not stimulate additional demand for goods and services. People had to spend an equal amount to the government subsidy to be eligible for the scheme. For those losing their jobs and running out of cash, they might not be able to survive without borrowing money, especially from informal sources. Even though the co-payment schemes were fully taken up, many shops eligible for half-half co-payment schemes were accessible largely to middle-class households, who might not have been hit hard by the Covid-19 crisis and so the programmes in some cases lowered

Figure 13.7
Year-on-Year GDP Growth in Selected Asian Countries, 2019Q2 to 2022Q2

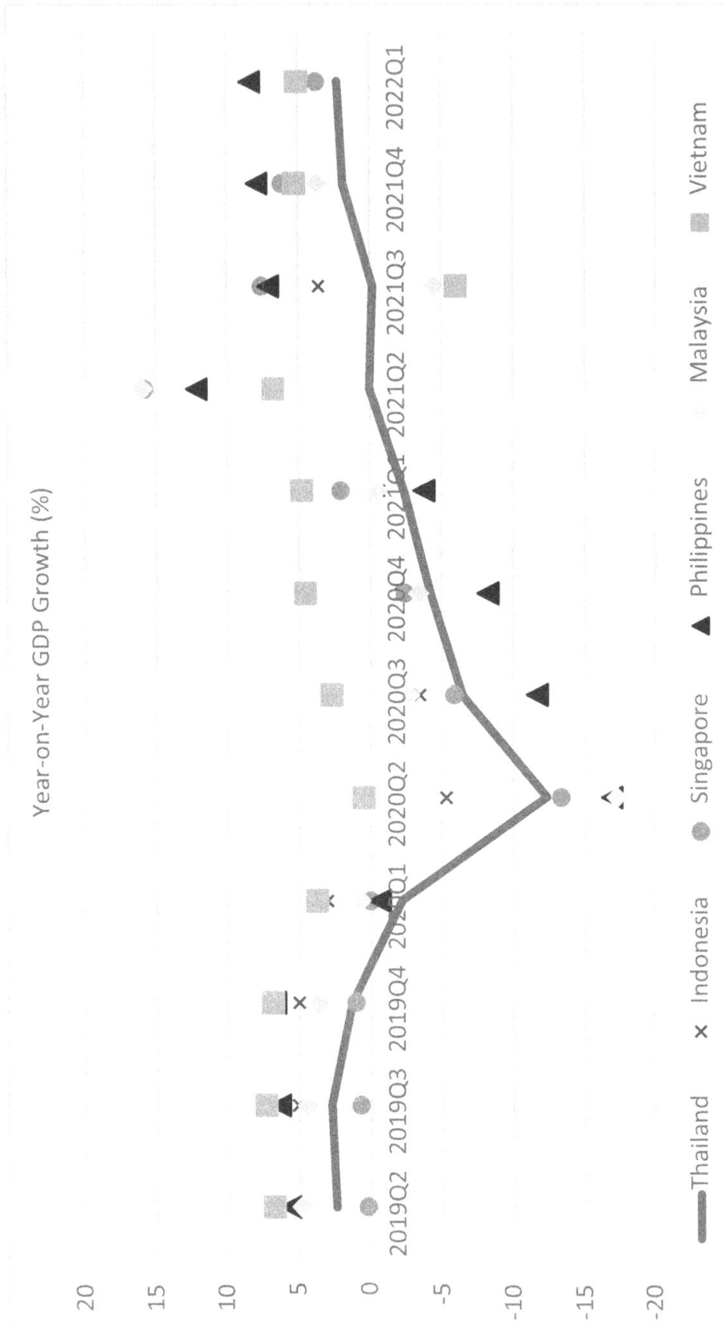

Source: Based on data from https://tradingeconomics.com

the prices of goods that were not necessities.[27] It may have acted as an economic stimulus but not economic relief, and the benefits and boost to economic growth were likely concentrated in urban areas with higher levels of digital literacy and fewer poor people, rather than countrywide.

Some programmes were not used as much as intended, while some were inadequately budgeted. Interestingly, the amount of stimulus that was initially set in July 2020 at THB358 billion was maintained. Its effect in stimulating overall demand was limited to cushioning shrinking demand induced by the Covid-19 crisis as it was only slowly utilized. By June 2022, the utilization rate was 81 per cent. Liquidity support, while rapidly deployed and filling a major need, was undermined by the limited credit guarantee. Even though the soft loan scheme was revised twice (October 2020 and April 2021), it remained unattractive for financial institutions to take up and assist firms in handling their liquidity constraints. A scheme assisting firms to keep their workers (Rao Rak*)* was later introduced in mid-2021, a year after Thailand was hit by the Covid-19 crisis. The amount of assistance was small, with a total budget of THB37 billion, equating to less than 2 per cent of total fiscal resources made available to combat the crisis.

The final remark is related to sector-specific policies. It is widely recognized that the effect of the Covid-19 crisis varies across sectors. For some sectors (food and electrical appliances), the Covid-19 crisis provided business opportunities. Nonetheless, policy packages failed to address this variation. This is especially true for tourism, which is one of Thailand's major economic activities and is highly export-oriented. While the government provided policies and special soft loan schemes for tourism businesses, the sector was generally treated the same as others in terms of loan requirements, for example additional collateral was also required.

CONCLUSION

This chapter examined the measures implemented by the Thai government to cushion the adverse economic effect of the Covid-19 crisis, with comparisons made with other nations. Thailand spent sizeable fiscal resources to maintain the economy in the Covid-19 crisis, but the net effect was limited in terms of GDP growth. Thailand was the slowest of ASEAN members to recover economically.

The analysis in this chapter suggests nearly three-quarters of fiscal resources deployed in response to the pandemic were spent to save people's livelihoods and to partially assist them in coping with the adverse effects of social distancing measures. The Covid-19 crisis was new, and Thailand faced steep hurdles in delivering relief and stimulus.

Thailand had substantial institutions and resources, and various economic stimulus and liquidity supports were launched to minimize the adverse effects on economic activity. Nonetheless, they arrived arguably too little and too late. In fact, most of the measures were designed under the assumption that the Covid-19 crisis was similar to previous economic crises experienced in the past decade, but the border closures and mobility restrictions were new, and both had adverse effects on the economy that Thailand had not experienced before. Also, the uncertainty and many unknowns surrounding recovery from the pandemic reduced the likelihood that standard economic stimulus could substantially boost demand. Thailand's administration appeared to expect the same level of responsiveness and recovery as experienced in preceding crises, such as SARS. The low uptake of liquidity support demonstrates the government's failure to account for the collapse of confidence. Government support mostly favoured small firms; it did not support large firms that faced bankruptcy due to the sudden stop in economic activity. This stop affected all firms, regardless of size. Job protection for employees, however, was offered to firms of all sizes. It is likely that such firms will need more credit support, to speed up economic recovery in the post Covid-19 era.

Thailand also faltered in not offering direct assistance to firms in sectors hit hardest by the Covid-19 crisis. Tourism is a clear example. The government provided subsidies to domestic travellers but not to the businesses themselves and the benefits were unevenly distributed. As the subsidy was applicable to all hotels, fierce price cuts from international chains and bigger hotels could drive smaller ones out of business. The insufficiency of sector-specific policies could explain the slow economic recovery of Thailand.

As Thailand slowly emerged from the pandemic, the post-crisis policy priority turned to job creation. Given weak domestic demand, exports have been the targeted growth engine; this will entail technological leapfrogging and the reforms necessary to realize this, potentially an opportunity for Thailand. The crisis has provided a platform for technological change, but upgrading takes time and incurs fixed costs, meaning its viability is questionable. This issue has been worsened by rising geopolitical tensions and anti-globalization sentiment. For a small, open economy like Thailand, pro-globalization stances, as well as collective action through regional cooperation, will be crucial for the country's pursuit of sustainable and resilient economic development.

Notes

1. Based on data from Worldometer, https://www.worldometers.info/coronavirus/#countries
2. On 1 August 2020 the border was opened for specific groups of foreigners only. These included medical tourists; film crews; holders of the Thailand Elite card, a long-stay multiple-entry visa; foreigners with work permits; foreigners married to Thai nationals and foreigners studying at educational institutions. These groups were allowed to enter but were subject to mandatory fourteen-day quarantine. All were required to take a Covid-19 test at the airport on arrival.
3. Incoming travellers from low-to-medium risk countries (as categorized by Thailand's Ministry of Public Health, including Taiwan, Australia, New Zealand, Singapore, Qatar, Israel and Norway) were required to be fully vaccinated at least fourteen days before their departure with vaccines registered with Thailand's Ministry of Public Health or approved by the World Health Organization (WHO). A vaccine certificate was required, as was a negative polymerase chain reaction (PCR) test result issued no more than seventy-two hours before departure. Visitors were also required to have insurance that would cover Covid-19 expenses, with a minimum cover of US$20,000 (Yuda 2021a).
4. See the announcement on Facebook at https://www.facebook.com/informationcovid19/photos/297007931917538
5. For example, the scheme in Hua Hin was called Hua Hin Recharge. Visitors were required to undergo three RT-PCR tests during their stay in the town—the first upon arrival, the second seven days later and the third on their thirteenth day. While awaiting the results of the first test, they were permitted to check in to their hotels, which were required to meet certain standards imposed by

the Safety and Health Administration, without stopovers en route. If testing negative for Covid-19, they were able to travel freely in the town or in 86.36 square kilometres of the district's territory without being quarantined. If testing negative in the second test, they were permitted to move to a new hotel of their choice. If testing negative in the third test, they were permitted to travel anywhere across Thailand, after completion of their fourteen-day stay in Hua Hin (Thai PBS 2021).

6. According to data released by the Tourism Authority of Thailand, Phuket received 25,886 international arrivals in the first sixty days (July and August 2021) following the launch of the sandbox scheme. This is far lower than the target of 100,000 arrivals (Nation 2021).
7. A state of emergency was instituted in Thailand on 26 March 2020 to help overcome the complexity of the country's bureaucracy. All administrative powers were transferred to the newly established Centre for Covid-19 Situation Administration (CCSA) chaired by Prime Minister Prayuth Chan-o-cha (Marome and Shaw 2021). It was the CCSA that conducted the monitoring.
8. Data taken from CEIC, accessed June 2023.
9. This figure is from IMF (2021) which is slightly above the estimate produced by the World Bank (2021). The sources differ in their calculation of foregone incomes from other economic relief such as tax relief, lower utility bills and the like.
10. The original figures reported on the IMF website are 11.4 per cent and 4.2 per cent of 2020 GDP for above-the-line and liquidity support measures respectively. Here, the 2019 nominal GDP figure of THB16.9 trillion is used.
11. In 2020, the minimum wage in Bangkok was THB331 a day. Under the assumption that these workers work five days a week for four weeks a month, the monthly return from the minimum wage would be THB6,620.
12. Many applicants found out they were not eligible for the scheme, raising questions on the cut-off points for qualifying for the assistance as well as the selection process (NNT 2020).
13. The poor were classified as those with taxable income in 2019 of less than THB300,000 and total savings of less than THB500,000 on 31 December 2019.
14. Bangkok, Nakhon Pathom, Nonthaburi, Pathum Thani, Samut Prakarn, Samut Sakhon, Narthiwat, Pattani, Yala and Songkhla. It covered nine sectors: construction; accommodation and food services; arts, entertainment and recreational activities; transportation and warehouses; wholesale and retail businesses; administration and support services; science and academic

activities; information and communications; and other services as stated by the Social Security Office.

15. On 25 May 2021 the government issued an emergency decree authorizing the Ministry of Finance to raise an additional THB0.5 trillion in loans to restore the economy and society from the effects of Covid-19.
16. Most people were eligible for this, aside from those who held social welfare cards as they had already received the assistance.
17. In fact, another measure was launched in March 2021 and was initially due to take effect from May 2021 to September 2021, the Tour Tiew Thai scheme. The government subsidized 40 per cent of package tours, up to THB5,000 per person. Tourists were required to buy packages from a domestic tour agency for three days and two nights, with a minimum price of THB12,500, and were required to travel from a Sunday to a Thursday. They were to be aged eighteen or over on the date of registration. The government targeted 1 million participants and budgeted THB5 billion. Due to the upward trend of new cases during the third wave, the scheme was postponed, beginning October 2021 and running to February 2022. The project underperformed, with a wide gap between budget and budget utilization. The budget was cut to THB1 billion, and it was extended to December 2022.
18. THB600 was offered to each person travelling at the weekend (Friday to Sunday) and THB900 for weekdays.
19. The phases of this measure were: round one from 15 July 2020 to October 2020, round two from December 2020 to April 2021, round three from October 2021 to February 2022, and round four from February 2022 to June 2022, with an extension to October 2022.
20. Initially, the target was set at 4 million participants. On 20 July 2021, the programme was extended to 30 November 2021, the ceiling was raised from THB7,000 to THB10,000 a day, and the targeted beneficiaries were reduced to 1.4 million.
21. See OECD (2020a) for the schemes applied in OECD countries.
22. Data retrieved from the Bank of Thailand website at https://www.bot.or.th/covid19/Pages/progress/property/default.aspx
23. A regular practice of the TCG in debt guarantee is if SME loans become non-performing loans, the TCG will provide compensation worth 80 per cent of the loss to lenders. The compensation increases to 90 per cent in the case of micro SMEs. The TCG charges micro-SMEs and SMEs a guarantee fee of 1.75 per cent a year. However, under the soft loan scheme, the fee is cut to 1 per cent a year (*Bangkok Post* 2021c).

24. Data from the Bank of Thailand website at https://www.bot.or.th/covid19/Pages/progress/property/default.aspx (accessed 5 July 2022).
25. Data from the Bank of Thailand available at https://www.bot.or.th/covid19/Pages/progress/property/default.aspx (accessed 13 September 2021).
26. Ibid.
27. Examples of eligible items not related to basic needs, sighted by the authors in online advertisements, included a Starbucks mug.

References

Archanun Kohpaiboon, Juthathip Jongwanich, Petharin Wongcharoen, and Panupong Sriudomkajorn. 2021. "Industrial Transformation after COVID 19: Evidence of Thai Manufacturing". Report submitted to Thailand Science Research and Innovation, Ministry of Higher Education, Science, Research and Innovation, February (in Thai).

Bangkok Post. 2020. "BoT Okays Extension of B500 Bn Soft Loan Plan". 20 October 2020. https://www.bangkokpost.com/business/2004827/bot-okays-extension-of-b500bn-soft-loan-plan (accessed 15 June 2022).

———. 2021a. "BoT Confident New Loan Scheme Will Help SMEs". 21 April 2021. https://www.bangkokpost.com/business/2103307/bot-confident-new-loan-scheme-will-help-smes (accessed 15 June 2022).

———. 2021b. "More Covid Relief in the Works". 3 May 2021. https://www.bangkokpost.com/business/2109259/more-covid-relief-in-the-works (accessed 15 June 2022).

———. 2021c. "TCG Expands Soft Loan Guarantee Allocation by B100bn". 18 September 2021. https://www.bangkokpost.com/business/2183755/tcg-expands-soft-loan-guarantee-allocation-by-b100bn (accessed 15 June 2022).

———. 2022a. "B43bn Generated from Phuket Sandbox". 22 February 2022. https://www.bangkokpost.com/travel/2268271/b43bn-generated-from-phuket-sandbox (accessed 15 June 2022).

———. 2022b. "Govt Drops Reports of ATK-Positive Cases". 29 May 2022. https://www.bangkokpost.com/thailand/general/2317454/govt-drops-reports-of-atk-positive-cases (accessed 15 June 2022).

———. 2022c. "What Are the Entry Rules from May 1?" 27 April 2022. https://www.bangkokpost.com/business/2301054/what-are-the-entry-rules-from-may-1- (accessed 15 June 2022).

Bank of Thailand. 2020. "Additional Measures to Assist SMEs Affected by COVID-19 and to Stabilize Corporate Bond Market". News Release.

https://www.mizuhogroup.com/binaries/content/assets/pdf/thailand/news/bot_press_release.pdf

———. 2021a. "Financial Rehabilitation Measures to Support Business Recovery Post-COVID-19". News Release. https://www.mizuhogroup.com/binaries/content/assets/pdf/thailand/news/bot_press_release.pdf

———. 2021b. "Performance of the Thai Banking System in the First Quarter of 2021". News Release. https://www.bot.or.th/content/dam/bot/documents/en/news-and-media/news/2021/n3564e.pdf

Gaspar, Vitor, Raphael Lam, Paolo Mauro, and Mehdi Raissi. 2021. "Government Support Is Vital as Countries Race to Vaccinate". International Monetary Fund. https://www.imf.org/en/Blogs/Articles/2021/01/28/blog-fm-update-government-support-is-vital-as-countries-race-to-vaccinate (accessed 15 June 2022).

International Monetary Fund (IMF). 2020. *Fiscal Monitor: April 2020.* Washington, DC: International Monetary Fund. https://www.imf.org/en/Publications/FM/Issues/2020/04/06/fiscal-monitor-april-2020

Marome, W., and R. Shaw. 2021. "Covid-19 Responses in Thailand and Its Implications on Future Preparedness". *International Journal of Environmental Research and Public Health* 18, no. 3: 1089. https://doi.org/10.3390/ijerph18031089

Ministry of Finance. 2021. "Performance of Half-Half and Ying Chai Ying Dai Schemes". News Release.

Nation. 2021. "Why Thailand's Tourism Sandbox Programmes Failed". 28 September 2021. https://www.nationthailand.com/in-focus/40006751

Nattadhanai Rajatanavin, Titiporn Tuangratananon, Rapeepong Suphanchaimat, and Viroj Tangcharoensathien. 2021. "Responding to the Covid-19 Second Wave in Thailand by Diversifying and Adapting Lessons from the First Wave". *BMJ Global Health* 6: e006178. https://gh.bmj.com/content/bmjgh/6/7/e006178.full.pdf

NNT (National News Bureau of Thailand). 2020. "5000-Baht Cash Relief Extended to 16 Million People". 28 April 2020. https://thainews.prd.go.th/en/news/detail/TCATG200428200905050 (accessed 15 June 2022).

OECD (Organization for Economic Co-operation and Development). 2020a. *COVID-19 Government Financing Support Programmes for Business.* http://dx.doi.org/www.oecd.org/finance/COVID-19-Government-Financing-Support-Programmes-for-Businesses.pdf

———. 2020b. "OECD Economic Surveys: Economic Assessment Thailand". Organization for Economic Cooperation and Development. https://www.

oecd-ilibrary.org/deliver/ad2e50fa-en.pdf?itemId=/content/publication/ad2e50fa-en&mimeType=pdf

———. 2021. *COVID-19 Emergency Government Support and Ensuring a Level Playing Field on the Road to Recovery*. https://read.oecd-ilibrary.org/view/?ref=1113_1113403-090x2f80uf&title=COVID-19-emergency-government-support-and-ensuring-a-level-playing-field-on-the-road-to-recovery

Subramaniam, R., A. Perdiguero, J. Rush, and P. Asis-Layugan, eds. 2021. *Policy Actions for COVID-19 Economic Recovery: A Compendium of Policy Briefs*. Manila: Asian Development Bank.

Thai PBS. 2021. "Thailand's Hua Hin Seeks to Reopen to Foreign Arrivals from October 1". 6 September 2021. https://www.thaipbsworld.com/thailands-hua-hin-set-to-reopen-to-foreign-arrivals-from-october-1/

WHO (World Health Organization). 2020. "Joint Intra-action Review of the Public Health Response to Covid-19 in Thailand". WHO, 20–24 July 2020. https://www.who.int/docs/default-source/searo/thailand/iar-covid19-en.pdf

———. 2022. "Covid-19 Situation, Thailand 15 June 2022". https://cdn.who.int/media/docs/default-source/searo/thailand/2022_06_15_tha-sitrep-240-covid-19.pdf?sfvrsn=6ee80816_1

———. 2021. *Thailand Economic Monitor: The Road to Recovery*. July 2021. Bangkok: World Bank. https://www.worldbank.org/en/country/thailand/publication/thailand-economic-monitor-july-2021-the-road-to-recovery

———. 2022a. *Thailand Economic Monitor: Building Back Greener: the Circular Economy*. June 2022. Bangkok: World Bank. https://www.worldbank.org/en/country/thailand/publication/thailand-economic-monitor-june-2022-building-back-greener-the-circular-economy#:~:text=The%20circular%20economy%20models%20offer,about%200.3%25%20of%20total%20employment

———. 2022b. *World Development Report 2022: Finance for an Equitable Recovery*. https://www.worldbank.org/en/publication/wdr2022#downloads

Yuda, M. 2020. "Thai Cash Handout Program Creates Risky Crowds amid Coronavirus". *Nikkei Asia*, 1 April 2020. https://asia.nikkei.com/Spotlight/Coronavirus/Thai-cash-handout-program-creates-risky-crowds-amid-coronavirus (accessed 15 June 2022).

———. 2021a. "Phuket to Reopen for Vaccinated Tourists without Quarantine: 5 Things to Know". *Nikkei Asia*, 25 June 2021. https://asia.nikkei.com/Business/Travel-Leisure/Phuket-to-reopen-for-vaccinated-tourists-without-quarantine-5-things-to-know2

COMPARATIVE SYNTHESIS

Economic Relief and Stimulus in Malaysia, Singapore and Thailand

Lee Hwok Aun

The experiences of Malaysia, Singapore and Thailand in providing relief and stimulus packages can be compared and contrasted in various ways (Nungsari, Ch 11 in this volume; Ho, Ch 12; Archanun, Juthathip, and Mayoon, Ch 13). We observed cross-country similarities and differences, and policy responses had country-specific elements. The scope of measures to remedy the pandemic-induced economic contraction is vast and, in general, common practices that yield positive results can be taken as examples worth serious consideration. This chapter synthesizes definitive and prescriptive findings while being mindful that policy options may be contingent on circumstances. Lessons can be drawn in three key areas: (1) objectives and transitions in policy focus, (2) targeting and mechanisms and (3) structural consequences.

OBJECTIVES AND TRANSITIONS

The urgency of providing job and income protection was readily apparent in the early phases of the pandemic, specifically when all three countries implemented nationwide lockdowns from March to May 2020. As mobility restrictions were scaled down, modified or localized, relief and stimulus measures remained important, but policy priority gravitated towards job creation and economic stimulus, especially as vaccination progressed. Amid these common threads, notable similarities and variations in the policy specifics provide lessons.

Cash transfers emerged as a necessary and impactful intervention for safeguarding well-being during the unprecedentedly extensive and state-imposed lockdown, meaning mobility restrictions. Cash transfers are worth reprising in the event of another pandemic, or any crisis that may entail shutdowns beyond the control of businesses, whether due to mobility restrictions or financial meltdown. The Covid-19 experience established a precedent of concerted, direct and effective means to protect jobs and income, both of which are of utmost importance to society. Malaysia and Singapore's informal economies are relatively small and hence formal mechanisms and existing social protection institutions were able to deliver assistance to broad swathes of the population. However, some communities remained marginalized and excluded, notably migrant workers, undocumented workers and refugees.

Policies in this thematic group's three countries were shaped by previous experience with epidemics or economic crises, availability of resources and observation of global Covid-19 responses. Singapore, as a high-income city-state with a formalized and open economy, has well-developed public institutions that were marshalled to provide household cash transfers and wage subsidies for workers, the latter channelled through employers. Singapore could also reference the Jobs Credit Scheme implemented to mitigate the 2008–9 global financial crisis, which hit the country harder than any other Southeast Asian counterpart. In Malaysia, additional cash assistance for low-income households was disbursed, and the wage subsidy was also introduced as a novel policy instrument that, despite a few teething problems, eventually gained considerable traction and broad participation. Like Singapore and Malaysia, Thailand also averted a steep hike in the official unemployment rate, but took a contrasting approach; its cash transfers prioritized informal economy workers and the worst-affected sectors, namely, tourism and farming, and businesses that temporarily closed down. The larger informal economy necessitated this approach to a significant extent and the country's method of electronic transfers is worth emulating, but wage subsidies could be considered during future crises.

Crises such as Covid-19 demand a focus on immediate survival and short-term priorities, but countries also need to transition to recovery mode and even restructure in response to the crisis. The array of interventions in the three countries, from loan moratoriums to grants, subsidies and fiscal incentives for job growth, provide useful case studies of varying paths to reactivating the economy. In the long term, a sustainable unemployment insurance scheme warrants serious consideration. In the case of Malaysia where far fewer Employment Insurance System claims were made than the estimated number of unemployed, a pressing challenge is to make the EIS the go-to scheme for the unemployed. For Singapore and Thailand, and countries that lack formal support for displaced workers in the form of allowances and job search and placement, the question is how such services can be provided. Singapore's initiatives in facilitating training and subsidizing new hires (especially workers aged over forty) demonstrate that crises are not a hindrance, and can indeed be a fillip, for policies that are aligned with long-term objectives of skills development and gainful employment, including for older workers.

TARGETING AND MECHANISMS

Substantial similarities and differences can be discerned in policy design and execution among the three countries. Programmes tended to work well when the government deployed and modified existing institutions and responded to changing circumstances. Singapore drew on its experiences from the Jobs Credit Scheme to devise the Jobs Support Scheme, which provided support at the onset of the pandemic by subsidizing employers to keep workers employed, at a modest initial rate of 8 per cent of wage costs. The subsidized portion was raised, and sectoral variations applied, with a focus on the most adversely impacted sectors, when the magnitude of potential job losses became more apparent. The qualifying wage thresholds in the Jobs Support Scheme were also raised, allowing more workers to be covered. Malaysia's decision to subsidize wages through the existing infrastructure of the Social Security Organisation (SOCSO) proved an enabling factor, given SOCSO's improvements in capacity in the years preceding the pandemic, exemplified in it being commissioned to handle the Employment Insurance System launched in 2019. Thailand, which provided income support mainly through cash transfers, advanced its transition to digital finance by using e-wallets as the mode of payment.

The means of targeting and funding varied in notable ways. Singapore's jobs support provided a proportion of workers' wages (initially 8 per cent, then 25 per cent, 50 per cent or 74 per cent depending on the sector), whereas Malaysia offered a fixed rate according to the company scale (MYR1,200 per employee for companies claiming the subsidy for fewer than 40 employees, MYR600 per employee for larger claims, up to a maximum of 200 subsidized employees per company). In both countries, receiving the support was conditional on employers maintaining employee wages—meaning no wage cuts. Singapore's jobs support was sector-based and could be claimed by companies in the target sector regardless of size, whereas Malaysia's wage subsidy granted automatic approval to small firms and required larger firms to show they had suffered a loss of income. The stringency of the approvals process and the verification of company financial records, however, remains unclear. Nonetheless, these operational differences hold out important case studies for social protection schemes that can apply to myriad situations, including severe recessions or shocks to particular industries. One cannot prescribe preferred options since these decisions are context-specific. Likewise, the amount of assistance and mode of determination—whether lump sum or proportional rate—are aspects of cash transfers that must also be flexibly applied. A key lesson from Covid-19, indeed, is adaptability, as exemplified in Singapore's broadening of those who were eligible for job protection via wage support (by raising the qualifying wage ceiling), and Malaysia's adjustments that also increased the number of beneficiaries and shifted to a focus on tourism. The Malaysia chapter in this section (Nungsari, Ch 11) argues that the sector should have been accorded more assistance from the onset of the pandemic. The countries' contrasting approaches, and questions over the adequacy of the wage subsidy amounts offered, constitute helpful reference points for drawing out policy lessons.

LONG-TERM CONSEQUENCES

Covid-19 relief and stimulus measures were necessarily concentrated on the immediate need to deliver assistance, with some leveraging on the opportunities presented for restructuring and change, particularly in the growth of the digital economy. At the same time, there are longer-term ramifications that warrant policy attention.

Given the unique circumstances of national self-imposed mobility restrictions—which decidedly induced a recession in each of the three countries—governments had to devise counteracting interventions outside the standard toolbox of fiscal or monetary policy. Public spending necessarily predominated, but some burden was also borne by households and the private sector, through tapping into reserves, deferring debt or rent payments, or other means—ideally, with a sense of collective solidarity.

Governments grappled with the spike in public spending and attendant deficit funding and debt implications. The protracted pandemic weighed on fiscal balances, especially as 2021 wore on and mobility restrictions remained in place. The extent to which social assistance was withheld due to real or perceived budget constraints, which may have caused longer-term consequences in household well-being, is a matter for national deliberation. Singapore's decision to draw on national reserves stands out, and both the past accumulation and ongoing replenishment merit further observation to understand how reserves can be used as a buffer in extreme situations.

In Malaysia, it must be noted that, while social spending did escalate, the amount was dwarfed by spending from the private savings of households and individuals or income sources unlocked by policy interventions. The loan moratorium provided relief, but allowing interest to continuously accrue gave a concession to a highly profitable sector that swiftly rebounded post-pandemic. The most voluminous cash injection came from Malaysia's decision to allow withdrawals from Employees Provident Fund individual accounts, including proportions of members' accumulated savings designated for old age income. Similarly, Thailand permitted Social Security System withdrawals, based on a proportion of monthly salary. The ensuing depletion of retirement income poses a colossal challenge for the coming decades.

The pandemic also deepened the challenges of inequality; prior to the pandemic, most Southeast Asian countries had been making positive strides to reduce inequality and promote more inclusive economic development. With the masses dependent on subsidized healthcare, the inadequacies of public health funding and the quantity and quality of public delivery demand robust action. The plight of marginalized communities was exacerbated by their formal exclusion from social assistance or the practical inaccessibility of such services. A further implication of inequality, specific to Singapore, concerns long-term wealth distribution in the wake of property price escalation.

CONCLUDING NOTE

Malaysia, Singapore and Thailand each sought to mitigate the recessionary impacts of Covid-19-induced lockdowns and mobility restrictions through expansive relief and stimulus measures. Their experiences underscore the paramount importance of supporting income, buffering the abrupt and widespread economic contraction and facilitating economic recovery. Inadequacies in the speed and amount of aid, as raised in the two Malaysia and two Thailand chapters in this volume, reinforce the imperative of having systems in place before crises strike and then mobilizing resources swiftly when they do. The world was tested on a massive scale in 2020–22 and there is no excuse for unpreparedness in the future.

This synthesis has zoomed in on salient similarities and differences, which have yielded valuable lessons—primarily in terms of prioritization of crisis response measures and the transition in focus, from relief to stimulus to recovery, and in variations of design and implementation, which call for responsiveness, flexibility and adaptation. The next crisis, whether triggered by financial markets, the real economy, political turmoil or even another pandemic, will require actions that the Covid-19 experience can substantially inform.

Theme 5

VACCINATION AND REOPENING
Country-Level and ASEAN Experiences

14

DETERMINANTS OF COVID-19 VACCINE ROLL-OUTS IN SOUTHEAST ASIA

Tham Siew Yean and Andrew Kam Jia Yi

INTRODUCTION

The emergence of the Covid-19 pandemic necessitated the administration of safe and effective vaccines. The vaccine also needed to be given to sufficient numbers of people to achieve the herd immunity required to halt transmission of the virus, as well as the health and mortality impacts and the negative effects on the economy. There was thus a rush to produce vaccines, but these had to be produced at scale, priced affordably and made available globally. Vaccines also had to be authorized or approved for human use. Each country had to choose whether to use only vaccines approved by the World Health Organization (WHO) or to expand their choices based on their assessment of the available vaccines and their country's needs. The supply of vaccines to a country, especially to developing countries with no capacity to produce their own, became a critical factor in managing the pandemic. Procuring vaccines has become a serious challenge for many developing countries (Sheikh et al. 2021), including those in Southeast Asia. Local production can also support supply since some developing countries do have the capacity to manufacture vaccines. Unfortunately, intellectual property rights and limited technology transfer can stand in the way of local production (OECD 2021). Vaccines were not accessible in most developing countries at the end of 2020 when they were first authorized for use, because high-income countries had pre-purchased a significant portion (Tagoe et al. 2021). Given budget constraints, developing countries had to consider different supply sources, including donations and aid.

In 2020, it was already established that several leading vaccines required ultra-cold storage and transport chains and had short shelf lives once removed from the ultra-cold conditions. Hence, the deployment of vaccines also depends on a country's logistics infrastructure, capacity and capability (OECD 2021). There can also be significant variations within a country, namely between better-developed urban areas and logistically challenged rural regions.

Another challenge that remains even once supplies are made available is the state's capacity to distribute and administer the vaccines to their entire populations, taking into account the risk factors of different age groups and vulnerabilities, geographical constraints and sociocultural factors (Tevdovski, Jolakoski, and Stojkoski 2022). A state's capacity to implement a viable and effective vaccination strategy is therefore another key factor that can influence a country's vaccine roll-out.

Besides these supply factors, demand is another crucial determinant of vaccination rates in a country. Vaccine hesitancy and acceptance can facilitate or deter the roll-out of vaccinations. The former can be influenced by misinformation about the nature and potential side effects and by prejudice against the country producing the vaccine. Misinformation may be home-grown or may have spread to Southeast Asia from outside the region.

The vaccination rates of a country depend on the combination of supply and demand factors (Deb et al. 2021): procurement, including from local production sources; state capacity; logistics infrastructure and the demand for vaccines as reflected by the extent of vaccine acceptance. The chapter discusses each of these determinants in the ten Southeast Asian countries to ascertain their influence on vaccination rates.

VACCINE PROCUREMENT

All countries in Southeast Asia obtained vaccines from multiple sources and through different channels: multilateral, bilateral, Covid-19 diplomacy, private purchase and domestic production. The number and type of vaccines approved for use varies from country to country, being subject to the regulatory approval body of each country (Table 14.1). By February 2022, Singapore and Brunei had approved the lowest number of vaccines, followed by Malaysia and Thailand (Table 14.1). Countries that were relatively more dependent on donations approved more types of vaccines. This included vaccines outside the list of those approved by the WHO, such as selected vaccines from China, Russia and Cuba. In particular, archipelagic countries such as Indonesia and the Philippines, where logistics are more complex, approved more vaccines (eleven in each country) than other Southeast Asian countries. This included single-shot vaccines and vaccines with less stringent storage requirements, which could therefore more easily reach the rural, less-developed and less-accessible parts of a country.

Multilateral Channel

The multilateral channel is provided by the Covid-19 Vaccines Global Access (or COVAX), a tripartite partnership between Gavi (the Vaccine Alliance), the Coalition for Epidemic Preparedness Innovations and the WHO (Berkley 2020), who also act as co-funders and cost-sharers. COVAX's role was twofold. First, it supported research, development and manufacture of Covid-19 vaccines. Second, it negotiated prices of vaccines through the COVAX facility, its risk-sharing mechanism for pooled procurement and equitable vaccine distribution for all countries worldwide. The vaccines could be procured from COVAX by self-financing or through the Advance Market Commitment, a COVAX financing instrument that aimed to provide free doses to ninety-two low- and middle-income economies that signed up to it. The Advance Market Commitment was a commitment by countries to buy vaccines and provided funding to pharmaceutical companies to help them put in place sufficient manufacturing capacity to ensure they could produce and supply at scale when regulatory approval and licences were obtained. Half of the doses produced were meant for lower-income countries to

TABLE 14.1
Vaccines Approved by Each Southeast Asian Country

Country	*Pfizer*	*Moderna*	*Astra Zeneca*	*Janssen (J&J)*	*Serum Institute of India (Covishield)*	*Covaxin*	*Sinovac*	*Sinopharm*	*Novavax (Australia)*	*Other Chinese Vaccines*[a]	*Russian Vaccines*[a]	*Others*
Brunei	X	X	X	0	0	0	0	X	0	0	0	0
Cambodia	0	0	X	X	0	0	X	X	0	0	Sputnik Light Sputnik V KoviVac EpiVacCorona	0
Laos	X	0	0	X	0	0	X	X	0	0	Sputnik Light Sputnik V	0
Indonesia	X	X	X	X	X	0	X	X	0	CanSino, ZF2001, KConvac	Sputnik V	0
Malaysia	X	X	X	X		0	X	X	0	CanSino	0	0
Myanmar	0	0	0	0	X	0		X	0	0	Sputnik V	0
Philippines	X	X	X	X	X	X	X	X (two types)	0	0	Sputnik Light, Sputnik V	0
Singapore	X	X	0	0	0	0	X	0	0	0	0	0
Thailand	X	X	X	X	0	0	X	X	0	0	0	0
Vietnam	X	X	X	X	0	X	0	X	0	0	Sputnik V	Abdala (Cuba)

Notes: X: Vaccine approved by country and by WHO; 0: Country did not approve the vaccine.
a. Vaccine not on approved list by WHO, as of February 2022.
Source: https://covid19.trackvaccines.org/agency/who (accessed 2 February 2022).

protect their front-line health workers and high-risk groups, such as senior citizens and those with comorbidities, and the other half for high- and middle-income countries.

The participation of Southeast Asian countries in the COVAX facility was determined by their income group; the ten countries were divided into three income groups based on the World Bank's Atlas method (World Bank n.d.). Brunei and Singapore are categorized as high-income countries, while Malaysia and Thailand fall into the upper-middle-income bracket. The remaining six Southeast Asian countries studied in this volume—Cambodia, Indonesia, Laos, Myanmar, Philippines and Vietnam—are classed as lower-middle-income countries.

Brunei and Singapore were among sixty-four high-income economies that had formally signed up with COVAX by 22 September 2020. Each country signed a legally binding agreement to buy vaccines and COVAX then started signing agreements with vaccine manufacturers and developers. Malaysia joined in November 2020, committing to buy and choosing the Optional Purchase arrangement, a scheme that allowed participants to decide which vaccines they bought. Thailand decided not to join COVAX in 2020 as it preferred to deal directly with manufacturers, and it also aimed for local production. Subsequently, in November 2020, Thailand arranged with AstraZeneca to supply Covid-19 vaccine and to transfer technology to local production in the country.

The list of the ninety-two lower-income countries that had signed up to the COVAX Advance Market Commitment was finalized by July 2020. The list included the six lower-middle-income countries in Southeast Asia studied in this volume. These countries were eligible to purchase vaccines based on two cost-sharing principles. Donor-funded, fully subsidized doses (i.e., free vaccines) were distributed across eligible countries until each country had enough to cover 20 per cent of its population (or until donor resources were exhausted). After 20 per cent coverage was achieved, eligible countries could purchase vaccines for 15 per cent to 20 per cent of the cost (Agarwal and Reed 2021).

In 2020, the COVAX Advance Market Commitment targeted to deliver to the ninety-two lower-income countries at least 1.3 billion donor-funded doses of approved vaccines by the end of 2021. Donations were crucial in COVAX supply; they funded 60 per cent of the doses delivered in 2021 (or 543 million doses out of 910 million delivered) (Bengy Puyvallée and Storeng 2022).

It should be noted that all countries in Southeast Asia country also bought directly from vaccine manufacturers because COVAX could not supply sufficient vaccines to cover their populations. There is no data on the direct purchases of each country.

Roll-out of COVAX Vaccines

Singapore had signed advanced purchase agreements through COVAX and approved the Pfizer vaccine by December 2020. It is therefore not surprising that it was the first country in Southeast Asia to receive COVAX vaccines: it received the first batch of the Pfizer vaccine in December 2020 (Table 14.2). Singapore also ordered two other types of vaccines, Moderna and Sinovac, through COVAX. It began vaccinating healthcare workers in December 2020, followed by seniors aged seventy and above in January 2021 and, subsequently, critical health workers (Amul et al. 2021).

Brunei, which also booked COVAX vaccines early, received its first batch of 240,000 doses of AstraZeneca in April 2021. Malaysia, which had signed later with COVAX, also received its first batch of COVAX AstraZeneca vaccines in April 2021. However, Malaysia received a batch of Pfizer vaccines in February 2021, having bought these directly from the Pfizer factory in Belgium.

The ninety-two lower-income countries of the Advance Market Commitment, including four of the six lower-middle-income countries in Southeast Asia studied in this volume, received their first batch of AstraZeneca vaccines from COVAX in March 2021. Vietnam received them in April 2021, while Myanmar did not receive its allocated vaccines due to the February 2021 coup and subsequent sanctions. There is no published information on whether the country actually received its COVAX vaccines.[1] As noted by Blanchet et al. (2021), sanctioned countries may have problems receiving vaccines from COVAX, which are delivered through formal channels. Sanctioned countries could also be hindered by limited access to goods and services including cold-storage equipment, fuel, software, insurance and logistics operators. Myanmar did manage to obtain vaccines through India and China.

TABLE 14.2
Vaccine Doses Allocated and Distributed to Southeast Asian Countries Participating in COVAX, as of January 2022

Country	*Advance Market Commitment Status*	*COVAX Doses Allocated*	*COVAX Doses Received*	*Per Capita Doses Allocated*	*Per Capita Doses Distributed*
Brunei	Self-financing	100,800	100,800	0.23	0.23
Singapore	Self-financing	938,400	938,400	0.17	0.17
Malaysia	Self-financing	1,840,300	1,387,200	0.06	0.04
Cambodia	Sponsored	3,925,260	3,925,260	0.23	0.23
Laos	Sponsored	6,557,300	5,088,150	0.90	0.70
Myanmar	Sponsored	12,252,600	—	0.23	—
Vietnam	Sponsored	68,341,910	49,606,820	0.70	0.51
Philippines	Sponsored	69,869,275	65,724,200	0.64	0.60
Indonesia	Sponsored	178,461,900	87,951,970	0.65	0.32

Note: Countries are ordered from lowest to highest in terms of COVAX doses allocated.
Source: Yoo et al. (2022).

By January 2022, COVAX had delivered more than 1 billion doses of Covid-19 vaccines to 144 participating economies, including more than 870 million to Advance Market Commitment economies, lower than the targeted 1.3 billion doses. This was due to intense competition for vaccines, which led to delays in the delivery of early doses under the contracts COVAX had signed with manufacturers. Furthermore, the majority of the donations were made in an ad hoc fashion and were provided with little notice and with a short shelf life, thereby making it difficult for the recipient countries to plan their vaccination programmes. Some of the donated doses were found to be earmarked to certain countries for political reasons, such as bilateral relations between donor and recipient countries, which violated the COVAX principle of equitable access (Bengy Puyvallée and Storeng 2022).

Out of the 870 million doses delivered to the ninety-two economies that had signed up to the Advance Market Commitment, East Asia and the Pacific received 216 million (or 24.6 per cent). The six Southeast Asian countries in the Advance Market Commitment received 98 per cent of the 216 million. Nevertheless, as shown in Table 14.2, as of January 2022, none of those Southeast Asian countries in the Advance Market Commitment had received their full allocation of vaccines. Table 14.2 also shows that Laos, Vietnam and the Philippines depended more on COVAX allocations per capita than did Cambodia and Indonesia.

Among the high-income self-paying countries, as of January 2022, Brunei and Singapore had received their entire allocation of doses and Malaysia had received 75 per cent. These three countries also made more direct purchases than the other countries in Southeast Asia, while Cambodia and Indonesia made more direct purchases than the other four Southeast Asian countries that had signed up to the Advance Market Commitment.

Vaccine Diplomacy: Multilateral and Bilateral

Vaccine diplomacy, meaning the use of vaccines to improve relations between donor and donee countries or to influence a donee, was widely practised during the Covid-19 pandemic.

China

China was the first to use the Covid-19 pandemic to strengthen bilateral ties in Southeast Asia. Before vaccines were in circulation, China donated masks and test kits and sent experts to Southeast Asia. For example, in the first quarter of 2020, China sent Malaysia personal protective equipment, hand sanitizers and other materials for the fight against the virus. Health authorities in Malaysia also held a teleconference with experts from China to discuss how to rein in infections. China also sent large shipments of aid packages, including N95 face masks, medical masks, goggles, protective suits, test kits and other items to the Philippines, Indonesia and Thailand (Vittachi 2023).

China had some early advantages in vaccine diplomacy. It had raced into vaccine development early in 2020 after the emergence of the virus in late 2019. Chinese state-owned and private companies, such as Sinopharm, Sinovac and Convidecia, with the Institute of Biology at the country's Academy of Military Medical Sciences, were mobilized in 2020 to accelerate the production of vaccines. China also has a sizeable vaccine manufacturing capacity which enabled speedy production at a large scale. It also gave conditional approval to vaccines for domestic use even before phase three trials had been completed. For example, in July 2020, China launched its controversial emergency use programme, distributing doses from Sinovac, Sinopharm and private Beijing firm CanSino to the Chinese population before the companies had completed phase 3 trials to test safety and efficacy in protecting from Covid-19. China also had vested commercial interests, and accelerating approvals meant the vaccines could be more quickly sold. China did indeed sell more doses than it donated. China's vaccine diplomacy is used for hard (material benefits) as well as soft (image-building) objectives (Bengy Puyvallée and Storeng 2022).

Thus, by October 2020, China had already started to supply vaccines, both through donations and commercial sales, to Southeast Asian countries. China's Foreign Minister Wang Yi conducted vaccine diplomacy by touring Southeast Asia in October 2020 and again in January 2021 (Yeremia and Raditio 2021). The use of China's vaccines was subsequently boosted when the WHO gave conditional approval in early May for the use of Sinopharm and in June 2021 for Sinovac. This was despite the lack of transparency on data about all China-made vaccines, especially regarding preliminary and peer-reviewed data proving their safety and efficacy. Sinopharm and Sinovac's conditional approval meant that these two vaccines could be used by COVAX to mitigate a shortfall left by a reduction in India's vaccine exports and meet its aim of supplying vaccines to the developing world.

Indonesia was the first country after China to issue fast-track authorization for the Sinovac vaccine, and the first country to receive Chinese vaccines. Its first batch of purchased Chinese vaccines, Sinovac, arrived in December 2020 and the influential Indonesian Ulema Council (Majelis Ulama Indonesia) issued a ruling confirming the vaccine's halal status. The President of Indonesia received an injection of Sinovac on live television on 13 January 2021, when the country's first mass vaccination programme began. Indonesia also received vaccine donations from China, but these began later, in September 2021.

Thailand was the second country in Southeast Asia to receive China's vaccines. It purchased its first batch, Sinovac, which arrived early in January 2021. The first donated batch of Sinovac arrived in February 2021. The next batch of Chinese Covid-19 vaccines arrived in Southeast Asia in February 2021 (Table 14.3), but Myanmar received China's vaccine donation later than the rest of Southeast Asia—they arrived in May 2021. This was due to the February 2021 coup and the ensuing sanctions which disrupted vaccine deliveries. However, India had already sent vaccines to Myanmar—it was the first country to do so—and these, produced by Serum Institute of India (Covishield), arrived in January 2021.

Although Brunei did not need donations, as it was in the high-income category, China did nevertheless donate vaccines in appreciation of the fact that at the outset of the pandemic, in March 2020, Brunei had provided financial assistance to China.

Malaysia received its first batch of vaccines purchased from China in February 2021 for bottling within the country. The then Minister of Science, Technology and Innovation, Khairy Jamaluddin, became the first person in Malaysia to receive a Sinovac vaccine on Thursday—he was vaccinated on 18 March 2021.

Singapore also received its first batch of advance purchased Sinovac in February 2021, though the vaccine had not yet been authorized by the country's regulators at the time of arrival and so could not be used immediately. Singapore approved Sinovac in June 2021 for private clinics, after the WHO approved the vaccine earlier that same month. Subsequently, Sinovac was added to the Singapore National Vaccination Programme in

TABLE 14.3
China's Vaccines in Southeast Asia, as of December 2021 and June 2022

Country	*First Arrival of China's Vaccines*	*Total Doses Purchased from and Donated by China*[a]	*Doses Purchased from China*	*Doses Donated by China*
Brunei	February 2021	—	—	—
Cambodia	February 2021	36.8 million (December 2021); 41.8 million (June 2022)	28.5 million (December 2021); 28.5 million (June 2022)	8.3 million (December 2021); 13.3 million (June 2022)
Laos	February 2021	8.7 million (December 2021); 9.1 million (June 2022)	0 (December 2021); 0 (June 2022)	8.7 million (December 2021); 9.1 million (June 2022)
Indonesia	December 2020 (purchased)	255 million (December 2021); 268.3 million (June 2022)	252 million (December 2021); 265.3 million (June 2022)	3 million (December 2021); 3 million (June 2021)
Malaysia	February 2021 (bulk purchase) July 2021 (donation)	10.9 million (December 2021); No change in June 2022	8.4 million (December 2021); No change in June 2022	2.5 million (December 2021); No change in June 2022
Myanmar	May 2021	44.0 million (December 2021); 54.3 million (June 2022)	33.4 million (December 2021); 33.7 million (June 2022)	10.6 million (December 2021); 20.64 million (June 2022)

continued on next page

TABLE 14.3 — *cont'd*

Country	*First Arrival of China's Vaccines*	*Total Doses Purchased from and Donated by China*[a]	*Doses Purchased from China*	*Doses Donated by China*
Philippines	February 2021	60 million (December 2021); No change in June 2022	55 million (December 2021); No change in June 2022	5 million (December 2021); No change in June 2022
Singapore	February 2021 (purchase, approved for use in June 2021)	—	—	—
Thailand	January 2021	29.9 million (December 2021); No change in June 2022	26.5 million (December 2021); No change in June 2022	3.4 million (December 2021); No change in June 2022
Vietnam	February 2021	37.7 million (December 2021); 41.5 million (June 2022)	36.2 million (December 2021); 36.2 million (June 2022)	1.5 million (December 2021); 5.3 million (June 2022)

Notes: The table covers only bilateral contributions directly from China as extracted from https://bridgebeijing.com/our-publications/our-publications-1/china-covid-19-vaccines-tracker/ for February 2022 and June 2022 (accessed 10 June 2022).
a. Data for Brunei and Singapore is unavailable.
Source: Media reports and embassy announcements.

October 2021 to cater to those who were medically ineligible for mRNA Covid-19 vaccines; Sinovac uses an inactivated form of the virus.

China's vaccines were among the first, whether purchased or donated, to assist Southeast Asian countries, arriving even before COVAX vaccines, except in the case of Singapore (Table 14.3). Further, purchased doses exceeded donations for all Southeast Asian countries except Laos, which bought no vaccines. Indonesia was the largest buyer, followed by the Philippines and Myanmar.

In 2022, Malaysia, the Philippines and Thailand continued to buy vaccines and receive vaccine donations. Purchases continued in 2022 for Cambodia, Indonesia, Myanmar and Vietnam. Cambodia, Laos, Myanmar and Vietnam also continued to receive donations in the same year.

United States

In June 2021, the Biden administration announced that it would share at least 80 million US vaccine doses (mostly Pfizer) globally by the end of June and the proposed allocation plan for the first 25 million doses. Specifically, the United States planned to share at least three-quarters of its donated doses through COVAX to countries in need. For doses shared through COVAX, the United States prioritized Latin America and the Caribbean, South Asia, Southeast Asia and Africa. Approximately 7 million doses were allocated to Asia, namely to India, Nepal, Bangladesh, Pakistan, Sri Lanka, Afghanistan, Maldives, Malaysia, Philippines, Vietnam, Indonesia, Thailand, Laos, Papua New Guinea, Taiwan and the Pacific Islands.

The United States did, however, invoke its Defense Protection Act to ensure American vaccine manufacturers prioritized deliveries to the US government, leading to virtually no exports or donations abroad in the first half of 2021 (Bengy Puyvallée and Storeng 2022). Moreover, President Biden also ensured that its donations would not impact its own vaccine supply by purchasing 1one billion doses for COVAX at cost, including the 700 million doses for donation. The donations were also bought from an American producer, guaranteeing production and employment in the country.

Overall, 45 per cent of the US vaccine donations were delivered via COVAX and 55 per cent were delivered direct, but there are no available regional or country breakdowns for the direct delivery. In 2021 and 2022, the countries that received significant US vaccine donations were Indonesia, the Philippines and Vietnam (Table 14.4). Although the delivery was slow and arrived late in 2021 and in 2022, it helped the region to fight the surge in Covid-19 cases that came with the Delta wave from April to August 2021 (*The Economist* 2021).

Other Countries

The European Union (EU) also conducted vaccine diplomacy (Table 14.5) The EU, with its member states, the European Investment Bank and the European Bank for Reconstruction and Development (the grouping is called Team Europe) was the second-largest donor, after the United States, to the COVAX Advance Market Commitment. Japan was another prominent donor to COVAX. Australia and China each contributed US$100 million. Some Southeast Asia countries also contributed, albeit in smaller amounts, with Singapore taking the lead.

In March 2021, the Quadrilateral Security Dialogue, an informal strategic forum comprising Australia, the United States, Japan and India, launched the Quad Vaccine Partnership to help enhance equitable access

TABLE 14.4
US Vaccine Diplomacy, as of September 2021 and February 2022

Country	*Cumulative Doses Received September 2021*	*Cumulative Doses Received February 2022*
Cambodia	1.1 million	1.1 million
Indonesia	4.5 million	35.8 million
Laos	1.1 million	2.7 million
Malaysia	1 million	1 million
Philippines	6.4 million	33.3 million
Thailand	1.5 million (Thailand negotiated this bilaterally with the United States, because it is not a member of COVAX.)	2.5 million
Vietnam	5 million	61.5 million

Note: US vaccine diplomacy covers only donations. Purchases were carried out privately between US producer companies and foreign governments.
Source: US International COVID-19 Vaccine Donations Tracker. https://www.kff.org/global-health-policy/issue-brief/u-s-international-covid-19-vaccine-donations-tracker/ (accessed 1 June 2022).

TABLE 14.5
Vaccine Donations (Including Donations from China and the United States, 2021–22, as of January 2022)

Country	*Direct Contributions (US$ million)*	*Total Contributions (US$ million)*
Australia	72	100
Canada	414	470
China	100 (August 2021)	100
Team Europe	–	3,220
European Union	489	489
Japan	1,000	1,000
Korea	210	210
United Kingdom	63	731
United States	3,500	4,000
Malaysia	0.1	0.1
Philippines	1.0	1.0
Singapore	5.0	5.0
Vietnam	0.5	0.5
Total donor[a] governments	8,444	10,377
Total foundations, corporations and organizations	443	473
Total pledged to date	8,887	10,849

Note: a. Data relating to individual countries grouped here can be found at Gavi (2022).
Source: Gavi (2022).

to safe and effective vaccines, first for the Indo-Pacific and then the rest of the world. The Quad Vaccine Partnership pledged to donate more than 1.2 billion vaccine doses globally, in addition to the doses they financed through COVAX. By September 2021, the Quad Vaccine Partnership had delivered nearly 79 million vaccine doses to the Indo-Pacific region. In February 2022, the Quad leaders announced that the countries of the Quad Vaccine Partnership had provided 500 million doses; they also increased their donations pledge by 0.1 billion to 1.3 billion doses (US Department of State 2022). Unfortunately, there is no detailed country breakdown by source and recipient countries.

Private Purchase

The relatively low vaccination rate in the first half of 2021 led private companies to try to supplement government purchases. Indonesia was the first in Southeast Asia to allow private companies to purchase vaccines, imported by the government, for their employees and their families (Table 14.6). However, this programme was terminated in July 2021 amid criticism from the public and civil society groups (Lai 2021).

As noted by Hudes and Chen (2021), the intention to use private purchasing to boost vaccinations would have widened gaps in access in each country, especially for informal workers, who were not covered at all under private purchase programmes. The COVAX facility was supposed to surmount this global vaccine inequity. Nevertheless, other Southeast

TABLE 14.6
Private Purchases of Covid Vaccines in Southeast Asia, 2021

Country	*Date of Purchase*	*Purchases by Private Companies*
Indonesia	25 February 2021	Gotong Royong scheme, funded by companies, allowed private and state-owned companies to purchase vaccine supplies from the government to inoculate workers and their family members.
Malaysia	June 2021	State governments and private hospitals permitted to buy Covid-19 vaccines from government and from vaccine manufacturers approved by the World Health Organization, such as Moderna and Sinopharm.
Myanmar	15 November 2021	Hemas Mandalar Pharmaceuticals Ltd imported 200,000 doses of filled and finished Sinovac from Malaysia.
Philippines	29 March 2021	Firms permitted to enter into tripartite deals with the national government and vaccine manufacturers.
Singapore	15 September 2021	Livingstone Health International, a private company, appointed by the Ministry of Health to lead in the procurement of Sinovac vaccines on behalf of private healthcare institutions.
Thailand	June 2021	Private organizations and local administrative organizations permitted to procure Covid-19 vaccines but only through government channels.
Vietnam	July 2021	T&T Group, a private company, permitted to purchase Sputnik V vaccines from Russia.

Source: Media reports.

Asian countries also permitted private companies to purchase from their governments, the importers, to supplement their vaccination programmes (Table 14.6).

Covid-19 Vaccine Production in Southeast Asia[2]

The 2019 ASEAN Vaccine Baseline Survey (ASEAN Secretariat 2019), conducted prior to Covid-19, found that Southeast Asia had four countries with vaccine production capacity: Indonesia, Myanmar, Thailand and Vietnam. It is therefore unsurprising that these countries—excluding Myanmar, which was struggling with the post-coup strife—were keen to develop vaccines, whether in partnership with existing producers from developed countries or alone. Domestic production was intended to ensure adequate supply for a country's own needs, reducing its dependency on imports and enhancing capabilities that would help the country cope with future health pandemics. The latter was especially important given uncertainties over the development of Covid-19 at the time, the time taken for the pandemic to move to endemic status and the need to learn to live with the virus.

Production with Existing Vaccine Producers

Indonesia was quick to act: the Indonesian embassy in Beijing sought to establish contact with Sinovac as early as March 2020, before any other country. In June 2020, Sinovac agreed to cooperate with Bio Farma, a state-owned Indonesian company, to conduct clinical trials and manufacture vaccines.[3] In August 2020, a phase 3 clinical trial for Sinovac's vaccine was conducted in Indonesia. Under the agreement with China, Bio Farma acquired the licence to produce Sinovac and was designated a production hub for the region. It was the only country in Southeast Asia to be so designated. Indonesia imported in bulk and Bio Farma filled and finished 15 million Sinovac doses for mid-January 2021 distribution.

Thailand's government also negotiated to produce Covid-19 vaccines, signing an advance agreement in November of 2020 to secure an undisclosed number of doses of the AstraZeneca vaccine. It also secured authorization for local production by the Thai private drug manufacturer Siam Bioscience, which had no prior experience in vaccine production (Tham 2022). Thailand considered it strategically important to gain from technology transfer and make the country self-reliant in vaccine production (Peter 2021). Domestic production would also promote the Thai pharmaceutical industry ahead of other Southeast Asian countries (Somkid 2021). The contract made Siam Bioscience the sole Southeast Asia production hub for the vaccine and permitted it to produce up to 200 million doses a year (Reed, Peel, and Kuchler 2021). The Thai government reserved about a third of those doses for Thailand, and the rest was exported to Indonesia, the Philippines, Vietnam and other neighbours (Peter 2021).

In June 2021, Siam Bioscience started the country's first production of a Covid-19 vaccine, using AstraZeneca's technology. However, there were teething problems, given the lack of prior experience, which led to a shortfall in the projected production (Satrusayang 2021). This affected the projected number of doses available for Thailand and for export. Siam Bioscience did surmount the problems and emerged as a major manufacturer of the AstraZeneca vaccine, producing 52.5 million doses in September 2021, compared with just 8.4 million in August 2021 (Global Commission for Post-Pandemic Policy n.d.).

Malaysia also signed a deal with Sinovac in January 2021 to fill and finish the vaccines in Malaysia through Pharmaniaga, a government-linked pharmaceutical company (*Sun Daily* 2021). Pharmaniaga imported bulk material from Sinovac and performed the fill and finish process at its LifeScience plant. This also involved the transfer of technology related to safety regulations and procedures and required testing of the equipment used. Subsequently, Pharmaniaga reported that it had supplied 12 million doses of the vaccine to the National Covid-19 Immunization Programme by 1 August 2021, following an agreement signed in January 2021 (Pharmaniaga 2021). There are subsequently two media reports of further collaboration with China on vaccine research, development and production, although the partners are not named (Bernama 2021). Moderna reportedly moved into vaccine production in Malaysia in 2022 (Adilla 2022).

Reportedly, Vietnamese conglomerate Vingroup teamed up with US vaccine maker Arcturus Therapeutics, based in the US city of San Diego, to begin production of the latter's Covid-19 vaccine in Vietnam in 2022 (Vingroup 2021). On 15 August 2021 Vingroup began phase one trials of the vaccine (Onishi 2021). Arcturus agreed to provide Vingroup with an exclusive licence to make its mRNA Covid-19 vaccine candidate—the same type as those developed by Pfizer and Moderna—solely for sale and use in Vietnam. Phase three trials were reported completed in April 2022 (Arcturus therapeutics 2022), but no further information has emerged regarding the start of production.

Producing Home-Made Covid-19 Vaccines

The desire to produce home-made Covid-19 vaccines was based on a wish to become self-sufficient, to improve coordination among research and development agencies and to enhance national capability in Covid-19 vaccine production. Four countries in Southeast Asia actively pursued the development of home-made vaccines.

Table 14.7 shows the home-grown vaccines that had advanced to clinical trials as of June 2022. Vietnam's Nanocovax, which was being developed by the Nanogen Pharmaceutical Biology Joint Stock Company in cooperation with the Military Medical Academy, had progressed to phase three trials. As of 12 January 2023, Nanocovax's expression of interest to provide the vaccine was still under review with the WHO (WHO 2022).

As of June 2022, Singapore's ARCT-021 vaccine was in phase two trials, while the Merah Putih vaccine in Indonesia entered into phase three trials in August 2022 (Bona 2022). Indonesia was pressing to launch the Merah Putih vaccine in the third quarter of 2022 (Yulisman 2022). Indonesia's Nusantara vaccine, however, was mired in domestic debates as it was being developed by an American company, Aivita Bio Medical Inc., and its vaccine technology was based on dendritic cells, components of blood cells that are part of the immune system (*Tempo* 2021). As of June 2022, no dendritic cell-based Covid-19 vaccines had entered into phase three clinical trials anywhere in the world, nor had any been approved by any drug regulatory authority.

As of June 2022, Thailand's two home-grown vaccines were still in phase two trials, with the Chula-Baiya vaccine being plant-based, while its developer Baiya was the first Thai company to collaborate with a university to develop the technology to manufacture recombinant proteins that can produce medicines and vaccines. The collaboration was with Chulalongkorn University's CU Innovation Hub, a Thai research centre for start-ups. Mass production of the vaccine Chula Cov-19 was expected to

TABLE 14.7
Vaccine Candidates under Development in Southeast Asia, as of 26 February 2022

	Candidate	*Mechanism*	*Sponsor*	*Trial Phase*	*Institution*
1	Nanocovax	Recombinant vaccine (spike protein)	Nanogen Biopharmaceutical	3	Military Medical Academy, Vietnam
2	ART-021	RNA vaccine	Arcturus Therapeutics and Duke Medical School	2	Duke–NUS Medical School, Singapore
3	Merah Putih	Inactivated vaccine	Ministry of Health, Indonesia; Airlangga University; Biotis Pharmaceuticals (from Indonesia)	2	Dr Soetomo General Hospital, Indonesia
4	Nusantara*	Dendritic cell vaccine	Aivita Bio Medical Inc	2	National Institute of Health and Development, Ministry of Health, Republic of Indonesia
5	ChulaCov19	mRNA-based vaccine	Chulalongkorn University's Center of Excellence in Vaccine Research and Development	2	Chula Vaccine Research Center, Faculty of Tropical Medicine, Mahidol University
6	Chula-Baiya	Protein subunit	Baiya Phytopharm Co Ltd, National Vaccine Institute, Thailand	2	Chula Clinical Research Center; Queen Saovabha Memorial Institute

Source: Regulatory Affairs Professionals Society at https://www.raps.org/news-and-articles/news-articles/2020/3/covid-19-vaccine-tracker (accessed 1 May 2024); * World Health Organization's COVID-19 Vaccine Tracker and Landscape at https://www.who.int/publications/m/item/draft-landscape-of-covid-19-candidate-vaccines (accessed 1 May 2024).

take place from June to September 2022, while the Chula-Baiya vaccine was expected to be approved for use in the third or fourth quarter of 2022 (Chulalongkorn University 2021).

In January 2022, the Institute of Medical Research (IMR), a biomedical research arm of the Ministry of Health, stated that two types of Covid-19 vaccines were being developed in Malaysia. The IMR was collaborating with Universiti Putra Malaysia and the Veterinary Research Institute on one (Asia News Network 2022), an inactivated vaccine, much like Sinovac. The second is an mRNA (messenger RNA) vaccine, which is solely an IMR initiative. The latter was scheduled for clinical trials in 2024.

The increase in production capacity in Southeast Asia, whether in collaboration with existing producers or through home-grown varieties, will increase future supply. However, demand for the latter may be low, according to an ISEAS report, *The State of Southeast Asia: 2022 Survey Report* (Seah et al. 2022). The survey indicates that trust in home-made vaccines is low. The most trusted vaccine brands among Southeast Asians—selected by 54.8 per cent of all respondents—are the mRNA vaccines Pfizer and Moderna. Domestic vaccines, on the other hand, are the second-least trusted, at 0.9 per cent, only slightly higher than the least trusted, the Russian-made vaccine Sputnik V. Even with the option of domestically made vaccines, citizens may still prefer to use established brands—unless imports of these are prohibited, priced too high or made unaffordable through domestic import taxes.

STATE CAPACITY

The proxy for a state's capacity to implement vaccine roll-outs is taken from the World Banks's World Governance Indicator database and compiles and summarizes information on the quality of different dimensions of governance. The information comes from data sources that report the views and experiences of citizens, entrepreneurs and experts in the public, private and non-profit sectors from around the world.

A study by Tatar et al. (2021) shows that good governance, in particular government effectiveness, voice and accountability, and regulatory quality, are the most important indicators in predicting the rate of Covid-19 vaccinations across countries. These indicators are shown in Table 14.8. *Government effectiveness* captures perceptions of the quality of public services, the quality of the civil service and the degree of its independence from political pressures, the quality of policy formulation and implementation, and the credibility of the government's commitment to such policies. *Voice and accountability* indicate perceptions of the extent

TABLE 14.8
Selected Governance Indicators Score[a]

Country	*Government Effectiveness*		*Voice and Accountability*		*Regulatory Quality*	
	2019	*2020*	*2019*	*2020*	*2019*	*2020*
Brunei	87	90.4	21.7	22.2	73.1	76.9
Cambodia	31.7	38	15	12.6	30.3	29.8
Indonesia	60.1	65.4	51.7	52.2	51.4	55.3
Laos	20.7	22.6	3.4	3.4	23.6	21.2
Malaysia	79.3	82.2	43.5	40.1	73.6	74
Myanmar	11.5	14.4	23.2	21.7	21.6	28.4
Philippines	54.8	56.3	45.4	41.1	55.3	53.4
Singapore	100	100	38.6	38.2	100	100
Thailand	66.3	63.5	23.7	26.1	60.1	58.7
Vietnam	53.4	61.5	11.6	12.1	41.8	46.6

Note: A government's score under each indicator is ranked from 0 to 100, with 100 being the highest.
a. This table presents composite indicators based on more than thirty data sources. These include surveys of households and firms, including the Afrobarometer surveys, the Gallup World Poll and the Global Competitiveness Report survey; commercial business information providers, including the Economist Intelligence Unit, IHS Markit, Political Risk Services; non-governmental organizations, including Global Integrity, Freedom House, Reporters Without Borders; and public sector organizations, including the Country Policy and Institutional Assessment (CPIA) assessments of the World Bank and regional development banks.
Source: World Bank's Worldwide Governance Indicators at http://info.worldbank.org/governance/wgi/ (accessed 1 April 2023).

to which a country's citizens can participate in selecting their government, and perceptions of freedom of expression, freedom of association, and free media. *Regulatory quality* covers perceptions of the ability of the government to formulate and implement sound policies and regulations that permit and promote private sector development.

Overall, state capacity is higher in Singapore, Brunei and Malaysia, relative to Thailand, Indonesia and the Philippines. Singapore has the highest score for government effectiveness and regulatory quality. The quick actions taken by the public service and the strong ability of the government to implement policies enabled Singapore to administer vaccines efficiently. Other countries with relatively strong governance are Brunei and Malaysia. Each executed its vaccination programme and movement control policies relatively efficiently. In the case of Malaysia, information dissemination via the MySejahtera app was current and trusted by people. Indonesia was the best performer in voice and accountability. A higher level of openness was shown with President Joko "Jokowi" Widodo acknowledged and encouraged criticisms on the handling of Covid-19 (Karmini 2021). The weakest performer was Myanmar, followed by Laos and Cambodia, though the latter was among the best performers in Covid-19 recovery.

However, the urgency called for in managing the pandemic, including rolling out vaccinations, gave rise to state digital innovations, which helped to overcome some of the weaknesses in state capacity, as occurred in Cambodia. Elsewhere, Lee, Ibrahim, and Zhang (2021) found that mobile apps released or updated with functions related to Covid-19 emerged and evolved in the first half of 2021 for some Southeast Asian countries, notably Indonesia, Malaysia, the Philippines, Thailand and Vietnam. These apps were used to complement public health measures for tracking Covid-19 cases, to disseminate information and to manage the vaccination programme. Although Brunei, Cambodia, Laos and Myanmar were not included in the study, mobile apps were also used effectively in these countries to manage the pandemic, including vaccinations. The use of digital technology enabled all countries in Southeast Asia, especially those with weaker state capacities, namely Laos, Myanmar and Cambodia, to conduct their vaccination programmes. These apps were also used to issue digital vaccination certificates.

LOGISTICS INFRASTRUCTURE

While the effectiveness of vaccine policies and government action plans are important, the deployment of vaccines requires good logistics infrastructure. Table 14.9 indicates the level of logistics infrastructure in Southeast Asian countries. Singapore, as a city-state, scores highest in the Logistics Performance Index (LPI). Other countries with larger and more challenging geographical conditions within the region score less well, while Thailand, Vietnam and Malaysia have relatively better LPI scores than the rest of Southeast Asia, aside from Singapore.

As many of these countries rely on imported vaccines, efficiency in customs and border management and competence and quality of logistics services—trucking, forwarding and customs brokerage—play a key role in vaccine deployment. Again, Singapore ranked highest in all these categories.

TABLE 14.9
Logistics Performance Index, 2018

	Overall LPI Score	*LPI Ranking out of 160 Countries*	*Customs*	*Infrastructure*	*International Shipments*	*Logistics Quality and Competence*	*Tracking and Tracing*	*Timelines*
			(A)	*(B)*	*(C)*	*(D)*	*(E)*	*(F)*
Singapore	4.00	7	6	6	15	3	8	6
Thailand	3.41	32	36	41	25	32	33	28
Vietnam	3.27	39	41	47	49	33	34	40
Malaysia	3.22	41	43	40	32	36	47	53
Indonesia	3.15	46	62	54	42	44	39	41
Philippines	2.90	60	85	67	37	69	57	100
Brunei Darussalam	2.71	80	73	89	113	77	88	80
Laos	2.70	82	74	91	85	83	69	117
Cambodia	2.58	98	109	130	71	111	111	84
Myanmar	2.30	137	131	143	144	128	143	108

Note: LPI: Logistics Performance Index.
Source: World Bank, Logistics Performance Index (2018).

The difference in ranking between Singapore and the next three countries, Thailand, Vietnam and Malaysia, is significant. In Thailand, Vietnam and Malaysia, the quality and competence of their logistic services are fairly similar.

However, the LPI (Table 14.9) only represents logistics and customs efficiency at the borders of a country. While seaport efficiency plays an important role in the speed of distribution of vaccines, equally important is the efficiency of land logistics in dispersing the vaccines throughout the country. The domestic LPI can be used here (Table 14.10) though unfortunately the dataset is limited and covers only eight of the ten Southeast Asian countries studied. The data indicates that country size can affect the distribution process. Smaller countries like Singapore and Brunei fare better compared to larger countries such as Thailand and Indonesia. Hence, the size of Brunei compensated for its weaker LPI score in Table 14.9 since it made domestic delivery easier to achieve. A landlocked country like Laos may face more challenges in transporting and dispersing the vaccines from the nearest seaport. Although Cambodia fares poorly in the LPI ranking in Table 14.9, and data on its domestic LPI is unavailable, its remarkable success in rolling out the vaccines to achieve the fifth-highest vaccination rate globally highlights the limitations of relying on these indicators alone.

TABLE 14.10
Import Distance (Land Supply Chain), 2018

	Distance (Kilometres)
Brunei	25
Indonesia	277
Laos	750
Malaysia	75
Myanmar	579
Singapore	33
Thailand	300
Vietnam	131

Note: This table shows the import distance from the point of origin (the seller's factory, typically located either in the capital city or in the largest commercial centre) to the buyer's warehouse in the same country, with the goods delivered with duty paid by the seller. The buyer pays transport costs.
Source: World Bank's Logistics Performance Index at https://lpi.worldbank.org/ (accessed 2 June 2022).

DEMAND FOR VACCINES

Vaccine acceptance in Southeast Asian countries followed a common pattern: greater hesitation in the early days of the pandemic before a gradual increase in vaccine acceptance (Figure 14.1). The Philippines, Thailand and Indonesia were generally below the Southeast Asian average for vaccine acceptance, according to YouGov (accessed 1 April 2023). The finding for the Philippines is supported by the World Bank's high-frequency monitoring surveys, which show that the Philippines had a significantly lower share of respondents who intended to be vaccinated compared with other countries in the region. This is attributed to a lack of information about vaccines, misinformation about their efficacy or side effects, mistrust, and underestimation of benefits compared to overestimation of risks and costs of vaccination (World Bank 2021).

Thailand initially had a high vaccine acceptance rate, but intention to be vaccinated fluctuated the most out of all Southeast Asian countries. In the second half of 2021, when citizens of other countries were gradually accepting vaccines, Thailand had one of the lowest vaccine acceptance rates in the region, alongside the Philippines and Indonesia. The reasons for vaccine hesitancy varied from widespread complaints at government disorganization and dissatisfaction with the military-backed government's vaccine strategy, to delays in getting vaccines and queries around the effectiveness of Sinovac and locally made AstraZeneca doses (Chayut 2021). Punchada (2022) also highlighted coordination failures among government agencies, which led poor management of the vaccination programme at the local level in 2021. Vaccine hesitation in Indonesia, on the other hand was due to uncertainty about the halal status of the vaccines (Rising and Tarigan 2021). However, vaccine acceptance rates in Malaysia, Singapore and Vietnam were above the Southeast Asia average.

Although there is no data for the four Southeast Asia countries excluded from Figure 14.1, Brunei, Cambodia, Laos and Myanmar, there is some anecdotal evidence of vaccine hesitancy in Myanmar due to a lack of trust in the administration (Liu 2022). On the other hand, 87 per cent of the population of Laos indicated their willingness to be vaccinated (Runde, Bandura, and McKeown 2022; World Bank 2021). Cambodia also had low vaccine hesitancy and a sense of communal responsibility (Macdonald 2021).

FIGURE 14.1
People Who Say They Will Take the Vaccine, or Who Already Have Done So, Percentage

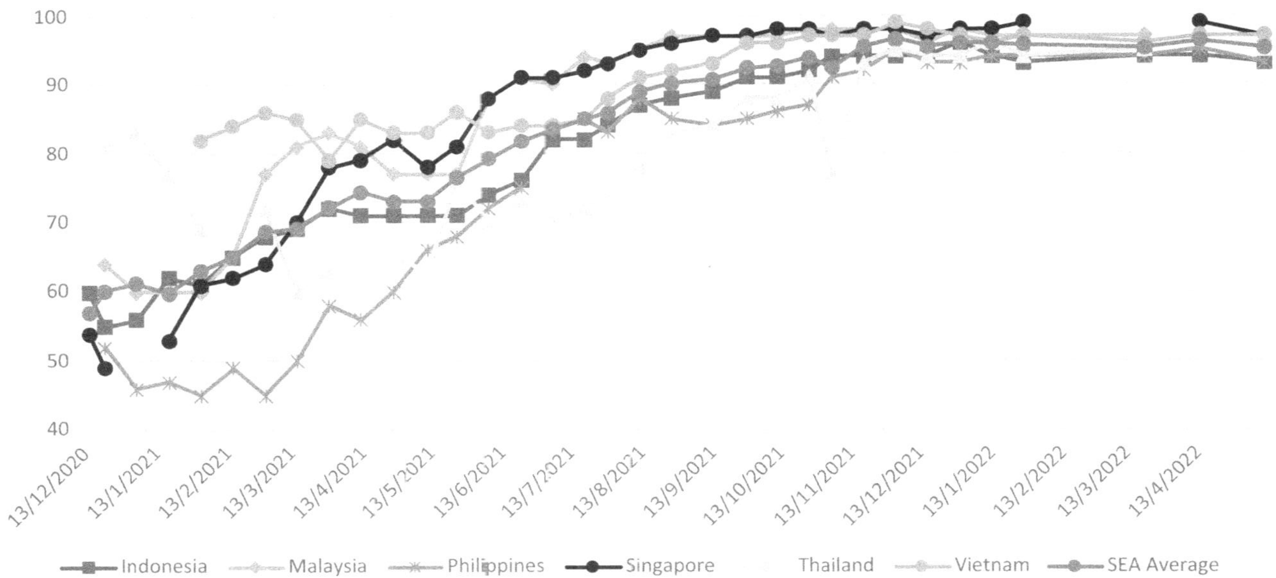

Note: There is no data for Brunei, Cambodia, Laos and Myanmar.
Source: YouGov. "COVID-19: Willingness to Be Vaccinated". https://yougov.co.uk/topics/international/articles-reports/2021/01/12/covid-19-willingness-be-vaccinated (accessed 1 April 2023).

VACCINATION RATES IN SOUTHEAST ASIA

The WHO's report, *Strategy to Achieve Global COVID-19 Vaccination by Mid-2022*, outlined its aim for 40 per cent of the total global population to be vaccinated by end-2021 and 70 per cent by June 2022 (WHO n.d.). The WHO's July 2022 update continued to uphold the numerical targets, although the deadline was made open-ended (WHO 2022). The targets are overall targets for all sources of supply, not just COVAX.

In Table 14.11, the target for 40 per cent of Southeast Asian populations to be fully vaccinated by end-2021 was achieved for all Southeast Asia countries except for Myanmar. Despite supply glitches throughout Southeast Asia in the first half of the year, supply eased towards the end of the year. Southeast Asia's strategy to procure different vaccines from multiple sources rather than through COVAX alone certainly helped, since COVAX supply constraints persisted until the fourth quarter of 2021. All the Southeast Asian countries studied fared better than the thirty-four countries of the ninety-two Advance Market Commitment countries that did not achieve the 40 per cent target—the thirty-four were the countries most dependent on COVAX vaccines (WHO 2021).

TABLE 14.11
Share of People Vaccinated against Covid-19, December 2021 and June 2022

	Partly Vaccinated (%)		*Fully Vaccinated (%)*	
	December 21	*June 22*	*December 21*	*June 22*
Brunei	92	100	91*	97
Cambodia	84	89	81*	85
Indonesia	58	73	41	61
Laos	51	79	42	69
Malaysia	79	85	78*	83
Myanmar	34	60	24	49
Philippines	51	68	34	63
Singapore	87	92	83*	92
Thailand	74	81	66	75
Vietnam	79	87	70*	81

Note: Countries that met the June 2022 target of the World Health Organization for vaccinating 70 per cent of the population.
Source: Our World in Data. https://ourworldindata.org/covid-vaccinations (accessed 1 April 2023).

In fact, by December 2021, five out of the ten Southeast Asia countries had already achieved the WHO's 70 per cent vaccination target. Brunei had the highest vaccination rate of 91 per cent in December 2021, followed by Singapore, Cambodia, Malaysia and Vietnam. Thailand achieved the WHO target of 70 per cent vaccination by June 2022, while Laos came close at 69 per cent. However, the Philippines (63 per cent), Indonesia (61 per cent) and Myanmar (49 per cent) missed the target.

The relatively high vaccination rates in Southeast Asia can be attributed in part to the sourcing strategy—different vaccines and multiple sources. The ninety-two countries of the COVAX Advance Market Commitment, in particular, benefited more from the supply of vaccines through Covid-diplomacy. Importantly, digital technology such as the use of mobile apps facilitated the roll-out of vaccination programmes in all countries in Southeast Asia. This greatly enabled countries with weaker state capacities to overcome some of their challenges.

Countries that were unable to meet the WHO's June 2022 target are those with logistics challenges, such as Indonesia and the Philippines. No detail was found on Laos and Myanmar (WHO 2022). The vaccine hesitancy in the Philippines and Indonesia, higher than the Southeast Asian average, was also a contributing factor.

Cambodia, on the other hand, overcame bureaucratic and logistic challenges during the crisis to achieve a high vaccination rate. This was due to support from China in vaccine procurement and the success of the Cambodian bureaucracy in administering the vaccines (Hutt 2021), as well as technical assistance from different international institutions. Cambodia, like most Southeast Asia countries, also used technology to overcome its challenges. A mobile app was used to help people register for vaccinations and for contact tracing (Munemo and Nyantakyi 2022). The app had substantial reach since reportedly 90 per cent of the population had mobile internet subscriptions in 2021 (ITU n.d.).

CONCLUSION

Southeast Asian countries, like all others, used vaccination as a tool to manage the Covid-19 pandemic. All Southeast Asian countries bought vaccines from multiple sources and, for some, this included vaccines that were not yet approved by the WHO, but that had been approved by domestic regulatory bodies for emergency use.

This made Southeast Asian countries less dependent on the COVAX facility, which only supplied WHO-approved vaccines and meant they fared better than developing countries that were dependent on COVAX as their main source of supply. COVAX had problems delivering to the ninety-two countries of the Advance Market Commitment in the first half of 2021 due to supply constraints and overbuying by the developed world. Over time, the situation eased and by 2022 vaccine supply was no longer as binding a constraint as it was in the first half of 2021. Vaccine hesitancy also eased over time, though each country still had remnants of anti-vaccination sentiment. The adoption of digital technology facilitated each country in managing the pandemic, including rolling out vaccinations and issuing digital vaccination certificates.

Nevertheless, logistical challenges as well as vaccine hesitancy continued to dog countries like Indonesia and the Philippines, so these countries did not achieve the WHO target of 70 per cent vaccination by June 2022. Myanmar's internal problems also held up vaccination in the country.

Notes

1. After the February 2021 coup, Myanmar's vaccinations and contact tracing efforts collapsed as the country descended into turmoil and thousands of doctors and healthcare workers walked out in protest against the takeover.
2. This section is based on Tham Siew Yean (2022).
3. In June 2021, Bio Farma was designated by the government to receive and distribute Covid-19 vaccines in Indonesia.
4. The LPI is constructed from six indicators using principal component analysis, a standard statistical technique used to reduce the dimensionality of a dataset. The output from the principal component analysis is a single indicator, the LPI, which is a weighted average of those scores. The weights are chosen to maximize the percentage of variation in the LPI's original six indicators, as accounted for by the summary indicators:
   (A) The efficiency of customs and border management clearance ("Customs"): 1 = very low, 5 = very high.
   (B) The quality of trade and transport infrastructure ("Infrastructure"): 1 = very low, 5 = very high.

(C) The ease of arranging competitively priced shipments ("Ease of arranging shipments"): 1 = very difficult, 1 = very difficult, 5 = very easy
(D) The competence and quality of logistics services—trucking, forwarding and customs brokerage ("Quality of logistics services"): 1 = low, 5 = very high.
(E) The ability to track and trace consignments ("Tracking and tracing"): 1 = very low, 5 = very high.
(F) The frequency with which shipments reach consignees within scheduled or expected delivery times ("Timeliness"): 1 = hardly ever, 5 = nearly always.

References

Adilla, F. 2022. "Moderna to Launch Malaysian Subsidiary, Seeks Partners in Vaccine Manufacturing & Development". *Business Times*, 16 February 2022. https://www.nst.com.my/business/2022/02/771792/moderna-launch-malaysian-subsidiary-seeks-partners-vaccine-manufacturing (accessed 23 May 2024).

Agarwal, Ruchir, and Tristan Reed. 2021. "How to End the Covid-19 Pandemic by March 2022". Policy Research Working Paper 9632, World Bank, Washington, DC, April 2021. https://documents1.worldbank.org/curated/en/181611618494084337/pdf/How-to-End-the-COVID-19-Pandemic-by-March-2022.pdf

Amul, Gianna Gayle, Michael Ang, Diya Kraybill, Suan Ee Ong, and Joanne Yoong. 2021. "Responses to Covid-19 in Southeast Asia: Diverse Paths and Ongoing Challenges". *Asian Economic Policy Review* 17, no. 1: 90–110. https://doi.org/10.1111/aepr.12362 (accessed 2 June 2022).

Arcturus Therapeutics. 2022. "Arcturus Announces Self-amplifying COVID-19 mRNA Vaccine Candidate ARCT-154 Meets Primary Efficacy Endpoint in Phase 3 Study". News Release, 20 April 2022. https://ir.arcturusrx.com/news-releases/news-release-details/arcturus-announces-self-amplifying-covid-19-mrna-vaccine

ASEAN Secretariat. 2019. *The ASEAN Vaccine Baseline Survey (AVBS) Current Situation and Gap Analysis*. Jakarta: ASEAN Secretariat. https://asean.org/wp-content/uploads/2021/10/Agd-6.3.a.i_AVBS_Final_23082019.pdf

Asia News Network. 2022. "Malaysian-Made Covid Vaccines Said to Offer Protection against New Variants". *Phnom Penh Post*, 16 January 2022. https://www.phnompenhpost.com/international/malaysian-made-covid-vaccines-said-offer-protection-against-new-variants (accessed 24 May 2024).

Bengy Puyvallée, A. de, and K.T. Storeng. 2022. "COVAX, Vaccine Donations and the Politics of Global Vaccine Inequity". *Global Health* 18: 26. https://doi.org/10.1186/s12992-022-00801-z (accessed 2 June 2022).

Berkley, Seth. 2020. "COVAX Explained". *Gavi.org*, 3 September 2020. https://www.gavi.org/vaccineswork/covax-explained (accessed 2 June 2022).

Bernama. 2021. "Malaysia, China to Collaborate in Vaccine R&D and Production". 4 December 2021. https://bernama.com/en/general/news_covid-19.php?id=2030133 (accessed 2 June 2022).

Blanchet, Karl, Grégoire Mallard, Erica Moret, and Jin Sun. 2021. "Sanctioned Countries in the Global Covid-19 Vaccination Campaign: The Forgotten 70%". *Conflict and Health* 15: 69. https://conflictandhealth.biomedcentral.com/track/pdf/10.1186/s13031-021-00404-2.pdf.

Bona, Fatima. 2022. "Kabar Baik, Uji Klinis Vaksin Merah Putih Fase Tiga Selesai September 2022" [Good news: the clinical trial of the Red and White vaccine in Phase Three will be completed by September 2022]. *Investor.id*, 27 August 2022. https://investor.id/national/304744/kabar-baik-uji-klinis-vaksin-merah-putih-fase-tiga-selesai-september-2022 (accessed 24 May 2024).

Chayut Setboonsarng. 2021. "Vaccine Hesitancy Grows Ahead of Thailand's Mass Inoculation Rollout". Reuters, 15 May 2021. https://www.reuters.com/world/asia-pacific/vaccine-hesitancy-grows-ahead-thailands-mass-inoculation-rollout-2021-05-25/ (accessed 2 June 2022).

Chulalongkorn University. 2021. "Chula Expects the 'ChulaCov19' mRNA vaccine and 'Chula-Baiya' Protein Subunit Vaccine to Be Ready in 2022". Newswise, 3 December 2021. https://www.newswise.com/coronavirus/chula-expects-the-chulacov19-mrna-vaccine-and-chula-baiya-protein-subunit-vaccine-to-be-ready-in-2022/?article_id=761704 (accessed 2 June 2022).

Deb, P., D. Furceri, D. Jimenez, S. Kothari, J. Ostry, and N. Tawk. 2021. "Determinants of Covid-19 Vaccine Rollouts and Their Effects on Health Outcomes". CEPR Discussion Paper No. 16681. https://cepr.org/publications/dp16681 (accessed 2 June 2022).

Economist, The. 2021. "What the Delta Variant Did to South-East Asia". 7 September 2021. https://www.economist.com/asia/what-the-delta-variant-did-to-south-east-asia/21804360 (accessed 2 June 2022).

Gavi. 2022. "Break Covid Now: The Gavi COVAX AMC Investment Opportunity". https://reliefweb.int/report/world/break-covid-now-gavi-covax-amc-investment-opportunity-enardeitjpzh.

Global Commission for Post-Pandemic Policy. n.d. "Covid-19 Vaccine Production, to September 30th 2021". https://globalcommissionforpostpandemicpolicy.org/covid-19-vaccine-production-to-september-30th-2021/ (accessed 2 June 2022).

Hutt, D. 2021. "China Isn't the Only Reason for Cambodia's Vaccination Success".

The Diplomat, 4 November 2021. https://thediplomat.com/2021/11/china-isnt-the-only-reason-for-cambodias-vaccination-success/ (accessed 2 June 2022).

ITU (International Telecommunication Union). N.d. "Facts and Figures 2021: Mobile Network Coverage". https://www.itu.int/itu-d/reports/statistics/2021/11/15/mobile-network-coverage/ (accessed 1 April 2021).

Karmini, Niniek. 2021. "President Widodo Says Pandemic Changed Indonesia's Culture". *Seattle Times*, 16 August 2021. https://www.seattletimes.com/business/president-widodo-says-pandemic-changed-indonesias-culture/ (accessed 2 June 2022).

Lai, Yerica. 2021. "Govt Drops Self-paid COVID-19 Vaccinations after Public Outcry". *Jakarta Post*, 17 July 2021. https://www.thejakartapost.com/news/2021/07/17/govt-drops-self-paid-covid-19-vaccinations-after-public-outcry.html (accessed 2 June 2022).

Lee, B., S.A. Ibrahim, and T. Zhang. 2021. "Mobile Apps Leveraged in the Covid-19 Pandemic in East and South-East Asia: Review and Content Analysis". *JMIR Mhealth Uhealth* 9, no. 11: e32093. https://doi.org/10.2196/32093

Liu, John. 2022. "Why People in Myanmar Don't Want the Junta's Jabs". *Frontier Myanmar*, 6 January 2022. https://www.frontiermyanmar.net/en/why-people-in-myanmar-dont-want-the-juntas-jabs/ (accessed 2 June 2022).

Macdonald, Sam. 2021. "Learning from Cambodia's Covid-19 Response". *Foreign Policy in Focus*, 22 September 2021. https://fpif.org/learning-from-cambodias-covid-19-response/

Munemo, Jonathan, and Eugene Bempong Nyantakyi. 2022. "Covid-19 Vaccination and Logistics Performance in Asia". *The Diplomat*, 2 March 2022. https://thediplomat.com/2022/03/covid-19-vaccination-and-logistics-performance-in-asia/ (accessed 2 June 2022).

OECD (Organisation for Economic Co-operation and Development). 2021. *Coronavirus (Covid-19) Vaccines for Developing Countries: An Equal Shot at Recovery*. https://read.oecd-ilibrary.org/view/?ref=1060_1060300-enj5o5xnwj&title=Coronavirus-COVID-19-vaccines-for-developing-countries-An-equal-shot-at-recovery

Onishi, Tomoya. 2021. "Vietnam's Homemade Vaccines Struggle to Debut as COVID Rages". 22 September 2021, *Nikkei Asia*. https://asia.nikkei.com/Spotlight/Coronavirus/COVID-vaccines/Vietnam-s-homemade-vaccines-struggle-to-debut-as-COVID-rages2 (accessed 2 June 2022).

Peter, Zsombor. 2021. "Thailand Considers Cap on Vaccine Exports as COVID Cases Surge". *VOA*, 27 July 2021. https://www.voanews.com/a/covid-19-pandemic_thailand-considers-cap-vaccine-exports-covid-cases-surge/6208775.html (accessed 2 June 2022).

Pharmaniaga. 2021. "Pharmaniaga Delivers Sinovac Covid-19 Vaccine on the 1st of August 2021, Ahead of Time as Requested by the Government to Accelerate National Covid-19 Immunisation Programme". News Release, 2 December 2021. https://pharmaniaga.com/wp-content/uploads/2021/12/Media-Release-No-Delays-in-Delivering-Vaccine.pdf

Punchada Sirivunnabood. 2022. "The Drama of Vaccine Politics: Covid-19 Inoculation Distribution in Thailand". Paper presented at the ISEAS – Yusof Ishak Institute Conference, "Covid-19 in Southeast Asia, 2020–2022: Restriction, Relief, Recovery", 28–29 July 2022, Singapore.

Reed, John, Michael Peel, and Hannah Kuchler. 2021. "A King's Vaccine: Thailand's Struggle to Deliver Jabs to Its People". *Financial Times*, 9 June 2021. https://www.ft.com/content/aaa8b820-68c7-408d-9486-222fe2d65634 (accessed 2 June 2022).

Rising, D., and E. Tarigan. 2021. "Concerns Rise Over Indonesia's Sputtering Virus Vaccinations". *The Diplomat*, 26 November 2021. https://thediplomat.com/2021/11/concerns-rise-over-indonesias-sputtering-virus-vaccinations/ (accessed 2 June 2022).

Runde, Daniel F., Romina Bandura, and Shannon McKeown. 2022. *Post-Covid-19 Economic and Health Recovery in Laos*. CSIS Briefs January 2022. https://csis-website-prod.s3.amazonaws.com/s3fs-public/publication/220119_Runde_Covid_Recovery.pdf?mUk23BihylQh29KrRptGFIpT17fRFsrr.(accessed 2 June 2022)

Satrusayang, Cod. 2021. "Opinion: Siam Bioscience Has Become an International Embarrassment". *Thai Enquirer*, 2 June 2021. https://www.thaienquirer.com/28152/opinion-siam-bioscience-has-become-an-international-embarrassment/ (accessed 2 June 2022).

Seah, Sharon, Joanne Lin, Sithanonxay Suvannaphakdy, Melinda Martinus, Pham Thi Phuong Thao, Farah Nadine Seth, and Hoang Thi Ha. 2022. *The State of Southeast Asia 2022 Survey Report*. https://www.iseas.edu.sg/wp-content/uploads/2022/02/The-State-of-SEA-2022_FA_Digital_FINAL.pdf

Sheikh, A.B., S. Pal, N. Javed, and R. Shekhar. 2021. "Covid-19 Vaccination in Developing Nations: Challenges and Opportunities for Innovation". *Infectious Disease Reports* 13, no. 2: 429–36. https://doi.org/10.3390/idr13020041

Somkid Puttasari. 2021. "The Failure of Vaccine Policy Pushed Thailand from the Best Recovering Country to the Worst". Observer Research Foundation (ORF), 19 August 2021. https://www.orfonline.org/expert-speak/failure-of-vaccine-policy-pushed-thailand/ (accessed 2 June 2022).

Sun Daily. 2021. "Pharmaniaga Buys Covid-19 Vaccine From Sinovac, Bottling To Be Done In Malaysia". 13 January 2021. http://www.insage.com.my/

Upload/MediaNews/PHARMA/PHARMA-TheSunDaily-13012021.pdf (accessed 2 June 2022).

Tagoe, E.T., N. Sheikh, A. Morton, J. Nonvignon, A.R. Sarker, L. Williams, and I. Megiddo. 2021. "Covid-19 Vaccination in Lower-Middle Income Countries: National Stakeholder Views on Challenges, Barriers, and Potential Solutions". *Frontiers in Public Health* 9: 709127. https://doi.org/10.3389/fpubh.2021.709127 (accessed 2 June 2022).

Tatar, Moosa, Mohammad Reza Faraji, Jalal Montazeri Shoorekchali, José A. Pagán, and Fernando Wilson. 2021. "The Role of Good Governance in the Race for Global Vaccination during the Covid-19 Pandemic". *Scientific Reports*, 11: 22440. https://doi.org/10.1038/s41598-021-01831-0 (accessed 2 June 2022).

Tempo. 2021. "Questioning Nusantara Vaccine". 12 March 2021 https://en.tempo.co/read/1441394/questioning-nusantara-vaccine (accessed 2 June 2022).

Tevdovski, D., P. Jolakoski, and V. Stojkoski. 2022. "The Impact of State Capacity on Cross-country Variations in Covid Vaccination Rates". *International Journal of Health Economics and Managemen*t 22: 237–55. https://doi.org/10.1007/s10754-021-09319-0 (accessed 2 June 2022).

Tham, Siew Yean. 2022. "The Race to Produce Covid-19 Vaccinations in South-East Asia". *ISEAS Perspective* no. 2022/29. https://www.iseas.edu.sg/articles-commentaries/iseas-perspective/2022-29-the-race-to-produce-covid-19-vaccines-in-southeast-asia-by-tham-siew-yean/ (accessed 23 May 2024).

US Department of State. 2022. "Joint Statement on Quad Cooperation in the Indo-Pacific". News release, 11 February 2022. https://www.state.gov/joint-statement-on-quad-cooperation-in-the-indo-pacific/ (accessed 2 June 2022).

Vingroup. 2021. "Vingroup Collaborates with Arcturus Therapeutics to Establish a Manufacturing Facility in Vietnam for Arcturus' mRNA Covid-19 vaccine". News Release, 2 August 2021. https://newsdirect.com/news/vingroup-collaborates-with-arcturus-therapeutics-to-establish-a-manufacturing-facility-in-vietnam-for-arcturus-mrna-covid-19-vaccine-866699795?category=Healthcare

Vittachi, Imran. 2023. "China Pursues 'Mask Diplomacy' With Asian Neighbors during COVID-19 Crisis". *Benar News*, 27 March 2023. https://www.benarnews.org/english/news/malaysian/China-mask-diplomacy-03272020121637.html (accessed 2 June 2022).

WHO (World Health Organization). N.d. *Strategy to Achieve Global Covid-19 Vaccination by Mid-2022*. https://cdn.who.int/media/docs/default-source/immunization/covid-19/strategy-to-achieve-global-covid-19-vaccination-by-mid-2022.pdf?sfvrsn=5a68433c_5 (accessed 2 June 2022).

———. 2021. "Achieving 70% COVID-19 Immunization Coverage by Mid-2022". 23 December 2021. https://www.who.int/news/item/23-12-2021-achieving-70-covid-19-immunization-coverage-by-mid-2022 (accessed 2 July 2022).

———. 2022. *Global COVID-19 Vaccination Strategy in a Changing World: July 2022 Update*. https://www.who.int/publications/m/item/global-covid-19-vaccination-strategy-in-a-changing-world--july-2022-update

World Bank. N.d. "The World by Income and Region: The World by Income". 2020. https://datatopics.worldbank.org/world-development-indicators/the-world-by-income-and-region.html (accessed 2 July 2022).

———. 2021. "Reducing Vaccine Hesitancy in the Philippines: Findings from a Survey Experiment". Philippines Covid-19 Monitoring Survey Policy Notes, September 2021. https://thedocs.worldbank.org/en/doc/9b206c064482a4fbb880ee23d6081d52-0070062021/original/Vaccine-Hesitancy-World-Bank-Policy-Note-September-2021.pdf (accessed 2 July 2022).

Yeremia, Ardhitya Eduard, and Klaus Heinrich Raditio. 2021. "Indonesia–China Vaccine Cooperation and South China Sea Diplomacy". *ISEAS Perspective*, no. 2021/55, 28 April 2021. https://www.iseas.edu.sg/wp-content/uploads/2021/03/ISEAS_Perspective_2021_55.pdf (accessed 2 July 2022).

Yoo, K.J., A. Mehta, J. Mak, D. Bishai, C. Chansa and B. Patenaude. 2022. "COVAX and Equitable Access to Covid-19 Vaccines". *Bull World Health Organ* 100: 315–28. https://pubmed.ncbi.nlm.nih.gov/35521037/ (accessed 2 July 2022).

Yulisman, Linda. 2022. "Indonesia Seeks to Launch Home-Grown Covid-19 Vaccine in Third Quarter". *The Star*, 20 February 2022. https://www.thestar.com.my/aseanplus/aseanplus-news/2022/02/20/indonesia-seeks-to-launch-home-grown-covid-19-vaccine-in-third-quarter (accessed 2 July 2022).

15

ASEAN'S RESPONSE TO COVID-19

Collaboration Towards Reopening

Sara Abdullah

In early 2020, Vietnam, as chair of the Association of Southeast Asian Nations (ASEAN) for the year, found itself in an uncomfortable and challenging position—it had to either sound the alarm on an increasingly threatening public health emergency or wait and see if the situation would allow for the country's best-laid plans for its chairmanship to come to fruition. Significantly, this decision-making was set against the backdrop of consecutive border closures and self-protecting national measures across the region.

ASEAN is an association of ten member nations. Since its establishment in 1967, it has gone through much change and development, in tandem with the growing global importance of the region on the political and economic fronts. With a combined population of over 620 million, the ASEAN region boasts an economic market of about US$2.3 trillion. On the political-security front, the region is the ostensible epicentre of the contested Indo-Pacific region. In the recent context of rivalry between the United States and China, many, if not most, ASEAN member states maintain a neutral position and hence are able to straddle both sides of the divide, often benefitting economically from this neutral position. While each ASEAN member state maintains its own bilateral relations with key partners around the world, the region as a whole possesses its own strengths and selling points. Therefore, ASEAN maintains relatively strong diplomatic relations with numerous different countries and international organizations.

This chapter outlines the ASEAN experience in countering and dealing with the Covid-19 pandemic. The regional response will be traced not only through the initiatives that ASEAN put in place in response to the pandemic but also through the collective sentiment that the ASEAN policies were espousing. The Covid-19 initiatives will be explored through case studies of two regional initiatives with a view to understanding the political, social and economic motivations behind the policies.

REGIONAL LANDSCAPE IN 2020

Border closures in the ASEAN region were the most visible sign of measures being put in place in response to the rapid spread of Covid-19. These all resulted in disruptions to supply chains, volatility in financial markets and warped market outlooks for industries and sectors such as tourism, services and manufacturing. Cognizant of the potential larger impact of border closures, Vietnam convened the Special Meeting of the ASEAN Coordinating Council (ASEAN 2022a) in Vientiane, Laos, on 20 February 2020. The ASEAN Coordinating Council is comprised of all ten ASEAN Foreign Ministers and is mandated to see through the decisions of the ASEAN Leaders. It also presides over all cross-cutting and multi-dimensional ASEAN issues. The meeting of the ASEAN Coordinating Council in 2020 was a signal to regional players and the wider global community that ASEAN recognized the threat of the pandemic to the region and would respond collectively. This would be achieved through multi-sectoral engagement and engagement of the whole ASEAN Community. Consequently, the ASEAN health sector—those working on matters involving regional public health security and policies in the member states—convened an ASEAN Plus Three Health Ministers

Meeting (ASEAN 2020b), the first of such meetings involving ASEAN's partner countries.

Perhaps the most significant moment in the region's undertakings in responding to the pandemic came in the form of the convening of a meeting of ASEAN Leaders, the Special ASEAN Summit (ASEAN 2020c), in April 2020. This was not part of the regular ASEAN timetable; its ad hoc nature denoted the significance of the situation, which required an ASEAN meeting at the highest level. The ASEAN Leaders met via videoconference for the first time in the organization's history and affirmed their commitment to regionalism in countering the impact of the pandemic. This was expounded upon in a commitment to ensure that critical economic and trade infrastructure and routes would remain open in the region, and that the flow of medicines, food and essential supplies would continue unhindered (ASEAN 2020c). In terms of tangible outcomes, the Leaders put in motion initiatives including a post-pandemic recovery plan and the COVID-19 ASEAN Response Fund. They reaffirmed the coordinating and oversight function of the ASEAN Coordinating Council and the ASEAN Coordinating Council Working Group on Public Health Emergencies (ACCWG-PHE) on all of ASEAN's Covid-19 initiatives and responses.

Alongside the Special ASEAN Summit, an ASEAN Plus Three Special Summit on Covid-19 was also convened. At this Summit, ASEAN and the three partner countries, the People's Republic of China, Japan and the Republic of Korea, reaffirmed their commitment to cooperation to maintain necessary interconnectedness by facilitating essential movement of people, including business travel, and keeping markets open for trade and investment. Most significantly, the Summit also sought to "encourage mutual support and assistance between ASEAN and the Plus Three Countries" and "to ensure adequate financing to contain the pandemic and protect our peoples" (ASEAN 2020d). The latter included the proposed establishment of the COVID-19 ASEAN Response Fund for public health emergencies, which would be funded by a budget reallocated from existing ASEAN Plus One and ASEAN Plus Three cooperation funds, with possible additional support from ASEAN's external partners (ASEAN 2020d). This Summit marked the beginning of the important role that ASEAN's partners would play in the regional response to Covid-19. ASEAN's partners played a pivotal role in supporting the region's efforts in countering Covid-19, but the effectiveness of the regional response was also affected by the strength of each relationship.

ASEAN'S INITIATIVES IN RESPONSE TO COVID-19

Given the active stewardship of Vietnam as ASEAN chair in 2020, and the close management of regional initiatives by the ASEAN Coordinating Council, supported by the ACCWG-PHE, ASEAN initiated a significant number of programmes and projects in 2020–22. Some of the more significant ones include the Covid-19 ASEAN Response Fund, the ASEAN Regional Reserve of Medical Supplies for Public Health Emergencies (ASEAN RRMS), the ASEAN Strategic Framework on Public Health Emergencies (ASF-PHE), the ASEAN Regional Centre for Public Health Emergencies (ACPHEED), the Post-Pandemic Recovery Plan, which was later renamed the ASEAN Comprehensive Recovery Framework (ACRF) and the ASEAN Travel Corridor Arrangement Framework (ATCAF) (Table 15.1). While the rest of this chapter will expound upon two of the more prominent initiatives, the others are also worthy of discussion in order to have a fuller understanding of ASEAN's commitment to regional response and recovery from the pandemic.

ASEAN Regional Reserve of Medical Supplies

The idea of establishing a warehouse or stockpile to cater to the needs of a public health emergency was first mooted by Vietnam as chair of ASEAN in 2020. In suggesting the establishment of such a warehouse, ASEAN member states were aware of the warehouses that were already in existence, serving the needs of the region. The experiences of setting these up informed the member states of the limitations of a physical warehouse, including the considerable costs involved. Given this and the fact that medical supplies generally have a shorter lifespan than generic life-saving emergency supplies, Vietnam envisioned that the ASEAN RRMS would stockpile earmarked essential medical supplies to support the region in addressing any future public health emergency. The premise of the ASEAN RRMS is that ASEAN member states set aside supplies

TABLE 15.1
ASEAN's Response to Covid-19: Regional Initiatives

Initiative	*Key Properties*	*Implementation*
1. ASEAN Regional Reserve of Medical Supplies (RRMS)	• Stockpile of medical supplies related to and useful in a public health emergency. • Each contributing country earmarks supplies for the RRMS. • The ASEAN Secretary-General is informed of contributions, while the ASEAN Secretariat maintains an inventory of all earmarked supplies.	• Launched at end-2020. • Current stockpile includes contributions from member states. • Several partners expressed interest in contributing, including ASEAN Plus Three (China, Japan and the Republic of Korea).
2. ASEAN Strategic Framework on Public Health Emergency (ASF-PHE)	• Standard operating procedures created to enhance ASEAN's preparedness for and resilience to public health emergencies. • Designed to complement and align with the existing ASEAN Public Health Emergencies Coordination System (ACPHECS) project.	• Launched in mid-2020. • Supported by ASEAN-USAID PROSPECT (a collaborative development project between ASEAN and the US government).
3. ASEAN Regional Centre for Public Health Emergencies (ACPHEED)	• Physical regional centre. • Strategic focus: (1) prevention and preparedness, (2) detection and risk assessment and (3) response. • Primarily funded and supported by Japan. • Australia's contribution arrived in 2021.	• Launch announced in November 2020. • Resolved in May 2022 that the Centre would be jointly hosted by Thailand, Indonesia and Vietnam, with all three member states focusing on different aspects of ACPHEED work.

continued on next page

TABLE 15.1 — *cont'd*

Initiative	*Key Properties*	*Implementation*
4. ASEAN Comprehensive Recovery Framework (ACRF)	• Large-scale post-pandemic recovery plan for the region. • Captures in one document initiatives being carried out on a longer-term scale with sectoral bodies in response to the pandemic. • A whole-of-community exit strategy from the Covid-19 crisis.	• The ACRF is explicated by an accompanying implementation plan. • Monitoring of the ACRF is conducted by the ACRF Support Unit. • Continuous updates on the progress of work of sectoral body initiatives under the ACRF are reported biannually to ASEAN member states.
5. ASEAN Travel Corridor Arrangement Framework (ATCAF)	• Created to enhance economic recovery by facilitating movement and travel for business and trade. • Anchored by the ASEAN Declaration on an ATCAF. • Will use an ASEAN QR code facility that was designed to digitally streamline health protocol across the region.	• Final iteration of the travel corridor was completed in August 2021 and announced in November 2021. • The ATCAF is conceived, managed and coordinated by a dedicated task force set up in 2021. • The ATCAF had not been trialled as of early 2024.
6. COVID-19 ASEAN Response Fund	• Dedicated funding mechanism to support ASEAN member states to mitigate the effects of Covid-19 and prevent it from spreading further. • The fund may be used to procure medicines and emergency supplies, and support research and development related to Covid-19.	• Launched in November 2020. • Funds held at and managed by the ASEAN Secretariat. • Received interest from ASEAN partners in contributing; has received approximately USD 30 million in contributions. • USD 10 million used to procure vaccines for the region, as of early 2021.

Source: Author's compilation.

from their national stockpiles and allocate them to the RRMS. These supplies would be physically held in the contributing member state, while the ASEAN Secretariat would maintain an inventory of all earmarked supplies in the region. If a member state needs a supply of a specific item, it can write to the Secretary-General of ASEAN who will identify the geographically closest source and request a physical transfer to be made. In this way, ASEAN saves costs on planning, building and maintaining a physical stockpile or warehouse.

Given the uniqueness and potential flexibility of the ASEAN RRMS, considerable attention and curiosity were focused on its set-up. Various ASEAN partners inquired about collaboration and engagement with ASEAN on the scheme, hoping to contribute to the reserves or use it to donate supplies such as vaccines to the region. In fact, shortly after the RRMS was set up, the ASEAN Plus Three countries (China, Japan and the Republic of Korea) drew up a concept note proposing a collaboration with ASEAN in expanding the ASEAN RRMS to include the Plus Three countries as contributors. However, for political and practical reasons there was surprisingly little interest among ASEAN member states themselves to earmark their own supplies for the RRMS once it had been set up. Given this and the general evolution of the pandemic, there was little occasion for the mechanism of the ASEAN RRMS to be tested or trialled. The ASEAN RRMS exists more on paper as a concept with a fully thought-out mechanism accompanying it.

ASEAN Strategic Framework on Public Health Emergency

The ASEAN Strategic Framework on Public Health Emergency (ASF-PHE) and the ASEAN Regional Centre for Public Health Emergencies and Emerging Diseases (ACPHEED) were conceived as initiatives that would inform one another. The ASF-PHE was a response to the ASEAN Leaders' advice to strengthen the implementation of the World Health Organization's International Health Regulations (IHR) (2005) in the region. Conceived as a set of standard operating procedures, the intention of the ASF-PHE was to enhance ASEAN's preparedness for and resilience to public health emergencies, thereby strengthening ASEAN's cooperation in health security. In 2021, the chair of the Senior Officials Meeting on Health Development, the body that discusses and manages health cooperation and health-related developments in the region, announced that the implementation of the ASF-PHE would be aligned with the ASEAN Public Health Emergencies Coordination System (ACPHECS) project and other complementary initiatives, forming a multi-year programme that is supported by the ASEAN-USAID Partnership for Regional Optimization within the Political-Security and Socio-Cultural Communities (PROSPECT).

Much like the ASF-PHE, the ACPHEED is significantly supported by an ASEAN Dialogue Partner. Early in 2021, at the beginning of the pandemic, Japan pledged to fund the establishment of the ACPHEED with almost US$50 million. The ACPHEED has three strategic focus pillars, specifically: (1) prevention and preparedness, (2) detection and risk assessment and (3) response. The launch of the ACPHEED was announced at the 37th ASEAN Summit in November 2020. However, at that point, ASEAN had yet to decide which of the shortlisted candidates among ASEAN member states would physically host the Centre. Japan stated that its proposed financial contribution to the ACPHEED would expire at the end of 2021. In the meantime, in May 2022, Australia announced that it would contribute AU$21,000,000. It was not until May 2022 that the final decision for Thailand, Indonesia and Vietnam to jointly host the Centre was made, allowing for its physical establishment to begin.

ASEAN Comprehensive Recovery Framework

The ACRF is posited as the post-pandemic recovery plan for the region. It captures the pandemic-response initiatives being carried out on a longer-term scale within sectoral bodies. The recovery plan was initially meant to include elements on mitigating a global economic recession and restoring the confidence of consumers, investors and the business community in the region. The ASEAN Secretariat proposed that the ACRF would serve as ASEAN's whole-of-community exit strategy from the Covid-19 crisis and would address the impact of the pandemic while also addressing reopening, recovery and long-term resilience. The Framework consists of five broad strategies: (1) enhancing health systems, (2) strengthening human security, (3) maximizing the potential of broader economic integration, (4) accelerating inclusive digital transformation and (5) advancing towards a more sustainable and resilient future. The ACRF is supported by the ACRF Support Unit, which is housed at the ASEAN Secretariat in Jakarta; the Support Unit monitors and evaluates the progress of the work of the ACRF and produces biannual reports for the ASEAN Coordinating Council.

CASE STUDY 1: COVID-19 ASEAN RESPONSE FUND AND ASEAN'S REGIONAL VACCINE PROCUREMENT

The COVID-19 ASEAN Response Fund has proven to be one of the more successful and more well-received regional Covid-19 initiatives. It was conceived as a way to re-channel funds from cooperation projects between ASEAN and partners that had stalled due to the pandemic (ASEAN 2022b). The COVID-19 ASEAN Response Fund is the funding mechanism for providing support to ASEAN member states in the mitigation and further spread of Covid-19. The ASEAN Coordinating Council mooted the idea that the fund could be used to procure medicines and emergency supplies to treat Covid-19. It stipulated that the fund can also support cooperation in research and development relevant to Covid-19, including research on virology, immunology and vaccines, and in harvesting and sharing of best practices related to the treatment and mitigation of the virus.

The fund was launched at the 37th ASEAN Summit in 2020 by the ASEAN Leaders. The funds are held at and managed by the ASEAN Secretariat. Since its launch, the fund has received much interest and contributions from ASEAN's partners. To date, it has received up to US$30 million in contributions from twenty-two countries—a considerable amount to have been raised in two years.

In early 2021, with Covid-19 a global problem, ASEAN member states called for the fund to be used to procure vaccines for the region. This was in the midst of the global roll-out of vaccines by the major pharmaceutical producers and the unprecedented scramble for doses by most countries around the world. In August 2021, the decision was made to contract the United Nations Children's Fund (UNICEF) as the procurement agent for ASEAN's regional purchasing.

In the course of negotiations with UNICEF to procure vaccines for the region, it became evident that ASEAN's purchase order of US$10 million worth of vaccines was not considered a priority to be expedited by UNICEF or the COVID-19 Vaccines Global Access (COVAX) programme.[1] This is because the amount of the purchase was considered small. Negotiations with UNICEF therefore spanned many months. In July 2022, the ASEAN Secretariat was finally able to report that the purchasing, delivery and administration of the vaccines procured through the fund was almost complete.

Given the amount of time that passed between ASEAN's decision to procure vaccines and their delivery to member states, developments in national vaccine administration overtook ASEAN's procurement. Many member states had no use for the ASEAN-procured vaccines for their own citizens as the majority of their populations had already been vaccinated through national schemes. These member states sought to redistribute their vaccine share via the fund to other ASEAN member states that seemed in more need. These redistribution requests slowed the completion of the initiative, while the political coup in Myanmar in early 2021 exacerbated distribution delays to the individual ASEAN member states, which needed to happen simultaneously.

ASEAN's regional vaccine procurement initiative was also mired in the global debate on vaccine diplomacy and discrimination (Minority Rights Group 2022). Aside from the issue of the relatively small number of vaccines the region was attempting to purchase, questions were raised on whether the severe delay in the delivery to the region was because Southeast Asia was considered by COVAX and the producing pharmaceutical companies as neither being in severe need nor a political priority, in comparison to Europe. Member states like Malaysia decried the delays as being evidence of greed by developed countries in buying vaccines in excess, causing global delivery and supply problems that negatively affected developing economies (Chan 2021). To exacerbate matters, these developed countries that had purchased vaccines in excess later tried to offload their near-expiring vaccines onto countries in Southeast Asia (*Straits Times* 2021). Similarly, UNICEF, as an agent procuring vaccines for ASEAN, was criticized as attempting to press onto ASEAN member states doses of the Pfizer vaccine, which in 2022 was in global supply excess, though they had requested other vaccines.

The conundrum that presents itself in ASEAN's attempt at regional vaccine procurement is manifold. While much may be said about the quick and generous contributions of ASEAN's partners to the COVID-19 ASEAN Response Fund, a mark of the strength of ASEAN's cooperative and diplomatic relations, the vaccine discrimination and supply disruptions that were ostensibly caused by some of these same partners brought into question the extent of ASEAN's strength on the global stage. At the core of the matter is the fact that diplomatic aid, whether it presents itself in the form of cooperation projects or financial contributions, needs to be carefully negotiated and ASEAN's ability to negotiate more favourable outcomes for itself is in fact dependent on many factors beyond the issue at hand, which in this case was the crisis brought about by the pandemic.

CASE STUDY 2: ASEAN TRAVEL CORRIDOR ARRANGEMENT FRAMEWORK AND REGIONAL REOPENING

ASEAN began thinking about regional reopening very early on in the pandemic. At the 36th ASEAN Summit in 2020, the ASEAN Leaders called for an enhanced effort to assist in ASEAN's economic recovery, including measures to facilitate movement and travel during the pandemic. Indonesia proposed the establishment of an ASEAN Travel Corridor and the ASEAN Declaration on an ASEAN Travel Corridor Arrangement Framework (ATCAF) (ASEAN 2020a) was adopted by the 37th ASEAN Summit in the same year.

To operationalize the travel corridor, the ad hoc Task Force on the Operationalization of the ASEAN Travel Corridor Arrangement Framework (TF-ATCAF) was set up by the ACCWG-PHE in March 2021. The goal was to draft and realize the travel corridor. As part of its initial discussions, the task force considered drafting a set of standard health protocols for travellers and sharing best practices and mechanisms that had been put in place by each member state in their efforts to reopen borders safely. It became evident that a feasible solution to harmonizing disparate systems lay in using digital technology. Singapore showcased its Digital Health Certificate and, later, TraceTogether, its application to track and trace the spread of Covid-19.

The final iteration of the ATCAF was realized in August 2021 and the existence of the facility was noted at the 38th ASEAN Summit in 2021. The design allows two ASEAN member states to set up a travel corridor between them, facilitating the movement of persons for business and official purposes between those two countries. Following the finalization of the ATCAF facility, the ACCWG-PHE directed the TF-ATCAF to work on the processes of implementing the travel corridor, including enabling a common approach to verifying digital vaccination certificates and potentially developing a common set of standards for non-digitally verifiable health documents.

Then, in 2022, the TF-ATCAF decided to use two existing systems from the Senior Officials Meeting on Health Development—Digitalization of Health Protocol: Recognition of COVID-19 Health Certificates for International Travel through the ASEAN Single Digital COVID-19 Health Certificate Verification Portal, and the Establishment of an ASEAN Single QR Code. Both initiatives seek to digitally represent verifiable health data, including the vaccination status of a particular individual. The QR code was intended to expedite travel in and around the ASEAN region, against the backdrop of the pandemic, by having the individual's health data already digitally parsed through a common set of regionally agreed standards.

By the time the ATCAF was ready to be used as an ASEAN mechanism for border reopening in late 2021, some countries outside the region had already begun to reopen their borders and economies. Many ASEAN member states had also tentatively followed suit—Cambodia and Singapore, for example, allowed travellers to enter for any purpose (whether business, official or tourism), albeit with some added requirements such as testing and minimal quarantine. Bilateral travel corridors had also become less relevant as borders became more porous, with layers of restrictions being peeled away to allow different types of admissions to varying degrees. Predictably then, the ATCAF, with its controlled use (limited to travel for business and official purposes) and rigid set-up (a corridor between two countries), became less relevant and work on its implementation began to fade.

The challenges of the ATCAF are immediately evident: the cumbersome processes of reaching consensus among all ten ASEAN member states could not keep up with the evolution of the pandemic. By the time the

ATCAF was ready for use, countries had naturally begun to open up without intermediary mechanisms like the ATCAF, thus rendering the ATCAF obsolete. The restrictive nature of the ATCAF also did not fit the needs of the twenty-first-century pandemic, where flexibility and adaptability proved to be key. Lastly, the ATCAF was also little known among the general ASEAN audience. While the ACCWG-PHE had mandated the Task Force to better publicize the ATCAF, it was not achieved swiftly enough to respond to the fast-changing pandemic.

The development of the ATCAF, however, was not a fruitless endeavour. When the ASEAN Leaders requested it to be set up, it was also considered from the longer-term perspective of having a mechanism on hand to use in similar circumstances in the future. The existence of the ATCAF, hence, is the beginning of securing the readiness and responsiveness of the region to emergencies, whether related to public health or otherwise.

DO MULTILATERAL SOLUTIONS WORK IN RESPONDING TO PANDEMICS?

ASEAN's steady growth and development are undeniable. Its global significance is growing in tandem with the general prominence of the individual economies of the member states. At the same time, the ASEAN Covid-19 response is the most ambitious and comprehensive regional response to a crisis to date. ASEAN member states instinctively sought to develop multifaceted responses that would not only address the impact of the pandemic but that would also mitigate its spread and see the region safely out of the crisis. In many ways, the attempt was complete, in that it was an attempt to respond, rebuild and recover from the pandemic. The questions that this ambition begets are whether ASEAN achieved success and whether the regional ambition was misplaced.

It may be argued that an individual living in an ASEAN country more keenly feels the pandemic response of their own government than that of ASEAN. However, the inherent premise of the organization must not be overlooked. ASEAN seeks to bring greater prosperity, security and success to the region through diplomacy and regional cooperation, thereby creating an ASEAN Community. Seen from this perspective, ASEAN's efforts take on a more positive sheen. In the desire to help the people of the region, ASEAN's partners were ready to contribute. The outpouring of aid and donations did not abate, as seen in the People's Republic of China's donation of 10 million vaccine doses to Myanmar in May 2022 (Xinhua 2022). If success is measured in this way, it is reassuring to know that ASEAN is offered immediate and substantial assistance and collaboration from its partners in times of crisis.

In looking ahead, the reasonable line of inquiry would be whether ASEAN is able to achieve success in enlarging the role of multilateralism and regionalism in dealing with crises and solving the major problems of the world. It is worthwhile to note that ASEAN may be the only multilateral organization or institution that has attempted to mount a comprehensive and multifaceted response to the Covid-19 pandemic. It may be argued that ASEAN is very different to the European Union in terms of its reasons for existence and its objectives, for example, the European Union's response to the pandemic has mostly been to enhance existing support systems to national governments, especially through funding facilities and the like (EU n.d.). The most significant European Union initiative in response to the pandemic has been its Recovery Plan for Europe, a plan for recovery from the economic fallout for the region. The European Union also made some small effort to fight disinformation during the pandemic, but its responses have mostly been to graft existing financial resources to individual government endeavours.

ASEAN's efforts hence are laudable even if only as an attempt to respond concertedly and holistically to the crisis. The organization was able to leverage its role as a multinational and intergovernmental organization, promising diplomatic cooperation to ten governments at once, and negotiating with its partners for aid and assistance. It is also noteworthy that this aid and assistance reached almost all aspects of the work of the organization. While this chapter mainly discussed the large-scale initiatives, the work of the sectoral bodies in the other pillars of the ASEAN Community (Political-Security, Economic and Socio-Cultural) was also responsive to the pandemic and benefitted from diplomatic cooperation and assistance from ASEAN's partners.

Looking ahead, it is also clear that the main challenge for ASEAN is to think of ways to hasten its decision-making processes to keep up with the fast pace of global developments. ASEAN's mode of building policy—

through consensus—has been a hurdle, as seen, for example, in developing the ATCAF. ASEAN's biggest selling point, that it is a multinational organization, is at times also a disadvantage; processes become unwieldy and initiatives ultimately irrelevant if they cannot keep up with the speed of change in global discourse.

The question that remains is whether there is still value to ideas enshrined within the concept of regionalism. One can reasonably argue that, on balance, ASEAN's efforts show that it embraced and leveraged its strengths for the benefit of the people. ASEAN's experience has also demonstrated that there is value to regionalism, as it is a different mode of diplomatic cooperation and community-building than national and bilateral engagements.

Note

1. UNICEF is a co-leader of the COVAX scheme.

References

ASEAN (Association of Southeast Asian Nations). 2020a. "ASEAN Declaration on an ASEAN Travel Corridor Arrangement Framework". 12 November 2020. https://asean.org/asean-declaration-on-an-asean-travel-corridor-arrangement-framework/

———. 2020b. "ASEAN Plus Three Health Ministers Reaffirm Collaboration to Address COVID-19 Pandemic". 7 April 2020. https://asean.org/asean-plus-three-health-ministers-reaffirm-collaboration-to-address-covid-19-pandemic/

———. 2020c. "Declaration of the Special ASEAN Summit on Coronavirus Disease 2019 (COVID-19)". 14 April 2020. https://asean.org/declaration-of-the-special-asean-summit-on-coronavirus-disease-2019-covid-19/

———. 2020d. "Joint Statement of the ASEAN Plus Three Summit on Coronavirus Disease 2019 (COVID-19)". 14 April 2020. https://asean.org/wp-content/uploads/2021/09/Final-Joint-Statement-of-the-Special-APT-Summit-on-COVID-19.pdf

———. 2022a. "Press Statement by the Chairman of the ASEAN Coordinating Council". News release, 20 February 2022. https://asean.org/wp-content/uploads/2021/09/Press-Statement-of-the_Special-ACC-20.2.2020.pdf

———. 2022b. "Terms of Reference: The COVID-19 ASEAN Response Fund". https://asean.org/wp-content/uploads/53-Finalised-and-APPROVED-TOR_COVID-19-ASEAN-Response-Fund.pdf

Chan, Dawn. 2021. "Khairy: 'Greedy' Countries Hoarding Vaccines led to Global Supply Problem, including in Malaysia". *New Straits Times*, 12 April 2021. https://www.nst.com.my/news/nation/2021/04/681731/khairy-greedy-countries-hoarding-vaccines-led-global-supply-problem (accessed 16 July 2022)

EU (European Union). n.d. "The Common EU Response to COVID-19". https://european-union.europa.eu/priorities-and-actions/common-eu-response-covid-19_en

Minority Rights Group. 2022. "UN Committee Decries Racial Discrimination in Global COVID-19 Vaccine Access". 29 April 2022. https://minorityrights.org/2022/04/29/covid-19-vaccine-access/

Straits Times. 2021. "US donation of 1 million Pfizer Covid-19 Vaccines Arrives in Malaysia". 5 July 2021. https://www.straitstimes.com/asia/se-asia/us-donation-of-one-million-pfizer-covid-19-vaccines-arrives-in-malaysia (accessed 16 July 2022).

Xinhua. 2022. "China Donates 10 million COVID-19 Vaccine Doses to Myanmar". 29 May 2022. https://english.www.gov.cn/news/international exchanges/202205/29/content_WS629363efc6d02e533532b775.html (accessed 16 July 2022).

INDEX

www.ingramcontent.com/pod-product-compliance
Ingram Content Group UK Ltd.
Pitfield, Milton Keynes, MK11 3LW, UK
UKHW022027041026
15591UKWH00012B/550

9 789815 20380